MATHEMATICS OF FINANCE

Mathematics of Finance

PAUL M. HUMMEL, Ph.D.
Professor of Statistics
University of Alabama

CHARLES L. SEEBECK, Jr., Ph.D.
Professor of Mathematics
University of Alabama

Third Edition

McGRAW-HILL BOOK COMPANY
NEW YORK   ST. LOUIS   SAN FRANCISCO   DÜSSELDORF
LONDON   MEXICO   PANAMA   SYDNEY   TORONTO

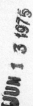

MATHEMATICS OF FINANCE

Library of Congress Catalog Card Number 75-115145
07-031161-7

567890 KPKP 7987654

Preface

There are several reasons why we have written this third edition. First, there have been vast improvements in computing equipment during the past twenty years, and this edition introduces several computing techniques that take advantage of the modern equipment.

Also, new problems have arisen, such as the amortization of debts using several rates of interest. Nearly all the states have small-loan legislation which allows the use of multiple rates, so we have included a treatment of this problem in this edition.

Finally, because of the recent trend toward higher interest rates, we have extended the tables to include the rates $8\frac{1}{2}$, 9, $9\frac{1}{2}$, 10, and $10\frac{1}{2}$ percent. We sincerely hope this extension will be adequate.

Otherwise, except for updated material, the text is very much like the earlier editions. It starts with the treatment of simple interest and simple discount; develops gradually and logically through the topics of compound interest, annuities with their many applications, perpetuities, bonds, and depreciation; and ends with an elementary treatment of the fundamentals of life insurance.

A chapter on computing techniques is included mainly for the benefit of new teachers and more mature students. It contains all the material in the earlier editions plus several new techniques that are geared to modern computing equipment. Much of the material in this chapter is not found elsewhere.

There are three appendixes, Appendix A on a short-cut method of multiplication; Appendix B, on the theory of logarithms, and Appendix C, on progressions, for students who need to review these topics.

As a prerequisite to this course, college algebra is highly desirable, although a very good background in high-school algebra should be sufficient. It is essential that the student be proficient in numerical computation involving both rational and decimal fractions.

v

Normally all the material in this book cannot be covered in one course. In those schools where the course is required and presupposes only college algebra or less, a five-quarter or three-semester-hour course should include practically all the material in the first nine chapters. Most of the starred material should be omitted in such a course. For a similar course given to more mature students, the first nine chapters (including much of the starred material) should be augmented by topics from the last three chapters. A short course should cover at least most of the material in Chaps. 1, 2, 3, 4, and 6 and selected topics from Chaps. 5, 7, 8, and 9. An advanced course of two semester or three quarter hours should consist of a brief review of the first nine chapters (including most of the starred material), followed by most of the material in the remaining chapters. Such a course should be a mixture of theory and practical problems. To get the maximum benefits from such a course, students should have access to computing machines.

Extreme care was exercised in compiling the tables, and we believe that they are as accurate as any in existence. The authors computed Tables 3 to 7. Where possible, these were compared with existing tables, discrepancies were investigated, and the correct results were determined and checked. For these tables, several internal-consistency checks were developed and applied, so the chance of their containing errors is small. Tables 8 to 12 were obtained by reducing to eight decimal places the corresponding entries in Kent and Kent's "Compound Interest and Annuity Tables," published by the McGraw-Hill Book Company. Table 15, with some corrections, was taken from the same source. The authors are indebted to the Kents for permission to use these tables.

Tables 13 and 14 are reproduced with the kind permission of the Society of Actuaries.

In our first edition, published in 1948, we introduced a new method of treating general annuities which we believed to be "the only teachable method of treating general annuities." We are therefore grateful to the many authors of similar texts who have obviously agreed with us by adopting our treatment.

We are also indebted to many friends and colleagues whose constructive criticism has been most helpful. There are far too many of these to list by name. Our main acknowledgment, however, is to the thousands of students—many of whom took the course by correspondence—who have convinced us by words and deeds that this text covers thoroughly and logically the mathematics of finance.

PAUL M. HUMMEL
CHARLES L. SEEBECK, Jr.

Contents

Interest.   Simple interest.   ★The 6 percent method of computing ordinary simple interest.   ★Ordinary and exact simple-interest tables.   The time between dates.   Notes.   Simple discount.

Compound amount and compound interest.   Notation.   The fundamental compound-amount formula.   Finding the compound amount.   Present value and compound discount.   Equivalent rates.   Compound amount and present value for a fractional period of time.   Determining the interest rate.   Finding the time.

Dated values.   Sets of dated values.   Nonequivalent dated values. Equivalent sets of payments.   ★Problems of occasional occurrence.

Definitions.   Present value and amount of an ordinary annuity. Annuities due.   Deferred annuities.   Identities relating $s_{\overline{n}|i}$ and

$a_{\overline{n}|i}$. Finding the payment of an annuity. Annuities with n unknown. *Determining the final payment by interpolation. Finding the interest rate.

The general annuity due.   The general case.   Finding the number of payments and the final payment.   Proof of the general interpolation theorem.   Other types of annuities.

Introduction.   Integral powers of numbers.   Fractional powers of numbers.   A recursion formula for powers and roots.   Proof of the recursion formulas.   Other methods of determining bond yield. Proof of the bond yield formulas.   The accuracy of interpolation.

Mortality tables.   Pure endowments.   Life annuities.   Whole-life annuities.   Deferred annuities.   Temporary annuities.   Equivalent annuities.   Other types of annuities.   Life insurance.   Whole-life insurance.   Term insurance.   Endowment insurance.   Reserves.   Concluding remarks.

Definition.   Rules for logarithms.   Logarithms of the numbers from 1 to 10.   Logarithms of other numbers.   Antilogarithms.   Multiplication and division.   Exponents and radicals.   Exponential equations.   Equations involving addition and subtraction.

Arithmetic progressions.   Geometric progressions.   The sum of the terms of an A.P.   The sum of the terms of a G.P.   The sum of a G.P. to infinity.

Tests and examinations.

MATHEMATICS OF FINANCE

1
Simple Interest

1 INTEREST

Interest is the income from invested capital; or in a narrower sense, it is the fee paid for the use of money. If a man owns a house in which he is not living, he may rent this house to another person. In the same way, a man who owns money that he is not using may loan (or rent) it to someone else. The fee (or rent) charged for the use of the money is interest. *The sum of money loaned is the* **principal.** An agreement is usually made concerning the period of time for which the money is loaned. *The sum of the interest and principal, due at the end of this time period, is called the* **amount.** *The interest rate per period is the ratio of the interest for the period to the principal.* This rate is always expressed as a percentage or the equivalent decimal.

Example The Smith Co. borrowed $150 from the First National Bank. If the bank charged $3.75 interest for the use of its money for the period of 6 months, what was the interest rate for this period?
Solution Call the interest rate for the 6-month period i. Then $i = 3.75/150 = 0.025 = 2\frac{1}{2}\%$.

2 SIMPLE INTEREST

Let P be the principal, r the interest rate for 1 year, and t the length of the time period in years. *If interest is computed by means of the formula*

$$I = Prt \tag{1}$$

and if the interest is due at the end of the time period, then the interest payment is called **simple interest.** In this case, the interest rate for the time period involved is rt. For simple interest, however, the interest rate is always given on a yearly basis.

If S represents the amount, then

$$S = P + I \tag{2}$$

Equations (1) and (2) are called the *fundamental equations* of simple interest. Every problem in simple interest can be solved by means of these two equations. It should be noted that they contain five different quantities, namely, S, P, I, r, and t. If any three, except the first three, are given, the remaining two can be found by means of Eqs. (1) and (2). For convenience, another one will be added. If I is eliminated from Eqs. (1) and (2),

$$S = P(1 + rt) \tag{3}$$

is obtained, an equation for the amount in terms of P, r, and t.

Since, for simple interest, r is always given as a yearly rate, t must be changed into years unless it is already given in this unit. When the time is given in months, t is simply the number of months divided by 12. When the time is given in days, two different methods are in use for computing t. The most commonly used method is to divide the number of days by 360. *When t is computed in this manner, the interest obtained is called* **ordinary simple interest.** A second method in use is to divide the number of days by 365 (366 in leap years). *When t is computed in this manner, the interest obtained is called* **exact simple interest.**

Example 1 Find the simple interest at 6% on $250 for 3 months.
Solution We have $P = 250$, $r = 0.06$, and $t = \frac{3}{12} = \frac{1}{4}$.

$$I = Prt = 250 \times 0.06 \times \frac{1}{4} = \$3.75$$

Example 2 Find the exact simple interest and the amount if $500 is loaned for 100 days at 4%.
Solution $P = 500$, $r = .04$, and $t = \frac{100}{365}$.

$$I = 500 \times 0.04 \times \frac{100}{365} = \$5.48 \qquad \text{and} \qquad S = 500 + 5.48 = \$505.48$$

Example 3 A man who invested $1000 had $1010 returned to him 45 days later. At what rate did his money earn ordinary simple interest?

Solution $P = 1000$, $S = 1010$, and $t = {}^{45}\!/\!_{360} = \frac{1}{8}$. Now, since $S = P + I$, $I = S - P = 1010 - 1000 = 10$. And, since $I = Prt$,

$$r = \frac{I}{Pt} = \frac{10}{1000 \times \frac{1}{8}} = 0.08 = 8\%$$

Example 4 Ninety days after borrowing money a man pays back exactly $100. How much was borrowed if the $100 payment includes the principal and ordinary simple interest at 8%?

Solution $S = 100$, $r = 0.08$, and $t = {}^{90}\!/\!_{360} = \frac{1}{4}$. Substituting these values in $S = P(1 + rt)$ gives

$$100 = P(1.02) \quad \text{and} \quad P = \frac{100}{1.02} = \$98.04$$

EXERCISE 1

1. Express the following percentages as proper fractions and as decimals correct to the nearest four places: (*a*) 4%, (*b*) $2\frac{1}{4}$%, (*c*) 3.2%, (*d*) $3\frac{1}{3}$%, (*e*) 0.8%, (*f*) $\frac{1}{6}$%.

2. Change each of the following fractions to a percentage, correct to the nearest hundredth percent: (*a*) 0.035, (*b*) $\frac{3}{40}$, (*c*) $0.04\frac{1}{3}$, (*d*) $\frac{5}{16}$, (*e*) $8.40/\$280$, (*f*) ${}^{40}\!/\!_{1250}$.

3. Find the value of $1 + rt$ and express the result in both fractional and decimal form: (*a*) $r = 6\%$, $t = \frac{1}{2}$; (*b*) $r = 1\frac{1}{4}\%$, $t = \frac{1}{3}$; (*c*) $r = 5\%$, $t = \frac{3}{4}$; (*d*) $r = 3.2\%$, $t = \frac{1}{12}$; (*e*) $r = 4.8\%$, $t = \frac{1}{8}$.

4. Compute $\$5000(1 + 0.03\frac{1}{3})$ correct to the nearest cent.

5. Find the value of $\$8000/(1 + 0.02\frac{2}{3})$ correct to the nearest cent.

6. Find the simple interest on $5000 for 3 months at 4%.

7. Find the simple interest and amount if $600 is invested for 4 months at $3\frac{1}{2}\%$.

8. Find the ordinary and exact simple interest on $2500 for 90 days at 5% in a normal year.

9. Find the ordinary simple interest and amount on $50,000 at $3\frac{1}{2}\%$ for 60 days.

10. A student charges his roommate $1 on a loan of $20 for 1 month. What simple-interest rate is he using?

11. A bank charges $3 ordinary simple interest for the use of $200 for 90 days. What simple-interest rate is in effect?

12. In payment for a shipment of goods, a businessman may pay either $600 cash or $610 at the end of 60 days. If he borrows the money to pay cash, what ordinary-simple-interest rate can he afford to pay?

13. A bill for $400 is payable at the end of 90 days or 2% off for cash. If the cash price is regarded as a 90-day investment, what ordinary-simple-interest rate does it earn?

14. Find P if $S = \$244.80$, $r = 8\%$, and $t = \frac{1}{4}$.

15. Find P if $S = \$406$, $r = 4.5\%$, and $t = \frac{1}{3}$.

16. What principal will amount to $2050 in 6 months if the rate is 5%?

17. What principal will amount to $4080 in 120 days at 6% ordinary simple interest?

18. How many days will it take for $900 to earn $6 if it is invested at 5% ordinary simple interest?

*3 THE 6 PERCENT METHOD OF COMPUTING ORDINARY SIMPLE INTEREST

Ordinary simple interest may be readily computed by using the following simple relations: 6 *percent ordinary simple interest on P for* 60 *days is* $P \times 0.06 \times {}^{60}\!/_{360} = 0.01P$, *and* 6 *percent ordinary simple interest on P for* 6 *days is one-tenth of the previous result, or* $0.001P$. Thus, moving the decimal point is all that is necessary to find the ordinary simple interest at 6 percent for either 6 or 60 days. For any other number of days, the proper multiples or fractional parts of the above results are used.

Example 1 Find the ordinary simple interest on $700 for 135 days at 6%.
Solution 135 may be represented as $(2 \times 60) + (2 \times 6) + (\frac{1}{2} \times 6)$. For 60 days, 6% interest on $700 is $7, and 6% interest on $700 for 6 days is $0.70. The interest then for 135 days will be

$$(2 \times 7) + (2 \times 0.70) + \left(\frac{1}{2} \times 0.70\right) = \$15.75$$

When the rate is not 6%, the procedure is to first find the interest at 6%, then take the proper multiple or fractional part of it.

Example 2 Find the ordinary simple interest on $800 for 78 days at 5%.
Solution First find the ordinary simple interest on $800 at 6%. Since

$$78 = 60 + (3 \times 6)$$

the interest at 6% will be

$$8 + (3 \times 0.80) = \$10.40$$

Interest at 1% would be one-sixth of the above result, or $1.73, and interest at 5% would be $10.40 - 1.73 = \$8.67$.

The 6 percent method applies only to ordinary simple interest. There is no comparable method for exact simple interest.

*4 ORDINARY AND EXACT SIMPLE-INTEREST TABLES

Various types of simple-interest tables have been compiled. Table 2 is such a table.† An example will illustrate its use.

Example Find the exact simple interest on $1250 for 93 days at 4%.
Solution Table 2 gives the exact (and ordinary) simple interest on $10,000 at 1% for any number of days up to 365. By moving the decimal point properly, one can readily obtain the interest on $1000, $100, $10, and $1. Thus, the exact simple interest on $1000 for 93 days at 1% is $2.54795, for $100 it is $0.25479, and for $10 it is $0.02548. Hence, the exact simple interest on $1250 for 93 days is

$$2.54795 + (2 \times 0.25479) + (5 \times 0.02548) = \$3.185$$

and the exact simple interest on $1250 for 93 days at 4% is

$$4 \times 3.185 = \$12.74$$

† All numbered tables will be found at the end of the book.

★EXERCISE 2

Find the ordinary simple interest, using the 6% method:

1. $P = \$750$, $r = 6\%$, and the time is 90 days.

2. $P = \$2000$, $r = 4\%$, and the time is 60 days.

3. $P = \$250$, $r = 2\%$, and the time is 36 days.

4. $P = \$800$, $r = 4\frac{1}{2}\%$, and the time is 54 days.

5. $P = \$1500$, $r = 7\frac{1}{2}\%$, and the time is 110 days.

6. $P = \$3000$, $r = 3\%$, and the time is 137 days.

Find the exact and ordinary simple interest, using Table 2:

7. $P = \$2000$, $r = 1\%$, and the time is 65 days.

8. $P = \$1500$, $r = 1\%$, and the time is 85 days.

9. $P = \$4000$, $r = 3\%$, and the time is 110 days.

10. $P = \$1750$, $r = 4\%$, and the time is 225 days.

11. $P = \$666.67$, $r = 5\%$, and the time is 173 days.

12. $P = \$2250$, $r = 4\frac{1}{2}\%$, and the time is 97 days.

5 THE TIME BETWEEN DATES

When the time is given indirectly as the time between dates, it is customary to count the exact number of days including either the first or the last day, but not both. When the time is computed in this manner, it is called the **exact time.** This custom makes it easy to determine the number of days between any two dates of the same year if a calendar that contains the number of the day of the year of each date is available. The exact number of days is the difference between the numbers of the days of the year of each date. Table 1 is essentially such a calendar. In leap years, the number of the day of the year is increased 1 for all dates after Feb. 28.

Another method of counting the number of days between dates consists of counting 30 days for each month. When this method is used, the time obtained is called the **approximate time.**

Regardless of which method of computing the number of days is used, either exact or ordinary simple interest may be used. Thus, there are four distinct methods of computing simple interest between dates, namely:

a. Using the exact time and ordinary simple interest
b. Using the exact time and exact simple interest
c. Using the approximate time and ordinary simple interest
d. Using the approximate time and exact simple interest

Of the four methods, *d* is almost never used, *b* and *c* are used occasionally, and *a* is nearly always used. Method *a* is frequently called the **bankers' rule** and will be used at all times in this text unless specified otherwise.

Example 1 Money is loaned on June 15 and repaid on Oct. 20. Find (a) the exact time, (b) the approximate time.

Solution a From Table 1, June 15 is the 166th day of the year and Oct. 20 is the 293d. So the exact number of days is 293 − 166 = 127.

Solution b For the approximate time, arrange the data as shown below:

Date	Month	Day
Oct. 20.....................	10	20
June 15...................	6	15
Difference...............	4	5

The difference is 4 months and 5 days, or 125 days, since each month is counted as having 30 days.

Example 2 A loan is made on Nov. 16, 1965, and repaid on the following Feb. 9. Find (a) the exact time, and (b) the approximate time.

Solution a From Table 1, Nov. 16 is the 320th day of the year and Feb. 9 is the 40th. One way to proceed is to find the time from Feb. 9 to Nov. 16, which is 280 days, and subtract this result from 365. Thus the desired time is 365 − 280 = 85. Alternately, we could add 40 to 365, then subtract 320. Thus 365 + 40 − 320 = 85, as before.

Solution b The data are arranged in a manner similar to that used in the preceding example. It is necessary, however, to alter the terminal date by first changing a year into months, then a month into days as shown in the table.

Date	Year	Month	Day
Feb. 9, 1966............	1966	2	9
Feb. 9, 1966............	1965	14	9
Feb. 9, 1966............	1965	13	39
Nov. 16, 1965...........	1965	11	16
Difference............	0	2	23

The approximate time is therefore 2 months and 23 days, or 83 days.

EXERCISE 3

1. Find the exact and the approximate time from Mar. 10 to Sept. 8.

2. Find the exact and the approximate time from June 6 to Feb. 20.

3. Money is loaned on Jan. 10, 1968, and repaid on Aug. 15, 1968. Find the exact and the approximate time.

4. On May 10, $800 is borrowed, and it is repaid on Dec. 15. If the interest rate is 6%, find how much simple interest is earned by each of the four methods.

5. Find the ordinary and the exact simple interest on $1200 at 5% from June 1 to July 16, using the exact time.

6. Using the bankers' rule, find the simple interest and the amount if $600 is invested at $4\frac{1}{2}\%$ from June 30 to Oct. 16.

7. Given $P = \$480$, $r = 4\frac{1}{4}\%$, and the time is from May 15 to July 26, find the ordinary simple interest and the amount.

8. Find the ordinary simple interest on $400 at 5%, using the approximate time from Aug. 31 to Oct. 15.

9. Find the ordinary-simple-interest rate which will cause $1200, invested on May 25, to amount to $1227 on Oct. 12.

10. What is the ordinary-simple-interest rate if $1000 earns $20 interest from Dec. 15, 1967, to Apr. 13, 1968?

11. How much should be invested at 6% ordinary simple interest on May 15 to obtain the amount of $1275 on Sept. 12?

12. What principal invested at 8% ordinary simple interest on Apr. 20 will amount to $803.40 on Sept. 2?

13. What principal invested on Feb. 20, 1968, will amount to $2777.50 on Apr. 21, 1968, if the rate is 6% and exact simple interest for the exact time is used?

6 NOTES

A note is essentially a written promise to pay a certain sum of money on a specified date.   The date on which the money is due is called the **date of maturity.**   The sum of money due is called **the maturity value.**   Although the maturity value and the date of maturity are the only essential features of a note, other information is usually given such as the date on which the note was made, the length of time until it matures, the sum of money borrowed, and an interest rate.   In fact, it is usually necessary to compute the maturity value and the date of maturity from the other information given.   For example, suppose Mr. A. B. Jones borrows $200 from Mr. C. D. Smith and agrees to pay back the loan with $6 interest at the end of 6 months.   The following note could be signed by Mr. Jones and given to Mr. Smith:

May 15, 1967

Six months after date I promise to pay to the order of Mr. C. D. Smith the sum of $200 and simple interest at the rate of 6% per annum.

(Signed) *Mr. A. B. Jones*

This note is essentially a promise to pay Mr. Smith $206 on Nov. 15, 1967.   The $200 is called the **face** of the note, and the 6-month period is called the **term** of the note.   The following note should satisfy Mr. Smith just as well as the preceding one:

                                                              May 15, 1967
       Six months after date I promise to pay to the order of Mr.
    C. D. Smith the sum of $206 without interest.
                                                    (Signed) *Mr. A. B. Jones*

   Clearly either of these notes calls for the payment of $206 on Nov.
15, 1967. The second form is rather common with banks when short
time loans are involved.

   When the term of the note is given in months, it normally matures on
the same day of the proper month. An exception would be a 3-month
note dated Nov. 30. Such a note would mature on the last day of
February. If the term of the note is given in days, it is customary to
count the exact number of days in computing the date of maturity, with
either the first or the last day counted, but not both. For example, a
90-day note dated Mar. 15 would mature on June 13. When the term is
given in days, Table 1 is useful in finding the date of maturity.

Example   Find the date of maturity for a 90-day note dated June 30, 1967.
Solution   From Table 1, June 30 is the 181st day of the year. Adding 90 gives the
date of maturity as the 271st day of the year. From Table 1, the 271st day of the
year is Sept. 28.

7   SIMPLE DISCOUNT

A discount is a deduction from an account, bill, debt, or the like, made
for various reasons. In the mathematics of finance, *a discount is a
deduction from the maturity value of an obligation made when the obligation
is sold before its date of maturity.* The sum remaining after the discount
is deducted from the maturity value is called the **proceeds.** For example,
suppose Mr. A holds a note for $400 on Mr. B that will mature in 10
months. Suppose Mr. A sells this note to a bank for $375. The discount
is $25, and the proceeds are $375.

   *The discount rate for a given period of time is the ratio of the discount
for the period to the maturity value.* As in simple interest, this rate is
always given as a percentage or the equivalent decimal and is usually
quoted on a yearly basis.

   Let S denote the maturity value, d the discount rate for 1 year, and
t the length of the time period in years. *If discount is computed by means
of the formula*

$$D = Sdt \tag{4}$$

it is called simple discount or bank discount. If P represents the proceeds, then

$$P = S - D \tag{5}$$

Equations (4) and (5) play the same role for simple or bank discount that Eqs. (1) and (2) do for simple interest. If D is eliminated from Eqs. (4) and (5),

$$P = S(1 - dt) \tag{6}$$

is obtained, an equation for the proceeds in terms of S, d, and t.

When an investor, such as the bank in the illustration above, buys a note before its maturity date, he is essentially loaning money to the seller. Thus the bank actually loans Mr. A \$375 for 10 months and keeps Mr. B's note as security. On the date of maturity, the bank will collect \$400 from Mr. B so that the bank realizes \$25 profit for the investment of \$375 for 10 months. Clearly the \$25 may be regarded as simple interest on the \$375 invested. *Thus, on the date of maturity, the discount on S becomes interest on P. Or stated differently, $S - P$ may be considered either discount on S or interest on P.* Clearly the discount rate and the interest rate will not be the same. In the example above the discount rate is (from $D = Sdt$)

$$d = \frac{D}{St} = \frac{25}{400 \times {}^{10}\!/_{12}} = 0.075$$

whereas the interest rate is (from $I = Prt$)

$$r = \frac{I}{Pt} = \frac{25}{375 \times {}^{10}\!/_{12}} = 0.08$$

The relation between the interest rate and the discount rate is easily obtained by equating the right-hand members of Eqs. (1) and (4) and dividing out t. This gives

$$Pr = Sd \tag{7}$$

The confusion in connection with problems concerning discount usually arises from misuse of the rates r and d. Equation (7) clearly shows that they are not the same and therefore not interchangeable.

When a note is bought before its date of maturity, the price P that an investor is willing to pay is usually determined by one of two methods:

a. The investor may state that a given discount rate d is to be used. In this case, S, t, and d are known and the simple-discount equations are used to find P. $P = S(1 - dt)$.

b. The investor may state the interest rate r that he wishes to realize on *his investment.   In this case, S, t, and r are known so that the simple-interest equations must be used to find P.   Therefore $P = S/(1 + rt)$.*

When the proceeds from the sale of a note are found by either of the above methods, the note is said to have been discounted.   If method a is used, the discount is called **bank discount** or discount at a discount rate. When method b is used, the discount is called **discount at an interest rate** or sometimes **true discount.**   It is unfortunate that the discount computed by either method is called simple discount by various financial institutions.

When a person borrows money and gives his note, he is essentially selling his own note before its date of maturity.   In the preceding section, Mr. Jones actually sells to Mr. Smith for $200 a note that will mature 6 months later for $206.   The proceeds are $200.   The $6 may be regarded as discount on the maturity value of $206.   Six months later when Mr. Jones pays back $206, the $6 is interest to Mr. Smith on his investment of $200.

Many banks use a discount rate on all small loans.   *However, they generally use the phrase* **interest in advance** *in the same sense as bank discount.*   For example, suppose Mr. Smith asks for a loan of $100 for 90 days from a bank that uses an 8 percent interest-in-advance rate. The bank computes the interest-in-advance charge by the formula $D = Sdt$, where $S = 100$, $d = 0.08$, and $t = \frac{1}{4}$, obtaining $2 as its fee, and gives Mr. Smith $98 as the proceeds of the loan.   Clearly the note for $100 due in 90 days that Mr. Smith signs is discounted by method a. *Thus, the phrase interest in advance is synonymous with bank discount and an interest-in-advance rate is banking terminology for discount rate.*

Example 1   On Mar. 10, 1967, Mr. Jones sold the following note to the City National Bank:

November 5, 1966

One year after date I promise to pay to the order of Mr. Jones the sum of $100 and simple interest at 5% per annum.

(Signed) *Mr. Adams*

If the City National Bank used a 6% interest-in-advance rate, (a) what were the proceeds?   (b) What interest rate did the bank realize on its investment?
Solution a   The note matured on Nov. 5, 1967, for $105.   From Mar. 10 to Nov. 5 is 240 days, so that $S = \$105$, $t = {}^{240}\!/_{360} = \frac{2}{3}$, and $d = 0.06$.

$$D = Sdt = 105 \times 0.06 \times \frac{2}{3} = \$4.20$$

and

$$P = S - D = 105 - 4.20 = \$100.80$$

Solution b $P = \$100.80$, $t = \frac{2}{3}$, and $I = \$4.20$.   From $I = Prt$,

$$r = \frac{I}{Pt} = \frac{4.20}{100.80 \times \frac{2}{3}} = 0.0625$$

Example 2   A note that will mature in 60 days for \$242 is sold to a bank that uses a 5% simple-interest rate for discounting purposes.   What are the proceeds?
Solution   Here $S = \$242$, $t = \frac{60}{360} = \frac{1}{6}$, and $r = 0.05$.   From $S = P(1 + rt)$,

$$P = \frac{S}{1 + rt} = \frac{242}{1 + (0.05 \times \frac{1}{6})} = \$240$$

Example 3   Mr. Brown intends to borrow money from the First National Bank for 90 days.   If the bank charges 6% interest in advance, for how much should he ask so as actually to get \$400?
Solution   We wish to determine S from the following data: $P = \$400$, $t = \frac{90}{360} = \frac{1}{4}$, and $d = 0.06$.   From $P = S(1 - dt)$,

$$S = \frac{P}{1 - dt} = \frac{400}{1 - (0.06 \times \frac{1}{4})} = \$406.09$$

Simple discount, like simple interest, is normally used only when short time periods are involved, usually less than a year.   In the majority of applications, a discount rate d is used, although the wide divergence of terminology used by different texts and financial institutions makes it difficult at times to determine whether the rate quoted is to be used as an interest rate r or as a discount rate d.   In the problems that follow, interest in advance means bank discount and should not be confused with interest, which is always computed on P and is paid at the end of the transaction.

EXERCISE 4

1. $S = \$1700$, $d = 4\%$, time $= 3$ months.   Find D and P.

2. $S = \$1500$, $d = 5\%$, the time is from May 15 to July 26.   Find D and P.

3. A note with a maturity value of \$320 is sold at a discount rate of $3\frac{1}{2}\%$ 75 days before maturity.   Find the discount and the proceeds.

4. Find the proceeds if the note in Prob. 3 is sold to yield an interest rate of $3\frac{1}{2}\%$.

5. A note maturing for \$600 on Aug. 15 is sold for \$595 on June 16.   What discount rate was used?   What interest rate will the purchaser realize on this investment?

6. Upon receipt of goods, a merchant signs a note promising to pay \$2400 in 90 days. Find the proceeds if the supplier sells the note to a bank that uses a $6\frac{1}{2}\%$ discount rate.   How much profit does the supplier make if the goods cost \$1900?

7. An investor lends \$3400 and receives a note promising to pay that amount plus 8% simple interest in 90 days.   The note is immediately sold to a bank that charges 6% bank discount.   How much does the bank pay for the note?   What is the investor's profit?   What interest rate will the bank realize on this investment when the note matures?

8. The Second National Bank pays \$441 for a note maturing for \$450 in 4 months. What is the discount rate?   What interest rate does the bank earn on this investment?

9. A 90-day note promises to pay $6000 and ordinary simple interest at $5\frac{1}{2}\%$. It is discounted at 6% bank discount 30 days before maturity. Find the maturity value of the note and the proceeds of the sale.

10.

April 1, 1970

One hundred and fifty days after date I promise to pay to Robert Dale or order the sum of $275 and ordinary simple interest at 6% per annum.

(Signed) *Dale Roberts*

Find the maturity value and the date of maturity. If the note is sold on May 31, 1970, at 5% bank discount, find the proceeds.

11.

June 1, 1968

Ninety days after date I promise to pay to the First National Bank or order exactly $250.

(Signed) *Archie Meedes*

On June 1 when Mr. Meedes signed the note he received $240. What ordinary-simple-interest rate does the bank realize? What bank-discount rate would give the same results?

12. A request for a loan of $650 for 3 months is made at a bank which charges 7% interest in advance. How much is the discount? What are the proceeds of the loan?

13. In order to receive $950 as proceeds, how much should a company request for a 6-month loan from a bank charging 6% bank discount?

14. On Apr. 18, 1969, Mr. Smith requests a loan of $325 for 60 days from a bank that charges $6\frac{1}{2}\%$ bank discount. How much does Mr. Smith receive? How much will he pay back and when? Make out a noninterest-bearing note that the bank would accept.

15. The City Savings and Loan Corp. buys notes at a price which enables it to realize 6% simple interest on its investment. How much will it offer for a note maturing in 75 days for $750?

16. A 6-month note for $400 and interest at 5% is sold 60 days before maturity to a bank that uses a 6% simple-interest rate. What are the proceeds? What is the equivalent bank-discount rate?

17. A note maturing for $1200 is to be sold 8 months before it is due. Which will offer the larger sum: the First National Bank, which uses a $6\frac{1}{4}\%$ simple-interest rate, or the Last National Bank, which uses a 6% bank-discount rate?

18. Mr. Jay owes Mr. Kay $500 due immediately. Mr. Kay agrees to accept as payment a noninterest-bearing note for 60 days which can be discounted immediately at a local bank which charges 6% interest in advance. What should the face of the note be so that Mr. Kay will receive $500 as proceeds?

19. A 6-month note maturing for $800 is sold to the First National Bank at 7% interest in advance 120 days before it is due. Thirty days later, this bank sells the note to the Second National Bank at 6% bank discount. How much profit did the First National Bank make, and what interest rate did it realize on this investment?

2
Compound Interest

8 COMPOUND AMOUNT AND COMPOUND INTEREST

When interest is periodically added to the principal and this new sum is used as the principal for the following time period and this procedure is repeated for a certain number of periods, the final amount is called the **compound amount.**   The difference between the compound amount and the original principal is called the **compound interest.**

The time period between two consecutive interest computations is called the **interest period,** or **conversion period,** and may be any convenient length of time.   The conversion period is usually taken as an exact divisor of the year, such as a month, 3 months, 6 months, or a year.

The interest rate is usually quoted on a yearly basis and must be changed to the interest rate per interest period for computational purposes.

Example   Find the compound amount at the end of 1 year on $1000 if the rate is 6% converted quarterly.
Solution   The phrase 6% *converted (or compounded) quarterly* means $1\frac{1}{2}\%$ per 3 months.   Thus, at the end of the first 3 months, $1\frac{1}{2}\%$ of $1000 is added on, giving

13

$1015 as the amount at the end of the first period.   This new sum is the principal for the second period.   At the end of the second 3-month period, $1\frac{1}{2}\%$ of $1015 is added on, giving $1030.23 as the amount at the end of the second period and the principal for the third period.   At the end of 3 more months, $1\frac{1}{2}\%$ of $1030.23 is added on, giving $1045.68 as the amount at the end of the third period.   And finally, at the end of the year, $1\frac{1}{2}\%$ of $1045.68 is added on, giving $1061.36 as the compound amount at the end of the year.   The compound interest for the year is $61.36, which is $1.36 more than simple interest would have been.

The direct method of computation used in the example becomes quite tedious as the number of interest periods gets larger, and quicker methods of getting the compound amount will be developed.

9   NOTATION

The following notation will be used:

P = the original principal, or the present values of S
S = the compound amount of P, or an amount due at a later date
n = the number of interest (or conversion) periods involved
m = the number of conversion periods per year
j = the yearly interest rate which is to be converted m times per year
i = the interest rate per conversion period; i *always equals* j/m

The yearly rate j is called the **yearly nominal rate,** or, more briefly the *nominal rate*, since it is the rate in name only involved in the transaction.   The rate $i\ (= j/m)$ is always used in the computation of compound amount.   Numerous methods of designating the nominal rate are in common usage and will be used.   For example, $j_4 = 0.08$ or $(8\%, m = 4)$ or $(j = 8\%, m = 4)$ means that a yearly nominal rate of 8% is converted 4 times per year and that $i = 0.02$ is the interest rate per 3-month period.

10   THE FUNDAMENTAL COMPOUND-AMOUNT FORMULA

If P represents the principal at the beginning of the first interest period and i is the interest rate per conversion period, then the interest earned during the first period is Pi, and the amount at the end of the first period is $P + Pi$, or $P(1 + i)$.   Thus, the amount at the end of the period is $(1 + i)$ times the principal at the beginning of the period.   Similar reasoning shows that the amount at the end of any period is $(1 + i)$ times the principal during that period, so that the amount at the end of the second period would be $P(1 + i)(1 + i) = P(1 + i)^2$, and continuing in this manner for n periods gives the final compound amount as

$$S = P(1 + i)^n \tag{1}$$

The equation above is called the **fundamental formula of compound interest.**   Every result in this chapter is obtained directly or indirectly from it.   Note that it contains four quantities, so if any three are given the fourth can be found.

11 FINDING THE COMPOUND AMOUNT

When P, n, and i are given, the compound amount can be obtained by numerous methods.   Some of these will now be discussed.

a. The simplest method of finding the compound amount is by the use of compound-amount tables.   Such tables give the values of $(1 + i)^n$, called the **accumulation factor,** for the common rates of interest and values of n.   Table 8 is a table of this type.   Its use will be illustrated by an example.

Example 1   Find the compound amount if \$500 is invested at $j_2 = 6\%$ for 10 years. *Solution* $j_2 = 6\%$ means that the nominal rate 6% is compounded semiannually and $i = 0.03$ per 6 months.   Thus $P = \$500$, $i = 0.03$, and $n = 20$, so that

$$S = 500(1.03)^{20}$$

In Table 8, the value of $(1.03)^{20}$ is given as 1.80611123.   Multiplying this value by 500 gives $S = \$903.06$, to the nearest cent.

Since compound-amount tables are not always available or may not contain the given value of i or n, it follows that for completeness, several other methods are desirable.

b. When the interest rate is in the table but the value of n is beyond the table limit, the compound amount can be found by using values given in the table and the law of exponents, $x^{a+b} = x^a x^b$.

Example 2   Find the value of $(1.01)^{220}$ correct to six decimal places. *Solution*   Using the law of exponents mentioned above, we may write

$$(1.01)^{220} = (1.01)^{120}(1.01)^{100}$$

Evaluating the factors on the right gives

$$(1.01)^{220} = 3.30038689 \times 2.70481383 = 8.926932$$

When multiplications such as the above are necessary, the student will profit greatly by learning and using the "bobtailed" method of multiplication outlined in Appendix A.

c. When the interest rate is not in the table but n is, an approximate value of the accumulation factor can be obtained by a method called **interpolation.**   This method is widely used in connection with tables of various types for finding values between those given in the table.

Interpolation in its simplest form is based on the assumption that the values in the table vary uniformly.   For example, since $3\frac{1}{4}$ percent is halfway between 3 percent and $3\frac{1}{2}$ percent, we expect $(1.0325)^n$ to be about halfway between $(1.03)^n$ and $(1.035)^n$. *While this is not exactly true, in many cases it is sufficiently accurate for the purpose at hand.*

Example 3 Find approximately the amount to which $1000 will accumulate in 20 years at $j_1 = 5.2\%$.

Solution We have $S = 1000(1.052)^{20}$, and the main problem is to evaluate the accumulation factor $(1.052)^{20}$. This will be done by interpolation, since an approximate solution is sufficient here. From Table 8, we find the value of $(1 + i)^{20}$ for values of i on either side of 5.2% and arrange the data as shown below:

$$
0.005 \left\{ 0.002 \left\{ \begin{array}{c|c}
i & (1 + i)^{20} \\
\hline
0.055 & 2.9178 \\
\hline
0.052 & X \\
\hline
0.050 & 2.6533 \\
\end{array} \right\} c \right\} 0.2645
$$

The entries in the right-hand column are written with only four decimals, since additional places will not appreciably increase the accuracy.

The method of interpolation is based on the assumption that the corresponding values in the two columns change proportionally. That is, the ratio of any two differences in one column equals the ratio of the corresponding differences in the other column. Thus,

$$\frac{X - 2.6533}{2.9178 - 2.6533} = \frac{0.052 - 0.050}{0.055 - 0.050}$$

The above equation is solved for X, giving $X = 2.7591$ as an approximate value of $(1.052)^{20}$. Hence $S = 1000 \times 2.7591 = \$2759.10$. The correct value to the nearest cent when computed by a more accurate method is $S = \$2756.22$.

In actual practice, the computer seldom bothers to set up the proportionality equation as was done in the example but uses only the differences involved. If we denote by c the correction to be applied to the tabular entry 2.6533, that is, the difference between X and 2.6533, and write down the other differences involved alongside the interpolation table as shown, then the proportionality equation takes the simple form

$$\frac{c}{0.2645} = \frac{0.002}{0.005}$$

This gives $c = 0.1058$ and $X = 2.6533 + c = 2.7591$ as before.

When an approximating method is used, it is important to know how accurate the result is. In Chap. 11, approximating methods and the corresponding errors are discussed in more detail. It is shown in

Chap. 11 that if $(1 + i)^n$ is evaluated by interpolating between the entries for i_1 and i_2, where i_1 is less than i_2, the value obtained is too large but the error is less than

$$E(i) = \frac{1}{4}[n(1 + i_2)^{n-1}(i_2 - i_1) - (1 + i_2)^n + (1 + i_1)^n]$$

If this error function is evaluated using the data of Example 3, we get 0.003 as an upper limit on the error. Thus, the error in S is less than $3. It is interesting to note that the error is actually $2.88, so that the error function gives a very satisfactory limit in this case.

d. When compound-amount tables are not available or do not apply, logarithms can be used to find S. Theoretically the logarithmic solution is exact, but actually the accuracy is limited to the accuracy of the table of mantissas used. If interpolation is used, the accuracy of logarithmic computation is usually to the same number of digits as the table used. That is, with six-place mantissas, the first five digits in the answer will be correct and the sixth, obtained by interpolation, is nearly always correct.

The first two pages of Table 15 contain seven-place mantissas for the numbers 10,000 through 11,009. This includes all numbers of the form $1 + i$ for all values of i up to and including 10.09 percent. The rest of Table 15 contains six-place mantissas for the numbers 1000 through 9999. The seven-place mantissas should always be used when log $(1 + i)$ is involved, not only for added accuracy but also because an additional digit is obtained without interpolation.

Example 4 Solve the preceding example by logarithms.
Solution Applying logarithms to the equation $S = 1000(1.052)^{20}$ gives

log S = log 1000 + 20 log 1.052

The mantissas of the numbers in the right-hand member of the equation are found in Table 15, and we have

log S = 3.000000 + (20 × 0.0220157) = 3.440314

Using Table 15 we next find the antilogarithm of the mantissa 0.440314. Interpolating, we get 275622; hence S = $2756.22. When seven-place mantissas are used, this result is found to be correct.

e. One more method of evaluating $(1 + i)^n$ will be described. Using the binomial expansion, we have

$$(1 + i)^n = 1 + \frac{ni}{1} + \frac{n(n-1)i^2}{1 \times 2} + \frac{n(n-1)(n-2)i^3}{1 \times 2 \times 3} + \cdots$$

To compute each term of this sum independently would repeat many multiplications unnecessarily. We can avoid this in the following manner.   We may write

$$(1 + i)^n = T_0 + T_1 + T_2 + \cdots + T_k + T_{k+1} + \cdots + T_n$$

where $T_0 = 1$, $T_1 = \dfrac{n}{1} i$, $T_2 = \dfrac{n(n-1)}{1 \times 2} i^2$, . . . , and in general

$$T_k = \frac{n(n-1)(n-2) \cdots (n-k+1)}{1 \times 2 \times 3 \cdots k} i^k$$

$$\text{for } k = 1, 2, \ldots, n$$

Inspection of the general term shows that successive terms may be computed from the preceding term and the relation

$$T_{k+1} = \frac{(n-k)i}{k+1} T_k$$

As soon as a new term is computed it is added to the sum of the preceding ones, giving a sequence of approximations each closer to the true value of $(1 + i)^n$ than the preceding one.   The number of terms to use will depend upon the desired accuracy and may be determined in the following way.   It can be shown that as soon as k is large enough so that

$$\frac{n-k}{k+1} i \text{ is less than } \frac{1}{2}$$

then the error due to omitting the remaining terms is less than the last term used.   An example will illustrate.

Example 5   Accumulate \$400 at $j_4 = 4.8\%$ for 5 years.
Solution   The binomial expansion will be used to evaluate the accumulation factor $(1.012)^{20}$.   Proceeding as just described we get

$$T_0 = 1 \qquad\qquad\qquad\qquad S_0 = 1$$

$$T_1 = \frac{20 \times 0.012}{1} T_0 = 0.24 \qquad\qquad S_1 = 1.24$$

$$T_2 = \frac{19 \times 0.012}{2} T_1 = 0.02736 \qquad S_2 = 1.26736$$

$$T_3 = \frac{18 \times 0.012}{3} T_2 = 0.00197 \qquad S_3 = 1.26933$$

$$T_4 = \frac{17 \times 0.012}{4} T_3 = 0.00010 \qquad S_4 = 1.26943$$

$$T_5 = \frac{16 \times 0.012}{5} T_4 = 0.000004 \qquad S_5 = 1.269434$$

According to the accuracy statement preceding this example, the sum of all the remaining terms will be less than 0.000004 and therefore using S_5 as an approximation for $(1.012)^{20}$ will give an answer accurate to the nearest cent.   Thus

$$S = 400 \times 1.269434 = \$507.77$$

Obviously, using the compound-amount tables is the simplest way of finding the value of the accumulation factor. However, such tables are not always at hand or do not always contain the necessary entries; thus it is desirable to master several of the methods discussed.

EXERCISE 5

Find the compound amount in the following problems by use of Table 8:

Problem	Principal	Nominal rate	Frequency of conversion	Time
1	$ 1,000	6%	Annually	6 years
2	$ 700	5%	Semiannually	8 years
3	$ 2,500	4½%	Quarterly	5 years 3 months
4	$ 112.50	7%	Monthly	15 years 7 months
5	$ 1,750	3%	Annually	12 years
6	$ 105	5½%	Semiannually	4 years 6 months
7	$20,000	6%	Quarterly	3 years 9 months
8	$ 1,250	5½%	Quarterly	12 years 9 months

Compute the value of $(1 + i)^n$ accurate to the nearest six decimal places using Table 8 and the laws of exponents:

9. $j_4 = 3\%$, time = 55 years.

10. $j_{12} = 6\%$, time = 30 years.

11. $j_{12} = 4\%$, time = 20 years.

12. $j_4 = 3\frac{1}{2}\%$, time = 60 years.

★Compute the value of $(1 + i)^n$ accurate to six decimal places by means of the binomial theorem:

13. $j_4 = 3.2\%$, time = 6 years.

14. $j_{12} = 4.8\%$, time = 5 years.

15. $j_{12} = 2.4\%$, time = 4 years 2 months.

Compute the value of $(1 + i)^n$ to four decimal places by interpolation:

16. $j_2 = 5.4\%$, time = 6 years.

17. $j_4 = 3.6\%$, time = 3 years 3 months.

18. $j_4 = 3.2\%$, time = 6 years.

19. $j_{12} = 4.8\%$, time = 5 years.

★**20.** $j_{52} = 2.6\%$, time = 2 years 6 months. (*Hint:* Use $i = 0$ as one of the rates.)

Find the compound amount in the following examples by logarithms:

21. $P = \$785$, $j_2 = 5.6\%$, time = 15 years.

22. $P = \$1250$, $j_4 = 3.92\%$, time = 10 years.

23. $P = \$999.95$, $j_{12} = 12.18\%$, time = 3 years.

24. $P = \$2995$, $j_{12} = 6.72\%$, time = 4 years.

Solve the remaining problems by any method which will give the answer accurately to the nearest cent.

25. Mr. Rose borrowed \$500 at $j_{12} = 4\%$ three years ago.   If no interest has been paid, how much will it require to repay the loan today?

26. How much will \$450 amount to at $j_1 = 8.5\%$ in 10 years?

27. How much will \$37.50 amount to at the end of 10 years if invested at $j_1 = 2.92\%$?

★28. Compute an upper limit for the interpolation error in Prob. 17.

★29. Compute an upper limit for the interpolation error in Prob. 19.

12 PRESENT VALUE AND COMPOUND DISCOUNT

Frequently it is necessary to know what principal P invested now at a given interest rate will accumulate to a specified amount S at some later date.   Under these conditions, P is called the **present value** of S.   Stated differently, *the present value P on a given date of a sum S due at a later date is that principal which if invested on the given date at the given interest rate will amount to S on the date that S is due.*   The difference $S - P$ may be thought of as **compound discount** on S, and the process of finding present value is called **discounting.**   Compound discount is practically always found by using an interest rate, although it need not be, and discounting at a compound discount rate will not be considered here.

Computing present value (or discounting S) means merely solving Eq. (1) for P when S, i, and n are given.   Equation (1) solved for P gives

$$P = \frac{S}{(1 + i)^n}$$

and the methods of computing $(1 + i)^n$ discussed in the preceding section could be used here.   However, it is desirable to avoid long division whenever possible, and this can always be done in numerical computations if a table of reciprocals is available.   To illustrate, multiplying by 0.5 gives the same result as dividing by 2; similarly, multiplying by 0.08 gives the same result as dividing by 12.5.   In fact, every number except zero has a reciprocal, obtained by dividing it into 1, which has the property that multiplying by the reciprocal gives the same result as dividing by the given number.

Table 9 is a table of reciprocal values of the numbers in Table 8. For example, Table 8 gives $(1.05)^{10} = 1.62889463$, whereas Table 9 gives $(1.05)^{-10} = 1/(1.05)^{10} = 0.61391325$, and multiplying by 0.61391325 gives the same result as dividing by 1.62889463.

When reciprocal tables are available, Eq. (1) is usually written in the form

$$P = S(1 + i)^{-n} \tag{2}$$

for discounting purposes.

Example 1   Find the present value of $10,000 due in 5 years if the interest rate is $j_2 = 5\%$.

Solution   We have S = $10,000, i = 0.025, and n = 10, so that

$$P = 10{,}000(1.025)^{-10}$$

From Table 9 we find that $(1.025)^{-10} = 0.78119840$, and hence

$$P = 10{,}000 \times 0.78119840 = \$7{,}811.98$$

When n is beyond the range of values given in Table 9, the law of exponents used in Example 2 of the preceding section may be used in an analogous manner here.

Example 2   Find the value of the discount factor $(1.01)^{-250}$.

Solution   We write

$$(1.01)^{-250} = (1.01)^{-150} \times (1.01)^{-100}$$

Table 9 gives the values of the factors on the right, hence

$$(1.01)^{-250} = 0.22479877 \times 0.36971121 = 0.08311063$$

The "bobtailed" method of multiplication outlined in Appendix A will greatly reduce the amount of work when multiplications of the above type are necessary.

When the interest rate is not in Table 9, we resort to interpolation if an approximate solution is adequate or use logarithms if a more exact solution is desired. The accuracy of a logarithmic solution depends upon the extensiveness of the logarithmic table used. Table 15 will, in general, give six-digit accuracy.

It is also possible to evaluate the discount factor by using the binomial expansion given in the preceding section. It can be shown that this expansion holds for all values of n, positive, negative, or fractional, as long as i is less than 100 percent.

Example 3   Find the present value of $1200 due in 5 years if interest is at (4.4%, m = 2).

Solution 1 S = $1200, i = 0.022, and n = 10, so that

$$P = 1200(1.022)^{-10}$$

Applying logarithms,

$$\log P = \log 1200 - 10 \log 1.022$$

Using Table 15, we get

$$\log P = 3.079181 - 10 \times 0.0094509 = 2.984672$$

Hence P = $965.32, correct to the nearest cent.

Solution 2 (*by interpolation*)   From Table 9 we obtain values of the discount factor for rates on either side of 0.022 and record as below:

$$
.0025 \left\{ .002 \left\{ \begin{array}{c|c} i & (1+i)^{-10} \\ \hline .02 & .82035 \\ \hline .022 & X \\ \hline .0225 & .80051 \end{array} \right\} c \right\} .01984
$$

The proportionality equation is

$$
\frac{c}{0.01984} = \frac{0.002}{0.0025}
$$

We get $c = 0.01587$, $X = 0.82035 - 0.01587$ (note that the correction is subtracted, since the tabular values are decreasing) $= 0.80448$, and finally,

$$
P = 1200 \times 0.80448 = \$965.38
$$

The error is 6 cents.

When interpolation is used, an upper limit for the error is highly desirable. In Chap. 11, it is shown that when the discount factor is evaluated by interpolating between the entries for i_1 and i_2, where i_1 is the smaller rate, the value obtained is too large but the error is less than

$$
E(i) = \frac{1}{4} \left[n(i_2 - i_1)(1 + i_1)^{-n-1} + (1 + i_2)^{-n} - (1 + i_1)^{-n} \right]
$$

If this error function is evaluated using the data of the example above, we find that the error in the discount factor cannot exceed 0.000067, and hence the error in P cannot exceed 8 cents.   Actually, the error is 6 cents.

EXERCISE 6

Find the present value in the following problems by use of Table 9:

Problem	Amount	Nominal rate	Frequency of conversion	Time
1	$ 300	6%	Semiannually	9 years
2	$ 1,500	4½%	Annually	7 years
3	$ 660	3½%	Quarterly	4 years 6 months
4	$ 1,250	3½%	Monthly	4 years 2 months
5	$ 8,500	4%	Monthly	6 years 3 months
6	$ 2,000	4½%	Quarterly	12 years 3 months
7	$10,000	3%	Monthly	5 years 5 months

Find the value of $(1 + i)^{-n}$ accurate to five decimal places, using Table 9 and the laws of exponents:

8. $j_{12} = 3\%$, time = 20 years.

9. $j_{12} = 6\%$, time = 25 years.

10. $j_4 = 5\%$, time = 30 years.

11. $j_2 = 7\%$, time = 55 years.

Find the value of P, using logarithms:

12. $S = \$2450$, $j_1 = 3.2\%$, time = 12 years.

13. $S = \$900$, $j_4 = 6.2\%$, time = 12 years 6 months.

14. $S = \$1225$, $j_{12} = 4.8\%$, time = 5 years.

15. $S = \$1750$, $j_{12} = 5.4\%$, time = 15 years.

Find the approximate value of P, using interpolation:

16. $S = \$2000$, $j_1 = 5\frac{1}{4}\%$, time = 10 years.

17. $S = \$1500$, $j_4 = 6\frac{1}{2}\%$, time = 7 years 6 months.

18. $S = \$800$, $j_{12} = 4.8\%$, time = 4 years 2 months.

★19. Find the value of $(1.003)^{-10}$ to five-decimal-place accuracy using the binomial theorem.

★20. Use the binomial theorem to find the value of $(1.004)^{-25}$ to four-decimal-place accuracy.

Solve the remaining problems, accurate to the nearest cent, by the best method available:

21. What sum will amount to $1000 in 10 years at $j_4 = 5\frac{1}{2}\%$?

22. On his sixteenth birthday a boy receives $5000 as the result of an investment his father made on the day he was born. How large was the investment if it earned interest at $j_2 = 3\frac{1}{2}\%$?

23. Discount $2500 for 25 years at $j_{12} = 6.6\%$.

24. A cash prize was invested 100 years ago at $j_1 = 4\%$ for the first solution of a problem which still remains unsolved. What was the original prize if the fund now contains $5050.50?

25. What sum of money invested 100 years ago at $j_1 = 7.15\%$ would amount to $1000 today?

13 EQUIVALENT RATES

It has been seen that the yearly nominal rate is meaningless until the frequency of conversion is specified. Below is given the amount to which $10,000 will accumulate in 1 year at a 6 percent nominal rate converted with different frequencies:

$m = 1$	$m = 2$	$m = 4$	$m = 12$
10,600.00	10,609.00	10,613.64	10,616.78

The table shows clearly why it is essential to specify the frequency of conversion. Since it is often desirable to know the total yearly growth of each unit of original principal, a new definition is next introduced.

The **yearly effective rate** *r corresponding to a given nominal rate j converted m times per year is the total amount of interest earned per year for each unit of principal at the beginning of the year.*

From the table above, the yearly effective rate corresponding to $j_1 = 6$ percent is 6 percent; for $j_2 = 6$ percent, the yearly effective rate is 6.09 percent; and for $j_{12} = 6$ percent, the yearly effective rate is 6.1678 percent.

It follows readily that the yearly effective rate, converted annually, will give the same compound amount at the end of any number of years as would be obtained by using the corresponding nominal rate compounded m times per year. Thus, \$1000 will earn the same amount of interest in 10 years at $j_1 = 6.09$ percent as at $j_2 = 6$ percent.

To find the yearly effective rate corresponding to a given nominal rate converted with a given frequency, it is sufficient to accumulate some principal for one year at each rate and equate the resulting amounts.

Example 1 What is the yearly effective rate corresponding to 8%, $m = 4$?
Solution Let r be the corresponding yearly effective rate. Then \$1 at rate r for 1 year will amount to $1 + r$, and \$1 at $j_4 = 0.08$ for 1 year will amount to $(1.02)^4$. Equating these amounts we have

$$1 + r = (1.02)^4 = 1.08243216 \qquad \text{(Table 8)}$$

and $r = 0.08243216$.

A general relationship between r, j, and m can be obtained exactly as above by finding the amount which \$1 will accumulate in 1 year at each rate and equating the results. Thus, the amount which \$1 will accumulate in 1 year at the effective rate r is $1 + r$, and the amount which \$1 will accumulate in 1 year at rate j, converted m times per year, is $(1 + i)^m$, where $i = j/m$. Equating these amounts gives

$$1 + r = (1 + i)^m \qquad \text{where} \qquad i = \frac{j}{m} \tag{3}$$

Equation (3) contains three quantities, so that if any two are known, the third can be found.

Example 2 Find the nominal rate that converted quarterly corresponds to an effective rate of 6%.
Solution Here $r = 0.06$, $m = 4$, and j is to be determined. Equating the amounts at the end of 1 year at each rate [or using Eq. (3)] gives

$$1.06 = (1 + i)^4 \qquad \text{where } i = \frac{j}{4}$$

Extracting the fourth root of each member of the above equation gives

$$1 + i = (1.06)^{1/4}$$

The fourth root of 1.06 can be extracted by logarithms; or if a table such as Table 3 is available, it can be looked up.   Table 3 gives the fourth root of 1.06 as 1.01467385. Hence $i = 0.01467385$, and $j = 4i = 0.0586954$.

*Any two interest rates, whether nominal or effective rates, that give the same compound amounts at the end of the year are called yearly equivalent or, more briefly, **equivalent**.* Thus a nominal rate converted monthly and a (different) nominal rate converted quarterly are equivalent, or *correspond*, if they produce the same amounts at the end of the year. The method of finding an equivalent rate when sufficient data are given is the same as above.

Example 3   What nominal rate converted monthly corresponds to $j_4 = 8\%$?
Solution   Let $(j, m = 12)$ be the desired rate, and let $i = j/12$. Equating the amounts which \$1 will accumulate in 1 year at each rate gives

$$(1 + i)^{12} = (1.02)^4$$

Extracting the twelfth root of each member of the above equation gives

$$1 + i = (1.02)^{1/3} = 1.00662271 \qquad \text{(Table 3)}$$

Hence $i = 0.00662271$, and $j = 12i = 0.07947252$, which should be rounded off to seven decimal places, since multiplying by 12 will in general reduce the accuracy of the result by one decimal place.

Example 4   What nominal rate converted quarterly is equivalent to $j_{12} = 8\%$?
Solution   Let $(j, m = 4)$ be the desired rate, and let $i = j/4$. Equating the amounts that \$1 will accumulate in 1 year at each rate gives

$$(1 + i)^4 = \left(1 + \frac{0.02}{3}\right)^{12}$$

Extracting the fourth root of both sides of the above equation gives

$$1 + i = \left(1 + \frac{0.02}{3}\right)^3 = 1.02013363 \qquad \text{(Table 8)}$$

Thus $i = 0.02013363$ per quarter, and $j = 4i = 0.08053452$.

The importance of equivalent rates cannot be overemphasized. Since equivalent rates give the same compound amounts on any principal at the end of any number of years, the following principle is logically sound: *In the mathematics of finance, it is always permissible to replace the given interest rate by an equivalent one.* The importance of this principle will become apparent in later work. For example, if the interest rate for a certain problem is $j_2 = 8$ percent, it is permissible to replace this rate by $j_1 = 8.16$ percent.

EXERCISE 7

Find the yearly effective rate, to the nearest hundredth percent, equivalent to the following rates:

1. $j_2 = 6\%$.   **2.** $j_4 = 3\%$.   **3.** $j_{12} = 7\%$.

4. $j_4 = 2\%$.   **5.** $j_2 = 3\frac{1}{2}\%$.   **6.** $j_{12} = 3\frac{1}{2}\%$.

7. $j_4 = 4\frac{1}{2}\%$.   **8.** $j_2 = 2\frac{1}{4}\%$.   **9.** $j_{12} = 6\%$.

Find the nominal rate, to the nearest hundredth percent, equivalent to the given yearly effective rate:

10. $r = 6\%$. Find j_4.   **11.** $r = 5\%$. Find j_4.

12. $r = 7\%$. Find j_{12}.   **13.** $r = 5\frac{1}{2}\%$. Find j_2.

14. $r = 4\%$. Find j_4.   **15.** $r = 4\frac{1}{2}\%$. Find j_{12}.

16. $r = 3\frac{1}{2}\%$. Find j_2.   **17.** $r = 3\%$. Find j_4.

Find the nominal rate equivalent to the given nominal rate:

18. $j_2 = 6\%$. Find j_4.   **19.** $j_4 = 6\%$. Find j_{12}.

20. $j_4 = 5\%$. Find j_2.   **21.** $j_{12} = 4\%$. Find j_4.

22. $j_{12} = 3\frac{1}{2}\%$. Find j_2.   **23.** $j_4 = 3\%$. Find j_2.

24. $j_2 = 5\frac{1}{2}\%$. Find j_{12}.   **25.** $j_2 = 7\%$. Find j_{12}.

In the remaining problems use the tables if they apply; otherwise use logarithms:

26. Find the yearly effective rate corresponding to $1\frac{1}{2}\%$, converted monthly.

27. Find the yearly effective rate corresponding to $4\frac{1}{2}\%$, converted monthly.

28. A sum of money is invested at $j_4 = 5\%$ for one year. What rate j_{12} would accumulate the same amount at the end of the year?

29. \$1000 is invested for 5 years at $j_{12} = 5\%$. What rate j_4 would accumulate the same amount in the same time?

30. Money is invested at $j_{12} = 2\%$ for 6 months. What rate j_4 would accumulate the same amount in the same time?

14 COMPOUND AMOUNT AND PRESENT VALUE FOR A FRACTIONAL PERIOD OF TIME

A statement such as "compound interest at $j_1 = 6$ percent for $2\frac{1}{2}$ years" does not have meaning at present, and an agreement must be made regarding how such cases are to be treated. The logical solution is to replace the given rate by an *equivalent rate* which is compounded with a frequency that makes the time involved a whole number of periods, then accumulating in the usual way with this new rate. Thus in the case just mentioned, $j_1 = 6$ percent could be replaced by an equivalent rate compounded monthly, quarterly, or semiannually. The time would then be an integral number of periods, and Eq. (1) would apply. An example will illustrate this technique.

Example 1 Find the compound amount if $1000 is accumulated for 15 years 3 months at $j_2 = 6\%$.

Solution The first step is to replace the rate $j_2 = 6\%$ by a rate compounded quarterly, since the time involved is an integer when expressed as quarters. So let i be the interest rate per quarter that is equivalent to $j_2 = 6\%$. Then

$$(1 + i)^4 = (1.03)^2 \quad \text{and} \quad 1 + i = (1.03)^{\frac{1}{2}}$$

Accumulating $1000 for 15 years 3 months at rate i gives

$$S = 1000(1 + i)^{61}$$

Substituting for $1 + i$ its value from the preceding equation gives

$$S = 1000[(1.03)^{\frac{1}{2}}]^{61} = 1000(1.03)^{30\frac{1}{2}} = 1000(1.03)^{30}(1.03)^{\frac{1}{2}}$$
$$= 1000 \times 2.42726247 \times 1.01488916 \qquad \text{(Tables 8 and 3)}$$
$$= 2463.40$$

The final result, $S = 1000(1.03)^{30\frac{1}{2}}$, could have been obtained by using $i = 0.03$ and $n = 30\frac{1}{2}$ in Eq. (1), so it appears that the compound-interest formula holds whether n is an integer or not.

The preceding example gives a logical foundation for the following rule: *The* **exact** **(or theoretical)** **method** *of accumulating or discounting consists of using the fundamental Eq.* (1) *or* (2) *regardless of whether the time is an integral number of periods or not.* It can be shown that the exact rule always gives the same result as that obtained by first replacing the given interest rate by an equivalent rate compounded with a frequency that would make the time an integral number of periods, then accumulating or discounting at this new rate. Thus it is unnecessary to *actually find* an equivalent rate, since the *final result* is the same as that obtained by merely substituting the original data into the appropriate Eq. (1) or (2).

Example 2 Using the exact method, find the present value of $600 due in 7 years 3 months at $j_1 = 5\%$.

Solution We have $S = 600$, $i = 0.05$, $n = 7\frac{1}{4}$, and

$$P = 600(1.05)^{-7\frac{1}{4}} = 600(1.05)^{-7}(1.05)^{-\frac{1}{4}}$$
$$= 600 \times 0.71068133 \times 0.98787655 \qquad \text{(Tables 9 and 4)}$$
$$= \$421.24$$

Because of the computational difficulties arising when irregular periods of time are encountered, approximate methods are frequently used for accumulating and discounting. Now it should be clear that any method that gives a result close to the true value is an approximating method. Consequently there is not one way, but usually numerous ways, of approximating a result. Finally, the choice between two approximating methods should be based largely upon the degree of accuracy and to some extent upon the ease of computation. Several approximating methods will now be illustrated by examples.

Example 3 Find an approximate answer for Example 1 (*a*) by using simple interest for the last 3 months (*b*) by using Table 8 and interpolation.
Solution a The $1000 is first accumulated for 15 years at $j_2 = 6\%$. Thus

$$S = 1000(1.03)^{30} = 2427.26$$

is the amount at the end of 15 years. This amount now becomes the new principal to be accumulated for 3 more months at simple interest. Using $S = P(1 + rt)$ gives

$$S = 2427.26\left(1 + 0.06 \times \frac{1}{4}\right) = 2427.26 \times 1.015 = \$2463.67$$

Solution b Here the problem is to approximate $(1.03)^{30\frac{1}{2}}$ by interpolation. Table 8 is used to get the table shown below.

$$1\left\{\tfrac{1}{2}\left\{\begin{array}{c|c} n & (1.03)^n \\ \hline 30 & 2.42726 \\ \hline 30\frac{1}{2} & ? \\ \hline 31 & 2.50008 \end{array}\right\}c\right\}0.07282$$

The proportionality equation is

$$\frac{c}{0.07282} = \frac{\frac{1}{2}}{1}$$

Thus $c = 0.03641$ and $(1.03)^{30\frac{1}{2}}$ is approximately equal to

$$2.42726 + 0.03641 = 2.46367$$

and finally

$$S = 1000 \times 2.46367 = \$2463.67$$

The example just solved illustrates several important facts. First, the answer obtained by interpolation is always the same as the one obtained by using simple interest for the fractional part of the interest period. It should also be observed that if the two computations in Solution *a* are merely indicated, the result is

$$S = 1000(1.03)^{30}(1.015)$$

Clearly the final result will be the same if the order of the two interest factors is reversed, giving

$$S = 1000(1.015)(1.03)^{30}$$

Consequently it does not matter whether the original principal is accumulated first at compound interest and then at simple interest, or vice versa; the result is the same. Finally, note that the answer obtained by the approximate method is slightly larger than the exact answer, and this is true in general.

Example 4 Find an approximate answer for Example 2 by interpolation.
Solution As in Example 2, we have $P = 600(1.05)^{-7\frac{1}{4}}$ and the problem is to approximate $(1.05)^{-7\frac{1}{4}}$. Table 9 is used to set up the interpolation table shown below.

	n	$(1.05)^{-n}$	
	7	.71068	
	$7\frac{1}{4}$	?	
	8	.67684	

(with brace grouping: $\frac{1}{4}$ and 1 on the left, c and .03384 on the right)

The proportionality equation is

$$\frac{c}{0.03384} = \frac{\frac{1}{4}}{1}$$

Thus $c = 0.00846$, and $(1.05)^{-7\frac{1}{4}}$ is approximately equal to

$$0.71068 - 0.00846 = 0.70222$$

The correction is subtracted since the discount factor decreases as n increases. Finally

$$P = 600 \times 0.70222 = \$421.33 \text{ approx.}$$

A comparison with Example 2 shows that this approximate answer is 9 cents larger than the exact answer.

Since using simple interest for the fractional part of the interest period gives the same result as interpolation when accumulating, the question arises: Is this also true when discounting? Suppose a sum of money is to be discounted $n + f$ interest periods, where n is an integer and f is a fraction between 0 and 1. Simple interest can be used in two different ways. (*a*) S can be accumulated at simple interest forward to the next interest period and then discounted $n + 1$ periods, and this is the usual procedure. Or (*b*), S can be discounted n periods, and then simple discount, as described in Sec. 7, Chap. 1, used for the fractional part of the period. An example will illustrate these procedures.

Example 5 Compute an approximate answer for Example 2 using simple interest in the following ways: (*a*) Accumulate S for 9 months at simple interest, then discount this amount for 8 years.   (*b*) Discount S for 7 years, then use simple discount for the remaining 3 months.

Solution a   The first step gives

$$S = 600\left(1 + 0.05 \times \frac{3}{4}\right) = 600 \times 1.0375 = 622.50$$

as the value 8 years from the present.   This amount is now discounted 8 years.

$$P = 622.50(1.05)^{-8} = 622.50 \times 0.67683936 = \$421.33$$

Solution b S is first discounted for 7 years, giving

$$P = 600(1.05)^{-7} = 600 \times 0.71068133 = 426.44$$

as the value 3 months from the present.   Using $P = S/(1 + rt)$ for the remaining 3 months gives the final result

$$P = \frac{426.41}{1 + 0.05 \times \frac{1}{4}} = \frac{426.41}{1.0125} = \$421.15$$

Note that the answer in Solution *a* is the same as that obtained in Example 4 by interpolation.   Also observe that the two steps can be combined into one equation:

$$P = S(1 + rt)(1 + i)^{-n}$$

which can be rearranged into

$$P = S(1 + i)^{-n}(1 + rt)$$

Thus, as in Example 3, it does not matter whether the simple interest accumulation is done before or after the discounting.   Finally, note that the fractional time periods in (*a*) and (*b*) are not the same, but are complementary.

When simple interest is used as in Solution *a* of Examples 3 and 5, the procedure is known as the **practical method** and may be formulated as follows: *To find by the practical method the amount or present value when a fractional period of time is involved, first, accumulate at simple interest the given sum from the given date to the nearest later date that is an integral number of periods from the desired date.   Then accumulate or discount this new sum to the desired date.*

The practical method always gives a result somewhat larger than that obtained by the exact method.   Also, the practical method always gives the same result as that obtained by interpolating in Table 8 or 9. It is probably due to this fact that the practical method has become the most widely used method when irregular periods of time are involved.

Concerning the two solutions to Example 5, it can be shown that they usually differ from the exact answer by about the same amount but on opposite sides.   Solution *b* gives a result too small, whereas Solution *a*, the practical method, gives a result too large.   While Solution *a* is more commonly employed, there can be no logical objection to Solution

b, and indeed it can be shown that in the majority of cases it gives a result closer to the exact answer than is obtained by the practical method.

The exact method is, of course, the proper one to use. However, when irregular periods of time are encountered, one of the foregoing approximating methods will usually be employed.

EXERCISE 8

Find the compound amount by the exact method:

1. $P = \$1000$, $j_2 = 7\%$, time = 7 years 1 month.
2. $P = \$200$, $j_4 = 4\%$, time = 6 years 1 month.
3. $P = \$5000$, $j_1 = 5\%$, time = 5 years 5 months.
4. $P = \$3000$, $j_2 = 3\frac{1}{2}\%$, time = 8 years 8 months.
5. $P = \$4000$, $j_4 = 6\%$, time = 9 years 11 months.
6. $P = \$2500$, $j_1 = 4\frac{1}{2}\%$, time = 2 years 9 months.

Find the present value by the exact method:

7. $S = \$1000$, $j_1 = 3\frac{1}{2}\%$, time = 4 years 6 months.
8. $S = \$2500$, $j_2 = 5\%$, time = 3 years 7 months.
9. $S = \$4000$, $j_4 = 3\%$, time = 10 years 4 months.
10. $S = \$5500$, $j_1 = 4\%$, time = 12 years 3 months.
11. $S = \$7000$, $j_2 = 2\frac{1}{2}\%$, time = 8 years 10 months.
12. $S = \$10,000$, $j_4 = 4\frac{1}{2}\%$, time = 9 years 5 months.

Find the compound amount by the practical method:

13. $P = \$1000$, $j_1 = 2\%$, time = 6 years 4 months.
14. $P = \$2000$, $j_2 = 6\%$, time = 4 years 4 months.
15. $P = \$1500$, $j_4 = 5\frac{1}{2}\%$, time = 2 years 7 months.
16. $P = \$10,000$, $j_1 = 3\%$, time = 7 years 9 months.

Find the present value by the practical method:

17. $S = \$10,000$, $j_2 = 4\%$, time = 4 years 3 months.
18. $S = \$3500$, $j_4 = 3\%$, time = 6 years 8 months.
19. $S = \$1000$, $j_1 = 5\frac{1}{2}\%$, time = 7 years 8 months.
20. $S = \$2000$, $j_2 = 5\%$, time = 5 years 4 months.

Solve the following problems using interpolation:

21. $P = \$8000$, $j_1 = 3\%$, time = 10 years 2 months.   Find S.
22. $P = \$5000$, $j_2 = 2\frac{1}{2}\%$, time = 20 years 5 months.   Find S.
23. $S = \$1000$, $j_4 = 4\frac{1}{2}\%$, time = 5 years 2 months.   Find P.
24. $S = \$2500$, $j_4 = 2\%$, time = 3 years 10 months.   Find P.

25. Solve Prob. 5 by both the practical method and interpolation, and compare the results with the answer to Prob. 5.
26. Solve Prob. 9 by both the practical method and interpolation, and compare the results with the answer to Prob. 9.
27. Solve Prob. 9 by the two methods used in the illustrative Example 5, and compare the results with the answer to Prob. 9.

15 DETERMINING THE INTEREST RATE

When S, P, and n are known, the interest rate is determined and can be found by substituting the known values into either Eq. (1) or (2) and solving for i. A logarithmic solution, though theoretically exact, is limited to the accuracy of the tables used; with Table 15, accuracy to the nearest thousandth percent is possible.   If interpolation is used, accuracy to the nearest hundredth percent is possible for the smaller rates and $\frac{1}{20}$ percent accuracy holds throughout the entire table.

Example Find the nominal rate, converted semiannually, at which $1500 will amount to $2400 in 9 years.
Solution 1 $S = 2400$, $P = 1500$, and $n = 18$. Let i be the interest rate per 6 months, then

$$1500(1 + i)^{18} = 2400$$

Taking logarithms of both members of the above equation gives

$$\log 1500 + 18 \log (1 + i) = \log 2400$$

Substituting the numerical values of $\log 1500$ and $\log 2400$ gives

$$3.176091 + 18 \log (1 + i) = 3.380211$$

Solving for $\log (1 + i)$ gives

$$\log (1 + i) = \frac{3.380211 - 3.176091}{18} = 0.0113400$$

From the first page of Table 15 we next find mantissas on either side of 0.0113400 and interpolate, getting $1 + i = 1.026455$, where only the last digit is in doubt. Consequently, $i = 0.026455$, and $j = 2i = 0.05291$.
Solution 2 (*by interpolation*)   Solve the first equation for $(1 + i)^{18}$.   Thus

$$(1 + i)^{18} = \frac{2400}{1500} = 1.60$$

From Table 8 find two consecutive rates that give values slightly larger and smaller than 1.60, and record as below.

	$(1 + i)^{18}$	i	j_2
	1.62957	0.0275	0.055
	1.60000	i	j
	1.55966	0.0250	0.050

$$0.06991 \left\{ 0.04034 \left\{ \quad\quad\quad\quad\quad\quad\quad\quad \right\} c \right\} 0.005$$

It should be observed that the interpolation table above contains a column that gives the yearly nominal rates corresponding to the given semiannual rates, and hence we can interpolate directly for j_2.   The proportionality equation is

$$\frac{c}{0.005} = \frac{0.04034}{0.06991}$$

Whence $c = 0.00289$, and $j_2 = 0.05289$.

It is shown in Chap. 11 that when i is found by interpolating between $(1 + i_1)^n$ and $(1 + i_2)^n$, where $i_1 < i_2$, the value obtained is too small, but the error is less than

$$E(i) = \frac{1}{4}\left[\frac{(1 + i_2)^n - (1 + i_1)^n}{n(1 + i_1)^{n-1}} - i_2 + i_1\right]$$

If this error function is evaluated using the data of the example, we get 0.000014 as an upper limit for the error in i, and hence the error in the interpolated value of j_2 cannot exceed $2 \times 0.000014 = 0.000028$.

It is also shown in Chap. 11 that when i is found by interpolating between $(1 + i_1)^{-n}$ and $(1 + i_2)^{-n}$, where $i_1 < i_2$, the value obtained is too large, but the error is less than

$$E(i) = \frac{1}{4}\left[\frac{(1 + i_1)^{-n} - (1 + i_2)^{-n}}{n(1 + i_2)^{-(n+1)}} - i_2 + i_1\right]$$

As a result, excellent accuracy can be had by interpolating for i in both tables, retaining six or more decimal places throughout, then averaging these results.

16 FINDING THE TIME

When S, P, and i are given, n is determined and can be found by methods similar to those used in the preceding section. Usually n will not be an integer, so the question arises whether the practical or theoretical method of accumulating (or discounting) is in effect. If the theoretical method is assumed, a logarithmic solution gives the correct value for n, whereas interpolation gives the true value for n if the practical method is in use. Since interpolation gives the correct answer when the practical method is assumed, the number of decimal places retained throughout the computations will depend upon the accuracy desired in the final result. Usually the difference in time obtained by the two methods is so small that unless large sums of money are involved, it does not matter which method of solution is used.

Example If the interest rate is $j_1 = 6\%$, how long will it take $1000 to amount to $1500?

Solution 1 If n represents the number of years, then

$$1000(1.06)^n = 1500$$

Taking logarithms, we have

$$\log 1000 + n \log 1.06 = \log 1500$$

Substituting the numerical values of the logarithms gives

$$3.000000 + n(0.0253059) = 3.176091 \qquad \text{(Table 15)}$$

Solving for n, we get

$$n = \frac{3.176091 - 3.000000}{0.0253059} = 6.9585 \text{ years}$$

or slightly over 6 years $11\frac{1}{2}$ months. This answer assumes that the theoretical method of accumulation is used.

Solution 2 If the practical method of accumulation is in effect, then the correct value of n is found by interpolation.

$$
1\left\{ c\left\{ \begin{array}{c|c}
n & (1.06)^n \\\hline
7 & 1.503630 \\
X & 1.500000 \\\hline
6 & 1.418519
\end{array}\right\} .081481 \right\} .085111
$$

The proportionality equation is

$$\frac{c}{1} = \frac{0.081481}{0.085111} = 0.95735$$

Hence the time is 6.95735 years, or 6 years 11.4882 months.

The difference in time between the two solutions is less than one-half day.

EXERCISE 9

Find the nominal rate by interpolation:

1. $P = \$5000$, $S = \$8888.72$, time $= 6$ years 5 months. Find j_{12}.
2. $P = \$2000$, $S = \$2564.86$, time $= 6$ years 3 months. Find j_4.
3. $P = \$1000$, $S = \$1600$, time $= 8$ years. Find j_2.
4. $P = \$500$, $S = \$1500$, time $= 20$ years. Find j_1.

Find the nominal rate by logarithms:

5. $P = \$1200$, $S = \$3000$, time $= 20$ years. Find j_1.
6. $P = \$375$, $S = \$1550$, time $= 25$ years. Find j_4.
7. $P = \$645.50$, $S = \$1125$, time $= 8$ years 4 months. Find j_{12}.
8. $P = \$100$, $S = \$10,000$, time $= 100$ years. Find j_2.

In the following examples find the time, assuming that the practical method is used to accumulate P to S:

9. $P = \$100$, $S = \$200$, $j_1 = 6\%$.
10. $P = \$1000$, $S = \$1300$, $j_2 = 5\%$.
11. $P = \$500$, $S = \$1300$, $j_4 = 4\frac{1}{2}\%$.
12. $P = \$2000$, $S = \$3000$, $j_{12} = 4\%$.

In the following examples find the time, assuming that the exact method is used to accumulate P to S.

13. $P = \$2250$, $S = \$4000$, $j_2 = 6\%$.
14. $P = \$118.50$, $S = \$181.50$, $j_4 = 5\%$.
15. $P = \$5425$, $S = \$8800$, $j_{12} = 5\frac{1}{2}\%$.
16. $P = \$150$, $S = \$350$, $j_1 = 3\%$.

17. A United States Bond costs $18.75 and pays $25 ten years later. What interest rate j_2 does it pay?

18. At what nominal rate j_4 will money double itself in 12 years?

19. At what nominal rate j_2 will money double itself in 15 years?

20. At a given interest rate j_2, $1000 will amount to $2500 in 20 years. What is the amount at the end of 10 years?

21. At a given interest rate j_4, $1000 will amount to $1500 at the end of 10 years. What is the amount at the end of 6 years?

The remaining examples require a knowledge of the calculus.

★22. Show that $\lim\limits_{m=\infty} (1 + j/m)^m = e^j$, where e is the natural base of logarithms. If j is the nominal rate of interest, e^j may be interpreted as the accumulation factor for 1 year with interest converted **continuously,** or instantaneously. Hence for continuous conversion, $S = Pe^{nj}$.

★23. Find the compound amount if $1000 is invested for 10 years at 6% converted continuously. Compare the result with that obtained by using $j_{12} = 6\%$. (*Hint:* Use logarithms and the fact that $e = 2.71828$.)

★24. For a fixed effective rate r, show that the corresponding j_∞, that is, $(j, m = \infty)$, is equal to $\log_e (1 + r)$. For a given r, the corresponding j_∞ is called the **force of interest.**

★25. When the nominal rate j is converted continuously, show that the instantaneous rate of change of S is equal to jS. (*Hint:* Find dS/dn.)

3
Equations of Equivalence

17 DATED VALUES

The value of a sum of money is meaningless unless the date on which it falls due is given. Clearly $1000 cash is more desirable than $2000 due in 95 years, and anyone with reasonable judgment would prefer the former. *The maturity value of an obligation together with its date of maturity is called a* **dated value.** Thus $500 due Jan. 2, 1970, is a dated value.

If two dated values are to be compared, it is necessary to decide on an interest rate for the comparison. If it is possible for any reasonable person to invest money at any time to earn 4 percent, compounded annually, we say money is worth $j_1 = 4$ percent. At this rate, $100 that is due 2 years from now and $100(1.04)^3 = \$112.49$ due 5 years from now would be considered equivalent since the $100 if collected when due and invested at $j_1 = 4$ percent would accumulate to the latter sum in the remaining 3 years. In the same way $100(1.04)^{-2} = \$92.46$ would be considered an equivalent sum at the present.

In general, dated values are compared by the following definition of equivalence: *P due on a given date is equivalent at a given compound interest rate to S due n periods later, if*

$$S = P(1 + i)^n \qquad or \qquad P = S(1 + i)^{-n}$$

Accumulating or discounting may be thought of as simply transferring a given dated value to a different date. The transferring is done in accordance with the time diagram below.

$D(1 + i)^{-n}$	D	$D(1 + i)^n$
Earlier date	Given date	Later date

The earlier and later sums are each equivalent to the dated value D.

An important and useful property of equivalent dated values is the following: **Property 1.** *At a given compound interest rate, if A is equivalent to B, and B is equivalent to C, then A is equivalent to C.*

To prove this statement we arrange the data on a time diagram as below

	A	B	C
0	n_1	n_2	n_3

where 0 represents "now" and the n's represent the number of interest conversion periods until the corresponding dates of maturity. If A is equivalent to B, then

$$B = A(1 + i)^{n_2 - n_1}$$

Similarly, if B is equivalent to C,

$$C = B(1 + i)^{n_3 - n_2}$$

Eliminating B from the two equations gives

$$C = A(1 + i)^{n_2 - n_1}(1 + i)^{n_3 - n_2} = A(1 + i)^{n_3 - n_1}$$

The final result is the condition that A be equivalent to C as was to be shown.†

This property does not hold for simple interest rates or simple discount rates, and in consequence the concept of equivalence at these rates lacks logical soundness.

Example 1 A debt of $1000 is due at the end of 10 years. If money is worth $j_1 = 5\%$, find an equivalent debt at the end of (*a*) 1 year and (*b*) 15 years.
Solution Arrange the data on a time diagram as below.

	X	1000	Y
0	1	10	15

† The fact that A, B, and C all appear to be due at future dates is not essential to the proof, as similar reasoning holds regardless of their maturity dates.

According to the definition of equivalence

$$X = 1000(1.05)^{-9} = \$644.61 \qquad \text{due at the end of 1 year}$$
$$Y = 1000(1.05)^{5} = \$1276.28 \qquad \text{due at the end of 15 years}$$

Property 1 may be illustrated by noting the equivalence of X and Y, since

$$644.61(1.05)^{14} = \$1276.28$$

Example 2   A note for $1000 with compound interest at $j_4 = 6\%$ for 3 years falls due at the end of 3 years.   What sum due at the end of 8 years is equivalent at $j_2 = 4\%$? *Solution*   The dated value of the given sum is $1000(1.015)^{12} = \$1195.62$ due at the end of 3 years.   We arrange the data on a time diagram as below:

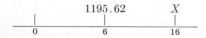

where the 6 and 16 represent the number of interest periods from the present.   When $1195.62 is transferred 10 interest periods to the right in accordance with the definition of equivalence, the result is

$$X = 1195.62(1.02)^{10} = \$1457.45 \qquad \text{due at the end of 8 years}$$

18   SETS OF DATED VALUES

The sum of a set of two or more dated values, due on different dates, has little or no meaning.   For example, suppose $1000 is due at the end of 2 years and $2000 is due at the end of 5 years.   The sum, $3000, is not associated with any date and consequently has little meaning.   However, if all the sums involved are replaced by equivalent dated values, due on the same date, the sum of these equivalent values is called **a dated value of the set.**   It will vary according to the date on which the equivalent values are summed.   The following property of the various dated values of the same set is true: **Property 2.**   *The various dated values of the same set are equivalent.*

A proof is given for a set of two dated values.   Let A and B be the two dated values due n_1 and n_2 interest periods from the present.†   Let U and V be any two dated values of the set, at t_1 and t_2 interest periods from the present.   We arrange the data on a time diagram as below.

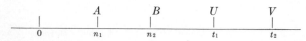

Transferring the values A and B to the time t_1 in accordance with the definition of equivalence and adding the results, we get

$$U = A(1 + i)^{t_1-n_1} + B(1 + i)^{t_1-n_2}$$

† Here, as in the preceding proof, the reasoning holds regardless of the various maturity dates.

Multiplying both sides of this equality by $(1 + i)^{t_2-t_1}$ and making obvious simplifications, we obtain

$$U(1 + i)^{t_2-t_1} = A(1 + i)^{t_2-n_1} + B(1 + i)^{t_2-n_2}$$

But the right-hand side of this equality is exactly V, so that

$$U(1 + i)^{t_2-t_1} = V$$

which is the condition that U and V be equivalent, and property 2 is true.

Example If money is worth $j_4 = 4\%$, find a single payment equivalent to the set $1000 due at the end of 2 years and $1500 due at the end of 5 years (a) at the present, (b) at the end of 2 years, and (c) at the end of 5 years.

Solution Represent the set on a time diagram as below.

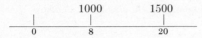

Next, compute equivalent values for both sums at the three times asked for, and arrange in tabular form as below.

Sums	At the present	At the end of 2 years	At the end of 5 years
First.....................	923.483	1000.000	1126.825
Second..................	1229.317	1331.174	1500.000
Value of the set............	2152.800	2331.174	2626.825

According to property 2, the three dated values of the set must be equivalent. This can be verified in the following manner. Place the dated values of the set on a time diagram as below.

2152.800   2331.174   2626.825

|_____|_____|
0   8   20

Since $2152.800(1.01)^8 = 2331.174$, the dated value of the set at the present is equivalent to the dated value of the set at the end of 2 years. Similarly, since

$$2331.174(1.01)^{12} = 2626.825$$

the second dated value of the set is equivalent to the third, and consequently all three dated values of the set are equivalent.

19 NONEQUIVALENT DATED VALUES

If two amounts are due on different dates, it is necessary to replace them by equivalent values on the same date for comparison purposes. Their differences will vary, depending on the date used to compare them. *In the same manner as with sums, the differences on various comparison dates will be equivalent.* The proof of this statement is similar to that of property 2 and is left as an exercise for the student.

Example   Compare the two obligations, $2000 with compound interest for 2 years at $j_4 = 5\%$ due at the end of 2 years and $1000 due at the end of 6 years if money is worth $j_2 = 6\%$, (a) at the present, (b) at the end of 2 years, and (c) at the end of 6 years.

Solution   The first dated value is $2000(1.0125)^8 = 2208.972$, due at the end of 2 years. We now arrange the maturity values on a time diagram as below.

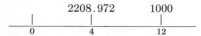

We transfer these two amounts to the three comparison dates in accordance with the definition of equivalence and arrange the results in tabular form as below.

Amounts	At the present	At the end of 2 years	At the end of 6 years
First......................	1962.643	2208.972	2798.260
Second...................	701.380	789.409	1000.000
Differences..............	1261.263	1419.563	1798.260

We can verify that these differences are equivalent, at $j_2 = 6\%$, by showing that $1261.263(1.03)^4 = 1419.563$ and $1419.563(1.03)^8 = 1798.260$.

EXERCISE 10

1. If money is worth $j_2 = 3\%$, find the dated value, due at the end of 12 years, equivalent to $2000 due at the end of 4 years.

2. If money is worth 4% effective, find the sum, due at the end of 10 years, equivalent to $1000 due at the end of 5 years.

3. What sum of money, due at the end of 4 years, is equivalent to $2500 due at the end of 9 years if money is worth $j_4 = 4\frac{1}{2}\%$?

4. If money is worth $j_2 = 5\frac{1}{2}\%$, find the sum, due at the end of 3 years, equivalent to $5000 due at the end of 10 years.

5. Find the dated value at the end of 3 years and at the end of 10 years of $1000 due at the end of 5 years if money is worth 4% effective.   Show that these sums are equivalent.

6. Find the dated value at the end of 2 years and at the end of 8 years of $2000 due at the end of 4 years if money is worth $j_2 = 3\frac{1}{2}\%$.   Show that these sums are equivalent.

7. $1000 with 10 years' interest at $j_2 = 5\%$ is due at the end of 10 years.   Find the equivalent sum, due at the end of 3 years, if money is worth 6% effective.

8. $500 with 8 years' interest at $j_4 = 4\%$ is due at the end of 5 years.   Find the equivalent sum, due at the end of 2 years, if money is worth $j_2 = 5\%$.

9. $1500 is due at the end of 3 years and $1600 is due at the end of 6 years. If money is worth $j_2 = 4\frac{1}{2}\%$, compare the debts (a) at the present and (b) at the end of 3 years. Show that the differences found in (a) and (b) are equivalent.

10. $1000 is due at the end of 4 years and $1500 is due at the end of 10 years. If money is worth $j_1 = 5\%$, compare these debts (a) at the present and (b) at the end of 4 years. Show that the differences found in (a) and (b) are equivalent.

11. If money is worth $j_4 = 3\%$, find the dated value at the end of 5 years of the set: $1000 due in 6 years and $2000 due in 10 years.

12. If money is worth $j_2 = 5\%$, find the dated value at the end of 3 years of the set: $500 due in 5 years and $800 due in 8 years.

13. If money is worth $j_2 = 4\%$, find the dated value at the end of 6 years of the set: $1000 due in 3 years and $1500 due in 8 years.

14. If money is worth $j_1 = 6\%$, find the dated value at the end of 7 years of the set: $600 due in 2 years and $900 due in 10 years.

15. Find the dated value at the present of the set: 4 obligations of $100 each due at the end of 3, 6, 9, and 12 months, if money is worth $j_4 = 4\%$.

16. Find the dated value at the end of the year of the set of obligations in the preceding problem.

17. Find the effective rate at which $1000 due now is equivalent to $2000 due at the end of 14 years.

18. Find the nominal rate, $m = 12$, for which $500 due at the end of 5 years is equivalent to $1500 due at the end of 25 years.

20 EQUIVALENT SETS OF PAYMENTS

One of the most important problems in the mathematics of finance concerns the replacing of a given set of payments, or obligations, by an equivalent set. For example, a car may be priced at $4000 cash. However, it can also be purchased for a moderate cash payment followed by a series of monthly payments.

In Sec. 18 we discussed the dated value of a set of payments or obligations. It was seen that the value of a set depended upon the interest rate used and the date on which the summing was done. It follows as a logical consequence to make the following definition: *For a given compound interest rate, two sets of payments are equivalent if the dated values of the sets, on any common date, are equal.* Thus, if the cash price of a car is $4000, any set of payments used to buy it must have a cash value (or present value) of $4000.

An equation stating that the dated values, on a common date, of two sets of payments are equal is called **an equation of equivalence** *or* **an equation of value.** The date used is called the **comparison date.** It follows from property 1 that *any date may be used as a comparison date.*

Example 1 A holds two notes signed by B, one maturing in 3 years at $1000 and the second maturing at $2000 in 8 years. A and B agree that money is worth $j_2 = 6\%$.

If A accepts \$500 now, how much will be required to liquidate B's obligations at the end of 5 years?

Solution   Let X, due at the end of 5 years, be the required amount.   The problem is to determine X so that the set: \$500 now and X at the end of 5 years is equivalent, at $j_2 = 6\%$, to the set: \$1000 at the end of 3 years and \$2000 at the end of 8 years.

We arrange the data on a time diagram as below, keeping one set above the line and the other set below the line.

We next choose a date on which to compare.   Any date may be used, so suppose we choose the end of 8 years, that is, 16 interest periods.   An equation of equivalence is now obtained by transferring all sums in both sets to the comparison date and equating the dated values of the sets.   This gives

$$500(1.03)^{16} + X(1.03)^6 = 1000(1.03)^{10} + 2000$$

Evaluating the accumulation factors gives

$$802.35 + 1.1940523X = 1343.92 + 2000$$

From this latter equation, $X = \$2128.52$.

Since any comparison date may be used on which the dated values of the two sets are equated, we could select the end of 5 years (10 periods) and avoid a long division.   The equation of equivalence in this case would be

$$X + 500(1.03)^{10} = 1000(1.03)^4 + 2000(1.03)^{-6}$$

Evaluating the interest factors and solving gives

$$X = 1125.51 + 1674.97 - 671.96 = \$2128.52$$

as before.

Example 2   If money is worth 5% effective, what equal payments at the end of 1 and 3 years will equitably replace the following set of obligations: \$1000 due at the end of 3 years and \$2000 with accumulated interest from today at $j_2 = 6\%$ due at the end of 4 years?

Solution   Let X be the maturity value of each of the desired payments.   Place the data on a time diagram as shown below, keeping the maturity values of one set above the line and the other set below the line.

We select the end of 4 years as a comparison date, although any other date would serve almost as well.   All sums are transferred to the comparison date, and the dated values of the sets are equated, giving the equation of equivalence

$$X(1.05)^3 + X(1.05)^1 = 1000(1.05)^1 + 2000(1.03)^8$$

that is,

$$1.157625X + 1.05X = 1050.00 + 2533.54$$

Solving this equation, we obtain

$$X = \frac{3583.54}{2.207625} = \$1623.26$$

*21 PROBLEMS OF OCCASIONAL OCCURRENCE

Careful study of an equation of equivalence shows that it involves several types of quantities: maturity values, maturity dates, and interest rates. In the preceding section, the unknown occurring in the equation of equivalence was always a maturity value, and this is the problem most frequently arising. Occasionally, however, the unknown in the equation of equivalence is a maturity date or the interest rate. While the technique used to obtain the equation of equivalence remains the same, the algebra involved in solving it is somewhat different and will be illustrated by examples.

Example 1 $1000 is due in 5 years, and $2000 is due in 10 years. If money is worth $j_1 = 4\%$, (a) on what date would $2500 equitably replace both obligations, and (b) on what date would $3000 replace both obligations?

Solution a Let n be the number of years from now to the date on which the $2500 should fall due. We arrange the data on a time diagram as shown below.

Since the relative position of n is not known, it is usually best to choose the present as a comparison date. Transferring all sums to the present and equating the results in an equation of equivalence, we obtain

$$2500(1.04)^{-n} = 1000(1.04)^{-5} + 2000(1.04)^{-10}$$

The right-hand side is evaluated, giving

$$2500(1.04)^{-n} = 821.927 + 1351.128 = 2173.055$$

We now solve for n as in the illustrative example in Sec. 16. If interpolation is used, we obtain $n = 3.578$ years, or approximately 3 years 6 months 28 days.

Solution b The procedure is exactly the same as in Solution a. The equation of equivalence is

$$3000(1.04)^{-n} = 1000(1.04)^{-5} + 2000(1.04)^{-10}$$

that is,

$$3000(1.04)^{-n} = 2173.055$$

By interpolation, we obtain $n = 8.226$ years, or approximately 8 years 2 months 21 days.

When a set of obligations is replaced by a single one whose maturity value is equal to the sum of the maturity values of all the members of the set, the time at which it must fall due in order to be an equitable replacement is called the **average due date** *or the* **equated date.**   In Solution *b* of the last example the average due date is approximately 8 years 2 months 21 days from the present.

Although solving for the equated date presents no particular difficulties, it is possible to simplify the computations if a rough approximation is sufficient.   Let S_1, S_2, S_3, . . . be the maturity values of the various obligations due at the ends of n_1, n_2, n_3, . . . interest periods, and let n be the number of interest periods until the average due date.   Then

$$n = \frac{n_1 \times S_1 + n_2 \times S_2 + n_3 \times S_3 + \cdots}{S_1 + S_2 + S_3 + \cdots}$$

is *an approximate formula for n.*   The formula may be obtained by writing an equation of equivalence using the latest of the various maturity dates for a comparison date and using simple interest instead of compound interest.

Example 2   Use the approximate formula to find the equated date for (*b*) of the preceding example.
Solution   According to the formula

$$n = \frac{5 \times 1000 + 10 \times 2000}{1000 + 2000} = \frac{25,000}{3000} = 8\frac{1}{3} \text{ years}$$

For completeness, we shall consider the problem of an unknown interest rate.   An example will illustrate.

Example 3   What effective interest rate will cause the following two sets of obligations to be equivalent: (*a*) \$300 due at the end of 2 years and \$1000 due at the end of 4 years and (*b*) \$400 due in 1 year and \$800 due in 3 years?
Solution   Arrange the data on a time diagram as below.

Choose 4 years as a comparison date, and write an equation of equivalence.

$$400(1 + i)^3 + 800(1 + i)^1 = 300(1 + i)^2 + 1000$$

To solve this equation we transpose all terms that contain i to the left-hand side of the equation and abbreviate it by $f(i)$, that is,

$$f(i) = 400(1 + i)^3 - 300(1 + i)^2 + 800(1 + i) = 1000$$

We seek a value of i that makes $f(i) = 1000$.   Using the tables, we compute $f(i)$ for various interest rates until two consecutive rates are found such that $f(i)$ exceeds 1000 for one of them and is less than 1000 for the other.　These values are then recorded in tabular form as below.

i	$f(i)$
.070	1002.5472
X	1000.0000
.065	994.9124

$$.005 \begin{cases} \begin{cases} \\ c \begin{cases} \\ \rule{0pt}{1em} \end{cases} \end{cases} \end{cases} \quad \left. \begin{matrix} \\ 5.0876 \end{matrix} \right\} 7.6348$$

We now interpolate, the proportionality equation being

$$\frac{c}{0.005} = \frac{5.0876}{7.6348}$$

Hence, $c = 0.0033$ and

$$X = 0.065 + c = 0.0683 \text{ approx.}$$

If greater accuracy is required, a more refined method of solving the equation of equivalence is necessary.

EXERCISE 11

Solve the following equations for X, in each case telling whether it is possible to avoid division:

1. $X(1.05)^6 = 1000$.

2. $X(1.03)^2 + 500(1.03)^{10} = 2000$.

3. $X(1.025)^{-5} + 1000(1.025)^{-10} = 1500$.

4. $X + X(1.015)^4 = 500$.

5. A debt of \$1000 is due at the end of 3 years.　If \$200 is paid on the debt today, what single payment at the end of 2 years would liquidate the obligation if money is worth $j_4 = 6\%$?　What comparison date gives the simplest arithmetic?

6. A debt of \$3000 is due at the end of 5 years.　If \$1000 is paid at the end of 2 years, what single payment at the end of 4 years would liquidate the debt if money is worth $j_2 = 5\%$?　What comparison date gives the simplest arithmetic?

7. A man borrows \$5000 today at $j_4 = 5\frac{1}{2}\%$.　He promises to pay \$1000 at the end of the first year, \$2000 at the end of the second year, and the balance at the end of the third year.　What will the final payment be?

8. A merchant buys goods worth \$1000 cash.　He pays \$200 down and will pay \$500 more at the end of 3 months.　If interest is charged on the unpaid balance at $j_{12} = 6\%$, what final payment will be necessary at the end of 6 months?

9. A man had \$1000 in a savings account 10 years ago.　The fund earned interest at $j_2 = 3\%$.　He withdrew \$200 five years ago and \$300 two years ago.　How much is in the fund today?

10. A man made the following deposits into a savings account that credits interest at $j_2 = 2\frac{1}{4}\%$: \$1000 five years ago and \$500 three years ago.　He withdrew \$200 one year ago and plans to withdraw the remainder one year from now. How much will he get?

11. A man buys a lot whose cash price is $2500. He pays $500 down and will pay the balance, including interest at $j_{12} = 6\%$, in two equal installments at the ends of 6 and 12 months. How large will these payments be?

12. A man has $1000 in a savings account that pays interest at $j_{12} = 3\%$. He will need $2000 a year from now to meet an obligation falling due at that time. What two equal deposits made at the ends of 3 and 9 months will serve the purpose?

13. Mr. Jones has a note falling due at the bank today for $1000 and accumulated interest for 1 year at $j_{12} = 6\%$. He wishes to pay $300 today and the balance in two equal installments to be made at the ends of 4 and 8 months. How much will each installment be?

14. Mr. Smith's note for $500 and 5 years' interest at $j_2 = 5\frac{1}{2}\%$ matures in 5 years, and a second note for $1000 matures at the end of 10 years. He wishes to pay $200 today and to complete the liquidation by two equal payments due at the ends of 5 and 10 years. If money is now worth $j_4 = 4\%$, what will these payments be?

Write an equation of equivalence for Probs. 15 to 18 (you need not solve it):

15. A debt of $1000 with interest at $j_4 = 6\%$ will be repaid by 4 equal payments at the ends of 3, 6, 9, and 12 months. What will these payments be?

16. Mr. Adams will need $1000 at the end of the year. What equal deposits, made at the ends of 3, 6, 9, and 12 months, will furnish the necessary amount if the deposits earn interest at $j_4 = 4\%$?

17. Mr. Rose has $10,000 in a savings fund that earns interest at $j_4 = 3\%$. What equal deposits at the end of each quarter will cause the fund to contain $30,000 in one more year?

18. A contract calls for the payment of $100 at the end of each quarter for the next year and a final payment of $500 at the end of 2 years. What is the cash value of the contract if money is worth $j_4 = 5\%$?

★19. $3000 is due in 4 years, $2000 is due in 6 years, and $1000 is due in 10 years. Money is worth 7% effective. (*a*) Find the equated date by the exact method. (*b*) Find the average due date by the approximate formula.

★20. $2000 is due in 5 years, $5000 is due in 15 years, and $10,000 is due in 25 years. Money is worth $j_1 = 5\%$. (*a*) Find the average due date by the exact method. (*b*) Find the equated date by the approximate formula.

★21. Find the date on which $5000 would equitably replace the three obligations in Prob. 19.

★22. Find the yearly interest rate that makes the following two sets of obligations equivalent: $500 due in 2 years and $250 due in 3 years, $800 due in 4 years.

★23. Find the yearly effective rate that makes the following two sets of obligations equivalent: $800 due in 3 years and $400 due in 5 years, $500 due in 4 years and $900 due in 8 years.

★24. Find the yearly rate that makes the following two sets of debts equivalent: $250 cash and $750 due in 5 years, $260 due in 2 years and $700 due in 3 years.

4

Simple Annuities

22 **DEFINITIONS**

An annuity is a sequence of periodic payments, usually equal, made at equal intervals of time.   Thus, payments of rent, life-insurance premiums, and installment payments are familiar examples of annuities.

The period of time between consecutive payments is called the **payment interval** and may be any convenient length.   Originally the word *annuity* referred only to yearly payments, but modern usage includes payment intervals of any length.

The **term** *of an annuity is the time from the beginning of the first payment interval to the end of the last.*   When the term of an annuity is fixed, that is, when the term starts and ends on definite dates, the annuity is called an **annuity certain.**   When the term of an annuity depends upon some uncertain event, such as the death of an individual, the annuity is called a **contingent annuity.**

When the payments are due or made at the ends of the payment intervals, the annuity is called an **ordinary annuity.**   When the payments are due or made at the beginnings of the payment intervals, the annuity is called an **annuity due.** Hereafter we will follow the conventional practice of using the word annuity to mean an ordinary annuity unless stated otherwise.

Illustration   Suppose Mrs. Jones buys a washing machine for a cash payment of $25 followed by 12 monthly installments of $15 each, the first due 1 month after the date of sale. The monthly installments constitute an ordinary annuity whose term starts on the day of sale and continues for 1 year. The payment interval is 1 month.

All problems involving annuities concern the total valuation of the set of payments on some given date. It would be possible to treat all such problems by the methods developed in the preceding chapter. However, due to the regularity of annuity payments, the computation of the total valuation can be greatly simplified.

23 PRESENT VALUE AND AMOUNT OF AN ORDINARY ANNUITY

The present value of an annuity is defined as an equivalent dated value of the set of payments due at the beginning of the term.   The amount of an annuity is defined as an equivalent dated value of the set of payments due at the end of the term.   Thus, the present value of an ordinary annuity is an equivalent value due one payment period before the date of the first payment, and the amount of an ordinary annuity is an equivalent value due on the date of the last payment.

Clearly both the present value and the amount of an annuity will depend upon the interest rate used in the equation of equivalence. Since the interest conversion period may or may not be the same as the payment interval, it is convenient to classify annuities according to this relationship. *When the payment interval and the interest conversion period coincide, the annuity is called a* **simple annuity;** *otherwise, a* **general annuity.**   In this chapter, we deal only with simple annuities.

Example 1   Find the present value and the amount of an ordinary annuity consisting of five semiannual payments of $100 each if money is worth $j_2 = 4\%$.
Solution   Let A represent the present value, and let S be the amount. Arrange the data on a time diagram as below.

To obtain A, we write an equation of equivalence using the beginning of the term as a comparison date. Thus,

$$A = 100(1.02)^{-1} + 100(1.02)^{-2} + 100(1.02)^{-3} + 100(1.02)^{-4}$$
$$+ 100(1.02)^{-5} = \$471.35$$

Similarly, to obtain S we write an equation of equivalence using the end of the term as a comparison date. This gives

$$S = 100 + 100(1.02) + 100(1.02)^2 + 100(1.02)^3 + 100(1.02)^4 = \$520.40$$

The method of computing A and S used in the example shows clearly the meaning of present value and amount but is too long when a large number of payments is involved. Shorter and easier methods will now be developed.

Let S be the amount of an ordinary simple annuity of n \$1 payments, let i be the interest rate per payment interval, and let A represent the present value of the same annuity. We arrange the data on a time diagram as below.

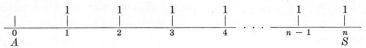

To find S we write an equation of equivalence using the end of the term as a comparison date. This gives

$$S = 1 + 1(1 + i) + 1(1 + i)^2 + 1(1 + i)^3 + \cdots + 1(1 + i)^{n-1}$$

The right-hand side is the sum of a geometric progression of n terms, whose first term is 1 and whose ratio is $(1 + i)$. Using a formula from algebra for such a sum,† we find

$$S = \frac{(1 + i)^n - 1}{i}$$

The right-hand side of this equation depends on n and i and is universally designated by the symbol $s_{\overline{n}|i}$, or $s_{\overline{n}|}$ at i, read "s angle n at i." Thus,

$$s_{\overline{n}|i} \text{ (or } s_{\overline{n}|} \text{ at } i) = \frac{(1 + i)^n - 1}{i}$$

If each payment of the annuity is R dollars, then the amount is R times as large and the formula for the amount is

$$S = Rs_{\overline{n}|i} \tag{1}$$

To obtain the present value A of the same annuity, we note that A and S are both dated values of the same set of payments and hence are equivalent to each other. Thus,

$$S = A(1 + i)^n \qquad \text{or} \qquad A = S(1 + i)^{-n} \tag{2}$$

Combining Eqs. (1) and (2) gives

$$A = Rs_{\overline{n}|i}(1 + i)^{-n} = R\,\frac{1 - (1 + i)^{-n}}{i}$$

† Appendix C contains a brief description of geometric progressions.

If we set

$$a_{\overline{n}|i} \text{ (or } a_{\overline{n}|} \text{ at } i) = \frac{1 - (1 + i)^{-n}}{i}$$

then the formula for the present value is

$$A = Ra_{\overline{n}|i} \tag{3}$$

Equations (1), (2), and (3) are the fundamental relations between S, A, and R. The two new symbols $s_{\overline{n}|i}$ and $a_{\overline{n}|i}$ have the property that they transfer a whole set of payments to a common date in one step. Their values are tabulated in Tables 10 and 11 for most of the values of n and i that occur in practice. If the desired rate is not in the tables, much tedious arithmetic is required to evaluate these symbols unless a modern computer is available. Interpolation is used only if a rough approximation is adequate.

Example 2 Mr. Smith will deposit $25 at the end of each quarter in a savings fund that earns interest at the rate 3%, compounded quarterly. How much will he have in the fund at the end of 10 years if (*a*) he has nothing in the account today, (*b*) he has $1000 in the fund at the present?
Solution a Arrange the data on a time diagram as below.

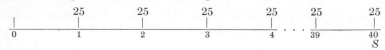

The time diagram is numbered from 0 to 40, representing payment intervals, and S is the sum at the end of the fortieth period equivalent to the annuity. Since $R = 25$, $i = \frac{3}{4}\%$ per period, and $n = 40$, we have

$$S = Rs_{\overline{n}|i} = 25s_{\overline{40}|\frac{3}{4}\%} = 25 \times 46.44648164 = \$1161.16$$

Solution b An additional sum of 1000 should be placed on the time diagram at the present. In this case the equation of equivalence is

$$S = 1000(1.0075)^{40} + 25s_{\overline{40}|\frac{3}{4}\%} = 1348.35 + 1161.16$$

and $S = \$2509.51$.

Example 3 A city is paying off a debt by making payments of $5000 at the end of each 6 months. Interest on the debt is at the rate $j_2 = 5\frac{1}{2}\%$. What is the outstanding debt at the present if (*a*) 30 payments will be needed to cancel it, (*b*) besides the 30 $5000 payments, an additional payment of $2000 will be needed 6 months later?
Solution a Arrange the given data on a time diagram as below.

The present value A of the debt is the present value of an annuity of $5000 payments for 30 periods, interest at $i = 2\frac{3}{4}\%$. An equation of equivalence gives

$$A = Ra_{\overline{n}|i} = 5000a_{\overline{30}|0.0275} = 5000 \times 20.24930130 = \$101,246.51$$

Solution b Here an additional sum of $2000 is placed on the time diagram at the end of the thirty-first period. A is equal to the sum of these payments all discounted back to the present. Therefore

$$A = 5000a_{\overline{30}|0.0275} + 2000(1.0275)^{-31} = 101,246.51 + 862.57 = \$102,109.08$$

EXERCISE 12

1. Find the amount and the present value of an annuity of 30 semiannual payments of $100 if the interest rate is $j_2 = 6\%$.

2. Find the amount of an annuity of $50 payable quarterly if there are 25 payments and the interest rate is $j_4 = 4\frac{1}{2}\%$. Next, find the present value by two methods.

3. A man deposits his bonus check of $250 in a savings bank at the end of each year. How much will he have at the end of 15 years if interest is computed at $2\frac{1}{2}\%$ effective?

4. A city puts $10,000 in a savings fund at the end of each year to prepare for a debt falling due in 10 years. If the fund earns interest at $j_1 = 3\%$, how much will the fund contain when the debt matures?

5. Find the cash value of a house which can be purchased for a $2500 down payment followed by $150 per month for 12 years if money is worth $j_{12} = 5\%$.

6. A used car can be purchased for $300 down and $45 per month for 3 years. Find its equivalent cash price if money is worth $j_{12} = 6\%$.

7. The present value of an annuity is $2500. Find the amount if the term is 20 years and the interest rate is $j_2 = 5\%$.

8. The amount of an annuity payable quarterly for 10 years is $5000. If money is worth $j_4 = 5\frac{1}{2}\%$, find its present value.

9. A television set worth $500 cash can be purchased by a down payment and monthly payments of $30 for 15 months. If interest is computed at $j_{12} = 4\%$, find the down payment.

10. A man buys a new car worth $4000 cash. If he gets $600 credit for his old car, what additional down payment will be necessary so that he can liquidate the balance, including interest at $j_{12} = 7\%$, by monthly payments of $150 for 2 years?

11. Mr. Smith deposits $150 at the end of each quarter in a savings fund that earns interest at $j_4 = 3\frac{1}{2}\%$. If he has $1000 in the fund today, how much will he have 12 years later?

12. A wealthy man wishes to deposit with a trust company a sum of money sufficient to provide his elderly sister with a monthly income of $500 for the next 16 years. How much is necessary if the fund earns interest at $j_{12} = 3\%$?

13. A contract calls for payments of $50 at the end of each quarter for 20 years and an additional payment of $2000 at that time. Find the equivalent cash value of the contract at $j_4 = 4\%$.

14. Mr. Jones has $500 in a savings fund that earns interest at the rate $j_{12} = 3\%$. If he continues to deposit $25 at the end of each month, how much will the fund contain 2 years from now?

15. If money is worth $j_{12} = 6\%$, which is more profitable—to pay $4200 cash for a car, or to pay $1000 down and $120 per month for $2\frac{1}{2}$ years?

16. Mr. Wilson deposits $30 at the end of each month in a savings fund that earns interest at $j_{12} = 3\frac{1}{2}\%$. After $3\frac{1}{2}$ years he increases the deposits to $40. How much will he have at the end of 5 years? (*Hint:* Consider the payments as forming two annuities.)

17. A man agrees to settle a debt by payments of $300 every 6 months for 4 years, followed by semiannual payments of $200 for the following 3 years. Find the present value of the debt if the interest rate is $j_2 = 3\frac{1}{2}\%$. (See hint to preceding problem.)

18. A contract calls for payments of $70 at the end of each quarter for 8 years. The debtor failed to make any payments until the end of the third year, at which time he wished to liquidate the entire contract with a single payment. What should this payment be if money is worth $j_4 = 4\frac{1}{2}\%$?

★19. Derive the expression for $a_{\overline{n}|i}$ by writing an equation of equivalence at the beginning of the term and sum the resulting geometric progression.

★20. Prove algebraically that $s_{\overline{n}|i}$ increases with increasing i whereas $a_{\overline{n}|i}$ decreases with increasing i.

24 ANNUITIES DUE

Frequently it is desirable to regard the term of an annuity as starting on the date of the first payment. Thus, the periodic payments are considered due or made at the beginnings of the payment intervals rather than at the ends. Under these conditions the annuity is called an **annuity due.** That is, *an annuity due consists of a set of periodic payments due or made at the beginnings of the payment intervals, with the term starting on the date of the first payment and ending one period after the last.* Since the present value of an annuity has been defined as an equivalent value at the beginning of the term, this means that *the present value of an annuity due is an equivalent value due on the date of the first payment.* Also, since the amount of an annuity is an equivalent value at the end of the term, it follows that *the amount of an annuity due is an equivalent value due on a date one period after the last payment.*

Let A represent the present value, S the amount, R the periodic payment, and i the interest rate per payment interval of an annuity due of n payments. We arrange the data on a time diagram as below.

A study of the time diagram shows that the essential difference between an annuity due and an ordinary annuity is that for the annuity due each payment is due one payment period earlier, relative to the equivalent values A and S, than for an ordinary annuity. The present value and amount of an annuity due may be computed by two methods.

To find A   *Method 1*   We write an equation of equivalence using the date one period before the present for the comparison. On this date the n payments of R may be considered an ordinary annuity. Therefore,

$$A(1 + i)^{-1} = Ra_{\overline{n}|i}$$

Solving this equation for A, we get, since $(1 + i)^{-1} = 1/(1 + i)$,

$$A = (1 + i)Ra_{\overline{n}|i} \tag{4}$$

Method 2 Write an equation of equivalence using the present as a comparison date. For this comparison date, we consider the first payment R a cash payment and the remaining $n - 1$ payments an ordinary annuity. Consequently,

$$A = R + Ra_{\overline{n-1}|i} = R(1 + a_{\overline{n-1}|i}) \tag{5}$$

To find S *Method* 1 Write an equation of equivalence using the date of the last payment as the comparison date. On this date, the payments may be considered an ordinary annuity. Consequently,

$$S(1 + i)^{-1} = Rs_{\overline{n}|i}$$

Solving this equation for S, we get

$$S = (1 + i)Rs_{\overline{n}|i} \tag{6}$$

Method 2 Referring back to the time diagram, we see that if an additional payment of R is added to the set at the end of the last period, the resulting set may be considered an ordinary annuity of $n + 1$ payments. This additional payment, however, will increase S by exactly R, since it occurs on the same date as S. Consequently,

$$S + R = Rs_{\overline{n+1}|i}$$

Solving this equation for S, we get

$$S = Rs_{\overline{n+1}|i} - R = R(s_{\overline{n+1}|i} - 1) \tag{7}$$

It is strongly recommended that the student master the methods used rather than apply the results as formulas. The formulas are extremely limited in their use, whereas the techniques involved have a wide application to various types of financial problems.

The examples that follow will illustrate the methods just described.

Example 1 Find the equivalent cash value of a refrigerator that can be purchased by payments of $20 at the beginning of each month for a year and a half if money is worth $j_{12} = 6\%$.

Solution Arrange the given data on a time diagram as below.

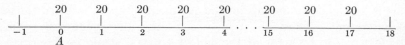

Method 1 From the date labeled *minus one*, the payments form an ordinary annuity of 18 payments and the equivalent value A is one period away. An equation of equivalence with this comparison date gives

$$A(1.005)^{-1} = 20a_{\overline{18}|\frac{1}{2}\%}$$

and therefore

$$A = (1.005) \times 20a_{\overline{18}|\frac{1}{2}\%} = 1.005 \times 20 \times 17.17276802 = \$345.17$$

Method 2   We regard the first payment as a cash payment and the remaining 17 payments as forming an ordinary annuity with its term starting at the present.   With the present as a comparison date, the equation of equivalence is

$$A = 20 + 20a_{\overline{17}|\frac{1}{2}\%} = 20(1 + 16.25863186) = \$345.17$$

Example 2   A savings fund earns interest at the rate $j_2 = 4\%$.   If \$500 is deposited at the beginning of each half year, how much will the fund contain at the end of 12 years?

Solution   Place the given data on a time diagram.

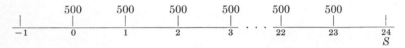

Method 1   Write an equation of equivalence using the last payment date as a comparison date.   On this date, the accumulated value of the payments equals the amount of an ordinary annuity, therefore

$$S(1.02)^{-1} = 500s_{\overline{24}|2\%}$$

Solving for S we get

$$S = 1.02 \times 500s_{\overline{24}|2\%} = 1.02 \times 500 \times 30.42186247 = \$15,515.15$$

Method 2   At the end of the twenty-fourth period, add an extra \$500 payment to the set of annuity payments and also add \$500 to the equivalent sum S.   An equation of equivalence on this date now gives

$$S + 500 = 500s_{\overline{25}|2\%}$$

Solving for S gives

$$S = 500s_{\overline{25}|2\%} - 500 = 500(32.03029972 - 1) = \$15,515.15$$

25   DEFERRED ANNUITIES

When the term of an annuity is to start at some future date, the annuity is called a deferred annuity.   It is customary to analyze all deferred annuities as deferred ordinary annuities, and henceforth the qualifying adjective "ordinary" will be omitted.

The length of time from the present to the beginning of the term, that is, to the beginning of the first payment interval, is called the **period of deferment.**   Thus, an annuity consisting of semiannual payments, the first one to be made at the end of 4 years, would be described as a deferred annuity, the period of deferment being $3\frac{1}{2}$ years.

To find the present value of a deferred annuity requires no new methods.   An equation of equivalence is used, as illustrated in the following example.

Example A certain sum is given a trust company in return for which it will pay $50 per month, the first payment to be made 2 years from today and the last one 5 years from today. How much should the trust company receive today if interest accumulates at the rate 6%, $m = 12$?

Solution Let A be the present value of the payments, and place the data on a time diagram as below.

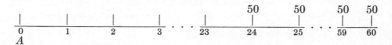

Method 1 The first payment is due at the end of the twenty-fourth month, and the last is due at the end of the sixtieth month, so there are 37 payments in all. Therefore we consider this an ordinary annuity of 37 payments with the term deferred 23 periods. We write an equation of equivalence with the end of the twenty-third month as the comparison date. This gives

$$A(1.005)^{23} = 50a_{\overline{37}|\frac{1}{2}\%}$$

Since dividing by $(1.005)^{23}$ is the same as multiplying by $(1.005)^{-23}$,

$$A = (1.005)^{-23}50a_{\overline{37}|\frac{1}{2}\%} = 0.89162160 \times 50 \times 33.70250372 = \$1502.49$$

Method 2 This method consists of a tricky but ingenious device. The time diagram is altered by adding $50 payments at the end of the 1st, 2d, 3d, . . . , 23d months to both the annuity and its equivalent value A. The new time diagram looks as follows:

	(50)	(50)	(50)	(50)	50	50	50	50
0	1	2	3	. . . 23	24	25	. . . 59	60
A	(50)	(50)	(50)	(50)				

Since A is equivalent to the deferred annuity, the two new systems are equivalent and an equation of equivalence with the present as a comparison date gives

$$A + 50a_{\overline{23}|\frac{1}{2}\%} = 50a_{\overline{60}|\frac{1}{2}\%}$$

Solving this equation for A, we get

$$A = 50(a_{\overline{60}|\frac{1}{2}\%} - a_{\overline{23}|\frac{1}{2}\%}) = 50(51.72556075 - 21.67568055) = \$1502.49$$

It will be observed that method 1 seems more natural but method 2 involves simpler arithmetic.

If these two methods of finding A are applied to an annuity of n payments of R dollars each with the term deferred for k periods and the interest rate is i per period, then method 1 gives

$$A = (1 + i)^{-k}Ra_{\overline{n}|i} \tag{8}$$

and method 2 gives

$$A = R(a_{\overline{n+k}|i} - a_{\overline{k}|i}) \tag{9}$$

Since the values of A obtained by the two methods must be the

same, we may equate the right-hand members of Eqs. (8) and (9) and
obtain the useful identity

$$a_{\overline{n+k}|i} - a_{\overline{k}|i} = (1 + i)^{-k}a_{\overline{n}|i} \tag{10}$$

It is strongly recommended that the student master the methods
used in the example rather than merely memorize Eqs. (8) and (9).
Always draw a time diagram and determine very carefully the number of
payments and the period of deferment.

EXERCISE 13

1. Find the amount and the present value of an annuity due of 20 payments of $500
each if the interest rate is $2\frac{1}{2}\%$ per period.

2. Find the amount and the present value of an annuity due of 25 quarterly payments
of $250 each if money is worth $j_4 = 3\%$.

3. A suit of clothes can be purchased for 12 monthly payments of $5 each, the first
one due on the day of sale. Find the equivalent cash price by two methods at $j_{12} = 9\%$.

4. A living-room suite can be purchased with 13 monthly payments of $25 each, the
first one due on the day of sale. Find the equivalent cash price at $j_{12} = 6\%$ by two
methods.

5. Deposits of $50 are made at the beginning of each half year into a fund bearing
interest at $j_2 = 3\frac{1}{2}\%$. How much is in the fund 6 months after the twelfth deposit?
Use two methods.

6. At the beginning of each quarter for 10 years a city placed $5000 in a fund earning
interest at $j_4 = 4\frac{1}{2}\%$. What additional deposit, made at the end of the tenth year,
is necessary to bring the fund up to $300,000?

7. Find the present value of an annuity of 15 annual payments of $1000, the first one
due at the end of 5 years, if money is worth $5\frac{1}{2}\%$ effective. Use two methods.

8. If money is worth $j_{12} = 3\%$, find the present value of an annuity of $50 monthly if
the first payment is due at the end of $1\frac{1}{2}$ years and the last one is due at the end of
5 years.

9. On the day of his son's birth, a man wishes to deposit with a trust company a sum
sufficient to provide the boy with regular monthly payments of $200 for the 4 years he
will attend college. What should this sum be if money is worth $j_{12} = 3\frac{1}{2}\%$ and the
first payment will be made one month after the boy's sixteenth birthday?

10. A teacher wishes to borrow some money on June 1 for repairing his house. He
can repay the loan by payments of $60 a month starting on Oct. 1 and continuing
through the following June 1. If the interest rate is $j_{12} = 6\%$, how much can he
borrow?

11. On his twenty-fifth birthday a man wishes to purchase an annuity of $300 per
month for 15 years, payments to start on his fortieth birthday. What will the annuity
cost if $j_{12} = 4\%$?

12. If money is worth 6% effective, which is the cheaper—to pay $30,000 cash for a
house, or to pay $10,000 cash and 24 annual payments of $2000, the first due at the
end of 5 years?

13. It is estimated that a mine will produce an income of $50,000 quarterly for 8
years. It will cost $10,000 to get the mine in operation, and the first income payment
will come at the end of 2 years. What is the equivalent cash value of the mine if
money is worth $j_4 = 7\%$?

14. A contract calls for payments of $1000 at the end of each 6 months for 4 years followed by semiannual payments of $500 for 6 more years. What is the present value of the contract at $j_2 = 5\frac{1}{2}\%$?

15. Find the equivalent cash value at $j_4 = 5\%$ of an annuity of $500 per quarter for 6 years followed by an annuity of $750 per quarter for 4 more years.

16. Merchandise was purchased for $50 down and $20 a month for 18 months. The first 5 monthly payments were paid when due. On the day of the sixth payment, the buyer wished to liquidate the remaining debt with a single payment. What was the necessary payment at $j_{12} = 8\%$?

17. What payments made at the end of each 6 months are equivalent to $50 payments made at the beginning of each month if money is worth $j_{12} = 3\frac{1}{2}\%$?

26 IDENTITIES RELATING $s_{\overline{n}|i}$ AND $a_{\overline{n}|i}$

There are two relationships existing between the two annuity symbols $s_{\overline{n}|i}$ and $a_{\overline{n}|i}$ that we shall frequently find useful. To obtain the first, we start with Eq. (2):

$$S = A(1 + i)^n$$

Replacing S and A by their formulas and dividing out R, we obtain

$$s_{\overline{n}|i} = (1 + i)^n a_{\overline{n}|i} \tag{11}$$

which is the first identity.

Since by definition

$$s_{\overline{n}|i} = \frac{(1 + i)^n - 1}{i}$$

it easily follows that

$$1 + i s_{\overline{n}|i} = (1 + i)^n$$

Dividing this equality by Eq. (11), we obtain the second identity

$$\frac{1}{s_{\overline{n}|i}} + i = \frac{1}{a_{\overline{n}|i}} \tag{12}$$

Both Eqs. (11) and (12) are valid for all values of n and i.

*In addition to the two fundamental identities just given, there are several others of occasional importance. These are given as problems in the following exercise. Their importance is apparent when we want the value of an annuity symbol for which n is not in the table. An example will illustrate.

Example A house can be purchased by paying $2000 down and $75 a month for the next 20 years. If money is worth $j_{12} = 6\%$, what is the equivalent cash price of the house?

Solution　Arrange the data on a time diagram as below.

$$
\begin{array}{ccccccc}
2000 & R & R & R & & R \\
| & | & | & | & \cdots & | \\
0 & 1 & 2 & 3 & & 240 \\
X
\end{array}
$$

An equation of equivalence with the present as comparison date gives

$$X = 2000 + Ra_{\overline{240}|\frac{1}{2}\%}$$

Since the tables run only to $n = 200$, the annuity symbol $a_{\overline{240}|\frac{1}{2}\%}$ cannot be obtained by direct means and must be evaluated in some other manner. To this end we use the identity in Prob. 4, Exercise 14, which is essentially Eq. (10), Sec. 25.

$$a_{\overline{n+k}|i} = (1+i)^{-k}a_{\overline{n}|i} + a_{\overline{k}|i}$$

With $n = 200$, $k = 40$, $i = \frac{1}{2}\%$, this identity gives

$$
\begin{aligned}
a_{\overline{240}|\frac{1}{2}\%} &= (1.005)^{-40}a_{\overline{200}|\frac{1}{2}\%} + a_{\overline{40}|\frac{1}{2}\%} \\
&= 0.81913886 \times 126.24055430 + 36.17222786 \\
&= 139.58077
\end{aligned}
$$

so that the equivalent cash price of the house is

$$X = 2000 + 75 \times 139.58077 = \$12,468.56$$

*EXERCISE 14

Prove by algebraic methods that the following equations are identities:

1. $(1+i)s_{\overline{n}|i} = s_{\overline{n+1}|i} - 1.$

2. $(1+i)a_{\overline{n}|i} = a_{\overline{n-1}|i} + 1.$

3. $s_{\overline{n+k}|i} = s_{\overline{n}|i} + (1+i)^n s_{\overline{k}|i} = (1+i)^k s_{\overline{n}|i} + s_{\overline{k}|i}.$

4. $a_{\overline{n+k}|i} = a_{\overline{n}|i} + (1+i)^{-n}a_{\overline{k}|i} = (1+i)^{-k}a_{\overline{n}|i} + a_{\overline{k}|i}.$

5. $s_{\overline{n-k}|i} = s_{\overline{n}|i} - (1+i)^n a_{\overline{k}|i} = (1+i)^{-k}s_{\overline{n}|i} - a_{\overline{k}|i}.$

6. $a_{\overline{n-k}|i} = a_{\overline{n}|i} - (1+i)^{-n}s_{\overline{k}|i} = (1+i)^k a_{\overline{n}|i} - s_{\overline{k}|i}.$

27　FINDING THE PAYMENT OF AN ANNUITY

The fundamental annuity equation (1) expresses a relation among S, R, n, and i. Similarly Eq. (3) expresses a relation among A, R, n, and i. In either case, if we know three of these quantities, it should be possible to solve for the remaining one. When S, n, and i are known, the periodic payment of the annuity is found by solving Eq. (1) for R. Thus,

$$R = \frac{S}{s_{\overline{n}|i}}$$

Here, as in the chapter on compound interest, it is highly desirable to avoid the indicated long division. For this purpose, a table of reciprocals of $s_{\overline{n}|i}$ is provided. The preceding equation is written in the form

$$R = S\frac{1}{s_{\overline{n}|i}} \tag{13}$$

The values of the fraction $1/s_{\overline{n}|i}$ are given in Table 12.

When A, n, and i are given, the formula for R is derived from Eq. (3). Thus,

$$R = A \, \frac{1}{a_{\overline{n}|i}} \tag{14}$$

It is not necessary to have a separate table for the values of $1/a_{\overline{n}|i}$, since these values are easily obtained by using Eq. (12) and Table 12. Adding i to the value of $1/s_{\overline{n}|i}$ gives the desired value of $1/a_{\overline{n}|i}$. For example, to find $1/a_{\overline{15}|5\%}$, get the value of $1/s_{\overline{15}|5\%} = 0.04634229$ from Table 12, add $i = 0.05$, and obtain 0.09634229 as the value of $1/a_{\overline{15}|5\%}$.

It should be noted that Eqs. (13) and (14) are valid only for ordinary annuities. When the payment of an annuity due or a deferred annuity is to be found, these equations cannot be used. The procedure in such cases is to write an equation of equivalence as in the preceding sections and then solve for R.

Example 1   A savings bank pays interest at $j_4 = 3\%$ on all deposits. What sequence of equal deposits made at the end of each quarter for 5 years would be necessary to accumulate \$1000 at the end of that time?

Solution   Arrange the data on a time diagram as below.

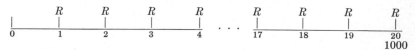

We write an equation of equivalence with the end of the twentieth period as comparison date. This gives

$$1000 = Rs_{\overline{20}|\frac{3}{4}\%}$$

Solving for R, we get

$$R = 1000 \, \frac{1}{s_{\overline{20}|\frac{3}{4}\%}} = 1000 \times 0.04653063 = \$46.53 \qquad \text{(Table 12)}$$

Example 2   The cash value of a piano is \$500. It may be purchased for a down payment of \$200 and the balance in equal monthly installments for 2 years. If money is worth $j_{12} = 3\frac{1}{2}\%$, find the monthly payment.

Solution   Arrange the data on a time diagram as below.

```
200      R      R      R      R          R      R      R
 |       |      |      |      |    ...    |      |      |
 0       1      2      3      4          22     23     24
500
```

The two methods of payment shown above and below the line are equivalent at the monthly rate of $\frac{7}{24}\%$. An equation of equivalence with the present as comparison date gives

$$500 = 200 + Ra_{\overline{24}|\frac{7}{24}\%}$$

Solving for R, we get

$$R = 300 \, \frac{1}{a_{\overline{24}|\frac{7}{24}\%}}$$

In view of Eq. (12)

$$\frac{1}{a_{\overline{24}|\frac{7}{24}\%}} = \frac{1}{s_{\overline{24}|\frac{7}{24}\%}} + \frac{7}{24} \%$$

We express $\frac{7}{24}\%$ as a decimal and use Table 12 to get the value of $1/s_{\overline{24}|\frac{7}{24}\%}$.   Thus,

$$\frac{1}{a_{\overline{24}|\frac{7}{24}\%}} = 0.04028606 + 0.00291667 = 0.04320273$$

Therefore, $R = 300 \times 0.04320273 = \$12.96$.

Example 3   A student borrows \$2000 to meet college expenses during his senior year. He promises to repay the loan with interest at $j_2 = 4\frac{1}{2}\%$ in 10 equal semiannual installments, the first payment to be made 3 years after the date of the loan.   What will these payments be?
Solution   Arrange the data on a time diagram as shown.

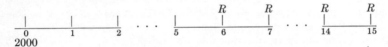

Method 1   Write an equation of equivalence using the end of the fifth half year as a comparison date.   This gives

$$Ra_{\overline{10}|2\frac{1}{4}\%} = 2000(1.0225)^5$$

Solving for R (and multiplying by $1/a_{\overline{10}|2\frac{1}{4}\%}$ instead of dividing by $a_{\overline{10}|2\frac{1}{4}\%}$) gives

$$R = 2000(1.0225)^5 \, \frac{1}{a_{\overline{10}|2\frac{1}{4}\%}} = 2000 \times 1.11767769 \times 0.11278768 = \$252.11$$

Method 2   Add payments of R at the ends of the first five periods to both the \$2000 and the deferred annuity.   The new time diagram appears below.

An equation of equivalence with the present as a comparison date now gives

$$Ra_{\overline{15}|2\frac{1}{4}\%} = 2000 + Ra_{\overline{5}|2\frac{1}{4}\%}$$

Solving for R, we get

$$R = \frac{2000}{a_{\overline{15}|2\frac{1}{4}\%} - a_{\overline{5}|2\frac{1}{4}\%}} = \frac{2000}{12.61216551 - 4.67945253} = \$252.11$$

If method 2 is used, the table of reciprocals does not apply and long division cannot be avoided.

EXERCISE 15

1. What quarterly deposits should be made into a savings bank paying $j_4 = 3\%$ in order to have $5000 at the end of 5 years?

2. Find the annual payment of an annuity whose amount is $2500, if the term is 10 years and the interest rate is $j_1 = 5\%$.

3. What equal payments at the end of each quarter for 20 years would purchase a house worth $20,000 cash if the interest rate is $j_4 = 5\%$?

4. A car worth $3500 cash may be purchased by paying $600 down and the rest in equal monthly payments for 3 years. If the interest rate is $j_{12} = 8\%$, what will the payments be?

5. A man will pay off a debt of $6000 with interest at $j_4 = 6\%$ by equal quarterly payments for 8 years. What will the payments be?

6. It is estimated that a machine will need replacing 15 years from now at a cost of $15,000. How much should the company save at the end of each year in order to replace the old machine if the savings can be invested at 4% per year?

7. A color TV set worth $750 is purchased for $150 down followed by equal monthly installments for $2\frac{1}{2}$ years. If the interest rate is $j_{12} = 5\%$, what will the payments be?

8. A firm has $10,000 in a savings fund. What annual deposits will it take to increase the fund to $50,000 at the end of 10 years if the fund earns interest at 3% per year?

9. An insurance policy will pay $10,000 cash to a beneficiary or a quarterly annuity for 10 years which is equivalent at $j_4 = 4\%$. Find the quarterly payment.

10. A young man borrows $2000 to help him through his final year in college. Interest accumulates on the loan at $j_{12} = 4\%$. What monthly payments for 2 years will liquidate the debt if the first payment is made 18 months after the loan?

11. On the day of his son's birth a man deposits $5000 with a trust company to finance the boy's education. The boy will receive 60 monthly payments starting on his fifteenth birthday. If the interest rate is $j_{12} = 4\%$, what will the payments be?

12. A contract requires the payment of $2000 at the beginning of each year. If money is worth 6%, $m = 12$, what payments at the end of each month would be an equitable substitute?

13. A contract calls for the payment of $1000 at the end of each year. If money is worth $j_4 = 5\%$, what quarterly payments would be equally satisfactory?

14. A young man borrows $2000 at the beginning of each year for 4 years from his rich uncle and will pay back the loan with interest at 6% per year in 6 equal annual payments starting 2 years after the last loan. What will the payments be?

15. A man borrows $10,000 at $j_2 = 5\%$ and starts repaying it with semiannual payments of $500. After making 10 payments he wishes to change the size of the payments in order to liquidate the debt with 15 more installments. How large should the new payments be?

16. A man has made quarterly deposits of $100 for 2 years into a savings fund paying interest at $j_4 = 3\%$. What quarterly deposits for the next 3 years will it take to bring the fund up to $2000?

28 ANNUITIES WITH n UNKNOWN

Illustration Suppose a man borrows $1000 and agrees to discharge the debt, with interest at $j_4 = 4$ percent, by payments of $50 at the end of each quarter for as long as is necessary. Clearly, the $50 payments will form an annuity, whose present value should equal the loan. That is,

$$1000 = 50a_{\overline{n}|1\%} \qquad \text{or} \qquad a_{\overline{n}|1\%} = 20$$

where n is unknown. If we now refer to Table 11, we find that

$$a_{\overline{22}|1\%} = 19.66037934 \qquad \text{and} \qquad a_{\overline{23}|1\%} = 20.45582113$$

Thus, there is no integer n such that $a_{\overline{n}|1\%} = 20$. Stated differently, there is no *proper annuity* with these given quantities. Clearly it would be possible to solve $a_{\overline{n}|1\%} = 20$ for n either by interpolation or by the use of logarithms. The only new point arising concerns the interpretation of nonintegral solutions. This point will be discussed in the next section.

In the above illustration, the customary practice would be to make 22 full payments of $50 each, followed by a smaller payment one period later, just sufficient to discharge the remaining debt.

In general, when A, R, and i are given, there is usually no proper annuity with these given quantities. Algebraically, this means that usually there is no integer n such that $A = Ra_{\overline{n}|i}$. Consequently, it is necessary to include one payment different from R in order to have equivalence. Normally, this odd payment is less than R and is dated one payment period after the last full payment of R, although this need not be the case.

When sufficient data are given, the number of full payments and the final payment are determined by solving a suitable equation of equivalence as illustrated in the following examples.

Example 1 Suppose the borrower in the last illustration signs a contract that calls for the payment of 22 quarterly payments of $50 each and a final payment F, due at the end of the twenty-third period, just sufficient to liquidate the debt. How large is F? *Solution* We arrange the data on a time diagram as shown.

	50	50	50		50	50	F
0	1	2	3	$\cdots$	21	22	23
1000							

Method 1 Write an equation of equivalence using the end of the twenty-second period as a comparison date. This gives

$$F(1.01)^{-1} + 50s_{\overline{22}|1\%} = 1000(1.01)^{22}$$

Solving for F gives

$$F(1.01)^{-1} = 1000(1.01)^{22} - 50s_{\overline{22}|1\%} = 1244.716 - 1223.579 = 21.137$$

and $F = 21.137(1.01)^1 = \$21.35$.

Method 2 Place two additional $50 payments on the time diagram, one above the line and one below the line at the end of the twenty-third period. Now write an equation of equivalence using this comparison date. This gives

$$F + 50s_{\overline{23}|1\%} = 1000(1.01)^{23} + 50$$
$$F = 1000(1.01)^{23} + 50 - 50s_{\overline{23}|1\%} = 1257.163 + 50 - 1285.815 = \$21.35$$

When S, R, and i are given, the situation is analogous and essentially the same procedure is followed.

Example 2 Deposits of \$100 will be made semiannually into a savings fund that earns interest at $j_2 = 3\%$. On what payment date will a final partial payment, less than \$100, cause the fund to contain exactly \$3000? What will this final deposit be?
Solution The deposits will form an annuity whose amount is to be \$3000. Therefore we should have

$$3000 = 100s_{\overline{n}|1\frac{1}{2}\%} \qquad \text{or} \qquad s_{\overline{n}|1\frac{1}{2}\%} = 30$$

where n is unknown. Referring to Table 10, we find that

$$s_{\overline{24}|1\frac{1}{2}\%} = 28.63352080 \qquad \text{and} \qquad s_{\overline{25}|1\frac{1}{2}\%} = 30.06302361$$

Consequently there will be 24 deposits of \$100 and a final deposit F, made at the end of the twenty-fifth period. We next arrange the data on a time diagram.

F is now determined by solving a suitable equation of equivalence.
Method 1 Using the end of the twenty-fourth period as a comparison date, we get

$$F(1.015)^{-1} + 100s_{\overline{24}|1\frac{1}{2}\%} = 3000(1.015)^{-1}$$

Solving for F gives

$$F = 3000 - 1.015 \times 100s_{\overline{24}|1\frac{1}{2}\%} = 3000 - 2906.30 = \$93.70$$

Method 2 We add \$100 to both F and the \$3000 and use the end of the twenty-fifth period as a comparison date. This gives

$$F + 100s_{\overline{25}|1\frac{1}{2}\%} = 3000 + 100$$

Solving for F gives

$$F = 3100 - 100s_{\overline{25}|1\frac{1}{2}\%} = 3100 - 100 \times 30.06302361 = \$93.70$$

It should be observed that when a savings fund is accumulating as in Example 2, interest is helping it to grow. Consequently, a final partial deposit will not always be necessary, as the interest for the final period may be enough, or more than enough, to attain the desired amount (see Prob. 13, Exercise 16).

*29 DETERMINING THE FINAL PAYMENT BY INTERPOLATION

When A, R, and i (or S, R, and i) are given, the annuity equation $A = Ra_{\overline{n}|i}$ (or $S = Rs_{\overline{n}|i}$) can be solved for n either by interpolation or by the use of logarithms. The algebra is not difficult. The only question that arises concerns the interpretation of nonintegral solutions. For example, if the annuity equation $a_{\overline{n}|1\%} = 20$, which arose in the illustration at the beginning of Sec. 28, is solved for n by interpolation, we get $n = 22.42696$. It is easily verified that if the fractional part of the solution is multiplied by the full payment, we get $50 \times 0.42696 = \$21.35$, which is exactly the value that was obtained for the final payment F. We shall now prove that this property holds in general.

Given A, R, and i. Let the value of n be determined by interpolation. Write n in the form $k + f$, where k is an integer and f is a fraction less than 1. Then $F = fR$ is the final payment, due one period after the last payment of R, necessary for equivalence. For if we set $a_{\overline{n}|i} = A/R$, this value in general will fall between two consecutive tabulated values $a_{\overline{k}|i}$ and $a_{\overline{k+1}|i}$. We write n in the form $n = k + f$ and set up an interpolation table.

$k + 1$	$a_{\overline{k+1}|i}$
$k + f$	A/R
k	$a_{\overline{k}|i}$

The proportionality equation is

$$\frac{f}{1} = \frac{A/R - a_{\overline{k}|i}}{a_{\overline{k+1}|i} - a_{\overline{k}|i}}$$

Using Eq. 10, Sec. 25, with $n = 1$ and the fact that $a_{\overline{1}|i} = (1 + i)^{-1}$, the denominator of the above fraction becomes $(1 + i)^{-k-1}$ and

$$f = \frac{A/R - a_{\overline{k}|i}}{(1 + i)^{-k-1}}$$

We now multiply both sides of the last equation by $R(1 + i)^{-k-1}$. This gives

$$fR(1 + i)^{-k-1} = A - Ra_{\overline{k}|i}$$

On the other hand, if F is determined by writing an equation of equivalence with the present as a comparison date, we get

$$A = Ra_{\overline{k}|i} + F(1 + i)^{-k-1}$$

Comparing these last two equations we see that

$$A - Ra_{\overline{k}|i} = fR(1 + i)^{-k-1} = F(1 + i)^{-k-1}$$

and consequently $F = fR$, as was to be proved.

Thus, when the annuity equation $a_{\overline{n}|i} = A/R$ is solved for n by interpolation, *the fractional part of n may be interpreted as the fractional part of R necessary for the final payment F, where F is dated one period after the last R.*

For completeness, it is stated without proof that while a solution of the annuity equation $a_{\overline{n}|i} = A/R$ (or $s_{\overline{n}|i} = S/R$) for n by logarithms is quite simple, the nonintegral solution does not have the same interpretation as above and is used only to find the number of payments. Consequently, a logarithmic solution is seldom used unless the interest rate is one not tabulated so that interpolation is impractical.

EXERCISE 16

1. The present value of an annuity of $100 per quarter is $5000. If the interest rate is $j_4 = 4\%$, find the number of full payments and the final partial payment.

2. The present value of an annuity of $1000 per year is $15,000. If the interest rate is $5\frac{1}{2}\%$ per year, find the number of full payments and the final partial payment.

3. The amount of an annuity of $100 per quarter is $2000. If the interest rate is $j_4 = 5\%$, find the number of full payments and the final partial payment if one is necessary.

4. The amount of an annuity of $1000 per year is $15,000. If the interest rate is 4% per year, find the number of full payments and the final partial payment if one is necessary.

5. A debt of $5000 bears interest at $j_2 = 5\%$. It is to be repaid by semiannual payments of $500. Find the number of full payments and the final partial payment.

6. Property worth $25,000 cash is purchased by paying $2000 down followed by $500 per quarter for as long as necessary. If the interest rate is $j_4 = 4\frac{1}{2}\%$, find the number of full payments and the final partial payment.

7. On the first of each month a man deposits $25 into a savings fund paying interest at $j_{12} = 3\frac{1}{2}\%$. How many deposits will it take to cause the fund to reach, or exceed, $3000 for the first time? How much will the fund contain if no deposit is made on this final date?

8. A city plans to make yearly deposits of $50,000 into a savings fund paying interest at $3\frac{1}{2}\%$ effective. How many full deposits and what final payment will it take to accumulate $1,000,000?

9. Find the number of $10 monthly payments and the final payment necessary to purchase a suit worth $90 cash, if the first payment is made on the day of sale and the interest rate is $j_{12} = 8\%$.

10. A student borrows $500 at the beginning of each quarter during his 4 years in college. He will repay the debt with quarterly payments of $200 starting one year after the last loan. If the interest rate is $j_4 = 4\frac{1}{2}\%$, how many full payments and what final payment will be required?

★11. Find the final payment in Prob. 1 by interpolation.

★12. Show that if $s_{\overline{n}|i} = S/R$ is solved for n by interpolation and if $n = k + f$, where k is an integer and f is a fraction less than 1, then an immediate deposit of fR followed by k regular deposits of R will amount to S.

★13. Suppose the value of n, from $s_{\overline{n}|i} = S/R$, is not integral. That is, S/R lies between $s_{\overline{k}|i}$ and $s_{\overline{k+1}|i}$ where k is an integer. Show that if $s_{\overline{k+1}|i} \geqq S/R + 1$, then no final partial deposit is necessary. The k deposits of R, with interest for one more period, will amount to S or more.

30 FINDING THE INTEREST RATE

When R, n, and either A or S are given, the interest rate is determined and may be found approximately by interpolation. Except in very special cases, there is no algebraic method of finding an exact solution for i. However, the solution obtained by interpolation is usually accurate enough for most purposes.

Example 1 Mr. Smith has deposited $25 in a savings fund at the end of each month for the past 5 years. He now has $1625 to his credit. What nominal rate, $m = 12$, did the fund earn?

Solution Let i be the monthly rate and $j_{12} = 12i$ the corresponding nominal rate. The $25 deposits form an annuity whose amount is $1625 as shown on the time diagram below.

The annuity equation is

$$25 s_{\overline{60}|i} = 1625.00$$

so that $s_{\overline{60}|i} = 65.00$.

We next enter Table 10 and find tabulated values of $s_{\overline{60}|i}$ on both sides of 65.00 and set up an interpolation table. These values may be rounded off to four or five decimal places, since additional places do not materially increase the accuracy.

	$s_{\overline{60}|i}$	i	j_{12}
	65.46611	$\frac{7}{24}\%$	$3\frac{1}{2}\%$
0.35329	65.00000	?	?
	64.64671	$\frac{1}{4}\%$	3%

0.81940 $\{$ ... $\}$ c $\}$ $\frac{1}{2}\%$

Interpolating for j_{12}, the proportionality equation is

$$\frac{c}{0.005} = \frac{0.35329}{0.81940}$$

Thus $c = 0.002156$, and $j_{12} = 0.032156$ or 0.03216.

Example 2 A firm sells $100 worth of goods on the following payment plan: $10 down and 10 monthly installments of $9.55 each, the first one due at the end of 3 months.

What nominal rate, $m = 12$, accurate to four decimal places, is included in the payment plan?

Solution   The 10 payments of \$9.55 form a deferred annuity whose present value is \$90 as shown on the time diagram below.

The annuity equation is (see method 2 of the example in Sec. 25)

$$90 = 9.55(a_{\overline{12}|i} - a_{\overline{2}|i})$$

so that $a_{\overline{12}|i} - a_{\overline{2}|i} = 9.4241$.

Using Table 11, we next compute $a_{\overline{12}|i} - a_{\overline{2}|i}$ for various values of i until we find two adjacent rates that produce values larger and smaller than 9.4241.   The data are now arranged in an interpolation table as shown below.

Interpolating for j_{12}, the proportionality equation is

$$\frac{c}{0.015} = \frac{0.0331}{0.0868}$$

Hence, $c = 0.0057$ and $j_{12} = 0.0957$.

Whenever approximating methods are used, a knowledge of the size of the error is of prime importance.   Consequently, we shall state several facts concerning the error resulting when i is found by interpolating in the annuity tables.   (*a*) When i is obtained by interpolation from $a_{\overline{n}|i}$, the result is slightly too large; when $s_{\overline{n}|i}$ is used, the resulting value of i is slightly too small.   (*b*) The error depends primarily on the difference between the two interest rates used and to a much less degree on the size of n.   Thus in the early part of the tables where adjacent rates differ very little, the accuracy is always excellent.   (*c*) Throughout the tables, the error seldom exceeds $n/10$ times the square of the difference of the rates used.   Thus, for Example 1, the error in i should not exceed $6(\frac{1}{24}\%)^2 = 0.00000104$, and the error in j_{12} should not exceed 12 times this, or 0.0000125.   With the use of more exact criteria developed in Chap. 11, it can be shown that the error in j_{12} is about 0.00001. Similarly, it can be shown that the value of j_{12} in Example 2, to six decimal places, is 0.095719.

In the following exercises, it will be sufficient to find i or j_m to the nearest four decimal places.

EXERCISE 17

1. A car worth $4000 cash is sold for $800 down followed by monthly payments of $100 for 3 years. What nominal rate, compounded monthly, does the buyer pay?

2. Goods worth $500 cash are purchased by paying $50 down followed by monthly payments of $40 for one year. What interest rate, compounded monthly, does the payment plan include?

3. Miss Smith has been depositing $100 at the end of each quarter in a savings account for the past 10 years. What rate j_4 did the fund earn if it now contains $4300?

4. Find the interest rate j_{12} earned by a mail-order house that sells goods worth $100 by collecting $10 down and $9 monthly for one year.

5. An insurance company will pay $10,000 to a beneficiary or quarterly payments of $300 for 10 years. What rate j_4 is the insurance company using?

6. Find the interest rate j_{12} charged by a loan company that lends $90 to be repaid by monthly payments of $10 for 10 months.

7. A savings bank advertises, "Starting on Jan. 15 if you will deposit $20 on the 15th of each month continuing through Nov. 15, on Dec. 15 we will give you $225 for Christmas shopping." What rate j_{12} is the bank paying?

8. What effective rate of interest must be earned for deposits of $500 at the end of each year to accumulate $9000 in 14 years?

SUMMARIZING PROBLEMS

1. A certain monthly magazine costs 25 cents on the newsstands. A 2-year subscription, however, costs only $5. If the first issue arrives one month after you mail your check, what interest rate j_{12} does your $5 earn?

2. A 3-year subscription for the magazine in the preceding problem costs $7. What rate j_{12} does a subscriber earn on this investment?

3. Mr. Smith borrows $10,000 from Mr. Jones and signs a contract promising to pay $600 interest at the end of each year for 10 years, at which time he will pay back the principal. Jones immediately sells this contract to a bank that is content to make 4% effective on its investments. How much will the bank pay for the contract and what is Mr. Jones's profit?

4. A contract calls for semiannual payments of $30 for 15 years and an additional $1000 at that time. If an investor is satisfied with $j_2 = 5\%$, how much will he offer for this contract?

5. On the day he is 10 years old, a boy is given $10,000 to finance his education. The money is deposited with an investment corporation that pays $j_{12} = 3\%$. The boy is to receive $200 per month, the first payment coming one month after his sixteenth birthday. How long will these payments continue, and what will the final partial payment be?

6. A boy has the option of receiving $5000 on his sixteenth birthday or a set of monthly payments, equivalent at $j_{12} = 3\frac{1}{2}\%$, during the 4 years he attends college. If he enters college at the age of eighteen and receives the first payment that day, how large will the payments be?

7. A schoolteacher receives $600 at the end of each month for the 9-month term. The school board has voted to change to a 12-month payment plan. If money is worth $j_{12} = 4\%$, what will the new salary be?

8. A contract calls for quarterly payments of $100 for 10 years. Both parties agree to change the contract, shortening the term to 5 years. If they agree that money is worth $j_4 = 5\frac{1}{2}\%$, what will the new payments be?

9. An investment company pays interest on deposits at $j_4 = 3\%$. A man deposits $100 at the end of each quarter for 20 years and then starts withdrawing $400 a quarter. How many full payments will he get, and what will the final partial payment be?

10. A man deposited $100 at the end of each quarter for 5 years in a savings fund that paid $j_4 = 4\%$. At that time the interest rate was changed to $j_4 = 3\%$. He continued his regular deposits for 4 more years. How much did the fund contain?

11. A town planned to make yearly deposits in a savings fund paying interest at 3% per year in order to accumulate $50,000 at the end of 20 years. The first 10 deposits were made according to schedule. Due to loss in revenue, the town was unable to make the next three deposits. How large should the last seven deposits be in order to attain the desired goal?

12. Work Prob. 11 assuming that the interest rate is changed to 2% per year at the end of the tenth year.

13. Mr. Adams owes the First National Bank $1000 due at the end of 5 years and $2000 due at the end of 10 years. He and the bank agree to replace these obligations by a set of quarterly payments for the next 12 years. What will the payments be if it is agreed that money is worth $j_4 = 6\%$?

14. A firm will need $50,000 at the end of 10 years to pay a debt falling due at that time. It can invest funds at 3% per year. What annual deposits, for the first 5 years only, will suffice to accumulate the desired amount?

15. A man agreed to repay a debt with quarterly payments of $100 for 5 years. He failed to make the first 5 payments. On the date that the sixth payment was due, he inherited some money and offered to liquidate the entire debt. How much did it take if money was worth $j_4 = 6\%$?

A knowledge of calculus is required for the remaining problems.

*16. Prove that $\lim\limits_{n=\infty} a_{\overline{n}|i} = 1/i$.

*17. Prove

$$\frac{d(s_{\overline{n}|i})}{di} = \frac{n(1+i)^{n-1} - s_{\overline{n}|i}}{i} = \frac{(n-1)s_{\overline{n}|i} - ns_{\overline{n-1}|i}}{i}$$

*18. Prove

$$\frac{d(a_{\overline{n}|i})}{di} = \frac{n(1+i)^{-n-1} - a_{\overline{n}|i}}{i} = \frac{na_{\overline{n+1}|i} - (n+1)a_{\overline{n}|i}}{i}$$

5
Ordinary General Annuities

31 INTRODUCTION

It has been seen that the fundamental problem in the mathematics of finance deals with the equivalence of sets of financial obligations. Thus, $100 due today is equivalent to $105 due a year from today if the interest rate is 5 percent. Likewise, a house worth $12,000 cash can be purchased for $2000 down and quarterly payments of $215.48 for the next 20 years if the interest rate is 6 percent, converted quarterly. The only essential tool for any problem in the mathematics of finance is an equation of equivalence. Numerous formulas have been developed and tables have been compiled for convenience rather than necessity, and the approach to each new type of problem should be an attempt to express it as simply as possible in terms of existing formulas and tables. A wide variety of symbols and tables is undesirable and should be introduced as sparingly as possible.

An annuity has been defined as a series of payments, usually equal, made at equal intervals of time. *It is called a simple annuity if the interest conversion period and the payment period are equal; otherwise it is called a general annuity.*   For example, suppose Herman Carpenter deposits $50 in a savings bank at the end of each 3 months.   If the bank compounds interest quarterly, the deposits form a simple annuity.   If the bank uses any other conversion period, the deposits form a general annuity.

The alert student will wonder if general annuities can be treated by replacing the given interest rate by an equivalent rate compounded with the desired frequency.   The answer is yes, but usually the new rate is not found in the annuity tables, and computational difficulties arise.

In order to make maximum use of the formulas and methods already developed, *the treatment of general annuities that follows will consist of replacing the given general annuity with an equivalent ordinary simple annuity with payments coming at the ends of the interest conversion periods.* In this chapter we treat only ordinary general annuities, that is, annuities with payments made at the ends of the payment intervals.

32 CONVERTING ORDINARY GENERAL ANNUITIES INTO SIMPLE ANNUITIES

Let W = the general annuity payment
$\quad\quad p$ = the number of general annuity payments per year
$\quad\quad i$ = the interest rate per conversion period
$\quad\quad m$ = the number of interest conversion periods per year
$\quad\quad R$ = the ordinary simple annuity payment, made m times per year, which equitably replaces the general annuity

If an annuity is to be replaced by another annuity, clearly two conditions must hold: (*a*) *the interest rates must be the same or equivalent, and* (*b*) *the values of the two annuities on any date must be the same.*

Given, then, an ordinary general annuity with payments of W made p times per year and an interest rate of i per conversion period, with m conversion periods per year.

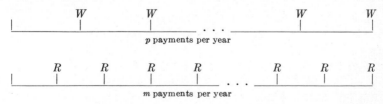

To determine the equivalent ordinary simple annuity of payments R, made m times per year, we proceed as follows: Let i' be the interest rate per general annuity payment period that is equivalent to i per interest conversion period.   Then (see Sec. 13, Chap. 2)

$$(1 + i')^p = (1 + i)^m \tag{1}$$

Now if we equate the amounts of the two annuities at the end of the year, we get

$$R s_{\overline{m}|i} = W s_{\overline{p}|i'} \tag{2}$$

If $s_{\overline{m}|i}$ and $s_{\overline{p}|i'}$ are replaced by the algebraic expressions for which they stand, Eq. (2) becomes

$$R \frac{(1 + i)^m - 1}{i} = W \frac{(1 + i')^p - 1}{i'} \tag{3}$$

In view of Eq. (1), the numerators of the above fractions are equal† and may be divided out, giving

$$\frac{R}{i} = \frac{W}{i'} \tag{4}$$

When Eq. (1) is solved for i', we get

$$i' = (1 + i)^{m/p} - 1$$

and Eq. (4) may be written in the form

$$R = W \frac{i}{(1 + i)^{m/p} - 1} \tag{5}$$

The fraction appearing in the above equation is precisely what one gets by substituting m/p for n in the expression for $1/s_{\overline{n}|i}$. Therefore no new symbol need be introduced. Thus, the preceding equation may be written in the abbreviated form

$$R = W \frac{1}{s_{\overline{m/p}|i}} \tag{6}$$

or the equivalent form

$$W = R s_{\overline{m/p}|i} \tag{7}$$

Clearly the fraction m/p could conceivably have almost any value. In nearly all applications, one of two situations holds: (a) m/p is an integer, in which case Tables 10 and 12 are used to evaluate Eq. (6) or (7); or (b) m/p is a fraction of the form $k/12$, $k = 1, 2, 3, 4$, or 6. In this latter case, Tables 5 and 6 are used to evaluate Eq. (6) or (7). Finally, it should be observed that m and p need not be yearly frequencies; all that is essential is that they both be obtained from the same time interval.

Example 1 Mr. Brown receives a pension of $1000 at the end of each year. What monthly payments are equivalent if money is worth $j_{12} = 6\%$?

† This would be true if present values or the amounts at the end of any number of years had been equated in Eq. (2) instead of the 1-year amounts.

Solution   Here $W = 1000$, $p = 1$, $i = \frac{1}{2}\%$, $m = 12$, and R is to be determined.

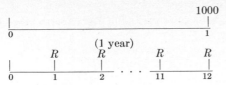

Using Eq. (6) gives

$$R = 1000 \, \frac{1}{s_{\overline{12}|\frac{1}{2}\%}} = \$81.07 \qquad \text{(Table 12)}$$

Thus, Mr. Brown should be willing to accept \$81.07 at the end of each month in place of \$1000 at the end of the year.   The same result is obtained by writing an equation of equivalence using the end of the year as a comparison date.

Example 2   If interest is at 5%, $m = 2$, replace payments of \$50 at the end of each quarter by semiannual payments.
Solution   We have $W = 50$, $p = 4$, $i = 2\frac{1}{2}\%$, and $m = 2$.

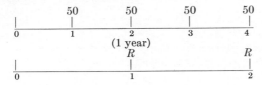

Equation (6) then gives

$$R = 50 \, \frac{1}{s_{\overline{1/2}|2\frac{1}{2}\%}} = 50 \times 2.01242284 = \$100.62 \qquad \text{(Table 5)}$$

Thus, semiannual payments of \$100.62 are equivalent to quarterly payments of \$50 if interest is at $j_2 = 5\%$.

EXERCISE 18

1. If the interest rate is $j_{12} = 5\%$, find the monthly annuity equivalent to \$200 per quarter.

2. Find the monthly annuity equivalent to semiannual payments of \$5000 at $j_{12} = 4\%$.

3. An annuity of \$150 per quarter is to be replaced by annual payments.   How large will they be if the interest rate is 6% per year?

4. A man pays \$80 at the end of each month as payments on a house.   Find the equivalent semiannual payments at $j_2 = 5\%$.

5. If \$500 is needed at the end of each year to overhaul a machine, what sum should be set aside at the end of each month for this purpose if money is worth 6% compounded monthly?

6. If money is worth $j_4 = 5\%$, replace an annual annuity of \$1000 by quarterly payments.

7. If the interest rate is $j_4 = 3\%$, replace yearly payments of \$300 by quarterly payments.

8. Convert a general annuity with semiannual payments of \$1000 into a simple annuity (*a*) if money is worth $j_1 = 6\%$, (*b*) if money is worth $j_4 = 6\%$.

9. Convert a general annuity with quarterly payments of $500 into a simple annuity (a) if the interest rate is $j_{12} = 5\%$, (b) if money is worth 5% per year.

10. An annuity requires payments of $10,000 at the end of every fourth year. Find an equivalent simple annuity at $j_2 = 2\frac{1}{2}\%$.

11. Find a simple annuity at $j_4 = 4\%$ equivalent to payments of $1500 every 5 years.

33 AMOUNT AND PRESENT VALUE OF AN ORDINARY GENERAL ANNUITY

To find the amount or present value of a general annuity, we first convert the general annuity into an ordinary simple annuity and then find the amount or present value of the simple annuity. The only new theory involved is the replacing of the general annuity by a simple one. As soon as this replacement is made, all the theory of the preceding chapter applies.

No additional theory is necessary for deferred general annuities. They are converted into simple annuities and then treated as in the preceding chapter.

Example 1 Mr. Jones deposits $100 at the end of each quarter in a fund that earns interest at $j_1 = 4\%$. How much will be in the fund at the end of 5 years?
Solution We first replace the general annuity by a simple annuity. $W = 100$, $p = 4$, $m = 1$, and $i = 4\%$.

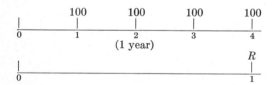

Using Eq. (6),

$$R = 100\,\frac{1}{s_{\overline{1/4}|4\%}} = 100 \times 4.05950975 = 405.950975 \qquad \text{(Table 5)}$$

The annuity is to run for five interest periods, so $n = 5$, and

$$S = Rs_{\overline{5}|4\%} = 405.950975 \times 5.41632256 = \$2198.76 \qquad \text{(Table 10)}$$

Example 2 Find the present value of a set of $500 payments to be made semiannually for 8 years, the first one due at the end of 5 years, if the interest rate is $j_4 = 5\%$.
Solution First replace the general annuity by an ordinary simple annuity. $W = 500$, $p = 2$, $m = 4$, and $i = 1\frac{1}{4}\%$.

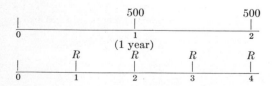

Using Eq. (6),

$$R = 500 \frac{1}{s_{\overline{2}|1\frac{1}{4}\%}} = 500 \times 0.49689441 = 248.4472 \qquad \text{(Table 12)}$$

which is the quarterly payment equivalent to $500 paid semiannually. The term of the annuity is 8 years and is deferred $4\frac{1}{2}$ years. Using the technique developed in the preceding chapter, we have

$$A = 248.4472(a_{\overline{50}|1\frac{1}{4}\%} - a_{\overline{18}|1\frac{1}{4}\%})$$
$$= 248.4472(37.01287574 - 16.02954893) = \$5213.25$$

It should be observed that as soon as the equivalent simple annuity is obtained, the interest period becomes the unit of time.

EXERCISE 19

1. Mr. Rose deposits $25 at the end of each month into a fund paying interest at $j_2 = 3\%$. How much will the fund contain at the end of 5 years?

2. If $100 is invested at the end of each quarter and the interest rate is $4\frac{1}{2}\%$ per year, what will the amount be at the end of 10 years?

3. A house can be purchased with a down payment of $2000 and $70 per month for 20 years. What is the equivalent cash price if the interest rate is 5% per year?

4. A suite of furniture can be purchased for $25 down and $20 per month for 18 months. Find the equivalent cash price at $j_4 = 8\%$.

5. Mr. Smith now has $1000 in a savings bank that pays interest at $j_{12} = 3\%$. If he continues to deposit $100 at the end of each quarter, how much will the fund contain at the end of 5 years?

6. Which is cheaper and by how much cash—to purchase a machine for $10,000, or to rent the machine for $1000 payable at the beginning of each year? In either case the machine will need replacing at the end of 11 years at the original cost and money is worth $j_4 = 3\frac{1}{2}\%$.

7. A contract calls for 12 quarterly payments of $10,000, the first one due at the end of $3\frac{1}{4}$ years. What is the present value of this contract if money is worth $2\frac{3}{4}\%$ per year?

8. Find the present value of a set of $2000 quarterly payments, the first one due at the end of $2\frac{1}{2}$ years and the last one due at the end of 5 years, if money is worth $j_{12} = 4\%$.

9. A contract calls for payments of $25 at the end of each 6 months for 10 years and an additional payment of $1000 at that time. What is the present value of the contract if money is worth 4% per year?

10. Find the present value of the contract in the preceding problem if the interest rate is 6% per year.

11. Find the present value of an annuity of $500 per quarter for 3 years followed by $400 per quarter for 3 more years at $j_2 = 4\%$.

12. Find the present value of the annuity in the preceding problem if the interest rate is 4% per year.

34 CONVERTING SIMPLE ANNUITIES INTO GENERAL ANNUITIES

It is frequently necessary to change ordinary simple annuities into ordinary general annuities. The change is readily made by using Eq. (7)

and Table 6 or 10.   This problem arises when we wish to find the payment of a general annuity.   *The procedure to be used in such a case is first to find the simple annuity that could be used and then to change this simple annuity into an equivalent general annuity.*

Example   A house worth $12,000 is sold for $2000 down and equal semiannual payments for the next 20 years.   How large will the payments be (*a*) if the interest rate is $j_1 = 4\frac{1}{2}\%$, (*b*) if the interest rate is $j_4 = 4\frac{1}{2}\%$?

Solution a   We first solve the simple annuity problem: What yearly payments would be required?   This problem was treated in the chapter on simple annuities, and we have

$$R = 10,000 \, \frac{1}{a_{\overline{20}|4\frac{1}{2}\%}} = 10,000 \times 0.07687614 = 768.7614$$

as the yearly payments that could be used.   We now change the simple annuity into the desired general annuity.   We have $R = 768.7614$, $m = 1$, $p = 2$, and $i = 4\frac{1}{2}\%$.

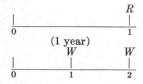

Using Eq. (7),

$$W = Rs_{\overline{1/2}|4\frac{1}{2}\%} = 768.7614 \times 0.49449811 \qquad \text{(Table 6)}$$
$$= \$380.15$$

the equivalent semiannual payments.

Solution b   As in (*a*), we first find the simple annuity, payable quarterly, which could be used.   Thus,

$$R = 10,000 \, \frac{1}{a_{\overline{80}|1\frac{1}{8}\%}} = 10,000 \times 0.01902323 = 190.2323$$

We now change this simple annuity into a general annuity with semiannual payments.

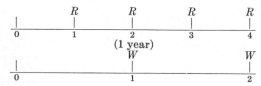

Using Eq. (7),

$$W = Rs_{\overline{2}|1\frac{1}{8}\%} = 190.2323 \times 2.01125000 = \$382.60$$

the equivalent semiannual payments.

EXERCISE 20

1. Replace a yearly annuity of $1000 by an equivalent general annuity payable quarterly if the interest rate is 6% per year.

2. If money is worth $j_4 = 6\%$, replace an annuity of $500 per quarter by an equivalent annuity payable (a) monthly, and (b) semiannually.

3. The cash price of a car is $2750. A purchaser is given credit for $950 on his trade-in, the balance to be paid by equal monthly installments for 30 months. What will these payments be if the interest rate is $j_4 = 5\frac{1}{2}\%$?

4. A house worth $20,000 cash is purchased by paying $5000 down followed by equal monthly installments for 20 years. What will these payments be if the interest rate is 5% per year?

5. A company will need $50,000 at the end of 10 years to pay a debt falling due at that time. It can make regular monthly deposits into a savings fund that earns interest at $j_4 = 3\%$. How large should these monthly deposits be?

6. A man makes semiannual payments into a savings fund paying interest at $3\frac{1}{2}\%$ per year. If he has $1000 in the fund now, how large should his payments be to cause the fund to amount to $6000 at the end of 5 years?

7. A debt of $10,000 is to be repaid by 48 equal monthly installments, the first one to be made 25 months from today. What will the payments be if the interest rate is $j_2 = 5\%$?

8. A lot worth $3000 cash is purchased by paying $1000 down, the balance to be paid by 24 equal monthly payments deferred one year. What will the monthly installment be if the interest rate is 6% per year?

9. Replace an annuity with semiannual payments of $10,000 by an equivalent monthly annuity if the interest rate is (a) $j_2 = 6\%$, (b) $j_{12} = 6\%$.

10. If money is worth $j_2 = 5\%$, replace payments of $500 made monthly by an equivalent set made annually.

11. A contract calls for payments of $1000 at the end of each year. What monthly payments are equivalent if the interest rate is $j_2 = 6\%$?

12. A house needs painting every third year at a cost of $500. The owner decides to make monthly deposits into a savings fund to accumulate this amount. What should these monthly deposits be if the fund bears interest at (a) $j_{12} = 5\%$, (b) $j_1 = 5\%$?

13. A sum of $50,000 is invested today to provide a man with a yearly income for 20 years, the first payment to be received 15 years from now. Find the annual payment if the interest rate is $j_4 = 3\%$.

35 FINDING THE INTEREST RATE FOR A GENERAL ANNUITY

When the interest rate for a general annuity is to be found, the simplest method is to determine first (as in the simple annuity chapter) what the interest rate per payment period would have to be, then to change this rate (as in Chap. 2) into an equivalent rate with the desired conversion period. If interpolation is used, first to determine the interest rate per payment period, then to find the equivalent rate, it is possible to combine the two into a single interpolation as illustrated in the following example.

Example 1 An ordinary annuity of $750 per quarter for 7 years can be purchased for $15,750. What nominal rate, compounded monthly, will the purchaser realize on his investment?

Solution   We first solve the simple annuity problem: What quarterly interest rate is in effect?   For this auxiliary problem we have

$$750a_{\overline{28}|i} = 15,750$$

where i is the rate per quarter.   Thus, $a_{\overline{28}|i} = 21.00$, and we set up an interpolation table as in the simple annuity chapter.   Only the first two columns of the table are formed at first.

	$a_{\overline{28}|i}$	i	j_{12}
	21.2813	2%	0.0795
	21.0000	i	j_{12}
	20.6078	$2\frac{1}{4}\%$	0.0893

$$0.6735\left\{0.2813\left\{\right.\right.$$ $$\left.\left.\right\}c\right\}0.0098$$

The interpolation equation for i is

$$\frac{c}{\frac{1}{4}\%} = \frac{0.2813}{0.6735}$$

where c is the correction to be added to 2%.   However, it is unnecessary actually to find i, as the next step is to determine what nominal rate j_{12} is equivalent to the quarterly rate i.   The equivalence relation is

$$\left(1 + \frac{j_{12}}{12}\right)^{12} = (1 + i)^4$$

Solving for j_{12} gives

$$j_{12} = 12[(1 + i)^{\frac{1}{3}} - 1]$$

The column for j_{12} is now added to the interpolation table.   This is done by substituting 2% and $2\frac{1}{4}\%$ for i in the above equation and using Table 3 to evaluate $(1 + i)^{\frac{1}{3}}$.   We now interpolate directly for j_{12}, using the first and third columns of the interpolation table.   The proportionality equation is

$$\frac{c}{0.0098} = \frac{0.2813}{0.6735}$$

Solving, $c = 0.0041$, and $j_{12} = 0.0795 + 0.0041 = 0.0836$.

Example 2   Solve the preceding example if the interest rate is converted semiannually.
Solution   The procedure is exactly as before except that the j_2 column is computed from the relation

$$\left(1 + \frac{j_2}{2}\right)^2 = (1 + i)^4 \qquad \text{or} \qquad j_2 = 2[(1 + i)^2 - 1]$$

$$0.6735 \left\{ 0.2813 \left\{ \begin{array}{c|c|c} a_{\overline{28}|i} & i & j_2 \\ \hline 21.2813 & 2\% & 0.0808 \\ \hline 21.0000 & i & j_2 \\ \hline 20.6078 & 2\frac{1}{4}\% & 0.0910 \end{array} \right\} c \right\} 0.0102$$

Interpolating between the first and last columns gives

$$\frac{c}{0.0102} = \frac{0.2813}{0.6735}$$

Hence, $c = 0.0043$, and $j_2 = 0.0808 + 0.0043 = 0.0851$.

36 FINDING THE TERM

The term of a general annuity may be found by first converting it into a simple annuity and then determining the term by the methods outlined in the chapter on simple annuities. Usually a final payment somewhat less than the regular payment is required to complete the annuity. The determination of the final payment will be taken up in Chap. 10. Here we shall simply determine the number of payments.

Example How many monthly payments of $50 each, the first due 1 month hence, will be required to liquidate a debt of $1000 if the interest rate is 6%, $m = 2$?
Solution The given annuity is equivalent to the ordinary simple annuity with semi-annual payments of

$$R = W \frac{1}{s_{\overline{1/6}|3\%}} = 50 \times 6.07456894 = 303.7284$$

The term is now determined from the simple annuity equation

$$303.7284 a_{\overline{n}|3\%} = 1000$$

and n may be found either by logarithms or by interpolation. Using interpolation, we have

$$a_{\overline{n}|3\%} = \frac{1000}{303.7284} = 3.2924$$

$$0.8885 \left\{ 0.4638 \left\{ \begin{array}{c|c|c} a_{\overline{n}|3\%} & n & \text{Months} \\ \hline 3.7171 & 4 & 24 \\ \hline 3.2924 & ? & X \\ \hline 2.8286 & 3 & 18 \end{array} \right\} c \right\} 6$$

Interpolating directly for months, gives

$$\frac{c}{6} = \frac{0.4638}{0.8885} \qquad c = 3.132 \qquad \text{and} \qquad X = 18 + 3.132 = 21.132 \text{ months}$$

The result means that 22 monthly payments will be required but that the last payment will not be a full one of $50.

Some labor could have been saved in the above solution if R had not actually been computed, but only indicated. Thus,

$$R = W \frac{1}{s_{\overline{\frac{1}{6}}|3\%}} \qquad \text{and} \qquad 1000 = R a_{\overline{n}|3\%}$$

are combined to give

$$1000 = W \frac{1}{s_{\overline{\frac{1}{6}}|3\%}} a_{\overline{n}|3\%}$$

which, solved for $a_{\overline{n}|3\%}$, gives

$$a_{\overline{n}|3\%} = \frac{1000}{W} s_{\overline{\frac{1}{6}}|3\%} = 20 \times 0.16462073 = 3.2924$$

From here the solution proceeds as before.

EXERCISE 21

1. Find the rate j_4 at which an annuity of $15 payable monthly into a savings fund will amount to $1100 in 5 years.

2. The amount of a semiannual annuity of $1000 is $200,000 at the end of 35 years. Find the rate j_{12}.

3. A debt of $1850 is to be paid off in 12 monthly installments of $160. Find the yearly rate.

4. A house worth $15,000 is purchased by paying $3000 down and $500 at the end of each quarter for 8 years. What rate j_{12} is paid on the debt?

5. A machine worth $10,000 cash is purchased by paying $1000 down and 10 semiannual payments of $1000. Find the interest rate j_4.

6. Furniture worth $350 is purchased by paying $35 down followed by monthly payments of $17.50 for 2 years. Find the interest rate j_2.

7. Find the yearly rate at which a set of quarterly deposits of $200 will amount to $9000 at the end of 8 years.

8. The amount of a $15 monthly annuity is $1000. If the interest rate is $j_2 = 5\%$, find the number of full payments.

9. A savings fund accumulates at $j_4 = 3\frac{1}{2}\%$. How many monthly deposits of $100 will it take to accumulate $5000?

10. How many $100 monthly payments will be necessary to pay off a debt of $4000 if the interest rate is 5% per year?

11. The present value of an annuity of $250 paid quarterly is $2500. If the interest rate is $j_{12} = 3\%$, find the number of full payments.

12. A debt of $100,000 will be repaid by annual payments of $20,000, the first one coming at the end of 10 years. How many full payments will it take if the interest rate is $j_4 = 4\%$?

6
Amortization and Sinking Funds

37 AMORTIZATION OF DEBTS

Originally, amortization meant the liquidation of a debt by any method. *In modern usage, the term* **amortization** *means the extinction of a debt, principal and interest, by means of a sequence of payments that are usually equal.* Thus each payment is large enough to pay the interest earned by the outstanding principal during the preceding time period and also to repay part of the outstanding principal. Usually the payments are all equal and form an annuity.

Example 1 A debt of $10,000 is to be amortized by equal payments at the end of each year for 5 years. If interest on the outstanding principal is computed at 5% effective, find the amount of each payment. Make out a schedule showing what part of each payment is interest, what part is principal repaid, and what the outstanding principal is at the end of each year.

Solution We first find what the payments must be. Since the five payments form an ordinary annuity whose present value is $10,000 (the original indebtedness), we have

$$10,000 = Ra_{\overline{5}|5\%} \quad \text{or} \quad R = 10,000 \,\frac{1}{a_{\overline{5}|5\%}} = \$2309.75$$

We now make out a schedule that shows the progress of the amortization of the debt. Since the entire debt of $10,000 is owed during the first year, the interest due at the end of the year is $10,000 \times 0.05 = 500$. A payment of $2309.75 is then made. Since the payment exceeds the interest due by $1809.75, the indebtedness is reduced to

$$10,000 - 1809.75 = \$8190.25$$

and this latter amount is the outstanding principal during the second year. At the end of the second year the interest due is 5% of $8190.25 or $409.51. Again a payment of $2309.75 is made. This payment is sufficient to pay the interest and further to reduce the indebtedness by $1900.24. The outstanding principal now becomes $6290.01. The same procedure is followed for thé remaining 3 years, when the debt will be completely liquidated. The schedule below gives a complete record of the progress of the amortization of the debt.

End of year	Interest due at 5%	Annual payment	Principal repaid	Outstanding principal
0				10,000.00
1	500.00	2,309.75	1,809.75	8,190.25
2	409.51	2,309.75	1,900.24	6,290.01
3	314.50	2,309.75	1,995.25	4,294.76
4	214.74	2,309.75	2,095.01	2,199.75
5	109.99	2,309.74*	2,199.75	0
Totals	1548.74	11,548.74	10,000.00	

*The final payment is $2309.74, as this is sufficient to liquidate the debt.

The totals at the bottom of the table are for check purposes. The total amount of principal repaid must equal the original indebtedness. Also, the total payments must equal the total interest plus the total principal returned.

A second type of amortization problem arises when the size of the payments is given and it is necessary to find how many payments will be required and what the final partial payment will be. An example will illustrate.

Example 2   A debt of $1000 with interest at $j_2 = 6\%$ will be amortized by payments of $200 at the end of each 6 months as long as necessary. Make out an amortization schedule showing the complete extinction of the debt.
Solution   The interest due at the end of the first 6 months is $1000 \times 0.03 = 30$. A payment of $200 made at this time will pay the interest and will also reduce the

outstanding principal by $170. Thus the first payment reduces the debt to $830. The procedure is repeated, and the results are tabulated below.

End of period	Interest due at 3%	Periodic payment	Principal repaid	Outstanding principal
0				1000.00
1	30.00	200.00	170.00	830.00
2	24.90	200.00	175.10	654.90
3	19.65	200.00	180.35	474.55
4	14.24	200.00	185.76	288.79
5	8.66	200.00	191.34	97.45
6	2.92	100.37	97.45	0
Totals	100.37	1100.37	1000.00	

It should be noticed that the sixth payment is only $100.37, since this amount completely liquidates the debt.

The foregoing examples indicate that the problems concerning amortization are essentially problems dealing with annuities whose present values are known and the amortization schedule is merely a record that shows the distribution of the payments as to interest and the repayment of principal.

EXERCISE 22

1. A debt of $1000 is to be amortized by equal monthly payments for 6 months. Find the payments if the interest rate is $j_{12} = 6\%$, and make out the complete amortization schedule.

2. A debt of $4000 is to be amortized by semiannual payments for $3\frac{1}{2}$ years. If the debt earns interest at $j_2 = 4\%$, find the payment and make out an amortization schedule.

3. After making a down payment on a house, the buyer will amortize the remaining principal of $10,000 at $j_{12} = 6\%$ by monthly payments for 15 years. Find the payment, and run the schedule for the first 4 months.

4. A company is amortizing a debt of $50,000 by annual payments for 20 years. If the debt earns interest at 4% per year, find the payment, and run the schedule for 4 years.

5. A debt of $1000 bearing interest at $j_2 = 4\%$ is amortized by payments of $240 every 6 months for as long as necessary. Make out the amortization schedule.

6. A debt of $3000 will be amortized by quarterly payments of $700 for as long as necessary. If interest is paid at $j_4 = 4\%$, make out the amortization schedule.

7. A debt of $5000 will be amortized by 12 semiannual payments, the first due at the end of $3\frac{1}{2}$ years. If money is worth $j_2 = 5\%$, find the amount of the debt 3 years from now and make out the schedule for the next 2 years.

8. A debt of $1000 will be repaid by monthly payments of $300 for as long as necessary, the first one to be made at the end of 7 months. If interest is paid at $j_{12} = 6\%$,

find the amount of the debt at the end of 6 months and make out the complete schedule starting at that time.

★9. A debt of \$1000 is to be amortized by three equal payments coming at the ends of the next 3 years. If the interest rate is 4%, $m = 4$, find the amortization payment. Construct an amortization schedule showing the outstanding principal before and after each payment.

★10. A debt of \$1000 will be amortized by 12 regular monthly payments. Find the necessary payment if the interest rate is 8% effective. Make out the schedule for the first 3 months.

38 FINDING THE OUTSTANDING PRINCIPAL

When a debt is amortized, the amount of principal remaining to be paid after any given number of payments can be found by making out an amortization schedule. When the number of payments is large, making out a complete schedule becomes tedious and short-cut methods are desirable. As will be seen, an appropriate equation of value can be used for this purpose.

The outstanding principal on any date represents the unpaid balance of the debt. Also on any given date, the present value of the payments that have not yet been made represents the unpaid balance of the debt. Thus we have the following equivalence relation: *The outstanding principal on any given date is equivalent to the payments yet to be made.*

Example 1 A debt of \$10,000 will be amortized by payments at the end of each quarter for 12½ years. If money is worth 3½%, $m = 4$, find the outstanding principal at the end of 7 years.

Solution *Method* 1 We first determine the necessary amortization payment. The payments form an ordinary annuity whose present value is \$10,000, hence

$$10,000 = Ra_{\overline{50}|\,7/8\%} \quad \text{and} \quad R = 10,000 \frac{1}{a_{\overline{50}|\,7/8\%}} = 247.79$$

Since the outstanding principal at the end of 7 years is equivalent to the payments yet to be made, we draw a time diagram for the last 5½ years only.

An equation of value now gives

$$P = Ra_{\overline{22}|\,7/8\%} = 247.79 \times 19.93310891 = \$4939.23$$

Method 2 A second method of finding the outstanding principal makes use of the first 7 years of the time diagram rather than the last 5½. The diagram appears below.

Note that P is placed on the time diagram at the end of the seventh year to replace the remaining payments.   We now write an equation of value using the end of the seventh year as a comparison date.   This gives

$$P + Rs_{\overline{28}|\frac{7}{8}\%} = 10,000(1.00875)^{28}$$

Solving for P, we get

$$P = 10,000(1.00875)^{28} - 247.79s_{\overline{28}|\frac{7}{8}\%} = \$4939.23$$

In finding the outstanding principal, we have the two methods illustrated in the example always available.   The first method makes use of the latter part of the time diagram and the payments yet to be made.   This is sometimes called the **prospective method,** since it uses the future history of the debt.   The second method makes use of the first part of the time diagram and the payments that have been made. Since this method makes use of the past history of the debt, it is sometimes called the **retrospective method.**   When all the payments including the final one are the same, it is usually simpler to use the first method, since the outstanding principal at any time is merely the present value of the annuity consisting of the payments yet to be made.   Thus, just after the kth payment has been made, the outstanding principal is

$$P = Ra_{\overline{n-k}|i} \tag{1}$$

However, when the final payment is an irregular one, it is usually simpler to use the second method.   Thus, just after the kth payment has been made, the outstanding principal is

$$P = A(1 + i)^k - Rs_{\overline{k}|i} \tag{2a}$$

By using the identity $(1 + i)^k = 1 + is_{\overline{k}|i}$, we can rewrite the preceding equation in the simpler form

$$P = A - (R - Ai)s_{\overline{k}|i} \tag{2b}$$

This second form has the advantage of requiring only one table.   It also shows that the amount of principal repaid is $(R - Ai)s_{\overline{k}|i}$.

Example 2   A debt of \$3000 and interest at $j_{12} = 6\%$ is to be amortized by payments of \$50 at the end of each month for as long as is necessary.   Find the outstanding principal at the end of 3 years.
Solution   Since the number of payments and the size of the final payment are not known, it is simpler to use the retrospective method.   Let P be the principal outstanding at the end of 3 years.   Then P is equivalent to all the payments made after 3 years and may be used to replace all these payments on the time diagram.   The time diagram appears below.

We now write an equation of value using the end of the thirty-sixth period as a comparison date and get

$$P + 50s_{\overline{36}|\frac{1}{2}\%} = 3000(1.005)^{36}$$

Solving for P gives $P = \$1623.24$.

The amortization method is often used to liquidate a debt incurred by the purchase of property. Under such conditions, the outstanding principal is frequently referred to as the **seller's equity.** The amount of principal that has been paid, including the down payment, if any, is called the **buyer's equity.** Thus we have the relation

$$\text{Buyer's equity} + \text{seller's equity} = \text{cash value of property} \qquad (3)$$

Cash value refers to the original selling price, which may or may not be its present market value.

Example 3 A house worth \$10,000 cash is purchased by a down payment of \$3000 and the balance in equal monthly installments for 15 years. If the interest rate is $j_{12} = 6\%$, find the buyer's and seller's equity in the house at the end of 6 years.
Solution Since \$7000 is to be amortized,

$$7000 = Ra_{\overline{180}|\frac{1}{2}\%}$$

and

$$R = 7000 \times \frac{1}{a_{\overline{180}|\frac{1}{2}\%}} = \$59.07$$

which is the required monthly payment. The outstanding principal at the end of 6 years is now found by either method, the prospective method being simpler in this case. We draw a time diagram for the last 9 years.

An equation of value gives

$$P = Ra_{\overline{108}|\frac{1}{2}\%} = 59.07 \times 83.29342446 = \$4920.14$$

which is the outstanding principal, or the seller's equity at the end of 6 years. Since the original price of the house was \$10,000, the buyer's equity is

$$10,000 - 4920.14 = \$5079.86$$

Example 4 Mr. Smith bought a tract of land worth \$10,000 cash by paying \$4000 down and the rest in monthly installments of \$50 for as long as necessary. If the interest rate is 5% effective, find Mr. Smith's equity at the end of 10 years.
Solution Since the number of payments is unknown, the second, or retrospective method will be used. The \$50 payments form a general annuity; hence we first find the equivalent yearly annuity. Thus we have (see Sec. 32)

$$R = W\frac{1}{s_{\overline{m/p}|i}} = 50\frac{1}{s_{\overline{1/12}|5\%}} = 50 \times 12.27257753 = \$613.6289$$

as the yearly payment equivalent to $50 monthly. We now draw a time diagram for the first 10 years.

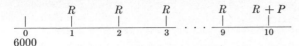

On the diagram, R is the yearly payment and P is the outstanding principal at the end of 10 years; hence it replaces all later payments. Writing an equation of value with the end of 10 years as a comparison date gives

$$P + Rs_{\overline{10}|5\%} = 6000(1.05)^{10}$$

whence

$$P = 6000 \times 1.62889463 - 613.6289 \times 12.57789254 = \$2055.21$$

Mr. Smith's equity is then

$$\text{Buyer's equity} = 10,000 - 2055.21 = \$7944.79$$

EXERCISE 23

1. A man buys property valued at $20,000 by paying $5000 down. The balance, with interest at 5% per year, will be amortized by annual payments for the next 20 years. What will the outstanding principal be at the end of 10 years? How much will the eleventh payment reduce the debt?

2. In buying a new car a man contracts a debt of $3000. This, with interest at $j_{12} = 6\%$, will be amortized by monthly payments for 2 years. What will the outstanding debt be just after the fifteenth payment? How much will the sixteenth payment reduce it?

3. A debt of $10,000 bearing interest at $j_4 = 4\%$ will be amortized by 60 quarterly payments. Find the outstanding principal just after the fifty-sixth payment, and run the amortization schedule from there on out.

4. A debt of $100,000 will be amortized by semiannual payments of $5000 for as long as necessary. If interest is paid at $j_2 = 3\%$, find the outstanding principal just after the twentieth payment.

5. A debt of $4000 bearing interest at $j_{12} = 6\%$ will be amortized by monthly payments of $50 for as long as necessary. Find the outstanding principal just after the last full payment and complete the last line of the amortization schedule.

6. A debt of $15,000 earning interest at $j_4 = 5\%$ will be amortized by quarterly payments of $1250 for as long as necessary. Find the outstanding principal just after the ninth payment. Complete the amortization schedule from there on out.

7. A house worth $15,000 cash is purchased by paying $4000 down. The balance, with interest at $j_{12} = 6\%$, will be amortized by monthly payments for 15 years. Find the buyer's and seller's equity at the end of 10 years.

8. A tract of land worth $50,000 is purchased with a down payment of $10,000 and yearly payments for 20 years. If the interest rate is $4\frac{1}{2}\%$ per year, find the equity of both buyer and seller at the end of 15 years.

9. A house worth $15,000 was purchased by Mr. Jones by a down payment of $3000, the balance, with interest at $j_4 = 5\frac{1}{2}\%$, to be amortized by quarterly payments for 20 years. Mr. Jones made his payments regularly for 15 years, at which time he sold the house for $20,000, part of which was needed to pay off the outstanding principal. How much did Mr. Jones have left?

10. A fraternity house worth $125,000 is purchased by paying $25,000 down. The balance, with interest at $j_1 = 6\%$, will be paid by quarterly installments of $2000 as long as necessary. Find the fraternity's equity at the end of 18 years.

11. A city borrows $800,000 to build a school. It will amortize this debt at $j_1 = 2\frac{1}{2}\%$ by semiannual payments of $30,000 for as long as necessary. Find the city's equity in the school at the end of 10 years.

39 INSTALLMENT BUYING

When an article is purchased and paid for by some installment plan, the buyer is essentially amortizing a debt incurred by the purchase of the article. Clearly the installment payments are equivalent to the cash price *at some rate of interest.* However, the interest rate that makes the two options (cash or the installment plan) equivalent is seldom given. In fact, the manner in which the payments are determined is usually such that it obscures the interest rate involved. There are two plans in common usage whereby the payments are determined in such a way that the interest rate is hidden. One is the **markup plan;** the other is the **carrying-charge plan.**

Under the markup plan, the dealer lists the article at the price for which he is willing to sell it by installment payments and allows a discount on this list price if the purchaser pays cash. For example, a piece of furniture is made to sell for $300 cash. The dealer will list the price at $360 and will allow a customer to buy it by paying $120 down and the balance ($240) by paying $20 a month for a year. If the customer wishes to pay cash, he is given a $16\frac{2}{3}$ percent discount on the list price. Thus he would be given a discount of $60 and would pay $300 for the merchandise. It should be noted that the markup is $^{60}\!/_{300} = 20$ percent of the cash selling price, whereas the cash discount is $^{60}\!/_{360} = 16\frac{2}{3}$ percent of the list price.

When the carrying-charge plan is used, the cash price of the merchandise is given. The installment payments are then determined as follows: A moderate down payment is usually required, after which a carrying charge is added to the unpaid balance to obtain the amount to be paid by installments. The carrying charge is usually a certain percentage of the unpaid balance. The amount obtained by adding the carrying charge to the unpaid balance is then divided into a certain number of installments, usually equal in size.

When either plan is used, the true interest rate is determined by writing an equation of equivalence stating that the cash price equals the down payment plus the present value of the annuity which the payments form. That is,

$$\text{Cash price} = \text{down payment} + Ra_{\overline{n}|i} \tag{4}$$

This equation is solved for $a_{\overline{n}|i}$, and the rate is then found by interpolation.

Example 1 Find the interest rate j_{12} paid by a purchaser who uses the installment plan described above.
Solution We draw a time diagram showing the two options.

Let i be the monthly interest rate that makes these two options equivalent. An equation of value with the present as a comparison date gives

$$300 = 120 + 20a_{\overline{12}|i} \quad \text{and} \quad a_{\overline{12}|i} = 9.00$$

We now use interpolation as described in Sec. 30 and obtain $j_{12} = 56.79\%$.

Example 2 Goods worth \$54 cash are purchased by the following carrying-charge plan: A down payment of \$14 is required, after which 20% of the unpaid balance is added on, and this amount is then divided into 12 equal monthly installments. What nominal rate, $m = 12$, does the installment plan include?
Solution The \$14 down payment leaves an unpaid balance of \$40. The carrying charge is 20% of \$40 or \$8. Thus \$48 is to be paid by installments, so that the monthly payments will be \$4 each.

The two options of buying the goods are shown on the time diagram below.

```
14      4      4      4          4      4
|       |      |      |          |      |
————————————————————————  . . .  ————————————
0       1      2      3          11     12
54
```

Let i be the monthly rate that makes these two options equivalent. An equation of value with the present as a comparison date gives

$$54 = 14 + 4a_{\overline{12}|i} \quad \text{and} \quad a_{\overline{12}|i} = 10.00$$

Using interpolation as in the preceding example, we get $j_{12} = 35.08\%$.

There are many variations of the two plans described in this section. For example, a recent mail-order catalog sells goods on the following *easy payment plan*.

Payment table*

If unpaid balance amounts to	We add for easy payments	Amount payable monthly is
\$40.01–45.00	\$4.00	\$5.00
45.01–50.00	4.50	5.00
50.01–55.00	5.00	5.00
55.01–60.00	5.50	6.00
60.01–65.00	6.00	6.00

* A down payment of at least 10 percent of the cash price must be included with the order.

EXERCISE 24

1. A man borrows $200 from a loan company, using his car as security. The company adds a 10% carrying charge and requires that the loan be repaid by 10 equal monthly payments. What interest rate j_{12} does the company realize?

2. A mail-order house uses a 20% carrying charge on goods paid for by monthly payments for 2 years. A 10% down payment is required. If goods worth $300 are financed by this plan, what interest rate j_{12} is the buyer paying?

3. A chair worth $48.50 is purchased from the company whose payment table appears in the text. If a down payment of $7.50 is made, what interest rate j_{12} does the buyer pay?

4. An auto-loan company uses a 30% carrying charge on a debt of $2000 incurred by purchasing a new car, the monthly payments to run for 3 years. What interest rate j_{12} is the purchaser paying?

5. What interest rate j_{12} is equivalent to a 10% carrying charge if the payments are monthly for one year? (*Note:* Use any convenient debt, such as $100.)

6. A suite of furniture is marked up to $600. If it is sold on time, a down payment of 15% is required and the balance paid in 12 equal monthly installments. If it is purchased for cash, a 25% discount on the list price is given. What interest rate j_{12} is the installment buyer paying? What percent markup is the company using?

7. Goods worth $200 cash are marked up 25%. If they are sold on time, a down payment of 20% of the list price is required and the balance paid in 12 equal monthly installments. What interest rate j_{12} does the installment buyer pay, and what is the cash discount?

8. A company sells goods for a down payment of 10% of the list price and the balance in 10 equal monthly installments. To a cash customer a 20% discount on the list price is given. What interest rate j_{12} does this payment plan include?

9. A company uses a 15% markup plan. A down payment of 30% of the list price is required and the balance paid in 10 equal monthly installments. What interest rate j_{12} is contained in this plan?

10. A certain firm uses a 12% markup plan. A down payment of 25% of the list price is collected and the balance paid in 10 equal monthly installments. What is the corresponding interest rate j_{12}?

11. A loan company charges 10% in advance and requires that the loan be repaid in 10 equal monthly installments. Thus, if a client asked for $250, he would receive $225 and repay $25 monthly for 10 months. What interest rate j_{12} does this company realize?

12. The Square Deal Loan Co. charges 8% "interest in advance" and allows the client to repay the loan in 12 equal monthly payments. What is the corresponding interest rate j_{12}?

40 SINKING FUNDS

In its simplest form, a sinking fund is a savings fund, productively invested, into which equal periodic payments are made. It is designed to accumulate a definite amount of money upon a specified date. Thus it differs from an ordinary savings fund only in that it is designed to accumulate a certain sum on a certain date and that regular payments are made into the fund. Sinking funds are established with a definite end in view,

such as to pay off a debt that will fall due at some later date, to buy a
new machine to replace an old one when it wears out, or to return the
principal invested in a mine when its stock of minerals has been depleted.
A schedule showing how such a fund accumulates the desired amount is
illustrated below.

Example The sum of \$5000 will be needed at the end of 5 years. If money can be
invested to earn 5% effective, find how much must be deposited in the fund at the
end of each year to accumulate the desired amount, and make out a schedule showing
the growth of the fund.
Solution The \$5000 is the amount of an ordinary annuity of five yearly payments.
Therefore

$$5000 = Rs_{\overline{5}|5\%} \quad \text{and} \quad R = 5000\,\frac{1}{s_{\overline{5}|5\%}} = \$904.87$$

We now construct a schedule showing the growth of the fund. At the end of the
first year, a deposit of 904.87 is made. Similarly, at the end of the second year,
another deposit is made. At this time, however, the first deposit has been earning
interest for one year; hence the fund is further increased by $904.87 \times 0.05 = 45.24$.
Thus the total increase at the end of the second year is $904.87 + 45.24 = 950.11$, and
the fund will contain 1854.98. This procedure is repeated, and the results are
tabulated.

End of year	Deposit	Interest on fund	Increase in fund	Amount in fund
1	904.87	0	904.87	904.87
2	904.87	45.24	950.11	1854.98
3	904.87	92.75	997.62	2852.60
4	904.87	142.63	1047.50	3900.10
5	904.87	195.01	1099.88	4999.98*
Totals†	4524.35	475.63	4999.98	

* The final amount is 2 cents short, since theoretically the deposits
should have been \$904.874, which was rounded to the nearest cent.
† The totals of the various columns are recorded only for check
purposes.

Occasionally it is desirable to know how much will be in the fund
on some specified date. While reference to the schedule will furnish the
answer, clearly this result can also be obtained by finding the amount
of an annuity whose periodic payment is the sinking-fund deposit and
whose term is the desired time. Thus, in the example above, the amount
in the fund at the end of the third year is $904.87s_{\overline{3}|5\%} = \$2852.60$.

EXERCISE 25

1. A sinking fund, bearing interest at $j_4 = 4\%$, is established to accumulate $1000 at the end of five quarters. Make out a schedule showing the growth of the fund.

2. Semiannual deposits are made into a sinking fund bearing interest at $j_2 = 4\%$. If the fund is to contain $2000 at the end of 3 years, make out a schedule showing the growth of the fund.

3. A city will need $100,000 at the end of 10 years to retire a bonded debt. What annual deposits into a sinking fund accumulating at 3% effective will be necessary? Make out the first four lines of the schedule.

4. A fraternity will need $6000 at the end of 5 years to replace worn-out furniture. What monthly deposits into a sinking fund earning interest at $j_{12} = 3\%$ will be necessary? Find the amount in the fund at the end of 4 years 8 months, and complete the rest of the schedule.

5. Find the quarterly deposits into a sinking fund with interest at $j_4 = 6\%$ necessary to accumulate $50,000 at the end of 10 years. Find the amount in the fund at the end of 9 years, and complete the rest of the schedule.

6. A sinking fund bearing interest at $j_4 = 3\%$ now contains $5000. What quarterly deposits for the next 8 years will cause the fund to amount to $50,000? How much is in the fund at the end of 5 years?

7. A company has $6000 in a sinking fund that earns interest at 5% per year. What annual deposits into this fund will cause it to amount to $25,000 at the end of 15 years? Find the amount in the fund at the end of 10 years.

8. What semiannual deposits into a sinking fund bearing interest at $j_4 = 4\%$ are necessary to accumulate $5000 in 15 years? How much will the fund contain at the end of 5 years?

9. What monthly deposits into a sinking fund earning $3\frac{1}{2}\%$ per year are necessary to accumulate $1000 in 4 years? How much will the fund contain at the end of 2 years?

★10. A city must pay off two debts, one of $50,000 due in 10 years and one of $10,000 due in 12 years. A sinking fund will be set up by equal annual deposits for 12 years to retire both debts when due. If the fund earns interest at 3% per year, what will the annual deposit be? Find the amount in the fund at the end of 9 years and complete the rest of the schedule.

★11. Show that the increase in the sinking fund at the end of the kth period is $R(1 + i)^{k-1}$.

41   THE SINKING-FUND METHOD OF RETIRING A DEBT

The amortization method of retiring a debt often creates a problem for the lender of the money. His principal is returned to him in small amounts and at frequent intervals. Since it is not always easy to invest small sums productively, he is very likely to have some of the returned principal lying idle for some time before it can be reinvested. For this reason, lenders sometimes require that all the principal be returned in a lump sum at the end of the term of the loan. Usually the interest is not allowed to accumulate but is paid at the end of each interest period. For example, a bank might loan $1000 for 5 years with interest at 6 percent effective and require that it be repaid as follows: At the end of each year a $60 interest payment is to be made, and at the end of the fifth year, in addition to the interest due at that time, the entire principal of $1000 is to be repaid.

When money is borrowed under the terms just described, the borrower usually prepares for the ultimate liquidation of the debt by establishing a sinking fund. Usually the sinking-fund payments are made on the same dates as the interest payments on the debt. When this is the case, the sum of these two payments is called the **periodic expense of the debt.**

Example A city borrows $10,000 for 10 years at 6% effective. The city will pay the interest at the end of each year and will establish a sinking fund to repay the principal. What annual sinking-fund payments are necessary if the fund earns interest at 4% effective? What is the annual expense of the debt? How much will the sinking fund contain at the end of 6 years?

Solution Since the sinking fund must amount, at 4% effective, to $10,000 in 10 years,

$$10,000 = Rs_{\overline{10}|4\%} \quad \text{and} \quad R = 10,000 \, \frac{1}{s_{\overline{10}|4\%}} = \$832.91$$

Interest on the debt at the end of each year will be 6% of 10,000 = $600. The total annual expense of the debt to the city is therefore

$$E = 832.91 + 600.00 = \$1432.91$$

At the end of 6 years, the fund will contain the amount of an ordinary annuity of six payments accumulated at 4%. Hence

$$S = 832.91 s_{\overline{6}|4\%} = \$5524.67$$

42 COMPARISON OF SINKING-FUND AND AMORTIZATION METHODS OF RETIRING A DEBT

It should be obvious by now that an experienced money lender will usually accept a somewhat lower interest rate when the sinking-fund method of retirement is to be used than he would demand if the debt is to be amortized. It should also be clear that the borrower will want to use the plan that is least expensive to him. Since there are usually several sources available from which to borrow, it is important for the borrower to determine which of the available loans will be cheapest. The method of determining which source to choose consists merely in computing what the periodic expense of the debt would be under the various plans offered.

Example A firm wishes to borrow $10,000 for 10 years. The First National Bank will lend the money at 6% effective and allow the debt to be amortized by annual payments. The Second National Bank will lend the money at 5% effective provided only the interest is paid annually and the principal is repaid at the end of the 10-year term. If the second source is used, the firm can set up a sinking fund that accumulates at 3% effective. How much can be saved each year by selecting the better method?

Solution If the money is borrowed from the First National Bank, the $10,000 is the present value of an annuity of 10 payments. If R is the necessary annual payment, then

$$10,000 = Ra_{\overline{10}|6\%} \quad \text{and} \quad R = 10,000\,\frac{1}{a_{\overline{10}|6\%}} = \$1358.68$$

The yearly expense of the debt to the firm in this case will be $1358.68. If the Second National Bank is used, the firm must pay $500 interest (5% of $10,000) and must also make a yearly deposit into a sinking fund for the purpose of retiring the principal. To find the sinking-fund deposit, we have

$$10,000 = Rs_{\overline{10}|3\%} \quad \text{and} \quad R = 10,000\,\frac{1}{s_{\overline{10}|3\%}} = \$872.31$$

Hence, the annual expense under the second plan would be

$$E = 500.00 + 872.31 = \$1372.31$$

Comparing the annual expenses of the two plans, we see that the firm would save $1372.31 − $1358.68 = $13.63 annually by borrowing from the First National Bank and amortizing the debt.

EXERCISE 26

1. A company borrows $10,000 for 5 years, paying interest semiannually at $j_2 = 5\%$. To retire the principal, equal semiannual deposits will be made into a sinking fund that earns interest at $j_2 = 4\%$. Find the semiannual expense of the debt.

2. A city borrows $100,000, paying interest annually on this sum at 4% per year. What annual deposits must be made into a sinking fund bearing interest at 3% per year in order to pay off the entire principal at the end of 20 years? Find the annual expense of the debt.

3. A company issues bonds that promise a semiannual interest payment on $1000 at $j_2 = 6\%$ and a redemption payment of $1000 at the end of 25 years. A sinking fund with semiannual deposits accumulating at $j_2 = 4\%$ is established to prepare for the redemption payment. If 50 bonds were issued, what is the semiannual expense of the debt?

4. On a debt of $1000, interest is paid monthly at $j_{12} = 4\%$ and monthly deposits are made into a sinking fund to retire the principal at the end of $2\frac{1}{2}$ years. If the sinking fund earns $j_{12} = 3\%$, what is the monthly expense of the debt?

5. A city wishes to borrow $500,000 for 20 years. The First National Bank will lend the money at 4% per year if the debt is amortized by annual payments. The bank is also willing to lend the money at $3\frac{1}{2}\%$ per year if only the interest is paid annually and the principal returned in a lump sum at the end of 20 years. If the second plan is used, a sinking fund that earns $j_1 = 3\%$ will be used to retire the principal. Which plan is cheaper, and how much is saved annually by using it?

6. A company wishes to borrow $10,000 for 5 years. One source will lend the money at $j_2 = 5\%$ if it is amortized by semiannual payments. A second source will lend the money at $j_2 = 4\%$ if only the interest is paid semiannually and the principal returned in a lump sum. If the second source is used, a sinking fund accumulating at $j_2 = 3\%$ will be used to accumulate the principal. How much can the company save semiannually by using the better plan?

7. In Prob. 5, which plan is cheaper if (*a*) all the rates are changed to $3\frac{1}{2}\%$ per year, (*b*) the sinking-fund rate is changed to $2\frac{1}{2}\%$ per year, the others remaining as given?

8. A company can borrow \$20,000 at 5% yearly and amortize the debt with annual payments for 15 years. From a second source the money can be borrowed at $4\frac{1}{2}$% per year if the interest is paid annually and the principal is repaid in a lump sum at the end of 15 years. If the second source is used and a sinking fund established to accumulate the principal, what yearly rate must the fund earn to keep the annual expense of the debt the same?

9. A company wishes to borrow \$10,000 for 20 years. From one source the money can be borrowed at $j_1 = 6$% and amortized by annual payments. From a second source, the money can be borrowed at $j_1 = 5$% if only the interest is paid annually and the principal repaid at the end of 20 years. If the second source is used, a sinking fund will be established by annual deposits that accumulate at $j_4 = 4$%. How much is saved annually by using the better plan?

10. A city can borrow \$50,000 for 20 years by issuing bonds on which interest will be paid semiannually at $j_2 = 4$%, and the principal will be retired by a sinking fund consisting of semiannual deposits invested at $j_2 = 3$%. Find the nominal rate j_2 at which the loan could be amortized with the same semiannual expense.

11. A company that can get 3% per year on sinking-fund deposits wishes to borrow \$50,000 for 25 years. If bonds are issued for this purpose, what yearly interest rate should the bonds pay in order to make the annual expense of the debt the same as a 5% amortization plan?

*43 AMORTIZATION USING SEVERAL INTEREST RATES

Many states have small-loan legislation which allows the use of two or more interest rates, depending on the size of the loan. For example, a company might charge 2 percent per month on unpaid principal of \$100 or less but only 1 percent per month on unpaid principal in excess of \$100. Thus, if \$250 were borrowed on such a plan, two interest rates would be used until the unpaid balance was reduced to \$100 or less, after which only one rate would be used. In a similar way a plan could use three or even more interest rates.

The following notation will be used:

A = the total amount of the original loan
A_1 = the amount of the loan which is amortized *first*
A_2 = the amount of the loan which is amortized *second*
i_1 = the interest rate paid on A_1
i_2 = the interest rate paid on A_2
$I_1 = A_1 i_1$, $I_2 = A_2 i_2$, and $I = I_1 + I_2$
n = the total number of payments
n_1 = the number of payments required to amortize A_1
n_2 = the number of additional payments required to amortize A_2.
    Clearly $n = n_1 + n_2$
R = the periodic payment which liquidates the debt
P_t = the outstanding principal just after the tth payment

We will first establish formulas for the outstanding principal at any time t. During the early part of the amortization, for $t \leqq n_1$, the payment R pays the interest I_2 on A_2 and amortizes A_1 (or slightly more than A_1) at i_1. Under the retrospective method, the outstanding principal will therefore be

$$P_t = A_2 + A_1(1 + i_1)^t - (R - I_2)s_{\overline{t}|i_1}$$

However, since $(1 + i)^t = 1 + is_{\overline{t}|i}$, the preceding equation can be written in the simpler form

$$P_t = A - (R - I)s_{\overline{t}|i_1} \qquad t = 1, 2, \ldots, n_1$$

After n_1 payments have been made, only one interest rate is involved and the outstanding principal, by the prospective method, is

$$P_t = Ra_{\overline{n-t}|i_2} \qquad t = n_1, n_1 + 1, \ldots$$

Since both formulas hold for $t = n_1$, they may be equated on this date and solved for R, giving

$$R = \frac{A + Is_{\overline{n_1}|i_1}}{a_{\overline{n_2}|i_2} + s_{\overline{n_1}|i_1}} \tag{5}$$

To determine n_1 and n_2, we note that since R must be at least large enough to pay I_2 and amortize A_1 at i_1 in n_1 periods,

$$R \geqq I_2 + A_1 \frac{1}{a_{\overline{n_1}|i_1}}$$

Moreover, since the first n_1 payments reduce the debt to A_2 or less, R will not exceed the payment necessary to amortize A_2 at i_2 in n_2 periods. Therefore

$$R \leqq A_2 \frac{1}{a_{\overline{n_2}|i_2}} = I_2 + A_2 \frac{1}{s_{\overline{n_2}|i_2}} \qquad \left(\text{using } \frac{1}{a_{\overline{n}|i}} = i + \frac{1}{s_{\overline{n}|i}}\right)$$

Combining the two inequalities gives

$$A_1 s_{\overline{n_2}|i_2} \leqq A_2 a_{\overline{n_1}|i_1} \tag{6}$$

n_1 is the *smallest integer* that satisfies inequality (6). To avoid checking numerous values of n_1 and n_2 in inequality (6), we may first estimate them as follows: Since $a_{\overline{n}|i} < n < s_{\overline{n}|i}$, inequality (6) may be replaced by the weaker one

$$A_1 n_2 < A_2 n_1$$

which leads easily to

$$n_1 > \frac{nA_1}{A} \quad \text{and} \quad n_2 < \frac{nA_2}{A} \tag{7}$$

In practice, n_1 and n_2 are estimated from (7), then determined exactly from (6), and then R is computed from Eq. (5).

Example 1 A lending agency charges interest at the rate of 3% per month on unpaid principal of $100 or less and 1% per month on unpaid principal in excess of $100. If $250 is borrowed from this agency and repaid with 6 equal monthly payments, find the size of the payment and make out an amortization schedule.

Solution Here $A_1 = 150$, $A_2 = 100$, $A = 250$, $i_1 = 1\%$, $i_2 = 3\%$, and $n = 6$. We first use inequality (7) to estimate n_1 and n_2.

$$n_1 > \frac{nA_1}{A} = \frac{6 \times 150}{250} = 3.6 \quad \text{and} \quad n_2 = n - n_1 < 2.4$$

We next verify that $n_1 = 4$ and $n_2 = 2$ do satisfy inequality (6) and are therefore the correct values. R is now computed from Eq. (5).

$$R = \frac{A + Is_{\overline{n_1}|i_1}}{a_{\overline{n_2}|i_2} + s_{\overline{n_1}|i_1}} = \frac{250 + 4.50s_{\overline{4}|1\%}}{a_{\overline{2}|3\%} + s_{\overline{4}|1\%}} = \$44.91$$

The amortization schedule is shown below.

End of period	Interest due at 3%	Interest due at 1%	Periodic payment	Principal repaid	Outstanding principal
0					250.00
1	3.00	1.50	44.91	40.41	209.59
2	3.00	1.10	44.91	40.81	168.78
3	3.00	.69	44.91	41.22	127.56
4	3.00	.28	44.91	41.63	85.93
5	2.58		44.91	42.33	43.60
6	1.31		44.91	43.60	0
Totals	15.89	3.57	269.46	250.00	

In order to compare multiple-rate plans with single-rate plans or other multiple-rate plans, it is convenient to define the **yield rate** of a plan. By definition, *it is the interest rate that a simple annuity with the same payments, term, and present value would include.* It is found by solving the equation $A = Ra_{\overline{n}|i}$ for i as discussed in Sec. 30, Chap. 4.

Example 2   Find the yield rate of the amortization plan in Example 1.
Solution   Let i be the yield rate, then

$$250 = 44.91a_{\overline{6}|i} \qquad a_{\overline{6}|i} = \frac{250}{44.91} = 5.5667$$

and by interpolation, $i = 2.185\%$ per month.

In multiple-rate plans, almost invariably i_1 is less than i_2, and this will be assumed in future statements.   The yield rate will always fall somewhere between the rates in use, and, in fact, it can be shown that it is greater than I/A.

When a plan uses three rates, our notation will be supplemented by A_3, i_3, and n_3, with their obvious meanings.   As before, A_1 is amortized first, then A_2, and A_3 last.   The outstanding principal during the first phase will be

$$P_t = A_2 + A_3 + A_1(1 + i_1)^t - (R - I_2 - I_3)s_{\overline{t}|i_1}$$

which may be simplified, as in the case of two rates, to

$$P_t = A - (R - I)s_{\overline{t}|i_1} \qquad t = 1, 2, \ldots, n_1$$

During the first phase, usually more than A_1 will be amortized so that P_{n_1} is usually less than $A_2 + A_3$.   If we set $A_2^* = P_{n_1} - A_3$, which simplifies to

$$A_2^* = A_1 + A_2 - (R - I)s_{\overline{n_1}|i_1}$$

then the problem remaining (after n_1 payments) is a two-rate problem involving A_2^* and A_3 at rates i_2 and i_3 with n_2 and n_3 payments.   Therefore the outstanding principal during the second phase can be written

$$P_t = A_2^* + A_3 - (R - I^*)s_{\overline{t-n_1}|i_2} \qquad \text{where } I^* = A_2^*i_2 + I_3$$

for $t = n_1 + 1, n_1 + 2, \ldots, n_1 + n_2$.

During the final phase, as in the case of two rates,

$$P_t = Ra_{\overline{n-t}|i_3} \qquad t = n_1 + n_2, \ldots, n - 1$$

Since the last two equations hold for $t = n_1 + n_2$, they may be equated on this date and solved for R.   Starting with

$$Ra_{\overline{n_3}|i_3} = A_2^* + A_3 - (R - I^*)s_{\overline{n_2}|i_2}$$

we substitute for A_2^* and I^* their values in terms of original data. The resulting equation will not be given since it is rather lengthy and can be reproduced by the reader if desired. The solution for R can be expressed in a variety of ways by using identities among the interest factors. The simplest of these is

$$R = \frac{A + A_3(i_3 - i_2)a_{\overline{n_2}|i_2} + Is_{\overline{n_1}|i_1}}{a_{\overline{n_3}|i_3}(1 + i_2)^{-n_2} + a_{\overline{n_2}|i_2} + s_{\overline{n_1}|i_1}} \tag{8}$$

In order to determine n_1, n_2, and n_3, the three-rate plan is compared with two different two-rate plans with the same amount and term. The two plans are:

a. To amortize $(A_1 + A_2)$ and A_3 at rates r_1 and i_3 with $(n_1 + n_2)$ and n_3 payments, where r_1 lies between i_1 and i_2

b. To amortize A_1 and $(A_2 + A_3)$ at i_1 and r_2 with n_1 and $(n_2 + n_3)$ payments, where r_2 is between i_2 and i_3

Inequalities (6) and (7) apply to the two-rate plans and from (7) it follows easily that

$$n_1 > \frac{nA_1}{A} \quad \text{and} \quad n_3 < \frac{nA_3}{A} \tag{9}$$

while the use of inequality (6) gives

$$(A_1 + A_2)s_{\overline{n_3}|i_3} \leqq A_3 a_{\overline{n_1+n_2}|r_1} \qquad \text{where } i_1 < r_1 < i_2 \tag{10a}$$
$$A_1 s_{\overline{n_2+n_3}|r_2} \leqq (A_2 + A_3)a_{\overline{n_1}|i_1} \qquad \text{where } i_2 < r_2 < i_3 \tag{10b}$$

An example will illustrate how these inequalities can be used to determine n_1, n_2, and n_3.

Example 3 A lending firm charges 3% per month on outstanding principal of $200 or less, 2% per month on that in excess of $200 but not exceeding $300, and 1% per month on all over $300. If $400 is borrowed from this firm and repaid with monthly payments for 1 year, find the size of the payment and make out the schedule. Find the yield rate.

Solution Here $A_1 = 100$, $A_2 = 100$, $A_3 = 200$, $i_1 = 1\%$, $i_2 = 2\%$, $i_3 = 3\%$, and $n = 12$.

Using inequality (9) gives

$$n_1 > \frac{12 \times 100}{400} = 3 \quad \text{and} \quad n_3 < \frac{12 \times 200}{400} = 6$$

Hence, n_1 is 4 or more, and n_3 is 5 or less.   Next, using inequalities (10a) and (10b), we get

$$200s_{\overline{n_3}|3\%} \leq 200a_{\overline{n_1+n_2}|r_1} \qquad \text{where} \qquad 1\% < r_1 < 2\%$$

and

$$100s_{\overline{n_2+n_3}|r_2} \leq 300a_{\overline{n_1}|1\%} \qquad \text{where} \qquad 2\% < r_2 < 3\%$$

Using the tables we verify that $n_1 + n_2 = 7$ is the smallest integer that satisfies the first inequality for any value of r_1 between 1% and 2%.   Likewise we find that $n_1 = 4$ from the second inequality.   Thus, $n_1 = 4$, $n_2 = 3$, and $n_3 = 5$.   The value of R is now found by using Eq. (8).

$$R = \frac{400 + 2a_{\overline{3}|2\%} + 9s_{\overline{4}|1\%}}{a_{\overline{5}|3\%}(1.02)^{-3} + a_{\overline{3}|2\%} + s_{\overline{4}|1\%}} = \$39.28$$

The amortization schedule is shown below.

End of period	Interest at 3%	Interest at 2%	Interest at 1%	Payment	Principal repaid	Out-standing principal
0						400.00
1	6.00	2.00	1.00	39.28	30.28	369.72
2	6.00	2.00	0.70	39.28	30.58	339.14
3	6.00	2.00	0.39	39.28	30.89	308.25
4	6.00	2.00	0.08	39.28	31.20	277.05
5	6.00	1.54		39.28	31.74	245.31
6	6.00	0.91		39.28	32.37	212.94
7	6.00	0.26		39.28	33.02	179.92
8	5.40			39.28	33.88	146.04
9	4.38			39.28	34.90	111.14
10	3.33			39.28	35.95	75.19
11	2.26			39.28	37.02	38.17
12	1.15			39.32*	38.17	0
Totals	58.52	10.71	2.17	471.40	400.00	

* The 4-cent difference is due to the accumulation of rounding errors.

To determine the yield rate, we have

$$39.28a_{\overline{12}|i} = 400 \qquad a_{\overline{12}|i} = \frac{400}{39.28} = 10.1833$$

and by interpolation $i = 2.62\%$ per month.

In most cases, inequalities (10a) and (10b) will uniquely determine n_1, n_2, and n_3.   However, it is possible that in order to get a unique solution we would need to know r_1 and r_2 more accurately.   While it is possible to narrow the range on these rates, there is an easier way.   If a fair

approximation of R is available, the formulas for the outstanding principal can be used to approximate the n's by using the fact that A_1 or more
is amortized during the first n_1 periods and A_3 or less is amortized during
the last n_3 periods. The values of n_1, n_2, and n_3 obtained in this fashion
are then used to compute a new value of R, and the procedure is repeated.
When the new R gives the same values to the n's that were used in computing it, the solution is complete. Obviously it is desirable to have computing equipment other than pencil and paper. We will illustrate the
procedure with a rather extreme example.

Example 4 Let $A_1 = 1000$, $A_2 = 500$, $A_3 = 500$, $i_1 = 1\%$, $i_2 = 3\%$, $i_3 = 8\%$, and
$n = 50$. Find R.
Solution From inequality (9) we have

$$n_1 > \frac{nA_1}{A} = \frac{50 \times 1000}{2000} = 25 \quad \text{and} \quad n_3 < \frac{nA_3}{A} = \frac{50 \times 500}{2000} = 12.5$$

We will start with $n_1 = 26$, $n_2 = 12$, and $n_3 = 12$ to compute R. A better choice
would be to take n_1 slightly larger and n_3 somewhat smaller, since inequality (9) gives
these values as *limits*. We are starting with the worst estimates to show that lucky
guessing is not essential. Carrying out the necessary computations gives $R = 93.11$
as a first approximation. To get improved values for n_1, n_2, and n_3, we use the
approximate value of R in the outstanding principal formulas. The principal repaid
during the first n_1 periods is

$$(R - I)s_{\overline{n_1}|i_1} = 28.11s_{\overline{n_1}|1\%} \geq 1000$$

which gives $s_{\overline{n_1}|1\%} \geq 35.5775$, and this requires that $n_1 \geq 31$. The principal repaid
during the final n_3 periods is

$$Ra_{\overline{n_3}|i_3} = 93.11a_{\overline{n_3}|8\%} \leq 500$$

from which $a_{\overline{n_3}|8\%} \leq 5.3700$, and this requires that $n_3 \leq 7$. R is now recomputed
using $n_1 = 31$, $n_2 = 12$, and $n_3 = 7$. The new approximation of R is 92.43. The
values of $s_{\overline{n_1}|i_1}$ and $a_{\overline{n_3}|i_3}$ are recomputed using the improved R. This gives

$$s_{\overline{n_1}|1\%} \geq 36.4564 \quad \text{and} \quad a_{\overline{n_3}|8\%} \leq 5.4095$$

which requires that $n_1 \geq 32$ and $n_3 \leq 7$. Again R is computed, this time with $n_1 = 32$,
$n_2 = 11$, and $n_3 = 7$. The new value of R is 92.43, which is the same as was obtained
at the preceding step (actually they differ by a fraction of a cent), so that n_1, n_2, n_3,
and R are all correct. If we had started with $n_1 = 30$, $n_2 = 10$, and $n_3 = 10$, the
final result would have been obtained one step earlier. Finally, we will check on how
much principal is repaid during the first and last phases. For the first phase we have

$$(R - I)s_{\overline{n_1}|i_1} = 27.43s_{\overline{32}|1\%} = 1028.46$$

and for the last phase

$$Ra_{\overline{n_3}|i_3} = 92.43a_{\overline{7}|8\%} = 481.28$$

Some selected entries of the amortization table are given below.

End of period	Interest at 8%	Interest at 3%	Interest at 1%	Payment	Principal repaid	Out-standing principal
0						2000.00
1	40.00	15.00	10.00	92.43	27.43	1972.57
2	40.00	15.00	9.73	92.43	27.70	1944.87
3	40.00	15.00	9.45	92.43	27.98	1916.89
..	....	......	......	....	....	....
31	40.00	15.00	0.46	92.43	36.97	1008.89
32	40.00	15.00	0.09	92.43	37.34	971.55
33	40.00	14.15		92.43	38.28	933.27
34	40.00	13.00		92.43	39.43	893.84
..	....	......	......	....	....	....
42	40.00	2.48		92.43	49.95	532.69
43	40.00	0.98		92.43	51.45	481.24
44	38.50			92.43	53.93	427.31
..	....	......	......	....	....	....
49	13.19			92.43	79.24	85.60
50	6.85			92.45*	85.60	0
Totals	1885.79	556.42	169.31	4621.52	2000.00	

* The 2-cent difference is due to the accumulation of rounding errors.

After some of the payments have been made in the amortization of a debt the question arises, What is the value of the remaining contract? The borrower can liquidate the debt on any date by paying the outstanding principal, plus perhaps a small close-out charge. However, when an amortization contract is sold by one investor to another, the price may differ considerably from that listed in the schedule as outstanding principal. For example, suppose the contract that involves the amortization in Example 3 is sold just after the fourth payment. The outstanding principal is listed as $277.05. If the contract were sold for exactly this amount, the transaction would be the same as the buyer lending the seller $277.05 under the exact conditions stated in Example 3, i.e., 3 percent per month on the first $200 and 2 percent per month on the remaining $77.05, to be liquidated by 8 monthly payments. It can be shown that the yield rate for the 8-month contract would be 2.85 percent per month, whereas the yield rate for the first 4 months was 2.21 percent per month. Since the original owner probably incurred some expense in obtaining the contract, he could rightfully reason that if he sold the contract for the figure listed as outstanding principal, the buyer would be getting a better deal than the seller. For this and other reasons, contracts of this type are usually sold at a price that will yield the purchaser some specified rate.

Example 5   What should the sale price of the contract in Example 3 be just after the fourth payment in order that it might yield the buyer (a) 2% per month?   (b) $1\frac{1}{2}\%$ per month?
Solution a   The buyer is getting an annuity of 8 monthly payments of $39.28.   To yield 2% per month the price should be

$$A = Ra_{\overline{n}|i} = 39.28a_{\overline{8}|2\%} = \$287.74$$

Solution b   To yield $1\frac{1}{2}\%$ per month the price should be

$$A = 39.28a_{\overline{8}|1\frac{1}{2}\%} = \$294.15$$

★EXERCISE 27

1. A lending agency charges 2% per month on outstanding principal of $300 or less and 1% per month on all in excess of $300.   If $500 is borrowed from this firm to be repaid by 12 monthly payments, find n_1, n_2, and R.

2. A lending firm charges $2\frac{1}{2}\%$ per month on outstanding principal of $200 or less and 1% per month on all in excess of $200.   If $400 is borrowed from this firm to be repaid by 8 monthly payments, find n_1, n_2, and R.

3. A lending firm charges 3% per month on outstanding principal of $150 or less, 2% per month on that in excess of $150 but not exceeding $300 and 1% per month on all in excess of $300.   If $500 is borrowed under these terms and is to be repaid by 12 monthly payments, find n_1, n_2, n_3, and R.

7
Perpetuities

44 ORDINARY SIMPLE AND GENERAL PERPETUITIES

A perpetuity is an annuity whose payments are to continue forever.   There
are many examples of perpetuities, perhaps the simplest being the interest
payments from any sum of money productively invested.   Qualifying
adjectives, such as simple, general, ordinary, deferred, etc., retain the
same meaning when applied to perpetuities as for annuities.   Thus an
ordinary simple perpetuity is a set of periodic payments, made at the
ends of consecutive interest periods, which are to continue forever.

A moment's reflection makes it clear that the amount of a perpetuity is meaningless, since payments are to continue indefinitely.   The
present value, however, of any type of perpetuity is a finite sum that
can readily be found as soon as sufficient data are known.

Let A be the present value of an ordinary simple perpetuity, let i
be the interest rate per period at which A is invested, and let R be the

perpetuity payment. Then A must be equivalent to the set of payments R as shown on the diagram below.

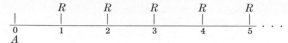

Since A will produce interest payments of Ai at the end of each interest period and will continue to do so as long as it remains invested at rate i, it follows that $R = Ai$, or

$$A = \frac{R}{i} \tag{1}$$

Clearly if any two of the three quantities A, R, and i are known, the other can be found by means of Eq. (1).

The relationship stated in Eq. (1) can also be obtained as the limiting case of an annuity as n becomes infinite. For when n is finite,

$$A = Ra_{\overline{n}|i} = R\,\frac{1 - (1 + i)^{-n}}{i}$$

As n increases, the fraction $(1 + i)^{-n} = 1/(1 + i)^n$ becomes smaller and approaches 0 as n becomes infinite, so that the present value equation above reduces to Eq. (1).

Example 1 How much money will it require to establish a permanent scholarship paying \$750 at the end of each year if money can be invested at 3% effective?
Solution Clearly the payments will form an ordinary simple perpetuity, and we have $R = 750$ and $i = 0.03$. From Eq. (1),

$$A = \frac{R}{i} = \frac{750}{0.03} = \$25{,}000$$

Frequently, as with annuities, the payment period is different from the interest conversion period. When this is the case, the perpetuity is called a **general perpetuity**. These are treated in essentially the same manner as general annuities. *The general perpetuity is changed into an equivalent simple perpetuity by the same formula used for annuities.* The formula

$$R = \frac{W}{s_{\overline{m/p}|i}} \tag{2}$$

which was developed in Sec. 32, is independent of the number of interest periods involved and therefore holds for perpetuities as well as annuities. Consequently an ordinary general perpetuity can be converted into a simple perpetuity by means of Eq. (2), after which Eq. (1) is used to find its present value.

Example 2   It costs a railroad company \$100 at the end of each month to guard a crossing.   How much should the company be willing to contribute toward the expense of building an underpass to be maintained by the state if the expense of guarding the crossing would be eliminated?   Money is worth 3% effective.

Solution   The \$100 at the end of each month forms an ordinary general perpetuity. The railroad can afford to pay an amount equal to the present value of this perpetuity. If R is the payment of the equivalent simple perpetuity, then by Eq. (2)

$$R = 100 \times \frac{1}{s_{\overline{1/12}|3\%}} = 100 \times 12.16411941 = 1216.411941$$

Then from Eq. (1),

$$A = \frac{R}{i} = \frac{1216.411941}{0.03} = \$40,547.06$$

45   PERPETUITIES DUE

When the payments of a perpetuity come at the beginnings of the payment periods, the perpetuity is a **perpetuity due.** Since these may be considered an immediate payment of R (or W) followed by an ordinary perpetuity of like payments, clearly the present value is simply R (or W) *more* than given by the formulas in the preceding section.   Hence the present value of a simple perpetuity due is given by

$$A = R + \frac{R}{i} \tag{3}$$

and the present value of the general perpetuity due may be found from

$$A = W + \frac{R}{i} \tag{4}$$

where R is obtained from Eq. (2).

It is sometimes desirable to express the present value of the general perpetuity due in somewhat different form.   To this end we substitute for R in Eq. (4) its value as given by Eq. (2).   This gives

$$A = W + \frac{W \times 1/s_{\overline{m/p}|i}}{i}$$

and

$$Ai = W\left(i + \frac{1}{s_{\overline{m/p}|i}}\right) = \frac{W}{a_{\overline{m/p}|i}} \qquad \text{[Eq. (12), Sec. 26]}$$

But from Eq. (1), $R = Ai$.   Hence a general perpetuity due whose payments are W may be replaced by an equivalent simple perpetuity whose payments are R by means of the formula

$$R = \frac{W}{a_{\overline{m/p}|i}} \tag{5}$$

The present value of the perpetuity is then found by means of Eq. (1).

It should be made clear that the values of R as given by Eqs. (2) and (4) *are not* the same. When R is computed from Eq. (2), the first W is not included, and consequently $A = W + R/i$. When R is computed from Eq. (5), however, the first W is included, and in terms of this R, we have $A = R/i$.

Equation (5) is valid for converting general annuities due into simple annuities and will be developed in a different manner in Sec. 68, Chap. 10.

Example A county and state together maintain a wooden highway bridge. The county pays \$5000 every 3 years as its share for replacing the bridge. If a new bridge is needed now and money is worth 5% effective, how much can the county afford to pay toward the construction of a steel and concrete bridge if the state agrees to pay all future replacement charges?

Solution The county can afford to pay the present value, at $j_1 = 5\%$, of the perpetuity formed by the triannual payments of \$5000. This is a general perpetuity due, since a bridge is needed immediately. The quantity m/p is the ratio of interest periods to payment periods and is therefore $3/1$; $W = 5000$, and $i = 0.05$.

a. If we consider the perpetuity due as an immediate payment of \$5000 followed by an ordinary perpetuity, then

$$R = \frac{W}{s_{\overline{m/p}|i}} = \frac{5000}{s_{\overline{3}|5\%}} = 5000 \times 0.31720856 = 1586.0428$$

The present value of the perpetuity is now given by Eq. (4).

$$A = W + \frac{R}{i} = 5000 + \frac{1586.0428}{0.05} = \$36{,}720.86$$

b. If we use Eq. (5) to replace the perpetuity due by an ordinary simple one, we get

$$R = \frac{W}{a_{\overline{m/p}|i}} = \frac{5000}{a_{\overline{3}|5\%}} = 5000 \times 0.36720856 = 1836.0428$$

The present value of the perpetuity is now given by Eq. (1).

$$A = \frac{R}{i} = \frac{1836.0428}{0.05} = \$36{,}720.86$$

*46 ALTERNATE TREATMENT OF GENERAL PERPETUITIES

When general annuities were first encountered, it was stated that they could be treated by replacing the given interest rate by an equivalent rate compounded with the frequency of the payments, thus obtaining simple annuities. The objection, however, was the fact that the new rate would usually not be tabulated and difficulty in evaluating the annuity symbols would arise. Since evaluating a simple perpetuity requires no annuity symbols, this objection disappears. Thus a second treatment of general perpetuities is as follows: *A general perpetuity may be converted into a simple perpetuity by replacing the given interest rate by an equivalent rate compounded with the frequency of the payments.* Examples will illustrate this technique.

Example 1 Solve Example 2, Sec. 44, by changing the given yearly rate into an equivalent monthly rate.
Solution Let i be the rate per month equivalent to 3% per year. Then

$$(1 + i)^{12} = 1.03 \qquad \text{(Sec. 13, Chap. 2)}$$
$$1 + i = (1.03)^{\frac{1}{12}} = 1.00246627 \qquad \text{(Table 3)}$$
$$i = 0.00246627 \text{ per month}$$

We now have an ordinary simple perpetuity consisting of payments of $100 monthly and an interest rate of $i = 0.00246627$ per month. Therefore

$$A = \frac{R}{i} = \frac{100}{0.00246627} = \$40{,}547.06$$

as before.

Example 2 Solve the example in Sec. 45 by replacing the given annual rate by an equivalent rate compounded every 3 years.
Solution Let i be the rate compounded every third year that is equivalent to 5% per year. Then

$$1 + i = (1.05)^3 = 1.15762500$$
$$i = 0.157625 \qquad \text{per 3 years}$$

We now have a simple perpetuity due consisting of payments of $5000 at the beginning of every third year and an interest rate of $i = 0.157625$ every third year. Therefore

$$A = R + \frac{R}{i} = 5000 + \frac{5000}{0.157625} = \$36{,}720.86$$

A comparison of the two techniques used in treating the general perpetuity shows that the changing-interest-rate method appears to be theoretically simpler. The main objection to this method is the fact that the necessary division is somewhat formidable. When mechanical computers are available, this objection disappears.

EXERCISE 28

1. Find the present value of a perpetuity with quarterly payments of $700 if money is worth $j_4 = 4\%$ and (*a*) the first payment is due in 3 months, (*b*) the first payment is due now.

2. Find the present value of a perpetuity with semiannual payments of $800 if the interest rate is $j_2 = 5\%$ and (*a*) the first payment is due in 6 months, (*b*) the first payment is due now.

3. Find the present value of perpetuity paying $1000 at the end of each year if money is worth (*a*) $j_1 = 6\%$, (*b*) $j_{12} = 6\%$.

4. Find the present value of a perpetuity that pays $500 at the end of each quarter if the interest rate is (a) $j_4 = 4\%$, (b) $j_1 = 4\%$.

5. Find the present value of a perpetuity of $50 due at the end of each month if the interest rate is $j_2 = 5\%$.

6. Payments of $500 are to be made at the end of each quarter indefinitely. Find the present value at 4% per year.

7. The Alpha Beta Gamma society wishes to donate to the university a fund to establish a scholarship prize of $300 to be awarded at the end of each year. How much will be required if the university can obtain $j_4 = 3\frac{1}{2}\%$ on investments?

8. A wealthy man wishes to set aside a fund for the purpose of awarding a prize of $10,000 at the end of each 10 years to the man making the greatest scientific discovery during that decade. How much will be required if the fund can be invested at 4% per year?

9. It costs $1000 every 3 years to paint the exterior of a church. A devout church member wishes to set aside a fund to keep the church painted indefinitely. How much will it take if the fund can be invested at $j_2 = 4\frac{1}{2}\%$?

10. The Alpha Pi scholarship for journalism students pays $1000 at the beginning of each year. How large must the fund be if it is invested at $j_4 = 3\%$?

11. The present value of a perpetuity is $30,000 which is invested at $j_2 = 5\%$. How much will it pay (a) at the end of each quarter, (b) at the beginning of each year?

12. A wealthy man leaves $50,000 to his alma mater to endow scholarships. If invested at $j_2 = 4\%$, how much will it furnish (a) at the end of each year, (b) at the beginning of each month?

★13. A college wishes to establish a permanent scholarship that will pay $100 at the beginning of each month during a 9-month school year, the first payment to be made on Sept. 1. How much should the fund contain on Sept. 1 if it is invested at $j_{12} = 3\%$?

★14. Solve Prob. 5 by changing the interest rate to an equivalent one, compounded monthly.

★15. Solve Prob. 7 by changing the interest rate into an equivalent rate, compounded annually.

47 CAPITALIZATION

The word capitalization has numerous meanings. For the purpose of this chapter we shall use the following restricted meaning: *The process of finding the present value of a set of periodic payments that are to continue indefinitely is called* **capitalization.** Thus to capitalize an income (or outgo) at a given interest rate is to find the present value of the perpetuity that will furnish the desired payments. For example, an income of $100 due at the end of each month capitalized at 3 percent, $m = 12$, is $40,000, since this is the present value of the perpetuity that will furnish $100 at the end of each month if invested at $j_{12} = 3$ percent.

In modern economic theory, capitalization is an extremely important device for the evaluation of various assets and liabilities, one of the most important applications being the determination of the capitalized investment cost, usually called the **capitalized cost,** of an asset. *The capitalized* *cost of an asset is defined as being the first cost plus the present value of infinitely many renewals.* The present value of infinitely many renewals is clearly the present value of a perpetuity that will furnish the desired renewal payments. Hence if C is the original cost and K is the capitalized cost, then

$$K = C + A \qquad (6)$$

where A is the present value of the perpetuity necessary for the renewal payments and is determined by Eq. (1). If the interest rate is such that the perpetuity is a simple one, R is taken as the renewal cost and we have

$$K = C + \frac{R}{i} \qquad (7)$$

If, however, the perpetuity is a general one, W is taken as the renewal cost and R is computed by means of Eq. (2) before Eq. (7) can be used.

Example 1 It cost an industrial concern $200 initially for drill points, after which it cost the company $100 at the end of each month to replace those which had been broken or worn out. If money is worth $4\frac{1}{2}\%$ effective, find the capitalized cost of the drill points.
Solution The $100 payments at the end of each month form a general perpetuity. If R is the equivalent simple perpetuity, then

$$R = 100 \, \frac{1}{s_{\overline{1/12}|\,4\frac{1}{2}\%}} = 100 \times 12.24553306 = 1224.553306$$

Then

$$K = C + \frac{R}{i} = 200 + \frac{1224.553306}{0.045} = \$27,412.30$$

If the original cost C is the same as the replacement charge, the computation can be simplified slightly by considering the original cost as the first payment of a perpetuity due. The following example will illustrate the procedure.

Example 2 Find the capitalized cost of a machine that cost $5000 and will need replacing, at the same cost, at the end of each 10 years. Money is worth 4% effective.
Solution The payments are shown on the time diagram below.

```
  5000        5000        5000        5000
   |           |           |           |
 ──┼───────────┼───────────┼───────────┼──  . . .
   0          10          20          30
   K
```

This general perpetuity due of $5000 payments may be replaced by a simple perpetuity whose payments are

$$R = W \, \frac{1}{a_{\overline{m/p}|\,i}} = 5000 \, \frac{1}{a_{\overline{10}|\,4\%}} = 5000 \times 0.12329094 = 616.4547$$

Then since K is the present value of this perpetuity,

$$K = \frac{R}{i} = \frac{616.4547}{0.04} = \$15,411.37$$

A term frequently encountered in capitalization theory is **periodic investment cost.** *The periodic investment cost of an asset is defined as the periodic interest on its capitalized cost.* For example, if the capitalized cost of an asset at $j_4 = 4$ percent is \$10,000, then the quarterly investment cost is \$100. Thus if we let H represent the periodic investment cost, then

$$H = Ki = Ci + R \tag{8}$$

where K, C, R, and i retain the same meaning as before.

The periodic investment cost has a rather simple interpretation. If K is the capitalized cost of an asset, then K will keep one supplied with that asset indefinitely. On the other hand, K invested now at rate i will yield Ki as interest payments indefinitely. Hence if K is used to keep one supplied with a certain asset, the Ki interest payments are lost as income and may logically be considered the periodic investment cost of owning the asset. The same conclusion can be reached by analyzing the formula $H = Ci + R$. The term Ci represents interest lost owing to the fact that the owner has used the money for the purchase of the asset rather than investing it at rate i. Moreover, if W is the cost of replacing the asset at the end of its useful life, then $R = W(1/s_{\overline{m/p}|i})$ placed in a savings fund at the end of each interest period will accumulate the principal that otherwise would be lost when the asset reaches the end of its useful life. Thus, the Ci lost as interest and the payment of R necessary to keep the original capital intact together comprise the actual periodic cost due to having the money invested in the asset rather than in a monetary investment and are therefore called the periodic investment cost.

Example 3 What is the semiannual investment cost of a hot-water heater that cost \$100 originally and needs replacing every 10 years at a cost of \$90 if money is worth $j_2 = 4\%$?

Solution The \$90 replacement charges are first replaced by an equivalent set due at the ends of the interest periods. From Eq. (2)

$$R = W \frac{1}{s_{\overline{m/p}|i}} = 90 \frac{1}{s_{\overline{20}|2\%}} = \$3.70$$

Thus, 20 semiannual payments of \$3.70 made into a savings fund will amount to \$90 at the end of 10 years and together with the old heater will buy a new one or return the original principal. The interest lost each period is $Ci = 100 \times 0.02 = \$2$. Hence,

$$H = Ci + R = 2.00 + 3.70 = \$5.70$$

is the semiannual investment cost of owning the heater.

48 COMPARISON OF ASSETS ON AN INVESTMENT–COST BASIS

A problem that frequently confronts the businessman is that of deciding which of several machines will prove most economical in the long run or when to replace old equipment with new or whether to repair a machine or buy a new one. To solve such a problem we need some method of comparing the values of different assets. Now all machines suffer a gradual loss of value due to wear, and the rate of loss is not the same for all. Consequently, it is inadequate merely to compare the original costs. However, since money spent for a machine is an investment, we can compare two different machines that do the same work by comparing either their capitalized costs or their periodic investment costs.

Example 1 One machine costs $1000 and must be replaced at the end of 10 years at a cost of $800. A second machine for the same purpose has an original cost of $1300 and must be replaced at the end of 15 years at a cost of $1000. If money is worth 5% effective, which machine is cheaper in the long run?
Solution Comparison by capitalized costs. By the methods developed in Sec. 47, we find that the capitalized cost of the first machine is

$$K_1 = \$2272.07$$

Similarly, the capitalized cost of the second machine is

$$K_2 = \$2226.85$$

Therefore the second machine is cheaper in the long run.
    If we compute the annual investment costs of the two machines, we obtain

$$H_1 = \$113.60 \qquad \text{and} \qquad H_2 = \$111.34$$

Therefore it costs $2.26 more per year to own the first machine than it does to own the second one.

Example 2 A machine costing $20,000 will last 40 years, at which time it can be sold as scrap for $1000. How much can a company afford to pay for a second machine for the same purpose that will last only 25 years and have no final scrap value if money is worth 4% effective?
Solution The two machines will be economically equivalent if their annual investment costs (or capitalized costs) are the same. For the first machine, we have

$$H_1 = Ci + R = 20,000 \times 0.04 + 19,000 \,\frac{1}{s_{\overline{40}|4\%}} = 999.94631$$

Let C be the original cost of the second machine. Then C is also the replacement cost, since the scrap value is zero. The annual investment cost of the second machine is

$$H_2 = Ci + C \frac{1}{s_{\overline{25}|4\%}} = C \frac{1}{a_{\overline{25}|4\%}} \qquad \text{[Eq. (12), Sec. 26]}$$

Equating H_1 and H_2 gives

$$C \frac{1}{a_{\overline{25}|4\%}} = 999.94631 \qquad \text{and} \qquad C = 999.94631 a_{\overline{25}|4\%} = \$15,621.24$$

This example could have been solved by equating the capitalized costs of the two machines. However, the algebra is usually slightly simpler when periodic investment costs are used.

EXERCISE 29

1. Find the capitalized cost and semiannual investment cost of a machine that costs $10,000 initially and needs replacing every 20 years at a cost of $8000 if money is worth $j_2 = 5\%$.

2. Find the capitalized cost and the annual investment cost of a machine that sells new for $1000 and needs replacing every 15 years at a cost of $800 if money is worth 4% per year.

3. Find the capitalized cost of a machine that sells for $5000 and must be replaced at the same cost every 10 years if money is worth $j_4 = 4\%$. Also find the quarterly investment charge.

4. Find the capitalized cost and the semiannual investment cost of a road surface which costs $100,000 and must be replaced every 25 years at the same price. Money is worth $j_2 = 3\%$.

5. A machine costs $2400 and will be worth $400 as scrap at the end of 10 years. A second machine for the same purpose costs $3000 and will have a scrap value of $500 in 12 years. If money is worth $5\frac{1}{2}\%$ effective, which is cheaper in the long run?

6. Compare the capitalized costs at 4% effective of the following two machines: Machine A costs $5000 and will have no scrap value at the end of 20 years. Machine B costs $7500 and will be worth $500 at the end of 25 years.

7. The annual investment cost for a machine is $500. It must be replaced every 5 years at the original cost. If money is worth 5% yearly, what is the original cost?

8. The semiannual cost of a machine is $400. It must be replaced and has no scrap value at the end of 6 years. Find the initial cost if money is worth $j_2 = 5\%$.

9. Certain equipment must be replaced every 5 years. Find the initial cost if the scrap value is $500, the annual investment cost is $1000, and the interest rate is 4% effective.

10. Mr. Smith wishes to paint his house. If grade A paint is used, it will cost $500 and last 4 years. It will cost $400 and last 3 years if grade B paint is used. Which is cheaper if money is worth 3% effective?

11. A machine costs $15,000, will last 25 years, and will have a scrap value of $3000. If money is worth $j_2 = 6\%$, how much can a company afford to pay for a cheaper model that lasts only 10 years and has no scrap value?

12. It cost \$5 to buy and install a railroad tie which must be replaced at the same cost every 5 years. If the tie is treated with a preservative, it will last 8 years. If money is worth 4% per year, how much can profitably be spent for the treatment?

13. A man pays \$4000 for a new car. If he keeps it for 4 years, its trade-in value will be \$1000. What should the trade-in value be at the end of 3 years so that trading at that time would be economically equivalent to keeping it 4 years if money is worth $j_2 = 5\%$?

14. If the trade-in value of the car in Prob. 13 is always set so that trading on any date is economically equivalent to trading on any other date, how old will the car be when the trade-in value becomes \$500?

*49 COMPARISON OF ASSETS ON A PRODUCTION-COST BASIS

In comparing the value of two machines that do the same type of work, operating and maintenance costs are equally as important as the investment cost. Also the number of units that each machine will produce per time period must be considered. Since it is possible to capitalize any sequence of periodic payments, we may capitalize the costs of maintenance and the costs of production per unit output, or, what is equivalent, we may find the periodic maintenance and production costs per unit output. These capitalized costs, or the corresponding periodic costs, provide a basis for deciding which of two machines is more economical to use.

Example A machine that costs \$5000 will last 20 years and have a scrap value at that time of \$500. Repairs will average \$300 per year. Operating expenses, including the operator, will be \$400 per month. A second machine will produce twice as many units per year. It costs \$50,000 and must be replaced at the end of 25 years at a cost of \$45,000. Repairs for this machine will average \$250 per year, and operating expenses will be \$500 per month. If money is worth 5% effective, how much will be saved each year by purchasing the most economical machine?

Solution Let H, R, and O be the annual costs equivalent, at 5% effective, to the investment costs, the repair costs, and the operational costs, respectively. Then

$$H_1 = 5000 \times 0.05 + 4500 \frac{1}{s_{\overline{20}|5\%}} = 250 + 136.09 = \$386.09$$

$$R_1 = \$300$$

$$O_1 = 400 \frac{1}{s_{\overline{1/12}|5\%}} = \$4909.03$$

Then the total annual production cost for the first machine is

$$H_1 + R_1 + O_1 = \$5595.12$$

We repeat these computations for the second machine and get

$$H_2 = 50,000 \times 0.05 + 45,000 \frac{1}{s_{\overline{25}|5\%}} = \$3442.86$$

$$R_2 = \$250$$

$$O_2 = 500 \frac{1}{s_{\overline{1/12}|5\%}} = \$6136.29$$

For the second machine,

$$H_2 + R_2 + O_2 = \$9829.15$$

Since the second machine does twice as much work as the first, two machines of the first type would be required to replace one of the second type. The annual charge for two of the first type would be $11,190.24. This is $1361.09 more than the annual charge for the second machine and consequently is the amount that would be saved annually on each machine of the second type that is purchased.

★EXERCISE 30

1. A manufacturing machine costs $25,000 and will last 18 years, at which time it will have a scrap value of $5000. It will cost $1000 every 6 months for maintenance and $500 a month to operate. A second machine, which does the same work, will last 15 years and will have a scrap value of zero at that time. Maintenance costs will be $300 each 3 months, and an operator will cost $400 per month. If money is worth 3% effective, how much should the second machine sell for to be economically equivalent to the first one?

2. A car for a salesman cost $3000 and should be replaced every 2 years at a cost of $1500. It costs the company $400 a month to operate the car. If a car is not furnished, the salesman must use hired transportation, that is, railroads, taxis, and airlines. If money is worth $j_{12} = 4\%$, how much can the company allow per month for hired transportation? (In either case, the salesman is reimbursed at the end of each month for expenditures during the month.)

3. A factory building large enough to manufacture 5000 units per month costs $500,000. It must be renovated every 10 years at a cost of $10,000, and the cost of maintaining the building is $4000 per year. How much could the company afford to pay to enlarge the building to produce 8000 units per month if the cost of renovation is increased by $1000 and the maintenance cost is likewise increased by $1000? Money is worth 4%, $m = 4$.

4. A house rents for $125 per month. It costs the owner about $75 every 3 months for routine repairs. It also costs $500 to paint it every 3 years. Finally, it requires major renovating costing $1500 every 10 years to keep it in good condition. If money is worth 5% effective, what is the equivalent cash price of the house?

5. A machine is invented that will replace five skilled workmen who receive $800 each at the end of each month. The machine has a life of 20 years and will have a scrap value of $2000 at that time. The machine will cost $1000 at the end of each month to operate and maintain. If money is worth 4% effective, what is the largest amount that can profitably be spent for the machine?

6. A large corporation employs highly trained trouble shooters who travel about the country for the purpose of eliminating bottlenecks of various types. These men receive a salary of $2000 at the end of each month and are also reimbursed at that time for expenditures during the month such as traveling expenses, hotels, etc. These monthly expenses average $1000. The corporation is considering the purchase of planes for transporting these agents around. If they use planes, one agent will be able to cover the territory now held by three agents. The planes under consideration, however, would require a trained pilot at $2000 a month, and operating expenses, including the agent's incidental expenses, would require $800 a month more. If the planes must be traded in every 2 years and the trade-in value is 20% of the original cost, how much can the corporation afford to pay for each plane? Money is worth 6%, $m = 12$.

8
Bonds

50 INTRODUCTION

When a large corporation wishes to borrow a sizable sum of money, such as $50,000,000, it usually cannot find a single financial company or even a small group of financial companies that would be able to lend the entire sum of money desired. Hence the money must be obtained from a great many investors both large and small. For convenience in dealing with a large number of investors, the corporation will have printed up in advance many notes or contracts each of which tells the amount of the loan, the date when the loan will be repaid, the rate at which interest will be paid on the loan, and the dates when these interest payments will be made. Each contract will also state where the payments can be collected and what security the company offers, if any, that the loan will be repaid. *Such a contract is called a* **bond.**

Since bonds are issued to borrow money, many devices are used to make them attractive to an investor. Most bonds are **unregistered** and can be transferred from one owner to another at will. The advantage

of such a bond is that it may be sold at any time the owner desires.
Other bonds are **registered** and can be transferred only by proper endorse-
ment and the consent of the issuer.   Thus the owner is protected against
loss or theft.   To facilitate the collection of interest, most bonds have
dated coupons attached, which can be cashed at any bank on or after
the date mentioned on the coupon.   Some registered bonds make the
interest payments directly to the owner by mail.

Some of the terminology relative to bonds will now be defined.
The sum of money named in the bond is called the **face value** or the
denomination.   This is usually $500, $1000, $5000, or $10,000.   The
date on which the loan will be repaid is called the **redemption date.**   The
amount that will be paid on the redemption date is called the **redemption
price.**   The redemption price is nearly always the same as the face value,
in which case the bond is said to be **redeemed at par.**   Some bonds contain a clause that allows the issuer to redeem the bond, that is, pay off
the loan, at a date earlier than the redemption date.   *Such a bond is said
to be* **callable.**   For example, a bond might be redeemable in 15 years and
callable at any time after 10 years.   Most callable bonds specify that
if they are called before the redemption date, they will be redeemed at a
premium, that is, for more than their face value.   For example, a bond
redeemable at par in 15 years might be callable at 105 percent of its face
value after 10 years.

51 THE INVESTMENT RATE

It should be clear by now that a bond is a contract that may be transferred from one person to another.   It should also be clear that when the
owner of a bond decides to sell it, he will naturally sell it to the highest
bidder.   *Consequently a bond is very seldom sold for exactly its face value.*
In fact when the bonds are first offered to the investing public, only
rarely does the issuer get exactly the face value of the bonds.   Owing to
this fact, various bond problems arise.   As an illustration, suppose that
a $1000 bond will be redeemed at par in 10 years and, in the meantime,
interest payments of $50 will be made at the end of each year.   Clearly
if a person buys this bond for $1000, his investment will earn interest at
5 percent effective.   Suppose, however, that this bond cannot be purchased for less than $1150.   Then the interest payments received will be
partially offset by the loss of $150 incurred when the bond is redeemed.
Thus the question naturally arises, How good an investment is this bond
if purchased for $1150?   Again suppose that an investor is willing to
invest money at 3 percent effective.   How much can he afford to offer for
the bond mentioned above?

The above illustrations are sufficient to make clear that when a bond is sold at a price other than its face value, *the purchaser is investing money but not at the rate stated in the bond.* For this reason, there are two interest rates associated with bonds: (a) *the rate at which the bond pays interest on its face value, hereinafter called the* **bond rate,** *and* (b) *the interest rate realized by the purchaser, called the* **investment or yield rate.**

52 PURCHASE PRICE TO YIELD A GIVEN INVESTMENT RATE

The first problem concerning bonds is to determine how much an investor should pay for a bond so that his investment earns interest at a specified investment rate.   Let

F = the face value, or par value, of the bond
C = the redemption price of the bond
n = the number of interest periods until the redemption date
r = the rate per period at which the bond pays interest on the face value.
$R = Fr$ = the amount of bond interest paid by the bond on interest dates
i = the investment rate, or yield rate, per interest period
P = the purchase price at which the bond will yield i

For simplicity it will be assumed for the present that the bond interest rate and the investment rate have the same conversion period.

When a person buys a bond, he receives a written contract that promises the following two types of payments: (a) *periodic interest payments, which form an annuity, and* (b) *the redemption price due on the redemption date.*   The time diagram below shows the payments promised by the bond.

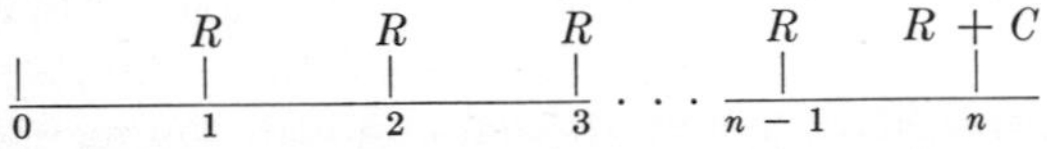

$$
\begin{array}{c|c|c|c|c|c|c}
 & R & R & R & & R & R + C \\
\hline
0 & 1 & 2 & 3 & \cdots & n-1 & n
\end{array}
$$

The investor who wishes to realize the investment rate i on his investment should pay a sum equivalent (at rate i) to these payments.   Thus P is the present value of the above set of payments at rate i.   Therefore

$$P = Ra_{\overline{n}|i} + C(1 + i)^{-n} \tag{1}$$

Example 1   A \$1000 bond that pays interest at 5%, $m = 2$, will be redeemed for \$1050 at the end of 15 years.   What should it sell for to yield an investor 4%, $m = 2$?
Solution   The bond interest payments will be

$$R = Fr = 1000 \times 0.025 = \$25$$

The bond will therefore furnish the following set of payments

$$
\begin{array}{ccccccc}
 & 25 & 25 & 25 & 25 & 25 + 1050 \\
| & | & | & | & \cdots & | & | \\
\hline
0 & 1 & 2 & 3 & & 29 & 30
\end{array}
$$

The purchase price is the present value, at 2%, of this set of payments. Therefore

$$P = 25a_{\overline{30}|2\%} + 1050(1.02)^{-30} = 559.911 + 579.674 = \$1139.59$$

Thus, a person who pays \$1139.59 for this bond is investing money at 4%, $m = 2$.

Example 2 A \$1000 bond with interest at 6% payable semiannually is callable at 110% of its face value on Mar. 1, 1992. If not called on this date, it will be redeemed at par on Mar. 1, 2002. Find the purchase price on Mar. 1, 1967, that will guarantee a yield of at least 7%, $m = 2$.

Solution If the bond is called on the given call date, it will furnish the set of payments listed on the diagram below.

$$
\begin{array}{ccccccc}
 & 30 & 30 & 30 & 30 & 30 + 1100 \\
| & | & | & | & \cdots & | & | \\
\hline
0 & 1 & 2 & 3 & & 49 & 50
\end{array}
$$

The purchase price should therefore be

$$P = 30a_{\overline{50}|3\frac{1}{2}\%} + 1100(1.035)^{-50} = 703.669 + 196.959 = \$900.63$$

If, however, the bond is not called, it will furnish the following set of payments:

$$
\begin{array}{ccccccc}
 & 30 & 30 & 30 & 30 & 30 + 1000 \\
| & | & | & | & \cdots & | & | \\
\hline
0 & 1 & 2 & 3 & & 69 & 70
\end{array}
$$

In this case, the purchase price should be

$$P = 30a_{\overline{70}|3\frac{1}{2}\%} + 1000(1.035)^{-70} = 780.012 + 89.986 = \$870.00$$

Since the purchaser does not know which set of payments he will receive, he must buy the bond for the smaller of these prices, \$870, to be sure of realizing 7%, $m = 2$, on his investment.

53 AN ALTERNATE PURCHASE-PRICE FORMULA

Although Eq. (1) is not difficult to use, it does require the use of two tables. A somewhat simpler formula will now be developed. To this end we recall that P is the present value, at rate i, of the set of payments promised by the bond. This equivalence is shown on the time diagram below.

$$
\begin{array}{ccccccc}
 & R & R & R & R & R + C \\
| & | & | & | & \cdots & | & | \\
\hline
0 & 1 & 2 & 3 & & n-1 & n \\
P
\end{array}
$$

(a)

On the other hand, C invested now at rate i will produce interest payments of Ci at the end of each interest period for n periods and a final payment of C at that time.   The diagram below shows this equivalence.

$$
\begin{array}{cccccc}
 & Ci & Ci & Ci & Ci & Ci + C \\
| & | & | & | & | & | \\
\hline
0 & 1 & 2 & 3 & \cdots & n-1 & n \\
C
\end{array}
\tag{b}
$$

We now subtract the sums on line (b) from those on line (a) and obtain the equivalence relation

$$
\begin{array}{cccccc}
 & R - Ci & R - Ci & R - Ci & R - Ci & R - Ci \\
| & | & | & | & | & | \\
\hline
0 & 1 & 2 & 3 & \cdots & n-1 & n \\
P - C
\end{array}
$$

An equation of value now gives $P - C = (R - Ci)a_{\overline{n}|i}$, or

$$P = C + (R - Ci)a_{\overline{n}|i} \tag{2}$$

The above equation can also be developed algebraically from Eq. (1) by using the identity

$$(1 + i)^{-n} = 1 - ia_{\overline{n}|i}$$

to eliminate the factor $(1 + i)^{-n}$.

An inspection of Eq. (2) shows that if $R = Ci$, the purchase price of the bond is the same as the redemption price; if R is larger than Ci, the purchase price is greater than the redemption price; and if R is less than Ci, then $R - Ci$ is negative and the purchase price is less than the redemption price.

Example 1   Solve Example 2 of the preceding section using Eq. (2).
Solution   If the bond is called on the given call date, $C = 1100$, $R = Fr = 1000 \times 0.03 = 30$, $Ci = 1100 \times 0.35 = 38.50$, and $n = 50$.   Equation (2) then gives

$$P = 1100 + (30 - 38.50)a_{\overline{50}|3\frac{1}{2}\%} = 1100 - 199.37 = \$900.63$$

If the bond is not called, then $C = 1000$, $Ci = 1000 \times 0.035 = 35$, $R = 30$, and $n = 70$.   In this case

$$P = 1000 + (30 - 35)a_{\overline{70}|3\frac{1}{2}\%} = 1000 - 130 = \$870$$

These are the same values of P obtained by using Eq. (1).

It is, of course, immaterial which purchase-price formula is used. Equation (1) seems more natural and is easier to remember, whereas Eq. (2) requires only an $a_{\overline{n}|i}$ table, which somewhat reduces the amount of arithmetical computation.

In the examples thus far, we have treated only the case where the bond interest payments form an ordinary simple annuity, that is, where the bond pays interest with the same frequency that the investment rate is converted.   Obviously this will not always be the case.   When these periods differ so that the bond interest payments form a general annuity, the general annuity is converted into an ordinary simple annuity by the technique developed in Chap. 5, after which either Eq. (1) or (2) may be used to find the purchase price. An example will illustrate the procedure.

Example 2 A $1000 bond that pays interest at 5%, $m = 2$, will be redeemed for $1050 at the end of 15 years. Find the purchase price to yield (a) 4%, $m = 1$, (b) 4%, $m = 4$.

Solution a The $25 bond interest payments form a general annuity with $W = 25$, $p = 2$, $i = 0.04$, and $m = 1$. Using Eq. (6), Sec. 32, we have

$$R = \frac{25}{s_{\overline{1/2}|4\%}} = 25 \times 2.01980390 = 50.495098$$

as the equivalent yearly annuity payment. The purchase price is now found by using either Eq. (1) or (2). Using Eq. (1), we get

$$P = 50.495098 a_{\overline{15}|4\%} + 1050(1.04)^{-15} = \$1144.45$$

Solution b The bond interest payments again form a general annuity with $W = 25$, $p = 2$, $i = 0.01$, and $m = 4$. Proceeding as in (a), we have

$$R = \frac{25}{s_{\overline{2}|1\%}} = 25 \times 0.49751244 = 12.437811$$

as the equivalent quarterly annuity payment. Now using Eq. (2) for the purchase price, we get

$$P = 1050 + (12.437811 - 10.50) a_{\overline{60}|1\%} = \$1137.11$$

When a bond is sold on a bond interest date, the interest payment due that day is considered the property of the seller, so that the purchaser buys only the future bond payments. Hence the bond interest payments that the purchaser will collect always form an ordinary annuity (simple or general) and the technique developed so far is complete. The case where bonds are purchased between bond interest payment dates will be discussed in a later section of this chapter.

EXERCISE 31

Find the purchase price of the following bonds, using either method (in each case the face of the bond is $1000):

Problem	Redemption price	Bond interest rate	Time until redemption, years	Yield rate
1	Par	6%, $m = 2$	10	4%, $m = 2$
2	Par	5%, $m = 2$	15	3%, $m = 2$
3	Par	4%, $m = 2$	20	5%, $m = 2$
4	Par	5%, $m = 1$	25	6%, $m = 1$
5	$1100	$3\frac{1}{2}\%$, $m = 1$	5	4%, $m = 1$
6	$1050	4%, $m = 2$	4	4%, $m = 2$
7	Par	5%, $m = 2$	12	4%, $m = 1$
8	Par	6%, $m = 1$	18	4%, $m = 2$

9. A $1000 bond, redeemable at par on July 1, 2000, pays bond interest annually at 5%. It is callable on July 1, 1990, at $1100. Find the maximum purchase price on July 1, 1970, to yield at least 4% effective on the investment.

10. A company issued $1000 bonds on Dec. 21, 1955, maturing at par 50 years later and paying bond interest semiannually at $j_2 = 4\%$. The bonds are callable at $1050 15 years before maturity. Find the purchase price on Dec. 21, 1970, to yield at least 5%, $m = 2$.

11. A $1000 bond, redeemable at par in 20 years, pays bond interest semiannually at $j_2 = 5\frac{1}{2}\%$. It is callable 5 years earlier at $1100. Find the purchase price to yield at least $j_2 = 5\%$.

12. A $1000 bond, redeemable at par in 25 years, pays bond interest at $j_2 = 4\%$. It is callable at $1100 on any date after 15 years. Find the purchase price to yield at least $j_2 = 3\frac{1}{2}\%$.

★13. Derive the formula

$$P = \frac{R}{i} + \left(C - \frac{R}{i}\right)(1 + i)^{-n}$$

a purchase-price formula that requires the use of only a discount table.

54 BOND SCHEDULES

When a bond is purchased for more than its final redemption price, the difference $P - C$ is called the **excess,** that is, the excess of purchase price over redemption price. Unless part of the bond interest payments is used to amortize this excess, it becomes a capital loss on the redemption date. As an illustration, suppose an investor buys a $1000 bond that pays bond interest at 5 percent, $m = 2$, and is redeemable at $1050 at the end of 3 years, to yield 4 percent, $m = 2$. By either Eq. (1) or (2), the purchase price is found to be $1072.41. At the end of each 6 months, the investor will receive a $25 bond interest payment. However, he does not actually gain $25 each 6 months, since at the end of 3 years he will receive only $1050 of the original $1072.41 invested in the bond. This excess of $22.41 must be saved out of the bond interest payments in order to recover the entire amount of principal originally invested in the bond. It is therefore important that some systematic plan be adopted whereby a certain portion of each bond interest payment is used to amortize this excess.

Although there are several methods used by accountants for amortizing the excess, *the most direct method is based on the fact that the bond was purchased to yield a given investment rate on the money invested in the bond.* In the illustration above, the purchase price was determined so that the bond would yield 2 percent each 6 months on the money invested in it. Thus at the end of the first half year, the **investor's interest** should be $1072.41 × 0.02 = $21.45. Since he actually receives $25, the difference $3.55 is regarded as part of the original principal being returned.   Consequently, the bond is now valued on the books at

$1072.41 − $3.55 = $1068.86

This **book value** is the same as the purchase price of the bond $2\frac{1}{2}$ years before maturity to yield 4 percent, $m = 2$, and may be computed independently by either of the purchase-price formulas.

Proceeding as above, we find that the investor's interest at the end of the second 6-month period should be

$1068.86 × 0.02 = $21.38

Thus $25 − $21.38 = $3.62 of the second bond interest payment is considered principal being returned, and the new book value is

$1068.86 − $3.62 = $1065.24

The above procedure is continued until the bond matures.   The final book value is $1050, the same as the redemption price.   This information may be arranged in the form of a table, and the result is called a **bond schedule.**   The following is a complete schedule for the bond just considered.

Schedule for a bond purchased at an excess

End of period	Bond interest payment	Investor's interest	For amortization of the excess	Book value
0				1072.41
1	25.00	21.45	3.55	1068.86
2	25.00	21.38	3.62	1065.24
3	25.00	21.30	3.70	1061.54
4	25.00	21.23	3.77	1057.77
5	25.00	21.16	3.84	1053.93
6	25.00	21.08	3.92	1050.01*
Totals	150.00	127.60	22.40	

* The 1-cent error is due to the accumulation of rounding errors.

When a bond is purchased for less than its redemption price, the difference $C − P$ is called the **deficiency.**   For example, suppose the bond in the preceding illustration had been purchased 3 years before maturity to yield 6 percent, $m = 2$.   In this case, either Eq. (1) or (2) gives $1014.79 as the required purchase price.   Since the bond will be redeemed at $1050, the deficiency is

$1050 − $1014.79 = $35.21

When a bond is purchased at a deficiency, the investor gains more than just the bond interest payments, since the bond is redeemed for more than its original purchase price. Good accounting practice requires that this increase in the value of the bond should accumulate gradually. Thus some systematic plan of **accumulating the deficiency** is necessary. There are several ways of doing this, *the most direct of which makes use of the fact that the bond should yield the given investment rate on the amount of money invested in the bond.* To illustrate this method, we shall construct a bond schedule for the bond used in the preceding illustration, but purchased at a price to yield 6 percent, $m = 2$. In this case, the purchase price would be \$1014.79; that is, the bond is purchased at a deficiency of \$35.21. Hence the *investor's interest* at the end of 6 months is $\$1014.79 \times 0.03 = \$30.44$. Since the bond interest payment is only \$25, the value of the bond is considered as having increased by

$$\$30.44 - \$25 = \$5.44$$

Thus it is valued on the books at \$1020.23. It should be observed that the investor's interest is considered as made up of two parts: (*a*) *the bond interest payment and* (*b*) *the increase in the value of the bond.* This latter part will be collected when the bond is redeemed.

At the end of the second interest period, the investor's interest will be $\$1020.23 \times 0.03 = \$30.61$; the increase in the value of the bond will be $\$30.61 - \$25.00 = \$5.61$; and the new book value will be

$$\$1020.23 + \$5.61 = \$1025.84$$

This procedure is repeated until the bond matures, at which time the final book value will be \$1050, the same as the redemption price. The following table is a complete schedule for the bond just considered.

Schedule for a bond purchased at a deficiency

End of period	Bond interest payment	Investor's interest	For accumulation of deficiency	Book value
0				1014.79
1	25.00	30.44	5.44	1020.23
2	25.00	30.61	5.61	1025.84
3	25.00	30.78	5.78	1031.62
4	25.00	30.95	5.95	1037.57
5	25.00	31.13	6.13	1043.70
6	25.00	31.31	6.31	1050.01*
Totals	150.00	185.22	35.22	

* The 1-cent error is due to the accumulation of rounding errors.

A few remarks are in order concerning modern terminology. The premium has been defined as $P - F$, whereas the excess is defined as $P - C$. When the bond is to be redeemed at par, the premium and the excess are the same; otherwise not. Since most bonds are redeemed at par, the process of writing off the excess of the purchase price over the redemption value is frequently called the *amortization of the premium*. Similarly, the discount $F - P$ and the deficiency $C - P$ are the same for bonds redeemable at par, so that the phrase "*accumulation of the discount*" is frequently used to mean the accumulation of the deficiency.

EXERCISE 32

Find the purchase price of the following bonds, and make out a complete bond schedule showing the amortization of the excess or the accumulation of the deficiency (the face value of each bond is $1000):

Problem	Redemption price	Bond interest rate	Time until redemption, years	Yield rate
1	Par	5%, $m = 1$	5	6%, $m = 1$
2	Par	4%, $m = 2$	3	6%, $m = 2$
3	Par	6%, $m = 1$	4	5%, $m = 1$
4	Par	5%, $m = 2$	$2\frac{1}{2}$	4%, $m = 2$
5	$1050	$5\frac{1}{2}$%, $m = 1$	4	6%, $m = 1$
6	$1100	5%, $m = 2$	$3\frac{1}{2}$	4%, $m = 2$

7. A $1000 bond, redeemable at $1050, pays bond interest at $j_2 = 3\frac{1}{2}\%$. It is purchased for $950.05 to yield 4%, $m = 2$. Make out a schedule for the next 2 years, and find its book value then.

8. The book value of a $1000 bond on a certain bond interest date is $1104.65. If the bond interest payments are $30 every 6 months and the yield rate is $j_2 = 5\%$, run the schedule for the next year and a half.

9. A $5000 bond, redeemable at par at the end of 25 years pays bond interest at $j_2 = 4\%$. Find the purchase price to earn $j_2 = 5\%$, and make out a schedule for the first 2 years.

10. A $10,000 bond, redeemable at par at the end of 35 years, pays bond interest at $j_2 = 5\%$. Find the purchase price to yield $j_2 = 3\%$, and make out a schedule for the first 2 years.

11. A $1000 bond, redeemable at par at the end of 25 years, is callable 10 years earlier at $1050. It pays bond interest at $j_2 = 6\%$. Find the purchase price to yield at least $j_2 = 4\%$. Find the book value of the bond at the end of the fourteenth year, and run the schedule one more year.

55 EVALUATING BONDS BETWEEN BOND INTEREST DATES

The purchase price formulas, Eqs. (1) and (2), were derived for bonds purchased on bond interest dates, in which case the seller keeps the bond interest payment due on that date and the purchaser receives the contract consisting of all future bond payments. Obviously bonds can be and are sold at any time. Consequently, we need methods of determining the value of a bond between bond interest dates.

As we have seen, the value attached to a bond depends upon the interest rate that it is to yield, and this is true whether the bond is purchased on a bond interest date or not. Suppose a bond is to be purchased between bond interest dates to yield the investor interest at rate i. Let P_0 represent the purchase price of the bond on the preceding interest date to yield i; let f be the fractional part of an interest period that has elapsed since the preceding interest date; and let P be its value on the date of sale. Then P_0 and P are values of the same contract on different dates and are therefore equivalent.

$$
\begin{array}{ccc}
P_0 & & P \\
| & & | \\
\hline
& f &
\end{array}
$$

An equation of equivalence now gives

$$P = P_0(1 + i)^f \tag{3}$$

as the **exact value** of the bond on the date of sale.

The student will recall from Sec. 14, Chap. 2, that when a fractional part of an interest period is involved, an approximation to the true result can be obtained by using simple interest in place of the exact compound interest law. In this case

$$P = P_0(1 + if) \tag{4}$$

gives an **approximate value** of P.

In actual practice, it is customary to use the approximate Eq. (4), and we shall follow this custom unless it is specifically stated otherwise. It is also customary to compute the time factor f by the approximate method, that is, on the assumption that the year consists of 12 months of 30 days each.

Example 1 Find the purchase price on June 16, 1970, of a $1000 bond, redeemable at par on Oct. 1, 1995, and paying bond interest at 7%, $m = 2$, to yield 6%, $m = 2$. *Solution* The preceding bond interest date is Apr. 1, 1970. The number of interest periods from this date until redemption is 51. The value of the bond on Apr. 1, 1970, is therefore

$$P_0 = 1000 + (35 - 30)a_{\overline{51}|3\%} = 1000 + 129.76 = \$1129.76$$

Counting 30 days to each month, from Apr. 1 to June 16 is 75 days, so that $f = {}^{75}\!/_{180} = {}^{5}\!/_{12}$. Equation (4) now gives

$$P = 1129.76\left(1 + 0.03 \times \frac{5}{12}\right) = 1129.76 \times 1.0125 = \$1143.88$$

Had the exact value of P been asked for, we should have used Eq. (3) and obtained

$$P = 1129.76(1.03)^{5/12} = 1129.76 \times 1.01239232 = \$1143.76$$

The difference between the two results is 12 cents.

An alternate method of approximating P is as follows. Let P_0 have the same meaning as before, and let P_1 be the purchase price of the bond on the forthcoming interest date. Now on the forthcoming interest date, the bond will make a bond interest payment of R and then be worth P_1. Consequently its value just before the bond interest payment is $P_1 + R$. If we assume that the change in value from P_0 to $P_1 + R$ is uniform during the interest period, then the value of the bond at an intermediate date can be found by interpolating between these values. The proof of this fact, though not difficult, will be omitted.

Example 2 Solve Example 1 by interpolation.
Solution As before, $P_0 = \$1129.76$. We now compute P_1.

$$P_1 = 1000 + (35 - 30)a_{\overline{50}|3\%} = \$1128.65$$

The value of the bond just before the next bond interest payment is therefore $\$1128.65 + \$35.00 = \$1163.65$. We now interpolate between $\$1129.76$ and $\$1163.65$. Thus

$$P = 1129.76 + \frac{5}{12}(1163.65 - 1129.76) = \$1143.88$$

as before.

Since the methods developed in this section require that the yield rate of the bond be known, these methods might accurately be described as methods of determining what price an investor should offer for a given bond in order that it yield a specified interest rate.

56 PURCHASING BONDS ON THE MARKET

Only rarely can a bond be purchased to yield a specified rate of interest. In most cases, bonds are purchased at a bond exchange, where they are auctioned off to the highest bidder. This is done through agents acting for the buyer and seller. A prospective seller instructs his agent as to the minimum price that he is willing to accept, whereas a prospective buyer tells his agent the maximum price that he is willing to pay. The agents work for a straight commission and naturally try to get their client the best price possible.

Now it has been pointed out that when a bond is sold on a bond interest date, the bond interest payment due that day is considered as belonging to the seller, so that the buyer purchases only the future earnings and does not share in those already accrued. For reasons that will become apparent, it is desirable to retain the concept that the purchaser is entitled to only the *future* earnings of the bond even when the bond is purchased between bond interest dates. *Thus the seller is considered as entitled to that part of the forthcoming bond interest payment which has already accrued.* Since the seller's share of the forthcoming bond interest payment is constantly changing, starting from zero on an interest date and increasing to R on the following interest date, the price at which he is willing to sell fluctuates according to the nearness of the forthcoming interest date. For this reason, it is undesirable to price bonds on the market at the actual price that the seller expects to receive. *Consequently bonds are "quoted" on the market at a price Q, with the understanding that the purchase price is Q plus that portion of the forthcoming bond interest payment which has already been earned.* Hence if Q is the **market price** and R' represents that part of the forthcoming bond interest payment which has already accrued (*hereinafter called the accrued bond interest*), then the total purchase price of the bond is

$$P = Q + R' \tag{5}$$

In actual practice, the accrued bond interest is computed by the simple formula $R' = fR$, where f is the fractional part of the interest period that has already elapsed. For example, if a bond pays $30 interest every 6 months, then 45 days after an interest date, the accrued bond interest would be $^{45}\!/_{180} \times 30.00 = \$7.50$.

Finally, since bonds are issued in various denominations, it is customary to give the **market quotation** on the basis of a $100 bond and rounded off to the nearest eighth. Thus if the market quotation is $105\frac{1}{4}$, then the market price of a $500 bond would be

$$5 \times 105\frac{1}{4} = \$526.25,$$

and the purchase price would be $526.25 plus the accrued bond interest, if any.

Example 1 A $500 bond pays $15 bond interest on Feb. 1 and Aug. 1. This bond was sold on Apr. 1 at a market quotation of $108\frac{1}{2}$. What did the purchaser pay? *Solution* The market price was $Q = 5 \times 108.50 = \$542.50$. Since it was sold on Apr. 1, $f = {}^{60}\!/_{180} = \frac{1}{3}$. Hence

$$R' = fR = \frac{1}{3} \times 15 = \$5$$

and finally

$$P = Q + R' = 542.50 + 5 = \$547.50$$

Example 2 A $1000 bond pays bond interest at the rate of 6%, $m = 2$. It is redeemable at par on Jan. 15, 1980. What should the market quotation be on Sept. 15, 1968, to yield the buyer $j_2 = 4\%$?

Solution The purchase price on July 15, 1968, to yield $j_2 = 4\%$ would be

$$P_0 = 1000 + (30 - 20)a_{\overline{23}|2\%} = 1000 + 182.92 = \$1182.92$$

On Sept. 15, 2 months later, the purchase price would be

$$P = P_0(1 + if) = 1182.92 \left(1 + 0.02 \times \frac{1}{3}\right) = \$1190.81$$

To determine Q we now use Eq. (5). The accrued bond interest is $R' = fR = \frac{1}{3} \times 30 = \$10$. Hence, from $P = Q + R'$,

$$Q = P - R' = 1190.81 - 10 = \$1180.81$$

Reducing this to a $100 bond, we get the market quotation as 118.081, and rounding off to the nearest eighth, 118⅛.

An alternate method of computing Q consists of interpolating between the values P_0 and P_1 where these letters retain the same meaning as in the preceding section.

It should be clearly understood that Eqs. (4) and (5) both give the same value for the purchase price P. The choice of which to use depends only on the known data. Thus, a prospective buyer who decides he is willing to buy a bond only if it yields, say, 4 percent or more would use Eq. (4) to determine the maximum price he can pay. Equation (5), or its equivalent, $Q = P - R'$, would then give the corresponding market price. A potential seller, however, usually decides upon a minimum price Q that he is willing to accept for the *future* earnings of the bond. This price *does not* include that part of the forthcoming bond interest payment R' that has already accrued, and consequently the total purchase price is given by Eq. (5).

A few remarks remain to be made concerning modern terminology. The quantity Q, which we have called the market price, is occasionally called the **book value** of the bond and is frequently called the **and interest price** of the bond. Both of these terms are in good usage, and the student should become familiar with them. Also, P, which we have called the purchase price, is almost always referred to as the **flat price** of the bond.

The methods discussed in the last two sections leave three important questions unanswered: (*a*) If the compound-interest law is used, what is the accrued bond interest? (*b*) What is an exact formula for Q? (*c*) How is an investment schedule made out for a bond purchased between interest dates? These questions will be answered in the next section.

*57 THE THEORETICAL TREATMENT OF BONDS BETWEEN INTEREST DATES

It has previously been observed that the **exact value** of a bond between interest dates is given by

$$P = P_0(1 + i)^f$$

where P_0 represents the value of the bond on the preceding interest date, i is the yield rate of the bond, and f is the fractional part of an interest period that has elapsed since the last interest date. We next develop an exact formula for the determination of the accrued bond interest R'.

If exact methods are to be used, it is clear that the buyer and seller should divide the forthcoming bond interest payment in a manner consistent with the compound-interest law. To this end, let R' be the seller's share, due on the date of sale, and let R'' be the buyer's share, due on the forthcoming interest date. These two shares must be equivalent to the bond interest payment R made at the end of the period as shown on the accompanying time diagram.

$$\begin{array}{c|c|c|c|}
 & R' & & R'' \\
\hline
f & & 1-f & R
\end{array}$$

An equation of value taken at the end of the period gives

$$R'(1 + i)^{1-f} + R'' = R \tag{a}$$

Since both R' and R'' are unknown, we need another relation between them in order to obtain their values. A second relation is obtained by observing that since the determination of R' and R'' is to be equitable to both the buyer and seller, interchanging the two times f and $1 - f$ would likewise interchange R' and R'' as shown on the following time diagram.

$$\begin{array}{c|c|c|}
 & R'' & R' \\
\hline
1-f & f & R
\end{array}$$

An equation of value now gives

$$R' + R''(1 + i)^f = R \tag{b}$$

If Eq. (a) is multiplied by $(1 + i)^f$, we get

$$R'(1 + i) + R''(1 + i)^f = R(1 + i)^f \tag{c}$$

We now subtract Eq. (b) from Eq. (c) and get

$$R'i = R(1 + i)^f - R$$

Solving for R' gives

$$R' = R\frac{(1 + i)^f - 1}{i} = Rs_{\overline{f}|i} \tag{6}$$

In a similar manner, $R'' = Rs_{\overline{1-f}|i}$.

Example A bond pays \$30 bond interest every 6 months. What is the accrued bond interest 2 months after an interest date if the yield rate is (a) 4%, $m = 2$, (b) 8%, $m = 2$?

Solution a Two months after an interest date, $f = \frac{1}{3}$. Hence

$$R' = Rs_{\overline{f}|i} = 30s_{\overline{1/3}|2\%} = 30 \times 0.33113548 = \$9.934$$

Solution b For a yield rate of 8%, $m = 2$, we have

$$R' = 30s_{\overline{1/3}|4\%} = 30 \times 0.32898510 = \$9.870$$

The practical method of computation gives $R' = fR = \frac{1}{3} \times 30 = \$10$.

It can be shown that the value of R' obtained from the exact equation (6) is always somewhat less than that given by the approximate (or practical) formula $R' = fR$. However, the difference is usually slight; and since the buyers on one date become sellers at a later date, no great injustice is enforced by use of the simpler formula.

Since Eq. (6) is an exact formula for R', it is now possible to develop an exact formula for Q. To this end, we start with $P = Q + R'$ or $Q = P - R'$. Using Eqs. (3) and (6) to eliminate P and R' gives

$$Q = P_0(1 + i)^f - Rs_{\overline{f}|i}$$

We now use Eq. (1) to eliminate P_0. This gives

$$Q = [C(1 + i)^{-n} + Ra_{\overline{n}|i}](1 + i)^f - Rs_{\overline{f}|i}$$

and after rearranging,

$$Q = C(1 + i)^{-n+f} + R[a_{\overline{n}|i}(1 + i)^f - s_{\overline{f}|i}]$$

By using the identity in Prob. 6, Exercise 14, Chap. 4, we reduce this last result to

$$Q = C(1 + i)^{-(n-f)} + Ra_{\overline{n-f}|i} \tag{7}$$

By using the same procedure as that used in Sec. 53, we can transform Eq. (7) into

$$Q = C + (R - Ci)a_{\overline{n-f}|i} \tag{8}$$

Thus Q is exactly what Eq. (1) or (2) gives when the time until maturity contains a fractional number of periods. In view of the meaning that will be attached to the symbol $a_{\overline{n}|i}$ in Sec. 69 for fractional values of n, Eq. (7) shows that Q is equal to the present value of the redemption price plus the present value of the *future* earnings of the bond and does not include the part of the current bond interest payment that has already been earned.   Hence the purchase price should be $P = Q + R'$.

We shall illustrate these theoretical formulas with a numerical example.   Suppose a \$1000 bond paying \$30 bond interest every 6 months and redeemable at par in 10 years 3 months is sold to yield $j_2 = 4$ percent.   We readily find that

$$P_0 = 1000 + 10a_{\overline{21}|2\%} = \$1170.112$$

and

$$P = P_0(1 + i)^f = 1170.112(1.02)^{\frac{1}{2}} = \$1181.755$$

Thus the purchase price of the bond should be \$1181.755.   This sum, however, should be regarded as consisting of two parts, namely, the accrued bond interest $R' = 30s_{\overline{\frac{1}{2}}|2\%} = \$14.926$ and the market price $Q = P - R' = \$1166.829$.   On the following interest date, the bond interest payment is likewise regarded as consisting of several parts. First, the new owner must recover R' with interest.   This will require $R'(1 + i)^{1-f} = 14.926(1.02)^{\frac{1}{2}} = \$15.075$.   Second, the owner is entitled to interest on Q.   The interest on Q will be

$$Q(1 + i)^{1-f} - Q = 1166.829(1.02)^{\frac{1}{2}} - 1166.829 = \$11.611$$

The rest of the bond interest payment, namely,

$$30.00 - 15.075 - 11.611 = \$3.314$$

is for the amortization of the premium and reduces the book value of the bond to $1166.829 - 3.314 = \$1163.515$.   It can be verified that the value obtained for Q is the same as that given by either Eq. (7) or (8) and that the final book value \$1163.51 is the value of P_1.

In actual practice, Q is usually given whereas only an approximate value of i is known.   Consequently, the exact formulas developed in this section are of little practical value.   However, these exact formulas justify the common accounting practice of treating Q and R' as separate transactions.   Therefore when the buyer of a bond considers R' a temporary loan that will be repaid out of the first bond interest payment and treats Q as the book value of the bond that is being purchased and consequently sets up an investment schedule with Q as the starting value of the bond, he is proceeding in a manner that is theoretically correct.

Finally, it should be observed that the approximate formulas used in the practical treatment are obtainable from the exact formulas in this section by replacing $(1 + i)^f$ by $1 + if$, and $s_{\overline{f}|i}$ by f.   Since f is a fraction, it can be shown that these replacements usually differ very little from the exact expressions.

EXERCISE 33

Find the purchase price and the corresponding market price of the following bonds, bought to yield the specified interest rate.

Prob-lem	Face value	Redemp-tion value	Bond interest rate	Yield rate	Redemp-tion date	Date of purchase
1	$1000	Par	$j_1 = 5\%$	$j_1 = 6\%$	4/1/1983	3/1/1969
2	$1000	Par	$j_2 = 6\%$	$j_2 = 5\%$	7/1/1998	3/1/1968
3	$5000	$5500	$j_2 = 4\frac{1}{2}\%$	$j_2 = 3\%$	10/1/2010	12/16/1974
4	$ 500	$ 525	$j_1 = 3\frac{1}{2}\%$	$j_1 = 4\frac{1}{2}\%$	2/1/1985	11/16/1971
5	$1000	$1100	$j_2 = 3\%$	$j_2 = 4\frac{1}{2}\%$	6/1/1990	4/25/1972
6	$1000	Par	$j_1 = 4\frac{1}{2}\%$	$j_2 = 2\frac{1}{2}\%$	1/1/1997	8/6/1968

Find the purchase price of the following bonds if bought at the given market quotation.

Prob-lem	Face value	Redemp-tion value	Bond interest rate	Market quotation	Redemp-tion date	Date of purchase
7	$1000	Par	$j_2 = 5\%$	105	3/1/2001	4/1/1973
8	$1000	Par	$j_1 = 5\frac{1}{2}\%$	$85\frac{1}{2}$	9/1/1979	8/1/1969
9	$ 500	$ 525	$j_1 = 3\%$	98	12/1/1989	3/10/1970
10	$1000	$1100	$j_2 = 3\frac{1}{4}\%$	$126\frac{1}{2}$	5/1/2006	7/11/1965
11	$1000	$1050	$j_2 = 2\frac{3}{4}\%$	$135\frac{1}{4}$	6/1/2008	4/21/1966
12	$5000	$5100	$j_2 = 3\frac{1}{4}\%$	$76\frac{1}{4}$	12/1/2015	3/7/1973

13. Find the purchase price of a $1000 bond, redeemable at par on June 1, 1986, paying bond interest at 6% effective, to yield $j_2 = 5\%$, if it is purchased on July 1, 1976.

14. Find the market price of a $1000 bond redeemable at $1050 on Mar. 1, 1976, paying bond interest at $j_2 = 6\%$, to yield 6% effective, if it is purchased on May 1, 1971.

⋆15. Find the exact purchase price and the exact market price for the bond in Prob. 2.

⋆16. Find the exact purchase price and the exact market price for the bond in Prob. 3.

⋆17. Prove that if n, integral or not, represents the number of interest periods from the date of purchase to the date of redemption, then an exact formula for Q, the market price, is

$$Q = \frac{Fr}{i} + \left(C - \frac{Fr}{i}\right)(1 + i)^{-n}$$

⋆18. Use the formula in Prob. 17 to find the exact market price of the bond in Prob. 1.

58 FINDING THE YIELD RATE

Perhaps the most important problem relative to bonds consists of finding the investment rate that a bond will yield when purchased for a given price. It is only by solving this problem that an investor can determine which of several bonds furnishes the best investment. Unfortunately, there is no direct solution, but numerous methods of varying degrees of accuracy and complexity are available for solving this important problem. Two of these will be discussed.

The method of averages   When a sum of money is invested for just one period, the interest rate can be found by dividing the interest earned by the amount invested. When more than one period is involved and the interest payments and invested principal both vary, *an approximate value of the rate can be obtained by dividing the average interest payment by the average amount invested.*   The procedure will be made clear by an example.

Example 1   A $1000 bond pays $30 bond interest on Jan. 15 and July 15. It will be redeemed at $1100 on Jan. 15, 1980. The market quotation on Jan. 15, 1970, is 120. What is the approximate yield rate if purchased on this date?
Solution   The purchase price of the bond is $1200, since the date of sale is a bond interest date. The benefits that the purchaser will receive if he holds the bond until maturity consist of 20 bond interest payments of $30 each, making a total of $600, and the redemption price of $1100. Thus he pays $1200 and receives a total of $600 + $1100 = $1700, or a net gain of $1700 − $1200 = $500. This total gain is realized over a period of 10 years, or 20 interest periods, so that the average gain per interest period is $500/20 = $25. Since the bond originally cost $1200 and is finally redeemed for $1100, its average value is

$$\frac{1}{2}(1200 + 1100) = \$1150$$

We now approximate the investment rate by dividing the average gain per period by the average amount invested in the bond. This gives $i = \frac{25}{1150} = 0.02174$ approximately, or a nominal rate of approximately $j_2 = 0.0435$.

Naturally the question of accuracy arises, and there is no satisfactory answer for the method just outlined. In most cases, the answer can be trusted to the nearest tenth percent, so that for the example just solved we can be almost certain that the nominal rate is between 4.3 percent and 4.4 percent. When greater accuracy is desired, the method of averages should be followed by the interpolation procedure described below.

The method of interpolation   This method consists of computing purchase prices to yield various investment rates until two such prices are obtained that enclose the actual purchase price, then interpolating between these two.   Clearly, only two purchase prices need be computed provided the right two investment rates are chosen.   This can nearly always be done if the rate is first approximated by the method of averages.

Example 2   Compute the yield rate for Example 1 by interpolation.
Solution   By the method of averages used in the solution of Example 1, we found that the rate was approximately $j_2 = 4.35\%$.   Hence we now compute the purchase prices to yield $j_2 = 4\%$ and $j_2 = 4\frac{1}{2}\%$.   The results are

$$P(\text{to yield } j_2 = 4\%) = 1100 + (30 - 22)a_{\overline{20}|\,2\%} = \$1230.81$$

and

$$P(\text{to yield } j_2 = 4\frac{1}{2}\%) = 1100 + (30 - 24.75)a_{\overline{20}|2\frac{1}{4}\%} = \$1183.81$$

Arranging the data in the form of a table, we have

		Purchase price	i	$j, m = 2$	
		1230.81	2%	4%	
	30.81	1200.00	i	j	$\frac{1}{2}\%$
		1183.81	$2\frac{1}{4}\%$	$4\frac{1}{2}\%$	

(bracketed as $47.00 \{ \ldots$, and $30.81\{$ for top two rows with $\}c$, and $\}\frac{1}{2}\%$)

The proportionality equation is

$$\frac{c}{\frac{1}{2}\%} = \frac{30.81}{47.00}$$

Hence $c = 0.328\%$ and $j_2 = 4.328\%$.

Concerning the accuracy of the yield rate as given by interpolation, the following "rule of thumb" almost always applies: When the yield rate of a bond is found by interpolation, the result is slightly too large. The error, however, seldom exceeds $n/5$ times the square of the difference of the rates used.

The rule of thumb just stated implies that the error in j for Example 2 should not exceed 0.00005.   Actually, it can be shown by more exact criteria developed in Chap. 11 that the error is almost exactly 0.00003.

Both methods described in this section apply equally well to bonds purchased between interest dates.   Naturally, the computations are somewhat more tedious, but the procedure is essentially the same.   If the method of averages is used, we may take either $\frac{1}{2}(P + C)$ or $\frac{1}{2}(Q + C)$ as the average value of the bond. Theoretical considerations imply that $\frac{1}{2}(Q + C)$ gives slightly better results.

EXERCISE 34

In Probs. 1 to 6, find the yield rate by the method of averages (in each case the face of the bond is $1000):

Problem	Redemption price	Bond interest	Time until redemption, years	Purchase price
1	Par	6%, $m = 1$	10	$1200
2	Par	5%, $m = 1$	15	$1100
3	Par	3%, $m = 2$	20	$ 900
4	Par	4%, $m = 2$	5	$ 900
5	$1100	$5\frac{1}{2}\%$, $m = 2$	25	$1300
6	$1050	$4\frac{1}{2}\%$, $m = 2$	10	$1100

7–12. Find the yield rate in Probs. 1 to 6 by the method of interpolation.

13. A $1000 bond redeemable at par at the end of 30 years and paying bond interest at $j_2 = 4\%$ is callable 15 years before maturity at $1050. Find the yield rate j_2 if quoted now at 110, assuming (a) that it is called, (b) that it is not called.

14. A $1000 bond, redeemable at par in 20 years, pays bond interest at $j_2 = 3\%$. It is callable at $1050 at the end of 10 years. If it is quoted at 95, find the yield rate j_2, assuming (a) that it is called, (b) that it is not called.

★59 BOND TABLES

Extensive bond tables have been prepared that give the purchase price of a bond for a wide variety of yield rates. A sample of such a table is shown on page 137.

When bond tables are available, many bond problems can be solved by direct reference to the tables. Moreover, since the yield rates are tabulated for values that differ by only $\frac{1}{20}$ percent, interpolation for intermediate values is highly accurate.

Since the various uses of bond tables are fairly obvious, no illustrative examples will be given. It should be emphasized, however, that not all bond problems are solvable by the use of bond tables, and consequently a thorough knowledge of the methods outlined in the earlier part of this chapter is highly desirable.

Purchase price of a $1000 par bond paying bond interest at $j_2 = 4\%$

Yield rate, $m = 2$	Time until redemption, years			
	8	$8\frac{1}{2}$	9	$9\frac{1}{2}$
3.25%	1052.46	1055.31	1058.12	1060.88
3.30%	1048.87	1051.52	1054.12	1056.69
3.35%	1045.29	1047.74	1050.15	1052.52
3.40%	1041.72	1043.97	1046.19	1048.36
3.45%	1038.17	1040.22	1042.24	1044.23
3.50%	1034.63	1036.49	1038.32	1040.12
3.55%	1031.10	1032.77	1034.41	1036.02
3.60%	1027.59	1029.07	1030.52	1031.94
3.65%	1024.09	1025.38	1026.64	1027.89
3.70%	1020.61	1021.71	1022.79	1023.85
3.75%	1017.14	1018.05	1018.95	1019.83
3.80%	1013.69	1014.41	1015.12	1015.82
3.85%	1010.24	1010.79	1011.32	1011.84
3.90%	1006.82	1007.18	1007.53	1007.88
3.95%	1003.40	1003.58	1003.76	1003.93
4.00%	1000.00	1000.00	1000.00	1000.00

*60 OTHER TYPES OF BONDS

When money is borrowed by means of an issue of bonds, there is no theoretical reason why the bonds should be redeemed in a single installment. Consequently, companies occasionally issue bonds specifying that they will be redeemed in installments. For example, a $10,000 bond paying bond interest at $j_2 = 6$ percent might state that it will be redeemed as follows: $2000 at the end of 10 years, $3000 at the end of 15 years, and $5000 at the end of 20 years. Naturally bond interest is paid only on the outstanding face value. Thus the bond just mentioned would pay $300 bond interest at the end of each 6 months for the first 10 years, $240 for the next 5 years, and $150 for the last 5 years. *Such bonds are called* serial bonds.

A moment's reflection makes it clear that the purchase of a serial bond is equivalent to buying several separate bonds simultaneously, and therefore the methods developed in the preceding sections are adequate for treating the various problems concerning serial bonds.

Example 1 Find the purchase price of the serial bond in the illustration above to yield 4%, $m = 2$.
Solution The given serial bond is equivalent to the following three 6%, $m = 2$, par bonds: $2000 redeemable in 10 years, $3000 redeemable in 15 years, and $5000

redeemable in 20 years. The corresponding purchase prices are

$$P_1 = 2000 + (60 - 40)a_{\overline{20}|2\%} = \$2327.029$$
$$P_2 = 3000 + (90 - 60)a_{\overline{30}|2\%} = \$3671.894$$
$$P_3 = 5000 + (150 - 100)a_{\overline{40}|2\%} = \$6367.774$$

The purchase price for the serial bond is therefore

$$P = P_1 + P_2 + P_3 = \$12,366.70$$

All bonds considered so far have been redeemed in one or more installments, with each installment an integral multiple of \$100. There is, however, no reason why the face of a bond should not be redeemed in such a manner that redemptions plus bond interest payments form an annuity. Thus, contracts that call for the extinction of a debt, principal and interest, by equal periodic payments are frequently called **annuity bonds**. *Stated differently, an annuity bond is a contract embodying an annuity written up in the form of a bond.*

Example 2 A \$10,000 annuity bond will be redeemed, principal and interest, at $j_1 = 5\%$, in 10 equal annual installments. What will a prospective buyer offer for this bond if he wishes to realize an effective investment rate of (*a*) 4%, (*b*) 5%, (*c*) 6%? *Solution* We first determine what the installment payments will be. Since these will form an ordinary annuity, we have

$$10,000 = Ra_{\overline{10}|5\%} \qquad \text{or} \qquad R = \frac{10,000}{a_{\overline{10}|5\%}} = \$1295.05$$

The benefits that this bond will furnish are shown on the time diagram below.

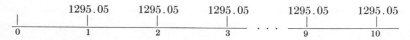

The price that will be bid for the bond is the present value of these payments computed at the desired investment rate. Consequently,

$$P = 1295.05a_{\overline{10}|4\%} = \$10,504.02 \qquad (a)$$
$$P = 1295.05a_{\overline{10}|5\%} = \$10,000.00 \qquad (b)$$
$$P = 1295.05a_{\overline{10}|6\%} = \$9,531.68 \qquad (c)$$

It should be fairly obvious that all problems concerning annuity bonds are merely annuity problems stated in bond phraseology, and consequently the methods developed in the annuity chapters are adequate for solving them.

★EXERCISE 35

1. A \$15,000 serial bond, paying bond interest semiannually at $j_2 = 5\%$, will be redeemed in 3 installments of \$5000 each, due at the ends of 5, 10, and 15 years. Find the purchase price to yield $j_2 = 3\%$.

2. Find the purchase price for the bond in Prob. 1 to yield the purchaser $j_2 = 7\%$.

3. A $10,000 serial bond paying bond interest semiannually at $j_2 = 6\%$ will be redeemed in 2 installments of $5000 each, due at the ends of 5 and 10 years. Find the yield rate by interpolation if it is quoted on the market at 110.

4. Find the yield rate by interpolation for the bond in Prob. 1 if it is quoted on the market at 105.

5. An annuity bond promises to repay $10,000 principal and interest at $j_1 = 5\%$ by equal payments at the end of each year for 15 years. How much will an investor offer for this bond if he wants to realize $j_1 = 4\%$ on his investment?

6. What will an investor offer for the bond in Prob. 5 if he wishes to realize $j_1 = 6\%$ on his investment?

9
Depreciation

61 DEFINITIONS

When a company is formed, a group of people, called stockholders, furnish capital for the purchase of property, machines, equipment, and other assets necessary for the operation of the company. Periodically thereafter the profits of the company are distributed to the stockholders. It is, of course, necessary to pay all operational costs, interest on loans, and other expenses before deciding what net profits have been earned.

One of the expenses of operating a business enterprise is the loss in value of physical property due to various causes not covered by current repairs. *Such a loss in value is called* **depreciation.** In fact, the United States Supreme Court in 1934 stated:

> Broadly speaking, depreciation is the loss, not restored by current maintenance, which is due to all the factors causing the ultimate retirement of the property. These factors embrace wear and tear, decay, inadequacy and obsolescence. Annual depreciation is the loss which takes place in a year.

Since it is a fundamental principle of economics that the capital invested in a business enterprise should be kept intact, some systematic plan to provide for depreciation should be an integral part of any good accounting system.

Depreciation is usually considered an operating expense and is treated more or less like any other expense. Thus annually (or oftener) a charge is made for the depreciation of the physical assets owned by the company. Occasionally depreciation is handled by setting up a special fund, called a **depreciation fund.** Yearly payments, equal to the depreciation, are then placed in this fund until the asset is eventually sold, replaced, or retired. The sum put into the depreciation fund is not necessarily a cash deposit placed in a savings account but may be invested in the company itself by being used to pay off debts or to purchase other assets. The important thing is that a charge equal to the depreciation be taken out of the gross income and invested in some manner so that the original capital remains intact. Thus at all times, the books of the company must show assets equal in value to the original capital invested.

Usually when a company purchases a new machine or similar asset, it decides immediately, according to the best available information, what the useful life of the machine will be and its probable scrap value at the end of this life. From this information and the cost of the machine, the company then sets up a depreciation schedule showing the depreciation for each year, the book value (or estimated value) at the end of each year, and the total depreciation. Although many methods are in use for deciding how much the depreciation for each year should be, for all methods the total depreciation plus the book value of the asset must always equal the original cost of the asset.

There are many methods of determining the depreciation of various assets. Some of these will be discussed in the following sections.

62 THE STRAIGHT–LINE METHOD, OR THE METHOD OF AVERAGES

One of the simplest and most popular methods of fixing the amount of depreciation is the method of averages, usually called the straight-line method. Under this method, it is assumed that the amount of depreciation for each year is the same, or constant. Thus, if C is the initial cost and S is the scrap value, or trade-in value, at the end of a useful life of n years, then the yearly depreciation is taken as

$$\frac{C - S}{n}$$

The following example will illustrate the method.

Example A machine costs a company $3300. It is estimated that the useful life of the machine will be 5 years and that the scrap value will be $300. Find the annual depreciation by the straight-line method, and make out a schedule that shows, for each year, the yearly depreciation, the book value of the machine, and the total depreciation.

Solution Since the machine depreciates $3300 − $300 = $3000 over a 5-year period, the average depreciation for each year is $3000/5 = $600. A depreciation schedule is now made out by decreasing the book value of the machine $600 each year and increasing the depreciation by the same amount.

End of year	Yearly depreciation	Total depreciation	Book value
0	0	0	3300
1	600	600	2700
2	600	1200	2100
3	600	1800	1500
4	600	2400	900
5	600	3000	300

It should be observed that the book value plus the total depreciation at the end of any year is equal to the original cost of the machine. Thus, on the books, the original investment has been preserved.

There are two main objections to the straight-line method. (*a*) It ignores interest on the depreciation fund when one is used. (*b*) Most equipment depreciates rapidly during the early years, so that the book values during these years are much higher than the actual market values. Consequently, the original investment only appears to remain intact. In spite of these objections, however, the method is widely used because of its simplicity.

63 THE SINKING–FUND METHOD

This method is a modification of the straight-line method to permit the depreciation fund to accumulate interest. Thus, a sinking fund is set up to accumulate a sum of money equal to the total depreciation $C - S$. If the sinking-fund rate is i per year and R is the annual payment into the fund, then

$$Rs_{\overline{n}|i} = C - S \quad \text{and} \quad R = (C - S)\frac{1}{s_{\overline{n}|i}}$$

Under this plan, the annual depreciation charge varies from year to year, since it equals the payment made at the end of the year plus the interest earned on the fund during the year. The book value of the asset is defined as the difference between the original cost and the total amount in the depreciation fund. The depreciation schedule contains two more columns than for the straight-line method: one, the annual payment into the fund, and the other, the interest earned on the fund during the year. These two items are added to get the yearly depreciation.

Example Find the annual payment into the depreciation fund, and make out a depreciation schedule for the machine in the example in the preceding section if the sinking-fund method is used and the fund accumulates at 4%, $m = 1$.
Solution Since the total depreciation is $3000, the sinking fund must accumulate this amount in 5 years, so that

$$Rs_{\overline{5}|4\%} = \$3000 \quad \text{and} \quad R = \frac{3000}{s_{\overline{5}|4\%}} = \$553.88$$

A schedule is now set up as below.

Year	Payment	Interest on fund	Yearly depreciation or increase in fund	Total depreciation	Book value
0	0	0	0	0	3300.00
1	553.88	0	553.88	553.88	2746.12
2	553.88	22.16	576.04	1129.92	2170.08
3	553.88	45.20	599.08	1729.00	1571.00
4	553.88	69.16	623.04	2352.04	947.96
5	553.88	94.08	647.96	3000.00	300.00

It should be observed that if the final column is omitted, the above is essentially a sinking-fund schedule. The final column of book values is obtained by subtracting the yearly depreciation from the book value at the end of the preceding year. Thus, at any time, the book value plus the total depreciation adds up to the original investment. In consequence, the original investment remains intact according to the books.

64 THE SUM–OF–THE–INTEGERS METHOD

Although both the straight-line and sinking-fund methods are used by accountants, these methods are considered unrealistic by a great many people. They reason that for many types of physical property, the depreciation is rapid during the early years and slow during the later years. Therefore, it is reasoned, the book value is a fictitious figure which most likely exceeds the market value of the asset, especially in the early years of its life. Consequently, the original investment remains intact only on the books and not in the sense that the market value of the asset plus the total depreciation is equal to the original investment.

If the foregoing reasoning is accepted as valid, then it follows that a more realistic method of depreciation must depreciate the asset rapidly at first and more slowly later on.   An argument in favor of this reasoning is the fact that most states use such a schedule in assigning a value to automobiles for taxation purposes.   One method of obtaining this result is the sum-of-the-integers method.   An example will illustrate how the method is used.

Example   Make out a depreciation schedule for the machine in the example in Sec. 62, using the sum-of-the-integers method.
Solution   Let s be the sum of the integers from 1 to n, n being the life of the machine. In this case, $n = 5$, and

$$s = 1 + 2 + 3 + 4 + 5 = 15$$

Next form the fractions $\frac{5}{15}$, $\frac{4}{15}$, $\frac{3}{15}$, $\frac{2}{15}$, and $\frac{1}{15}$.   Notice that the numerators are the integers 1, 2, 3, 4, and 5 in reverse order.   The total depreciation $3000 is now multiplied by these fractions to get the yearly depreciation charges.   Thus, $\frac{5}{15} \times 3000 = \$1000$ is the depreciation for the first year; $\frac{4}{15} \times 3000 = \$800$ is the depreciation for the second year; etc.   A depreciation schedule is now made out as shown below.

Year	Yearly depreciation	Total depreciation	Book value
0	0	0	3300
1	1000	1000	2300
2	800	1800	1500
3	600	2400	900
4	400	2800	500
5	200	3000	300

It is easy to show that the fractions formed in the manner illustrated in the example will always total 1, regardless of the value of n; consequently, the sum of the yearly depreciation charges will always be the total depreciation.

EXERCISE 36

1. A machine costs $10,000 and will have a scrap value of $2000 at the end of 5 years. Make out depreciation schedules for the machine by (*a*) the straight-line method, (*b*) the sinking-fund method with money worth 5% effective, (*c*) the sum-of-the-integers method.

2. A machine costing $50,000 will depreciate to $10,000 in 4 years.   Make out depreciation schedules for the machine by (*a*) the straight-line method, (*b*) the sinking-fund method with interest at $j_1 = 4\%$, (*c*) the sum-of-the-integers method.

3. A machine costing $25,000 will have a useful life of 20 years and no scrap value at that time.   Find the total depreciation and the book value at the end of 12 years by (*a*) the straight-line method, (*b*) the sinking-fund method with money worth $4\frac{1}{2}\%$ effective.

4. A machine costing \$3000 will have no scrap value at the end of its useful life of 15 years. Find the total depreciation and the book value at the end of 10 years by (*a*) the straight-line method, (*b*) the sinking-fund method with money worth $3\frac{1}{2}\%$ per year.

5. A machine depreciates from its purchase price of \$2000 to \$300 at the end of 10 years. Find its book value at the end of 7 years by (*a*) the straight-line method, (*b*) the sum-of-the-integers method.

6. A machine depreciates from an original cost of \$12,000 to a scrap value of \$2000 in 8 years. Find its book value at the end of 3 years by (*a*) the straight-line method, (*b*) the sum-of-the-integers method.

7. The sinking-fund method at $j_1 = 5\%$ is used to depreciate a machine from its purchase price of \$40,000 to a scrap value of \$5000 at the end of 30 years. Find (*a*) the amount in the sinking fund at the end of 15 years, (*b*) the book value, (*c*) the depreciation charge for the sixteenth year.

★8. If R is the annual payment into the sinking fund, show that the book value at the end of k years is $B_k = C - Rs_{\overline{k}|i}$.

65   THE CONSTANT-PERCENTAGE METHOD

Another method of determining the yearly depreciation charges so that they are largest during the early years is the constant-percentage method. Under this plan, each year's depreciation is a fixed percentage of the preceding book value. When this method is used, it is customary to assign a value to the rate of depreciation rather than to estimate the life and scrap value. The rate is usually determined after a careful analysis of the equipment under consideration.

Example 1   A certain type of machine loses 10% of its value each year. The machine costs \$2000 originally. Make out a schedule showing the yearly depreciation, the total depreciation, and the book value at the end of each year for 5 years.
Solution   The depreciation charge for the first year is

   10% of \$2000 = \$200

The book value at the end of the first year will be \$2000 − \$200 = \$1800. For the second year, the depreciation charge will be 10% of \$1800 = \$180, and the book value will be \$1800 − \$180 = \$1620. Continuing in this manner, we find the depreciation charge and book value for each year. The total depreciation at any time is the sum of the depreciation charges made so far, or it is the difference between the original cost and the book value. The completed schedule appears below.

Year	Yearly depreciation	Total depreciation	Book value
0	0	0	2000.00
1	200.00	200.00	1800.00
2	180.00	380.00	1620.00
3	162.00	542.00	1458.00
4	145.80	687.80	1312.20
5	131.22	819.02	1180.98

It should be noted that since the machine loses 10% of its value each year, 90% of the value remains.   Consequently each book value is 90% of the preceding one. This fact makes it possible to set up the schedule by finding the column of book values first.

The procedure followed in the example will now be translated into formulas.   Let d be the constant rate of depreciation and B_k the book value at the end of k years.   The depreciation for the next year is then dB_k.   If this depreciation is subtracted from the book value B_k, the new book value is obtained.   Therefore

$$B_{k+1} = B_k - dB_k = B_k(1 - d)$$

This formula states, in effect, that if an article loses a fractional part d of its value, then the fractional part of the value that remains is $1 - d$. Therefore, since each new book value is $1 - d$ times the preceding one, the book value at the end of n years can be found by multiplying the original cost C by $1 - d$ and multiplying each successive result by $1 - d$ until n multiplications have been made.   Therefore

$$B_n = C(1 - d)^n \tag{1}$$

The formula can be used to find the book value at the end of any number of years without first finding the preceding ones.

Example 2   Find the book value, at the end of 20 years, of the machine in Example 1. *Solution*   We have $C = \$2000$, $d = 0.1$, and $n = 20$.   Substituting these values in the formula gives

$$B_{20} = 2000(1 - 0.1)^{20} = 2000(0.9)^{20}$$

This computation is readily carried out with the aid of logarithms.

$$\log B_{20} = \log 2000 + 20 \log 0.9$$
$$= 3.301030 + 20(9.954243 - 10) = 2.385890$$

Hence, $B_{20} = \$243.16$.

It was stated earlier that when the constant-percentage method is used, it is customary to estimate the rate of depreciation and then compute the successive book values and depreciation charges.   This procedure is not necessary, however, as the method works equally well if we prefer to estimate the useful life and scrap value of the asset.   In this case, it is necessary first to compute the rate of depreciation, using Eq. (1), after which the procedure is the same as before.   Logarithms are usually needed to determine the rate.

Example 3   Equipment costing $15,000 is assumed to have a useful life of 6 years and will have a scrap value of $2000 at that time.   If the constant-percentage method of depreciation is to be used, find the rate.

Solution We have $C = \$15,000$, $B_6 = \$2000$, and $n = 6$. Substituting these values in Eq. (1) gives

$$2000 = 15,000(1 - d)^6 \quad \text{and} \quad (1 - d)^6 = \frac{2000}{15,000} = \frac{2}{15}$$

Applying logarithms to the last equation gives

$$6 \log (1 - d) = \log 2 - \log 15$$

$$\begin{array}{lll} \log 2 = 10.301030 - 10 & & \\ \log 15 = \ \ 1.176091 & & \text{(subtract)} \\ \hline 6 \log (1 - d) = \ \ 9.124939 - 10 = 59.124939 - 60 & & \\ \log (1 - d) = \ \ 9.854156 - 10 & & \text{(dividing by 6)} \\ 1 - d = \ \ 0.71475 & & \\ d = 1 - 0.71475 = 0.28525 = 28.525\% \end{array}$$

The schedule can now be set up in the same manner as was used in Example 1. Some labor can be saved if the successive book values are computed by logarithms. When logarithms are used, the logarithm of C is added to the logarithm of $1 - d$ to get the logarithm of B_1; adding the logarithm of $1 - d$ to the logarithm of B_1 gives the logarithm of B_2; etc. The book values are then obtained and the schedule completed.

EXERCISE 37

1. Equipment costing $10,000 depreciates 25% of its value each year. Make out a depreciation schedule for the first 4 years. Without running the schedule further, find what the book value would be at the end of 10 years.

2. A machine that costs $5000 depreciates 15% of its value each year. Make out a depreciation schedule for the first 4 years, and find its book value at the end of 12 years.

3. A car costing $4000 depreciates 20% of its value each year. Make out a depreciation schedule for the first 3 years, and find the book value at the end of 7 years.

4. Find the book value at the end of 8 years of a machine that costs $20,000 and depreciates 30% of its value each year.

5. A taxicab costing $4500 will depreciate to $500 in 3 years. Find the rate of depreciation and make out the schedule.

6. A $7000 truck depreciates to $1500 in 4 years. Find the rate of depreciation and make out the schedule.

7. An $800 machine depreciates to $50 in 12 years. Find the rate of depreciation and the book value at the end of 5 years.

8. A machine costs $22,000 and will have a scrap value of $2000 at the end of 9 years. Find its book value at the end of 6 years and the depreciation charge for the seventh year.

9. A machine that costs $60,000 will depreciate to $5000 in 15 years. Find the book value at the end of 10 years and the depreciation charge for the eleventh year.

★**10.** A race-track crowd has $1,000,000 to start with and bets half its wealth on each race. Since, under the pari-mutuel system, the track takes 10% of all money bet before paying off the winners, the wealth of the crowd is decreased 10% of the amount bet after each race. Find how much money the crowd has left after the seventh race.

★**11.** Solve Prob. 10 if the crowd bets 25% of its wealth each time.

*66 THE ANNUAL CHARGE FOR DEPRECIATION AND INTEREST

A charge frequently encountered in accounting is one that, in order to avoid ambiguity, we shall call the annual charge for depreciation and interest. *This charge, as its name implies, is comprised of a charge for depreciation plus an interest charge on the book value.* The yearly interest charge is computed on the book value during that year, that is, on the book value at the end of the preceding year.

Although any method of depreciation could be used, in actual practice the sinking-fund method is almost invariably employed. However, the rate of interest that the sinking fund earns is not necessarily the same as the rate used for computing interest on the book value of the asset.

Example A company pays $3300 for a new machine. It is estimated that the useful life of the machine will be 5 years and that the scrap value at that time will be $300. Find the annual charges for depreciation and interest if a 4% sinking fund is used for depreciating the machine, and interest on the book values is computed at 6% effective. *Solution* The annual depreciation charges for this machine were computed in the example in Sec. 63. The annual interest charges are found by multiplying the successive book values by 6%. Thus, the interest charge at the end of the first year is 6% of $3300 = $198; the interest charge at the end of the second year is 6% of $2746.12 = $164.77; etc. The total annual charges are now found by combining the interest and depreciation charges. The schedule appears below.

Year	Annual depreciation charge	Book value	Interest on book value at 6%	Total annual charge
0	0	3300.00	0	0
1	553.88	2746.12	198.00	751.88
2	576.04	2170.08	164.77	740.81
3	599.08	1571.00	130.20	729.28
4	623.04	947.96	94.26	717.30
5	647.96	300.00	56.88	704.84

The method used in the example for computing the annual charge for depreciation and interest is frequently called *the compound-interest method of depreciation*, although only part of the annual charge is depreciation.

A formula for the annual charge for depreciation and interest can easily be developed when the sinking-fund method of depreciation is used. To this end we recall (see Prob. 11, Exercise 25) that the increase in the sinking fund at the end of the kth year is $R(1 + i)^{k-1}$. Also (see Prob. 8, Exercise 36) the book value of the asset at the end of the $(k - 1)$st year is $C - Rs_{\overline{k-1}|i}$. Therefore if i' is the yearly rate used for computing interest on the book value, then the total annual charge at the end of the kth year is

$$R(1 + i)^{k-1} + (C - Rs_{\overline{k-1}|i})i'$$

It is left as an exercise for the student to show that when $i' = i$, the above expression can be simplified to $R + Ci$.

When the annual charge for depreciation and interest is computed with $i' = i$, the total yearly charge is frequently called *the depreciation charge by the annuity method*, although only part of this charge is assigned to depreciation. In fact this precise charge, $R + Ci$, was discussed in Sec. 47, where it was interpreted as an investment charge.

*67 DEPLETION

A coal mine in operation suffers a gradual loss in value due to the fact that the coal is being used up. A similar loss in value applies to oil wells, timber tracts, and various other types of income-producing assets. *The loss in value due to using up the asset is called* **depletion.**

Just as in the case of depreciation, some systematic plan should be used to restore the loss of capital due to depletion. This is usually done by making annual payments into a sinking fund, called the *depletion reserve*. Thus if P is the purchase price of a depletable asset that will have a scrap value of S at the end of n years, then the depletion reserve must amount to $P - S$ at that time. If R is the annual payment into the sinking fund, then

$$Rs_{\overline{n}|i} = P - S \qquad \text{or} \qquad R = \frac{P - S}{s_{\overline{n}|i}}$$

When a sinking fund is used to care for depletion, the *yearly depletion* is defined as the increase in the sinking fund for the year, and the *amount of depletion* at any time is the amount in the depletion reserve. The *book value* of the asset is the difference between the original investment and the amount in the depletion reserve.

If the annual income from a depletable asset is I, then $I - R$ represents the profit for the year and may be considered as interest on the investment. This fact may be stated as follows:

Income = (interest on investment) + (depletion payment)

One of the main problems regarding depletable assets concerns their evaluation. Let r be the yearly rate that a prospective buyer wishes to realize on his investment, I the yearly income that the asset will produce, S the scrap value after n years, and P the purchase price that can be paid. If depletion is to be cared for by a sinking fund accumulating at rate i, then P should be determined so that

$$I = Pr + R \qquad \text{where } R = \frac{P - S}{s_{\overline{n}|i}}$$

Eliminating R between these two equations gives

$$I = Pr + \frac{P - S}{s_{\overline{n}|i}} \tag{2}$$

If the above equation is solved for P, the result is

$$P = \frac{I s_{\overline{n}|i} + S}{1 + r s_{\overline{n}|i}} = \frac{I + S/s_{\overline{n}|i}}{r + 1/s_{\overline{n}|i}} \tag{3}$$

These formulas can be simplified somewhat when the two rates r and i are the same. The rate r, however, is usually higher than i owing to the risk element in this kind of business venture.

Example It is estimated that a mine will furnish an income of \$50,000 a year for 25 years, at which time the property will be worth \$10,000. Find the purchase price to yield 8% on the investment if the depletion fund accumulates at $3\frac{1}{2}\%$. Also find the yearly depletion for the fifth year.

Solution The purchase price may be obtained by direct substitution into Eq. (3). However, it will be more instructive to solve the problem using fundamental principles. Let P be the purchase price. Then the payments into the depletion fund will be $R = 50{,}000 - 0.08P$, and these payments must accumulate $P - \$10{,}000$ by the end of the twenty-fifth year. Therefore

$$P - 10{,}000 = (50{,}000 - 0.08P)s_{\overline{25}|3\frac{1}{2}\%}$$
$$P(1 + 0.08s_{\overline{25}|3\frac{1}{2}\%}) = 10{,}000 + 50{,}000s_{\overline{25}|3\frac{1}{2}\%}$$

Solving for P gives

$$P = \$475{,}582.67$$

The yearly payment into the depletion reserve is given by

$$R = I - Pr = 50{,}000 - 0.08 \times 475{,}582.67 = \$11{,}953.39$$

To find the yearly depletion for the fifth year, we first find the amount in the depletion reserve at the end of the fourth year. This amount will be

$$11{,}953.39s_{\overline{4}|3\frac{1}{2}\%} = \$50{,}382.86$$

The increase in the fund 1 year later will be interest, at $3\frac{1}{2}\%$, on the amount just found plus a regular depletion payment of \$11,953.39. Depletion for the fifth year is therefore

$$50{,}382.86 \times 0.035 + 11{,}953.39 = \$13{,}716.79$$

This result could have been obtained by using the formula given in Prob. 11, Exercise 25.

1. A certain machine costs $1200 and will have a scrap value of $200 and a probable life of 5 years.   Find the annual charge for depreciation and interest if 4% effective is used as the sinking-fund rate as well as the investment rate.

2. A certain type of taxicab costs $4000 and will have a trade-in value of $500 at the end of 3 years.   Find the annual charges for depreciation and interest if 5% effective is used as both the sinking-fund rate and the investment rate.   Make out the complete schedule.

3. Make out the first three lines of the schedule for Prob. 1 if the sinking-fund rate is 3% and the investment rate is 6%.

4. Solve Prob. 2 if the sinking-fund rate is 4% and the investment rate is 7%.

5. A certain mine, according to mining experts, will produce an income of $100,000 annually and will be worthless at the end of 20 years.   Find the purchase price to yield an investor 10% if 4% can be earned on payments placed in a depletion reserve.

6. It is estimated that the annual income from an oil well will be $60,000 and that the well will be worthless at the end of 10 years.   Find the purchase price to yield 9% on the investment if 3% interest is available for a sinking fund.   Find the depletion for the eighth year.

7. Mr. Jones owns a 10-acre tract of land that contains a vein of coal.   It is estimated that $3000 will be required to start operating, after which coal worth $1500 over expenses can be sold each month for 5 years.   At the end of this time, the land will be worth $10 per acre.   Because of the risks involved, a prospective buyer offers to buy at a price that, if these estimates are correct, will yield 18%, $m = 12$.   What price does he offer if depletion is to be cared for by a 4%, $m = 12$, sinking fund?

8. Show that Eq. (2) can be changed into the purchase-price formula for a bond by taking $r = i$ and interpreting I as the bond interest payment and S as the redemption price.   [*Hint:* Make use of Eq. (12), Sec. 26.]

*10
General Annuities—Advanced Topics

68 THE GENERAL ANNUITY DUE

An annuity is called a general annuity due if the payment period is different from the interest period and payments are made at the beginnings of the payment periods. The treatment of general annuities due is analogous to that of ordinary general annuities in that the general annuity due is converted into an ordinary simple annuity, then treated as in Chap. 5.

Let W be the general annuity payment, i the interest rate per interest period, m the number of interest conversions per year, p the number of annuity payments per year, and R the equivalent simple annuity payment. The time diagram below shows the two equivalent annuities for a 1-year period.

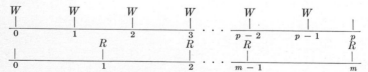

The relationship between the payments of the two annuities can be established by the following simple reasoning. If the first W on the diagram above were transferred to the end of the year, the general annuity would be an ordinary one and the relationship would be Eq. (6) of Chap. 5. Hence the amount at the end of the year of the annuity above exceeds the 1-year amount of an ordinary general annuity by the compound interest that accrues when one W payment is accumulated for 1 year. The compound interest would be $W(1 + i)^m - W$, which can be written in the form $Wis_{\overline{m}|i}$. But this is the amount of an ordinary annuity of Wi per interest period for 1 year. Therefore the R payments corresponding to the annuity due are each Wi more than they would be if the general annuity were an ordinary one. Hence we conclude

$$R = W \frac{1}{s_{\overline{m/p}|i}} + Wi = W\left(\frac{1}{s_{\overline{m/p}|i}} + i\right) = W \frac{1}{a_{\overline{m/p}|i}} \tag{1}$$

or the equivalent form

$$W = Ra_{\overline{m/p}|i} \tag{2}$$

This formula was developed in a somewhat different manner in Sec. 45, Chap. 7. It is left as an exercise for the student to prove Eqs. (1) and (2) by the technique used in Sec. 32, Chap. 5, using either the present or the end of the year as a comparison date.

When m/p is fractional, Table 7 gives the values of $a_{\overline{m/p}|i}$, whereas no new table is needed for the values of $1/a_{\overline{m/p}|i}$, since these can be readily obtained by adding i to the values of $1/s_{\overline{m/p}|i}$ given in Table 5.

Example 1   If the interest rate is $j_2 = 5\%$, what annuity payable at the end of each half year is equivalent to \$50 payable at the beginning of each month?
Solution   The given payments form a general annuity due with $W = 50$ and $p = 12$. The desired payments will form an ordinary simple annuity. Since $m = 2$ and $i = 0.025$, we have

$$R = W \frac{1}{a_{\overline{m/p}|i}} = 50 \frac{1}{a_{\overline{1/6}|2\frac{1}{2}\%}}$$

Now

$$\frac{1}{a_{\overline{1/6}|2\frac{1}{2}\%}} = \frac{1}{s_{\overline{1/6}|2\frac{1}{2}\%}} + 0.025 = 6.06219991 + 0.025 = 6.08719991$$

and consequently $R = 50 \times 6.08719991 = \$304.36$ is the desired semiannual payment.

Example 2   If the interest rate is $j_4 = 4\%$, find the annuity payable at the beginning of each month equivalent to \$1000 payments at the beginning of each 5-year period.
Solution   Here, a general annuity due is to be replaced by a second general annuity due. This is done by first replacing the given annuity by an ordinary simple annuity, payable quarterly, then converting the simple annuity into a general annuity due payable monthly. For the first part of the solution, we take 5 years as the basic

unit of time instead of 1 year. Then $p = 1$ and $m = 20$. The time diagrams are shown below.

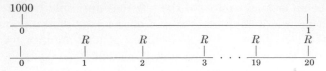

Since $W = 1000$, $i = 1\%$, and $m/p = 20$, we have

$$R = W \frac{1}{a_{\overline{m/p}|i}} = 1000 \frac{1}{a_{\overline{20}|1\%}} = 1000 \times 0.05541531 = \$55.41531$$

as the equivalent simple annuity payable quarterly. We next replace this simple annuity by a general annuity due payable at the beginning of each month. For this conversion a 1-year time diagram is shown below.

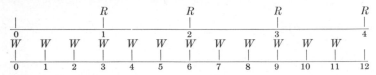

We have $p = 12$, $m = 4$, $i = 1\%$, $R = 55.41531$, and

$$W = Ra_{\overline{m/p}|i} = 55.41531a_{\overline{1/3}|1\%} = 55.41531 \times 0.33112825 = \$18.35$$

Other problems concerning the general annuity due, such as finding an interest rate or the term, are treated in the same manner as in Chap. 5. The only essential difference is the use of Eqs. (1) and (2) for converting the given annuity into an equivalent one instead of Eq. (6) or (7) of Chap. 5.

EXERCISE 39

1. Replace a set of $200 payments made at the beginning of each quarter by an equivalent set made at the end of each month if money is worth 6%, $m = 12$.

2. Replace a set of $500 payments made at the beginning of each month by an equivalent set made at the end of each half year if money is worth 4%, $m = 2$.

3. Find the present value of a set of $25 payments made at the beginning of each month for 6 years if interest is at $j_2 = 5\%$.

4. Find the amount of an annuity of $1000 payable at the beginning of each year for 10 years if money is worth $j_4 = 3\%$.

5. A man owes $2800 and agrees to pay off the debt in 30 monthly installments starting now. If he pays interest at the rate $j_4 = 4\%$, how large will these payments be?

6. A man will need $2000 at the end of 6 years. To this end, he will make 12 semi-annual deposits starting now. How large should these deposits be if the fund accumulates at $j_{12} = 3\frac{1}{2}\%$?

7. Merchandise worth $500 is sold on a payment plan that calls for monthly payments of $25 for as long as is necessary, the first payment due on the date of sale. If the interest rate is $j_1 = 7\%$, how many payments will be necessary?

8. A debt of \$1000 is to be paid off by quarterly payments of \$120 for 3 years, the first one due immediately. What effective interest rate is being paid on the debt?

69 THE GENERAL CASE

It has been seen that the formulas

$$S = Rs_{\overline{n}|i} \quad \text{and} \quad A = Ra_{\overline{n}|i}$$

can be used for the evaluation of general annuities after R has been determined by

$$R = W\frac{1}{s_{\overline{m/p}|i}} \quad \text{or} \quad R = W\frac{1}{a_{\overline{m/p}|i}}$$

according as the general annuity is an ordinary one or an annuity due. However, it has been tacitly assumed so far that n, the number of interest periods involved, is a whole number. For example, if interest were converted yearly and payments made monthly, the formulas would be used only if the number of payments were a multiple of 12. Thus they would be used for 24 or 36 payments but not for 37. *It will now be shown that these formulas are valid whether n is an integer or not.* For example, if the interest rate is yearly and there are 37 monthly payments, the above formulas apply with $n = 3\frac{1}{12}$.

Let W be the payment of an ordinary general annuity, q the total number of payments, and i the interest rate per interest period. Let p be the number of payments and m the number of interest periods for any convenient time interval. Finally, let i' be the interest rate per payment interval that is equivalent to i per interest period. Since i' is the rate per payment period and there are q payments, clearly the amount of the annuity is

$$S = Ws_{\overline{q}|i'} = W\frac{(1 + i')^q - 1}{i'}$$

Since i and i' are equivalent rates, we have

$$(1 + i')^p = (1 + i)^m \quad \text{or} \quad 1 + i' = (1 + i)^{m/p}$$

If we now eliminate i' in terms of the given rate i, we get

$$S = W\frac{(1 + i)^{(m/p)q} - 1}{(1 + i)^{m/p} - 1} = W\frac{i}{(1 + i)^{m/p} - 1} \times \frac{(1 + i)^{mq/p} - 1}{i}$$

Therefore

$$S = W\frac{1}{s_{\overline{m/p}|i}}\, s_{\overline{mq/p}|i}$$

Now if n is the number of interest periods corresponding to q payment periods, then $n/q = m/p$ or $n = mq/p$. Hence the last equation may be written $S = Rs_{\overline{n}|i}$, where $R = W(1/s_{\overline{m/p}|i})$, and $n = mq/p$ is the number of interest periods in the term of the annuity, and this formula is valid whether n is an integer or not.

The proof for the present value formula is similar in nature and will not be given. Likewise, similar proofs may be given for the general annuity due.

The only difficulty in using these formulas for all cases lies in the fact that tables do not exist for all possible choices of n. However, most of the cases that arise in practice can be evaluated by means of Tables 3 to 11 and the following identities, which were given as Probs. 3 to 6 in Exercise 14.

$$s_{\overline{k+f}|i} = (1 + i)^f s_{\overline{k}|i} + s_{\overline{f}|i} \tag{3}$$
$$a_{\overline{k+f}|i} = (1 + i)^{-f} a_{\overline{k}|i} + a_{\overline{f}|i} \tag{4}$$
$$s_{\overline{k-f}|i} = (1 + i)^{-f} s_{\overline{k}|i} - a_{\overline{f}|i} \tag{5}$$
$$a_{\overline{k-f}|i} = (1 + i)^f a_{\overline{k}|i} - s_{\overline{f}|i} \tag{6}$$

Example 1 A contract calls for the payment of \$100 at the end of each month for 29 months. Find the present value if interest is at 6% effective.

Solution. Method 1 By use of identities. The payments form an ordinary general annuity with $W = 100$, $p = 12$, $i = 6\%$, and $m = 1$. Exactly as in Chap. 5 we find that the equivalent yearly payment is

$$R = W \frac{1}{s_{\overline{m/p}|i}} = 100 \frac{1}{s_{\overline{1/12}|6\%}} = 1232.652834$$

Since the term of the annuity is 29 months, $n = 2\frac{5}{12}$ years, or interest periods, and

$$A = Ra_{\overline{n}|i} = 1232.652834 a_{\overline{2\frac{5}{12}}|6\%}$$

We now evaluate the symbol $a_{\overline{2\frac{5}{12}}|6\%}$ by means of Eq. (4).

$$a_{\overline{2+\frac{5}{12}}|6\%} = (1.06)^{-\frac{5}{12}} a_{\overline{2}|6\%} + a_{\overline{\frac{5}{12}}|6\%}$$

All the symbols occurring in the right-hand member of the above equation are tabulated, and we have

$$a_{\overline{2+\frac{5}{12}}|6\%} = 0.97601365 \times 1.83339267 + 0.39977258 = 2.1891888$$

Therefore $A = 1232.652834 \times 2.1891888 = \$2698.51$.

Method 2 This method consists of writing an equation of equivalence using as a comparison date the end of the interest period nearest the end of the term of the annuity. Since the term is 29 months, the end of 2 years will be used as a comparison date.

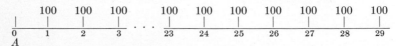

We first find R, the equivalent yearly payment, exactly as in the first solution. Then our equivalence equation becomes

$$A(1.06)^2 = Rs_{\overline{2}|6\%} + Ra_{\overline{\frac{5}{12}}|6\%}$$

since all times are expressed in terms of the yearly interest period. Evaluating the above equation gives

$$A(1.06)^2 = 1232.652834(2.06 + 0.39977258) = 3032.0457$$

Therefore $A = 3032.0457(1.06)^{-2} = \$2698.51$.

Example 2 If a man deposits \$100 at the end of each 4 months for 3 years 8 months in a savings fund that earns interest at 4% effective, how much will he have to his credit at that time?

Solution. *Method* 1 We desire the amount of an ordinary general annuity for which $W = \$100$, $p = 3$, $m = 1$, $i = 4\%$, and n, the number of interest periods, is $3\frac{2}{3}$. Exactly as in Chap. 5, we first find the equivalent simple annuity payable yearly. Thus,

$$R = W \frac{1}{s_{\overline{m/p}|i}} = 100 \frac{1}{s_{\overline{1/3}|4\%}} = 100 \times 3.03965138 = 303.965138$$

The amount of the annuity is then

$$S = Rs_{\overline{n}|i} = 303.965138 s_{\overline{3\frac{2}{3}}|4\%}$$

To evaluate the symbol $s_{\overline{3\frac{2}{3}}|4\%}$ we use Eq. (5). Thus,

$$s_{\overline{4-1/3}|4\%} = (1.04)^{-1/3} s_{\overline{4}|4\%} - a_{\overline{1/3}|4\%}$$

All symbols on the right are tabulated, and we have

$$s_{\overline{4-1/3}|4\%} = 0.98701152 \times 4.24646400 - 0.32471208 = 3.86659681$$

Hence, $S = 303.965138 \times 3.86659681 = \$1175.31$.

Method 2 We write an equation of equivalence using the end of 4 years as a comparison date, since this is the end of the interest period nearest the end of the term of the annuity.

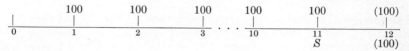

We add an additional \$100 to both the annuity and the equivalent value S at the end of 4 years (12 interest periods). The equivalence equation for this date is

$$S(1.04)^{1/3} + 100 = Rs_{\overline{4}|4\%}$$

where R has the same value as in the preceding solution. Hence

$$S(1.04)^{1/3} = 303.965138 \times 4.246464 - 100 = 1190.777024$$

and

$$S = 1190.777024(1.04)^{-1/3} = 1190.777024 \times 0.98701152 = \$1175.31$$

When the payment of a general annuity is to be found, essentially the same procedure is used as in Chap. 5. However, for simplest computation the comparison date should be chosen as the end of the interest period nearest the date on which the equivalent value of the annuity is known.

Example 3 The cash value of a car is \$4000. It is purchased for \$500 cash and the balance in equal payments at the end of each month for 20 months. What should these payments be if the interest rate is $7\frac{1}{2}\%$ effective.

Solution The payments will form an ordinary general annuity with present value $A = \$3500$, $p = 12$, $m = 1$, and $i = 7\frac{1}{2}\%$. Since the term of the annuity is 20 months, or $1\frac{2}{3}$ years, the end of the interest period nearest the equivalent value $A = 3500$ is 4 months in the past. We next draw a time diagram including this date.

We add four payments (W) to both the annuity and the equivalent value A as shown. Let R be the equivalent yearly payment, and write an equation of equivalence using 4 months ago as the comparison date. Since all times must be expressed in years, we get

$$Ra_{\overline{2}|7\frac{1}{2}\%} = Ra_{\overline{\frac{1}{3}}|7\frac{1}{2}\%} + A(1.075)^{-\frac{1}{3}}$$

or

$$R(a_{\overline{2}|7\frac{1}{2}\%} - a_{\overline{\frac{1}{3}}|7\frac{1}{2}\%}) = 3500(1.075)^{-\frac{1}{3}}$$

Hence, $R(1.4779833) = 3416.63476$, and $R = 2311.687$. We now convert these yearly payments of R into monthly payments. Thus,

$$W = Rs_{\overline{\frac{1}{12}}|7\frac{1}{2}\%} = 2311.687 \times 0.08059892 = \$186.32$$

Example 4 A man borrows \$800 on June 1 which he will repay in 10 equal monthly installments, the first one due Sept. 1. If money is worth $j_2 = 8\%$, what should these payments be?

Solution The time diagram is shown below.

Two additional payments of (W) are added to both the annuity and the equivalent value 800 as shown. We write an equation of value with the present as the comparison date, getting

$$Ra_{\overline{2}|4\%} = 800 + Ra_{\overline{\frac{1}{3}}|4\%}$$

where R is the equivalent semiannual payment and the times are expressed in terms of half years. Evaluating the symbols and solving for R,

$$R(a_{\overline{2}|4\%} - a_{\overline{\frac{1}{3}}|4\%}) = R(1.56138259) = 800 \quad \text{and} \quad R = 512.36641$$

Then $W = Rs_{\overline{\frac{1}{6}}|4\%} = 512.36641 \times 0.16395492 = \$84.00$.

The methods illustrated in the examples can be used even when tables are not available. In this case, logarithms may be used to evaluate the annuity symbols.

Example 5 A contract calls for the payment of \$2 at the end of each 2 weeks for 100 weeks. Find the equivalent cash value of this contract if money is worth $j_{12} = 7.2\%$

Solution   Here $W = 2.00$, $q = 50$, $p = 26$, $i = 0.006$, $m = 12$, and

$$n = q\frac{m}{p} = 23\tfrac{1}{13}$$

The present value of this ordinary general annuity will be

$$A = Ra_{\overline{n}|i} \qquad \text{where } R = W\frac{1}{s_{\overline{m/p}|i}}$$

The tables do not contain the necessary entries, so the evaluation of the annuity symbols will be done by logarithms. To this end, we combine the last two equations and replace the annuity symbols by the expressions for which they stand. Thus,

$$A = W\frac{1}{s_{\overline{m/p}|i}}\,a_{\overline{n}|i} = W\left[\frac{i}{(1+i)^{m/p}-1}\right]\left[\frac{1-(1+i)^{-n}}{i}\right]$$

Therefore

$$A = 2\frac{1-(1.006)^{-23\tfrac{1}{13}}}{(1.006)^{\tfrac{9}{13}}-1}$$

We use logarithms to evaluate the interest factors and get

$$(1.006)^{\tfrac{9}{13}} = 1.002765 \qquad \text{and} \qquad (1.006)^{-23\tfrac{1}{13}} = 0.871056$$

Therefore

$$A = 2\frac{1-0.871056}{1.002765-1} = \$93.27$$

EXERCISE 40

1. Find the amount and present value of an annuity of 13 quarterly payments of $500 each if money is worth 4%, $m = 2$.

2. A radio can be purchased for $20 down and 10 monthly payments of $5 each. Find the equivalent cash price if money is worth $j_4 = 4\tfrac{1}{2}\%$.

3. A sells B a lot worth $1000 cash. B will pay for the lot by making 10 equal monthly payments. What should these payments be if money is worth $j_1 = 5\tfrac{1}{2}\%$ and (*a*) the first payment is due on the day of sale, (*b*) the first payment is due 1 month after the day of sale?

4. What regular quarterly deposits would be necessary to accumulate $1000 at the end of 5 years 9 months if the deposits earn interest at 5% effective?

5. A man places $10 a month into a savings bank, making the first deposit on Jan. 1, 1968. What additional deposit on Dec. 1, 1968, would be necessary to increase his account to $2000 if the savings bank pays interest at the rate $j_4 = 2\%$?

6. A car worth $4000 is purchased by paying $500 down and monthly payments for 18 months. An additional $150 is added to the present value of the debt to pay for insurance. What will the monthly payments be if the finance company makes 8% effective on the loan?

70   FINDING THE NUMBER OF PAYMENTS AND THE FINAL PAYMENT

If q is the number of general annuity payment periods, n is the number of interest periods in the term of an annuity, and p and m are the number of payment periods and interest periods, respectively, per year, then clearly $q/n = p/m$. In all general annuity problems, p and m are given so that if q is known, n is easily determined and conversely. We now consider the problem of finding q when sufficient data are known. As in the case of simple annuities, if A or S, i, and W are given, assuming, of course, that m and p are known, usually no *proper annuity* exists with these given quantities and it is necessary to include one payment different from W in order to satisfy the equivalence relation. It is customary, as in the case of simple annuities, to have this odd payment be the final payment and fall due one payment period after the last regular payment of W. *Henceforth it is understood that all improper annuities include a final payment F, which is less than W and is dated one payment period after the last regular payment of W.*

When sufficient data are given, the number of payments and the final payment are found by solving suitable equations of equivalence. The methods are best illustrated by means of examples.

Example 1 Find the number of full payments and the final payment necessary to cancel a debt of \$1000 if \$100 is to be paid at the end of each year and the interest rate is 6%, $m = 4$.
Solution Since $m = 4$, $p = 1$, and $W = 100$, we have for the equivalent simple annuity

$$R = W \frac{1}{s_{\overline{m/p}|i}} = 100 \frac{1}{s_{\overline{4}|1\frac{1}{2}\%}}$$

Since the debt is \$1000, $A = 1000$ and

$$1000 = Ra_{\overline{n}|1\frac{1}{2}\%}$$

Solving for $a_{\overline{n}|1\frac{1}{2}\%}$, we get

$$a_{\overline{n}|1\frac{1}{2}\%} = \frac{1000}{R} = 10s_{\overline{4}|1\frac{1}{2}\%} = 40.9090338$$

Referring to the tables, we find that this value lies between those tabulated for $n = 63$ and $n = 64$. Since there are four interest periods for each payment period, we conclude that 16 full payments of \$100 would be more than enough to discharge the debt and consequently the annuity consists of 15 full payments of \$100 and a final payment F, less that \$100, due at the end of the sixteenth year.

To find F, we next draw time diagrams showing the known data.

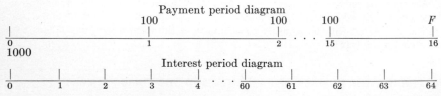

The quantity F can now be found by the methods used in Sec. 28, Chap. 4. If we add 100 to both the general annuity and its equivalent value at the end of the sixteenth year (sixty-fourth interest period) and write an equation of equivalence with this as a comparison date, we get

$$F + Rs_{\overline{64}|1\frac{1}{2}\%} = 100 + 1000(1.015)^{64}$$

where $R = 100(1/s_{\overline{4}|1\frac{1}{2}\%}) = 24.444479$. Solving for F, we get

$$F = 100 + 1000 \times 2.59314442 - 24.444479 \times 106.20962774 = \$96.91$$

The quantity F can also be found by interpolation in a manner similar to that described in Sec. 29, Chap. 4. This method consists of determining the number of general annuity payments q (not the number of interest periods n) by interpolation between consecutive integral values of q, then multiplying the fractional part of the solution thus obtained by W to get F. A general proof of the validity of this method will be given in the next section.

Example 2   Find F in the preceding example by interpolation.
Solution   As in the preceding solution, we find that

$$a_{\overline{n}|1\frac{1}{2}\%} = 40.9090338$$

and that this value lies between those tabulated for $n = 63$ and $n = 64$. However, since the interpolation must be between consecutive integral values of q, we use $n = 60$ and $n = 64$ for the interpolation table as shown below.

q	n	$a_{\overline{n}|1\frac{1}{2}\%}$
16	64	40.957853
$15 + f$		40.909034
15	60	39.380269

Interpolating, we get $f = 0.1528765/0.1577584 = 0.969055$ and

$$F = fW = \$96.91$$

Example 3   A man purchases a used car worth \$1500 by means of a \$500 down payment and \$50 at the end of each month for as long as necessary. Find the number of payments and the final payment if money is worth 6%, $m = 2$.
Solution.   *Method* 1   The monthly payments will form an annuity for which the present value $A = 1000$, $W = 50$, $p = 12$, $m = 2$, and $i = 3$ percent. Therefore

$$1000 = Ra_{\overline{n}|3\%} \qquad \text{where} \qquad R = 50\,\frac{1}{s_{\overline{\frac{1}{6}}|3\%}} = 303.728447$$

Solving for $a_{\overline{n}|3\%}$, we get

$$a_{\overline{n}|3\%} = \frac{1000}{R} = 20s_{\overline{\frac{1}{6}}|3\%} = 3.2924146 \qquad (a)$$

If we wished to do so, we could now find the term and hence the number of payments by the method used in Example 1. However, less computation is necessary if the following procedure is used. Determine by inspection which tabulated entry is nearest to the value of $a_{\overline{n}|i}$ obtained at the last step, then use one of the following identities:

$$a_{\overline{n+k}|i} = a_{\overline{n}|i} + (1 + i)^{-n}a_{\overline{k}|i} \qquad \text{(Prob. 4, Exercise 14)} \qquad (b)$$

$$a_{\overline{n-k}|i} = a_{\overline{n}|i} - (1 + i)^{-n}s_{\overline{k}|i} \qquad \text{(Prob. 6, Exercise 14)} \qquad (c)$$

Choose n as the integer nearest the end of the term of the annuity so that k will not exceed $\frac{1}{2}$. In our case, $a_{\overline{n}|i} = 3.2924146$ is closer to the value given for $n = 4$ than for $n = 3$, so we choose Eq. (c). Thus

$$a_{\overline{n}|3\%} = a_{\overline{4}|3\%} - (1.03)^{-4}s_{\overline{k}|3\%}$$

where we are writing n in place of $n - k$ for the nonintegral solution of Eq. (a) and k is the fractional part remaining in the fourth interest period. Solving for $s_{\overline{k}|3\%}$, we get

$$s_{\overline{k}|3\%} = (a_{\overline{4}|3\%} - a_{\overline{n}|3\%})(1.03)^4 = 0.477985 \qquad (d)$$

We now refer to Table 6 and find that k lies between $\frac{2}{6}$ and $\frac{3}{6}$. Thus n lies between $4 - \frac{1}{3} = 3\frac{2}{3}$ and $4 - \frac{1}{2} = 3\frac{1}{2}$. Since there are 6 payments per interest period there will be $6 \times 3\frac{1}{2} = 21$ full payments and a twenty-second partial payment. Had we used the wrong identity in this last step, the value of $s_{\overline{k}|i}$ (or $a_{\overline{k}|i}$) obtained would not be found in Table 6 or 7, thereby indicating that the value of k exceeds $\frac{1}{2}$. To determine F we next draw the following time diagrams.

Adding three payments of W to both the annuity and its equivalent value and writing an equation of equivalence with the end of the fourth interest period as a comparison date give

$$F(1.03)^{\frac{1}{3}} + Rs_{\overline{4}|3\%} = 1000(1.03)^4 + Rs_{\overline{1/2}|3\%}$$

Now since $1000 = Ra_{\overline{n}|3\%}$ and $s_{\overline{4}|3\%} = (1.03)^4 a_{\overline{4}|3\%}$, this last equation may be written

$$F(1.03)^{\frac{1}{3}} = Rs_{\overline{1/2}|3\%} - R(a_{\overline{4}|3\%} - a_{\overline{n}|3\%})(1.03)^4$$

In view of Eq. (d), the second term in the right-hand member is $Rs_{\overline{k}|3\%}$, so that

$$F = R(s_{\overline{1/2}|3\%} - s_{\overline{k}|3\%})(1.03)^{-\frac{1}{3}} = \$5.51$$

Method 2 (by interpolation) As in the preceding solution we first determine how many payments are necessary. Since there will be 21 full payments and a twenty-second partial payment, the interpolation is between values corresponding to $q = 21$ and $q = 22$. Therefore we shall determine n, hence q, by interpolating between the values $a_{\overline{3\frac{1}{2}}|3\%}$ and $a_{\overline{3\frac{2}{3}}|3\%}$. However, it is not necessary to compute these symbols, since it is apparent from the identities

$$a_{\overline{3\frac{1}{2}}|3\%} = a_{\overline{4}|3\%} - (1.03)^{-4}s_{\overline{1/2}|3\%}$$

$$a_{\overline{3\frac{2}{3}}|3\%} = a_{\overline{4}|3\%} - (1.03)^{-4}s_{\overline{1/3}|3\%}$$

that interpolating between the left-hand members for n is equivalent to interpolating for k between the values $s_{\overline{1/2}|3\%}$ and $s_{\overline{1/3}|3\%}$.   Using the value $s_{\overline{k}|3\%} = 0.477985$ as found in the preceding solution, we form the following interpolation table.

$$
1\left\{f\left\{
\begin{array}{c|c|c}
q & k & s_{\overline{k}|3\%} \\
\hline
21 & \tfrac{1}{2} & .496305 \\
\hline
21+f & & .477985 \\
\hline
22 & \tfrac{1}{3} & .330054
\end{array}
\right.\Big\}.018320\right\}.166251
$$

Interpolating, we get $f = 0.018320/0.166251 = 0.11019$ and

$$F = fW = \$5.51$$

While it appears that either solution of the last example seems long, it will be observed that most of the solution is descriptive and only a few computations are necessary.   Moreover, all symbols occurring in the computations are tabulated to eight-decimal-place accuracy, thereby ensuring accuracy in the final result of at least seven significant digits.

71 PROOF OF THE GENERAL INTERPOLATION THEOREM

Let A be the present value of an annuity, W the periodic payment, p the number of payments per year, i the interest rate per conversion period, and m the number of conversion periods per year.   When the above data are given, the annuity is usually an improper one, so that a final payment F, dated one payment period after the last W payment, is necessary for equivalence.   *If q, the number of payments, is determined by interpolating between values corresponding to consecutive integral values of q, then the fractional part f of this solution multiplied by W gives the final payment F.*

Proof   Suppose first that the annuity is an ordinary annuity so that the time diagrams appear as below.

where $n' = q(m/p)$ and $n'' = (q + 1)m/p$.   An equation of equivalence with the present as comparison date gives

$$A = Ra_{\overline{n'}|i} + F(1 + i)^{-n''} \qquad \text{where } R = W\frac{1}{s_{\overline{m/p}|i}}$$

Therefore

$$F = (A - Ra_{\overline{n'}|i})(1 + i)^{n''} \qquad (a)$$

If we set $a_{\overline{n}|i} = A/R$, then $n = (q + f)m/p$, where f lies between 0 and 1. Interpolating for n between n' and n'' is equivalent to interpolating for f, and we get

$$f = \frac{A/R - a_{\overline{n'}|i}}{a_{\overline{n''}|i} - a_{\overline{n'}|i}}$$

Hence

$$A - Ra_{\overline{n'}|i} = fR(a_{\overline{n''}|i} - a_{\overline{n'}|i}) \qquad (b)$$

Combining Eqs. (a) and (b) gives

$$F = fR(a_{\overline{n''}|i} - a_{\overline{n'}|i})(1 + i)^{n''}$$

Now in view of Eq. (10), Sec. 25,

$$a_{\overline{n''}|i} - a_{\overline{n'}|i} = a_{\overline{n''-n'}|i}(1 + i)^{-n'}$$

and consequently

$$F = fRa_{\overline{n''-n'}|i}(1 + i)^{n''-n'} = fRs_{\overline{n''-n'}|i} \qquad (c)$$

But $n'' - n' = m/p$ and $Rs_{\overline{m/p}|i} = W$; therefore $F = fW$.

If the annuity is an annuity due, each payment, including F, falls due one period earlier and Eq. (a) becomes

$$F = (A - Ra_{\overline{n'}|i})(1 + i)^{n'} \qquad \text{where } R = W\,\frac{1}{a_{\overline{m/p}|i}}$$

Equation (c) then becomes

$$F = fRa_{\overline{n''-n'}|i} = fRa_{\overline{m/p}|i} = fW$$

EXERCISE 41

1. A debt of \$1000 will be repaid by semiannual payments of \$100 for as long as necessary. If the interest rate is 6%, $m = 12$, find the number of payments and the final payment.

2. A man borrows \$3000 with interest at 5% effective. He will repay the loan by payments of \$50 at the end of each month for as long as necessary. Find the number of payments and the final payment.

3. A company owes a debt of \$100,000 on which interest accumulates at 4%, $m = 4$. They plan to pay \$20,000 at the end of each year. How many payments will be required, and what will the final payment be?

4. How many monthly deposits of \$25 will be necessary to accumulate \$1000 if interest at 2%, $m = 4$, is paid on the deposits? What final deposit will be required to bring the account to exactly \$1000?

5. A divorce decree awards a woman $40,000 cash or an annuity that is equivalent to this sum at $4\frac{1}{2}\%$, $m = 2$, and pays $500 at the end of each month. How many payments will she receive, and what will the final payment be?

6. How many quarterly payments of $1000 will be necessary to pay off a debt of $10,000 if money is worth $3\frac{1}{2}\%$ effective and the first payment is made 1 year after the debt was incurred? What will the final payment be?

7. A finance company makes loans at the rate of 8% effective and requires that the debt be retired by payments at the end of each month equal to 15% of the borrowed principal. How many full payments are necessary, and what percentage of a full payment is the final partial payment?

8. Merchandise worth $100 may be purchased by monthly payments of $10, the first one due on the date of sale. If the payment plan includes interest at $j_2 = 9\%$, how many payments will be required and what will the final partial payment be?

72 OTHER TYPES OF ANNUITIES

There are several other types of annuities that are occasionally encountered. Some of these will be discussed briefly.

Increasing annuities This term is applied to a sequence of periodic payments of W, $2W$, $3W$, . . . , qW, each payment being W more than the preceding one until q payments have been made. As usual, let i be the interest rate per conversion period, m the number of conversion periods per year, p the number of payments per year, and $n = qm/p$ the number of interest periods in the term of the annuity. To find the amount of such an annuity, we consider it as consisting of q separate annuities as follows: one annuity with q payments of W, a second annuity with $q - 1$ payments of W, a third annuity with $q - 2$ payments of W, etc., all of them terminating at the same time as shown on the time diagram below.

payment diagram

Each of the annuities above will be equivalent to a simple annuity with payments of $R = W/s_{\overline{m/p}|i}$ and with terms of $qm/p\ (= n)$, $(q - 1)m/p$, $(q - 2)m/p$, . . . , $2m/p$ and finally, m/p. Consequently, the amount of the increasing annuity is

$$S = Rs_{\overline{n}|i} + Rs_{\overline{(q-1)m/p}|i} + Rs_{\overline{(q-2)m/p}|i} + \cdot\cdot\cdot + rs_{\overline{m/p}|i}$$

If the annuity symbols are replaced by their algebraic equivalents and obvious simplifications made, there results

$$S = \frac{R}{i}[(1 + i)^n + (1 + i)^{(q-1)m/p} + (1 + i)^{(q-2)m/p} + \cdots$$
$$+ (1 + i)^{m/p} - q]$$

The expression above contains a geometric progression of q terms with first term $(1 + i)^n$ and ratio $= (1 + i)^{-m/p}$. Using the formula for the sum of a geometric progression, we get

$$S = \frac{R}{i}\left[\frac{(1 + i)^n - 1}{1 - (1 + i)^{-m/p}} - q\right] = \frac{R}{i}\left(\frac{s_{\overline{n}|i}}{a_{\overline{m/p}|i}} - q\right) \tag{7}$$

the last simplification being possible after dividing the numerator and denominator of the preceding fraction by i.

If the present or some other equivalent value of an increasing annuity is wanted, it is best to first determine its amount by Eq. (7) and then transfer this value to the desired date.

Decreasing annuities   A decreasing annuity differs from the increasing annuity only in that *the first payment is qW and each succeeding payment is W less than the preceding one until a final payment of W is reached.* Since this annuity may be considered as the sum of q distinct annuities all starting at the present, it is simpler to determine a formula for its present value than for its amount.   The formula is

$$A = \frac{R}{i}\left(q - \frac{a_{\overline{n}|i}}{s_{\overline{m/p}|i}}\right) \qquad \text{where } R = \frac{W}{s_{\overline{m/p}|i}} \tag{8}$$

The proof is similar to that for increasing annuities and is left as an exercise for the student.   If a decreasing annuity is to be evaluated at some other date than the present, it is simplest to compute its present value first, then transfer this value to the required date.

Finally, it should be observed that if the annuity is either an increasing or decreasing annuity due, the R occurring in Eq. (7) or (8) should be computed by Eq. (1) of Chap. 10, $R = W/a_{\overline{m/p}|i}$.

Annuities payable continuously   This type of annuity refers to *the collection of a finite sum of money T, each interest period, where the money is collected in a continuous flow during the period.*   Although continuous annuities do not actually occur in business, they are closely approximated in certain practical cases such as the flow of coins in a city subway system.

To derive formulas for the present value and amount of such an annuity, two results from the calculus are needed.

$$\lim_{p=\infty} p[(1+i)^{m/p} - 1] = m \log_e (1+i)$$

$$\text{where } e = 2.71828 \ldots \quad (9)$$

$$\lim_{x=\infty} \left(1 + \frac{1}{x}\right)^x = e = 2.71828 \ldots \quad (10)$$

The present value of an ordinary general annuity can be written in the form

$$A = W \frac{1}{s_{\overline{m/p}|i}} a_{\overline{n}|i} \quad (11)$$

Let $T = pW$ be the total annuity payments per year. Then

$$A = T \frac{i}{p[(1+i)^{m/p} - 1]} a_{\overline{n}|i}$$

If we let p become infinite and use the limit from Eq. (9), we get

$$\lim_{p=\infty} A = T \frac{i}{m \log_e (1+i)} a_{\overline{n}|i} \quad (12)$$

Similarly,

$$\lim_{p=\infty} S = T \frac{i}{m \log_e (1+i)} s_{\overline{n}|i} \quad (13)$$

Annuities with interest converted continuously Returning to Eq. (11), let p be constant, $i = j/m$, $n = tm$ where t is the total time in years. Then

$$A = W \frac{j/m}{(1+j/m)^{m/p} - 1} \frac{1 - (1+j/m)^{-tm}}{j/m}$$

This last relation may be written in the form

$$A = W \frac{1 - [(1+j/m)^{m/j}]^{-jt}}{[(1+j/m)^{m/j}]^{j/p} - 1}$$

If we now let m become infinite, Eq. (10) with x replaced by m/j gives us

$$\lim_{m=\infty} A = W \frac{1 - e^{-jt}}{e^{j/p} - 1} \quad \text{and} \quad \lim_{m=\infty} S = W \frac{e^{jt} - 1}{e^{j/p} - 1} \quad (14)$$

The above formulas apply to annuities for which payments are made a finite number of times per year but interest is converted continuously.

Annuities payable continuously and interest converted continuously As a final type, let us consider an annuity for which both payments and interest are continuous. Let $T = pW$ be the total yearly payment, and let $n = tm$ where t is the total time in years. If m and p are both allowed to become infinite, the use of Eqs. (9) and (10) gives

$$\lim_{m,p = \infty} A = T \frac{1 - e^{-jt}}{j} \quad \text{and} \quad \lim_{m,p = \infty} S = T \frac{e^{jt} - 1}{j} \quad (15)$$

If we do not insist that the payments of an annuity all be equal, clearly the number of different types theoretically possible is almost unlimited. While it would be possible to develop formulas for almost any type of situation that may arise, we feel that a clear understanding of the underlying principles is of far more importance.

EXERCISE 42

1. A man borrows \$10,000 and signs a contract promising to pay \$200 on the principal at the end of each year for 50 years and interest at 5% at the end of each year on the amount owed during the year. After 10 years, the contract is sold to an investor who wishes to make 6% effective on his investment. Find the selling price. (*Hint:* The payments of principal form an ordinary annuity, and the interest payments form a decreasing annuity.)

2. A man deposits \$1000 at the beginning of each year in a fund paying interest at 5% effective. The principal will be divided among his three daughters at the end of 10 years. His son receives all the interest from the fund at the end of each year. If the son invests his interest payments in a savings fund that accumulates at 3%, $m = 4$, how much will he have at the end of 10 years?

3. A city subway system collects 100,000 dimes during each day in a practically continuous flow. Find the present value of this income for the next 365 days if money is worth (*a*) 4% effective, (*b*) 3% converted continuously. [*Hint:* $\log_e (1 + i) = \log_{10} (1 + i)/\log_{10} e$.]

4. Find the amount and present value of an annuity of \$1000 at the end of each year for 20 years if interest is converted continuously at 3%.

5. A contract calls for the payment of \$50 at the end of each month for a year, \$45 at the end of each month during the second year, etc., the monthly payments being \$5 less each year than the preceding year for a total of 10 years. Find the present value of this contract if money is worth 6%, $m = 12$. (*Hint:* The amounts of each of these 10 ordinary annuities form a decreasing annuity.)

MISCELLANEOUS EXERCISES ON GENERAL ANNUITIES

1. A mail-order house sells goods on the following plan: 10% of the cash price down and 10% of the cash price per month for 10 months. What effective rate of interest does the company receive?

2. A contract calls for the payment of \$50 at the end of each half year for $7\frac{1}{2}$ years and an additional \$1000 at that time. What is the present value of the contract if money is worth $j_1 = 5\%$?

3. An insurance policy requires the payment of \$7 at the beginning of each quarter for 25 years and will pay \$1000 at the death of the insured. How long must the insured live for the company to break even if money is worth 4% effective?

4. A high-school teacher borrows $100 on July 1 and a like amount on Aug. 15.   He agrees to pay off these loans in eight equal monthly installments beginning on Nov. 1. If interest at 8%, $m = 2$, is included, what should the payments be?

5. How many quarterly payments of $300 will it take to complete the purchase of a car worth $4500 if $800 cash is paid and interest is computed at $j_{12} = 5\%$?   What will the final payment be?

6. A furniture company sells goods by either of the following plans: a 25% discount on the list price for cash or 25% down and the rest in 12 equal monthly installments with no interest added.   What effective rate makes the two plans equivalent?

7. A teacher receives a salary of $600 per month for 9 months.   If money is worth 5% effective, what monthly payments should he receive if the payments are continued the year round?

8. A fraternity house is worth $80,000.   The chapter pays $5000 down and will pay off the balance of the debt during the next 50 years by equal payments on Dec. 1, Mar. 1, and June 1 of each year.   What will these payments be if the house is purchased on Sept. 1 and the interest rate is 6% effective?

9. A fraternity house worth $90,000 is purchased on Sept. 1 by paying $10,000, the balance to be paid by installments of $2000 on Dec. 1, Mar. 1, and June 1 of each year for as long as is necessary.   If the interest rate is 5% effective, find the date of the final payment and how large it should be.

*11
Computing Techniques

73 INTRODUCTION

In the mathematics of finance there are essentially two different types of computations that can lead to much tedious arithmetic. The first is the evaluation of some interest function for an interest rate not included in the tables. The other is the inverse problem of finding an interest rate which satisfies a given function. The methods employed in solving these problems will usually depend upon the computing equipment available and the desired accuracy of the final result. Various methods of computing the different interest functions will be discussed, and for those methods which give approximations, limits for the error will be given when practical.

74 INTEGRAL POWERS OF NUMBERS

Finding the value of expressions such as $(1.053)^{146}$ or $(0.9875)^{25}$ requires relatively few multiplications when these are carried out in a manner related to the binary representation of the exponent. The procedure is readily adapted to a desk computer and is easily programmed for an electronic computer. When using a desk computer, set up a table with three columns labeled A, B, and N. Given then x and n, to find x^n, enter the numbers 1.0, x, and n in the first row of the table, and then complete the table by following the steps listed below.

Step 1   If the last number entered in column N is an odd integer, multiply the last numbers entered in columns A and B and enter the product in column A. If the number in column N is even, omit step 1.

Step 2   Square the number in column B and enter the result in column B.

Step 3   Divide the integer in column N by 2 and enter the integral part of the quotient in column N.

Step 4   If the integer just placed in column N is 1, the final result is now obtained by multiplying the last entries in columns A and B. Otherwise repeat steps 1 through 4.

Example 1   Compute the value of $(1.031)^{50}$.
Solution   A table is started as described, and successive lines are then formed in accordance with steps 1 through 4.

Since 50 is an even integer, step 1 is omitted and steps 2 and 3 give the second line. Since 25 is an odd integer, step 1 is performed during the second iteration. After five iterations, a 1 appears in column N of row 6. The final step is to multiply the last entries in columns A and B.

A	B	N
1.0	1.031	50
	1.0629 61	25
1.0629 61	1.1298 8608 7521	12
	1.2766 4257 0773	6
	1.6298 1625 3509	3
1.7324 3111 4646	2.6563 0102 0202	1

$(1.031)^{50}$ = (1.7324 3111 4646) $\times$ (2.6563 0102 0202) = 4.6018 5854 which has been rounded to eight decimal places.

In the example just solved the computations were made on a thirteen-digit desk computer in approximately three minutes. Since some of the latest desk computers have means of storing several factors until needed, it is not necessary to record the intermediate results as was done in the example just worked, and the final result can be obtained in less than one minute.

The theory behind the method used in the example is based on binary arithmetic. When expressed in powers of 2, $50 = 32 + 16 + 2$, and its binary representation is 110010. The 1s, reading from right to left, tell which powers of 2 to use. To get $(1.031)^{50}$ we need $(1.031)^2$, $(1.031)^{16}$, and $(1.031)^{32}$. The last entry in column B is $(1.031)^{32}$ and the last entry in column A is the product of $(1.031)^2$ and $(1.031)^{16}$.

When the accumulation factor is evaluated in the manner just described some round-off error may enter into the computations. Usually about half of the roundings will be up and the other half down, and the accumulated error will be negligible. Occasionally, nearly all roundings will be in the same direction and the resulting error may be noticeable. However, the number of significant digits lost due to round-off error will rarely exceed half the number of multiplications made.

Another method that can be used to evaluate expressions of the type under discussion is the binomial expansion. It may be written

$$(a + b)^n = a^n + na^{n-1}b + \frac{n(n-1)a^{n-2}b^2}{1 \times 2}$$
$$+ \frac{n(n-1)(n-2)a^{n-3}b^3}{1 \times 2 \times 3} + \cdots \quad (1)$$

To evaluate x^n, choose a and b so that $a + b = x$, then compute as many terms as necessary to obtain the desired accuracy. By choosing b relatively small, the number of terms required may be quite moderate.

Example 2 Compute the value of $(1.031)^{50}$ accurate to seven decimal places.
Solution We could take $a = 1$ and $b = 0.031$ and use Eq. (1). However, since n is fairly large the terms would diminish slowly and quite a few terms would be necessary to give the desired accuracy. A much quicker method is possible if tables are available for the powers of 1.03. In this case, we take $a = 1.03$ and $b = 0.001$ and get the expansion

$$(1.031)^{50} = (1.03)^{50} + 50(1.03)^{49}(0.001) + \frac{50 \times 49(1.03)^{48}(0.001)^2}{1 \times 2}$$
$$+ \frac{50 \times 49 \times 48(1.03)^{47}(0.001)^3}{1 \times 2 \times 3} + \frac{50 \times 49 \times 48 \times 47(1.03)^{46}(0.001)^4}{1 \times 2 \times 3 \times 4}$$
$$+ \cdots$$

Using tables for the powers of 1.03, we obtain the successive terms as 4.38390602, 0.21281097, 0.00506201, 0.00007863, and 0.00000090. Although these five terms appear to be sufficient for seven-decimal-place accuracy, for safety we compute the next term and get 0.00000001. Adding these values, we get $(1.031)^{50} = 4.60185854$ or 4.6018585. Actually, the answer is accurate to eight decimal places, but we should allow for some round-off error.

The binomial expansion is quite useful because it is valid for all values of n, positive or negative, integral or fractional, provided the numerical value of a exceeds that of b. It also can be used to evaluate the annuity symbols $a_{\overline{n}|i}$ and $s_{\overline{n}|i}$. It is left as an exercise for the student to verify the following formulas.

$$s_{\overline{n}|i} = n + \frac{n(n-1)i}{1 \times 2} + \frac{n(n-1)(n-2)i^2}{1 \times 2 \times 3} + \cdots \tag{2}$$

$$a_{\overline{n}|i} = n - \frac{n(n+1)i}{1 \times 2} + \frac{n(n+1)(n+2)i^2}{1 \times 2 \times 3} - \cdots \tag{3}$$

(signs alternating)

It can be shown that once the terms of the expansion start decreasing in numerical value, they continue to decrease so that it is not difficult to determine how many terms are necessary for accuracy to the desired number of decimal places.

75 FRACTIONAL POWERS OF NUMBERS

Solving for a compound-interest rate usually involves finding some fractional power of a number. Solutions by logarithms or interpolation are commonly used and have been discussed earlier in this text. Several other methods will now be discussed.

Quite often the binomial expansion can be used to obtain a solution as accurate as desired with relatively little computation.

Example 1 Find the nominal rate, compounded monthly, equivalent to an effective rate of 7.2%.

Solution Let i be the monthly rate. Then

$$(1 + i)^{12} = 1.072 \quad \text{and} \quad 1 + i = (1.072)^{1/12}$$

Using the binomial expansion, we get

$$(1 + 0.072)^{1/12} = 1 + \frac{1}{12} \times 0.072 + \frac{\frac{1}{12}(-\frac{11}{12})(0.072)^2}{1 \times 2}$$
$$+ \frac{\frac{1}{12}(-\frac{11}{12})(-\frac{23}{12})(0.072)^3}{1 \times 2 \times 3} + \cdots$$

Computing the terms by the method described in Sec. 11 gives

$$(1.072)^{1/12} = 1 + 0.006 - 0.000198 + 0.000009108$$
$$- 0.00000047817 + 0.000000026968788 - \cdots.$$

$1 + i = 1.00581066$ to eight-decimal-place accuracy. Consequently $i = 0.00581066$ and $j_{12} = 0.06972792$, accurate to seven decimal places.

When the binomial expansion is used with a fractional exponent, after at most a few terms, the signs will start alternating and the terms will diminish numerically so that the error due to stopping with a given term is less than the last term used. An even closer estimate of the error is possible after a moderate number of terms are used.

In Sec. 11 we wrote

$$(1 + i)^n = T_0 + T_1 + T_2 + \cdots$$

where

$$T_0 = 1 \quad \text{and} \quad T_{k+1} = \frac{(n-k)i}{k+1} T_k, \; k = 0, 1, 2, \ldots$$

As k increases, the value of T_{k+1} will approach $-iT_k$, and we write $T_{k+1} \to -iT_k$. In a similar way $T_{k+2} \to -iT_{k+1} \to i^2 T_k$, $T_{k+3} \to -i^3 T_k$, etc., so that

$$T_{k+1} + T_{k+2} + T_{k+3} + \cdots$$

$$\to (-i + i^2 - i^3 + \cdots)T_k = \frac{-i}{1+i} T_k$$

Thus the expression $E_k = \dfrac{-i}{1+i} T_k$ may be used to estimate the error due to stopping with the term T_k.

Consider again Example 1. Since the terms are decreasing numerically and the signs alternate, we can use the results just developed to discuss the error. The table below shows, for different values of k, the value of T_k, the sum of the series ending with T_k, the actual error and the approximate error E_k, all results to eight-decimal-place accuracy.

k	T_k	Sum of terms through T_k	Actual error	E_k
1	0.006	1.006	−0.00018934	−0.00040299
2	−0.000198	1.005802	0.00000866	0.00001329
3	0.00000911	1.00581111	−0.00000045	−0.00000061
4	−0.00000048	1.00581063	0.00000003	0.00000003
5	0.00000003	1.00581066		

While the binomial expansion works nicely in many cases, there are times when terms diminish slowly and a considerable number of terms are needed for the degree of accuracy desired. For example,

$$(1.6)^{1/18} = 1 + \frac{1}{18} \times 0.6 + \frac{\frac{1}{18}(-\frac{17}{18})(0.6)^2}{1 \times 2} + \cdots$$

$$= 1 + 0.03333333 - 0.00944444 + 0.00367284 - \cdots$$

It would require nearly twenty terms to obtain eight-decimal-place accuracy. This, of course, is no objection to the method if we have programmed a computer to do the work. When, however, some or all of the computations are to be done manually, other methods may be quicker. We will describe two other methods of finding fractional powers of numbers; the choice of these will usually depend upon the computing equipment available.

There are electronic desk computers that have a built-in square root routine. These computers are also capable of storing several factors until needed. With a computer of this type, fractional powers of numbers can be approximated to a high degree of accuracy quickly and easily by the **repeated-square-root method.** An example will illustrate the method.

Example 2 Find the value of i if $(1 + i)^{51} = 13.50$.

Solution We will approximate the value of $(13.50)^{1/51}$ by the repeated-square-root method. We first convert the exponent into a binary decimal. This can be done by long division. Since in binary $51 = 110011$ and 1 may be written either as 1.0 or 0.1111111111111 . . . , we have

$$
\begin{array}{r}
0.0000010100000101 \text{ etc.} = \frac{1}{51} \text{ as a binary decimal} \\
110011 \overline{)0.1111111111111111 \text{ etc.}} \\
\underline{110011} \\
110011 \\
\underline{110011} \\
111111 \\
\underline{110011} \\
110011 \\
110011 \text{ etc.}
\end{array}
$$

Another way to get the binary decimal is to start with its base 10 decimal representation, which is 0.01960784313 . . . . This decimal is doubled repeatedly. At each step, a 1 or a 0 is added to the binary decimal representation according to whether there is a carry over the decimal point or not.

We next take the square root of 13.50, then the square root of this result, and continue repeating the procedure. Each result is associated with the corresponding integer in the binary decimal representation of the exponent as shown in the table below.

Binary integer	Results of repeated square roots
0	3.6742 3461 4175
0	1.9108 2931 2738
0	1.3844 9605 0098
0	1.1766 4610 2317
0	1.0847 3319 4609
1	1.0415 0525 3980
0	1.0205 4164 7352
1	1.0102 1861 3643

The first approximation is the result associated with the first binary integer 1, namely 1.0415 0525 3980.   The second approximation is obtained by multiplying the preceding result with the factor associated with the second binary integer 1.   Thus,

$$1.041505253980 \times 1.010218613643 = 1.0521\ 4799\ 3777$$

is the second approximation.   To obtain further approximations, we continue the above table, getting

Binary integer	Results of repeated square roots
0	1.0050 9632 0579
0	1.0025 4492 1975
0	1.0012 7165 2437
0	1.0006 3562 4209
0	1.0003 1776 1618
1	1.0001 5886 8189
0	1.0000 7943 0939
1	1.0000 3971 4680

The third approximation is now obtained by multiplying the second approximation by the factor associated with the next binary integer 1. Thus

$$1.052147993777 \times 1.000158868189 = 1.0523\ 1514\ 6623$$

is the third approximation and the fourth approximation is

$$1.052315146623 \times 1.000039714680 = 1.0523\ 5693\ 8982$$

If we continue through one more cycle, the next factors associated with binary integer 1s are

1.0000 0062 0529   and   1.0000 0015 5131

These give closer approximations of

1.0523 5759 1999   and   1.0523 5775 5252

The procedure may be repeated as many times as desired, with the knowledge that each approximation is closer than the preceding ones. Moreover each approximation is too small, so they approach the true value *from below*.

There is a simple accuracy check associated with this method.   If any approximation is multiplied by a factor associated with a binary zero which precedes the next binary 1, the product is too large and therefore gives an upper limit to the answer.   To illustrate, if we take the square root of the last factor used, we get 1.0000 0007 7565, and multiplying the last approximation by this result gives

$$(1.0000\ 0007\ 7565) \times (1.0523\ 5775\ 5252) = 1.0523\ 5783\ 6878$$

This result is too large and consequently we know that

$$1.0523\ 5775\ 5252 < 1 + i < 1.0523\ 5783\ 6878$$

and $i = 0.0523578$ is accurate to seven decimal places.

The example just solved contains much detail that can be omitted in practice. With a desk computer of the type mentioned earlier it is only necessary to enter the original number and then punch the keys marked SQRT, MULT, REPEAT, STORE, and RECALL repeatedly in a sequence determined by the binary decimal representation of the exponent.

The method can be shortened even more. At the end of the first cycle when we get the product of the factors associated with the binary 1s in the first cycle (in the example 1.0521 4799 3777), repeated square roots of this number will give the product of the factors associated with the binary 1s in the second cycle (in the example, the product of 1.0001 5886 8189 and 1.0000 3971 4680). Only one multiplication is then needed after each cycle.

Since the method just described requires rather special computing equipment that is not available to everyone, we will describe one more way of finding roots and powers of numbers.

76   A RECURSION FORMULA FOR POWERS AND ROOTS

Frequently it is necessary to evaluate the accumulation (or discount) factor for an interest rate not tabulated. Or the value of the factor is known and the interest rate is to be found.   In this section, we shall give recursion formulas that are simple to use and usually give excellent results.   Formulas for determining the accuracy are included.

For simplicity of expression, throughout the section the following notation will be used; i represents a rate not tabulated, i_0 is the nearest tabulated rate to i, x stands for $1 + i$, a represents $1 + i_0$, and n can be positive or negative, integral or fractional.

Suppose that n, x, a, and a^n are given and we wish to determine the approximate value of x^n.   In the next section, we shall prove that

$$x^n = \frac{2a + (n+1)(x-a)}{2x - (n+1)(x-a)}a^n - E \tag{4}$$

where

$$E = \frac{n(n^2 - 1)(x - a)^3 t^{n-2}}{6[2x - (n + 1)(x - a)]} \tag{5}$$

and t lies between a and x. By ignoring E in Eq. (4), we obtain an approximate value for x^n. Equation (5) may be used to determine the accuracy of this approximation. An example will illustrate the use of these formulas.

Example 1 Compute the approximate value of $(1.031)^{50}$ by Eq. (4), and determine the accuracy.
Solution Here we have $x = 1.031$, $n = 50$, and we take $a = 1.03$, since this is the nearest tabulated value. Equation (4) then gives

$$(1.031)^{50} = \frac{2 \times 1.03 + 51(0.001)}{2 \times 1.031 - 51(0.001)} \times (1.03)^{50} - E$$

$$= \frac{2.111}{2.011} \times 4.38390602 - E$$

$$= 4.60190234 - E$$

Thus $(1.031)^{50} = 4.60190234$ approximately, with the degree of accuracy unknown. To determine the accuracy, we evaluate the error function, Eq. (5). This gives

$$E = \frac{50 \times 2499(0.001)^3 t^{48}}{6 \times 2.011}$$

where t lies between 1.03 and 1.031. To obtain limits for E, we evaluate the above expression for $t = 1.03$ and also for $t = 1.035$. Making the necessary computations, we find that E lies between 0.00004279 and 0.00005399. Thus our approximate value is too large by about 0.00005; in fact it lies between the values 4.6018483 and 4.6018596. It is possible to get sharper limits by using a better upper limit for t than 1.035. If we evaluate $(1.031)^{48}$ by interpolation, the value obtained will be too large (Sec. 11) and may be used as an upper limit for t^{48} in the error function. If this is done, we find that $t^{48} < 4.35$, and the corresponding improved limits for $(1.031)^{50}$ are 4.6018573 and 4.6018596. Actually, the correct value lies about halfway between these last two values as may be seen by referring to Example 1, Sec. 74. When $(1.031)^{50}$ is evaluated by interpolation, the error exceeds 0.02225.

When the accumulation (or discount) factor is given and we wish to find the interest rate, Eq. (4) can be put into a somewhat more convenient form. Using the same notation, suppose n, a, a^n, and x^n are known and we wish to find i (or x). In the next section, we shall prove that

$$i = i_0 + \frac{2a(x^n - a^n)}{(n + 1)(x^n + a^n) - 2x^n} + E \tag{6}$$

where

$$E = \frac{n(n^2 - 1)(x - a)^3 t^{n-2}}{6[(n + 1)(x^n + a^n) - 2x^n]} \tag{7}$$

and t lies between a and x.

These formulas are used in a manner similar to Eqs. (4) and (5). Equation (6), by ignoring E, gives an approximate value of i, and Eq. (7) furnishes a check on the accuracy.

Example 2 Find the approximate value of i if $(1 + i)^{51} = 13.50$, and discuss the accuracy.

Solution From Table 8 we find that $(1.05)^{51} = 12.04076978$ is the nearest tabulated value and is taken as a^n. Thus we take $a = 1.05$, $i_0 = 0.05$, $x^n = 13.50$, and $n = 51$ and substitute these in Eq. (6). This gives

$$i = 0.05 + \frac{2 \times 1.05(13.50 - 12.04076978)}{52(13.50 + 12.04076978) - 2 \times 13.50} + E$$

$$= 0.05 + \frac{3.06438346}{1301.12002856} + E$$

$$= 0.05235519 + E$$

Thus, 0.05235519 is an approximate value of i, the degree of accuracy being unknown. To determine how accurate this result is, we evaluate Eq. (7). This gives

$$E = \frac{51 \times 2600(x - a)^3 t^{49}}{6 \times 1301.12002856} \qquad \text{where } t \text{ lies between } a \text{ and } x$$

We next compute limits for E by taking $t = 1.05$ and 1.055. Making the necessary computations, we get

$$185.50(x - a)^3 < E < 234.13(x - a)^3$$

Rough limits are now obtained for E by taking $x = 1.05$ in the left-hand member of the above inequality and $x = 1.055$ in the right-hand member. This gives

$$0 < E < 0.00003$$

Using these limits for E, we now know that the true value of i lies between 0.05235519 and 0.05238519. Much closer limits can now be obtained by using these improved values in the error function. Since x lies between 1.0523 and 1.0524, $x - a$ lies between 0.0023 and 0.0024. When these improved values are used in the error function, we get

$$0.00000225 < E < 0.00000324$$

and consequently i lies between 0.05235744 and 0.0523843. By referring to Example 2, Sec. 75, we find that the error is 0.0000026 to seven decimal places. It is interesting to note that when this problem is solved by interpolation, the error is more than fifty times as large.

Practical experience indicates that the results obtained by the use of Eqs. (4) and (6) are usually accurate to one or two more places than given by interpolation. Consequently for solving problems that are usually done by interpolation, these formulas may be used with confidence that the accuracy will be better than the interpolation method and the evaluation of the error function, Eq. (5) or (7), may be omitted.

It will be shown in the next section that Eqs. (4) and (6) are both derived from the same relationship and are valid for all values of a, x, and n except a combination that would give a zero denominator. This condition, however, is almost impossible if the data are from a standard mathematics of finance problem.

EXERCISE 43

1. Evaluate $s_{\overline{20}|3\%}$ by using the first 6 terms of the binomial expansion and check the accuracy by the tables.

2. Compute the value of $a_{\overline{25}|4\%}$ by using the first 6 terms of the binomial expansion and check the accuracy by the tables.

3. Evaluate $(1.042)^{30}$ by the binomial expansion, using enough terms to ensure five-decimal-place accuracy.

4. Compute the value of $(1.053)^{-20}$ by the binomial expansion, using enough terms to give five-decimal-place accuracy.

5. Find the value of $(1.003)^{99}$ by Eq. (4).

6. Using Eq. (6) find the nominal rate, converted semiannually, at which \$1500 will amount to \$2400 in 9 years. Compare your result with the example in Sec. 15.

7. Determine the accuracy of the answer to Prob. 5 by the use of Eq. (5).

8. Determine the accuracy of the answer in Prob. 6 by the use of Eq. (7).

77 PROOF OF THE RECURSION FORMULAS

An algebraic proof† of the formulas in the preceding section when n is a positive integer will be briefly outlined. We start with the expression

$$(n + 1)(x - a)(x^n + a^n) - 2(x^{n+1} - a^{n+1}) \tag{8}$$

By algebraic manipulation this expression can be factored and written as follows:

$$(x - a)^3 \sum_{k=1}^{n-1} \sum_{p=1}^{n-k} \sum_{q=1}^{k} x^{n-p-q} a^{p+q-2}$$

† A general proof using the calculus is as follows: Let $f(x)$ be given and define $F(x) = \int_a^x f'''(u)(u - a)(x - u)du$. Repeated integration by parts gives

$$F(x) = (x - a)[f'(x) + f'(a)] - 2[f(x) - f(a)]$$

However, since the expression $(u - a)(x - u)$ is nonnegative throughout the interval of integration, the integral mean value theorem (see Ivan S. Sokolnikoff, "Advanced Calculus," McGraw-Hill Book Company, Inc., New York, 1939, p. 113) applies and we can write

$$F(x) = f'''(t) \int_a^x (u - a)(x - u)du = \frac{1}{6}(x - a)^3 f'''(t)$$

where t lies between a and x. Equating these two expressions for $F(x)$ and taking $f(x) = x^{n+1}$ readily gives Eq. (9).

The number of terms in the triple summation can be shown to be

$$N = \frac{1}{6} n(n^2 - 1)$$

and each term is of the form $x^{n-m}a^{m-2}$. If we set $t_m^{n-2} = x^{n-m}a^{m-2}$, it follows that t_m will lie between a and x. There will also be a number t between t_1 and t_N, and therefore between a and x, such that

$$\sum_{m=1}^{N} t_m^{n-2} = \frac{1}{6} n(n^2 - 1)t^{n-2}$$

Consequently expression (8) can be put into the form of an equation as follows:

$$(n+1)(x-a)(x^n + a^n) - 2(x^{n+1} - a^{n+1})$$
$$= \frac{1}{6} n(n^2 - 1)(x - a)^3 t^{n-2} \quad (9)$$

where t lies between a and x. Equation (9) may be rewritten in the following manner

$$x^n[2x - (n+1)(x-a)] = a^n[2a + (n+1)(x-a)]$$
$$- \frac{1}{6} n(n^2 - 1)(x - a)^3 t^{n-2}$$

If both members of this last equation are divided by $2x - (n+1)(x-a)$, the result is Eq. (4) of the preceding section.

If 1 is added to both members of Eq. (6), $1 + i$ replaced by x, $1 + i_0$ replaced by a, E replaced by the right-hand member of Eq. (7), then both members of this equation multiplied by

$$(n+1)(x^n + a^n) - 2x^n$$

the result is Eq. (9), thereby establishing Eq. (6).

78 OTHER METHODS OF DETERMINING BOND YIELD

In Sec. 58, two methods of determining the yield rate of a bond were given. There are numerous other methods of approximating bond yield, several of which we shall now discuss. It will be recalled that "the method of averages" was introduced in Sec. 58. This method is one of several that make use of the relationship

$$i = \frac{I}{B} \tag{10}$$

where I is the average income and B is the average book value of the bond. It will be proved in the next section that the average income is given by

$$I = R - \frac{P - C}{n} \tag{11}$$

whereas the average book value B cannot be exactly determined unless the investment rate is known. Consequently, the various methods of approximating the yield rate based on Eq. (10) are, in reality, methods of approximating B. The simplest of these approximates the average book value by

$$B_1 = \frac{1}{2}(P + C) \tag{12}$$

When B_1 is substituted in Eq. (10) for B, the value obtained for i is fairly accurate unless the excess (or deficiency) is moderately large. Also, as n increases, the accuracy gets worse. It is easily verified that the approximate yield rate given by I/B_1 is exactly the same as that obtained by the method of averages discussed in Sec. 58.

A more accurate value of B than that given by Eq. (12) can be obtained by averaging the value of the bond during the first interest period (that is, the purchase price) with the value of the bond during the last interest period before redemption. Now the value of a bond decreases each period approximately $(P - C)/n$ if it is purchased at an excess and increases each period approximately $(C - P)/n$ if it is purchased at a deficiency. In either case, the value of the bond at the beginning of the final interest period before redemption is approximately $C + (P - C)/n$. Thus a more accurate value for B is given by

$$B_2 = \frac{1}{2}\left(P + C + \frac{P - C}{n}\right) \tag{13}$$

When B_2 is substituted in Eq. (10) for B, the value of i obtained is almost always correct to the nearest tenth percent and is usually better than this.

Still more accurate results may be had as follows: Let i_0 be an approximation to the yield rate; i_0 can be found by Eq. (10) with either B_1 or B_2 used for the average book value. Now compute

$$B_3 = B_2 + (P - C)\frac{n^2 - 1}{12n}i_0 \tag{14}$$

If B_3 is used in Eq. (10), the value obtained for i is nearly always accurate to the nearest hundredth percent and is usually better than this.

Example 1 A \$1000 bond, redeemable at \$1100 on Jan. 15, 1980, pays bond interest semiannually at 6%, $m = 2$. The market quotation is 120 on Jan. 15, 1970. Find the approximate yield rate by Eq. (10), using B_1, B_2, and B_3 as the average book value.

Solution Here we have $P = 1200$, $C = 1100$, $R = 30$, and $n = 20$. The average income from the bond as given by Eq. (11) is

$$I = R - \frac{P - C}{n} = 30 - \frac{100}{20} = 25$$

The approximate book value as given by Eq. (12) is

$$B_1 = \frac{1}{2}(P + C) = 1150$$

These values are now substituted in Eq. (10) to obtain an approximate value for i. Thus

$$i = \frac{I}{B_1} = \frac{25}{1150} = 0.02174$$

is a rough approximation of the yield rate. The accuracy is probably to the nearest tenth percent, so that the true value of i is probably between 0.021 and 0.022. To get a more accurate result, we compute B_2. Using Eq. (13), we get

$$B_2 = \frac{1}{2}\left(P + C + \frac{P - C}{n}\right) = 1152.50$$

Equation (10) now gives

$$i = \frac{I}{B_2} = \frac{25}{1152.50} = 0.02169$$

as a better approximation than the preceding one. This value indicates that the true value of i is probably between 0.0216 and 0.0217. To get still a better value, we take $i_0 = 0.0217$ and compute B_3. Equation (14) gives

$$B_3 = B_2 + (P - C)\frac{n^2 - 1}{12n} i_0 = 1152.50 + 3.61 = 1156.11$$

Substituting B_3 in Eq. (10), we get

$$i = \frac{I}{B_3} = \frac{25}{1156.11} = 0.021624$$

as an approximate value for i. By more advanced methods, it is found that the true value of i, correct to six decimal places, is 0.021625. Thus our third approximation is in error only 1 in the sixth decimal place and is therefore more accurate than the result obtained when this example was solved by interpolation in Sec. 58 (Example 2).

The main objection to the formulas just discussed is that an adequate check for accuracy is difficult. However, since they are easy to use, require no tables, and prove reasonably accurate in practice, the objection just mentioned is relatively unimportant.

Another excellent method of approximating bond yield consists of repeated use of the recursion formula

$$i = \frac{R - (P - C)/s_{\overline{n}|i}}{P} \tag{15}$$

This formula is used by estimating the bond yield, then using the estimated value to evaluate the right-hand member of Eq. (15). The result is an approximation of i. In fact, it can be shown that Eq. (15) has the following properties: (*a*) For a bond purchased at an excess, the value of i obtained from Eq. (15) always lies between the true value of i and the estimated value used to evaluate the right member. (*b*) For a bond purchased at a deficiency, the value of i obtained from Eq. (15) and the estimated value lie on opposite sides of the true i. (*c*) In either case, unless the deficiency exceeds $\frac{1}{2}C$, the value obtained by Eq. (15) is closer to the true i than the estimated value. If the deficiency exceeds $\frac{1}{2}C$, the value given by Eq. (15) may be further from the true value than the estimated value. However, a bond purchased at so great a deficiency is purely a speculative bond, and the yield rate is not nearly so important as whether or not it will pay off at all. We shall illustrate the use of the formula.

Example 2   Solve Example 1 by the use of Eq. (15).
Solution   We have $P = 1200$, $C = 1100$, $R = 30$, $n = 20$, and the bond rate is 3%. Since the bond is purchased at an excess, we shall take $2\frac{1}{2}\%$ as our first estimate. Evaluating Eq. (15) gives

$$i = \frac{30 - 100/s_{\overline{20}|2\frac{1}{2}\%}}{1200} = \frac{26.085287}{1200} = 0.02174$$

Since the use of Eq. (15) gives, for a bond purchased at an excess, a value that lies between the true value and the estimated value, it follows that 0.02174 is too large. We therefore repeat the procedure using 2% as our estimated value. This gives

$$i = \frac{30 - 100/s_{\overline{20}|2\%}}{1200} = \frac{25.884328}{1200} = 0.02157$$

We are now certain that the true rate lies between 0.02157 and 0.02174. In order to narrow this interval, we compute the value of $1/s_{\overline{20}|i}$ for $i = 0.0216$ and for $i = 0.0217$. These symbols are found to have the values $1/s_{\overline{20}|0.0216} = 0.04050507$ and $1/s_{\overline{20}|0.0217} = 0.04046451$. When these values are substituted for $1/s_{\overline{n}|i}$ in Eq. (15), we find that the true value of i must lie between 0.02162^+ and 0.02163^-. Actually the true value is about halfway between these limits.

The main objection to the use of Eq. (15) is the fact that in order to attain a high degree of accuracy, estimated rates must be used for which $1/s_{\overline{n}|i}$ is not tabulated and must be computed. The main advantage of using Eq. (15) is that results can be made as accurate as the computer pleases by repeated application of the formula, using a better estimate each time.

79 PROOF OF THE BOND YIELD FORMULAS

Equation (11), for the average income from a bond, can be proved intuitively as follows: The bond costs P, will make n bond interest payments of R, and then will be redeemed for C. Thus the total profit is $nR + C - P$. Dividing the total profit by n to get the average per period gives Eq. (11).

In order to determine the average book value of a bond, we start with the fact that the book value k periods before redemption can be written [see Eq. (2), Sec. 53]

$$B_k = C + (R - Ci)a_{\overline{k}|i}$$

If k is given the values $1, 2, 3, \ldots, n$ and the resulting equations added, we get

$$B_1 + B_2 + \cdots + B_n$$
$$= nC + (R - Ci)(a_{\overline{1}|i} + a_{\overline{2}|i} + \cdots + a_{\overline{n}|i})$$

It is not difficult to verify that

$$a_{\overline{1}|i} + a_{\overline{2}|i} + \cdots + a_{\overline{n}|i} = \frac{1}{i}(n - a_{\overline{n}|i})$$

Moreover, from Eq. (2), Sec. 53, we readily see that

$$R - Ci = \frac{P - C}{a_{\overline{n}|i}}$$

Therefore the sum of the book values may be written

$$B_1 + B_2 + \cdots + B_n = nC + \left(\frac{P - C}{a_{\overline{n}|i}}\right)\left(\frac{n - a_{\overline{n}|i}}{i}\right)$$

Dividing both sides by n to get the average book value gives

$$B = C + (P - C)\frac{n - a_{\overline{n}|i}}{nia_{\overline{n}|i}} \tag{16}$$

It can be shown that the fraction

$$\frac{n - a_{\overline{n}|i}}{nia_{\overline{n}|i}}$$

is greater than $(n + 1)/2n$ but is less than $(n + 1)/2n + (n^2 - 1)i/12n$. Using these limits in Eq. (16) gives

$$\frac{1}{2}\left(P + C + \frac{P - C}{n}\right) < B < \frac{1}{2}\left(P + C + \frac{P - C}{n}\right)$$
$$+ (P - C)\frac{(n^2 - 1)i}{12n}$$

The left member of the above inequality is B_2 as given by Eq. (13) and the right member differs from B_3 as given by Eq. (14) in that it contains i rather than i_0.

In order to establish Eq. (15), we start with the bond formula

$$P = C + (R - Ci)a_{\overline{n}|i}$$

By division, it readily follows that

$$\frac{P - C}{a_{\overline{n}|i}} = R - Ci$$

By making use of the relation $1/a_{\overline{n}|i} = i + 1/s_{\overline{n}|i}$, we can change the preceding equation into

$$Pi + \frac{P - C}{s_{\overline{n}|i}} = R$$

whence

$$i = \frac{R - (P - C)/s_{\overline{n}|i}}{P} \tag{15}$$

Let r be an approximation to i, and let us call i_1 the value obtained when r is used to evaluate the right-hand member of Eq. (15). Thus

$$i_1 = \frac{R - (P - C)/s_{\overline{n}|r}}{P} \tag{17}$$

By subtracting Eq. (17) from Eq. (15), we get

$$i - i_1 = \frac{(P - C)\left(\dfrac{1}{s_{\overline{n}|r}} - \dfrac{1}{s_{\overline{n}|i}}\right)}{P}$$

Now suppose $r < i$. Then $1/s_{\overline{n}|r} > 1/s_{\overline{n}|i}$ and i is greater than i_1 if $P > C$, whereas i is less than i_1 if $P < C$. If $r > i$, all inequality signs are reversed. This proves statements (a) and (b) made in the preceding section concerning Eq. (15). To prove statement (c), we rewrite the preceding equation in the form

$$|i - i_1| = \frac{|P - C|}{P}\left|\frac{1}{s_{\overline{n}|r}} - \frac{1}{s_{\overline{n}|i}}\right|$$

where the notation $|x|$ means the numerical value of x, disregarding sign. Now it is easily shown that $|P - C|/P$ is less than 1 unless $P \leq \frac{1}{2}C$. Thus unless $P \leq \frac{1}{2}C$,

$$|i - i_1| \leq \left|\frac{1}{s_{\overline{n}|r}} - \frac{1}{s_{\overline{n}|i}}\right|$$

It is easily shown that

$$\left|\frac{1}{s_{\overline{n}|r}} - \frac{1}{s_{\overline{n}|i}}\right| = |r - i| - \left|\frac{1}{a_{\overline{n}|r}} - \frac{1}{a_{\overline{n}|i}}\right|$$

and therefore

$$|i - i_1| < |r - i|$$

Thus i_1 as given by Eq. (17) is closer to i than r is unless the bond is purchased at a price $\leq \frac{1}{2}C$. In fact the preceding statement is true unless P is well below $\frac{1}{2}C$.

EXERCISE 44

In Probs. 1 to 4, find the yield rate by using Eq. (10) with B replaced by B_2 as given by Eq. (13) (the face of each bond is $1000):

Problem	Redemption price	Bond interest	Time until redemption, years	Purchase price
1	Par	6%, $m = 2$	10	$1100
2	Par	5%, $m = 1$	20	$ 900
3	$1100	4%, $m = 1$	25	$ 950
4	$1100	5%, $m = 2$	15	$1300

5. Find the yield rate for Prob. 1 by using Eq. (10) with B replaced by B_3 as given by Eq. (14), using the result of Prob. 1 as i_0.

6. Find the yield rate for Prob. 3 by using Eq. (10) with B replaced by B_3 as given by Eq. (14), using the result of Prob. 3 as i_0.

7. Find the approximate yield rate for Prob. 1 by using Eq. (15) with $2\frac{1}{4}\%$ as the estimated rate.

8. Find the approximate yield rate for Prob. 3 by using Eq. (15) with $4\frac{1}{2}\%$ as the estimated rate.

80 THE ACCURACY OF INTERPOLATION

Whenever interpolation is used, the accuracy of the result is in question. Sometimes a fairly accurate knowledge of the error involved for a given type of problem can be obtained by trial-and-error methods, that is, by solving several similar problems with known answers by the interpolation technique and noting the size of the errors. Furthermore, a high degree of accuracy is seldom a matter of life and death, so that it has become common practice to use interpolation to add an extra digit or two and to leave the question of accuracy unanswered. There are times, however, when it is highly desirable to know how accurate a result is. If the problem has been solved by interpolation, this means that some sort of error function is necessary. In Chap. 2, four such error functions were given. We shall now list several other such functions for types of problems that are normally solved by interpolation.

In all these functions, i_1 represents the smaller of the two rates used.

Let $s_{\overline{n}|i}$ be given, and let i be determined by interpolating between the values of $s_{\overline{n}|i_1}$ and $s_{\overline{n}|i_2}$, which for brevity we shall abbreviate by s_1 and s_2, respectively. The value of i obtained by interpolation is too small, but the error is less than

$$\frac{1}{4}\left[\frac{(s_2 - s_1)i_1}{n(1 + i_1)^{n-1} - s_1} - i_2 + i_1\right]$$

If $a_{\overline{n}|i}$ is given and i is determined by interpolating between $a_{\overline{n}|i_2} = a_2$ and $a_{\overline{n}|i_1} = a_1$, the value of i obtained is too large but the error is less than

$$\frac{1}{4}\left[\frac{(a_1 - a_2)i_2}{a_2 - n(1 + i_2)^{-n-1}} - i_2 + i_1\right]$$

Let $P_1, P,$ and P_2 be the purchase prices of a bond to yield $i_1, i,$ and i_2, respectively. If P lies between P_1 and P_2 and i is determined by interpolation, the value obtained is too large but the error is less than

$$\frac{1}{4}\left[\frac{(P_1 - P_2)i_2}{Ra_2 - n(R - Ci_2)(1 + i_2)^{-n-1}} - i_2 + i_1\right]$$

where a_2 stands for $a_{\overline{n}|i_2}$ and $R, C,$ and n have their usual meaning.

All the error functions listed here and in Chap. 2 are special cases of the following rather general theorem:

Theorem   *Let $f(x)$ be a function that together with its first three derivatives is continuous throughout the interval $a \leqq x \leqq b$. Moreover, let $f''(x)$ and $f'''(x)$ be of constant sign throughout the interval. If $a, b, f(a), f(b),$ and x are given and $f(x)$ is determined by interpolation, the difference between the value obtained by interpolation and the true value*

$$E = interpolated\ value - true\ value$$

satisfies the inequalities

$$\frac{(b - x)(x - a)}{(b - a)^2}[f(b) - f(a) - (b - a)f'(a)] \leqq E$$

$$\leqq \frac{(b - x)(x - a)}{(b - a)^2}[(b - a)f'(b) - f(b) + f(a)]$$

or these inequalities reversed according as $f'''(x)$ is positive or negative.

The proof of this theorem is beyond the scope of this book and will not be given here.† Its use allows the computer to determine both an upper and a lower limit for the error. Here we have given only an upper

---

† The proof will be found in the *American Mathematical Monthly*, vol. 53, no. 7, p. 364, August-September, 1946.

limit for the numerical value of the error and have stated whether the interpolated value is too large or too small. We have also weakened these results slightly by replacing the factor $(b - x)(x - a)/(b - a)^2$ by $\frac{1}{4}$, which is its maximum value.

For the student with a knowledge of the calculus, the following theorem is frequently simpler to use:

Theorem *With the same conditions holding as for the preceding theorem,*

$$E = \frac{1}{2}(b - x)(x - a)f''(t)$$

where t is some value between a and b.†

By giving t values for which $f''(t)$ assumes its maximum and minimum values in the interval (a,b), both an upper and a lower limit are obtained for the error.

EXERCISE 45

1. Find an upper limit for the error for Prob. 1, Exercise 17.

2. Find an upper limit for the error for Prob. 3, Exercise 17.

3. Find an upper limit for the error for Prob. 7, Exercise 34.

† For a proof see the *American Mathematical Monthly,* vol. 54, no. 4, p. 218, April, 1947.

*12

Life Annuities and Life Insurance

81 MORTALITY TABLES

A mortality table is essentially a record, based on past experience, that shows the number of persons living at successive ages out of an original group of a given size. For convenience, the original group is usually taken as 100,000 or 1,000,000 at age one. The table also includes information other than the number of persons living at successive ages. The value of this additional information we shall see as we progress.

One of the widely used mortality tables at the present time is the Commissioners 1941 Standard Ordinary Mortality Table (usually referred to as the CSO table). This table is based on the experience of a group of insurance companies during the decade 1930 to 1940. A brief excerpt of this table is given on page 191, the complete table being given as Table 13 in the tables.

If we denote by l_x the number of persons from the original group who live to attain the age x, then the table shows that $l_5 = 983,817$, $l_{50} = 810,900$, etc. Clearly the number that die in any year can be

Age	Number living	Number of deaths	Yearly death rate	Yearly rate of survival
x	l_x	d_x	q_x	p_x
1	1,000,000	5,770	0.00577	0.99423
2	994,230	4,116	0.00414	0.99586
3	990,114	3,347	0.00338	0.99662
4	986,767	2,950	0.00299	0.99701
5	983,817	2,715	0.00276	0.99724
10	971,804	1,914	0.00197	0.99803
11	969,890	1,852	0.00191	0.99809
20	951,483	2,312	0.00243	0.99757
21	949,171	2,382	0.00251	0.99749
50	810,900	9,990	0.01232	0.98768
71	427,593	27,481	0.06427	0.93573
98	454	329	0.72467	0.27533
99	125	125	1.00000	0.00000

obtained as the difference in the numbers living at consecutive ages. Thus

$$l_{10} - l_{11} = 971,804 - 969,890 = 1914$$

persons died between the ages of ten and eleven.

If we denote by d_x the number of persons in the original group that attain age x but die before reaching age $x + 1$, then clearly

$$d_x = l_x - l_{x+1} \tag{1}$$

Thus, $d_{50} = 9990$ means that 9990 persons out of the original 1,000,000 died during their fiftieth year of life.

Since l_x persons attain age x and l_{x+1} of these also reach age $x + 1$, the ratio

$$p_x = \frac{l_{x+1}}{l_x} \tag{2}$$

is called the rate of survival for persons of age x.   Likewise, since d_x persons die between the ages x and $x + 1$, the ratio

$$q_x = \frac{d_x}{l_x} \tag{3}$$

is called the rate of mortality, or death rate, for persons of age x.

The mortality table is the foundation of life insurance and life annuities and is therefore of fundamental importance. It should be clear that a mortality table based on a given group will not agree exactly with another table based on a different group. For example, wide differences are found in the rate of mortality according to race, sex, occupation, standard of living, and various other factors. Consequently, there are numerous mortality tables in actual use, and many of these are revised from time to time as medical science progresses and general health conditions improve, thus increasing the span of life. Most life insurance companies use at least two mortality tables: one for life insurance and a different one for life annuities. For if people die more rapidly than predicted by the mortality table, the company pays out faster on insurance policies than it has provided for but pays out less on life annuities than it has provided for. If people die less rapidly than predicted by the mortality table, the situation is reversed. Thus to be safe, a company should use different mortality tables for life-insurance policies and life annuities. Since the choice of mortality table does not affect the theory, in this text all computations will be based on the CSO mortality table.

The fundamental principle that makes life insurance and life annuities sound is that persons of a given class do tend to die with approximately the same regularity as indicated by a mortality table made up of such a group.

Example   The graduating class of a university contained 500 students aged twenty-one. According to the CSO table, how many of these will be alive to celebrate the fiftieth reunion of their class?

Solution   The question is, essentially, how many of these 500 students will live to attain the age of seventy-one. The CSO table gives $l_{21} = 949{,}171$ and $l_{71} = 427{,}593$. Consequently the expected number is

$$500 \frac{l_{71}}{l_{21}} = 500 \frac{427{,}593}{949{,}171} = 225 \text{ approx.}$$

EXERCISE 46

1. A certain county has 10,000 fifth-grade pupils all aged ten. How many of these will live to enroll in high school (ninth grade), assuming that all pass each year?

2. How many of the students in Prob. 1 will die during their twentieth year of life?

3. Out of 1000 persons aged twenty-one, how many are expected to reach age fifty?

4. Show that $l_x - l_{x+n} = d_x + d_{x+1} + d_{x+2} + \cdots + d_{x+n-1}$.

82   PURE ENDOWMENTS

A contract that promises a person at age x to pay S dollars if and when he reaches age $x + n$ is called a pure endowment. We shall denote by $_nE_x$ the net charge, to be made at age x, for a pure endowment of \$1 to be

paid at age $x + n$. The value of this symbol is easily found as follows:
Assume that l_x persons of age x each purchase such a \$1 pure endowment.
The issuing company will collect the amount $l_x \times {}_nE_x$. If the company
invests this amount at the effective rate i, then in n years the accumulated
amount will be $l_x \times {}_nE_x(1 + i)^n$. Since there will be l_{x+n} persons alive
at that time to collect \$1 each, we get the equation

$$l_{x+n} = l_x \times {}_nE_x(1 + i)^n$$

Solving for ${}_nE_x$ gives

$${}_nE_x = \frac{l_{x+n}}{l_x(1 + i)^n} = \frac{l_{x+n}(1 + i)^{-n}}{l_x}$$

Since a life insurance company usually evaluates all contracts at the
same interest rate, and since the discount factor is used more frequently
than the accumulation factor, it is customary to designate $(1 + i)^{-1}$ by
the letter v. Then $(1 + i)^{-n} = v^n$, and the preceding formula can be
written as

$${}_nE_x = \frac{v^n l_{x+n}}{l_x}$$

Clearly the value of ${}_nE_x$ is readily computed as soon as the interest
rate is given and the mortality table chosen. However, since the concept of a pure endowment is so important, it is desirable to express
${}_nE_x$ in a more convenient form. This can be done by multiplying both
numerator and denominator of the right-hand member above by v^x.
This gives the more symmetric form

$${}_nE_x = \frac{v^{x+n} l_{x+n}}{v^x l_x}$$

We now introduce one of the numerous so-called "commutation symbols." Let us denote the product $v^k l_k$ by D_k. Then the preceding formula can be written as

$${}_nE_x = \frac{D_{x+n}}{D_x} \tag{4}$$

If the endowment is for S dollars, then the present value, or net single
premium, is given by

$$A = S({}_nE_x) \tag{5}$$

The values of the commutation symbols are given in Table 14.
These values were computed on the basis of the CSO table with a yearly
interest rate of $2\frac{1}{2}$ percent.

Example A young man at age twenty wishes to buy a pure endowment that will pay him $1000 if he lives to attain the age of fifty.   How much should he pay for this contract?

Solution This is a 30-year pure endowment, and the net single premium should be

$$A = S(_nE_x) = 1000(_{30}E_{20}) = 1000 \frac{D_{50}}{D_{20}}$$

From Table 14 we find that $D_{50} = 235,925$ and $D_{20} = 580,662$.   Consequently,

$$A = 1000 \frac{235,925}{580,662} = \$406.30$$

83 LIFE ANNUITIES

A life annuity consists of a set of periodic payments, usually equal in size, made over a period of years with each payment being contingent upon the survival of a designated life.   The person whose life the payments are contingent upon is called the *annuitant*.   All the qualifying adjectives used relative to annuities in earlier chapters of this text retain their same meaning when applied to life annuities.   We shall limit our discussion, however, to life annuities with equal annual payments with an annual interest rate of $2\frac{1}{2}$ percent.   Moreover, since in life-insurance work the annuity due occurs more frequently than the ordinary annuity, the theory will be developed in terms of annuities due, that is, annuities for which the payments are considered as due at the beginnings of the years.

84 WHOLE–LIFE ANNUITIES

A whole-life annuity (due) is a set of yearly payments of R dollars each, to continue as long as the annuitant lives, with the first one due immediately.

The present value, or the net single premium, of a $1 whole-life annuity contingent on the life of (x)† is designated by the symbol $\ddot{a}_x$. Clearly a whole-life annuity can be thought of as a set of pure endowments.   Thus we have

$$\ddot{a}_x = {}_0E_x + {}_1E_x + {}_2E_x + \cdots \text{ to the end of the table}$$

If the endowment symbols are replaced by the commutation symbols [Eq. (4)], we obtain

$$\ddot{a}_x = \frac{D_x + D_{x+1} + D_{x+2} + \cdots \text{ to the end of the table}}{D_x}$$

We now introduce a second commutation symbol defined by the relation

$$N_k = D_k + D_{k+1} + D_{k+2} + \cdots \text{ to the end of the table}$$

† It is customary to refer to a person aged x as simply (x).

In terms of commutation symbols, the annuity symbol can be written

$$\ddot{a}_x = \frac{N_x}{D_x} \tag{6}$$

If the annuity is to pay R dollars instead of $1, then the present value, or the net single premium, is given by

$$A = R\ddot{a}_x = R\frac{N_x}{D_x} \tag{7}$$

Example A 30-year-old person wishes to buy a whole-life annuity that will pay $100 yearly. What should the net single premium be?

Solution Using Eq. (7), we have

$$A = R\ddot{a}_x = 100\ddot{a}_{30} = 100\frac{N_{30}}{D_{30}}$$

From Table 14 we find that $N_{30} = 10{,}594{,}280$ and $D_{30} = 440{,}801$. Consequently,

$$A = 100\frac{10{,}594{,}280}{440{,}801} = \$2403.42$$

It should be clearly understood that the net single premium is the actual cost of the annuity, assuming that annuitants die exactly as predicted by the mortality table used and that all funds are invested at the interest rate used in computing the commutation symbols. The gross premiums, or actual premiums, for which companies sell annuities are somewhat higher than the net premiums and are obtained by a process called *loading*. A discussion of gross premiums and loading will not be given here.

Naturally the premiums vary according to the mortality table and the interest rate used. Thus, if the example just worked is solved using the 1937 Standard Annuity Mortality Table at $2\frac{1}{2}$ percent, the net single premium is $2560.23 if the annuitant is a male, and $2717.99 if the annuitant is a female.

EXERCISE 47

1. Find the net single premium of a pure endowment of $5000 due at the end of 20 years and purchased (*a*) at age twenty, (*b*) at age fifty.

2. Find the present value of $1000 due at the end of 15 years (*a*) if the payment is certain to be made, (*b*) if the payment is contingent on the life of a person now aged twenty-five.

3. How large a pure endowment, payable at age sixty, can a man aged thirty buy with $1000 cash?

4. Compute the net single premium for a whole-life annuity of $1000 per year, purchased (*a*) at age twenty-five, (*b*) at age sixty.

5. A schoolteacher receives $5000 from his retirement fund at age sixty. If he uses this to buy a whole-life annuity, what annual payments will he receive?

6. By how much would the answers in Prob. 4 be changed if the first annuity payment is not due until 1 year after the date of purchase?

85 DEFERRED ANNUITIES

A life annuity (due), deferred n years, is a contract contingent on the life of the annuitant that will pay R dollars annually, with the first payment coming at the end of the nth year. Here as with annuities, it is the term of the annuity that is deferred. Thus if (x) buys such a contract, he will receive the first payment at the end of the year that he attains the age $x + n$. Just as in the preceding section, an annuity of this type may be thought of as a set of pure endowments for the purpose of evaluation. If we use the symbol $_n \mid \ddot{a}_x$ to represent the present value, or the net single premium, of a $1 annuity, deferred n years and contingent upon the life of (x), then

$$_n \mid \ddot{a}_x = {_nE_x} + {_{n+1}E_x} + {_{n+2}E_x} + \cdots \text{ to the end of the table}$$

This equation can be put into commutation symbols as in the preceding section, and we obtain

$$_n \mid \ddot{a}_x = \frac{N_{x+n}}{D_x} \tag{8}$$

If the annuity is to pay R dollars instead of $1, then the present value, or the net single premium, is

$$A = R(_n \mid \ddot{a}_x) = R\frac{N_{x+n}}{D_x} \tag{9}$$

Example A 35-year-old person wishes to buy an annuity that will pay $500 annually, the first payment to be deferred 25 years. What is the net single premium?
Solution Using Eq. (9) we have

$$A = R(_n \mid \ddot{a}_x) = 500(_{25} \mid \ddot{a}_{35}) = 500\frac{N_{60}}{D_{35}}$$

From Table 14, we find that $N_{60} = 1,865,613.6$ and $D_{35} = 381,996$. Therefore

$$A = 500\frac{1,865,613.6}{381,996} = \$2441.93$$

86 TEMPORARY ANNUITIES

A temporary life annuity differs from a whole-life annuity in that it terminates after a certain number of payments even though the annuitant is still alive. Thus a temporary annuity of 10 payments contingent upon the life of (x) would consist of annual payments until either a total of 10 payments have been made or (x) dies. The present value, or the net single premium, of a temporary annuity is found as in the preceding sections by considering the annuity as consisting of a set of pure endowments. Thus if we denote by $\ddot{a}_{x:\overline{n}|}$ the present value of a \$1 temporary annuity of n payments contingent upon the life of (x), then

$$\ddot{a}_{x:\overline{n}|} = {}_0E_x + {}_1E_x + {}_2E_x + \cdots + {}_{n-1}E_x$$

This equation may be expressed in commutation symbols, the result being

$$\ddot{a}_{x:\overline{n}|} = \frac{N_x - N_{x+n}}{D_x} \tag{10}$$

If the payments are R dollars instead of \$1, then the present value, or the net single premium, is

$$A = R\ddot{a}_{x:\overline{n}|} = R\frac{N_x - N_{x+n}}{D_x} \tag{11}$$

Example Find the net single premium of a temporary annuity of 20 payments of \$500 each, contingent upon a life of 30 years.
Solution Using Eq. (11), we have

$$A = R\ddot{a}_{x:\overline{n}|} = 500\ddot{a}_{30:\overline{20}|} = 500\frac{N_{30} - N_{50}}{D_{30}}$$

From Table 14, we find that $N_{30} = 10,594,280$, $N_{50} = 3,849,487.6$, and $D_{30} = 440,801$. Consequently,

$$A = 500\frac{10,594,280 - 3,849,487.6}{440,801} = \$7650.61$$

In connection with the example just solved, it is interesting to note that the present value of an annuity due *certain* of 20 payments of \$500 each at $2\frac{1}{2}$ percent effective is \$7989.45. Thus it appears that a temporary annuity is not a very attractive contract to an investor. This type of contract, however, is widely used for the purpose of buying insurance, as will be discussed later.

EXERCISE 48

1. A person aged forty pays \$5000 for a deferred annuity, the first payment to be received on his sixtieth birthday. Find how large the payments will be.

2. Mr. Smith, aged forty-five, wishes to retire at age sixty with an annual income of \$2000. How much should he pay for a deferred annuity that will furnish this income?

3. In his will, Mr. Jones specifies that his son, aged fifteen, is to receive a temporary annuity of \$1000 per year with the last payment to be made when he reaches twenty-five. What is the cash value of this bequest?

4. A certain insurance policy for a person aged thirty requires 20 premiums of $100 each. What net single premium would buy the policy?

5. Show algebraically that $\ddot{a}_x = \ddot{a}_{x:\overline{n}|} + {}_n|\,\ddot{a}_x$.

6. Prove algebraically that $\ddot{a}_x = \ddot{a}_{x:\overline{n}|} + {}_nE_x \cdot \ddot{a}_{x+n}$.

87 EQUIVALENT ANNUITIES

It frequently is desirable to replace one type of annuity by another type or to use one type to buy a different type. For this purpose, *two annuities are considered equivalent if their present values, or their net single premiums, are the same.* For example, a temporary annuity of n payments of R' would be equivalent to an annuity with payments of R'', deferred m years, if $R'\ddot{a}_{x:\overline{n}|} = R''({}_m|\,\ddot{a}_x)$.

Example A person aged twenty wishes to retire when he is sixty years old. He wishes to buy an annuity that will pay him $1000 on his sixtieth birthday and the same amount annually thereafter. He wishes to buy this annuity by making annual payments starting now and ending on his fifty-ninth birthday. What annual payments will be required?

Solution The annuity consisting of his payments is a temporary annuity of 40 payments. The annuity that he will receive is a deferred annuity, deferred 40 years. Let R be the required annual payment of the temporary annuity. We now equate the present values of the two annuities and get

$$R\ddot{a}_{20:\overline{40}|} = 1000({}_{40}|\,\ddot{a}_{20})$$

Replacing the annuity symbols by commutation symbols and solving for R gives

$$R = 1000\,\frac{N_{60}}{N_{20} - N_{60}} = 1000\,\frac{1{,}865{,}613.6}{15{,}744{,}216 - 1{,}865{,}613.6} = \$134.42$$

88 OTHER TYPES OF ANNUITIES

One of the assumptions underlying the development of pure life annuities is that the payments are contingent upon the life of the annuitant. Thus if a person purchased a deferred annuity and died before the period of deferment had elapsed, his beneficiaries would receive nothing. This is not an unjust contract as it may appear at first sight, since it is based precisely on the assumption that payments are dependent on survival. It is possible, however, by slightly increasing the cost of the annuity to guarantee certain benefits. Thus there are annuity contracts that guarantee to pay back at least as much as they cost, others that guarantee a certain minimum number of payments, and still others that provide for various types of death benefits. Most persons when buying annuities prefer one with some such guarantee even though the payments that they will receive are smaller, relative to the cost, than for a similar type of pure annuity.

Although it is possible to develop the theory of life annuities with a wide variety of guaranteed benefits along lines similar to that used in the preceding sections, we shall illustrate only one type, namely, a whole-life annuity with a guaranteed number of payments.

Example Solve the example in Sec. 84 if the first 20 payments are guaranteed.
Solution Since the first 20 payments are guaranteed, they may be considered an annuity due certain of 20 payments, and the present value of this part of the contract is found by the technique developed in Sec. 24. The remaining payments, those which are dependent upon the survival of the annuitant, form a deferred life annuity, deferred 20 years. The present value of these payments is found as in Sec. 85. Hence the present value of the first 20 payments is

$$A = R(1 + a_{\overline{n-1}|i}) = 100(1 + a_{\overline{19}|2\frac{1}{2}\%}) = \$1597.889$$

Using Eq. (9) for the present value of the remaining payments, we have

$$A = R({}_n \mid \ddot{a}_x) = 100({}_{20} \mid \ddot{a}_{30}) = 100\,\frac{N_{50}}{D_{30}} = \$873.294$$

The total value of the contract is therefore

$$\$1597.889 + \$873.294 = \$2471.18$$

This result is \$67.76 more than the answer to the example in Sec. 84. Thus for a person aged thirty, a \$100-payment whole-life annuity with the first 20 payments guaranteed costs \$67.76 more than a pure whole-life annuity of \$100 payments. Obviously, most people would be willing to pay the small extra amount for the guaranteed payments.

EXERCISE 49

1. A person aged twenty-five wishes to receive \$2000 annually, the first payment to be made on his sixty-fifth birthday. In order to buy such an annuity, what yearly payments should he make if the first one is made immediately and the last one on his sixty-fourth birthday?

2. A person aged thirty pays \$100 each year into a retirement fund. These payments will continue until he reaches sixty. Starting on his sixty-fifth birthday, he will receive an annual pension for life. What payments will he receive?

3. Find the difference in the present values of a pure whole-life annuity of \$500 payments for a person aged thirty and a similar contract with the first 25 payments guaranteed.

4. Solve Prob. 1 if the first 10 payments of \$2000 are guaranteed.

89 LIFE INSURANCE

The main purpose of life insurance is the protection of the dependents of the insured person. Thus a man with a wife and children should carry sufficient insurance so that if he were to die, his family would not suffer financial hardship. The person to whom the payment is made upon the death of the insured is called the *beneficiary*.

There are many types of insurance policies, differing according to the kind of protection that is desired and also according to the manner in which the insurance is to be paid for. For example, a policy that will pay \$1000 upon the death of the insured may be purchased by making a single payment, by making annual payments for 20 years, or by making annual payments for the rest of the insured's life. Again, a policy may pay \$10,000 if the insured dies within 10 years but only \$5000 if death occurs at a later date. Actually the number of different types of policies is practically unlimited. We shall restrict our discussion, however, to only a few of the commonest types of policies.

For simplicity, we shall assume that death claims are paid at the end of the year in which death occurs instead of immediately afterward as is actually the case. Also, we shall consider only the net premiums. The gross premiums, or actual premiums, for which companies sell policies are slightly higher than the net premiums and are obtained by a process called *loading*. A discussion of loading and gross premiums will not be given here.

90 WHOLE-LIFE INSURANCE

A whole-life insurance policy on the life of (x) is a contract that promises to pay a specified amount to the beneficiary of (x) at the end of the year in which (x) dies, provided, of course, that (x) pays the premiums as called for in the contract.

We shall denote by A_x the net single premium that such a \$1 policy should cost. Thus A_x is the cost, at age x, of a policy that will pay \$1 at the end of the year in which (x) dies. To evaluate this symbol assume that l_x persons, all aged x, buy such a \$1 policy. The issuing company will receive $l_x A_x$ dollars. The number of death claims that must be paid at the ends of successive years will be

$$d_x, \ d_{x+1}, \ d_{x+2}, \ d_{x+3}, \ \ldots$$

The present value of all these claims must equal the amount collected by the company. Hence

$$l_x A_x = vd_x + v^2 d_{x+1} + v^3 d_{x+2} + \ \cdots \ \text{to the end of the table}$$

This equation may be solved for A_x. However, to obtain a more convenient expression for A_x, we multiply both sides of the above equation by v^x and introduce another commutation symbol defined by the relation $C_k = v^{k+1} d_k$. Solving for A_x now gives

$$A_x = \frac{C_x + C_{x+1} + C_{x+2} + \ \cdots \ \text{to the end of the table}}{D_x}$$

We define still another commutation symbol by the relation

$$M_k = C_k + C_{k+1} + C_{k+2} + \cdots \text{ to the end of the table}$$

We can now write

$$A_x = \frac{M_x}{D_x} \tag{12}$$

If the policy is for S dollars, then clearly the net single premium will be S times the value given by Eq. (12).

Example 1 Find the net single premium for a $1000 policy for a person aged twenty-five.
Solution The net single premium will be

$$1000 A_{25} = 1000 \frac{M_{25}}{D_{25}} = 1000 \frac{189,700.9}{506,597} = \$374.46$$

Actually not much insurance is purchased by a single premium. Most policies are paid for by either a temporary or a whole-life annuity. To compute the annual payments when an annuity is used to purchase the insurance, it is necessary only to equate the net single premium for the insurance to the present value of the annuity to be used, then solve for the annuity payment.

Let P_x be the net annual premium for a $1 whole-life policy issued at age x, these premiums to be paid as long as (x) lives. These annual premiums will form a whole-life annuity whose present value must equal the net single premium of the policy. Hence

$$P_x \ddot{a}_x = A_x$$

so that

$$P_x = \frac{A_x}{\ddot{a}_x} \tag{13}$$

If the right-hand side of Eq. (13) is expressed in terms of commutation symbols, we easily obtain

$$P_x = \frac{M_x}{N_x} \tag{14}$$

Similarly, let $_nP_x$ denote the net annual premium for a $1 whole-life policy, these premiums to be paid for only n years. A policy of this type is usually referred to as an n-payment life policy. In this case, the payments form a temporary annuity whose present value must equal the net single premium of the policy. Therefore

$$_nP_x \ddot{a}_{x:\overline{n}|} = A_x$$

and consequently

$$_nP_x = \frac{A_x}{\ddot{a}_{x:\overline{n}|}} \qquad (15)$$

or, in terms of commutation symbols,

$$_nP_x = \frac{M_x}{N_x - N_{x+n}} \qquad (16)$$

Example 2   Find the net annual premium for the policy in the preceding example if the payments are to continue (a) for life, (b) for 20 years.
Solution a   Using Eq. (14), we have

$$P_x = \frac{M_x}{N_x} = \frac{M_{25}}{N_{25}} = \frac{189,700.9}{12,992,619} = 0.014601$$

as the net annual premium for a \$1 policy.   For a \$1000 policy the net annual premium would therefore be \$14.60.
Solution b   In this case, the net annual premium is given by Eq. (16).   Hence

$$_nP_x = \frac{M_{25}}{N_{25} - N_{45}} = \frac{189,700.9}{12,992,619 - 5,161,996} = 0.024226$$

as the net annual premium for a \$1 policy.   For a \$1000 policy it would therefore be \$24.23.

91   TERM INSURANCE

Frequently it is desirable to take out insurance for a limited time rather than for a person's whole life.   For example, a man buying a new house that he is financing on a 20-year loan could carry a term policy on his life so that, in the case of his death, the money would be available to pay off the loan.   *Insurance that pays a benefit only if the insured dies within a specified time is called term insurance.*   The net single premium for term insurance of \$1 for n years on the life of (x) is denoted by the symbol $A^1_{x:\overline{n}|}$.   The small "1" placed above the letter x means that (x) must die before n years has elapsed in order that the benefits be paid.†

In exactly the same manner as in the preceding section, it is easily shown that

$$A^1_{x:\overline{n}|} = \frac{C_x + C_{x+1} + \cdots + C_{x+n-1}}{D_x} = \frac{M_x - M_{x+n}}{D_x} \qquad (17)$$

When the term is 1 year, the above formula reduces to $A^1_{x:\overline{1}|} = C_x/D_x$, called the *natural premium* and usually denoted by the simpler symbol c_x.

---

† The symbol for term insurance should not be confused with $A_{x:\overline{n}|}$ or $A_{x:\overline{n}|}^{\;\;1}$, both of which are used in life insurance to represent the present value of certain types of benefits.

Example (a) Find the net single premium for a $1000 policy issued at age thirty for a term of 20 years. (b) What would the net annual premium, payable for 15 years, be for this policy?

Solution a From Eq. (17), the net single premium for a $1 policy of this type is

$$A^1_{30:\overline{20}|} = \frac{M_{30} - M_{50}}{D_{30}} = \frac{182,403.5 - 142,035.1}{440,801} = 0.091580$$

Hence for a $1000 policy the net single premium is $91.58.

Solution b Let P be the net annual premium payable for 15 years. The premiums will form a temporary annuity whose present value must equal the present value of the policy being purchased. Hence

$$P\ddot{a}_{30:\overline{15}|} = 1000 A^1_{30:\overline{20}|}$$

Substituting commutation symbols and solving for P gives

$$P = 1000 \frac{M_{30} - M_{50}}{N_{30} - N_{45}} = 1000 \frac{182,403.5 - 142,035.1}{10,594,280 - 5,161,996} = \$7.43$$

In a more extensive treatment of life insurance, the natural premium c_x as well as the commutation symbol C_x occur sufficiently often that their values have been computed and tabulated. For a brief discussion such as this is, we have omitted tables for these symbols. The commutation symbol C_x can be obtained from Table 14, and the relation

$$C_x = M_x - M_{x+1}$$

and the natural premium is then easily obtained from the relation

$$c_x = C_x/D_x$$

92 ENDOWMENT INSURANCE

A rather popular type of insurance policy consists of a term insurance policy and a pure endowment payable to the insured, if he is still alive, at the end of the insurance term. When these two contracts are combined in this manner, the result is called *endowment insurance*. Thus a 20-year endowment insurance policy for $5000 would pay $5000 to the insured's beneficiary if the insured died before the 20 years had elapsed and would pay $5000 to the insured if he survived the 20-year term.

The symbol $A_{x:\overline{n}|}$ is used to denote the net single premium for an n-year endowment insurance policy of $1 for a person aged x. This symbol differs from the one for term insurance in that the "1" is omitted above the x.

Since endowment insurance is a combination of term insurance and a pure endowment, it follows readily that

$$A_{x:\overline{n}|} = A^1_{x:\overline{n}|} + {}_nE_x \tag{18}$$

For symmetry, the present value of a pure endowment is sometimes written as $A_{x:\overline{n}|}^{1}$ instead of $_nE_x$. The preceding equation is then written in the form

$$A_{x:\overline{n}|} = A_{x:\overline{n}|}^{1} + A_{x:\overline{n}|}^{1}$$

If the right-hand member of Eq. (18) is expressed in commutation symbols, we easily obtain

$$A_{x:\overline{n}|} = \frac{M_x - M_{x+n} + D_{x+n}}{D_x} \tag{19}$$

Example (*a*) Find the net single premium for a 20-year endowment insurance policy of $1000 issued at age twenty-five. (*b*) Find the net annual premium payable, for 15 years, for this policy.

Solution a   Using Eq. (19), we have

$$A_{25:\overline{20}|} = \frac{M_{25} - M_{45} + D_{45}}{D_{25}} = \frac{189,700.9 - 154,736.6 + 280,639}{506,594} = 0.62299$$

for a $1 policy, and consequently the net single premium for a $1000 policy would be $622.99.

Solution b   Let P be the net annual premium, payable for 15 years, for this policy. These premiums will form a temporary annuity whose present value is $622.99. We therefore have

$$P\ddot{a}_{25:\overline{15}|} = 622.99$$

Solving for P gives

$$P = \frac{622.99}{\ddot{a}_{25:\overline{15}|}} = 622.99\,\frac{D_{25}}{N_{25} - N_{40}} = \$50.22$$

EXERCISE 50

1. Find the net single premium for a whole-life insurance of $5000 for a person (*a*) aged twenty-five, (*b*) aged seventy-five.

2. Find the net single premium for a whole-life insurance of $3000 for a person (*a*) aged fifteen, (*b*) aged fifty, (*c*) aged ninety.

3. How much whole-life insurance can a person aged thirty-five buy with $3000 cash?

4. Find the net single premium for a 5-year term insurance of $10,000 issued to a person aged forty.

5. Compute the net single premium at age twenty for a 25-year endowment insurance policy of $5000.

6. Compute the net annual premium for the policy in (*a*), Prob. 1.

7. Find the net annual premium for the policy in (*b*), Prob. 2.

8. Compute the net annual premium, payable for 20 years, for the policy in (*a*), Prob. 2.

9. Find the net annual premium, payable for 20 years, for the policy in Prob. 5.

10. An insurance policy requires annual premiums of $100 payable for 20 years. What is the amount of insurance if the insured is thirty years old and (*a*) it is a whole-life policy, (b) it is a 20-year endowment insurance policy, (c) it is a 20-year term insurance policy?

93 RESERVES

In Sec. 91 brief mention was made of the *natural premium* of insurance, that is, the cost of insuring a life for 1 year. This natural premium $c_x = C_x/D_x$ increases with the age of the insured. However, insurance is usually purchased by equal annual payments. A comparison of the natural premium and the net level premium for a whole-life policy of $1000 issued at age twenty is given in the accompanying table.

Age	Net level premium at age twenty	Natural premium
20	12.49	2.37
30	12.49	3.47
40	12.49	6.03
50	12.49	12.02
51	12.49	12.95
60	12.49	25.94
80	12.49	128.64
95	12.49	386.55

This table shows that a person aged twenty who agrees to pay $12.49 every year for a whole-life policy actually pays more than year-by-year term insurance would cost until he reaches age fifty-one, after which year-by-year term insurance becomes more expensive. The excess of the level premium over the actual cost of insurance, accumulated with interest, builds up a *reserve* on the policy. Contrary to widespread belief, the reserve *does not* accumulate in early years to be depleted in later years but constantly grows regardless of how long the insured lives. The reason for this will now be explained. First, it must be clearly understood that a policy, say a whole-life policy for $1000, promises a *total* death benefit of $1000 and does not promise to insure the individual each year for $1000. If this latter were the case, the total death benefit should be $1000 plus the reserve. Consequently, when the reserve on a policy reaches, say, $200, the company carries only $800 insurance on the life involved, and in case of death pays $800 insurance and the $200 reserve, making a total of $1000 as promised.   In order to illustrate how reserves accumulate, suppose l_{20} persons aged twenty buy a whole-life policy for $1000 by making annual payments.   The annual net level premium for this policy is $12.49.   On the date of issue, the company would collect

$$l_{20}(1000P_{20}) = 951{,}483 \times 12.49 = \$11{,}884{,}022.67$$

At the end of the year, this sum would amount to

$$\$11{,}884{,}022.67 \times 1.025 = \$12{,}181{,}123.24$$

At this time, the company would pay $d_{20} = 2312$ death claims of $1000 each, which would reduce the preceding amount to

$$\$12{,}181{,}123.24 - \$2{,}312{,}000 = \$9{,}869{,}123.24$$

This last sum of money actually belongs to the $l_{21} = 949{,}171$ survivors. Thus, at the end of the first year, each of the l_{21} survivors would have a reserve to his credit of

$$\frac{\$9{,}869{,}123.24}{949{,}171} = \$10.40$$

At the beginning of the second year, each of these l_{21} persons would pay another premium of $12.49, or a total of

$$949{,}171 \times 12.49 = \$11{,}855{,}145.79$$

which would increase the fund to

$$\$9{,}869{,}123.24 + \$11{,}855{,}145.79 = \$21{,}724{,}269.03$$

By the end of the second year, this would have accumulated to

$$\$21{,}724{,}269.03 \times 1.025 = \$22{,}267{,}375.76$$

Since the company would have to pay $d_{21} = 2382$ death claims at the end of the second year, there would remain

$$\$22{,}267{,}375.76 - \$2{,}382{,}000 = \$19{,}885{,}375.76$$

as the total reserve for the $l_{22} = 946{,}789$ survivors.   Thus each survivor would now have a reserve of

$$\frac{\$19{,}885{,}375.76}{946{,}789} = \$21.00$$

This method may be continued until we reach the end of the mortality table.   For the policy under consideration, the reserves at the end of the 3d, 4th, 5th, 20th, 50th, and 70th years are found to be $31.84, $42.88, $54.13, $247.95, $499.31, and $762.53, respectively.

The method of computing reserves just used, though enlightening, becomes tedious, and shorter methods will now be discussed. Let $_tV$ be the reserve at the end of the tth policy year for a policy of $1 issued at age x. (It is customary to denote the type of policy by the use of subscripts on the V. Thus $_tV_x$ represents the reserve for a whole-life policy, $_tV_{x:\overline{n}|}$ would be the reserve for an endowment insurance policy, etc.) The reserve at the end of any year, called the *terminal reserve*, can be found in a manner similar to the prospective method of finding the outstanding indebtedness used in Sec. 38, Chap. 6. An equation of value taken at the end of the tth policy year requires that

$$\begin{pmatrix} t\text{th terminal} \\ \text{reserve} \end{pmatrix} + \begin{pmatrix} \text{present value of} \\ \text{future premiums} \end{pmatrix} = \begin{pmatrix} \text{present value of} \\ \text{future benefits} \end{pmatrix} \quad (20)$$

Thus for a whole-life policy with annual net level premiums of P_x, the present value of future premiums, t years after issue, would be $P_x\ddot{a}_{x+t}$. The present value of future benefits would be A_{x+t}. Hence, according to the above equation,

$$_tV_x + P_x\ddot{a}_{x+t} = A_{x+t}$$

or, after transposing,

$$_tV_x = A_{x+t} - P_x\ddot{a}_{x+t} \quad (21)$$

Expressions similar to Eq. (21) can readily be obtained from Eq. (20) for other types of policies such as endowment insurance or term insurance. It is left as an exercise for the student to show that

$$_tV_{x:\overline{n}|} = A_{x+t:\overline{n-t}|} - P_{x:\overline{n}|}\ddot{a}_{x+t:\overline{n-t}|} \quad (22)$$

gives the tth terminal reserve for endowment insurance and

$$_tV^1_{x:\overline{n}|} = A^1_{x+t:\overline{n-t}|} - P^1_{x:\overline{n}|}\ddot{a}_{x+t:\overline{n-t}|} \quad (23)$$

holds for term insurance.

Example Find the fifth terminal reserve for a whole-life policy for $1000 issued at age twenty.

Solution Using Eq. (21), we have

$$_5V_{20} = A_{25} - P_{20}\ddot{a}_{25}$$

as the reserve for a $1 policy of this type. We replace each of the symbols in the right-hand member of the above equation by commutation symbols and get

$$_5V_{20} = \frac{M_{25}}{D_{25}} - \frac{M_{20}}{N_{20}} \cdot \frac{N_{25}}{D_{25}}$$

When the commutation symbols are evaluated and the indicated computations made, we get $_5V_{20} = 0.05413$, so that the reserve for a policy of \$1000 would be \$54.13.

The computation of reserves is greatly facilitated by the use of more elaborate tables. For example, tables have been compiled for the symbols A_x, P_x, and $\ddot{a}_x$. With such tables available, the reserves for a whole-life policy can be computed directly from Eq. (21) by making one multiplication and one subtraction.

A second method of computing reserves, known as "Fackler's accumulation formula," can be derived as follows: Suppose that l_x persons buy a given type of policy for \$1 at age x. t years later each of the survivors will have a reserve of $_tV$. At the beginning of the $(t + 1)$st year each will pay a premium of P. This total, $(_tV + P)l_{x+t}$, will accumulate until the end of the year, at which time the company will pay death claims amounting to d_{x+t}. What remains constitutes the total reserve for the remaining l_{x+t+1} persons. Translating these statements into equation form, we have

$$(_tV + P)(1 + i) - d_{x+t} = _{t+1}Vl_{x+t+1}$$

If we divide through by l_{x+t+1}, setting

$$\frac{d_{x+t}}{l_{x+t+1}} = k_{x+t} \quad \text{and} \quad l_{x+t}\frac{1 + i}{l_{x+t+1}} = u_{x+t}$$

the preceding equation may be written

$$_{t+1}V = (_tV + P)u_{x+t} - k_{x+t} \tag{24}$$

This final equation is usually referred to as Fackler's accumulation formula. Since obviously $_0V = 0$, the first terminal reserve is given by

$$_1V = Pu_x - k_x$$

Equation (24) is then used to get the second reserve, then the third, then the fourth, etc. Tables have been compiled that give the values of u_x and k_x. Consequently, by means of Eq. (24), the reserves may be computed consecutively by performing an addition, followed by a multiplication, followed by a subtraction.

EXERCISE 51

1. Find the tenth terminal reserve for a whole-life policy for \$1000 issued at age twenty-five.

2. Find the sixtieth terminal reserve for a whole-life policy for \$1000 issued at age thirty.

3. Compute the tenth terminal reserve for a 20-year term insurance policy for \$1000 issued at age thirty-five.

4. For a 20-payment life policy for $1000 issued at age forty, find (*a*) the fifteenth terminal reserve, (*b*) the twenty-fifth terminal reserve. [*Hint:* For part (*b*), use Eq. (20).]

5. Express in commutation symbols the tenth terminal reserve for a 15-payment 20-year endowment policy issued at age twenty-five.

6. Express in commutation symbols the fifteenth terminal reserve for a 10-payment 20-year term insurance policy for a person aged twenty-eight.

7. Prove algebraically that $_tV_x = (A_{x+t} - A_x)/(1 - A_x)$.

8. Use the result of Prob. 7 to show that $_{t+1}V_x > {_t}V_x$.

94 CONCLUDING REMARKS

As we have seen in the preceding sections, when a policy is purchased by annual net level premiums, reserves are built up for the policy.   Naturally the question arises, How are these reserves disposed of in case the insurance is dropped before the premiums are all paid or before the insured dies?   It has been pointed out that these reserves belong essentially to the policyholder.   Consequently if a policyholder discontinues his insurance, he is entitled to recover practically all the reserve held on his policy.   When a policy is discontinued, or *surrendered*, the policyholder usually has his choice of one of the following three options:

A cash payment   Under this option, the insured receives a payment of cash, called the *cash surrender value*, which is somewhat less than the reserve at that time.   In most states, the law allows the company to make a *surrender charge* not exceeding $25 per $1000 of insurance.   The cash surrender value is also the amount of money that the company is willing to loan on the policy.

Paid-up insurance   Under this plan, the reserve, minus a surrender charge, is used to buy a fully paid-up policy of the same type for a reduced amount of insurance.

Extended insurance   In this case, the reserve, minus a surrender charge, is used to buy the original amount of insurance for a temporary period.

As an illustration, a whole-life policy for $1000 might offer if surrendered at the end of 12 years (*a*) $100 cash, (*b*) a fully paid-up life insurance of $250, or (*c*) a temporary life insurance of $1000 for 14 years. These three options are usually actuarial equivalents or nearly so.

All states have rigid regulations governing insurance companies to protect the policyholders.   Thus there is very little doubt that benefits will be paid.   Consequently, premiums are always sufficiently high to ensure the safety or soundness of the policy.   As a result, under normal conditions the company earns more on invested funds and receives more in premiums from policyholders than required to meet death benefits and build up the required reserves. If the company is a mutual company, this surplus belongs to the policyholders and is returned to them in the form of dividends. A policy that is eligible to receive dividends is called a *participating* policy. There are also stock companies, in contrast to mutual companies, which issue nonparticipating policies. In order to compete with mutual companies, the gross premiums in a stock company are usually substantially lower than in a mutual company. Thus the stock company appears cheaper unless the mutual company pays substantial dividends.

appendix A
Bobtailed Multiplication

When numbers with many digits are multiplied together and then the result is rounded down to fewer digits than the actual product contains, it is quite possible that a considerable amount of unnecessary work is performed.

Example   Accumulate $875.89 for 19 years 3 months at $j_4 = 7\%$.
Solution   Here $P = 875.89$, $i = 0.0175$, $n = 77$, and

$$S = 875.89(1.0175)^{77} = 875.89 \times 3.80320888$$

Multiplying in the usual way gives

```
        3.803208 88
            875.89
       34 228879 92
      3 04 256710 4
     19 01 604440
    266 22 46216
    3042 56 7104
    3331.19 262590 32
```

So that $S = \$3331.19$ to the nearest cent.

Since the final result is rounded from 10 decimal places down to 2, it is clear that many of the digits in the right part of the diagram above do not enter into the final result and could have been omitted. A method will now be described that omits many of the unnecessary multiplications.

It is usually best to select the longer number as the multiplicand and the one with the fewer digits as the multiplier. It is also convenient to adjust the decimal points so that the multiplicand has them all and the multiplier has none. In the example this means that we will multiply 0.0380320888 by 87589. We proceed as follows: Write down the multiplicand and draw a vertical line at the decimal point. Next, if d is the number of decimal places to be retained in the final answer, draw a second vertical line $d + 2$ digits to the right of the decimal point. This is called the **cutoff line.** Now write the multiplier, *with the digits in reverse order*, under the multiplicand so that the first digit of the reversed number is placed just to the left of the cutoff line as shown below.

1.		0380	320888	the multiplicand
2.		9	8578	the multiplier, digits reversed
3.	3042	5664		3803208 × 8
4.	266	2240		380320 × 7
5.	19	0160		38032 × 5
6.	3	0424		3803 × 8
7.		3420		380 × 9
8.	3331	1908	or 3331.19	add

The multiplication proceeds from right to left as in ordinary multiplication. However, the multiplication always starts with the digit directly above the line-2 digit being used in the multiplication. Line 3 is obtained by multiplying 8 by the part of the multiplicand that ends with the 8 immediately above the 8. Line 4 is obtained by multiplying 7 by that part of the multiplicand that ends with the 0 immediately above the 7. The procedure continues through all the digits in the multiplier. The results of each multiplication are placed to the left of the cutoff line as in the diagram. After the addition is made, the last two decimal places are rounded off.

Common Logarithms

1 DEFINITION

Let n be a positive number, and let b be positive and different from 1. Then the logarithm x of the number n to the base b is defined as the exponent on b such that $b^x = n$.

When logarithms are used for computation, the base b is taken to be 10 and the exponent x is called a *common logarithm*. In this appendix, we shall consider only common logarithms and shall use the word logarithm to mean the common logarithm.

For common logarithms, x is the logarithm of n if $10^x = n$. Thus, 2 is the logarithm of 100, since $10^2 = 100$. The statement that x is the logarithm of n is written more briefly as $x = \log n$. For example, since $10^3 = 1000$, we write $\log 1000 = 3$.

It should be clear that since logarithms are exponents, they are not new; only the notation is new. For a clear understanding of logarithms, it is essential that the student be familiar with both the exponential and the logarithmic notation and be able to write equations in either form.

Example 1   Find log 1,000,000.
Solution   Since $10^6 = 1,000,000$, log 1,000,000 = 6.

Example 2   If log $n = 0.5$, find n.
Solution   log $n = 0.5$ means that $10^{0.5} = n$.   Hence

$$n = 10^{\frac{1}{2}} = \sqrt{10}$$

EXERCISE 1

1. Find log 10,000.
2. Prove that log 0.01 = -2.
3. Find n if log $n = -1$.
4. Prove that log 1 = 0.
5. If log 2 = 0.30103, find $10^{0.30103}$.
6. If $10^{0.47712} = 3$, find log 3.
7. If log $10^{\frac{1}{2}} = x$, find x.
8. If log $100^x = 2$, find x.

9. Using the laws of exponents, prove that if log $a = x$ and log $b = y$, then $ab = 10^{x+y}$.

2 RULES FOR LOGARITHMS

If $10^x = n$ and $10^y = m$, then by a law of exponents, $10^{x+y} = mn$.   In terms of logarithmic notation, this statement would be written: If log $n = x$ and log $m = y$, then log $mn = x + y$ or

$$\log mn = \log m + \log n \tag{1}$$

Similarly, since $n/m = 10^{x-y}$, we write log $(n/m) = x - y$ or

$$\log \frac{n}{m} = \log n - \log m \tag{2}$$

Moreover, since $n^p = (10^x)^p = 10^{px}$, $px = \log n^p$, or

$$\log n^p = p \log n \tag{3}$$

Equations (1), (2), and (3) state symbolically the three fundamental laws of logarithms.   They are merely restatements of laws of exponents. Thus, Eq. (1) states in effect that when the bases are alike, adding exponents (or logarithms) multiplies the numbers.

Example   Given that log 2 = 0.30103, find log 5.
Solution   Since $10^1 = 10$, log 10 = 1.   By rule 2,

$$\log \frac{10}{2} = \log 10 - \log 2 = 1.00000 - 0.30103$$

Therefore

$$\log 5 = 0.69897$$

EXERCISE 2

Given log 2 = .30103 and log 3 = .47712, find the following:

1. log 6.	**2.** log 1.5.	**3.** log 20.
4. log 9.	**5.** log 2^5.	**6.** log 128.
7. log 810.	**8.** log 1200.	**9.** $10^{0.60206}$.
10. $10^{1.47712}$.	**11.** log 10n.	**12.** log 10^pn.

3 LOGARITHMS OF THE NUMBERS FROM 1 TO 10

Since $x = \log n$ if $10^x = n$, the logarithms of the integral powers of 10 are easily determined. However, the computation of the logarithms of other numbers is a more difficult task. It is beoynd the scope of this book to discuss the computation of the logarithms of numbers in general. Suffice it to say that the equation $10^x = n$ has been solved for x for all values of n, including fractions to three decimal places, from 1 to 10. The results, accurate to six decimal places, are recorded in Table 15. When we have learned to read the logarithms of these numbers, we shall obtain from these the logarithms of numbers above and below the range of the table.

Table 15 contains all the numbers from 1.000 to 9.999 with their logarithms. The decimal point has been omitted from behind the first digit of the number and also from in front of its logarithm. The sixth digit of the logarithm, in general, is not exact, since the logarithm has been rounded off to six places. The first three digits of the number appear below n, and the last digit appears in the row at the top of the page. The logarithm of the number is given in the row and column determined by the four digits of the number.

Example 1 Find log 3.245.
Solution For the moment, ignore the decimal point. Follow the row across from 324 until the column under 5 is reached. The digits 1215 are found. For compactness, the first two digits of the logarithm are printed only in the first column under 0. Thus the digits 51 must be placed before the 1215, so that the complete logarithm consists of the digits 511215. A decimal point is understood to precede all six digits, so that the complete logarithm is 0.511215 and we write

log 3.245 = 0.511215

Example 2 Find log 2.345.
Solution The row and column determined by 234 and 5 contain the entry *0143. The asterisk indicates that the first two digits are to be taken from the next line. Thus, 37 rather than 36 are the first two digits of the logarithm. Consequently, log 2.345 = 0.370143.

When a number is given accurate to five digits, it lies between two entries in the table and interpolation can be used to find the logarithm. An example will illustrate the method.

Example 3 Find log 3.5516.

Solution The number 3.5516 lies between 3.5510 and 3.5520, both of which are in the tables. The numbers and their logarithms are arranged in tabular form below. Decimal points have been omitted.

n	$\log n$
35520	550473
35516	?
35510	550351

$$10\left\{6\left\{\right\}c\right\}122$$

Assuming that corresponding differences are proportional, we get

$$\frac{c}{122} = \frac{6}{10}$$

Solving for c, we find that $c = 73$ when rounded off to the nearest whole number. Consequently we find that log 3.5516 = 0.550424.

EXERCISE 3

Find the logarithms of the following numbers, using interpolation when necessary:

1. 1.244.	**2.** 3.75.	**3.** 5.6.
4. 7.	**5.** 8.7765.	**6.** 3.091.
7. 6.4331.	**8.** 8.4444.	**9.** 3.1416.
10. 2½.	**11.** 2.4536.	**12.** 6.37.
13. 9.3578.	**14.** 7.7004.	**15.** 5.0007.

4 LOGARITHMS OF OTHER NUMBERS

The logarithms of the numbers from 1 to 10 are readily found from the tables. The logarithms of other numbers can be found rather easily from these. For if n is any number,

$$\log 10n = 1 + \log n \tag{4}$$

$$\log \frac{n}{10} = \log n - 1 \tag{5}$$

Thus, multiplying a number by 10 adds 1 to its logarithm and dividing a number by 10 subtracts 1 from its logarithm. By repeated use of Eqs. (4) and (5) the logarithm of any number can be obtained from the logarithm of a basic number by the addition or subtraction of an integer. For example, 23.7 is obtained from 2.37 by multiplying by 10 once. Hence log 23.7 = 1 + log 2.37.   Similarly, 2370 = 2.37 × 1000.   Therefore log 2370 = 3 + log 2.37.

The logarithm of any number may be thought of as consisting of two parts: one the logarithm of the basic number and the other the integer added to or subtracted from this logarithm. *The logarithm of the basic number is called the mantissa of the logarithm of the number. The integer added to or subtracted from the mantissa is called the characteristic of the logarithm of the number.* If the decimal point lies between the first and second significant digits of a number, the characteristic of the logarithm is 0. This position of the decimal point is called the *standard position*. Since multiplying or dividing a number by 10 merely moves the decimal point, the following rule for the characteristic of its logarithm can be used: *The characteristic of the logarithm of a number is equal to the number of moves necessary to change the decimal point from the standard position to its actual position. The characteristic is positive if the moves are to the right, negative if to the left.*

The logarithm of any number is obtained by combining its characteristic and its mantissa. Its characteristic is found by the rule above. Its mantissa is equal to the logarithm of the basic number, that is, the number with the decimal point in the standard position.

Example 1 Find log 324.5.
Solution To find the mantissa, find the logarithm of the basic number 3.245. Since log 3.245 = 0.511215, this is the desired mantissa. The number of moves necessary to change the decimal point from standard position to its actual position is two to the right. Therefore the characteristic is +2 and log 324.5 = 2.511215.

Example 2 Find log 0.02345.
Solution Since log 2.345 = 0.370143, the mantissa is 0.370143. The decimal point requires two moves to the left to change it from standard position to its actual position. Therefore the characteristic is −2, and log 0.02345 = 0.370143 − 2.

When the logarithm of a number is negative, as in Example 2, it is technically correct to combine the characteristic and mantissa so that we could write log 0.02345 = −1.629857. This form, however, is seldom used, since it contains a negative decimal, −0.629857, which is not listed in the tables. It is a common practice, however, to write the characteristic −2 in the form 8.000000 − 10. Thus we could write

$$\log 0.02345 = 8.370143 - 10$$

It should be clear that all three of these forms are numerically equivalent. Thus

$$\log 0.02345 = 0.370143 - 2 = 8.370143 - 10 = -1.629857$$

are all correct, but the first two forms are preferred.

EXERCISE 4

Given $\log 3.5516 = 0.550424$ and $\log 2 = 0.301030$, find the following (to be done orally):

1. $\log 35.516$.	**2.** $\log 2000$.	**3.** $\log 0.35516$.
4. $\log 355.16$.	**5.** $\log 0.2$.	**6.** $\log 20$.
7. $\log 35516$.	**8.** $\log 0.00002$.	**9.** $\log 3551.6$.

In each of the remaining problems, find the complete logarithm, using the table and interpolating when necessary (to be written out):

10. $\log 45.45$.	**11.** $\log 57$.	**12.** $\log 0.789$.
13. $\log 0.0606$.	**14.** $\log 3500$.	**15.** $\log 10,000$.
16. $\log 0.005$.	**17.** $\log 0.025$.	**18.** $\log 500.25$.
19. $\log 32,642$.	**20.** $\log 0.79875$.	**21.** $\log 0.301030$.

5 ANTILOGARITHMS

So far, we have concerned ourselves with the problem: given a number, to find its logarithm. We proceed now to the converse problem: given the logarithm of a number, to find the number. The number that corresponds to a given logarithm is called the *antilogarithm*.

The procedure is to search the body of Table 15 in an attempt to find the mantissa listed there. If it is found there, the basic number corresponding to it is determined by the row and column in which the mantissa stands. When just the matissa is considered, the decimal point is understood to be in standard position, that is, just after the first digit of the number. It is now necessary to move the decimal point to its actual position in accordance with the rule for characteristics as stated in the preceding section.

If the given mantissa is not found in the table, it will lie between two mantissas that are in the table and the number can be found by interpolation.

Example 1 If $\log n = 2.877544$, find n.
Solution The mantissa 0.877544 is found in the body of the table in the row opposite the number 754 and in the column under 3. Therefore the number with the decimal point in the standard position is 7.543. Since the characteristic is $+2$, the actual position of the decimal point is two places to the right of the standard position. Therefore $n = 754.3$.

Example 2 If $\log n = 9.770360 - 10$, find n.
Solution The mantissa 0.770360 lies between the mantissas 0.770410 and 0.770336. Therefore interpolation is necessary. The mantissas and the corresponding numbers are arranged in the form of a table as shown on page 219. All decimal points are omitted. Assuming that corresponding differences are proportional, we have

$$\frac{c}{100} = \frac{24}{74}$$

	Mantissa	Number	
	770410	589400	
	770360	?	
	770336	589300	

$$74 \left\{ 24 \left\{ \right. \right\} c \right\} 100$$

Therefore $c = 32.4$, or 32 to the nearest whole number. Adding this to 589300, we get as the basic number with the decimal point in standard position, 5.89332. The characteristic is $9 - 10 = -1$. Therefore the actual position of the decimal point is one place to the left of the standard position. Therefore $n = 0.598332$.

It must be remembered that the last digits of the mantissas listed in the table are not exact. Moreover, the interpolation procedure is based on the assumption that corresponding differences are proportional, which is only approximately true. Consequently, the last digit of the number found by interpolation may contain a small error.

Example 3 If $\log n = -1.383$, find n.
Solution This logarithm is negative and not in the conventional characteristic-mantissa form. It must be changed to this form before the tables can be used. This is done by adding and subtracting 10 from the given logarithm. Thus

$$-1.383 = (10 - 1.383) - 10 = 8.617000 - 10$$

It is now possible to find the basic number 4.14 from the table. Since the characteristic is -2, the decimal point is moved two places to the left and $n = 0.0414$.

EXERCISE 5

If $\log 3.122 = 0.494433$, $\log 7 = 0.845098$, and $\log 8.2 = 0.913814$, find n in the following problems (to be done orally):

1. $\log n = 1.494433$.   **2.** $\log n = 4.845098$.
3. $\log n = 2.913814$.   **4.** $\log n = 3.913814$.
5. $\log n = -0.505567$.   **6.** $\log n = -1.086186$.
7. $\log n = 2.494433$.   **8.** $\log n = 7.845098 - 10$.
9. $\log n = 8.845098 - 10$.

In each of the remaining problems, find n if $\log n$ is as follows, using interpolation when necessary (to be written out):

10. 0.934751.   **11.** 1.883207.   **12.** 0.860428.
13. 3.936182.   **14.** 9.903090 − 10.   **15.** 7.707570 − 10.
16. 8.637750 − 10.   **17.** 9.461398 − 10.   **18.** 4.210051.
19. −1.749824.   **20.** −2.476675.   **21.** 3.141590.

6 MULTIPLICATION AND DIVISION

Logarithms may be used to simplify the arithmetic processes of multiplication and division. For suppose we wish to compute the value of $(2.375 \times 8.24) \div 10.3$. Using the table of logarithms, we find that $\log 2.375 = 0.375664$. This means that $10^{0.375664} = 2.375$. Similarly we find that $8.24 = 10^{0.915927}$ and $10.3 = 10^{1.012837}$. We now replace the numbers in the problem by their equals and obtain

$$
\begin{aligned}
2.375 \times 8.24 \div 10.3 &= 10^{0.375664} \times 10^{0.915927} \div 10^{1.012837} \\
&= 10^{0.375664+0.915927-1.012837} \\
&= 10^{0.278754}
\end{aligned}
$$

Since 0.278754 is an exponent of 10, it is the logarithm of the answer to our problem. Using the technique of the preceding section, we find that the number 1.9 corresponds to this logarithm. Thus

$$2.375 \times 8.24 \div 10.3 = 1.9$$

It should be observed that the problem was solved by using only tables and addition and subtraction. Actually the procedure may be further simplified by using logarithmic notation throughout. Thus if we set $n = 2.375 \times 8.24 \div 10.3$ and take logarithms of this equation, we get, using Eqs. (1) and (2),

$$\log n = \log 2.375 + \log 8.24 - \log 10.3$$

Substituting the logarithms of the given numbers in the above equation, we get

$$\log n = 0.375664 + 0.915927 - 1.012837 = 0.278754$$

Now using the tables to find the number corresponding to the logarithm 0.278754, we obtain $n = 1.9$. The only difference in the two solutions is the form of presentation. The logarithmic notation becomes more advantageous as the complexity of the problem increases.

Example 1 Using logarithms, compute $n = 43.73 \times 0.01326$.
Solution Taking logarithms of both sides of the given equality, we get

$$\log n = \log 43.73 + \log 0.01326$$

Finding the logarithms of the given numbers and substituting them in the logarithmic equation gives

$$\log n = 1.640779 + (8.122544 - 10) = 9.763323 - 10$$

The characteristic of this logarithm is -1, and the mantissa is 0.763323. This mantissa lies between the two mantissas 0.763353 and 0.763278. By interpolation, we find that the number corresponding to the given mantissa is 5.79860. Since the characteristic is -1, the decimal point must be moved one place to the left, so that $n = 0.579860$.

Example 2 Using logarithms, compute $n = 3.914/16.48$.

Solution Taking logarithms of both sides of the given equality gives

$$\log n = \log 3.914 - \log 16.48$$

Substituting the logarithms of the given numbers gives

$$\log n = 0.592621 - 1.216957$$

The logarithm is negative and equal to -0.624336. We can change the form of this negative logarithm to $9.375664 - 10$ by adding and subtracting 10 as was done in Example 3 of the preceding section. However, the same result is obtained more quickly by adding and subtracting 10 from the smaller of the two logarithms in the preceding logarithmic equation. Thus

$$\log n = 10.592621 - 10 - 1.216957 = 9.375664 - 10$$

The number corresponding to the mantissa 0.375664 is 2.375. Since the characteristic is -1, the decimal point must be moved one place to the left, so that $n = 0.2375$.

If $n = 10^x$, it follows readily that n is positive regardless of whether x is positive or negative. Therefore logarithms for negative values of n do not exist in the usual sense. However, computations involving negative factors can be performed by first determining the sign of the answer by inspection, then computing the numerical value of the answer by ignoring all negative signs.

EXERCISE 6

Use logarithms to perform the following computations:

1. 1.275×5.24.

2. 0.8625×46.4.

3. 0.564×0.1725.

4. $\dfrac{19.57}{8.24}$.

5. $\dfrac{0.105}{0.00112}$.

6. $\dfrac{59.67}{0.153}$.

7. $\dfrac{2.457}{182}$.

8. $\dfrac{23.1 \times 0.005668}{0.7235}$.

9. $\dfrac{4205 \times 1.034}{78.42 \times 0.672}$.

10. $\dfrac{358.75}{56 \times 2.07}$.

11. $512.42 \times \dfrac{51}{73} \times 0.0355$.

12. $\dfrac{15.86 \times 67360}{172.66}$.

13. $\dfrac{55.2 \times 27.5 \times 16.6}{1728}$.

14. $\dfrac{0.332 \times 0.096 \times 144}{0.23671}$.

15. $\dfrac{563.29}{72.669 \times 5280\%_{3600}}$

7 EXPONENTS AND RADICALS

In performing computations involving powers and roots of numbers, we use the same procedure as before. The logarithmic equation is first written, the logarithms are then substituted into this equation, and the indicated computations are made. In order to use Eq. (3), all roots are changed to exponential form.

Example 1 Using logarithms, find $n = \sqrt{40.5}$.
Solution We first write $n = (40.5)^{1/2}$. Taking logarithms of both sides of this equation gives

$$\log n = \frac{1}{2} \log 40.5$$

$$\log n = \frac{1}{2} (1.607455) = 0.803728$$

Using interpolation to find the antilogarithm gives $n = 6.36397$.

Example 2 Using logarithms, find $S = 1246(1.043)^{25}$.
Solution Taking logarithms of both sides of the equation gives

$$\log S = \log 1246 + 25 \log 1.043$$

Looking up these logarithms, we get

$$\log S = 3.095518 + 25(0.018284) = 3.552618$$

Using the tables and interpolation to obtain the antilogarithm, we now find that $S = 3569.59$.

Example 3 Compute by logarithms $n = 1/(7.92)^8$.
Solution We rewrite the equation as $n = (7.92)^{-8}$. The corresponding logarithmic equation is

$$\log n = -8 \log 7.92 = -8(0.898725) = -7.189800$$

It must be remembered that the mantissas in the logarithmic tables are all positive. Therefore it is necessary to change the form as was done in Example 3, Sec. 5. Thus

$$\log n = 10 - 7.189800 - 10 = 2.810200 - 10$$

Finding the antilogarithm, we get $n = 0.0000000645951$.

Example 4 Compute by logarithms $r = \sqrt[3]{0.055}$.
Solution We first write $r = (0.055)^{1/3}$. Then

$$\log r = \frac{1}{3} \log 0.055 = \frac{1}{3} (8.740363 - 10)$$

If the indicated division is performed, we obtain

$$\log r = 2.913454 - 3.333333 = -0.419879$$

This result is now changed into the characteristic-mantissa form as in previous examples, and we get $\log r = 9.580121 - 10$. The foregoing arithmetic can be materially simplified by changing the form of the characteristic before the division. Thus, the characteristic -2 may be written as $8 - 10$, $1 - 3$, $28 - 30$, or innumerable ways.   Using the latter form, we have

$$\log r = \frac{1}{3} (28.740363 - 30) = 9.580121 - 10$$

In either case, the antilogarithm is $r = 0.380296$.

EXERCISE 7

Compute each of the following by logarithms:

1. $(1.026)^7$.

2. $\sqrt{305.6}$.

3. $\sqrt[4]{6.32}$.

4. $25.76(1.032)^{22}$.

5. $15,000(0.6316)^{30}$.

6. $152.50(1.068)^{-8}$.

7. $3200(1.0025)^{-20}$.

8. $\sqrt[3]{0.2}$.

9. $\sqrt[3]{0.0468}$.

10. $\sqrt[5]{\dfrac{135}{3113}}$.

11. $\sqrt[15]{\dfrac{24.60}{396}}$.

12. $(1.095)^{-10}$.

13. $(0.8663)^{-12}$.

14. $\sqrt{0.231 \times 3.1416}$.

15. $\dfrac{\sqrt{1.6}}{0.77317}$.

8   EXPONENTIAL EQUATIONS

Logarithms may be used to solve equations of the form $a^x = b$, for the exponent x when a and b are known.   No new technique is required. Equate the logarithms of each side, substitute the known logarithms in this equation, and solve the resulting equation for x by ordinary algebraic methods.

Example 1   Solve the equation $(1.033)^x = 2.5$ for x.
Solution   Taking logarithms of both sides of the given equation gives

$$x \log 1.033 = \log 2.5$$

Substituting the logarithms of the given numbers into this equation yields

$$x(0.014100) = 0.397940$$

This is a simple algebraic equation and can be solved in the same manner as similar equations encountered by the student in previous work.   If both sides of this equation are divided by 0.0141, we obtain

$$x = \frac{0.39794}{0.0141} = 28.223$$

the final result being obtained by long division.   In cases where this final long division becomes tedious, logarithms may be used to perform this division.   Thus, if we take logarithms of the equation

$$x = \frac{0.39794}{0.0141}$$

we get

$$\log x = \log 0.39794 - \log 0.0141$$

Looking these logarithms up, we have

$$\log x = (9.599818 - 10) - (8.149219 - 10) = 1.450599$$

The antilogarithm of this value is $x = 28.2227$, or 28.223.

Example 2 Solve the following equation for n.

$$875(1.02)^n = 1800$$

Solution Taking logarithms of both sides, we obtain

$$\log 875 + n \log 1.02 = \log 1800$$

Substituting the logarithms of the given numbers gives

$$2.942008 + n(0.008600) = 3.255273$$

This equation is solved for n by ordinary algebraic methods. We subtract 2.942008 from both sides of the equation, then divide by 0.0086. The result is

$$n = \frac{3.255273 - 2.942008}{0.0086} = 36.426$$

Example 3 Solve the equation $2350(0.785)^x = 365$ for x.
Solution Taking logarithms of both sides, we get

$$\log 2350 + x \log 0.785 = \log 365$$

Substituting the known logarithms gives

$$3.371068 + x(9.894870 - 10) = 2.562293$$

Since the unknown in this equation is x, and not $\log x$, it is no longer necessary or desirable to write the logarithm of 0.785 in the customary characteristic-mantissa form. This form is necessary only when antilogarithms are to be found. If we change this logarithm to its negative equivalent, we get

$$3.371068 - 0.105130x = 2.562293$$

Solving for x by ordinary methods gives

$$x = \frac{2.562293 - 3.371068}{-0.105130} = \frac{-0.808775}{-0.105130} = 7.693$$

EXERCISE 8

In each case, solve for x:

1. $(1.024)^x = 2.256$.
2. $2^x = 65536$.
3. $6950(1.073)^x = 15480$.
4. $825.25(1.044)^x = 1000$.
5. $(0.8531)^x = 0.05$.
6. $(0.9)^x = 0.09$.
7. $126(0.75)^x = 30$.
8. $150(0.626)^x = 15$.
9. $2^{2x+1} = 2048$.
10. $3^x = 5 \times 2^x$.
11. $2^{x-1} = 12 \times 3^{2x}$.
12. $\log_2 10 = x$.

9 EQUATIONS INVOLVING ADDITION AND SUBTRACTION

It will be remembered that the three rules of logarithms provide a means for multiplying numbers, dividing numbers, and raising numbers to powers. Even the simplest addition or subtraction cannot be done by means of logarithms. However, logarithms can be used in solving many equations involving addition and subtraction provided either (a) the form of the equation can be changed to avoid the addition or subtraction, or (b) a part of the problem does not involve addition or subtraction. Factoring can often be used to change the form of an equation.

Example 1 Find $n = \sqrt{(2.75)^2 - (1.065)^2}$.
Solution The form of the equation can be changed by factoring. Since $a^2 - b^2 = (a + b)(a - b)$,

$$(2.75)^2 - (1.065)^2 = (2.75 + 1.065)(2.75 - 1.065) = 3.815 \times 1.685$$

Therefore $n = (3.815 \times 1.685)^{1/2}$. We now take logarithms and get

$$\log n = \frac{1}{2}(\log 3.815 + \log 1.685) = \frac{1}{2}(0.581495 + 0.226600) = 0.404048$$

Finding the antilogarithm, we get $n = 2.53541$.

Example 2 Solve for x. $[(1.044)^x - 1]/0.044 = 10.5$.
Solution In this example, some preliminary arithmetic work is necessary to eliminate the subtraction in the numerator. We multiply both sides of the given equation by 0.044. This gives

$$(1.044)^x - 1 = 10.5 \times 0.044 = 0.462$$

Adding 1 to both sides gives

$$(1.044)^x = 1.462$$

This equation is now solved by logarithms in the same manner as Example 1, Sec. 8. We have

$$x \log 1.044 = \log 1.462$$
$$x(0.018700) = 0.164947$$
$$x = \frac{0.164947}{0.0187} = 8.821$$

Example 3 Compute the value of $a = [1 - (1.052)^{-20}]/0.052$.
Solution The subtraction in the numerator prevents the direct use of logarithms. However, the most difficult part of the computation, finding the value of $(1.052)^{-20}$, can be done with the aid of logarithms. To this end we set $x = (1.052)^{-20}$. Then

$$\log x = -20 \log 1.052 = -20(0.022016)$$
and
$$\log x = -0.440320 = (10 - 0.440320) - 10 = 9.559680 - 10$$

Finding the antilogarithm, we get $x = 0.362811$. This value, 0.362811, is now substituted in the original equation for $(1.052)^{-20}$. Thus,

$$a = \frac{1 - 0.362811}{0.052} = \frac{0.637189}{0.052} = 12.254$$

EXERCISE 9

Find the unknown quantity with the aid of logarithms:

1. $x^2 = (25.15)^2 - (17.65)^2$.

2. $x + 1 = \sqrt[5]{1.72}$.

3. $1 - x = \sqrt[3]{0.1025}$.

4. $(x/4 + 1)^4 = 1.0648$.

5. $\dfrac{2x^6 - 1}{5} = 13$.

6. $s = \dfrac{(1.026)^{1/4} - 1}{0.026}$.

7. $a = \dfrac{1 - (1.003)^{-25}}{0.003}$.

8. $\dfrac{(1.09)^n - 1}{0.09} = 50$.

9. $\left(1 + \dfrac{j}{12}\right)^{12} = \left(1 + \dfrac{0.07}{52}\right)^{52}$.

10. $\dfrac{1 - (1.087)^{-n}}{0.087} = 4.5$.

Progressions

1 ARITHMETIC PROGRESSIONS

Suppose we start with the number 7 and count by fives up to 32. The following sequence of numbers results: 7, 12, 17, 22, 27, 32. Each number of this sequence can be obtained from the preceding number by adding a constant number, in this case 5. This is an example of an arithmetic progression. *Any sequence of numbers with the property that each number in the sequence, after the first, can be obtained from the preceding one by adding the same constant is called an arithmetic progression, or, more briefly, an A.P.* The numbers of the sequence are called the *terms* of the progression, and the difference between each number and the preceding one is called the *common difference.* If the common difference is negative, the terms of the A.P. decrease as in the progression 21, 17, 13, 9, 5. In this case, the common difference is −4, and we can obtain any term, after the first, by adding −4 to the preceding one.

Let us write eight terms of an A.P. whose first term is a and whose common difference is d.   We obtain the sequence

$$\underset{a,}{\overset{(1)}{}} \quad \underset{a + d,}{\overset{(2)}{}} \quad \underset{a + 2d,}{\overset{(3)}{}} \quad \underset{a + 3d,}{\overset{(4)}{}} \quad \underset{a + 4d,}{\overset{(5)}{}} \quad \underset{a + 5d,}{\overset{(6)}{}} \quad \underset{a + 6d,}{\overset{(7)}{}} \quad \underset{a + 7d}{\overset{(8)}{}}$$

Above each term is written the number, or *index*, of the term.   It should be noted that the coefficient of d in any term is always one less than the index, or the number of the term.   Thus if the sequence were continued, the seventeenth term would be $a + 16d$ and the sixtieth term would be $a + 59d$.   Hence by observing this rule, any term can be written without writing the intermediate ones.   If there are n terms in the progression, the coefficient of d for the last term will be $n - 1$.   If this last term is called l, then

$$l = a + (n - 1)d \tag{1}$$

If we are given any three of the four letters l, a, n, and d, it is possible to solve this equation for the remaining one.

If an A.P. contains more than two terms, the terms between the first and last are called *arithmetic means*.   If the first and last terms are given, it is possible to insert any number of arithmetic means between these two.   For since a and l are given and n is two more than the number of means to be inserted, Eq. (1) can be solved for d.   The progression can then be written by starting with a and adding d repeatedly.

Example 1   A boy swims 100 yd one day and increases the distance by 20 yd each day.   What distance does he swim on the fourteenth day?
Solution   The problem is that of determining the fourteenth term of the A.P. 100, 120, 140, ...   We have $a = 100$, $d = 20$, $n = 14$, and we are to find l.   Substituting these values in Eq. (1) gives

$$l = 100 + 13 \times 20 = 360 \text{ yd}$$

Example 2   Insert three arithmetic means between 17 and 33.
Solution   We have $a = 17$, $l = 33$, and $n = 5$, since three means are to be inserted between a and l.   Substituting these values in Eq. (1) gives

$$33 = 17 + 4d \qquad \text{and} \qquad d = 4$$

Now starting with 17 and repeatedly adding 4, we get the entire progression

$$17, 21, 25, 29, 33$$

The three means are 21, 25, and 29.

Example 3   The third term of an A.P. is 6, and the seventh term is -14.   Write the first three terms of the progression.
Solution.   Since the third term is 6,

$$a + 2d = 6$$

Similarly

$$a + 6d = -14$$

Thus we have two linear equations to be solved for the two unknowns a and d. Subtracting the second equation from the first gives

$$-4d = 20 \quad \text{and} \quad d = -5$$

Substituting this value for d in the first equation gives

$$a + 2(-5) = 6 \quad \text{and} \quad a = 16$$

Since a and d are known, we can now write as many terms of the progression as we please; in particular, the first three terms are 16, 11, and 6.

2 GEOMETRIC PROGRESSIONS

Let us consider the sequence of three numbers: 36, 48, 64. Since the difference between the second and the first is 12 and the difference between the third and the second is 16, there is no common difference and the numbers do not form an A.P. However, the ratio of the second to the first is $48/36 = 4/3$, and the ratio of the third to the second is $64/48 = 4/3$. Thus the ratio of each term to the preceding one is constant. *A sequence of numbers with the property that the ratio of each term to the preceding one is constant is called a geometric progression, or a G.P.*

Multiplying any term of a G.P. by the common ratio gives the following term. Thus, in the example above, $36 \times \frac{4}{3} = 48$, and $48 \times \frac{4}{3} = 64$. The progression's fourth term would be $64 \times \frac{4}{3} = 85\frac{1}{3}$. If the common ratio is negative, the terms of the G.P. will alternate in sign as in the G.P. 3, -6, 12, -24, 48. Here the common ratio is -2.

If we write eight terms of the G.P. whose first term is a and whose common ratio is r, we obtain the sequence

(1)	(2)	(3)	(4)	(5)	(6)	(7)	(8)
a,	ar,	ar^2,	ar^3,	ar^4,	ar^5,	ar^6,	ar^7

Above each term is written the number, or *index*, of the term. It should be noted that the exponent of r is always one less than the index, or number of the term. Thus if the sequence were continued, the seventeenth term would be ar^{16} and the sixtieth term would be ar^{59}. Hence by observing this rule, any term can be written without writing the intermediate ones. If there are n terms in the progression, the exponent of r for the last term will be $n - 1$. If this last term is called l, then

$$l = ar^{n-1} \tag{2}$$

If any three of the four letters l, a, r, and n are given, it is possible to solve Eq. (2) for the remaining one, although in certain cases the solution will be imaginary. Progressions with imaginary solutions will not be considered here. Since Eq. (2) involves an exponent, logarithms are frequently useful for solving Eq. (2).

If the G.P. contains more than two terms, the terms between the first and the last are called *geometric means*. The problems of inserting a given number of geometric means between two numbers is essentially that of solving Eq. (2) for r when a, l, and n are given.

Example 1 The value of a certain machine at the end of each year is one-half as much as its value at the beginning of the year. If the machine originally cost $10,000, find its value at the end of 10 years.

Solution The value at the end of the first year is $5000; at the end of the second year, $2500; at the end of the third year, $1250; etc., each successive value being one-half of the preceding one. These numbers form a G.P. in which $a = 5000$, $r = \frac{1}{2}$, and $n = 10$. The tenth term is therefore

$$l = ar^9 = 5000 \left(\frac{1}{2}\right)^9 = \frac{5000}{512} = \$9.77$$

Example 2 Insert three geometric means between 16 and 81.

Solution We have $a = 16$ and $l = 81$. Since three means are to be placed between these numbers, $n = 5$. Substituting these values in Eq. (2), we get

$$81 = 16r^4 \qquad \text{or} \qquad r^4 = \frac{81}{16}$$

Taking the fourth root of both sides of this last equation gives $r = \frac{3}{2}$. The complete progression can now be written. It is 16, 24, 36, 54, 81. The three geometric means are 24, 36, and 54. Since $r = -\frac{3}{2}$ is also a solution of the above equation, a second set of geometric means is -24, 36, and -54.

EXERCISE 1

Determine which of the following progressions are arithmetic, which are geometric; write the fourth term of each; and find the term indicated:

1. 1, -2, 4, . . . 8th term.

2. -2, 1, 4, . . . 20th term.

3. 32, 48, 72, . . . 5th term.

4. 36, 48, 60, . . . 9th term.

5. -32, -48, -72, . . . nth term.

6. -36, -48, -60, . . . 10th term.

7. $\frac{1}{3}$, $\frac{1}{12}$, $-\frac{1}{6}$, . . . 12th term.

8. $\frac{2}{3}$, $\frac{1}{3}$, $\frac{1}{6}$, . . . 7th term.

9. 100, 101, 102.01, . . . 6th term.

10. 35.2, 34, 32.8, . . . 25th term.

Insert the indicated number of arithmetic means between the given numbers:

11. 6 and 9, six means.

12. 12 and 27, one mean.

13. 27 and 81, two means.

14. 48 and -32, three means.

15. -12 and 28, four means.

16. 56.6 and 11.6, nine means.

Insert the indicated number of geometric means between the given numbers:

17. 12 and 27, one mean.

18. 24 and 81, two means.

19. 625 and 256, three means.

20. 16 and $\frac{1}{2}$, four means.

21. Prove that if one arithmetic mean is inserted between a and l, it is the average of a and l.

22. How many odd integers are there from 87 to 143 inclusive?

23. In a G.P., $r = \frac{1}{3}$ and the fifth term is $\frac{1}{18}$. Find the first term.

24. The seventh term of an A.P. is 71, and the thirteenth term is 32. Find the first term.

25. The first term of a G.P. is 125, and $r = 1.025$. Find the fifteenth term.

3 THE SUM OF THE TERMS OF AN A.P.

It is often necessary to find the sum of the terms of an A.P. To illustrate the method of deriving a formula for this sum, we shall find the sum of the integers from 1 to 100 inclusive. These integers form an A.P. for which $a = 1, d = 1, n = 100,$ and $l = 100.$ The sum of the first and last terms is 101. The sum of the second term, 2, and the second from the last, 99, is likewise 101. The sum of the third term and the third from the last is also 101. Proceeding in this manner, the sum of each kth term and the kth from the last is always 101. If these sums are formed for each of the 100 terms and all of these sums added, the result is $100 \times 101 = 10,100.$ This sum, 10,100, contains each term of the progression twice. Therefore the sum of the terms of the progression is one-half of this, or $\frac{1}{2} \times 10,100 = 5,050.$

Consider now the general A.P. with first term a, last term l, common difference d, and number of terms n. The sum of the first and last terms is $a + l$. Since the second term is $a + d$ and the second from the last is $l - d$, the sum of these two terms is also $a + l$. Since successive terms increase by d as we count from the first and decrease by d as we count from the last, the sum of any kth term and the kth from the last will always be $a + l$. If these sums are made for each of the n terms of the progression and all of them added together, the result will be $n(a + l)$. Each term, however, has been counted twice, so that the sum of the terms of the progression is one-half of this; or letting S represent this sum, we have

$$S = \frac{1}{2} n(a + l) \tag{3}$$

An alternate formula can be obtained by replacing l in Eq. (3) by its equal $a + (n - 1)d$, from Eq. (1). If this is done, we easily obtain

$$S = \frac{1}{2} n[2a + (n - 1)d] \tag{4}$$

This second form is useful when l is not involved in the problem.

Example 1   A certain pile of logs contains 20 in the top row, 21 in the next lower row, and one more log in each lower row until 50 logs are reached in the bottom row. Find the number of logs in the pile.

Solution   The number of logs in each row, counting from the top, form an A.P. with $a = 20$, $d = 1$, and $l = 50$.   We must first find the number of terms.   Using Eq. (1),

$$50 = 20 + (n - 1)1$$

Solving this equation for n, we obtain $n = 31$.   Therefore

$$S = \frac{1}{2} n(a + l) = \frac{1}{2} \times 31(20 + 50) = \frac{1}{2} \times 31 \times 70 = 1085 \text{ logs}$$

Example 2   Prove that the sum of the first n odd integers is equal to n^2.†
Solution   The odd integers form the A.P. 1, 3, 5, . . . , to n terms.   Hence $a = 1$, $d = 2$, and $n = n$.   Substituting these values in Eq. (4) gives

$$S = \frac{1}{2} n[2 + (n - 1)2] = \frac{1}{2} n(2 + 2n - 2) = \frac{1}{2} n(2n) = n^2$$

4   THE SUM OF THE TERMS OF A G.P.

Let S stand for the sum of the n terms of a G.P. whose first term is a and whose common ratio is r.   Then

$$S = a + ar + ar^2 + \cdots + ar^{n-1}$$

where the dots stand for the terms omitted, if any.   If we multiply both sides of this equation by $-r$, we get

$$-rS = -ar - ar^2 - \cdots - ar^{n-1} - ar^n$$

The first sum contains terms with every power of r from 1 to $n - 1$, and the second contains terms with every power of r from 1 to n.   Consequently, if the two sums are added, all terms containing powers of r from 1 to $n - 1$ will cancel out and the result will be

$$S - rS = a - ar^n \qquad \text{or} \qquad S(1 - r) = a - ar^n$$

Dividing both sides by $1 - r$, we obtain the formula for the sum

$$S = \frac{a - ar^n}{1 - r} \qquad \text{or} \qquad S = \frac{ar^n - a}{r - 1} \tag{5}$$

An alternate formula for the sum can be obtained as follows: multiply both sides of the equation $l = ar^{n-1}$ by r.   This gives

$$rl = ar^n$$

† This property of the odd integers is used in the standard method of finding the square root of a number on a computing machine.

Substituting rl in Eq. (5) for ar^n gives

$$S = \frac{a - rl}{1 - r} \quad \text{or} \quad S = \frac{rl - a}{r - 1} \tag{6}$$

Example 1 If a person were offered a job paying 1 cent the first day, 2 cents the second day, 4 cents the third day, etc., each day's salary being double that for the preceding day, how much would he receive for a 30-day month?

Solution The sequence of daily wages forms the progression 0.01, 0.02, 0.04, 0.08, $\cdots$, to 30 terms. This is a G.P. with $a = 0.01$, $r = 2$, and $n = 30$. The total 30-day salary will be the sum of these terms. Substituting in Eq. (5) gives

$$S = \frac{0.01(2)^{30} - 0.01}{2 - 1}$$

To compute 2^{30}, we note that $2^5 = 32$. Then

$$2^{10} = 2^5 \times 2^5 = 32 \times 32 = 1024$$

Also $2^{30} = 2^{10} \times 2^{10} \times 2^{10} = 1024 \times 1024 \times 1024 = 1,073,741,824$. Therefore

$$S = \frac{10,737,418.24 - 0.01}{1} = \$10,737,418.23$$

Example 2 Find the sum of the progression 240, 240(1.025), 240(1.025)^2, $\ldots$, 240(1.025)^{50}.

Solution This is a G.P. with $a = 240$, $r = 1.025$, and

$$l = 240(1.025)^{50}$$

Using Eq. (6),

$$S = \frac{rl - a}{r - 1} = \frac{(1.025)240(1.025)^{50} - 240}{1.025 - 1} = \frac{240(1.025)^{51} - 240}{0.025}$$

A part of the computation can be done with the aid of logarithms. Let $x = 240(1.025)^{51}$. Then

$$\log x = \log 240 + 51 \log 1.025$$
$$= 2.380211 + 51 \times 0.010724 = 2.927135$$

and $x = 845.541$. We now substitute 845.541 for 240(1.025)^{51} in the formula for S and get

$$S = \frac{845.541 - 240}{0.025} = \frac{605.541}{0.025} = 24,221.6$$

EXERCISE 2

Find the sums of the following progressions:

1. 100, 40, 16, $\ldots$, to 10 terms.
2. 1, 3, 9, $\ldots$, to 7 terms.
3. 20, $18\frac{1}{2}$, 17, $\ldots$, 2.
4. 3, 0.9, 0.27, $\ldots$, 0.0243.
5. 1000, 1100, 1210, $\ldots$, 1610.51.

6. 55, 57, 59, . . . , 173.

7. 130, 160, 190, . . . to 20 terms.

8. 16.1, 48.3, 80.5, . . . to 10 terms.

9. A ball rolling down an inclined plane rolls 2 ft the first second, 6 ft the second second, 10 ft the third second, etc. Find the total distance it will roll in 15 sec.

10. In a potato race, 10 potatoes and a basket are placed in a line. The potatoes are 15 ft apart, and the basket is 25 ft from the first potato. A runner starting at the basket must get each potato and return with it to the basket, making a complete round trip for each potato. Find the total distance traveled.

11. Find the total number of ancestors a person has in the 10 generations preceding him, assuming there are no duplicates.

12. Find the sum of the progression 75, 75(1.02), 75(1.02)^2, . . . , to 60 terms.

13. There are 50 members present at a fraternity convention. If each member shakes hands with each other member just once, how many handshakes are there in all?

14. A rubber ball falls from 729 ft above the ground. If it always bounces back two-thirds of the height from which it falls, find the total distance it has traveled when it hits the ground for the eighth time.

15. Seventy-five tickets, numbered from 1 to 75, are sold for a turkey raffle. The tickets are sold by a punchboard method, the even tickets being free and the odd-numbered tickets costing the same number of cents as the number of the ticket. How much money is collected?

16. A man donates a dime to a certain charity and writes five letters to friends asking each to donate a dime and write five letters to friends making the same request. Assuming that everyone cooperates and that there are no duplicates, how much money will be collected by 10 sets of letters?

17. Each stroke of a vacuum pump extracts 4% of the air in a container. What (decimal) fraction of the original air remains after 55 strokes?

18. A man received $2000 the first year, an annual increase of $100, and $5000 for the last year. Find the total amount that he received.

5 THE SUM OF A G.P. TO INFINITY

Consider the sum of the terms of the G.P. $\frac{1}{2}$, $\frac{1}{4}$, $\frac{1}{8}$, $\frac{1}{16}$, . . . , $(\frac{1}{2})^n$. The sum of the first three terms is $\frac{7}{8}$; the sum of the first four terms is $\frac{15}{16}$; and the sum of the first five terms is $\frac{31}{32}$. In each case, the result is a fraction with its numerator one less than its denominator. The sum of the first n terms is, by Eq. (5) or (6)

$$S = \frac{\frac{1}{2} - \frac{1}{2}(\frac{1}{2})^n}{1 - \frac{1}{2}} = 1 - \left(\frac{1}{2}\right)^n = \frac{2^n - 1}{2^n}$$

This shows that the sum is a fraction with its numerator one less than its denominator for any value of n. Now let us think of n as a large number and one that may be increased at will. Clearly the larger n is the closer S is to 1; and by taking n larger and larger, we can make S lie as close to 1 as we please. An example will help clarify this last statement.

Example 1 How large must n be so that the sum of the terms of the progression $\frac{1}{2}, \frac{1}{4}, \frac{1}{8}, \frac{1}{16}, \ldots, (\frac{1}{2})^n$ differs from 1 by less than 0.0001?
Solution The sum of the first n terms of this progression has just been written in several forms, one of which was

$$S = 1 - \left(\frac{1}{2}\right)^n$$

Since this shows that S is always less than 1, our problem requires that $1 - S < 0.0001$ This condition requires that

$$\left(\frac{1}{2}\right)^n < 0.0001$$

Taking logarithms of both sides gives

$$n(\log 1 - \log 2) < \log 0.0001$$
$$n(0 - 0.301030) < -4$$

Consequently $n > 4/0.30103 = 14^-$. Thus, the sum of the progression $\frac{1}{2}, \frac{1}{4}, \frac{1}{8}$, $\ldots, (\frac{1}{2})^{14}$ differs from 1 by less than 0.0001.

Whenever it is possible by taking n sufficiently large to make the sum of a progression of n terms lie as near as we please to some fixed value, we say that the sum of the progression "to infinity" is the given fixed value. In the case just considered, we say that the sum of the progression $\frac{1}{2}, \frac{1}{4}, \frac{1}{8}, \frac{1}{16}, \ldots$, to infinity is 1.

It should be clearly understood that all progressions cannot be summed to infinity. For example, the sum of the progression 1, 2, 4, 8, 16, . . . , does not approach a fixed value as the number of terms increases. For this progression, the sum can be made as large as you please by taking sufficiently many terms.

Theorem *Whenever the ratio of a geometric progression, whether positive or negative, is numerically less than* 1, *the progression can be summed to infinity, and the sum is*

$$S = \frac{a}{1 - r} \tag{7}$$

An A.P. can never be summed to infinity unless $a = 0$ and $d = 0$.

The proof follows from the fact that if r is numerically less than 1, then $r^2, r^3, \ldots, r^n$ form a sequence of numbers that decrease in numerical value; and by taking n sufficiently large, r^n can be made as small as we please. Consequently, the formula for S:

$$S = \frac{a - ar^n}{1 - r} = \frac{a}{1 - r}(1 - r^n)$$

can be made as close to $a/(1 - r)$ as we please by choosing n sufficiently large.

Example 2 Find the sum to infinity of the G.P. 100, 40, 16, ...
Solution For this G.P., $a = 100$ and $r = \frac{2}{5}$. Using Eq. (7), we have

$$S = \frac{100}{1 - \frac{2}{5}} = \frac{100}{\frac{3}{5}} = 166\frac{2}{3}$$

Example 3 Change the following decimal fraction to a proper fraction, 0.1363636
. . . repeating to infinity.
Solution Any decimal fraction that repeats a set of numbers can be written as a
sum that includes the terms of a G.P. Here we may write

$$f = 0.1363636 \cdots = 0.1 + 0.036 + 0.00036 + 0.0000036 + \cdots$$

or

$$f = \frac{1}{10} + S \qquad \text{where} \qquad S = 0.036 + 0.036(0.01) + 0.036(0.01)^2 + \cdots$$

S is the sum to infinity of a G.P. whose first term is 0.036 and whose common ratio
is 0.01. By Eq. (7)

$$S = \frac{0.036}{1 - 0.01} = \frac{0.036}{0.99} = \frac{2}{55}$$

Therefore

$$f = \frac{1}{10} + \frac{2}{55} = \frac{11 + 4}{110} = \frac{3}{22}$$

Check. By long division, $\frac{3}{22} = 0.1363636$ . . . .

EXERCISE 3

Find the sum to infinity of the following G.P.'s:

1. 8, 4, 2, 1, ...
2. $\frac{1}{2}$, $\frac{1}{3}$, $\frac{2}{9}$, $\frac{4}{27}$, ...
3. 7, 0.7, 0.07, 0.007, ...
4. 1, $-\frac{1}{2}$, $\frac{1}{4}$, $-\frac{1}{8}$, ...
5. $8\frac{1}{3}$, 5, 3, $1\frac{4}{5}$, ...
6. 1, $(1.01)^{-1}$, $(1.01)^{-2}$, ...

Change to a proper fraction or mixed number:

7. 0.33333 . . . .
8. 0.066666 . . . .
9. 1.133333 . . . .
10. 0.454545 . . . .
11. 2.2272727 . . . .
12. 0.342342342 . . . .

13. A rubber ball always rebounds one-third of the height from which it is dropped.
If it is first dropped from a height of 30 ft, find the total distance it travels before
coming to rest.

14. A man can walk halfway home in 10 min, half of the remaining distance in 5 min,
half of the remaining distance in $2\frac{1}{2}$ min, etc. How long does it take him to walk the
entire distance?

15. Find the sum to infinity of 1, $(1 + i)^{-1}$, $(1 + i)^{-2}$, . . . , where i is any positive
number.

Review Exercises

1. $2190 is loaned out on June 15 and is repaid on Aug. 27. How much interest is due if the rate is 5% and (a) exact interest for the exact time is charged, (b) the bankers' rule is used?

2. A debt of $5000 will be repaid, principal and interest at 8%, $m = 4$, by payments of $300 at the end of each quarter for as long as necessary. Find the number of payments and the final partial payment, and construct the first two lines of the appropriate schedule.

3. A $1000 bond pays $30 bond interest on each Jan. 15 and July 15. It will be redeemed at 110% on Jan. 15, 1990. The market quotation on Jan. 15, 1970, is 120. Find the yield rate by interpolation if purchased on this date.

4. In payment for a certain lot, Mr. Smith promises to make a series of quarterly payments of $100 each, the first one due at the end of 2 years and the last one due at the end of 5 years. If money is worth 6%, $m = 4$, what is the cash value of the lot?

5. $1000 is due at the end of 5 years, and $2000 is due at the end of 10 years. If money is worth 6%, $m = 2$, (a) find the equivalent single payment due at the end of 7 years; (b) write an equation of equivalence, but do not solve it, that will determine two equal payments due at the ends of 6 and 8 years.

6. (a) What nominal rate, $m = 2$, is equivalent to 6%, $m = 12$? (b) What nominal rate, $m = 4$, is equivalent to 8%, $m = 2$?

7. Discount $2325 for 6 years 8 months at 2.4%, $m = 12$.

8. A contract calls for payments of $500 at the end of each year for 10 years followed by yearly payments of $1000 for the next 5 years. What is the cash value of this contract if money is worth 4% effective?

9. A machine worth $8000 will last 10 years and have a salvage value of $500. Find the first year's depreciation charge by the constant-percentage method.

10. A certain improvement will cause the machine in Prob. 9 to last 5 years longer, with a final salvage value of zero. If money is worth 5% effective, how much is the improvement worth?

11. A bill demands the payment of $500 in 90 days or 2% off for cash. If a man borrows the money to pay cash, (a) what is the highest simple-interest rate that he can afford to pay? (b) What is the highest "interest-in-advance" rate that he can afford to pay?

12. What yearly payments on a debt of $1000 will reduce it to $100 in 5 years if money is worth 5% effective?

13. A man agrees to settle a debt by making payments of $50 at the end of each quarter for 7 years. He fails to make any of these payments for the first 3 years, at which time he wishes to liquidate the entire obligation with a single payment. If money is worth 6%, $m = 4$, what should this payment be?

14. A note maturing for $450 in 120 days is sold to the City National Bank at 8% bank discount 90 days before it is due. This bank sells the note 30 days later to a Federal Reserve Bank that discounts notes at 6% bank discount. Find the profit made by the City National Bank and the rate at which its money earned interest on this investment.

15. Discount $10,000 for 4 years 9 months at $j_1 = 8\%$ (a) by the approximate method and (b) by the exact method, omitting the final arithmetic computation.

16. A man buys a car worth $4000. If he gets $800 credit for his old car, what additional cash payment will be necessary so that the balance can be liquidated by payments of $100 at the end of each month for 30 months? The interest rate is 6%, $m = 12$.

17. A woman purchased a washing machine by making a cash payment of $30 and promising to pay $25 at the end of each quarter for the next 2 years. She made the first two payments when due. On the date that the third payment is due, what single payment will cancel the contract if interest is computed at $j_4 = 5\%$?

18. (a) An interest charge of $20 is made for the use of $1000 for 4 months. What is the simple-interest rate? (b) How many days will it take $600 to earn $4 ordinary simple interest if the rate is 5%?

19. A city wishes to borrow $100,000 for 20 years. It can borrow the money from one source at 7%, $m = 2$, and repay the loan, principal and interest, by equal semiannual payments. From another source, it can borrow the money at 5½%, $m = 2$, if it pays the interest when due and returns the principal in a lump sum at the end of 20 years. If a sinking fund is available at 2½%, $m = 2$, how much can be saved semiannually by choosing the better plan?

20. Accumulate $2375.50 for 10½ years at 6.2%, $m = 4$.

21. A $1000 5% bond with semiannual interest payments will be redeemed at 110% in 10 years. Find the purchase price to yield 4%, $m = 2$, and construct the first two lines of the proper investment schedule.

22. A wealthy church member wishes to give his church an endowment that will be sufficient to paint the church every 5 years at a cost of $1000 and also to replace lost hymnals every year at a cost of $100. If both services are needed immediately and 3%, $m = 1$, investments are available, what sum of money will be required?

23. A suite of furniture can be purchased for $270 cash or $60 down and $20 per month for a year. At what nominal rate, $m = 12$, are these two options equivalent?

24. A machine worth $1200 depreciates 12½% of its value each year. Make out a schedule showing the depreciation for the first 2 years. What is the book value at the end of 20 years?

25. On his son's fifth birthday, a man wishes to deposit with a trust company a sum sufficient to provide the boy with regular monthly payments of $100 for 4 years, the first one coming 1 month after his sixteenth birthday. If money is worth 6%, $m = 12$, what should this sum be?

26. Mr. Jones has two notes outstanding. One of them matures in 3 months for $900 plus simple interest at 5% for 10 months, and the other matures at the end of 6 months for $1000. He will pay $500 today and $500 more at the end of 3 months. If money is worth $j_4 = 5\frac{1}{2}\%$, what equal payments at the ends of 9 and 12 months would liquidate the remaining debt?

27. A debt is to be retired by monthly payments of $50, the first to be made at the end of 2½ years and the last at the end of 6 years. How large is the debt if the interest rate is 5% converted monthly?

28. Mr. Jones sold the following note on Feb. 8, 1967, to a bank that charged $7\frac{1}{2}\%$ bank discount:

December 5, 1966

One year after date I promise to pay to Mr. A. B. Jones or order the sum of \$800 and simple interest at 5% per year.

(Signed) *Mr. C. D. Smith*

Find (*a*) the proceeds, (*b*) the interest rate realized by the bank on this investment.

29. Mr. Smith desires \$1500 as the proceeds of an 8-month loan. How much will he pay back if the bank uses a (*a*) 6% discount rate, (*b*) $6\frac{1}{4}\%$ simple interest rate?

30. \$1000 is borrowed at 6%, $m = 2$. It will be amortized by semiannual payments of \$50 for as long as necessary. (*a*) How many full \$50 payments will be required? (*b*) What is the outstanding principal just after the last full payment? (*c*) What final payment, made one period after the last full payment, will be required?

31. How long will it take \$1250 to amount to \$1750 if the interest rate is $j_2 = 5\frac{1}{2}\%$? Use logarithms.

32. What nominal rate j_4 will cause \$1234.50 to amount to \$5432.10 in 25 years? Use logarithms.

33. The amount of an ordinary annuity payable monthly for 10 years is \$10,000. Find the present value if the interest rate is 5%, $m = 12$.

34. A owes B \$1000 due at the end of 5 years and \$2000 due at the end of 10 years. What equal payments at the end of each year for 8 years would B be willing to accept if money is worth $4\frac{1}{2}\%$ effective?

35. A signal system for University Hall would cost \$1000 now and require overhauling every 5 years at a cost of \$200. In addition, \$50 would be needed at the end of each year for maintenance. What sum of money would be required to endow such a system if it can be invested at 4% effective?

36. A sinking fund is being accumulated at $4\frac{1}{2}\%$, $m = 2$, to pay off a debt of \$15,000 due in 12 years. How much is in the fund at the end of 7 years?

37. A staunch Democrat wishes to contribute \$1000 to the presidential campaign every 4 years perpetually. Money is worth 4% effective. How much is needed if the first contribution is needed (*a*) in 4 years, (*b*) immediately, (*c*) in 2 years?

38. A contract calls for payments of \$1000 at the end of each quarter. (*a*) What yearly payments are equivalent at 8%, $m = 1$? (*b*) What semiannual payments are equivalent at 7%, $m = 4$?

39. Just before Christmas a finance company advertises, "Borrow \$100 for a total cost of only \$5. You repay the loan in seven easy monthly installments of \$15 each, the first one due 1 month after the loan." What interest rate j_{12} does this finance company realize?

40. A debt with interest at $j_4 = 6\%$ is to be amortized by payments of \$1000 at the end of each quarter for 5 years. What regular quarterly payments would it take to liquidate this debt if payments are to continue for 8 years?

41. \$1460 is borrowed on Sept. 10 and repaid on Nov. 21. How much interest is due if the rate is 5% and (*a*) the bankers' rule is used, (*b*) exact interest for the exact time is used?

42. A farm is worth $12,000 cash. It is purchased by paying $2000 down and the balance in quarterly installments for 15 years. What will these payments be (a) if the interest rate is 7%, $m = 4$, (b) if the interest rate is 7% effective?

43. A stove can be purchased by making 10 monthly payments of $10 each, the first one due on the date of sale. What is the equivalent cash price if money is worth 7%, $m = 12$?

44. A $1000 bond, paying $25 bond interest every Jan. 1 and July 1, will be redeemed at par on July 1, 1985. On Aug. 16, 1968, the owner offers the bond for sale at a price that will yield the purchaser 3%, $m = 2$. Find the flat price and the market quotation.

45. Jones has $1000 in a savings bank that credits interest at $j_4 = 3\%$. If he deposits $25 at the end of each quarter for the next 5 years, how much will he have if no withdrawals are made?

46. A contract calls for the payment of $100 at the end of each year for 10 years and an additional payment of $1000 1 year later. If money is worth $3\frac{1}{2}\%$ effective, what is the cash value of this contract?

47. For discounting notes the First National Bank uses an 8% bank discount rate while the Second National Bank uses an 8.1% simple-interest rate. On a note maturing for $1000 in 6 months, how much can the seller save by choosing the proper bank?

48. Mr. Green owes Mr. Brown $1000 due now. Brown agrees to accept as payment of this debt a noninterest-bearing note for 60 days, which can be discounted immediately at the Second National Bank for $1000. If the bank charges $7\frac{1}{2}\%$ bank discount, what should the face of the note be?

49. A man receives two offers for a certain piece of real estate: (a) $3000 cash and $1500 at the end of each year for 2 years and (b) $3025 cash and $1000 at the end of each year for 3 years. Which offer is better if money is worth 5% effective?

50. A $10,000 5% serial bond, with semiannual bond interest payments, will be redeemed as follows: $2000 at the end of 5 years, $3000 at the end of 10 years, and $5000 at the end of 20 years. What is the purchase price to yield 4%, $m = 2$?

★51. A man desires to accumulate $5000 at the end of 8 years by making semiannual deposits in a bank that pays 4%, $m = 2$. (a) What deposits must he make? (b) If at the end of 3 years the bank changes its interest rate to 3%, $m = 2$, how much will he have to increase his deposits?

52. Mr. and Mrs. Newlywed plan to take a trip around the world on their tenth anniversary. For this purpose, they will make equal deposits at the end of each month in a savings fund that earns 3%, $m = 1$. How much should these monthly deposits be if the proposed trip will cost $5000?

53. A debt of $1000 with interest at $j_2 = 4\%$ will be liquidated by semiannual payments of $50 for as long as necessary. Find the outstanding principal at the end of 10 years. Construct a schedule for the first year.

54. If money is worth 4%, $m = 1$, what would it cost to endow a university to provide for a scholarship (a) of $500 per year, (b) of $100 per quarter for four quarters per year, the payments in either case to start immediately?

55. A house worth $15,000 cash can be purchased by making an adequate down payment, followed by equal monthly payments for the next 20 years. What down payment will be required if the interest rate is $j_1 = 4\frac{1}{2}\%$ and the monthly payments are $80 each?

56. A machine costs $10,000, will last 12 years, and will have a salvage value at that time of $2000. Find (a) the constant rate of depreciation, (b) the capitalized cost of the machine at $j_2 = 3\%$.

57. A $500 bond, redeemable at par, pays bond interest annually at 6%. It is quoted at 116 on the market 33 years before maturity. Find the yield rate.

58. A contract calls for payments of $500 at the end of each quarter for 5 years. (a) What monthly payments are equivalent if the interest rate is 4%, $m = 4$? (b) What yearly payments are equivalent if the interest rate is 5%, $m = 1$?

★59. $1000 is due at the end of 3 years, $2000 is due at the end of 5 years, and $5000 is due at the end of 10 years. If money is worth 5%, $m = 2$, find the average due date (or equated time) (a) by the approximate method, (b) by an equation of equivalence and interpolation.

60. Mr. Smith has been depositing $25 at the end of each quarter for the past 10 years. He now has $1300 to his credit. At what rate j_1 did his money earn interest?

61. Find the nominal rate j_{12} at which $3512 will amount to $5994 in 10 years.

62. A $1000 7% bond, paying bond interest on June 20 and Dec. 20, will be redeemed at 110% on Dec. 20, 1990. What is the purchase price on Dec. 20, 1968, to yield $j_2 = 5\%$? What is the book value of this bond on Mar. 20, 1969?

63. What annual deposits into a sinking fund accumulating at $j_1 = 5\%$ would be necessary to furnish $5000 at the end of 3 years? Make out the complete schedule showing the growth of the fund.

64. Discount $10,000 for 5 years 3 months at 4% effective using the bankers' approximate method. Write an equation that will give the exact present value of this sum, but do not evaluate it.

65. (a) What nominal rate j_4 is equivalent to 6%, $m = 1$? (b) What nominal rate j_2 is equivalent to 7%, $m = 12$?

66. $5000 can be borrowed from either of two sources. Bank A charges $5\frac{1}{2}\%$, $m = 2$, and will allow the debt to be amortized by semiannual payments for the next 10 years. Bank B charges interest at the rate 5%, $m = 2$, but requires that only the interest be paid when due and the entire principal be returned in one lump sum at the end of 10 years. If bank B is used, a sinking fund will be established to repay the principal at the end of the term. What is the lowest acceptable rate for the sinking fund?

67. A contract calls for semiannual payments of $100 each, the first one due on July 1, 1970, and the last one due on July 1, 1980. If money is worth 5%, $m = 2$, find the value of this contract (a) on July 1, 1970, (b) on Jan. 1, 1970, (c) on Jan. 1, 1968.

68. A debt of $6000 with compound interest from today at $j_4 = 5\%$ is due at the end of 3 years. If $3000 is paid at the end of 1 year, how much will it take to liquidate the debt at the end of the third year? Money is worth $j_1 = 4\frac{1}{2}\%$ for the equivalence.

69. A company will need $10,000 at the end of 12 years to retire a debt falling due at that time. This sum will be accumulated by quarterly deposits into a fund that earns 4%, $m = 4$. Find the size of the payments, and construct the first three lines of the appropriate schedule.

70. A debt of $1000 will be amortized by monthly payments of $50 for as long as necessary. If the interest rate is $j_{12} = 6\%$, (a) find the number of payments required, (b) find the final partial payment, (c) construct the first three lines of the amortization schedule.

71. A contract calls for payments of $500 at the end of each 6 months for 10 years. If the interest rate is $j_2 = 7\%$, (a) what yearly payments would be equally satisfactory? (b) What would the equivalent monthly payments be?

72. A $1000 6% bond with semiannual bond interest payments will mature at par in 15 years. Find the purchase price to yield 4%, $m = 2$, and construct the first three lines of an appropriate bond schedule.

73. Solve Prob. 72 if the yield rate is 8%, $m = 2$.

74. (a) Solve the following equation for X:

$$X(1.03)^{-4} = 100a_{\overline{5}|3\%} + 1000(1.03)^{-6}$$

(b) Make up a problem for which this equation gives the answer.

75. A machine costing $8000 will last 10 years and have a final salvage value of $750. Find the first year's depreciation charge by the constant-percentage method.

76. A certain improvement will extend the life of the machine in Prob. 75 an additional 5 years but reduce its salvage value to zero. If the interest rate is 4% effective, how much is the improvement worth?

77. Show that amortizing a $1000 debt at 5%, $m = 1$, by equal annual payments for 10 years costs the same as paying interest annually at 5% and retiring the principal at the end of 10 years by means of a 5% sinking fund.

78. Make out an amortization and a sinking-fund schedule for the first 2 years for Prob. 77.

79. Mr. Smith has formerly purchased a make of car that sells for $5500, driven them for 5 years, then traded them in for $2500 on a new one. He wishes to buy cheaper cars more often. Ignoring operational costs, what priced car should he choose if he intends to trade every 3 years? Money is worth 5% effective and the trade-in value of the used car is 30% of its original cost.

80. A woman buys a piano worth $625. She pays $125 cash and will pay the balance in two equal installments at the ends of 6 months and 1 year. What will these payments be if money is worth $j_4 = 6\%$?

81. A contract requires payments of $1000 at the end of each year for 12 years. If the interest rate is $5\frac{1}{2}\%$, $m = 2$, what equivalent payments could be made (a) at the end of each 6 months, (b) at the beginning of each year?

82. A piece of furniture is listed at $100. If cash is paid, a 15% discount is allowed. If the furniture is purchased on the installment plan, a $20 down payment is required, followed by eight monthly payments of $10 each. What effective interest rate does the installment plan contain?

83. A car worth $4000 will depreciate to $1000 in 4 years. (a) Find the first year's depreciation charge by the straight-line method, the sinking-fund method at 4%, the sum-of-the-integers method. (b) Construct the complete schedule for the straight-line method and the sum-of-the-integers method.

84. A house worth $20,000 is purchased by paying $2000 down and agreeing to pay $100 at the end of each month for as long as necessary. If the interest rate is $j_1 = 4\frac{1}{2}\%$, find how many monthly payments will be required.

85. The H-S Real Estate Co. sells lots on time using its own "5% plan," which works as follows: On a $1000 lot, 5% is immediately added, giving $1050. A down payment of 20% of this, or $210, is required. The balance, $840, is then divided into 12 easy monthly payments of $70 each. What effective interest rate does the company realize on this plan?

★86. A contract calls for the payment of $1000 at the end of each year for the next 3 years. If money is worth $j_1 = 6\%$, on what date would $3000 be equivalent? Use logarithms to solve for the time.

87. $10,000 is to be discounted for $5\frac{1}{2}$ years at $j_1 = 8\%$. How much difference is there in the answers obtained by the exact method and the practical method?

★88. Mr. I. M. Wealthy wishes to will his favorite charity an annual income of $1000 perpetually. He realizes, however, that $1000 buys less year after year due to uncontrollable inflation. Hence he decides to endow this charity with a fund that will furnish it with $1000 at the end of the first year; $1100 the second year; $1200 the third year; etc.—each year's payment to be $100 more than the preceding year. How large an endowment fund is necessary if it can be invested at 4% effective?

★89. At his son's birth, Mr. Jones decides to guarantee that his son will have sufficient funds for a college education. He decides that his son will enroll in college on his eighteenth birthday and will need $200 on that date followed by 11 monthly payments of $100. On his nineteenth birthday, he will require $250 followed by 11 monthly payments of $150. On his twentieth birthday he will need $300 followed by 11 monthly payments of $200. And on his twenty-first birthday, he will need $350 followed by 11 monthly payments of $250. If investments are available at $j_1 = 5\%$, how much should Mr. Jones invest on the day of his son's birth to provide for these payments?

★90. What interest rate j_{12} is equivalent to 6% converted continuously?

91. Construct depreciation schedules that reduce the value of an asset from $1000 to $300 in 4 years by the straight-line method and the sum-of-the-integers method.

★92. What interest rate j_4 is equivalent to $j_2 = 4.3\%$? Use logarithms for solving this problem.

★93. What single payment, due at the end of the year, is equivalent to monthly payments of $100 each if 6% simple interest is used to establish the equivalence?

★94. A bank makes loans on personal property up to $1000 on the following conditions: $6 payable in advance is charged for each $100 loan, and the principal is repaid in 10 monthly payments of $10 each (for each $100 loan), the first payment due 1 month after the date of the loan. (a) What effective rate of interest does this bank realize on loans of this type? (b) If the payment in advance is eliminated, what should the monthly payments be in order to amortize the loan with the same profit to the bank?

★95. Two $1000 bonds, redeemable at par on the same date, are purchased to yield 3%, $m = 2$. One of them pays bond interest at the rate $j_2 = 4\%$, and the other pays bond interest at the rate $j_2 = 2\%$. One of the bonds cost $1126.34; what did the other one cost?

★96. On June 1, 1950, Mr. Smith had $1000 in a bank that credits interest at 3% effective. At the end of each year thereafter, he deposited $500 except on June 1, 1962, when he withdrew $1000 instead of making a deposit. How much is in his fund on June 1, 1970, just after his regular deposit?

★97. A man owes $2000, due in 2 years, upon which he has agreed to pay interest, when due, at $j_2 = 6\%$. He has another debt of $1000, due at the end of 3 years, upon which he has agreed to pay interest, when due, at $j_4 = 4\%$. What sum of money should he invest at $j_{12} = 3\%$ to provide for the liquidation of both these obligations?

★98. $10,000 is borrowed at 5% effective. It is to be repaid by 15 annual installments, the first one due at the end of 5 years. The first five payments are to be one-half as large as the remaining 10 payments. How large should these payments be?

★**99.** (*a*) In order to accumulate $5000 at the end of 10 years, what annual deposits should be made into a fund that credits interest at 4% effective? (*b*) If at the end of 4 years the interest rate is changed to 3% effective and the same sized deposits are continued, how much will be in the fund at the end of 8 years?

★**100.** A man deposits $100 at the end of each quarter for 20 years in a savings fund that pays 4%, $m = 4$. He then starts withdrawing $500 each quarter. How many withdrawals can he make and what will the final partial withdrawal be?

TESTS AND EXAMINATIONS

For obvious reasons we feel that each instructor should make out his own tests and final examinations and should change these constantly. However, for the benefit of teachers who have had little experience in teaching this course, and for the benefit of students in reviewing the course, we list various combinations of problems taken from this list of review problems that we consider adequate tests for the different chapters and final examinations for the course. These are listed in tests of varying lengths to allow the individual instructor as much leeway as possible. We suggest that five 1-hr tests, or their equivalent, be given during the term, followed by a 2- or 3-hr final.

Test 1   Simple interest, ½ hr: 1, 18, 28.
Test 2   Simple interest, 1 hr: 28, 41, 47, 48.
Test 3   Compound interest, 1 hr: 6, 15, 20, 31, 32, work four.
Test 4   Equations of equivalence, ½ hr: 5, 68, 80.
Test 5   Equations of equivalence, 1 hr: 5, 26, 68, 80.
Test 6   Simple annuities, 1 hr: 4, 16, 17, 23, 33, work four.
Test 7   Simple annuities, 1 hr: 27, 39, 43, 46, 67, work four.
Test 8   General annuities, ½ hr: 55, 58.
Test 9   General annuities, 1 hr: 38, 52, 60, 84.
Test 10   Perpetuities, ½ hr: 22, 79.
Test 11   Perpetuities, 1 hr: 35, 37 (*a*) and (*b*), 54, 76.
Test 12   Amortization and sinking funds, ½ hr: 30, 69.
Test 13   Amortization and sinking funds, 1 hr: 30, 53, 63, 66.
Test 14   Bonds, 1 hr: 3, 21, 44, 50.
Test 15   Depreciation, 1 hr: 9, 24, 83.

Examination 1   Three hr: 7, 8, 22, 23, 28, 34, 52, 53, 62, 75, 76, work ten.
Examination 2   Three hr: 11, 12, 16, 24, 30, 39, 40, 54, 57, 77, 78, work ten.
Examination 3   Two hr: Omit Prob. 34 in Examination 1 and work 8 of the remaining 10.
Examination 4   Two hr: Omit Prob. 12 in Examination 2 and work 8 of the remaining 10.

Answers to Odd-numbered Problems

Exercise 1

1. (a) $\frac{1}{25}$, 0.04; (b) $\frac{9}{400}$, 0.0225; (c) $\frac{4}{125}$, 0.032; (d) $\frac{1}{30}$, 0.0333; (e) $\frac{1}{125}$, 0.008; (f) $\frac{1}{600}$, 0.0017. **3.** (a) $\frac{103}{100}$, 1.03; (b) $\frac{241}{240}$, 1.0042; (c) $\frac{83}{80}$, 1.0375; (d) $\frac{376}{375}$, 1.0027; (e) $\frac{503}{500}$, 1.006. **5.** \$7792.21. **7.** \$7, \$607.
9. \$291.67, \$50,291.67. **11.** 6%. **13.** 8.16%. **15.** \$400. **17.** \$4000.

Exercise 2

1. \$11.25. **3.** \$0.50. **5.** \$34.38. **7.** \$3.56, \$3.61. **9.** \$36.16, \$36.67.
11. \$15.80, \$16.02.

Exercise 3

1. 182 days, 178 days. **3.** 218 days, 215 days. **5.** \$7.50, \$7.61. **7.** \$4.08, \$484.08.
9. $5\frac{11}{14}$%. **11.** \$1250. **13.** \$2750.

Exercise 4

1. \$17, \$1683. **3.** \$2.33, \$317.67. **5.** 5%, 5.04%. **7.** \$3415.98, \$15.98, 6.09%.
9. \$6082.50, \$6052.09. **11.** $16\frac{2}{3}$%, 16%. **13.** \$979.38. **15.** \$740.74.
17. Same, \$1152. **19.** \$6.67, 10.24%.

Exercise 5

1. \$1418.52. **3.** \$3162.05. **5.** \$2495.08. **7.** \$25,004.64. **9.** 5.175020.
11. 2.222582. **13.** 1.210745. **15.** 1.105061. **17.** 1.1235. **19.** 1.2709.
21. \$1797.48. **23.** \$1438.37. **25.** \$563.64. **27.** \$50.01. **29.** 0.0004.

Exercise 6

1. \$176.22. **3.** \$564.21. **5.** \$6622.56. **7.** \$8501.88. **9.** 0.22397. **11.** 0.02273.
13. \$417.11. **15.** \$779.93. **17.** \$925.51. **19.** 0.97049. **21.** \$579.12.
23. \$482.29. **25.** \$1.00.

Exercise 7

1. 6.09%. **3.** 7.23%. **5.** 3.53%. **7.** 4.58%. **9.** 6.17%. **11.** 4.91%. **13.** 5.43%.
15. 4.41%. **17.** 2.97%. **19.** 5.97%. **21.** 4.01%. **23.** 3.01%. **25.** 6.90%.
27. 4.59%. **29.** 5.02%.

Exercise 8

1. \$1628.00. **3.** \$6512.46. **5.** \$7220.15. **7.** \$856.58. **9.** \$2937.18.
11. \$5620.64. **13.** \$1133.67. **15.** \$1727.37. **17.** \$8451.23. **19.** \$663.54.
21. \$10,805.09. **23.** \$793.59. **25.** \$7220.33. **27.** \$2937.17, \$2937.20.

Exercise 9

1. 9%. **3.** 5.96%. **5.** 4.69%. **7.** 6.68%. **9.** 11 years 10.70 months.
11. 21 years 4.23 months. **13.** 9 years 8.79 months. **15.** 8 years 9.78 months.
17. 2.90%. **19.** 4.67%. **21.** $1275.42.

Exercise 10

1. $2537.97. **3.** $1998.80. **5.** $924.56, $1216.65. **7.** $1089.78.
9. (a) $87.47, (b) $99.96. **11.** $2692.93. **13.** $2511.93. **15.** $390.20. **17.** 5.07%.

Exercise 11

1. 746.22. **3.** 813.26. **5.** $716.88. **7.** $2662.61. **9.** $796.34. **11.** $1045.79.
13. $392.39. **15.** $259.44. **17.** $4869.10. **19.** (a) 5 years 6.35 months,
   (b) 5 years 8 months. **21.** 2 years 9.97 months. **23.** 5.60%.

Exercise 12

1. $4757.54, $1960.04. **3.** $4482.98. **5.** $18,718.14. **7.** $6712.66. **9.** $61.78.
11. $10,419.47. **13.** $3646.65. **15.** Cash, $135.29 cheaper. **17.** $3204.91.

Exercise 13

1. $13,091.64, $7989.45. **3.** $57.60. **5.** $672.83. **7.** $8102.50. **9.** $5114.29.
11. $22,355. **13.** $1,067,999.36. **15.** $18,339.14. **17.** $303.08.

Exercise 15

1. $232.65. **3.** $396.93. **5.** $237.46. **7.** $21.32. **9.** $304.56. **11.** $167.06.
13. $245.36. **15.** $581.45.

Exercise 16

1. 69, $66.19. **3.** 17, $95.38. **5.** 11, $326.67. **7.** 104, $3007.30. **9.** 9, $2.49.
11. $66.19.

Exercise 17

1. 7.81%. **3.** 1.47%. **5.** 3.69%. **7.** 4.49%.

Summarizing problems

1. 18.16%. **3.** $11,622.18, $1622.18. **5.** 65 months, $181.84. **7.** $452.24.
9. 30, $248.63. **11.** $2783.94. **13.** $54.20. **15.** $1877.29.

Exercise 18

1. $66.39. **3.** $613.34. **5.** $40.53. **7.** $74.16. **9.** (a) $165.97, (b) $2037.12.
11. $68.12.

Exercise 19

1. $1615.41. **3.** $12,706.04. **5.** $3311.13. **7.** $105,878.87. **9.** $1085.12.
11. $9628.22.

Exercise 20

1. $244.56. **3.** $64.34. **5.** $357.94. **7.** $253.94. **9.** (a) $1646.21, (b) $1645.95.
11. $81.09. **13.** $5123.00.

Exercise 21

1. 7.98%. **3.** 7.14%. **5.** 3.91%. **7.** 8.67%. **9.** 46 + a partial payment.
11. 10 + a partial payment.

Exercise 22

1. $169.60.   **3.** $84.39.   **7.** $5798.47, payments = $565.28.

Exercise 23

1. $9294.18, $738.93.   **3.** $867.96.   **5.** $20.94.   **7.** $10,198.61, $4801.39.
9. $15,684.73.   **11.** $452,310.61.

Exercise 24

1. 21.26%.   **3.** 22.85%.   **5.** 17.97%.   **7.** 56.79%, 20%.   **9.** 47.25%.   **11.** 23.56%.

Exercise 25

1. Payments = $196.04.   **3.** $8723.05.   **5.** $921.36, $43,558.19.
7. $580.50, $17,074.83.   **9.** $19.46, $482.78.

Exercise 26

1. $1163.27.   **3.** $2091.16.   **5.** $683.03, second plan.
7. (a) Neither, (b) the first by $282.68.   **9.** $38.13.   **11.** 4.35%.

Exercise 27

1. 6, 6, $46.73.   **3.** 6, 3, 3, $48.09.

Exercise 28

1. (a) $70,000, (b) $70,700.   **3.** (a) $16,666.67, (b) $16,213.29.   **5.** $12,124.40.
7. $8459.75.   **9.** $7001.55.   **11.** (a) $372.69, (b) $1445.57.   **13.** $30,187.36.

Exercise 29

1. $14,747.59, $368.69.   **3.** (a) $15,227.80, (b) $152.28.   **5.** First machine saves
$30.24 annually.   **7.** $2164.74.   **9.** $4862.79.   **11.** $8277.62.   **13.** $1806.44.

Exercise 30

1. $43,239.80.   **3.** $344,707.15.   **5.** $499,070.62.

Exercise 31

1. $1163.51.   **3.** $874.49.   **5.** $1059.93.   **7.** $1098.50.   **9.** $1172.92 when not
called.   **11.** $1062.76 when not called.

Exercise 32

1. $957.88.   **3.** $1035.46.   **5.** $1022.28.   **7.** $956.23.   **9.** $4290.94.
11. $1251.57, $1067.47.

Exercise 33

1. $952.54, $906.70.   **3.** $6857.94, $6811.06.   **5.** $872.32, $860.32.   **7.** $1054.17.
9. $494.12.   **11.** $1363.19.   **13.** $1076.64.   **15.** $1165.20, $1155.29.

Exercise 34

1. 3.6%.   **3.** $j_2 = 3.7\%$.   **5.** $j_2 = 3.9\%$.   **7.** 3.59%.   **9.** $j_2 = 3.72\%$.
11. $j_2 = 3.86\%$.   **13.** (a) 3.40%, (b) 3.46%.

Exercise 35

1. $17,520.33.   **3.** 4.4%.   **5.** $10,711.68.

Exercise 36

3. (a) \$15,000, \$10,000; (b) \$12,323.34, \$12,676.66.   5. (a) \$810, (b) \$485.45.
7. (a) \$11,367.59, (b) \$28,632.41, (c) \$1095.18.

Exercise 37

1. \$563.13.   3. \$838.86.   5. 51.925%.   7. 20.63%, \$251.98.
9. \$11,447.00, \$1747.40.   11. \$837,596.

Exercise 38

1. \$232.63.   5. \$748,605.25.   7. \$46,911.87.

Exercise 39

1. \$67.33.   3. \$1561.03.   5. \$97.89.   7. 22.

Exercise 40

1. \$6902.59, \$6068.91.   3. (a) \$102.02, (b) \$102.48.   5. \$525.19.

Exercise 41

1. 13, \$10.09.   3. 6, \$14,112.38.   5. 96, \$56.45.   7. 6, 83.6%.

Exercise 42

1. \$7168.21.   3. (a) \$3,579,000, (b) \$3,596,000.   5. \$2698.07.

Miscellaneous exercises on general annuities

1. 26.28%.   3. $22\frac{1}{4}$ years.   5. 14, \$145.52.   7. \$452.73.   9. End of $21\frac{1}{2}$ years, \$1313.98.

Exercise 43

3. 3.43583.   5. 1.34521713.   7. $0.000000062 < E < 0.000000065$.

Exercise 44

1. $j_2 = 0.0475$.   3. 0.0450.   5. $j_2 = 0.047328$.   7. $j_2 = 0.0472$.

Exercise 45

1. Error in j_{12} less than 0.00003.   3. 0.000032.

Exercise 46

1. 9922.   3. 854.

Exercise 47

1. (a) \$2832.84, (b) \$1710.43.   3. \$2861.49.   5. \$412.86.

Exercise 48

1. \$881.70.   3. \$9645.47.

Exercise 49

1. \$198.32.   3. Diff = \$550.14.

Exercise 50

1. (a) \$1872.32, (b) \$4201.66.   3. \$6570.14.   5. \$2777.52.   7. \$110.69.
9. \$178.49.

Exercise 51

1. $131.32.   **3.** $28.67.   **5.** $\dfrac{M_{35} - M_{45} + D_{45}}{D_{35}} - \dfrac{M_{25} - M_{45} + D_{45}}{N_{25} - N_{40}}\,\dfrac{N_{35} - N_{40}}{D_{35}}.$

APPENDIX B

Exercise 1

1. 4.   **3.** 0.1.   **5.** 2.   **7.** $\frac{1}{2}$.

Exercise 2

1. 0.77815.   **3.** 1.30103.   **5.** 1.50515.   **7.** 2.90848.   **9.** 4.   **11.** $1 + \log n$.

Exercise 3

1. 0.094820.   **3.** 0.748188.   **5.** 0.943322.   **7.** 0.808421.   **9.** 0.497151.
11. 0.389804.   **13.** 0.971174.   **15.** 0.699031.

Exercise 4

11. 1.755875.   **13.** 8.782473 − 10.   **15.** 4.   **17.** 8.397940 − 10.   **19.** 4.513777.
21. 9.478610 − 10.

Exercise 5

11. 76.42.   **13.** 8633.40.   **15.** 0.0051.   **17.** 0.289333.   **19.** 0.01779.   **21.** 1385.45.

Exercise 6

1. 6.681.   **3.** 0.09729.   **5.** 93.75.   **7.** 0.0135.   **9.** 82.5070.   **11.** 12.7087.
13. 14.5826.   **15.** 5.28509.

Exercise 7

1. 1.19682.   **3.** 1.58555.   **5.** .0154651.   **7.** 3044.18.   **9.** 0.360370.   **11.** 0.830900.
13. 5.59737.   **15.** 1.63601.

Exercise 8

1. 34.305.   **3.** 11.366.   **5.** 18.856.   **7.** 4.988.   **9.** 5.   **11.** −2.113.

Exercise 9

1. 17.9164.   **3.** 0.532005.   **5.** 1.79096.   **7.** 24.052.   **9.** 0.0702.

APPENDIX C

Exercise 1

1. G.P., −8, −128.   **3.** G.P., 108, 162.   **5.** G.P., −108, $-32(\frac{3}{2})^{n-1}$.
7. A.P., $-\frac{5}{12}$, $-2\frac{9}{12}$.   **9.** G.P., 103.0301, 105.10100501.
11. $6\frac{3}{7}$, $6\frac{6}{7}$, $7\frac{2}{7}$, $7\frac{5}{7}$, $8\frac{1}{7}$, $8\frac{4}{7}$.   **13.** 45, 63.   **15.** −4, 4, 12, 20.   **17.** ±18.
19. ±500, 400, ±320.   **23.** $4\frac{1}{2}$.   **25.** 176.622.

Exercise 2

1. 166.649⁺.   **3.** 143.   **5.** 7715.61.   **7.** 8300.   **9.** 450 ft.   **11.** 2046.   **13.** 1225.
15. $14.44.   **17.** 0.1059.

Exercise 3

1. 16.   **3.** $7\frac{7}{9}$.   **5.** $20\frac{5}{6}$.   **7.** $\frac{1}{3}$.   **9.** $1\frac{2}{15}$.   **11.** $2\frac{5}{22}$.   **13.** 60 ft.   **15.** $\dfrac{1 + i}{i}.$

Tables

Tables 1 through 7 were computed and rigorously checked by the authors. Tables 8 through 12 were obtained by rounding off to eight decimal places the corresponding ten-place entries in Kent and Kent's "Compound Interest and Annuity Tables," published by the McGraw-Hill Book Company. Tables 13 and 14 are reproduced through the courtesy of the Society of Actuaries. Table 15 was taken from the Kent tables.

Extreme care was exercised to make this set of tables as accurate as possible, and we feel that they are as free from error as any in existence. We are indebted to the Kents for permission to use the Kent tables and to Mrs. Marion Hawley for her help in compiling these tables.

Because of current increases in interest rates, all tables have been extended to include the rates $8\frac{1}{2}\%$, 9%, $9\frac{1}{2}\%$, 10%, and $10\frac{1}{2}\%$. The computations were made in double-precision arithmetic on the University of Alabama's electronic digital computer.

CONTENTS

Table 1   The number of each day of the year*

Day of month	Jan.	Feb.	Mar.	April	May	June	July	Aug.	Sept.	Oct.	Nov.	Dec.	Day of month
1	1	32	60	91	121	152	182	213	244	274	305	335	1
2	2	33	61	92	122	153	183	214	245	275	306	336	2
3	3	34	62	93	123	154	184	215	246	276	307	337	3
4	4	35	63	94	124	155	185	216	247	277	308	338	4
5	5	36	64	95	125	156	186	217	248	278	309	339	5
6	6	37	65	96	126	157	187	218	249	279	310	340	6
7	7	38	66	97	127	158	188	219	250	280	311	341	7
8	8	39	67	98	128	159	189	220	251	281	312	342	8
9	9	40	68	99	129	160	190	221	252	282	313	343	9
10	10	41	69	100	130	161	191	222	253	283	314	344	10
11	11	42	70	101	131	162	192	223	254	284	315	345	11
12	12	43	71	102	132	163	193	224	255	285	316	346	12
13	13	44	72	103	133	164	194	225	256	286	317	347	13
14	14	45	73	104	134	165	195	226	257	287	318	348	14
15	15	46	74	105	135	166	196	227	258	288	319	349	15
16	16	47	75	106	136	167	197	228	259	289	320	350	16
17	17	48	76	107	137	168	198	229	260	290	321	351	17
18	18	49	77	108	138	169	199	230	261	291	322	352	18
19	19	50	78	109	139	170	200	231	262	292	323	353	19
20	20	51	79	110	140	171	201	232	263	293	324	354	20
21	21	52	80	111	141	172	202	233	264	294	325	355	21
22	22	53	81	112	142	173	203	234	265	295	326	356	22
23	23	54	82	113	143	174	204	235	266	296	327	357	23
24	24	55	83	114	144	175	205	236	267	297	328	358	24
25	25	56	84	115	145	176	206	237	268	298	329	359	25
26	26	57	85	116	146	177	207	238	269	299	330	360	26
27	27	58	86	117	147	178	208	239	270	300	331	361	27
28	28	59	87	118	148	179	209	240	271	301	332	362	28
29	29		88	119	149	180	210	241	272	302	333	363	29
30	30		89	120	150	181	211	242	273	303	334	364	30
31	31		90		151		212	243		304		365	31

* For leap year add 1 to the tabulated number after Feb. 28.   The number designating a leap year is divisible by 4.

Table 2

Ordinary interest on $10,000 at 1%

Days	Interest	For days below add to interest column			
		$20	$40	$60	$80
1	.2777778	73	145	217	289
2	.5555556	74	146	218	290
3	.8333333	75	147	219	291
4	1.1111111	76	148	220	292
5	1.3888889	77	149	221	293
6	1.6666667	78	150	222	294
7	1.9444444	79	151	223	295
8	2.2222222	80	152	224	296
9	2.5000000	81	153	225	297
10	2.7777778	82	154	226	298
11	3.0555556	83	155	227	299
12	3.3333333	84	156	228	300
13	3.6111111	85	157	229	301
14	3.8888889	86	158	230	302
15	4.1666667	87	159	231	303
16	4.4444444	88	160	232	304
17	4.7222222	89	161	233	305
18	5.0000000	90	162	234	306
19	5.2777778	91	163	235	307
20	5.5555556	92	164	236	308
21	5.8333333	93	165	237	309
22	6.1111111	94	166	238	310
23	6.3888889	95	167	239	311
24	6.6666667	96	168	240	312
25	6.9444444	97	169	241	313
26	7.2222222	98	170	242	314
27	7.5000000	99	171	243	315
28	7.7777778	100	172	244	316
29	8.0555556	101	173	245	317
30	8.3333333	102	174	246	318
31	8.6111111	103	175	247	319
32	8.8888889	104	176	248	320
33	9.1666667	105	177	249	321
34	9.4444444	106	178	250	322
35	9.7222222	107	179	251	323

Exact interest on $10,000 at 1%

Days	Interest	For days below add to interest column			
		$20	$40	$60	$80
1	.2739726	74	147	220	293
2	.5479452	75	148	221	294
3	.8219178	76	149	222	295
4	1.0958904	77	150	223	296
5	1.3698630	78	151	224	297
6	1.6438356	79	152	225	298
7	1.9178082	80	153	226	299
8	2.1917808	81	154	227	300
9	2.4657534	82	155	228	301
10	2.7397260	83	156	229	302
11	3.0136986	84	157	230	303
12	3.2876712	85	158	231	304
13	3.5616438	86	159	232	305
14	3.8356164	87	160	233	306
15	4.1095890	88	161	234	307
16	4.3835616	89	162	235	308
17	4.6575342	90	163	236	309
18	4.9315068	91	164	237	310
19	5.2054795	92	165	238	311
20	5.4794521	93	166	239	312
21	5.7534247	94	167	240	313
22	6.0273973	95	168	241	314
23	6.3013699	96	169	242	315
24	6.5753425	97	170	243	316
25	6.8493151	98	171	244	317
26	7.1232877	99	172	245	318
27	7.3972603	100	173	246	319
28	7.6712329	101	174	247	320
29	7.9452055	102	175	248	321
30	8.2191781	103	176	249	322
31	8.4931507	104	177	250	323
32	8.7671233	105	178	251	324
33	9.0410959	106	179	252	325
34	9.3150685	107	180	253	326
35	9.5890411	108	181	254	327

Table 2 (*Continued*)

36	10.0000000	108	180	252	324
37	10.2777778	109	181	253	325
38	10.5555556	110	182	254	326
39	10.8333333	111	183	255	327
40	11.1111111	112	184	256	328
41	11.3888889	113	185	257	329
42	11.6666667	114	186	258	330
43	11.9444444	115	187	259	331
44	12.2222222	116	188	260	332
45	12.5000000	117	189	261	333
46	12.7777778	118	190	262	334
47	13.0555556	119	191	263	335
48	13.3333333	120	192	264	336
49	13.6111111	121	193	265	337
50	13.8888889	122	194	266	338
51	14.1666667	123	195	267	339
52	14.4444444	124	196	268	340
53	14.7222222	125	197	269	341
54	15.0000000	126	198	270	342
55	15.2777778	127	199	271	343
56	15.5555556	128	200	272	344
57	15.8333333	129	201	273	345
58	16.1111111	130	202	274	346
59	16.3888889	131	203	275	347
60	16.6666667	132	204	276	348
61	16.9444444	133	205	277	349
62	17.2222222	134	306	278	350
63	17.5000000	135	207	279	351
64	17.7777778	136	208	280	352
65	18.0555556	137	209	281	353
66	18.3333333	138	210	282	354
67	18.6111111	139	211	283	355
68	18.8888889	140	212	284	356
69	19.1666667	141	213	285	357
70	19.4444444	142	214	286	358
71	19.7222222	143	215	287	359
72	20.0000000	144	216	288	360

36	9.8630137	109	182	255	328
37	10.1369863	110	183	256	329
38	10.4109589	111	184	257	330
39	10.6849315	112	185	258	331
40	10.9589041	113	186	259	332
41	11.2328767	114	187	260	333
42	11.5068493	115	188	261	334
43	11.7808219	116	189	262	335
44	12.0547945	117	190	263	336
45	12.3287671	118	191	264	337
46	12.6027397	119	192	265	338
47	12.8767123	120	193	266	339
48	13.1506849	121	194	267	340
49	13.4246575	122	195	268	341
50	13.6986301	123	196	269	342
51	13.9726027	124	197	270	343
52	14.2465753	125	198	271	344
53	14.5205479	126	199	272	345
54	14.7945206	127	200	273	346
55	15.0684932	128	201	274	347
56	15.3424658	129	202	275	348
57	15.6164384	130	203	276	349
58	15.8904111	131	204	277	350
59	16.1643836	132	205	278	351
60	16.4383562	133	206	279	352
61	16.7123288	134	207	280	353
62	16.9863014	135	208	281	354
63	17.2602740	136	209	282	355
64	17.5342466	137	210	283	356
65	17.8082192	138	211	284	357
66	18.0821918	139	212	285	358
67	18.3561644	140	213	286	359
68	18.6301370	141	214	287	360
69	18.9041096	142	215	288	361
70	19.1780822	143	216	289	362
71	19.4520548	144	217	290	363
72	19.7260274	145	218	291	364
73	20.0000000	146	219	292	365

Table 3
$(1 + i)^k$, k fractional

k		$\frac{1}{4}\%$	$\frac{7}{24}\%$	$\frac{1}{3}\%$	$\frac{5}{12}\%$	$\frac{1}{2}\%$
$\frac{1}{12}$	$\frac{1}{12}$	1.0002 0809	1.0002 4273	1.0002 7735	1.0003 4656	1.0004 1571
$\frac{1}{6}$	$\frac{2}{12}$	1.0004 1623	1.0004 8552	1.0005 5479	1.0006 9324	1.0008 3160
$\frac{1}{4}$	$\frac{3}{12}$	1.0006 2441	1.0007 2837	1.0008 3229	1.0010 4004	1.0012 4766
$\frac{1}{3}$	$\frac{4}{12}$	1.0008 3264	1.0009 7128	1.0011 0988	1.0013 8696	1.0016 6390
$\frac{5}{12}$	$\frac{5}{12}$	1.0010 4091	1.0012 1425	1.0013 8754	1.0017 3401	1.0020 8030
$\frac{1}{2}$	$\frac{6}{12}$	1.0012 4922	1.0014 5727	1.0016 6528	1.0020 8117	1.0024 9688

k		$\frac{7}{12}\%$	$\frac{2}{3}\%$	$\frac{3}{4}\%$	$\frac{7}{8}\%$	1%
$\frac{1}{12}$	$\frac{1}{12}$	1.0004 8482	1.0005 5387	1.0006 2286	1.0007 2626	1.0008 2954
$\frac{1}{6}$	$\frac{2}{12}$	1.0009 6987	1.0011 0804	1.0012 4611	1.0014 5304	1.0016 5976
$\frac{1}{4}$	$\frac{3}{12}$	1.0014 5515	1.0016 6252	1.0018 6975	1.0021 8036	1.0024 9068
$\frac{1}{3}$	$\frac{4}{12}$	1.0019 4068	1.0022 1730	1.0024 9378	1.0029 0820	1.0033 2228
$\frac{5}{12}$	$\frac{5}{12}$	1.0024 2643	1.0027 7240	1.0031 1819	1.0036 3657	1.0041 5458
$\frac{1}{2}$	$\frac{6}{12}$	1.0029 1243	1.0033 2780	1.0037 4299	1.0043 6547	1.0049 8756

k		$1\frac{1}{8}\%$	$1\frac{1}{4}\%$	$1\frac{3}{8}\%$	$1\frac{1}{2}\%$	$1\frac{3}{4}\%$
$\frac{1}{12}$	$\frac{1}{12}$	1.0009 3270	1.0010 3575	1.0011 3868	1.0012 4149	1.0014 4677
$\frac{1}{6}$	$\frac{2}{12}$	1.0018 6627	1.0020 7256	1.0022 7865	1.0024 8452	1.0028 9562
$\frac{1}{4}$	$\frac{3}{12}$	1.0028 0071	1.0031 1046	1.0034 1992	1.0037 2909	1.0043 4658
$\frac{1}{3}$	$\frac{4}{12}$	1.0037 3602	1.0041 4943	1.0045 6249	1.0049 7521	1.0057 9963
$\frac{5}{12}$	$\frac{5}{12}$	1.0046 7221	1.0051 8947	1.0057 0636	1.0062 2287	1.0072 5479
$\frac{1}{2}$	$\frac{6}{12}$	1.0056 0927	1.0062 3059	1.0068 5153	1.0074 7208	1.0087 1205

k		2%	$2\frac{1}{4}\%$	$2\frac{1}{2}\%$	$2\frac{3}{4}\%$	3%
$\frac{1}{12}$	$\frac{1}{12}$	1.0016 5158	1.0018 5594	1.0020 5984	1.0022 6328	1.0024 6627
$\frac{1}{6}$	$\frac{2}{12}$	1.0033 0589	1.0037 1532	1.0041 2392	1.0045 3168	1.0049 3862
$\frac{1}{4}$	$\frac{3}{12}$	1.0049 6293	1.0055 7815	1.0061 9225	1.0068 0522	1.0074 1707
$\frac{1}{3}$	$\frac{4}{12}$	1.0066 2271	1.0074 4444	1.0082 6484	1.0090 8390	1.0099 0163
$\frac{5}{12}$	$\frac{5}{12}$	1.0082 8523	1.0093 1420	1.0103 4170	1.0113 6774	1.0123 9232
$\frac{1}{2}$	$\frac{6}{12}$	1.0099 5049	1.0111 8742	1.0124 2284	1.0136 5675	1.0148 8916

k		$3\frac{1}{2}\%$	4%	$4\frac{1}{2}\%$	5%	$5\frac{1}{2}\%$
$\frac{1}{12}$	$\frac{1}{12}$	1.0028 7090	1.0032 7374	1.0036 7481	1.0040 7412	1.0044 7170
$\frac{1}{6}$	$\frac{2}{12}$	1.0057 5004	1.0065 5820	1.0073 6312	1.0081 6485	1.0089 6339
$\frac{1}{4}$	$\frac{3}{12}$	1.0086 3745	1.0098 5341	1.0110 6499	1.0122 7223	1.0134 7517
$\frac{1}{3}$	$\frac{4}{12}$	1.0115 3314	1.0131 5940	1.0147 8046	1.0163 9636	1.0180 0713
$\frac{5}{12}$	$\frac{5}{12}$	1.0144 3715	1.0164 7622	1.0185 0959	1.0205 3728	1.0225 5935
$\frac{1}{2}$	$\frac{6}{12}$	1.0173 4950	1.0198 0390	1.0222 5242	1.0246 9508	1.0271 3193

k		6%	$6\frac{1}{2}\%$	7%	$7\frac{1}{2}\%$	8%
$\frac{1}{12}$	$\frac{1}{12}$	1.0048 6755	1.0052 6169	1.0056 5415	1.0060 4492	1.0064 3403
$\frac{1}{6}$	$\frac{2}{12}$	1.0097 5879	1.0105 5107	1.0113 4026	1.0121 2638	1.0129 0946
$\frac{1}{4}$	$\frac{3}{12}$	1.0146 7385	1.0158 6828	1.0170 5853	1.0182 4460	1.0194 2655
$\frac{1}{3}$	$\frac{4}{12}$	1.0196 1282	1.0212 1347	1.0228 0912	1.0243 9981	1.0259 8557
$\frac{5}{12}$	$\frac{5}{12}$	1.0245 7584	1.0265 8679	1.0285 9223	1.0305 9222	1.0325 8679
$\frac{1}{2}$	$\frac{6}{12}$	1.0295 6301	1.0319 8837	1.0344 0804	1.0368 2207	1.0392 3048

k		$8\frac{1}{2}\%$	9%	$9\frac{1}{2}\%$	10%	$10\frac{1}{2}\%$
$\frac{1}{12}$	$\frac{1}{12}$	1.0068 2149	1.0072 0732	1.0075 9153	1.0079 7414	1.0083 5516
$\frac{1}{6}$	$\frac{2}{12}$	1.0136 8952	1.0144 6659	1.0152 4070	1.0160 1187	1.0167 8012
$\frac{1}{4}$	$\frac{3}{12}$	1.0206 0440	1.0217 7818	1.0229 4793	1.0241 1369	1.0252 7548
$\frac{1}{3}$	$\frac{4}{12}$	1.0275 6644	1.0291 4247	1.0307 1368	1.0322 8012	1.0338 4181
$\frac{5}{12}$	$\frac{5}{12}$	1.0345 7598	1.0365 5983	1.0385 3838	1.0405 1166	1.0424 7972
$\frac{1}{2}$	$\frac{6}{12}$	1.0416 3333	1.0440 3065	1.0464 2248	1.0488 0885	1.0511 8980

Table 4
$(1 + i)^{-k}$, k fractional

k		$\frac{1}{4}\%$	$\frac{7}{24}\%$	$\frac{1}{3}\%$	$\frac{5}{12}\%$	$\frac{1}{2}\%$
$\frac{1}{12}$	$\frac{1}{12}$	0.9997 9195	0.9997 5733	0.9997 2272	0.9996 5356	0.9995 8446
$\frac{1}{6}$	$\frac{2}{12}$	0.9995 8394	0.9995 1471	0.9994 4552	0.9993 0724	0.9991 6909
$\frac{1}{4}$	$\frac{3}{12}$	0.9993 7597	0.9992 7216	0.9991 6840	0.9989 6104	0.9987 5389
$\frac{1}{3}$	$\frac{4}{12}$	0.9991 6805	0.9990 2966	0.9988 9135	0.9986 1496	0.9983 3887
$\frac{5}{12}$	$\frac{5}{12}$	0.9989 6017	0.9987 8723	0.9986 1438	0.9982 6900	0.9979 2402
$\frac{1}{2}$	$\frac{6}{12}$	0.9987 5234	0.9985 4485	0.9983 3749	0.9979 2315	0.9975 0934

k		$\frac{7}{12}\%$	$\frac{2}{3}\%$	$\frac{3}{4}\%$	$\frac{7}{8}\%$	1%
$\frac{1}{12}$	$\frac{1}{12}$	0.9995 1542	0.9994 4644	0.9993 7753	0.9992 7427	0.9991 7115
$\frac{1}{6}$	$\frac{2}{12}$	0.9990 3107	0.9988 9319	0.9987 5544	0.9985 4906	0.9983 4299
$\frac{1}{4}$	$\frac{3}{12}$	0.9985 4696	0.9983 4024	0.9981 3374	0.9978 2438	0.9975 1551
$\frac{1}{3}$	$\frac{4}{12}$	0.9980 6308	0.9977 8760	0.9975 1243	0.9971 0023	0.9966 8872
$\frac{5}{12}$	$\frac{5}{12}$	0.9975 7944	0.9972 3527	0.9968 9150	0.9963 7661	0.9958 6261
$\frac{1}{2}$	$\frac{6}{12}$	0.9970 9603	0.9966 8324	0.9962 7096	0.9956 5350	0.9950 3719

k		$1\frac{1}{8}\%$	$1\frac{1}{4}\%$	$1\frac{3}{8}\%$	$1\frac{1}{2}\%$	$1\frac{3}{4}\%$
$\frac{1}{12}$	$\frac{1}{12}$	0.9990 6817	0.9989 6533	0.9988 6262	0.9987 6005	0.9985 5532
$\frac{1}{6}$	$\frac{2}{12}$	0.9981 3721	0.9979 3172	0.9977 2653	0.9975 2164	0.9971 1274
$\frac{1}{4}$	$\frac{3}{12}$	0.9972 0711	0.9968 9919	0.9965 9174	0.9962 8477	0.9956 7223
$\frac{1}{3}$	$\frac{4}{12}$	0.9962 7788	0.9958 6772	0.9954 5824	0.9950 4942	0.9942 3381
$\frac{5}{12}$	$\frac{5}{12}$	0.9953 4952	0.9948 3732	0.9943 2602	0.9938 1561	0.9927 9746
$\frac{1}{2}$	$\frac{6}{12}$	0.9944 2202	0.9938 0799	0.9931 9510	0.9925 8333	0.9913 6319

k		2%	$2\frac{1}{4}\%$	$2\frac{1}{2}\%$	$2\frac{3}{4}\%$	3%
$\frac{1}{12}$	$\frac{1}{12}$	0.9983 5114	0.9981 4750	0.9979 4440	0.9977 4183	0.9975 3980
$\frac{1}{6}$	$\frac{2}{12}$	0.9967 0500	0.9962 9843	0.9958 9302	0.9954 8876	0.9950 8565
$\frac{1}{4}$	$\frac{3}{12}$	0.9950 6158	0.9944 5279	0.9938 4586	0.9932 4078	0.9926 3754
$\frac{1}{3}$	$\frac{4}{12}$	0.9934 2086	0.9926 1057	0.9918 0291	0.9909 9787	0.9901 9545
$\frac{5}{12}$	$\frac{5}{12}$	0.9917 8285	0.9907 7176	0.9897 6416	0.9887 6003	0.9877 5937
$\frac{1}{2}$	$\frac{6}{12}$	0.9901 4754	0.9889 3635	0.9877 2960	0.9865 2725	0.9853 2928

k		$3\frac{1}{2}\%$	4%	$4\frac{1}{2}\%$	5%	$5\frac{1}{2}\%$
$\frac{1}{12}$	$\frac{1}{12}$	0.9971 3732	0.9967 3694	0.9963 3865	0.9959 4241	0.9955 4821
$\frac{1}{6}$	$\frac{2}{12}$	0.9942 8283	0.9934 8453	0.9926 9070	0.9919 0128	0.9911 1623
$\frac{1}{4}$	$\frac{3}{12}$	0.9914 3652	0.9902 4274	0.9890 5610	0.9878 7655	0.9867 0399
$\frac{1}{3}$	$\frac{4}{12}$	0.9885 9835	0.9870 1152	0.9854 3482	0.9838 6815	0.9823 1139
$\frac{5}{12}$	$\frac{5}{12}$	0.9857 6831	0.9837 9084	0.9818 2679	0.9798 7601	0.9779 3834
$\frac{1}{2}$	$\frac{6}{12}$	0.9829 4637	0.9805 8068	0.9782 3198	0.9759 0007	0.9735 8477

k		6%	$6\frac{1}{2}\%$	7%	$7\frac{1}{2}\%$	8%
$\frac{1}{12}$	$\frac{1}{12}$	0.9951 5603	0.9947 6585	0.9943 7764	0.9939 9140	0.9936 0710
$\frac{1}{6}$	$\frac{2}{12}$	0.9903 3552	0.9895 5909	0.9887 8690	0.9880 1891	0.9872 5507
$\frac{1}{4}$	$\frac{3}{12}$	0.9855 3836	0.9843 7958	0.9832 2759	0.9820 8230	0.9809 4365
$\frac{1}{3}$	$\frac{4}{12}$	0.9807 6444	0.9792 2719	0.9776 9953	0.9761 8136	0.9746 7258
$\frac{5}{12}$	$\frac{5}{12}$	0.9760 1365	0.9741 0176	0.9722 0256	0.9703 1588	0.9684 4160
$\frac{1}{2}$	$\frac{6}{12}$	0.9712 8586	0.9690 0317	0.9667 3649	0.9644 8564	0.9622 5045

k		$8\frac{1}{2}\%$	9%	$9\frac{1}{2}\%$	10%	$10\frac{1}{2}\%$
$\frac{1}{12}$	$\frac{1}{12}$	0.9932 2472	0.9928 4425	0.9924 6566	0.9920 8894	0.9917 1407
$\frac{1}{6}$	$\frac{2}{12}$	0.9864 9535	0.9857 3971	0.9849 8809	0.9842 4047	0.9834 9681
$\frac{1}{4}$	$\frac{3}{12}$	0.9798 1157	0.9786 8600	0.9775 6686	0.9764 5409	0.9753 4762
$\frac{1}{3}$	$\frac{4}{12}$	0.9731 7308	0.9716 8277	0.9702 0154	0.9687 2931	0.9672 6597
$\frac{5}{12}$	$\frac{5}{12}$	0.9665 7956	0.9647 2965	0.9628 9172	0.9610 6563	0.9592 5127
$\frac{1}{2}$	$\frac{6}{12}$	0.9600 3072	0.9578 2629	0.9556 3697	0.9534 6259	0.9513 0299

Table 5

$$\frac{1}{s_{\overline{k}|i}}, \ k \text{ fractional} \left(\frac{1}{a_{\overline{k}|i}} = \frac{1}{s_{\overline{k}|i}} + i\right)$$

k		$\frac{1}{4}\%$	$\frac{7}{24}\%$	$\frac{1}{3}\%$	$\frac{5}{12}\%$	$\frac{1}{2}\%$
$\frac{1}{12}$	$\frac{1}{12}$	12.0137 4384	12.0160 3328	12.0183 2234	12.0228 9946	12.0274 7526
$\frac{1}{6}$	$\frac{2}{12}$	6.0062 4696	6.0072 8756	6.0083 2795	6.0104 0824	6.0124 8788
$\frac{1}{4}$	$\frac{3}{12}$	4.0037 4805	4.0043 7235	4.0049 9654	4.0062 4459	4.0074 9221
$\frac{1}{3}$	$\frac{4}{12}$	3.0024 9861	3.0029 1478	3.0033 3087	3.0041 6282	3.0049 9446
$\frac{5}{12}$	$\frac{5}{12}$	2.4017 4897	2.4020 4026	2.4023 3150	2.4029 1380	2.4034 9588
$\frac{1}{2}$	$\frac{6}{12}$	2.0012 4922	2.0014 5727	2.0016 6528	2.0020 8117	2.0024 9688

k		$\frac{7}{12}\%$	$\frac{2}{3}\%$	$\frac{3}{4}\%$	$\frac{7}{8}\%$	1%
$\frac{1}{12}$	$\frac{1}{12}$	12.0320 4968	12.0366 2270	12.0411 9435	12.0480 4930	12.0549 0119
$\frac{1}{6}$	$\frac{2}{12}$	6.0145 6684	6.0166 4513	6.0187 2276	6.0218 3795	6.0249 5163
$\frac{1}{4}$	$\frac{3}{12}$	4.0087 3940	4.0099 8616	4.0112 3249	4.0131 0118	4.0149 6891
$\frac{1}{3}$	$\frac{4}{12}$	3.0058 2579	3.0066 5682	3.0074 8755	3.0087 3306	3.0099 7789
$\frac{5}{12}$	$\frac{5}{12}$	2.4040 7773	2.4046 5934	2.4052 4074	2.4061 1240	2.4069 8355
$\frac{1}{2}$	$\frac{6}{12}$	2.0029 1243	2.0033 2780	2.0037 4300	2.0043 6547	2.0049 8756

k		$1\frac{1}{8}\%$	$1\frac{1}{4}\%$	$1\frac{3}{8}\%$	$1\frac{1}{2}\%$	$1\frac{3}{4}\%$
$\frac{1}{12}$	$\frac{1}{12}$	12.0617 5002	12.0685 9580	12.0754 3856	12.0822 7820	12.0959 4852
$\frac{1}{6}$	$\frac{2}{12}$	6.0280 6382	6.0311 7452	6.0342 8372	6.0373 9144	6.0436 0242
$\frac{1}{4}$	$\frac{3}{12}$	4.0168 3567	4.0187 0147	4.0205 6632	4.0224 3021	4.0261 5513
$\frac{1}{3}$	$\frac{4}{12}$	3.0112 2203	3.0124 6549	3.0137 0827	3.0149 5037	3.0174 3253
$\frac{5}{12}$	$\frac{5}{12}$	2.4078 5420	2.4087 2434	2.4095 9397	2.4104 6309	2.4121 9982
$\frac{1}{2}$	$\frac{6}{12}$	2.0056 0927	2.0062 3059	2.0068 5153	2.0074 7208	2.0087 1205

k		2%	$2\frac{1}{4}\%$	$2\frac{1}{2}\%$	$2\frac{3}{4}\%$	3%
$\frac{1}{12}$	$\frac{1}{12}$	12.1096 0670	12.1232 5281	12.1368 8697	12.1505 0916	12.1641 1941
$\frac{1}{6}$	$\frac{2}{12}$	6.0498 0747	6.0560 0662	6.0621 9991	6.0683 8735	6.0745 6894
$\frac{1}{4}$	$\frac{3}{12}$	4.0298 7623	4.0335 9356	4.0373 0709	4.0410 1686	4.0447 2289
$\frac{1}{3}$	$\frac{4}{12}$	3.0199 1199	3.0223 8875	3.0248 6282	3.0273 3422	3.0298 0294
$\frac{5}{12}$	$\frac{5}{12}$	2.4139 3454	2.4156 6726	2.4173 9797	2.4191 2670	2.4208 5344
$\frac{1}{2}$	$\frac{6}{12}$	2.0099 5049	2.0111 8742	2.0124 2284	2.0136 5675	2.0148 8916

k		$3\frac{1}{2}\%$	4%	$4\frac{1}{2}\%$	5%	$5\frac{1}{2}\%$
$\frac{1}{12}$	$\frac{1}{12}$	12.1913 0434	12.2184 4211	12.2455 3306	12.2725 7753	12.2995 7585
$\frac{1}{6}$	$\frac{2}{12}$	6.0869 1471	6.0992 3739	6.1115 3716	6.1238 1418	6.1360 6860
$\frac{1}{4}$	$\frac{3}{12}$	4.0521 2374	4.0595 0975	4.0668 8103	4.0742 3769	4.0815 7982
$\frac{1}{3}$	$\frac{4}{12}$	3.0347 3244	3.0396 5138	3.0445 5985	3.0494 5791	3.0543 4565
$\frac{5}{12}$	$\frac{5}{12}$	2.4243 0100	2.4277 4071	2.4311 7264	2.4345 9682	2.4380 1333
$\frac{1}{2}$	$\frac{6}{12}$	2.0173 4950	2.0198 0390	2.0222 5241	2.0246 9508	2.0271 3193

k		6%	$6\frac{1}{2}\%$	7%	$7\frac{1}{2}\%$	8%
$\frac{1}{12}$	$\frac{1}{12}$	12.3265 2834	12.3534 3534	12.3802 9716	12.4071 1409	12.4338 8648
$\frac{1}{6}$	$\frac{2}{12}$	6.1483 0059	6.1605 1031	6.1726 9791	6.1848 6355	6.1970 0737
$\frac{1}{4}$	$\frac{3}{12}$	4.0889 0752	4.0962 2091	4.1035 2009	4.1108 0514	4.1180 7618
$\frac{1}{3}$	$\frac{4}{12}$	3.0592 2313	3.0640 9043	3.0689 4762	3.0737 9477	3.0786 3195
$\frac{5}{12}$	$\frac{5}{12}$	2.4414 2221	2.4448 2351	2.4482 1730	2.4516 0362	2.4549 8252
$\frac{1}{2}$	$\frac{6}{12}$	2.0295 6301	2.0319 8837	2.0344 0804	2.0368 2207	2.0392 3048

k		$8\frac{1}{2}\%$	9%	$9\frac{1}{2}\%$	10%	$10\frac{1}{2}\%$
$\frac{1}{12}$	$\frac{1}{12}$	12.4606 1463	12.4872 9883	12.5139 3939	12.5405 3661	12.5670 9079
$\frac{1}{6}$	$\frac{2}{12}$	6.2091 2954	6.2212 3021	6.2333 0950	6.2453 6759	6.2574 0460
$\frac{1}{4}$	$\frac{3}{12}$	4.1253 3329	4.1325 7657	4.1398 0612	4.1470 2204	4.1542 2440
$\frac{1}{3}$	$\frac{4}{12}$	3.0834 5923	3.0882 7668	3.0930 8437	3.0978 8235	3.1026 7071
$\frac{5}{12}$	$\frac{5}{12}$	2.4583 5406	2.4617 1829	2.4650 7526	2.4684 2501	2.4717 6761
$\frac{1}{2}$	$\frac{6}{12}$	2.0416 3333	2.0440 3065	2.0464 2248	2.0488 0885	2.0511 8980

Table 6
Values of $s_{\overline{k}|i}$, k fractional

k	$\frac{1}{4}\%$	$\frac{7}{24}\%$	$\frac{1}{3}\%$	$\frac{5}{12}\%$	$\frac{1}{2}\%$
$\frac{1}{12}$ $\frac{1}{12}$	0.0832 3800	0.0832 2214	0.0832 0629	0.0831 7461	0.0831 4297
$\frac{1}{6}$ $\frac{2}{12}$	0.1664 9332	0.1664 6448	0.1664 3566	0.1663 7805	0.1663 2050
$\frac{1}{4}$ $\frac{3}{12}$	0.2497 6597	0.2497 2703	0.2496 8811	0.2496 1032	0.2495 3261
$\frac{1}{3}$ $\frac{4}{12}$	0.3330 5594	0.3330 0978	0.3329 6365	0.3328 7144	0.3327 7932
$\frac{5}{12}$ $\frac{5}{12}$	0.4163 6325	0.4163 1276	0.4162 6229	0.4161 6141	0.4160 6063
$\frac{1}{2}$ $\frac{6}{12}$	0.4996 8789	0.4996 3595	0.4995 8403	0.4994 8025	0.4993 7656

k	$\frac{7}{12}\%$	$\frac{2}{3}\%$	$\frac{3}{4}\%$	$\frac{7}{8}\%$	1%
$\frac{1}{12}$ $\frac{1}{12}$	0.0831 1136	0.0830 7978	0.0830 4824	0.0830 0099	0.0829 5381
$\frac{1}{6}$ $\frac{2}{12}$	0.1662 6301	0.1662 0558	0.1661 4821	0.1660 6226	0.1659 7644
$\frac{1}{4}$ $\frac{3}{12}$	0.2494 5498	0.2493 7742	0.2492 9994	0.2491 8385	0.2490 6793
$\frac{1}{3}$ $\frac{4}{12}$	0.3326 8728	0.3325 9532	0.3325 0345	0.3323 6581	0.3322 2835
$\frac{5}{12}$ $\frac{5}{12}$	0.4159 5993	0.4158 5932	0.4157 5880	0.4156 0818	0.4154 5776
$\frac{1}{2}$ $\frac{6}{12}$	0.4992 7295	0.4991 6943	0.4990 6600	0.4989 1101	0.4987 5621

k	$1\frac{1}{8}\%$	$1\frac{1}{4}\%$	$1\frac{3}{8}\%$	$1\frac{1}{2}\%$	$1\frac{3}{4}\%$
$\frac{1}{12}$ $\frac{1}{12}$	0.0829 0671	0.0828 5968	0.0828 1273	0.0827 6585	0.0826 7231
$\frac{1}{6}$ $\frac{2}{12}$	0.1658 9075	0.1658 0518	0.1657 1975	0.1656 3445	0.1654 6423
$\frac{1}{4}$ $\frac{3}{12}$	0.2489 5218	0.2488 3660	0.2487 2118	0.2486 0593	0.2483 7592
$\frac{1}{3}$ $\frac{4}{12}$	0.3320 9109	0.3319 5401	0.3318 1712	0.3316 8042	0.3314 0758
$\frac{5}{12}$ $\frac{5}{12}$	0.4153 0754	0.4151 5751	0.4150 0768	0.4148 5804	0.4145 5935
$\frac{1}{2}$ $\frac{6}{12}$	0.4986 0160	0.4984 4719	0.4982 9297	0.4981 3893	0.4978 3143

k	2%	$2\frac{1}{4}\%$	$2\frac{1}{2}\%$	$2\frac{3}{4}\%$	3%
$\frac{1}{12}$ $\frac{1}{12}$	0.0825 7907	0.0824 8611	0.0823 9345	0.0823 0108	0.0822 0899
$\frac{1}{6}$ $\frac{2}{12}$	0.1652 9452	0.1651 2531	0.1649 5662	0.1647 8843	0.1646 2073
$\frac{1}{4}$ $\frac{3}{12}$	0.2481 4658	0.2479 1789	0.2476 8985	0.2474 6247	0.2472 3573
$\frac{1}{3}$ $\frac{4}{12}$	0.3311 3548	0.3308 6412	0.3305 9350	0.3303 2362	0.3300 5447
$\frac{5}{12}$ $\frac{5}{12}$	0.4142 6144	0.4139 6430	0.4136 6792	0.4133 7231	0.4130 7746
$\frac{1}{2}$ $\frac{6}{12}$	0.4975 2469	0.4972 1870	0.4969 1346	0.4966 0897	0.4963 0522

k	$3\frac{1}{2}\%$	4%	$4\frac{1}{2}\%$	5%	$5\frac{1}{2}\%$
$\frac{1}{12}$ $\frac{1}{12}$	0.0820 2568	0.0818 4349	0.0816 6243	0.0814 8248	0.0813 0362
$\frac{1}{6}$ $\frac{2}{12}$	0.1642 8684	0.1639 5492	0.1636 2496	0.1632 9692	0.1629 7080
$\frac{1}{4}$ $\frac{3}{12}$	0.2467 8417	0.2463 3516	0.2458 8868	0.2454 4469	0.2450 0317
$\frac{1}{3}$ $\frac{4}{12}$	0.3295 1834	0.3289 8510	0.3284 5470	0.3279 2714	0.3274 0237
$\frac{5}{12}$ $\frac{5}{12}$	0.4124 9003	0.4119 0560	0.4113 2414	0.4107 4563	0.4101 7003
$\frac{1}{2}$ $\frac{6}{12}$	0.4956 9993	0.4950 9757	0.4944 9811	0.4939 0153	0.4933 0780

k	6%	$6\frac{1}{2}\%$	7%	$7\frac{1}{2}\%$	8%
$\frac{1}{12}$ $\frac{1}{12}$	0.0811 2584	0.0809 4914	0.0807 7351	0.0805 9892	0.0804 2538
$\frac{1}{6}$ $\frac{2}{12}$	0.1626 4657	0.1623 2422	0.1620 0372	0.1616 8505	0.1613 6821
$\frac{1}{4}$ $\frac{3}{12}$	0.2445 6410	0.2441 2746	0.2436 9321	0.2432 6135	0.2428 3184
$\frac{1}{3}$ $\frac{4}{12}$	0.3268 8037	0.3263 6112	0.3258 4460	0.3253 3076	0.3248 1960
$\frac{5}{12}$ $\frac{5}{12}$	0.4095 9732	0.4090 2748	0.4084 6047	0.4078 9628	0.4073 3488
$\frac{1}{2}$ $\frac{6}{12}$	0.4927 1690	0.4921 2880	0.4915 4348	0.4909 6090	0.4903 8106

k	$8\frac{1}{2}\%$	9%	$9\frac{1}{2}\%$	10%	$10\frac{1}{2}\%$
$\frac{1}{12}$ $\frac{1}{12}$	0.0802 5286	0.0800 8137	0.0799 1089	0.0797 4140	0.0795 7291
$\frac{1}{6}$ $\frac{2}{12}$	0.1610 5317	0.1607 3991	0.1604 2842	0.1601 1868	0.1598 1067
$\frac{1}{4}$ $\frac{3}{12}$	0.2424 0466	0.2419 7979	0.2415 5721	0.2411 3689	0.2407 1882
$\frac{1}{3}$ $\frac{4}{12}$	0.3243 1108	0.3238 0518	0.3233 0188	0.3228 0115	0.3223 0298
$\frac{5}{12}$ $\frac{5}{12}$	0.4067 7623	0.4062 2032	0.4056 6713	0.4051 1662	0.4045 6878
$\frac{1}{2}$ $\frac{6}{12}$	0.4898 0392	0.4892 2945	0.4886 5765	0.4880 8848	0.4875 2192

Table 7

$a_{\overline{k}|i}$, k fractional

k	$\frac{1}{4}\%$	$\frac{7}{24}\%$	$\frac{1}{3}\%$	$\frac{5}{12}\%$	$\frac{1}{2}\%$
$\frac{1}{12}$ $\frac{1}{12}$	0.0832 2068	0.0832 0194	0.0831 8322	0.0831 4580	0.0831 0842
$\frac{1}{6}$ $\frac{2}{12}$	0.1664 2405	0.1663 8370	0.1663 4337	0.1662 6279	0.1661 8230
$\frac{1}{4}$ $\frac{3}{12}$	0.2496 1011	0.2495 4527	0.2494 8047	0.2493 5099	0.2492 2167
$\frac{1}{3}$ $\frac{4}{12}$	0.3327 7886	0.3326 8665	0.3325 9451	0.3324 1040	0.3322 2653
$\frac{5}{12}$ $\frac{5}{12}$	0.4159 3030	0.4158 0786	0.4156 8550	0.4154 4103	0.4151 9689
$\frac{1}{2}$ $\frac{6}{12}$	0.4990 6445	0.4989 0890	0.4987 5346	0.4984 4291	0.4981 3278

k	$\frac{7}{12}\%$	$\frac{2}{3}\%$	$\frac{3}{4}\%$	$\frac{7}{8}\%$	1%
$\frac{1}{12}$ $\frac{1}{12}$	0.0830 7108	0.0830 3379	0.0829 9654	0.0829 4075	0.0828 8506
$\frac{1}{6}$ $\frac{2}{12}$	0.1661 0192	0.1660 2162	0.1659 4143	0.1658 2131	0.1657 0141
$\frac{1}{4}$ $\frac{3}{12}$	0.2490 9251	0.2489 6351	0.2488 3468	0.2486 4172	0.2484 4912
$\frac{1}{3}$ $\frac{4}{12}$	0.3320 4289	0.3318 5949	0.3316 7633	0.3314 0203	0.3311 2825
$\frac{5}{12}$ $\frac{5}{12}$	0.4149 5307	0.4147 0958	0.4144 6641	0.4141 0227	0.4137 3885
$\frac{1}{2}$ $\frac{6}{12}$	0.4978 2308	0.4975 1381	0.4972 0496	0.4967 4249	0.4962 8098

k	$1\frac{1}{8}\%$	$1\frac{1}{4}\%$	$1\frac{3}{8}\%$	$1\frac{1}{2}\%$	$1\frac{3}{4}\%$
$\frac{1}{12}$ $\frac{1}{12}$	0.0828 2945	0.0827 7395	0.0827 1854	0.0826 6322	0.0825 5287
$\frac{1}{6}$ $\frac{2}{12}$	0.1655 8172	0.1654 6225	0.1653 4299	0.1652 2395	0.1649 8649
$\frac{1}{4}$ $\frac{3}{12}$	0.2482 5688	0.2480 6500	0.2478 7347	0.2476 8230	0.2473 0101
$\frac{1}{3}$ $\frac{4}{12}$	0.3308 5501	0.3305 8228	0.3303 1009	0.3300 3841	0.3294 9662
$\frac{5}{12}$ $\frac{5}{12}$	0.4133 7616	0.4130 1419	0.4126 5294	0.4122 9240	0.4115 7348
$\frac{1}{2}$ $\frac{6}{12}$	0.4958 2042	0.4953 6080	0.4949 0213	0.4944 4440	0.4935 3176

k	2%	$2\frac{1}{4}\%$	$2\frac{1}{2}\%$	$2\frac{3}{4}\%$	3%
$\frac{1}{12}$ $\frac{1}{12}$	0.0824 4290	0.0823 3331	0.0822 2408	0.0821 1523	0.0820 0674
$\frac{1}{6}$ $\frac{2}{12}$	0.1647 4987	0.1645 1409	0.1642 7915	0.1640 4503	0.1638 1173
$\frac{1}{4}$ $\frac{3}{12}$	0.2469 2113	0.2465 4264	0.2461 6554	0.2457 8981	0.2454 1546
$\frac{1}{3}$ $\frac{4}{12}$	0.3289 5689	0.3284 1922	0.3278 8360	0.3273 5001	0.3268 1843
$\frac{5}{12}$ $\frac{5}{12}$	0.4108 5739	0.4101 4413	0.4094 3368	0.4087 2602	0.4080 2113
$\frac{1}{2}$ $\frac{6}{12}$	0.4926 2285	0.4917 1765	0.4908 1613	0.4899 1828	0.4890 2406

k	$3\frac{1}{2}\%$	4%	$4\frac{1}{2}\%$	5%	$5\frac{1}{2}\%$
$\frac{1}{12}$ $\frac{1}{12}$	0.0817 9086	0.0815 7643	0.0813 6344	0.0811 5185	0.0809 4167
$\frac{1}{6}$ $\frac{2}{12}$	0.1633 4759	0.1628 8668	0.1624 2897	0.1619 7442	0.1615 2300
$\frac{1}{4}$ $\frac{3}{12}$	0.2446 7084	0.2439 3161	0.2431 9770	0.2424 6905	0.2417 4561
$\frac{1}{3}$ $\frac{4}{12}$	0.3257 6129	0.3247 1208	0.3236 7070	0.3226 3706	0.3216 1108
$\frac{5}{12}$ $\frac{5}{12}$	0.4066 1960	0.4052 2896	0.4038 4906	0.4024 7979	0.4011 2100
$\frac{1}{2}$ $\frac{6}{12}$	0.4872 4645	0.4854 8311	0.4837 3386	0.4819 9854	0.4802 7696

k	6%	$6\frac{1}{2}\%$	7%	$7\frac{1}{2}\%$	8%
$\frac{1}{12}$ $\frac{1}{12}$	0.0807 3287	0.0805 2544	0.0803 1937	0.0801 1463	0.0799 1123
$\frac{1}{6}$ $\frac{2}{12}$	0.1610 7468	0.1606 2940	0.1601 8715	0.1597 4789	0.1593 1159
$\frac{1}{4}$ $\frac{3}{12}$	0.2410 2731	0.2403 1409	0.2396 0589	0.2389 0266	0.2382 0435
$\frac{1}{3}$ $\frac{4}{12}$	0.3205 9265	0.3195 8169	0.3185 7811	0.3175 8183	0.3165 9276
$\frac{5}{12}$ $\frac{5}{12}$	0.3997 7258	0.3984 3439	0.3971 0632	0.3957 8824	0.3944 8004
$\frac{1}{2}$ $\frac{6}{12}$	0.4785 6896	0.4768 7437	0.4751 9301	0.4735 2474	0.4718 6939

k	$8\frac{1}{2}\%$	9%	$9\frac{1}{2}\%$	10%	$10\frac{1}{2}\%$
$\frac{1}{12}$ $\frac{1}{12}$	0.0797 0913	0.0795 0833	0.0793 0881	0.0791 1057	0.0789 1358
$\frac{1}{6}$ $\frac{2}{12}$	0.1588 7820	0.1584 4771	0.1580 2008	0.1575 9528	0.1571 7328
$\frac{1}{4}$ $\frac{3}{12}$	0.2375 1089	0.2368 2223	0.2361 3832	0.2354 5910	0.2347 8453
$\frac{1}{3}$ $\frac{4}{12}$	0.3156 1081	0.3146 3592	0.3136 6799	0.3127 0694	0.3117 5270
$\frac{5}{12}$ $\frac{5}{12}$	0.3931 8159	0.3918 9279	0.3906 1352	0.3893 4366	0.3880 8312
$\frac{1}{2}$ $\frac{6}{12}$	0.4702 2681	0.4685 9683	0.4669 7932	0.4653 7411	0.4637 8106

Table 8
$(1 + i)^n$

n	$\frac{1}{4}\%$	$\frac{7}{24}\%$	$\frac{1}{3}\%$	$\frac{5}{12}\%$	$\frac{1}{2}\%$
1	1.0025 0000	1.0029 1667	1.0033 3333	1.0041 6667	1.0050 0000
2	1.0050 0625	1.0058 4184	1.0066 7778	1.0083 5069	1.0100 2500
3	1.0075 1877	1.0087 7555	1.0100 3337	1.0125 5216	1.0150 7513
4	1.0100 3756	1.0117 1781	1.0134 0015	1.0167 7112	1.0201 5050
5	1.0125 6266	1.0146 6865	1.0167 7815	1.0210 0767	1.0252 5125
6	1.0150 9406	1.0176 2810	1.0201 6741	1.0252 6187	1.0303 7751
7	1.0176 3180	1.0205 9618	1.0235 6797	1.0295 3379	1.0355 2940
8	1.0201 7588	1.0235 7292	1.0269 7986	1.0338 2352	1.0407 0704
9	1.0227 2632	1.0265 5834	1.0304 0313	1.0381 3111	1.0459 1058
10	1.0252 8313	1.0295 5247	1.0338 3780	1.0424 5666	1.0511 4013
11	1.0278 4634	1.0325 5533	1.0372 8393	1.0468 0023	1.0563 9583
12	1.0304 1596	1.0355 6695	1.0407 4154	1.0511 6190	1.0616 7781
13	1.0329 9200	1.0385 8736	1.0442 1068	1.0555 4174	1.0669 8620
14	1.0355 7448	1.0416 1657	1.0476 9138	1.0599 3983	1.0723 2113
15	1.0381 6341	1.0446 5462	1.0511 8369	1.0643 5625	1.0776 8274
16	1.0407 5882	1.0477 0153	1.0546 8763	1.0687 9106	1.0830 7115
17	1.0433 6072	1.0507 5732	1.0582 0326	1.0732 4436	1.0884 8651
18	1.0459 6912	1.0538 2203	1.0617 3060	1.0777 1621	1.0939 2894
19	1.0485 8404	1.0568 9568	1.0652 6971	1.0822 0670	1.0993 9858
20	1.0512 0550	1.0599 7829	1.0688 2060	1.0867 1589	1.1048 9558
21	1.0538 3352	1.0630 6990	1.0723 8334	1.0912 4387	1.1104 2006
22	1.0564 6810	1.0661 7052	1.0759 5795	1.0957 9072	1.1159 7216
23	1.0591 0927	1.0692 8018	1.0795 4448	1.1003 5652	1.1215 5202
24	1.0617 5704	1.0723 9891	1.0831 4296	1.1049 4134	1.1271 5978
25	1.0644 1144	1.0755 2674	1.0867 5344	1.1095 4526	1.1327 9558
26	1.0670 7247	1.0786 6370	1.0903 7595	1.1141 6836	1.1384 5955
27	1.0697 4015	1.0818 0980	1.0940 1053	1.1188 1073	1.1441 5185
28	1.0724 1450	1.0849 6508	1.0976 5724	1.1234 7244	1.1498 7261
29	1.0750 9553	1.0881 2956	1.1013 1609	1.1281 5358	1.1556 2197
30	1.0777 8327	1.0913 0327	1.1049 8715	1.1328 5422	1.1614 0008
31	1.0804 7773	1.0944 8624	1.1086 7044	1.1375 7444	1.1672 0708
32	1.0831 7892	1.0976 7849	1.1123 6601	1.1423 1434	1.1730 4312
33	1.0858 8687	1.1008 8005	1.1160 7389	1.1470 7398	1.1789 0833
34	1.0886 0159	1.1040 9095	1.1197 9414	1.1518 5346	1.1848 0288
35	1.0913 2309	1.1073 1122	1.1235 2679	1.1566 5284	1.1907 2689
36	1.0940 5140	1.1105 4088	1.1272 7187	1.1614 7223	1.1966 8052
37	1.0967 8653	1.1137 7995	1.1310 2945	1.1663 1170	1.2026 6393
38	1.0995 2850	1.1170 2848	1.1347 9955	1.1711 7133	1.2086 7725
39	1.1022 7732	1.1202 8648	1.1385 8221	1.1760 5121	1.2147 2063
40	1.1050 3301	1.1235 5398	1.1423 7748	1.1809 5142	1.2207 9424
41	1.1077 9559	1.1268 3101	1.1461 8541	1.1858 7206	1.2268 9821
42	1.1105 6508	1.1301 1760	1.1500 0603	1.1908 1319	1.2330 3270
43	1.1133 4149	1.1334 1378	1.1538 3938	1.1957 7491	1.2391 9786
44	1.1161 2485	1.1367 1957	1.1576 8551	1.2007 5731	1.2453 9385
45	1.1189 1516	1.1400 3500	1.1615 4446	1.2057 6046	1.2516 2082
46	1.1217 1245	1.1433 6010	1.1654 1628	1.2107 8446	1.2578 7892
47	1.1245 1673	1.1466 9490	1.1693 0100	1.2158 2940	1.2641 6832
48	1.1273 2802	1.1500 3943	1.1731 9867	1.2208 9536	1.2704 8916
49	1.1301 4634	1.1533 9371	1.1771 0933	1.2259 8242	1.2768 4161
50	1.1329 7171	1.1567 5778	1.1810 3303	1.2310 9068	1.2832 2581

Table 8 (*Continued*)

$$(1 + i)^n$$

n	$\frac{1}{4}\%$	$\frac{7}{24}\%$	$\frac{1}{3}\%$	$\frac{5}{12}\%$	$\frac{1}{2}\%$
51	1.1358 0414	1.1601 3165	1.1849 6981	1.2362 2022	1.2896 4194
52	1.1386 4365	1.1635 1537	1.1889 1971	1.2413 7114	1.2960 9015
53	1.1414 9026	1.1669 0896	1.1928 8277	1.2465 4352	1.3025 7060
54	1.1443 4398	1.1703 1244	1.1968 5905	1.2517 3745	1.3090 8346
55	1.1472 0484	1.1737 2585	1.2008 4858	1.2569 5302	1.3156 2887
56	1.1500 7285	1.1771 4922	1.2048 5141	1.2621 9033	1.3222 0702
57	1.1529 4804	1.1805 8257	1.2088 6758	1.2674 4946	1.3288 1805
58	1.1558 3041	1.1840 2594	1.2128 9714	1.2727 3050	1.3354 6214
59	1.1587 1998	1.1874 7935	1.2169 4013	1.2780 3354	1.3421 3946
60	1.1616 1678	1.1909 4283	1.2209 9659	1.2833 5868	1.3488 5015
61	1.1645 2082	1.1944 1641	1.2250 6658	1.2887 0601	1.3555 9440
62	1.1674 3213	1.1979 0013	1.2291 5014	1.2940 7561	1.3623 7238
63	1.1703 5071	1.2013 9400	1.2332 4730	1.2994 6760	1.3691 8424
64	1.1732 7658	1.2048 9807	1.2373 5813	1.3048 8204	1.3760 3016
65	1.1762 0977	1.2084 1235	1.2414 8266	1.3103 1905	1.3829 1031
66	1.1791 5030	1.2119 3689	1.2456 2093	1.3157 7872	1.3898 2486
67	1.1820 9817	1.2154 7171	1.2497 7300	1.3212 6113	1.3967 7399
68	1.1850 5342	1.2190 1683	1.2539 3891	1.3267 6638	1.4037 5785
69	1.1880 1605	1.2225 7230	1.2581 1871	1.3322 9458	1.4107 7664
70	1.1909 8609	1.2261 3813	1.2623 1244	1.3378 4580	1.4178 3053
71	1.1939 6356	1.2297 1437	1.2665 2015	1.3434 2016	1.4249 1968
72	1.1969 4847	1.2333 0104	1.2707 4188	1.3490 1774	1.4320 4428
73	1.1999 4084	1.2368 9816	1.2749 7769	1.3546 3865	1.4392 0450
74	1.2029 4069	1.2405 0578	1.2792 2761	1.3602 8298	1.4464 0052
75	1.2059 4804	1.2441 2393	1.2834 9170	1.3659 5082	1.4536 3252
76	1.2089 6291	1.2477 5262	1.2877 7001	1.3716 4229	1.4609 0069
77	1.2119 8532	1.2513 9190	1.2920 6258	1.3773 5746	1.4682 0519
78	1.2150 1528	1.2550 4179	1.2963 6945	1.3830 9645	1.4755 4622
79	1.2180 5282	1.2587 0233	1.3006 9068	1.3888 5935	1.4829 2395
80	1.2210 9795	1.2623 7355	1.3050 2632	1.3946 4627	1.4903 3857
81	1.2241 5070	1.2660 5547	1.3093 7641	1.4004 5729	1.4977 9026
82	1.2272 1108	1.2697 4813	1.3137 4099	1.4062 9253	1.5052 7921
83	1.2302 7910	1.2734 5156	1.3181 2013	1.4121 5209	1.5128 0561
84	1.2333 5480	1.2771 6580	1.3225 1386	1.4180 3605	1.5203 6964
85	1.2364 3819	1.2808 9086	1.3269 2224	1.4239 4454	1.5279 7148
86	1.2395 2928	1.2846 2680	1.3313 4532	1.4298 7764	1.5356 1134
87	1.2426 2811	1.2883 7362	1.3357 8314	1.4358 3546	1.5432 8940
88	1.2457 3468	1.2921 3138	1.3402 3575	1.4418 1811	1.5510 0585
89	1.2488 4901	1.2959 0010	1.3447 0320	1.4478 2568	1.5587 6087
90	1.2519 7114	1.2996 7980	1.3491 8554	1.4538 5829	1.5665 5468
91	1.2551 0106	1.3034 7054	1.3536 8283	1.4599 1603	1.5743 8745
92	1.2582 3882	1.3072 7233	1.3581 9510	1.4659 9902	1.5822 5939
93	1.2613 8441	1.3110 8520	1.3627 2242	1.4721 0735	1.5901 7069
94	1.2645 3787	1.3149 0920	1.3672 6483	1.4782 4113	1.5981 2154
95	1.2676 9922	1.3187 4435	1.3718 2238	1.4844 0047	1.6061 1215
96	1.2708 6847	1.3225 9069	1.3763 9512	1.4905 8547	1.6141 4271
97	1.2740 4564	1.3264 4825	1.3809 8310	1.4967 9624	1.6222 1342
98	1.2772 3075	1.3303 1706	1.3855 8638	1.5030 3289	1.6303 2449
99	1.2804 2383	1.3341 9715	1.3902 0500	1.5092 9553	1.6387 7611
100	1.2836 2489	1.3380 8856	1.3948 3902	1.5155 8426	1.6466 6849

Table 8 *(Continued)*
$(1 + i)^n$

n	$\frac{1}{4}\%$	$\frac{7}{24}\%$	$\frac{1}{3}\%$	$\frac{5}{12}\%$	$\frac{1}{2}\%$
101	1.2868 3395	1.3419 9131	1.3994 8848	1.5218 9919	1.6549 0183
102	1.2900 5104	1.3459 0546	1.4041 5344	1.5282 4044	1.6631 7634
103	1.2932 7616	1.3498 3101	1.4088 3395	1.5346 0811	1.6714 9223
104	1.2965 0935	1.3537 6802	1.4135 3007	1.5410 0231	1.6798 4969
105	1.2997 5063	1.3577 1651	1.4182 4183	1.5474 2315	1.6882 4894
106	1.3030 0000	1.3616 7652	1.4229 6931	1.5538 7075	1.6966 9018
107	1.3062 5750	1.3656 4807	1.4277 1254	1.5603 4521	1.7051 7363
108	1.3095 2315	1.3696 3121	1.4324 7158	1.5668 4665	1.7136 9950
109	1.3127 9696	1.3736 2597	1.4372 4649	1.5733 7518	1.7222 6800
110	1.3160 7895	1.3776 3238	1.4420 3731	1.5799 3091	1.7308 7934
111	1.3193 6915	1.3816 5047	1.4468 4410	1.5865 1395	1.7395 3373
112	1.3226 6757	1.3856 8029	1.4516 6691	1.5931 2443	1.7482 3140
113	1.3259 7424	1.3897 2186	1.4565 0580	1.5997 6245	1.7569 7256
114	1.3292 8917	1.3937 7521	1.4613 6082	1.6064 2812	1.7657 5742
115	1.3326 1240	1.3978 4039	1.4662 3202	1.6131 2157	1.7745 8621
116	1.3359 4393	1.4019 1742	1.4711 1946	1.6198 4291	1.7834 5914
117	1.3392 8379	1.4060 0635	1.4760 2320	1.6265 9226	1.7923 7644
118	1.3426 3200	1.4101 0720	1.4809 4327	1.6333 6973	1.8013 3832
119	1.3459 8858	1.4142 2001	1.4858 7975	1.6401 7543	1.8103 4501
120	1.3493 5355	1.4183 4482	1.4908 3268	1.6470 0950	1.8193 9673
121	1.3527 2693	1.4224 8166	1.4958 0212	1.6538 7204	1.8284 9372
122	1.3561 0875	1.4266 3057	1.5007 8813	1.6607 6317	1.8376 3619
123	1.3594 9902	1.4307 9157	1.5057 9076	1.6676 8302	1.8468 2437
124	1.3628 9777	1.4349 6471	1.5108 1006	1.6746 3170	1.8560 5849
125	1.3663 0501	1.4391 5003	1.5158 4609	1.6816 0933	1.8653 3878
126	1.3697 2077	1.4433 4755	1.5208 9892	1.6886 1603	1.8746 6548
127	1.3731 4508	1.4475 5731	1.5259 6858	1.6956 5193	1.8840 3880
128	1.3765 7794	1.4517 7935	1.5310 5514	1.7027 1715	1.8934 5900
129	1.3800 1938	1.4560 1371	1.5361 5866	1.7098 1181	1.9029 2629
130	1.3834 6943	1.4602 6042	1.5412 7919	1.7169 3602	1.9124 4092
131	1.3869 2811	1.4645 1951	1.5464 1678	1.7240 8992	1.9220 0313
132	1.3903 9543	1.4687 9103	1.5515 7151	1.7312 7363	1.9316 1314
133	1.3938 7142	1.4730 7500	1.5567 4341	1.7384 8727	1.9412 7121
134	1.3973 5609	1.4773 7147	1.5619 3256	1.7457 3097	1.9509 7757
135	1.4008 4948	1.4816 8047	1.5671 3900	1.7530 0485	1.9607 3245
136	1.4043 5161	1.4860 0204	1.5723 6279	1.7603 0903	1.9705 3612
137	1.4078 6249	1.4903 3621	1.5776 0400	1.7676 4365	1.9803 8880
138	1.4113 8214	1.4946 8302	1.5828 6268	1.7750 0884	1.9902 9074
139	1.4149 1060	1.4990 4252	1.5881 3889	1.7824 0471	2.0002 4219
140	1.4184 4787	1.5034 1472	1.5934 3269	1.7898 3139	2.0102 4340
141	1.4219 9399	1.5077 9968	1.5987 4413	1.7972 8902	2.0202 9462
142	1.4255 4898	1.5121 9743	1.6040 7328	1.8047 7773	2.0303 9609
143	1.4291 1285	1.5166 0801	1.6094 2019	1.8122 9763	2.0405 4808
144	1.4326 8563	1.5210 3145	1.6147 8492	1.8198 4887	2.0507 5082
145	1.4362 6735	1.5254 6779	1.6201 6754	1.8274 3158	2.0610 0457
146	1.4398 5802	1.5299 1707	1.6255 6810	1.8350 4588	2.0713 0959
147	1.4434 5766	1.5343 7933	1.6309 8666	1.8426 9190	2.0816 6614
148	1.4470 6631	1.5388 5460	1.6364 2328	1.8503 6978	2.0920 7447
149	1.4506 8397	1.5433 4293	1.6418 7802	1.8580 7966	2.1025 3484
150	1.4543 1068	1.5478 4434	1.6473 5095	1.8658 2166	2.1130 4752

Table 8 (*Continued*)

$$(1 + i)^n$$

n	$\frac{1}{4}\%$	$\frac{7}{24}\%$	$\frac{1}{3}\%$	$\frac{5}{12}\%$	$\frac{1}{2}\%$
151	1.4579 4646	1.5523 5889	1.6528 4212	1.8735 9591	2.1236 1276
152	1.4615 9132	1.5568 8660	1.6583 5160	1.8814 0256	2.1342 3082
153	1.4652 4530	1.5614 2752	1.6638 7943	1.8892 4174	2.1449 0197
154	1.4689 0842	1.5659 8169	1.6694 2570	1.8971 1358	2.1556 2648
155	1.4725 8069	1.5705 4913	1.6749 9045	1.9050 1822	2.1664 0462
156	1.4762 6214	1.5751 2990	1.6805 7375	1.9129 5580	2.1772 3664
157	1.4799 5279	1.5797 2403	1.6861 7567	1.9209 2645	2.1881 2282
158	1.4836 5268	1.5843 3156	1.6917 9625	1.9289 3031	2.1990 6344
159	1.4873 6181	1.5889 5253	1.6974 3557	1.9369 6752	2.2100 58⁻⁵
160	1.4910 8021	1.5935 8697	1.7030 9369	1.9450 3821	2.2211 0905
161	1.4948 0791	1.5982 3493	1.7087 7067	1.9531 4254	2.2322 1459
162	1.4985 4493	1.6028 9645	1.7144 6657	1.9612 8063	2.2433 756ᶜ
163	1.5022 9129	1.6075 7157	1.7201 8146	1.9694 5264	2.2545 9254
164	1.5060 4702	1.6122 6032	1.7259 1540	1.9776 5869	2.2658 6551
165	1.5098 1214	1.6169 6274	1.7316 6845	1.9858 9893	2.2771 9483
166	1.5135 8667	1.6216 7888	1.7374 4068	1.9941 7351	2.2885 8081
167	1.5173 7064	1.6264 0878	1.7432 3215	2.0024 8257	2.3000 2371
168	1.5211 6406	1.6311 5247	1.7490 4292	2.0108 2625	2.3115 2383
169	1.5249 6697	1.6359 1000	1.7548 7306	2.0192 0469	2.3230 8145
170	1.5287 7939	1.6406 8140	1.7607 2264	2.0276 1804	2.3346 9686
171	1.5326 0134	1.6454 6673	1.7665 9172	2.0360 6645	2.3463 7034
172	1.5364 3284	1.6502 6600	1.7724 8035	2.0445 5006	2.3581 0219
173	1.5402 7393	1.6550 7928	1.7783 8862	2.0530 6902	2.3698 9270
174	1.5441 2461	1.6599 0659	1.7843 1658	2.0616 2347	2.3817 4217
175	1.5479 8492	1.6647 4799	1.7902 6431	2.0702 1357	2.3936 5088
176	1.5518 5488	1.6696 0350	1.7962 3185	2.0788 3946	2.4056 1913
177	1.5557 3452	1.6744 7318	1.8022 1929	2.0875 0129	2.4176 4723
178	1.5596 2386	1.6793 5706	1.8082 2669	2.0961 9921	2.4297 3546
179	1.5635 2292	1.6842 5518	1.8142 5411	2.1049 3338	2.4418 8414
180	1.5674 3172	1.6891 6760	1.8203 0163	2.1137 0393	2.4540 9356
181	1.5713 5030	1.6940 9433	1.8263 6930	2.1225 1103	2.4663 6403
182	1.5752 7868	1.6990 3544	1.8324 5720	2.1313 5483	2.4786 9585
183	1.5792 1688	1.7039 9096	1.8385 6539	2.1402 3547	2.4910 8933
184	1.5831 6492	1.7089 6094	1.8446 9394	2.1491 5312	2.5035 4478
185	1.5871 2283	1.7139 4541	1.8508 4292	2.1581 0793	2.5160 6250
186	1.5910 9064	1.7189 4441	1.8570 1240	2.1671 0004	2.5286 4281
187	1.5950 6836	1.7239 5800	1.8632 0244	2.1761 2963	2.5412 8603
188	1.5990 5604	1.7289 8621	1.8694 1311	2.1851 9683	2.5539 9246
189	1.6030 5368	1.7340 2909	1.8756 4449	2.1943 0182	2.5667 6242
190	1.6070 6131	1.7390 8667	1.8818 9664	2.2034 4474	2.5795 9623
191	1.6110 7896	1.7441 5901	1.8881 6963	2.2126 2576	2.5924 9421
192	1.6151 0666	1.7492 4614	1.8944 6352	2.2218 4504	2.6054 5668
193	1.6191 4443	1.7543 4811	1.9007 7840	2.2311 0272	2.6184 8397
194	1.6231 9229	1.7594 6496	1.9071 1433	2.2403 9899	2.6315 7639
195	1.6272 5027	1.7645 9673	1.9134 7138	2.2497 3398	2.6447 3427
196	1.6313 1839	1.7697 4347	1.9198 4962	2.2591 0787	2.6579 5794
197	1.6353 9669	1.7749 0522	1.9262 4912	2.2685 2082	2.6712 4773
198	1.6394 8518	1.7800 8203	1.9326 6995	2.2779 7299	2.6846 0397
199	1.6435 8390	1.7852 7393	1.9391 1218	2.2874 6455	2.6980 2699
200	1.6476 9285	1.7904 8098	1.9455 7589	2.2969 9565	2.7115 1712

Table 8   (*Continued*)

$(1 + i)^n$

n	$\frac{7}{12}\%$	$\frac{2}{3}\%$	$\frac{3}{4}\%$	$\frac{7}{8}\%$	1%
1	1.0058 3333	1.0066 6667	1.0075 0000	1.0087 5000	1.0100 0000
2	1.0117 0069	1.0133 7778	1.0150 5625	1.0175 7656	1.0201 0000
3	1.0176 0228	1.0201 3363	1.0226 6917	1.0264 8036	1.0303 0100
4	1.0235 3830	1.0269 3452	1.0303 3919	1.0354 6206	1.0406 0401
5	1.0295 0894	1.0337 8075	1.0380 6673	1.0445 2235	1.0510 1005
6	1.0355 1440	1.0406 7262	1.0458 5224	1.0536 6192	1.0615 2015
7	1.0415 5490	1.0476 1044	1.0536 9613	1.0628 8147	1.0721 3535
8	1.0476 3064	1.0545 9451	1.0615 9885	1.0721 8168	1.0828 5671
9	1.0537 4182	1.0616 2514	1.0695 6084	1.0815 6327	1.0936 8527
10	1.0598 8865	1.0687 0264	1.0775 8255	1.0910 2695	1.1046 2213
11	1.0660 7133	1.0758 2732	1.0856 6441	1.1005 7343	1.1156 6835
12	1.0722 9008	1.0829 9951	1.0938 0690	1.1102 0345	1.1268 2503
13	1.0785 4511	1.0902 1950	1.1020 1045	1.1199 1773	1.1380 9328
14	1.0848 3662	1.0974 8763	1.1102 7553	1.1297 1701	1.1494 7421
15	1.0911 6483	1.1048 0422	1.1186 0259	1.1396 0203	1.1609 6896
16	1.0975 2996	1.1121 6958	1.1269 9211	1.1495 7355	1.1725 7864
17	1.1039 3222	1.1195 8404	1.1354 4455	1.1596 3232	1.1843 0443
18	1.1103 7182	1.1270 4794	1.1439 6039	1.1697 7910	1.1961 4748
19	1.1168 4899	1.1345 6159	1.1525 4009	1.1800 1467	1.2081 0895
20	1.1233 6395	1.1421 2533	1.1611 8414	1.1903 3980	1.2201 9004
21	1.1299 1690	1.1497 3950	1.1698 9302	1.2007 5527	1.2323 9194
22	1.1365 0808	1.1574 0443	1.1786 6722	1.2112 6188	1.2447 1586
23	1.1431 3771	1.1651 2046	1.1875 0723	1.2218 6042	1.2571 6302
24	1.1498 0602	1.1728 8793	1.1964 1353	1.2325 5170	1.2697 3465
25	1.1565 1322	1.1807 0718	1.2053 8663	1.2433 3653	1.2824 3200
26	1.1632 5955	1.1885 7857	1.2144 2703	1.2542 1572	1.2952 5631
27	1.1700 4523	1.1965 0242	1.2235 3523	1.2651 9011	1.3082 0888
28	1.1768 7049	1.2044 7911	1.2327 1175	1.2762 6052	1.3212 9097
29	1.1837 3557	1.2125 0897	1.2419 5709	1.2874 2780	1.3345 0388
30	1.1906 4069	1.2205 9236	1.2512 7176	1.2986 9280	1.3478 4892
31	1.1975 8610	1.2287 2964	1.2606 5630	1.3100 5636	1.3613 2740
32	1.2045 7202	1.2369 2117	1.2701 1122	1.3215 1935	1.3749 4068
33	1.2115 9869	1.2451 6731	1.2796 3706	1.3330 8265	1.3886 9009
34	1.2186 6634	1.2534 6843	1.2892 3434	1.3447 4712	1.4025 7699
35	1.2257 7523	1.2618 2489	1.2989 0359	1.3565 1366	1.4166 0276
36	1.2329 2559	1.2702 3705	1.3086 4537	1.3683 8315	1.4307 6878
37	1.2401 1765	1.2787 0530	1.3184 6021	1.3803 5650	1.4450 7647
38	1.2473 5167	1.2872 3000	1.3283 4866	1.3924 3462	1.4595 2724
39	1.2546 2789	1.2958 1153	1.3383 1128	1.4046 1843	1.4741 2251
40	1.2619 4655	1.3044 5028	1.3483 4861	1.4169 0884	1.4888 6373
41	1.2693 0791	1.3131 4661	1.3584 6123	1.4293 0679	1.5037 5237
42	1.2767 1220	1.3219 0092	1.3686 4969	1.4418 1322	1.5187 8989
43	1.2841 5969	1.3307 1360	1.3789 1456	1.4544 2909	1.5339 7779
44	1.2916 5062	1.3395 8502	1.3892 5642	1.4671 5534	1.5493 1757
45	1.2991 8525	1.3485 1559	1.3996 7584	1.4799 9295	1.5648 1075
46	1.3067 6383	1.3575 0569	1.4101 7341	1.4929 4289	1.5804 5885
47	1.3143 8662	1.3665 5573	1.4207 4971	1.5060 0614	1.5962 6344
48	1.3220 5388	1.3756 6610	1.4314 0533	1.5191 8370	1.6122 2608
49	1.3297 6586	1.3848 3721	1.4421 4087	1.5324 7655	1.6283 4834
50	1.3375 2283	1.3940 6946	1.4529 5693	1.5458 8572	1.6446 3182

Table 8 *(Continued)*

$$(1 + i)^n$$

n	$7\!\!/\!12\%$	$2\!\!/\!3\%$	$3\!\!/\!4\%$	$7\!\!/\!8\%$	1%
51	1.3453 2504	1.4033 6325	1.4638 5411	1.5594 1222	1.6610 7814
52	1.3531 7277	1.4127 1901	1.4748 3301	1.5730 5708	1.6776 8892
53	1.3610 6628	1.4221 3713	1.4858 9426	1.5868 2133	1.6944 6581
54	1.3690 0583	1.4316 1805	1.4970 3847	1.6007 0602	1.7114 1047
55	1.3769 9170	1.4411 6217	1.5082 6626	1.6147 1219	1.7285 2457
56	1.3850 2415	1.4507 6992	1.5195 7825	1.6288 4093	1.7458 0982
57	1.3931 0346	1.4604 4172	1.5309 7509	1.6430 9328	1.7632 6792
58	1.4012 2990	1.4701 7799	1.5424 5740	1.6574 7035	1.7809 0060
59	1.4094 0374	1.4799 7918	1.5540 2583	1.6719 7322	1.7987 0960
60	1.4176 2526	1.4898 4571	1.5656 8103	1.6866 0298	1.8166 9670
61	1.4258 9474	1.4997 7801	1.5774 2363	1.7013 6076	1.8348 6367
62	1.4342 1246	1.5097 7653	1.5892 5431	1.7162 4766	1.8532 1230
63	1.4425 7870	1.5198 4171	1.6011 7372	1.7312 6483	1.8717 4443
64	1.4509 9374	1.5299 7399	1.6131 8252	1.7464 1340	1.8904 6187
65	1.4594 5787	1.5401 7381	1.6252 8139	1.7616 9452	1.9093 6649
66	1.4679 7138	1.5504 4164	1.6374 7100	1.7771 0934	1.9284 6015
67	1.4765 3454	1.5607 7792	1.6497 5203	1.7926 5905	1.9477 4475
68	1.4851 4766	1.5711 8310	1.6621 2517	1.8083 4482	1.9672 2220
69	1.4938 1102	1.5816 5766	1.6745 9111	1.8241 6783	1.9868 9442
70	1.5025 2492	1.5922 0204	1.6871 5055	1.8401 2930	2.0067 6337
71	1.5112 8965	1.6028 1672	1.6998 0418	1.8562 3043	2.0268 3100
72	1.5201 0550	1.6135 0217	1.7125 5271	1.8724 7245	2.0470 9931
73	1.5289 7279	1.6242 5885	1.7253 9685	1.8888 5658	2.0675 7031
74	1.5378 9179	1.6350 8724	1.7383 3733	1.9053 8408	2.0882 4601
75	1.5468 6283	1.6459 8782	1.7513 7486	1.9220 5619	2.1091 2847
76	1.5558 8620	1.6569 6107	1.7645 1017	1.9388 7418	2.1302 1975
77	1.5649 6220	1.6680 0748	1.7777 4400	1.9558 3933	2.1515 2195
78	1.5740 9115	1.6791 2753	1.7910 7708	1.9729 5292	2.1730 3717
79	1.5832 7334	1.6903 2172	1.8045 1015	1.9902 1626	2.1947 6754
80	1.5925 0910	1.7015 9053	1.8180 4398	2.0076 3066	2.2167 1522
81	1.6017 9874	1.7129 3446	1.8316 7931	2.0251 9742	2.2388 8237
82	1.6111 4257	1.7243 5403	1.8454 1691	2.0429 1790	2.2612 7119
83	1.6205 4090	1.7358 4972	1.8592 5753	2.0607 9343	2.2838 8390
84	1.6299 9405	1.7474 2205	1.8732 0196	2.0788 2537	2.3067 2274
85	1.6395 0235	1.7590 7153	1.8872 5098	2.0970 1510	2.3297 8997
86	1.6490 6612	1.7707 9868	1.9014 0536	2.1153 6398	2.3530 8787
87	1.6586 8567	1.7826 0400	1.9156 6590	2.1338 7341	2.3766 1875
88	1.6683 6134	1.7944 8803	1.9300 3339	2.1525 4481	2.4003 8494
89	1.6780 9344	1.8064 5128	1.9445 0865	2.1713 7957	2.4243 8879
90	1.6878 8232	1.8184 9429	1.9590 9246	2.1903 7914	2.4486 3267
91	1.6977 2830	1.8306 1758	1.9737 8565	2.2095 4496	2.4731 1900
92	1.7076 3172	1.8428 2170	1.9885 8905	2.2288 7848	2.4978 5019
93	1.7175 9290	1.8551 0718	2.0035 0346	2.2483 8117	2.5228 2869
94	1.7276 1219	1.8674 7456	2.0185 2974	2.2680 5450	2.5480 5698
95	1.7376 8993	1.8799 2439	2.0336 6871	2.2878 9998	2.5735 3755
96	1.7478 2646	1.8924 5722	2.0489 2123	2.3079 1910	2.5992 7293
97	1.7580 2211	1.9050 7360	2.0642 8814	2.3281 1340	2.6252 6565
98	1.7682 7724	1.9177 7409	2.0797 7030	2.3484 8439	2.6515 1831
99	1.7785 9219	1.9305 5925	2.0953 6858	2.3690 3363	2.6780 3349
100	1.7889 6731	1.9434 2965	2.1110 8384	2.3897 6267	2.7048 1383

Table 8   (*Continued*)

$$(1 + i)^n$$

n	$\frac{7}{12}\%$	$\frac{2}{3}\%$	$\frac{3}{4}\%$	$\frac{7}{8}\%$	1%
101	1.7994 0295	1.9563 8585	2.1269 1697	2.4106 7309	2.7318 6197
102	1.8098 9947	1.9694 2842	2.1428 6885	2.4317 6648	2.7591 8059
103	1.8204 5722	1.9825 5794	2.1589 4036	2.4530 4444	2.7867 7239
104	1.8310 7655	1.9957 7499	2.1751 3242	2.4745 0858	2.8146 4012
105	1.8417 5783	2.0090 8016	2.1914 4591	2.4961 6053	2.8427 8652
106	1.8525 0142	2.0224 7403	2.2078 8175	2.5180 0193	2.8712 1438
107	1.8633 0768	2.0359 5719	2.2244 4087	2.5400 3445	2.8999 2653
108	1.8741 7697	2.0495 3024	2.2411 2417	2.5622 5975	2.9289 2579
109	1.8851 0967	2.0631 9377	2.2579 3260	2.5846 7953	2.9582 1505
110	1.8961 0614	2.0769 4840	2.2748 6710	2.6072 9547	2.9877 9720
111	1.9071 6676	2.0907 9472	2.2919 2860	2.6301 0931	3.0176 7517
112	1.9182 9190	2.1047 3335	2.3091 1807	2.6531 2276	3.0478 5192
113	1.9294 8194	2.1187 6491	2.3264 3645	2.6763 3759	3.0783 3044
114	1.9407 3725	2.1328 9000	2.3438 8472	2.6997 5554	3.1091 1375
115	1.9520 5822	2.1471 0927	2.3614 6386	2.7233 7840	3.1402 0489
116	1.9634 4522	2.1614 2333	2.3791 7484	2.7472 0796	3.1716 0693
117	1.9748 9865	2.1758 3282	2.3970 1865	2.7712 4603	3.2033 2300
118	1.9864 1890	2.1903 3837	2.4149 9629	2.7954 9444	3.2353 5623
119	1.9980 0634	2.2049 4063	2.4331 0876	2.8199 5501	3.2677 0980
120	2.0096 6138	2.2196 4023	2.4513 5708	2.8446 2962	3.3003 8689
121	2.0213 8440	2.2344 3784	2.4697 4226	2.8695 2013	3.3333 9076
122	2.0331 7581	2.2493 3409	2.4882 6532	2.8946 2843	3.3667 2467
123	2.0450 3600	2.2643 2965	2.5069 2731	2.9199 5643	3.4003 9192
124	2.0569 6538	2.2794 2518	2.5257 2927	2.9455 0605	3.4343 9584
125	2.0689 6434	2.2946 2135	2.5446 7224	2.9712 7922	3.4687 3980
126	2.0810 3330	2.3099 1882	2.5637 5728	2.9972 7792	3.5034 2719
127	2.0931 7266	2.3253 1828	2.5829 8546	3.0235 0410	3.5384 6147
128	2.1053 8284	2.3408 2040	2.6023 5785	3.0499 5976	3.5738 4608
129	2.1176 6424	2.3564 2587	2.6218 7553	3.0766 4691	3.6095 8454
130	2.1300 1728	2.3721 3538	2.6415 3960	3.1035 6757	3.6456 8039
131	2.1424 4238	2.3879 4962	2.6613 5115	3.1307 2378	3.6821 3719
132	2.1549 3996	2.4038 6928	2.6813 1128	3.1581 1762	3.7189 5856
133	2.1675 1044	2.4198 9507	2.7014 2112	3.1857 5115	3.7561 4815
134	2.1801 5425	2.4360 2771	2.7216 8177	3.2136 2647	3.7937 0963
135	2.1928 7182	2.4522 6789	2.7420 9439	3.2417 4570	3.8316 4673
136	2.2056 6357	2.4686 1635	2.7626 6009	3.2701 1098	3.8699 6319
137	2.2185 2994	2.4850 7379	2.7833 8005	3.2987 2445	3.9086 6282
138	2.2314 7137	2.5016 4095	2.8042 5540	3.3275 8829	3.9477 4945
139	2.2444 8828	2.5183 1855	2.8252 8731	3.3567 0468	3.9872 2695
140	2.2575 8113	2.5351 0734	2.8464 7697	3.3860 7585	4.0270 9922
141	2.2707 5036	2.5520 0806	2.8678 2554	3.4157 0401	4.0673 7021
142	2.2839 9640	2.5690 2145	2.8893 3424	3.4455 9142	4.1080 4391
143	2.2973 1971	2.5861 4826	2.9110 0424	3.4757 4035	4.1491 2435
144	2.3107 2074	2.6033 8924	2.9328 3677	3.5061 5308	4.1906 1559
145	2.3241 9995	2.6207 4517	2.9548 3305	3.5368 3192	4.2325 2175
146	2.3377 5778	2.6382 1681	2.9769 9430	3.5677 7919	4.2748 4697
147	2.3513 9470	2.6558 0492	2.9993 2175	3.5989 9726	4.3175 9544
148	2.3651 1117	2.6735 1028	3.0218 1667	3.6304 8849	4.3607 7139
149	2.3789 0765	2.6913 3369	3.0444 8029	3.6622 5526	4.4043 7910
150	2.3927 8461	2.7092 7591	3.0673 1389	3.6943 0000	4.4484 2290

Table 8 (*Continued*)

$$(1 + i)^n$$

n	$\frac{7}{12}\%$	$\frac{2}{3}\%$	$\frac{3}{4}\%$	$\frac{7}{8}\%$	1%
151	2.4067 4252	2.7273 3775	3.0903 1875	3.7266 2512	4.4929 0712
152	2.4207 8186	2.7455 2000	3.1134 9614	3.7592 3309	4.5378 3620
153	2.4349 0308	2.7638 2347	3.1368 4736	3.7921 2638	4.5832 1456
154	2.4491 0668	2.7822 4896	3.1603 7372	3.8253 0749	4.6290 4670
155	2.4633 9314	2.8007 9729	3.1840 7652	3.8587 7893	4.6753 3717
156	2.4777 6293	2.8194 6927	3.2079 5709	3.8925 4324	4.7220 9054
157	2.4922 1655	2.8382 6573	3.2320 1677	3.9266 0300	4.7693 1145
158	2.5067 5448	2.8571 8750	3.2562 5690	3.9609 6077	4.8170 0456
159	2.5213 7721	2.8762 3542	3.2806 7882	3.9956 1918	4.8651 7461
160	2.5360 8525	2.8954 1032	3.3052 8391	4.0305 8085	4.9138 2635
161	2.5508 7908	2.9147 1306	3.3300 7354	4.0658 4843	4.9629 6462
162	2.5657 5921	2.9341 4448	3.3550 4910	4.1014 2460	5.0125 9426
163	2.5807 2614	2.9537 0544	3.3802 1196	4.1373 1207	5.0627 2021
164	2.5957 8037	2.9733 9681	3.4055 6355	4.1735 1355	5.1133 4741
165	2.6109 2242	2.9932 1945	3.4311 0528	4.2100 3179	5.1644 8088
166	2.6261 5280	3.0131 7425	3.4568 3857	4.2468 6957	5.2161 2569
167	2.6414 7203	3.0332 6208	3.4827 6486	4.2840 2968	5.2682 8695
168	2.6568 8062	3.0534 8383	3.5088 8560	4.3215 1494	5.3209 6982
169	2.6723 7909	3.0738 4038	3.5352 0224	4.3593 2819	5.3741 7952
170	2.6879 6796	3.0943 3265	3.5617 1625	4.3974 7232	5.4279 2131
171	2.7036 4778	3.1149 6154	3.5884 2913	4.4359 5020	5.4822 0052
172	2.7194 1906	3.1357 2795	3.6153 4234	4.4747 6476	5.5370 2253
173	2.7352 8233	3.1566 3280	3.6424 5741	4.5139 1896	5.5923 9275
174	2.7512 3815	3.1776 7702	3.6697 7584	4.5534 1575	5.6483 1668
175	2.7672 8704	3.1988 6153	3.6972 9916	4.5932 5813	5.7047 9985
176	2.7834 2954	3.2201 8728	3.7250 2891	4.6334 4914	5.7618 4785
177	2.7996 6622	3.2416 5519	3.7529 6662	4.6739 9182	5.8194 6633
178	2.8159 9760	3.2632 6623	3.7811 1387	4.7148 8925	5.8776 6099
179	2.8324 2426	3.2850 2134	3.8094 7223	4.7561 4453	5.9364 3760
180	2.8489 4673	3.3069 2148	3.8380 4327	4.7977 6080	5.9958 0198
181	2.8655 6559	3.3289 6762	3.8668 2859	4.8397 4120	6.0557 6000
182	2.8822 8139	3.3511 6074	3.8958 2981	4.8820 8894	6.1163 1760
183	2.8990 9469	3.3735 0181	3.9250 4853	4.9248 0722	6.1774 8077
184	2.9160 0608	3.3959 9182	3.9544 8639	4.9678 9928	6.2392 5558
185	2.9330 1612	3.4186 3177	3.9841 4504	5.0113 6840	6.3016 4813
186	2.9501 2538	3.4414 2265	4.0140 2613	5.0552 1787	6.3646 6462
187	2.9673 3444	3.4643 6546	4.0441 3133	5.0994 5103	6.4283 1126
188	2.9846 4389	3.4874 6123	4.0744 6231	5.1440 7123	6.4925 9437
189	3.0020 5431	3.5107 1097	4.1050 2078	5.1890 8185	6.5575 2032
190	3.0195 6630	3.5341 1571	4.1358 0843	5.2344 8631	6.6230 9552
191	3.0371 8043	3.5576 7649	4.1668 2700	5.2802 8807	6.6893 2648
192	3.0548 9732	3.5813 9433	4.1980 7820	5.3264 9059	6.7562 1974
193	3.0727 1755	3.6052 7029	4.2295 6379	5.3730 9738	6.8237 8194
194	3.0906 4174	3.6293 0543	4.2612 8551	5.4201 1199	6.8920 1976
195	3.1086 7048	3.6535 0080	4.2932 4516	5.4675 3797	6.9609 3996
196	3.1268 0440	3.6778 5747	4.3254 4449	5.5153 7892	7.0305 4936
197	3.1450 4409	3.7023 7652	4.3578 8533	5.5636 3849	7.1008 5485
198	3.1633 9018	3.7270 5903	4.3905 6947	5.6123 2033	7.1718 6340
199	3.1818 4329	3.7519 0609	4.4234 9874	5.6614 2813	7.2435 8203
200	3.2004 0404	3.7769 1880	4.4566 7498	5.7109 6562	7.3160 1785

Table 8 (*Continued*)

$$(1 + i)^n$$

n	$1\frac{1}{8}\%$	$1\frac{1}{4}\%$	$1\frac{3}{8}\%$	$1\frac{1}{2}\%$	$1\frac{3}{4}\%$
1	1.0112 5000	1.0125 0000	1.0137 5000	1.0150 0000	1.0175 0000
2	1.0226 2656	1.0251 5625	1.0276 8906	1.0302 2500	1.0353 0625
3	1.0341 3111	1.0379 7070	1.0418 1979	1.0456 7838	1.0534 2411
4	1.0457 6509	1.0509 4534	1.0561 4481	1.0613 6355	1.0718 5903
5	1.0575 2994	1.0640 8215	1.0706 6680	1.0772 8400	1.0906 1656
6	1.0694 2716	1.0773 8318	1.0853 8847	1.0934 4326	1.1097 0235
7	1.0814 5821	1.0908 5047	1.1003 1256	1.1098 4491	1.1291 2215
8	1.0936 2462	1.1044 8610	1.1154 4186	1.1264 9259	1.1488 8178
9	1.1059 2789	1.1182 9218	1.1307 7918	1.1433 8998	1.1689 8721
10	1.1183 6958	1.1322 7083	1.1463 2740	1.1605 4083	1.1894 4449
11	1.1309 5124	1.1464 2422	1.1620 8940	1.1779 4894	1.2102 5977
12	1.1436 7444	1.1607 5452	1.1780 6813	1.1956 1817	1.2314 3931
13	1.1565 4078	1.1752 6395	1.1942 6656	1.2135 5244	1.2529 8950
14	1.1695 5186	1.1899 5475	1.2106 8773	1.2317 5573	1.2749 1682
15	1.1827 0932	1.2048 2918	1.2273 3469	1.2502 3207	1.2972 2786
16	1.1960 1480	1.2198 8955	1.2442 1054	1.2689 8555	1.3199 2935
17	1.2094 6997	1.2351 3817	1.2613 1843	1.2880 2033	1.3430 2811
18	1.2230 7650	1.2505 7739	1.2786 6156	1.3073 4064	1.3665 3111
19	1.2368 3611	1.2662 0961	1.2962 4316	1.3269 5075	1.3904 4540
20	1.2507 5052	1.2820 3723	1.3140 6650	1.3468 5501	1.4147 7820
21	1.2648 2146	1.2980 6270	1.3321 3492	1.3670 5783	1.4395 3681
22	1.2790 5071	1.3142 8848	1.3504 5177	1.3875 6370	1.4647 2871
23	1.2934 4003	1.3307 1709	1.3690 2048	1.4083 7715	1.4903 6146
24	1.3079 9123	1.3473 5105	1.3878 4451	1.4295 0281	1.5164 4279
25	1.3227 0613	1.3641 9294	1.4069 2738	1.4509 4535	1.5429 8054
26	1.3375 8657	1.3812 4535	1.4262 7263	1.4727 0953	1.5699 8269
27	1.3526 3442	1.3985 1092	1.4458 8388	1.4948 0018	1.5974 5739
28	1.3678 5156	1.4159 9230	1.4657 6478	1.5172 2218	1.6254 1290
29	1.3832 3989	1.4336 9221	1.4859 1905	1.5399 8051	1.6538 5762
30	1.3988 0134	1.4516 1336	1.5063 5043	1.5630 8022	1.6828 0013
31	1.4145 3785	1.4697 5853	1.5270 6275	1.5865 2642	1.7122 4913
32	1.4304 5140	1.4881 3051	1.5480 5986	1.6103 2432	1.7422 1349
33	1.4465 4398	1.5067 3214	1.5693 4569	1.6344 7918	1.7727 0223
34	1.4628 1760	1.5255 6629	1.5909 2419	1.6589 9637	1.8037 2452
35	1.4792 7430	1.5446 3587	1.6127 9940	1.6838 8132	1.8352 8970
36	1.4959 1613	1.5639 4382	1.6349 7539	1.7091 3954	1.8674 0727
37	1.5127 4519	1.5834 9312	1.6574 5630	1.7347 7663	1.9000 8689
38	1.5297 6357	1.6032 8678	1.6802 4633	1.7607 9828	1.9333 3841
39	1.5469 7341	1.6233 2787	1.7033 4971	1.7872 1025	1.9671 7184
40	1.5643 7687	1.6436 1946	1.7267 7077	1.8140 1841	2.0015 9734
41	1.5819 7611	1.6641 6471	1.7505 1387	1.8412 2868	2.0366 2530
42	1.5997 7334	1.6849 6677	1.7745 8343	1.8688 4712	2.0722 6624
43	1.6177 7079	1.7060 2885	1.7989 8396	1.8968 7982	2.1085 3090
44	1.6359 7071	1.7273 5421	1.8237 1999	1.9253 3302	2.1454 3019
45	1.6543 7538	1.7489 4614	1.8487 9614	1.9542 1301	2.1829 7522
46	1.6729 8710	1.7708 0797	1.8742 1708	1.9835 2621	2.2211 7728
47	1.6918 0821	1.7929 4306	1.8999 8757	2.0132 7910	2.2600 4789
48	1.7108 4105	1.8153 5485	1.9261 1240	2.0434 7829	2.2995 9872
49	1.7300 8801	1.8380 4679	1.9525 9644	2.0741 3046	2.3398 4170
50	1.7495 5150	1.8610 2237	1.9794 4464	2.1052 4242	2.3807 8893

Table 8 *(Continued)*
$(1 + i)^n$

n	$1\frac{1}{8}\%$	$1\frac{1}{4}\%$	$1\frac{3}{8}\%$	$1\frac{1}{2}\%$	$1\frac{3}{4}\%$
51	1.7692 3395	1.8842 8515	2.0066 6201	2.1368 2106	2.4224 5274
52	1.7891 3784	1.9078 3872	2.0342 5361	2.1688 7337	2.4648 4566
53	1.8092 6564	1.9316 8670	2.0622 2460	2.2014 0647	2.5079 8046
54	1.8296 1988	1.9558 3279	2.0905 8019	2.2344 2757	2.5518 7012
55	1.8502 0310	1.9802 8070	2.1193 2566	2.2679 4398	2.5965 2785
56	1.8710 1788	2.0050 3420	2.1484 6639	2.3019 6314	2.6419 6708
57	1.8920 6684	2.0300 9713	2.1780 0780	2.3364 9259	2.6882 0151
58	1.9133 5259	2.0554 7335	2.2079 5541	2.3715 3998	2.7352 4503
59	1.9348 7780	2.0811 6676	2.2383 1480	2.4071 1308	2.7831 1182
60	1.9566 4518	2.1071 8135	2.2690 9163	2.4432 1978	2.8318 1628
61	1.9786 5744	2.1335 2111	2.3002 9164	2.4798 6807	2.8813 7306
62	2.0009 1733	2.1601 9013	2.3319 2065	2.5170 6609	2.9317 9709
63	2.0234 2765	2.1871 9250	2.3639 8456	2.5548 2208	2.9831 0354
64	2.0461 9121	2.2145 3241	2.3964 8934	2.5931 4442	3.0353 0785
65	2.0692 1087	2.2422 1407	2.4294 4107	2.6320 4158	3.0884 2574
66	2.0924 8949	2.2702 4174	2.4628 4589	2.6715 2221	3.1424 7319
67	2.1160 2999	2.2986 1976	2.4967 1002	2.7115 9504	3.1974 6647
68	2.1398 3533	2.3273 5251	2.5310 3978	2.7522 6896	3.2534 2213
69	2.1639 0848	2.3564 4442	2.5658 4158	2.7935 5300	3.3103 5702
70	2.1882 5245	2.3858 9997	2.6011 2190	2.8354 5629	3.3682 8827
71	2.2128 7029	2.4157 2372	2.6368 8732	2.8779 8814	3.4272 3331
72	2.2377 6508	2.4459 2027	2.6731 4453	2.9211 5796	3.4872 0990
73	2.2629 3994	2.4764 9427	2.7099 0026	2.9649 7533	3.5482 3607
74	2.2883 9801	2.5074 5045	2.7471 6139	3.0094 4996	3.6103 3020
75	2.3141 4249	2.5387 9358	2.7849 3486	3.0545 9171	3.6735 1098
76	2.3401 7659	2.5705 2850	2.8232 2771	3.1004 1059	3.7377 9742
77	2.3665 0358	2.6026 6011	2.8620 4710	3.1469 1674	3.8032 0888
78	2.3931 2675	2.6351 9336	2.9014 0024	3.1941 2050	3.8697 6503
79	2.4200 4942	2.6681 3327	2.9412 9450	3.2420 3230	3.9374 8592
80	2.4472 7498	2.7014 8494	2.9817 3730	3.2906 6279	4.0063 9192
81	2.4748 0682	2.7352 5350	3.0227 3618	3.3400 2273	4.0765 0378
82	2.5026 4840	2.7694 4417	3.0642 9881	3.3901 2307	4.1478 4260
83	2.5308 0319	2.8040 6222	3.1064 3291	3.4409 7492	4.2204 2984
84	2.5592 7473	2.8391 1300	3.1491 4637	3.4925 8954	4.2942 8737
85	2.5880 6657	2.8746 0191	3.1924 4713	3.5449 7838	4.3694 3740
86	2.6171 8232	2.9105 3444	3.2363 4328	3.5981 5306	4.4459 0255
87	2.6466 2562	2.9469 1612	3.2808 4300	3.6521 2535	4.5237 0584
88	2.6764 0016	2.9837 5257	3.3259 5459	3.7069 0723	4.6028 7070
89	2.7065 0966	3.0210 4948	3.3716 8646	3.7625 1084	4.6834 2093
90	2.7369 5789	3.0588 1260	3.4180 4715	3.8189 4851	4.7653 8080
91	2.7677 4867	3.0970 4775	3.4650 4530	3.8762 3273	4.8487 7496
92	2.7988 8584	3.1357 6085	3.5126 8967	3.9343 7622	4.9336 2853
93	2.8303 7331	3.1749 5786	3.5609 8916	3.9933 9187	5.0199 6703
94	2.8622 1501	3.2146 4483	3.6099 5276	4.0532 9275	5.1078 1645
95	2.8944 1492	3.2548 2789	3.6595 8961	4.1140 9214	5.1972 0324
96	2.9269 7709	3.2955 1324	3.7099 0897	4.1758 0352	5.2881 5429
97	2.9599 0559	3.3367 0716	3.7609 2021	4.2384 4057	5.3806 9699
98	2.9932 0452	3.3784 1600	3.8126 3287	4.3020 1718	5.4748 5919
99	3.0268 7807	3.4206 4620	3.8650 5657	4.3665 4744	5.5706 6923
100	3.0609 3045	3.4634 0427	3.9182 0110	4.4320 4565	5.6681 5594

Table 8   (*Continued*)

$$(1 + i)^n$$

n	2%	$2\frac{1}{4}\%$	$2\frac{1}{2}\%$	$2\frac{3}{4}\%$	3%
1	1.0200 0000	1.0225 0000	1.0250 0000	1.0275 0000	1.0300 0000
2	1.0404 0000	1.0455 0625	1.0506 2500	1.0557 5625	1.0609 0000
3	1.0612 0800	1.0690 3014	1.0768 9063	1.0847 8955	1.0927 2700
4	1.0824 3216	1.0930 8332	1.1038 1289	1.1146 2126	1.1255 0881
5	1.1040 8080	1.1176 7769	1.1314 0821	1.1452 7334	1.1592 7407
6	1.1261 6242	1.1428 2544	1.1596 9342	1.1767 6836	1.1940 5230
7	1.1486 8567	1.1685 3901	1.1886 8575	1.2091 2949	1.2298 7387
8	1.1716 5938	1.1948 3114	1.2184 0290	1.2423 8055	1.2667 7008
9	1.1950 9257	1.2217 1484	1.2488 6297	1.2765 4602	1.3047 7318
10	1.2189 9442	1.2492 0343	1.2800 8454	1.3116 5103	1.3439 1638
11	1.2433 7431	1.2773 1050	1.3120 8666	1.3477 2144	1.3842 3387
12	1.2682 4179	1.3060 4999	1.3448 8882	1.3847 8378	1.4257 6089
13	1.2936 0663	1.3354 3611	1.3785 1104	1.4228 6533	1.4685 3371
14	1.3194 7876	1.3654 8343	1.4129 7382	1.4619 9413	1.5125 8972
15	1.3458 6834	1.3962 0680	1.4482 9817	1.5021 9896	1.5579 6742
16	1.3727 8571	1.4276 2146	1.4845 0562	1.5435 0944	1.6047 0644
17	1.4002 4142	1.4597 4294	1.5216 1826	1.5859 5595	1.6528 4763
18	1.4282 4625	1.4925 8716	1.5596 5872	1.6295 6973	1.7024 3306
19	1.4568 1117	1.5261 7037	1.5986 5019	1.6743 8290	1.7535 0605
20	1.4859 4740	1.5605 0920	1.6386 1644	1.7204 2843	1.8061 1123
21	1.5156 6634	1.5956 2066	1.6795 8185	1.7677 4021	1.8602 9457
22	1.5459 7967	1.6315 2212	1.7215 7140	1.8163 5307	1.9161 0341
23	1.5768 9926	1.6682 3137	1.7646 1068	1.8663 0278	1.9735 8651
24	1.6084 3725	1.7057 6658	1.8087 2595	1.9176 2610	2.0327 9411
25	1.6406 0599	1.7441 4632	1.8539 4410	1.9703 6082	2.0937 7793
26	1.6734 1811	1.7833 8962	1.9002 9270	2.0245 4575	2.1565 9127
27	1.7068 8648	1.8235 1588	1.9478 0002	2.0802 2075	2.2212 8901
28	1.7410 2421	1.8645 4499	1.9964 9502	2.1374 2682	2.2879 2768
29	1.7758 4469	1.9064 9725	2.0464 0739	2.1962 0606	2.3565 6551
30	1.8113 6158	1.9493 9344	2.0975 6758	2.2566 0173	2.4272 6247
31	1.8475 8882	1.9932 5479	2.1500 0677	2.3186 5828	2.5000 8035
32	1.8845 4059	2.0381 0303	2.2037 5694	2.3824 2138	2.5750 8276
33	1.9222 3140	2.0839 6034	2.2588 5086	2.4479 3797	2.6523 3524
34	1.9606 7603	2.1308 4945	2.3153 2213	2.5152 5626	2.7319 0530
35	1.9998 8955	2.1787 9356	2.3732 0519	2.5844 2581	2.8138 6245
36	2.0398 8734	2.2278 1642	2.4325 3532	2.6554 9752	2.8982 7833
37	2.0806 8509	2.2779 4229	2.4933 4870	2.7285 2370	2.9852 2668
38	2.1222 9879	2.3291 9599	2.5556 8242	2.8035 5810	3.0747 8348
39	2.1647 4477	2.3816 0290	2.6195 7448	2.8806 5595	3.1670 2698
40	2.2080 3966	2.4351 8897	2.6850 6384	2.9598 7399	3.2620 3779
41	2.2522 0046	2.4899 8072	2.7521 9043	3.0412 7052	3.3598 9893
42	2.2972 4447	2.5460 0528	2.8209 9520	3.1249 0546	3.4606 9589
43	2.3431 8936	2.6032 9040	2.8915 2008	3.2108 4036	3.5645 1677
44	2.3900 5314	2.6618 6444	2.9638 0808	3.2991 3847	3.6714 5227
45	2.4378 5421	2.7217 5639	3.0379 0328	3.3898 6478	3.7815 9584
46	2.4866 1129	2.7829 9590	3.1138 5086	3.4830 8606	3.8950 4372
47	2.5363 4352	2.8456 1331	3.1916 9713	3.5788 7093	4.0118 9503
48	2.5870 7039	2.9096 3961	3.2714 8956	3.6772 8988	4.1322 5188
49	2.6388 1179	2.9751 0650	3.3532 7680	3.7784 1535	4.2562 1944
50	2.6915 8803	3.0420 4640	3.4371 0872	3.8823 2177	4.3839 0602

Table 8 *(Continued)*

$$(1 + i)^n$$

n	2%	$2\tfrac{1}{4}\%$	$2\tfrac{1}{2}\%$	$2\tfrac{3}{4}\%$	3%
51	2.7454 1979	3.1104 9244	3.5230 3644	3.9890 8562	4.5154 2320
52	2.8003 2819	3.1804 7852	3.6111 1235	4.0987 8547	4 6508 8590
53	2.8563 3475	3.2520 3929	3.7013 9016	4.2115 0208	4.7904 1247
54	2.9134 6144	3.3252 1017	3.7939 2491	4.3273 1838	4.9341 2485
55	2.9717 3067	3.4000 2740	3.8887 7303	4.4463 1964	5.0821 4859
56	3.0311 6529	3.4765 2802	3.9859 9236	4.5685 9343	5.2346 1305
57	3.0917 8859	3.5547 4990	4.0856 4217	4.6942 2975	5.3916 5144
58	3.1536 2436	3.6347 3177	4.1877 8322	4.8233 2107	5.5534 0098
59	3.2166 9685	3.7165 1324	4.2924 7780	4.9559 6239	5.7200 0301
60	3.2810 3079	3.8001 3479	4.3997 8975	5.0922 5136	5.8916 0310
61	3.3466 5140	3.8856 3782	4.5097 8449	5.2322 8827	6.0683 5120
62	3.4135 8443	3.9730 6467	4.6225 2910	5.3761 7620	6.2504 0173
63	3.4818 5612	4.0624 5862	4.7380 9233	5.5240 2105	6.4379 1379
64	3.5514 9324	4.1538 6394	4.8565 4464	5.6759 3162	6.6310 5120
65	3.6225 2311	4.2473 2588	4.9779 5826	5.8320 1974	6.8299 8273
66	3.6949 7357	4.3428 9071	5.1024 0721	5.9924 0029	7.0348 8222
67	3.7688 7304	4.4406 0576	5.2299 6739	6.1571 9130	7.2459 2868
68	3.8442 5050	4.5405 1939	5.3607 1658	6.3265 1406	7.4633 0654
69	3.9211 3551	4.6426 8107	5.4947 3449	6.5004 9319	7.6872 0574
70	3.9995 5822	4.7471 4140	5.6321 0286	6.6792 5676	7.9178 2191
71	4.0795 4939	4.8539 5208	5.7729 0543	6.8629 3632	8.1553 5657
72	4.1611 4038	4.9631 6600	5.9172 2806	7.0516 6706	8.4000 1727
73	4.2443 6318	5.0748 3723	6.0651 5876	7.2455 8791	8.6520 1778
74	4.3292 5045	5.1890 2107	6.2167 8773	7.4448 4158	8.9115 7832
75	4.4158 3546	5.3057 7405	6.3722 0743	7.6495 7472	9.1789 2567
76	4.5041 5216	5.4251 5396	6.5315 1261	7.8599 3802	9.4542 9344
77	4.5942 3521	5.5472 1993	6.6948 0043	8.0760 8632	9.7379 2224
78	4.6861 1991	5.6720 3237	6.8621 7044	8.2981 7869	10.0300 5991
79	4.7798 4231	5.7996 5310	7.0337 2470	8.5263 7861	10.3309 6171
80	4.8754 3916	5.9301 4530	7.2095 6782	8.7608 5402	10.6408 9056
81	4.9729 4794	6.0635 7357	7.3898 0701	9.0017 7751	10.9601 1727
82	5.0724 0690	6.2000 0397	7.5745 5219	9.2493 2639	11.2889 2079
83	5.1738 5504	6.3395 0406	7.7639 1599	9.5036 8286	11.6275 8842
84	5.2773 3214	6.4821 4290	7.9580 1389	9.7650 3414	11.9764 1607
85	5.3828 7878	6.6279 9112	8.1569 6424	10.0335 7258	12.3357 0855
86	5.4905 3636	6.7771 2092	8.3608 8834	10.3094 9583	12.7057 7981
87	5.6003 4708	6.9296 0614	8.5699 1055	10.5930 0696	13.0869 5320
88	5.7123 5402	7.0855 2228	8.7841 5832	10.8843 1465	13.4795 6180
89	5.8266 0110	7.2449 4653	9.0037 6228	11.1836 3331	13.8839 4865
90	5.9431 3313	7.4079 5782	9.2288 5633	11.4911 8322	14.3004 6711
91	6.0619 9579	7.5746 3688	9.4595 7774	11.8071 9076	14.7294 8112
92	6.1832 3570	7.7450 6621	9.6960 6718	12.1318 8851	15.1713 6556
93	6.3069 0042	7.9193 3020	9.9384 6886	12.4655 1544	15.6265 0652
94	6.4330 3843	8.0975 1512	10.1869 3058	12.8083 1711	16.0953 0172
95	6.5616 9920	8.2797 0921	10.4416 0385	13.1605 4584	16.5781 6077
96	6.6929 3318	8.4660 0267	10.7026 4395	13.5224 6085	17.0755 0559
97	6.8267 9184	8.6564 8773	10.9702 1004	13.8943 2852	17.5877 7076
98	6.9633 2768	8.8512 5871	11.2444 6530	14.2764 2255	18.1154 0388
99	7.1025 9423	9.0504 1203	11.5255 7693	14.6690 2417	18.6588 6600
100	7.2446 4612	9.2540 4630	11.8137 1635	15.0724 2234	19.2186 3198

Table 8 $(Continued)$
$$(1 + i)^n$$

n	$3\frac{1}{2}\%$	4%	$4\frac{1}{2}\%$	5%	$5\frac{1}{2}\%$
1	1.0350 0000	1.0400 0000	1.0450 0000	1.0500 0000	1.0550 0000
2	1.0712 2500	1.0816 0000	1.0920 2500	1.1025 0000	1.1130 2500
3	1.1087 1788	1.1248 6400	1.1411 6613	1.1576 2500	1.1742 4138
4	1.1475 2300	1.1698 5856	1.1925 1860	1.2155 0625	1.2388 2465
5	1.1876 8631	1.2166 5290	1.2461 8194	1.2762 8156	1.3069 6001
6	1.2292 5533	1.2653 1902	1.3022 6012	1.3400 9564	1.3788 4281
7	1.2722 7926	1.3159 3178	1.3608 6183	1.4071 0042	1.4546 7916
8	1.3168 0904	1.3685 6905	1.4221 0061	1.4774 5544	1.5346 8651
9	1.3628 9735	1.4233 1181	1.4860 9514	1.5513 2822	1.6190 9427
10	1.4105 9876	1.4802 4428	1.5529 6942	1.6288 9463	1.7081 4446
11	1.4599 6972	1.5394 5406	1.6228 5305	1.7103 3936	1.8020 9240
12	1.5110 6866	1.6010 3222	1.6958 8143	1.7958 5633	1.9012 0749
13	1.5639 5606	1.6650 7351	1.7721 9610	1.8856 4914	2.0057 7390
14	1.6186 9452	1.7316 7645	1.8519 4492	1.9799 3160	2.1160 9146
15	1.6753 4883	1.8009 4351	1.9352 8244	2.0789 2818	2.2324 7649
16	1.7339 8604	1.8729 8125	2.0223 7015	2.1828 7459	2.3552 6270
17	1.7946 7555	1.9479 0050	2.1133 7681	2.2920 1832	2.4848 0215
18	1.8574 8920	2.0258 1652	2.2084 7877	2.4066 1923	2.6214 6627
19	1.9225 0132	2.1068 4918	2.3078 6031	2.5269 5020	2.7656 4691
20	1.9897 8886	2.1911 2314	2.4117 1402	2.6532 9771	2.9177 5749
21	2.0594 3147	2.2787 6807	2.5202 4116	2.7859 6259	3.0782 3415
22	2.1315 1158	2.3699 1879	2.6336 5201	2.9252 6072	3.2475 3703
23	2.2061 1448	2.4647 1554	2.7521 6635	3.0715 2376	3.4261 5157
24	2.2833 2849	2.5633 0416	2 8760 1383	3.2250 9994	3.6145 8990
25	2.3632 4498	2.6658 3633	3.0054 3446	3.3863 5494	3.8133 9235
26	2.4459 5856	2.7724 6978	3.1406 7901	3.5556 7269	4.0231 2893
27	2.5315 6711	2.8833 6858	3.2820 0956	3.7334 5632	4.2444 0102
28	2.6201 7196	2.9987 0332	3.4296 9999	3.9201 2914	4.4778 4307
29	2.7118 7798	3.1186 5145	3.5840 3649	4.1161 3560	4.7241 2444
30	2.8067 9370	3.2433 9751	3.7453 1813	4.3219 4238	4.9839 5129
31	2.9050 3148	3.3731 3341	3.9138 5745	4.5380 3949	5.2580 6861
32	3.0067 0759	3.5080 5875	4.0899 8104	4.7649 4147	5.5472 6238
33	3.1119 4235	3.6483 8110	4.2740 3018	5.0031 8854	5.8523 6181
34	3.2208 6033	3.7943 1634	4.4663 6154	5.2533 4797	6.1742 4171
35	3.3335 9045	3.9460 8899	4.6673 4781	5.5160 1537	6.5138 2501
36	3.4502 6611	4.1039 3255	4.8773 7846	5.7918 1614	6.8720 8538
37	3.5710 2543	4.2680 8986	5.0968 6049	6.0814 0694	7.2500 5008
38	3.6960 1132	4.4388 1345	5.3262 1921	6.3854 7729	7.6488 0283
39	3.8253 7171	4.6163 6599	5.5658 9908	6.7047 5115	8.0694 8699
40	3.9592 5972	4.8010 2063	5.8163 6454	7.0399 8871	8.5133 0877
41	4.0978 3381	4.9930 6145	6.0781 0094	7.3919 8815	8.9815 4076
42	4.2412 5799	5.1927 8391	6.3516 1548	7.7615 8756	9.4755 2550
43	4.3897 0202	5.4004 9527	6.6374 3818	8.1496 6693	9.9966 7940
44	4.5433 4160	5.6165 1508	6.9361 2290	8.5571 5028	10.5464 9677
45	4.7023 5855	5.8411 7568	7.2482 4843	8.9850 0779	11.1265 5409
46	4.8669 4110	6.0748 2271	7.5744 1961	9.4342 5818	11.7385 1456
47	5.0372 8404	6.3178 1562	7.9152 6849	9.9059 7109	12.3841 3287
48	5.2135 8898	6.5705 2824	8.2714 5557	10.4012 6965	13.0652 6017
49	5.3960 6459	6.8333 4937	8.6436 7107	10.9213 3313	13.7838 4948
50	5.5849 2686	7.1066 8335	9.0326 3627	11.4673 9979	14.5419 6120

Table 8 *(Continued)*

$$(1 + i)^n$$

n	$3\frac{1}{2}\%$	4%	$4\frac{1}{2}\%$	5%	$5\frac{1}{2}\%$
51	5.7803 9930	7.3909 5068	9.4391 0490	12.0407 6978	15.3417 6907
52	5.9827 1327	7.6865 8871	9.8638 6463	12.6428 0826	16.1855 6637
53	6.1921 0824	7.9940 5226	10.3077 3853	13.2749 4868	17.0757 7252
54	6.4088 3202	8.3138 1435	10.7715 8677	13.9386 9611	18.0149 4001
55	6.6331 4114	8.6463 6692	11.2563 0817	14.6356 3092	19.0057 6171
56	6.8653 0108	8.9922 2160	11.7628 4204	15.3674 1246	20.0510 7860
57	7.1055 8662	9.3519 1046	12.2921 6993	16.1357 8309	21.1538 8793
58	7.3542 8215	9.7259 8688	12.8453 1758	16.9425 7224	22.3173 5176
59	7.6116 8203	10.1150 2635	13.4233 5687	17.7897 0085	23.5448 0611
60	7.8780 9090	10.5196 2741	14.0274 0793	18.6791 8589	24.8397 7045
61	8.1538 2408	10.9404 1250	14.6586 4129	19.6131 4519	26.2059 5782
62	8.4392 0793	11.3780 2900	15.3182 8014	20.5938 0245	27.6472 8550
63	8.7345 8020	11.8331 5016	16.0076 0275	21.6234 9257	29.1678 8620
64	9.0402 9051	12.3064 7617	16.7279 4487	22.7046 6720	30.7721 1994
65	9.3567 0068	12.7987 3522	17.4807 0239	23.8399 0056	32.4645 8654
66	9.6841 8520	13.3106 8463	18.2673 3400	25.0318 9559	34.2501 3880
67	10.0231 3168	13.8431 1201	19.0893 6403	26.2834 9037	36.1338 9643
68	10.3739 4129	14.3968 3649	19.9483 8541	27.5976 6488	38.1212 6074
69	10.7370 2924	14.9727 0995	20.8460 6276	28.9775 4813	40.2179 3008
70	11.1128 2526	15.5716 1835	21.7841 3558	30.4264 2554	42.4299 1623
71	11.5017 7414	16.1944 8308	22.7644 2168	31.9477 4681	44.7635 6163
72	11.9043 3624	16.8422 6241	23.7888 2066	33.5451 3415	47.2255 5751
73	12.3209 8801	17.5159 5290	24.8593 1759	35.2223 9086	49.8229 6318
74	12.7522 2259	18.2165 9102	25.9779 8688	36.9835 1040	52.5632 2615
75	13.1985 5038	18.9452 5466	27.1469 9629	38.8326 8592	55.4542 0359
76	13.6604 9964	19.7030 6485	28.3686 1112	40.7743 2022	58.5041 8479
77	14.1386 1713	20.4911 8744	29.6451 9862	42.8130 3623	61.7219 1495
78	14.6334 6873	21.3108 3494	30.9792 3256	44.9536 8804	65.1166 2027
79	15.1456 4013	22.1632 6834	32.3732 9802	47.2013 7244	68.6980 3439
80	15.6757 3754	23.0497 9907	33.8300 9643	49.5614 4107	72.4764 2628
81	16.2243 8835	23.9717 9103	35.3524 5077	52.0395 3132	76.4626 2973
82	16.7922 4195	24.9306 6267	36.9433 1106	54.6414 8878	80.6680 7436
83	17.3799 7041	25.9278 8918	38.6057 6006	57.3735 6322	85.1048 1845
84	17.9882 6938	26.9650 0475	40.3430 1926	60.2422 4138	89.7855 8347
85	18.6178 5881	28.0436 0494	42.1584 5513	63.2543 5344	94.7237 9056
86	19.2694 8387	29.1653 4914	44.0555 8561	66.4170 7112	99.9335 9904
87	19.9439 1580	30.3319 6310	46.0380 8696	69.7379 2467	105.4299 4698
88	20.6419 5285	31.5452 4163	48.1098 0087	73.2248 2091	111.2285 9407
89	21.3644 2120	32.8070 5129	50.2747 4191	76.8860 6195	117.3461 6674
90	22.1121 7595	34.1193 3334	52.5371 0530	80.7303 6505	123.8002 0591
91	22.8861 0210	35.4841 0668	54.9012 7503	84.7668 8330	130.6092 1724
92	23.6871 1568	36.9034 7094	57.3718 3241	89.0052 2747	137.7927 2419
93	24.5161 6473	38.3796 0978	59.9535 6487	93.4554 8884	145.3713 2402
94	25.3742 3049	39.9147 9417	62.6514 7529	98.1282 6328	153.3667 4684
95	26.2623 2856	41.5113 8594	65.4707 9168	103.0346 7645	161.8019 1791
96	27.1815 1006	43.1718 4138	68.4169 7730	108.1864 1027	170.7010 2340
97	28.1328 6291	44.8987 1503	71.4957 4128	113.5957 3078	180.0895 7969
98	29.1175 1311	46.6946 6363	74.7130 4964	119.2755 1732	189.9945 0657
99	30.1366 2607	48.5624 5018	78.0751 3687	125.2392 9319	200.4442 0443
100	31.1914 0798	50.5049 4818	81.5885 1803	131.5012 5785	211.4686 3567

Table 8 *(Continued)*

$$(1 + i)^n$$

n	6%	6½%	7%	7½%	8%
1	1.0600 0000	1.0650 0000	1.0700 0000	1.0750 0000	1.0800 0000
2	1.1236 0000	1.1342 2500	1.1449 0000	1.1556 2500	1.1664 0000
3	1.1910 1600	1.2079 4963	1.2250 4300	1.2422 9688	1.2597 1200
4	1.2624 7696	1.2864 6635	1.3107 9601	1.3354 6914	1.3604 8896
5	1.3382 2558	1.3700 8666	1.4025 5173	1.4356 2933	1.4693 2808
6	1.4185 1911	1.4591 4230	1.5007 3035	1.5433 0153	1.5868 7432
7	1.5036 3026	1.5539 8655	1.6057 8148	1.6590 4914	1.7138 2427
8	1.5938 4807	1.6549 9567	1.7181 8618	1.7834 7783	1.8509 3021
9	1.6894 7896	1.7625 7039	1.8384 5921	1.9172 3866	1.9990 0463
10	1.7908 4770	1.8771 3747	1.9671 5136	2.0610 3156	2.1589 2500
11	1.8982 9856	1.9991 5140	2.1048 5195	2.2156 0893	2.3316 3900
12	2.0121 9647	2.1290 9624	2.2521 9159	2.3817 7960	2.5181 7012
13	2.1329 2826	2.2674 8750	2.4098 4500	2.5604 1307	2.7196 2373
14	2.2609 0396	2.4148 7418	2.5785 3415	2.7524 4405	2.9371 9362
15	2.3965 5819	2.5718 4101	2.7590 3154	2.9588 7735	3.1721 6911
16	2.5403 5168	2.7390 1067	2.9521 6375	3.1807 9315	3.4259 4264
17	2.6927 7279	2.9170 4637	3.1588 1521	3.4193 5264	3.7000 1805
18	2.8543 3915	3.1066 5438	3.3799 3228	3.6758 0409	3.9960 1950
19	3.0255 9950	3.3085 8691	3.6165 2754	3.9514 8940	4.3157 0106
20	3.2071 3547	3.5236 4506	3.8696 8446	4.2478 5110	4.6609 5714
21	3.3995 6360	3.7526 8199	4.1405 6237	4.5664 3993	5.0338 3372
22	3.6035 3742	3.9966 0632	4.4304 0174	4.9089 2293	5.4365 4041
23	3.8197 4966	4.2563 8573	4.7405 2986	5.2770 9215	5.8714 6365
24	4.0489 3464	4.5330 5081	5.0723 6695	5.6728 7406	6.3411 8074
25	4.2918 7072	4.8276 9911	5.4274 3264	6.0983 3961	6.8484 7520
26	4.5493 8296	5.1414 9955	5.8073 5292	6.5557 1508	7.3963 5321
27	4.8223 4594	5.4756 9702	6.2138 6763	7.0473 9371	7.9880 6147
28	5.1116 8670	5.8316 1733	6.6488 3836	7.5759 4824	8.6271 0639
29	5.4183 8790	6.2106 7245	7.1142 5705	8.1441 4436	9.3172 7490
30	5.7434 9117	6.6143 6616	7.6122 5504	8.7549 5519	10.0626 5689
31	6.0881 0064	7.0442 9996	8.1451 1290	9.4115 7683	10.8676 6944
32	6.4533 8668	7.5021 7946	8.7152 7080	10.1174 4509	11.7370 8300
33	6.8405 8988	7.9898 2113	9.3253 3975	10.8762 5347	12.6760 4964
34	7.2510 2528	8.5091 5950	9.9781 1354	11.6919 7248	13.6901 3361
35	7.6860 8679	9.0622 5487	10.6765 8148	12.5688 7042	14.7853 4429
36	8.1472 5200	9.6513 0143	11.4239 4219	13.5115 3570	15.9681 7184
37	8.6360 8712	10.2786 3603	12.2236 1814	14.5249 0088	17.2456 2558
38	9.1542 5235	10.9467 4737	13.0792 7141	15.6142 6844	18.6252 7563
39	9.7035 0749	11.6582 8595	13.9948 2041	16.7853 3858	20.1152 9768
40	10.2857 1794	12.4160 7453	14.9744 5784	18.0442 3897	21.7245 2150
41	10.9028 6101	13.2231 1938	16.0226 6989	19.3975 5689	23.4624 8322
42	11.5570 3267	14.0826 2214	17.1442 5678	20.8523 7366	25.3394 8187
43	12.2504 5463	14.9979 9258	18.3443 5475	22.4163 0168	27.3666 4042
44	12.9854 8191	15.9728 6209	19.6284 5959	24.0975 2431	29.5559 7166
45	13.7646 1083	17.0110 9813	21.0024 5176	25.9048 3863	31.9204 4939
46	14.5904 8748	18.1168 1951	22.4726 2338	27.8477 0153	34.4740 8534
47	15.4659 1673	19.2944 1278	24.0457 0702	29.9362 7915	37.2320 1217
48	16.3938 7173	20.5485 4961	25.7289 0651	32.1815 0008	40.2105 7314
49	17.3775 0403	21.8842 0533	27.5299 2997	34.5951 1259	43.4274 1899
50	18.4201 5427	23.3066 7868	29.4570 2506	37.1897 4603	46.9016 1251

Table 8 (*Continued*)

$$(1 + i)^n$$

n	$8\frac{1}{2}\%$	9%	$9\frac{1}{2}\%$	10%	$10\frac{1}{2}\%$
1	1.0850 0000	1.0900 0000	1.0950 0000	1.1000 0000	1.1050 0000
2	1.1772 2500	1.1881 0000	1.1990 2500	1.2100 0000	1.2210 2500
3	1.2772 8913	1.2950 2900	1.3129 3238	1.3310 0000	1.3492 3263
4	1.3858 5870	1.4115 8161	1.4376 6095	1.4641 0000	1.4909 0205
5	1.5036 5669	1.5386 2395	1.5742 3874	1.6105 1000	1.6474 4677
6	1.6314 6751	1.6771 0011	1.7237 9142	1.7715 6100	1.8204 2868
7	1.7701 4225	1.8280 3912	1.8875 5161	1.9487 1710	2.0115 7369
8	1.9206 0434	1.9925 6264	2.0668 6901	2.1435 8881	2.2227 8892
9	2.0838 5571	2.1718 9328	2.2632 2156	2.3579 4769	2.4561 8176
10	2.2609 8344	2.3673 6367	2.4782 2761	2.5937 4246	2.7140 8085
11	2.4531 6703	2.5804 2641	2.7136 5924	2.8531 1671	2.9990 5934
12	2.6616 8623	2.8126 6478	2.9714 5686	3.1384 2838	3.3139 6057
13	2.8879 2956	3.0658 0461	3.2537 4527	3.4522 7121	3.6619 2643
14	3.1334 0357	3.3417 2703	3.5628 5107	3.7974 9834	4.0464 2870
15	3.3997 4288	3.6424 8246	3.9013 2192	4.1772 4817	4.4713 0371
16	3.6887 2102	3.9703 0588	4.2719 4750	4.5949 7299	4.9407 9060
17	4.0022 6231	4.3276 3341	4.6777 8251	5.0544 7028	5.4595 7362
18	4.3424 5461	4.7171 2042	5.1221 7185	5.5599 1731	6.0328 2885
19	4.7115 6325	5.1416 6125	5.6087 7818	6.1159 0904	6.6662 7588
20	5.1120 4612	5.6044 1077	6.1416 1210	6.7274 9995	7.3662 3484
21	5.5465 7005	6.1088 0774	6.7250 6525	7.4002 4994	8.1396 8950
22	6.0180 2850	6.6586 0043	7.3639 4645	8.1402 7494	8.9943 5690
23	6.5295 6092	7.2578 7447	8.0635 2137	8.9543 0243	9.9387 6437
24	7.0845 7360	7.9110 8317	8.8295 5590	9.8497 3268	10.9823 3463
25	7.6867 6236	8.6230 8066	9.6683 6371	10.8347 0594	12.1354 7977
26	8.3401 3716	9.3991 5792	10.5868 5826	11.9181 7654	13.4097 0514
27	9.0490 4881	10.2450 8213	11.5926 0979	13.1099 9419	14.8177 2418
28	9.8182 1796	11.1671 3952	12.6939 0772	14.4209 9361	16.3735 8522
29	10.6527 6649	12.1721 8208	13.8998 2896	15.8630 9297	18.0928 1167
30	11.5582 5164	13.2676 7847	15.2203 1271	17.4494 0227	19.9925 5690
31	12.5407 0303	14.4617 6953	16.6662 4241	19.1943 4250	22.0917 7537
32	13.6066 6279	15.7633 2879	18.2495 3544	21.1137 7675	24.4114 1178
33	14.7632 2913	17.1820 2838	19.9832 4131	23.2251 5442	26.9746 1002
34	16.0181 0360	18.7284 1093	21.8816 4924	25.5476 6986	29.8069 4407
35	17.3796 4241	20.4139 6792	23.9604 0591	28.1024 3685	32.9366 7320
36	18.8569 1201	22.2512 2503	26.2366 4448	30.9126 8053	36.3950 2389
37	20.4597 4953	24.2538 3528	28.7291 2570	34.0039 4859	40.2165 0140
38	22.1988 2824	26.4366 8046	31.4583 9264	37.4043 4344	44.4392 3404
39	24.0857 2865	28.8159 8170	34.4469 3994	41.1447 7779	49.1053 5362
40	26.1330 1558	31.4094 2005	37.7193 9924	45.2592 5557	54.2614 1575
41	28.3543 2190	34.2362 6786	41.3027 4216	49.7851 8113	59.9588 6440
42	30.7644 3927	37.3175 3197	45.2265 0267	54.7636 9924	66.2545 4516
43	33.3794 1660	40.6761 0984	49.5230 2042	60.2400 6916	73.2112 7240
44	36.2166 6702	44.3369 5973	54.2277 0736	66.2640 7608	80.8984 5601
45	39.2950 8371	48.3272 8610	59.3793 3956	72.8904 8369	89.3927 9389
46	42.6351 6583	52.6767 4185	65.0203 7682	80.1795 3205	98.7790 3724
47	46.2591 5492	57.4176 4862	71.1973 1262	88.1974 8526	109.1508 3616
48	50.1911 8309	62.5852 3700	77.9610 5732	97.0172 3378	120.6116 7395
49	54.4574 3365	68.2179 0833	85.3673 5777	106.7189 5716	133.2758 9972
50	59.0863 1551	74.3575 2008	93.4772 5675	117.3908 5288	147.2698 6919

Table 9

$$v^n = (1 + i)^{-n}$$

n	$\frac{1}{4}\%$	$\frac{7}{24}\%$	$\frac{1}{3}\%$	$\frac{5}{12}\%$	$\frac{1}{2}\%$
1	0.9975 0623	0.9970 9182	0.9966 7774	0.9958 5062	0.9950 2488
2	0.9950 1869	0.9941 9209	0.9933 6652	0.9917 1846	0.9900 7450
3	0.9925 3734	0.9913 0079	0.9900 6630	0.9876 0345	0.9851 4876
4	0.9900 6219	0.9884 1791	0.9867 7704	0.9835 0551	0.9802 4752
5	0.9875 9321	0.9855 4341	0.9834 9871	0.9794 2457	0.9753 7067
6	0.9851 3038	0.9826 7727	0.9802 3127	0.9753 6057	0.9705 1808
7	0.9826 7370	0.9798 1946	0.9769 7469	0.9713 1343	0.9656 8963
8	0.9802 2314	0.9769 6996	0.9737 2893	0.9672 8308	0.9608 8520
9	0.9777 7869	0.9741 2875	0.9704 9395	0.9632 6946	0.9561 0468
10	0.9753 4034	0.9712 9581	0.9672 6972	0.9592 7249	0.9513 4794
11	0.9729 0807	0.9684 7110	0.9640 5620	0.9552 9211	0.9466 1487
12	0.9704 8187	0.9656 5461	0.9608 5335	0.9513 2824	0.9419 0534
13	0.9680 6171	0.9628 4631	0.9576 6115	0.9473 8082	0.9372 1924
14	0.9656 4759	0.9600 4617	0.9544 7955	0.9434 4978	0.9325 5646
15	0.9632 3949	0.9572 5418	0.9513 0852	0.9395 3505	0.9279 1688
16	0.9608 3740	0.9544 7031	0.9481 4803	0.9356 3657	0.9233 0037
17	0.9584 4130	0.9516 9453	0.9449 9803	0.9317 5426	0.9187 0684
18	0.9560 5117	0.9489 2683	0.9418 5851	0.9278 8806	0.9141 3616
19	0.9536 6700	0.9461 6718	0.9387 2941	0.9240 3790	0.9095 8822
20	0.9512 8878	0.9434 1555	0.9356 1071	0.9202 0372	0.9050 6290
21	0.9489 1649	0.9406 7192	0.9325 0236	0.9163 8544	0.9005 6010
22	0.9465 5011	0.9379 3627	0.9294 0435	0.9125 8301	0.8960 7971
23	0.9441 8964	0.9352 0858	0.9263 1663	0.9087 9636	0.8916 2160
24	0.9418 3505	0.9324 8882	0.9232 3916	0.9050 2542	0.8871 8567
25	0.9394 8634	0.9297 7697	0.9201 7192	0.9012 7013	0.8827 7181
26	0.9371 4348	0.9270 7301	0.9171 1487	0.8975 3042	0.8783 7991
27	0.9348 0646	0.9243 7691	0.9140 6798	0.8938 0623	0.8740 0986
28	0.9324 7527	0.9216 8865	0.9110 3121	0.8900 9749	0.8696 6155
29	0.9301 4990	0.9190 0821	0.9080 0453	0.8864 0414	0.8653 3488
30	0.9278 3032	0.9163 3557	0.9049 8790	0.8827 2611	0.8610 2973
31	0.9255 1653	0.9136 7069	0.9019 8130	0.8790 6335	0.8567 4600
32	0.9232 0851	0.9110 1357	0.8989 8468	0.8754 1578	0.8524 8358
33	0.9209 0624	0.9083 6417	0.8959 9802	0.8717 8335	0.8482 4237
34	0.9186 0972	0.9057 2248	0.8930 2128	0.8681 6599	0.8440 2226
35	0.9163 1892	0.9030 8848	0.8900 5444	0.8645 6365	0.8398 2314
36	0.9140 3384	0.9004 6213	0.8870 9745	0.8609 7624	0.8356 4492
37	0.9117 5445	0.8978 4342	0.8841 5028	0.8574 0373	0.8314 8748
38	0.9094 8075	0.8952 3232	0.8812 1290	0.8538 4604	0.8273 5073
39	0.9072 1272	0.8926 2882	0.8782 8528	0.8503 0311	0.8232 3455
40	0.9049 5034	0.8900 3289	0.8753 6739	0.8467 7488	0.8191 3886
41	0.9026 9361	0.8874 4451	0.8724 5920	0.8432 6129	0.8150 6354
42	0.9004 4250	0.8848 6366	0.8695 6066	0.8397 6228	0.8110 0850
43	0.8981 9701	0.8822 9031	0.8666 7175	0.8362 7779	0.8069 7363
44	0.8959 5712	0.8797 2445	0.8637 9245	0.8328 0776	0.8029 5884
45	0.8937 2281	0.8771 6605	0.8609 2270	0.8293 5212	0.7989 6402
46	0.8914 9407	0.8746 1509	0.8580 6249	0.8259 1083	0.7949 8907
47	0.8892 7090	0.8720 7155	0.8552 1179	0.8224 8381	0.7910 3390
48	0.8870 5326	0.8695 3540	0.8523 7055	0.8190 7102	0.7870 9841
49	0.8848 4116	0.8670 0663	0.8495 3876	0.8156 7238	0.7831 8250
50	0.8826 3457	0.8644 8522	0.8467 1637	0.8122 8785	0.7792 8607

Table 9 *(Continued)*

$v^n = (1 + i)^{-n}$

n	¼ %	⁷⁄₂₄ %	⅓ %	⁵⁄₁₂ %	½ %
51	0.8804 3349	0.8619 7114	0.8439 0336	0.8089 1736	0.7754 0902
52	0.8782 3790	0.8594 6436	0.8410 9969	0.8055 6086	0.7715 5127
53	0.8760 4778	0.8569 6488	0.8383 0534	0.8022 1828	0.7677 1270
54	0.8738 6312	0.8544 7267	0.8355 2027	0.7988 8957	0.7638 9324
55	0.8716 8391	0.8519 8771	0.8327 4446	0.7955 7468	0.7600 9277
56	0.8695 1013	0.8495 0997	0.8299 7787	0.7922 7354	0.7563 1122
57	0.8673 4178	0.8470 3944	0.8272 2047	0.7889 8610	0.7525 4847
58	0.8651 7883	0.8445 7609	0.8244 7222	0.7857 1230	0.7488 0445
59	0.8630 2128	0.8421 1991	0.8217 3311	0.7824 5208	0.7450 7906
60	0.8608 6911	0.8396 7087	0.8190 0310	0.7792 0539	0.7413 7220
61	0.8587 2230	0.8372 2895	0.8162 8216	0.7759 7217	0.7376 8378
62	0.8565 8085	0.8347 9413	0.8135 7026	0.7727 5237	0.7340 1371
63	0.8544 4474	0.8323 6640	0.8108 6737	0.7695 4593	0.7303 6190
64	0.8523 1395	0.8299 4572	0.8081 7346	0.7663 5279	0.7267 2826
65	0.8501 8848	0.8275 3209	0.8054 8850	0.7631 7291	0.7231 1269
66	0.8480 6831	0.8251 2547	0.8028 1246	0.7600 0621	0.7195 1512
67	0.8459 5343	0.8227 2586	0.8001 4531	0.7568 5266	0.7159 3544
68	0.8438 4382	0.8203 3322	0.7974 8702	0.7537 1219	0.7123 7357
69	0.8417 3947	0.8179 4754	0.7948 3756	0.7505 8476	0.7088 2943
70	0.8396 4037	0.8155 6879	0.7921 9690	0.7474 7030	0.7053 0291
71	0.8375 4650	0.8131 9697	0.7895 6502	0.7443 6876	0.7017 9394
72	0.8354 5786	0.8108 3204	0.7869 4188	0.7412 8009	0.6983 0243
73	0.8333 7442	0.8084 7399	0.7843 2745	0.7382 0424	0.6948 2829
74	0.8312 9618	0.8061 2280	0.7817 2171	0.7351 4115	0.6913 7143
75	0.8292 2312	0.8037 7845	0.7791 2463	0.7320 9078	0.6879 3177
76	0.8271 5523	0.8014 4091	0.7765 3618	0.7290 5306	0.6845 0923
77	0.8250 9250	0.7991 1018	0.7739 5632	0.7260 2794	0.6811 0371
78	0.8230 3491	0.7967 8622	0.7713 8504	0.7230 1537	0.6777 1513
79	0.8209 8246	0.7944 6901	0.7688 2230	0.7200 1531	0.6743 4342
80	0.8189 3512	0.7921 5855	0.7662 6807	0.7170 2770	0.6709 8847
81	0.8168 9289	0.7898 5481	0.7637 2233	0.7140 5248	0.6676 5022
82	0.8148 5575	0.7875 5776	0.7611 8505	0.7110 8960	0.6643 2858
83	0.8128 2369	0.7852 6740	0.7586 5619	0.7081 3902	0.6610 2346
84	0.8107 9670	0.7829 8370	0.7561 3574	0.7052 0069	0.6577 3479
85	0.8087 7476	0.7807 0664	0.7536 2366	0.7022 7454	0.6544 6248
86	0.8067 5787	0.7784 3620	0.7511 1993	0.6993 6054	0.6512 0644
87	0.8047 4600	0.7761 7236	0.7486 2451	0.6964 5863	0.6479 6661
88	0.8027 3915	0.7739 1511	0.7461 3739	0.6935 6876	0.6447 4290
89	0.8007 3731	0.7716 6442	0.7436 5853	0.6906 9088	0.6415 3522
90	0.7987 4046	0.7694 2028	0.7411 8790	0.6878 2495	0.6383 4350
91	0.7967 4859	0.7671 8266	0.7387 2548	0.6849 7090	0.6351 6766
92	0.7947 6168	0.7649 5156	0.7362 7125	0.6821 2870	0.6320 0763
93	0.7927 7973	0.7627 2694	0.7338 2516	0.6792 9829	0.6288 6331
94	0.7908 0273	0.7605 0878	0.7313 8720	0.6764 7962	0.6257 3464
95	0.7888 3065	0.7582 9708	0.7289 5735	0.6736 7265	0.6226 2153
96	0.7868 6349	0.7560 9182	0.7265 3556	0.6708 7733	0.6195 2391
97	0.7849 0124	0.7538 9296	0.7241 2182	0.6680 9361	0.6164 4170
98	0.7829 4388	0.7517 0050	0.7217 1610	0.6653 2143	0.6133 7483
99	0.7809 9140	0.7495 1442	0.7193 1837	0.6625 6076	0.6103 2321
100	0.7790 4379	0.7473 3469	0.7169 2861	0.6598 1155	0.6072 8678

Table 9 ($Continued$)

$$v^n = (1 + i)^{-n}$$

n	$\frac{1}{4}\%$	$\frac{7}{24}\%$	$\frac{1}{3}\%$	$\frac{5}{12}\%$	$\frac{1}{2}\%$
101	0.7771 0104	0.7451 6131	0.7145 4679	0.6570 7374	0.6042 6545
102	0.7751 6313	0.7429 9424	0.7121 7288	0.6543 4730	0.6012 5915
103	0.7732 3006	0.7408 3348	0.7098 0686	0.6516 3216	0.5982 6781
104	0.7713 0180	0.7386 7899	0.7074 4869	0.6489 2829	0.5952 9136
105	0.7693 7836	0.7365 3078	0.7050 9837	0.6462 3565	0.5923 2971
106	0.7674 5971	0.7343 8881	0.7027 5585	0.6435 5417	0.5893 8279
107	0.7655 4584	0.7322 5307	0.7004 2111	0.6408 8382	0.5864 5054
108	0.7636 3675	0.7301 2355	0.6980 9413	0.6382 2455	0.5835 3288
109	0.7617 3242	0.7280 0021	0.6957 7488	0.6355 7632	0.5806 2973
110	0.7598 3284	0.7258 8305	0.6934 6334	0.6329 3907	0.5777 4102
111	0.7579 3799	0.7237 7205	0.6911 5947	0.6303 1277	0.5748 6669
112	0.7560 4787	0.7216 6719	0.6888 6326	0.6276 9736	0.5720 0666
113	0.7541 6247	0.7195 6845	0.6865 7468	0.6250 9281	0.5691 6085
114	0.7522 8176	0.7174 7581	0.6842 9370	0.6224 9906	0.5663 2921
115	0.7504 0575	0.7153 8926	0.6820 2030	0.6199 1608	0.5635 1165
116	0.7485 3441	0.7133 0878	0.6797 5445	0.6173 4381	0.5607 0811
117	0.7466 6774	0.7112 3434	0.6774 9613	0.6147 8222	0.5579 1852
118	0.7448 0573	0.7091 6594	0.6752 4531	0.6122 3126	0.5551 4280
119	0.7429 4836	0.7071 0356	0.6730 0197	0.6096 9088	0.5523 8090
120	0.7410 9562	0.7050 4717	0.6707 6608	0.6071 6104	0.5496 3273
121	0.7392 4750	0.7029 9676	0.6685 3763	0.6046 4170	0.5468 9824
122	0.7374 0399	0.7009 5232	0.6663 1657	0.6021 3281	0.5441 7736
123	0.7355 6508	0.6989 1382	0.6641 0289	0.5996 3434	0.5414 7001
124	0.7337 3075	0.6968 8125	0.6618 9657	0.5971 4623	0.5387 7612
125	0.7319 0100	0.6948 5459	0.6596 9758	0.5946 6844	0.5360 9565
126	0.7300 7581	0.6928 3382	0.6575 0589	0.5922 0094	0.5334 2850
127	0.7282 5517	0.6908 1893	0.6553 2149	0.5897 4367	0.5307 7463
128	0.7264 3907	0.6888 0991	0.6531 4434	0.5872 9660	0.5281 3396
129	0.7246 2750	0.6868 0672	0.6509 7443	0.5848 5969	0.5255 0643
130	0.7228 2045	0.6848 0936	0.6488 1172	0.5824 3288	0.5228 9197
131	0.7210 1791	0.6828 1781	0.6466 5620	0.5800 1615	0.5202 9052
132	0.7192 1986	0.6808 3205	0.6445 0784	0.5776 0944	0.5177 0201
133	0.7174 2629	0.6788 5206	0.6423 6662	0.5752 1273	0.5151 2637
134	0.7156 3720	0.6768 7783	0.6402 3251	0.5728 2595	0.5125 6356
135	0.7138 5257	0.6749 0935	0.6381 0549	0.5704 4908	0.5100 1349
136	0.7120 7239	0.6729 4659	0.6359 8554	0.5680 8207	0.5074 7611
137	0.7102 9664	0.6709 8954	0.6338 7263	0.5657 2488	0.5049 5135
138	0.7085 2533	0.6690 3817	0.6317 6674	0.5633 7748	0.5024 3916
139	0.7067 5843	0.6670 9249	0.6296 6785	0.5610 3981	0.4999 3946
140	0.7049 9595	0.6651 5246	0.6275 7593	0.5587 1185	0.4974 5220
141	0.7032 3785	0.6632 1807	0.6254 9096	0.5563 9354	0.4949 7731
142	0.7014 8414	0.6612 8931	0.6234 1292	0.5540 8485	0.4925 1474
143	0.6997 3480	0.6593 6616	0.6213 4178	0.5517 8574	0.4900 6442
144	0.6979 8983	0.6574 4860	0.6192 7752	0.5494 9618	0.4876 2628
145	0.6962 4921	0.6555 3662	0.6172 2012	0.5472 1611	0.4852 0028
146	0.6945 1292	0.6536 3020	0.6151 6955	0.5449 4550	0.4827 8635
147	0.6927 8097	0.6517 2932	0.6131 2580	0.5426 8432	0.4803 8443
148	0.6910 5334	0.6498 3397	0.6110 8884	0.5404 3252	0.4779 9446
149	0.6893 3001	0.6479 4414	0.6090 5864	0.5381 9006	0.4756 1637
150	0.6876 1098	0.6460 5980	0.6070 3519	0.5359 5690	0.4732 5012

Table 9   (*Continued*)

$$v^n = (1 + i)^{-n}$$

n	$\frac{1}{4}\%$	$\frac{7}{24}\%$	$\frac{1}{3}\%$	$\frac{5}{12}\%$	$\frac{1}{2}\%$
151	0.6858 9624	0.6441 8093	0.6050 1846	0.5337 3302	0.4708 9565
152	0.6841 8578	0.6423 0754	0.6030 0843	0.5315 1836	0.4685 5288
153	0.6824 7958	0.6404 3959	0.6010 0508	0.5293 1289	0.4662 2177
154	0.6807 7764	0.6385 7707	0.5990 0839	0.5271 1657	0.4639 0226
155	0.6790 7994	0.6367 1997	0.5970 1833	0.5249 2936	0.4615 9429
156	0.6773 8647	0.6348 6827	0.5950 3488	0.5227 5123	0.4592 9780
157	0.6756 9723	0.6330 2196	0.5930 5802	0.5205 8214	0.4570 1274
158	0.6740 1220	0.6311 8101	0.5910 8773	0.5184 2205	0.4547 3904
159	0.6723 3137	0.6293 4542	0.5891 2398	0.5162 7092	0.4524 7666
160	0.6706 5473	0.6275 1517	0.5871 6676	0.5141 2872	0.4502 2553
161	0.6689 8228	0.6256 9024	0.5852 1604	0.5119 9540	0.4479 8560
162	0.6673 1399	0.6238 7062	0.5832 7180	0.5098 7094	0.4457 5682
163	0.6656 4987	0.6220 5629	0.5813 3402	0.5077 5529	0.4435 3912
164	0.6639 8989	0.6202 4723	0.5794 0268	0.5056 4842	0.4413 3246
165	0.6623 3406	0.6184 4344	0.5774 7775	0.5035 5030	0.4391 3678
166	0.6606 8235	0.6166 4489	0.5755 5922	0.5014 6088	0.4369 5202
167	0.6590 3476	0.6148 5158	0.5736 4706	0.4993 8013	0.4347 7813
168	0.6573 9129	0.6130 6347	0.5717 4126	0.4973 0801	0.4326 1505
169	0.6557 5191	0.6112 8057	0.5698 4179	0.4952 4449	0.4304 6274
170	0.6541 1661	0.6095 0285	0.5679 4862	0.4931 8954	0.4283 2113
171	0.6524 8540	0.6077 3031	0.5660 6175	0.4911 4311	0.4261 9018
172	0.6508 5826	0.6059 6292	0.5641 8115	0.4891 0517	0.4240 6983
173	0.6492 3517	0.6042 0066	0.5623 0679	0.4870 7569	0.4219 6003
174	0.6476 1613	0.6024 4354	0.5604 3866	0.4850 5462	0.4198 6073
175	0.6460 0112	0.6006 9152	0.5585 7674	0.4830 4195	0.4177 7187
176	0.6443 9015	0.5989 4460	0.5567 2100	0.4810 3763	0.4156 9340
177	0.6427 8319	0.5972 0276	0.5548 7143	0.4790 4162	0.4136 2528
178	0.6411 8024	0.5954 6598	0.5530 2801	0.4770 5390	0.4115 6744
179	0.6395 8129	0.5937 3426	0.5511 9070	0.4750 7442	0.4095 1984
180	0.6379 8632	0.5920 0757	0.5493 5950	0.4731 0316	0.4074 8243
181	0.6363 9533	0.5902 8590	0.5475 3439	0.4711 4007	0.4054 5515
182	0.6348 0831	0.5885 6924	0.5457 1534	0.4691 8513	0.4034 3796
183	0.6332 2525	0.5868 5757	0.5439 0233	0.4672 3831	0.4014 3081
184	0.6316 4613	0.5851 5088	0.5420 9535	0.4652 9956	0.3994 3364
185	0.6300 7096	0.5834 4916	0.5402 9437	0.4633 6886	0.3974 4641
186	0.6284 9971	0.5817 5238	0.5384 9937	0.4614 4616	0.3954 6906
187	0.6269 3238	0.5800 6053	0.5367 1033	0.4595 3145	0.3935 0155
188	0.6253 6895	0.5783 7361	0.5349 2724	0.4576 2468	0.3915 4383
189	0.6238 0943	0.5766 9159	0.5331 5008	0.4557 2582	0.3895 9586
190	0.6222 5380	0.5750 1447	0.5313 7881	0.4538 3484	0.3876 5757
191	0.6207 0204	0.5733 4222	0.5296 1343	0.4519 5171	0.3857 2892
192	0.6191 5416	0.5716 7484	0.5278 5392	0.4500 7639	0.3838 0987
193	0.6176 1013	0.5700 1230	0.5261 0025	0.4482 0886	0.3819 0037
194	0.6160 6996	0.5683 5460	0.5243 5241	0.4463 4907	0.3800 0037
195	0.6145 3362	0.5667 0172	0.5226 1038	0.4444 9700	0.3781 0982
196	0.6130 0112	0.5650 5365	0.5208 7413	0.4426 5261	0.3762 2868
197	0.6114 7244	0.5634 1037	0.5191 4365	0.4408 1588	0.3743 5689
198	0.6099 4757	0.5617 7186	0.5174 1892	0.4389 8677	0.3724 9442
199	0.6084 2650	0.5601 3813	0.5156 9992	0.4371 6525	0.3706 4121
200	0.6069 0923	0.5585 0914	0.5139 8663	0.4353 5128	0.3687 9723

Table 9 *(Continued)*

$$v^n = (1 + i)^{-n}$$

n	$\frac{7}{12}\%$	$\frac{2}{3}\%$	$\frac{3}{4}\%$	$\frac{7}{8}\%$	1%
1	0.9942 0050	0.9933 7748	0.9925 5583	0.9913 2590	0.9900 9901
2	0.9884 3463	0.9867 9882	0.9851 6708	0.9827 2704	0.9802 9605
3	0.9827 0220	0.9802 6373	0.9778 3333	0.9742 0276	0.9705 9015
4	0.9770 0301	0.9737 7192	0.9705 5417	0.9657 5243	0.9609 8034
5	0.9713 3688	0.9673 2310	0.9633 2920	0.9573 7539	0.9514 6569
6	0.9657 0361	0.9609 1699	0.9561 5802	0.9490 7102	0.9420 4524
7	0.9601 0301	0.9545 5330	0.9490 4022	0.9408 3868	0.9327 1805
8	0.9545 3489	0.9482 3175	0.9419 7540	0.9326 7775	0.9234 8322
9	0.9489 9906	0.9419 5207	0.9349 6318	0.9245 8761	0.9143 3982
10	0.9434 9534	0.9357 1398	0.9280 0315	0.9165 6765	0.9052 8695
11	0.9380 2354	0.9295 1720	0.9210 9494	0.9086 1724	0.8963 2372
12	0.9325 8347	0.9233 6145	0.9142 3815	0.9007 3581	0.8874 4923
13	0.9271 7495	0.9172 4648	0.9074 3241	0.8929 2273	0.8786 6260
14	0.9217 9779	0.9111 7200	0.9006 7733	0.8851 7743	0.8699 6297
15	0.9164 5182	0.9051 3775	0.8939 7254	0.8774 9931	0.8613 4947
16	0.9111 3686	0.8991 4346	0.8873 1766	0.8698 8779	0.8528 2126
17	0.9058 5272	0.8931 8886	0.8807 1231	0.8623 4230	0.8443 7749
18	0.9005 9922	0.8872 7371	0.8741 5614	0.8548 6225	0.8360 1731
19	0.8953 7619	0.8813 9772	0.8676 4878	0.8474 4709	0.8277 3992
20	0.8901 8346	0.8755 6065	0.8611 8985	0.8400 9625	0.8195 4447
21	0.8850 2084	0.8697 6224	0.8547 7901	0.8328 0917	0.8114 3017
22	0.8798 8815	0.8640 0222	0.8484 1589	0.8255 8530	0.8033 9621
23	0.8747 8524	0.8582 8035	0.8421 0014	0.8184 2409	0.7954 4179
24	0.8697 1192	0.8525 9638	0.8358 3140	0.8113 2499	0.7875 6613
25	0.8646 6802	0.8469 5004	0.8296 0933	0.8042 8748	0.7797 6844
26	0.8596 5338	0.8413 4110	0.8234 3358	0.7973 1101	0.7720 4796
27	0.8546 6782	0.8357 6931	0.8173 0380	0.7903 9505	0.7644 0392
28	0.8497 1117	0.8302 3441	0.8112 1966	0.7835 3908	0.7568 3557
29	0.8447 8327	0.8247 3617	0.8051 8080	0.7767 4258	0.7493 4215
30	0.8398 8394	0.8192 7434	0.7991 8690	0.7700 0504	0.7419 2292
31	0.8350 1303	0.8138 4868	0.7932 3762	0.7633 2594	0.7345 7715
32	0.8301 7037	0.8084 5896	0.7873 3262	0.7567 0477	0.7273 0411
33	0.8253 5580	0.8031 0492	0.7814 7158	0.7501 4104	0.7201 0307
34	0.8205 6914	0.7977 8635	0.7756 5418	0.7436 3424	0.7129 7334
35	0.8158 1025	0.7925 0299	0.7698 8008	0.7371 8388	0.7059 1420
36	0.8110 7896	0.7872 5463	0.7641 4896	0.7307 8947	0.6989 2495
37	0.8063 7510	0.7820 4102	0.7584 6051	0.7244 5053	0.6920 0490
38	0.8016 9853	0.7768 6194	0.7528 1440	0.7181 6657	0.6851 5337
39	0.7970 4907	0.7717 1716	0.7472 1032	0.7119 3712	0.6783 6967
40	0.7924 2659	0.7666 0645	0.7416 4796	0.7057 6171	0.6716 5314
41	0.7878 3091	0.7615 2959	0.7361 2701	0.6996 3986	0.6650 0311
42	0.7832 6188	0.7564 8635	0.7306 4716	0.6935 7111	0.6584 1892
43	0.7787 1935	0.7514 7650	0.7252 0809	0.6875 5500	0.6518 9992
44	0.7742 0316	0.7464 9984	0.7198 0952	0.6815 9108	0.6454 4546
45	0.7697 1317	0.7415 5613	0.7144 5114	0.6756 7889	0.6390 5492
46	0.7652 4922	0.7366 4516	0.7091 3264	0.6698 1798	0.6327 2764
47	0.7608 1115	0.7317 6672	0.7038 5374	0.6640 0792	0.6264 6301
48	0.7563 9883	0.7269 2058	0.6986 1414	0.6582 4824	0.6202 6041
49	0.7520 1209	0.7221 0654	0.6934 1353	0.6525 3853	0.6141 1921
50	0.7476 5079	0.7173 2437	0.6882 5165	0.6468 7835	0.6080 3882

Table 9 (*Continued*)

$$v^n = (1 + i)^{-n}$$

n	$\frac{7}{12}\%$	$\frac{2}{3}\%$	$\frac{3}{4}\%$	$\frac{7}{8}\%$	1%
51	0.7433 1479	0.7125 7388	0.6831 2819	0.6412 6726	0.6020 1864
52	0.7390 0393	0.7078 5485	0.6780 4286	0.6357 0484	0.5960 5806
53	0.7347 1808	0.7031 6707	0.6729 9540	0.6301 9067	0.5901 5649
54	0.7304 5708	0.6985 1033	0.6679 8551	0.6247 2433	0.5843 1336
55	0.7262 2079	0.6938 8444	0.6630 1291	0.6193 0541	0.5785 2808
56	0.7220 0907	0.6892 8918	0.6580 7733	0.6139 3349	0.5728 0008
57	0.7178 2178	0.6847 2435	0.6531 7849	0.6086 0817	0.5671 2879
58	0.7136 5877	0.6801 8975	0.6483 1612	0.6033 2904	0.5615 1365
59	0.7095 1990	0.6756 8518	0.6434 8995	0.5980 9571	0.5559 5411
60	0.7054 0504	0.6712 1044	0.6386 9970	0.5929 0776	0.5504 4962
61	0.7013 1404	0.6667 6534	0.6339 4511	0.5877 6482	0.5449 9962
62	0.6972 4677	0.6623 4968	0.6292 2592	0.5826 6649	0.5396 0358
63	0.6932 0308	0.6579 6326	0.6245 4185	0.5776 1238	0.5342 6097
64	0.6891 8285	0.6536 0588	0.6198 9266	0.5726 0211	0.5289 7126
65	0.6851 8593	0.6492 7737	0.6152 7807	0.5676 3530	0.5237 3392
66	0.6812 1219	0.6449 7752	0.6106 9784	0.5627 1158	0.5185 4844
67	0.6772 6150	0.6407 0614	0.6061 5170	0.5578 3056	0.5134 1429
68	0.6733 3372	0.6364 6306	0.6016 3940	0.5529 9188	0.5083 3099
69	0.6694 2872	0.6322 4807	0.5971 6070	0.5481 9517	0.5032 9801
70	0.6655 4637	0.6280 6100	0.5927 1533	0.5434 4007	0.4983 1486
71	0.6616 8653	0.6239 0165	0.5883 0306	0.5387 2622	0.4933 8105
72	0.6578 4908	0.6197 6985	0.5839 2363	0.5340 5325	0.4884 9609
73	0.6540 3388	0.6156 6542	0.5795 7681	0.5294 2082	0.4836 5949
74	0.6502 4081	0.6115 8816	0.5752 6234	0.5248 2857	0.4788 7078
75	0.6464 6973	0.6075 3791	0.5709 7999	0.5202 7615	0.4741 2949
76	0.6427 2053	0.6035 1448	0.5667 2952	0.5157 6322	0.4694 3514
77	0.6389 9307	0.5995 1769	0.5625 1069	0.5112 8944	0.4647 8726
78	0.6352 8723	0.5955 4738	0.5583 2326	0.5068 5447	0.4601 8541
79	0.6316 0288	0.5916 0336	0.5541 6701	0.5024 5796	0.4556 2912
80	0.6279 3990	0.5876 8545	0.5500 4170	0.4980 9959	0.4511 1794
81	0.6242 9816	0.5837 9350	0.5459 4710	0.4937 7902	0.4466 5142
82	0.6206 7754	0.5799 2731	0.5418 8297	0.4894 9593	0.4422 2913
83	0.6170 7792	0.5760 8674	0.5378 4911	0.4852 4999	0.4378 5063
84	0.6134 9917	0.5722 7159	0.5338 4527	0.4810 4089	0.4335 1547
85	0.6099 4118	0.5684 8171	0.5298 7123	0.4768 6829	0.4292 2324
86	0.6064 0382	0.5647 1693	0.5259 2678	0.4727 3188	0.4249 7350
87	0.6028 8698	0.5609 7709	0.5220 1169	0.4686 3136	0.4207 6585
88	0.5993 9054	0.5572 6201	0.5181 2575	0.4645 6640	0.4165 9985
89	0.5959 1437	0.5535 7153	0.5142 6873	0.4605 3671	0.4124 7510
90	0.5924 5836	0.5499 0549	0.5104 4043	0.4565 4197	0.4083 9119
91	0.5890 2240	0.5462 6374	0.5066 4063	0.4525 8187	0.4043 4771
92	0.5856 0636	0.5426 4610	0.5028 6911	0.4486 5613	0.4003 4427
93	0.5822 1014	0.5390 5241	0.4991 2567	0.4447 6444	0.3963 8046
94	0.5788 3361	0.5354 8253	0.4954 1009	0.4409 0651	0.3924 5590
95	0.5754 7666	0.5319 3629	0.4917 2217	0.4370 8204	0.3885 7020
96	0.5721 3918	0.5284 1353	0.4880 6171	0.4332 9075	0.3847 2297
97	0.5688 2106	0.5249 1410	0.4844 2850	0.4295 3234	0.3809 1383
98	0.5655 2218	0.5214 3785	0.4808 2233	0.4258 0654	0.3771 4241
99	0.5622 4243	0.5179 8462	0.4772 4301	0.4221 1305	0.3734 0832
100	9.5589 8171	0.5145 5426	0.4736 9033	0.4184 5159	0.3697 1121

Table 9 *(Continued)*

$$v^n = (1 + i)^{-n}$$

n	$7\!/\!12\,\%$	$2\!/\!3\,\%$	$3\!/\!4\,\%$	$7\!/\!8\,\%$	$1\,\%$
101	0.5557 3989	0.5111 4661	0.4701 6410	0.4148 2190	0.3660 5071
102	0.5525 1688	0.5077 6154	0.4666 6412	0.4112 2370	0.3624 2644
103	0.5493 1255	0.5043 9888	0.4631 9019	0.4076 5670	0.3588 3806
104	0.5461 2681	0.5010 5849	0.4597 4213	0.4041 2064	0.3552 8521
105	0.5429 5955	0.4977 4022	0.4563 1973	0.4006 1526	0.3517 6753
106	0.5398 1065	0.4944 4393	0.4529 2281	0.3971 4028	0.3482 8469
107	0.5366 8002	0.4911 6946	0.4495 5117	0.3936 9545	0.3448 3632
108	0.5335 6754	0.4879 1669	0.4462 0464	0.3902 8049	0.3414 2210
109	0.5304 7312	0.4846 8545	0.4428 8302	0.3868 9516	0.3380 4168
110	0.5273 9664	0.4814 7561	0.4395 8612	0.3835 3919	0.3346 9474
111	0.5243 3800	0.4782 8703	0.4363 1377	0.3802 1233	0.3313 8093
112	0.5212 9710	0.4751 1957	0.4330 6577	0.3769 1433	0.3280 9993
113	0.5182 7383	0.4719 7308	0.4298 4196	0.3736 4494	0.3248 5141
114	0.5152 6810	0.4688 4743	0.4266 4214	0.3704 0391	0.3216 3506
115	0.5122 7980	0.4657 4248	0.4234 6615	0.3671 9099	0.3184 5056
116	0.5093 0884	0.4626 5809	0.4203 1379	0.3640 0593	0.3152 9758
117	0.5063 5510	0.4595 9413	0.4171 8491	0.3608 4851	0.3121 7582
118	0.5034 1849	0.4565 5046	0.4140 7931	0.3577 1847	0.3090 8497
119	0.5004 9891	0.4535 2695	0.4109 9683	0.3546 1559	0.3060 2473
120	0.4975 9627	0.4505 2346	0.4079 3730	0.3515 3961	0.3029 9478
121	0.4947 1046	0.4475 3986	0.4049 0055	0.3484 9032	0.2999 9483
122	0.4918 4138	0.4445 7602	0.4018 8640	0.3454 6748	0.2970 2459
123	0.4889 8895	0.4416 3181	0.3988 9469	0.3424 7086	0.2940 8375
124	0.4861 5305	0.4387 0710	0.3959 2524	0.3395 0024	0.2911 7203
125	0.4833 3361	0.4358 0175	0.3929 7792	0.3365 5538	0.2882 8914
126	0.4805 3051	0.4329 1565	0.3900 5252	0.3336 3606	0.2854 3479
127	0.4777 4367	0.4300 4866	0.3871 4891	0.3307 4207	0.2826 0870
128	0.4749 7300	0.4272 0065	0.3842 6691	0.3278 7318	0.2798 1060
129	0.4722 1839	0.4243 7151	0.3814 0636	0.3250 2917	0.2770 4019
130	0.4694 7976	0.4215 6110	0.3785 6711	0.3222 0984	0.2742 9722
131	0.4667 5701	0.4187 6930	0.3757 4899	0.3194 1496	0.2715 8141
132	0.4640 5005	0.4159 9600	0.3729 5185	0.3166 4432	0.2688 9248
133	0.4613 5879	0.4132 4106	0.3701 7553	0.3138 9771	0.2662 3108
134	0.4586 8314	0.4105 0436	0.3674 1988	0.3111 7493	0.2635 9424
135	0.4560 2301	0.4077 8579	0.3646 8475	0.3084 7577	0.2609 8439
136	0.4533 7830	0.4050 8522	0.3619 6997	0.3058 0002	0.2584 0039
137	0.4507 4893	0.4024 0254	0.3592 7541	0.3031 4748	0.2558 4197
138	0.4481 3481	0.3997 3762	0.3566 0090	0.3005 1795	0.2533 0888
139	0.4455 3585	0.3970 9035	0.3539 4630	0.2979 1122	0.2508 0087
140	0.4429 5197	0.3944 6061	0.3513 1147	0.2953 2711	0.2483 1770
141	0.4403 8306	0.3918 4829	0.3486 9625	0.2927 6541	0.2458 5911
142	0.4378 2906	0.3892 5327	0.3461 0049	0.2902 2594	0.2434 2486
143	0.4352 8987	0.3866 7543	0.3435 2406	0.2877 0849	0.2410 1471
144	0.4327 6541	0.3841 1467	0.3409 6681	0.2852 1288	0.2386 2843
145	0.4302 5558	0.3815 7086	0.3384 2860	0.2827 3891	0.2362 6577
146	0.4277 6031	0.3790 4390	0.3359 0928	0.2802 8640	0.2339 2650
147	0.4252 7952	0.3765 3368	0.3334 0871	0.2778 5517	0.2316 1040
148	0.4228 1311	0.3740 4008	0.3309 2676	0.2754 4503	0.2293 1723
149	0.4203 6100	0.3715 6299	0.3284 6329	0.2730 5579	0.2270 4676
150	0.4179 2312	0.3691 0231	0.3260 1815	0.2706 8728	0.2247 9877

Table 9 (*Continued*)
$$v^n = (1 + i)^{-n}$$

n	$\frac{7}{12}\%$	$\frac{2}{3}\%$	$\frac{3}{4}\%$	$\frac{7}{8}\%$	1%
151	0.4154 9937	0.3666 5792	0.3235 9122	0.2683 3931	0.2225 7304
152	0.4130 8968	0.3642 2973	0.3211 8235	0.2660 1170	0.2203 6935
153	0.4106 9396	0.3618 1761	0.3187 9141	0.2637 0429	0.2181 8747
154	0.4083 1214	0.3594 2147	0.3164 1828	0.2614 1689	0.2160 2720
155	0.4059 4414	0.3570 4119	0.3140 6280	0.2591 4934	0.2138 8832
156	0.4035 8986	0.3546 7668	0.3117 2487	0.2569 0145	0.2117 7061
157	0.4012 4924	0.3523 2783	0.3094 0434	0.2546 7306	0.2096 7387
158	0.3989 2220	0.3499 9453	0.3071 0108	0.2524 6400	0.2075 9789
159	0.3966 0864	0.3476 7669	0.3048 1496	0.2502 7410	0.2055 4247
160	0.3943 0851	0.3453 7419	0.3025 4587	0.2481 0320	0.2035 0739
161	0.3920 2172	0.3430 8695	0.3002 9367	0.2459 5113	0.2014 9247
162	0.3897 4819	0.3408 1485	0.2980 5823	0.2438 1772	0.1994 9750
163	0.3874 8784	0.3385 5779	0.2958 3944	0.2417 0282	0.1975 2227
164	0.3852 4060	0.3363 1569	0.2936 3716	0.2396 0627	0.1955 6661
165	0.3830 0640	0.3340 8843	0.2914 5127	0.2375 2790	0.1936 3030
166	0.3807 8515	0.3318 7593	0.2892 8166	0.2354 6756	0.1917 1317
167	0.3785 7679	0.3296 7807	0.2871 2820	0.2334 2509	0.1898 1502
168	0.3763 8123	0.3274 9478	0.2849 9077	0.2314 0033	0.1879 3566
169	0.3741 9841	0.3253 2594	0.2828 6925	0.2293 9314	0.1860 7492
170	0.3720 2824	0.3231 7146	0.2807 6352	0.2274 0336	0.1842 3259
171	0.3698 7066	0.3210 3125	0.2786 7347	0.2254 3084	0.1824 0850
172	0.3677 2560	0.3189 0522	0.2765 9898	0.2234 7543	0.1806 0248
173	0.3655 9297	0.3167 9326	0.2745 3993	0.2215 3699	0.1788 1434
174	0.3634 7272	0.3146 9529	0.2724 9621	0.2196 1535	0.1770 4390
175	0.3613 6475	0.3126 1122	0.2704 6770	0.2177 1039	0.1752 9099
176	0.3592 6902	0.3105 4094	0.2684 5429	0.2158 2194	0.1735 5543
177	0.3571 8544	0.3084 8438	0.2664 5587	0.2139 4988	0.1718 3706
178	0.3551 1394	0.3064 4144	0.2644 7233	0.2120 9406	0.1701 3571
179	0.3530 5445	0.3044 1203	0.2625 0355	0.2102 5433	0.1684 5119
180	0.3510 0691	0.3023 9605	0.2605 4943	0.2084 3057	0.1667 8336
181	0.3489 7125	0.3003 9343	0.2586 0986	0.2066 2262	0.1651 3204
182	0.3469 4739	0.2984 0407	0.2566 8472	0.2048 3035	0.1634 9707
183	0.3449 3527	0.2964 2788	0.2547 7392	0.2030 5363	0.1618 7829
184	0.3429 3481	0.2944 6478	0.2528 7734	0.2012 9233	0.1602 7553
185	0.3409 4596	0.2925 1469	0.2509 9488	0.1995 4630	0.1586 8864
186	0.3389 6864	0.2905 7750	0.2491 2643	0.1978 1541	0.1571 1747
187	0.3370 0279	0.2886 5315	0.2472 7189	0.1960 9954	0.1555 6185
188	0.3350 4835	0.2867 4154	0.2454 3116	0.1943 9855	0.1540 2163
189	0.3331 0523	0.2848 4259	0.2436 0413	0.1927 1232	0.1524 9667
190	0.3311 7339	0.2829 5621	0.2417 9070	0.1910 4071	0.1509 8680
191	0.3292 5275	0.2810 8233	0.2399 9077	0.1893 8361	0.1494 9188
192	0.3273 4324	0.2792 2086	0.2382 0423	0.1877 4087	0.1480 1176
193	0.3254 4482	0.2773 7171	0.2364 3100	0.1861 1239	0.1465 4630
194	0.3235 5740	0.2755 3482	0.2346 7097	0.1844 9803	0.1450 9535
195	0.3216 8093	0.2737 1008	0.2329 2404	0.1828 9768	0.1436 5876
196	0.3198 1534	0.2718 9743	0.2311 9011	0.1813 1121	0.1422 3640
197	0.3179 6057	0.2700 9679	0.2294 6909	0.1797 3849	0.1408 2811
198	0.3161 1655	0.2683 0807	0.2277 6089	0.1781 7942	0.1394 3378
199	0.3142 8323	0.2665 3119	0.2260 6540	0.1766 3388	0.1380 5324
200	0.3124 6055	0.2647 6608	0.2243 8253	0.1751 0174	0.1366 8638

Table 9 (*Continued*)

$$v^n = (1 + i)^{-n}$$

n	$1\frac{1}{8}\%$	$1\frac{1}{4}\%$	$1\frac{3}{8}\%$	$1\frac{1}{2}\%$	$1\frac{3}{4}\%$
1	0.9888 7515	0.9876 5432	0.9864 365C	0.9852 2167	0.9828 0098
2	0.9778 7407	0.9754 6106	0.9730 5696	0.9706 6175	0.9658 9777
3	0.9669 9537	0.9634 1833	0.9598 5890	0.9563 1699	0.9492 8528
4	0.9562 3770	0.9515 2428	0.9468 3986	0.9421 8423	0.9329 5851
5	0.9455 9970	0.9397 7706	0.9339 9739	0.9282 6033	0.9169 1254
6	0.9350 8005	0.9281 7488	0.9213 2912	0.9145 4219	0.9011 4254
7	0.9246 7743	0.9167 1593	0.9088 3267	0.9010 2679	0.8856 4378
8	0.9143 9054	0.9053 9845	0.8965 0571	0.8877 1112	0.8704 1157
9	0.9042 1808	0.8942 2069	0.8843 4596	0.8745 9224	0.8554 4135
10	0.8941· 5880	0.8831 8093	0.8723 5113	0.8616 6723	0.8407 2860
11	0.8842 1142	0.8722 7746	0.8605 1899	0.8489 3323	0.8262 6889
12	0.8743 7470	0.8615 0860	0.8488 4734	0.8363 8742	0.8120 5788
13	0.8646 4742	0.8508 7269	0.8373 3400	0.8240 2702	0.7980 9128
14	0.8550 2835	0.8403 6809	0.8259 7682	0.8118 4928	0.7843 6490
15	0.8455 1629	0.8299 9318	0.8147 7368	0.7998 5150	0.7708 7459
16	0.8361 1005	0.8197 4635	0.8037 2250	0.7880 3104	0.7576 1631
17	0.8268 0846	0.8096 2602	0.7928 2120	0.7763 8526	0.7445 8605
18	0.8176 1034	0.7996 3064	0.7820 6777	0.7649 1159	0.7317 7990
19	0.8085 1455	0.7897 5866	0.7714 6020	0.7536 0747	0.7191 9401
20	0.7995 1995	0.7800 0855	0.7609 9649	0.7424 7042	0.7068 2458
21	0.7906 2542	0.7703 7881	0.7506 7472	0.7314 9795	0.6946 6789
22	0.7818 2983	0.7608 6796	0.7404 9294	0.7206 8763	0.6827 2028
23	0.7731 3210	0.7514 7453	0.7304 4926	0.7100 3708	0.6709 7817
24	0.7645 3112	0.7421 9707	0.7205 4181	0.6995 4392	0.6594 3800
25	0.7560 2583	0.7330 3414	0.7107 6874	0.6892 0583	0.6480 9632
26	0.7476 1516	0.7239 8434	0.7011 2823	0.6790 2052	0.6369 4970
27	0.7392 9806	0.7150 4626	0.6916 1847	0.6689 8574	0.6259 9479
28	0.7310 7348	0.7062 1853	0.6822 3771	0.6590 9925	0.6152 2829
29	0.7229 4040	0.6974 9978	0.6729 8417	0.6493 5887	0.6046 4697
30	0.7148 9780	0.6888 8867	0.6638 5615	0.6397 6243	0.5942 4764
31	0.7069 4467	0.6803 8387	0.6548 5194	0.6303 0781	0.5840 2716
32	0.6990 8002	0.6719 8407	0.6459 6985	0.6209 9292	0.5739 8247
33	0.6913 0287	0.6636 8797	0.6372 0824	0.6118 1568	0.5641 1053
34	0.6836 1223	0.6554 9429	0.6285 6546	0.6027 7407	0.5544 0839
35	0.6760 0715	0.6474 0177	0.6200 3991	0.5938 6608	0.5448 7311
36	0.6684 8667	0.6394 0916	0.6116 3000	0.5850 8974	0.5355 0183
37	0.6610 4986	0.6315 1522	0.6033 3416	0.5764 4309	0.5262 9172
38	0.6536 9578	0.6237 1873	0.5951 5083	0.5679 2423	0.5172 4002
39	0.6464 2352	0.6160 1850	0.5870 7850	0.5595 3126	0.5083 4400
40	0.6392 3216	0.6084 1334	0.5791 1566	0.5512 6232	0.4996 0098
41	0.6321 2080	0.6009 0206	0.5712 6083	0.5431 1559	0.4910 0834
42	0.6250 8855	0.5934 8352	0.5635 1253	0.5350 8925	0.4825 6348
43	0.6181 3454	0.5861 5656	0.5558 6933	0.5271 8153	0.4742 6386
44	0.6112 5789	0.5789 2006	0.5483 2979	0.5193 9067	0.4661 0699
45	0.6044 5774	0.5717 7290	0.5408 9252	0.5117 1494	0.4580 9040
46	0.5977 3324	0.5647 1397	0.5335 5612	0.5041 5265	0.4502 1170
47	0.5910 8355	0.5577 4219	0.5263 1923	0.4967 0212	0.4424 6850
48	0.5845 0784	0.5508 5649	0.5191 8050	0.4893 6170	0.4348 5848
49	0.5780 0528	0.5440 5579	0.5121 3860	0.4821 2975	0.4273 7934
50	0.5715 7506	0.5373 3905	0.5051 9220	0.4750 0468	0.4200 2883

Table 9   (*Continued*)

$$v^n = (1 + i)^{-n}$$

n	$1\frac{1}{8}\%$	$1\frac{1}{4}\%$	$1\frac{3}{8}\%$	$1\frac{1}{2}\%$	$1\frac{3}{4}\%$
51	0.5652 1637	0.5307 0524	0.4983 4003	0.4679 8491	0.4128 0475
52	0.5589 2843	0.5241 5332	0.4915 8079	0.4610 6887	0.4057 0492
53	0.5527 1044	0.5176 8229	0.4849 1323	0.4542 5505	0.3987 2719
54	0.5465 6162	0.5112 9115	0.4783 3611	0.4475 4192	0.3918 6947
55	0.5404 8120	0.5049 7892	0.4718 4820	0.4409 2800	0.3851 2970
56	0.5344 6843	0.4987 4461	0.4654 4829	0.4344 1182	0.3785 0585
57	0.5285 2256	0.4925 8727	0.4591 3518	0.4279 9194	0.3719 9592
58	0.5226 4282	0.4865 0594	0.4529 0770	0.4216 6694	0.3655 9796
59	0.5168 2850	0.4804 9970	0.4467 6468	0.4154 3541	0.3593 1003
60	0.5110 7887	0.4745 6760	0.4407 0499	0.4092 9597	0.3531 3025
61	0.5053 9319	0.4687 0874	0.4347 2749	0.4032 4726	0.3470 5676
62	0.4997 7077	0.4629 2222	0.4288 3106	0.3972 8794	0.3410 8772
63	0.4942 1090	0.4572 0713	0.4230 1461	0.3914 1669	0.3352 2135
64	0.4887 1288	0.4515 6259	0.4172 7705	0.3856 3221	0.3294 5587
65	0.4832 7602	0.4459 8775	0.4116 1731	0.3799 3321	0.3237 8956
66	0.4778 9965	0.4404 8173	0.4060 3434	0.3743 1843	0.3182 2069
67	0.4725 8309	0.4350 4368	0.4005 2709	0.3687 8663	0.3127 4761
68	0.4673 2568	0.4296 7277	0.3950 9454	0.3633 3658	0.3073 6866
69	0.4621 2675	0.4243 6817	0.3897 3568	0.3579 6708	0.3020 8222
70	0.4569 8566	0.4191 2905	0.3844 4949	0.3526 7692	0.2968 8670
71	0.4519 0177	0.4139 5462	0.3792 3501	0.3474 6495	0.2917 8054
72	0.4468 7443	0.4088 4407	0.3740 9126	0.3423 3000	0.2867 6221
73	0.4419 0302	0.4037 9661	0.3690 1727	0.3372 7093	0.2818 3018
74	0.4369 8692	0.3988 1147	0.3640 1210	0.3322 8663	0.2769 8298
75	0.4321 2551	0.3938 8787	0.3590 7483	0.3273 7599	0.2722 1914
76	0.4273 1818	0.3890 2506	0.3542 0451	0.3225 3793	0.2675 3724
77	0.4225 6433	0.3842 2228	0.3494 0026	0.3177 7136	0.2629 3586
78	0.4178 6337	0.3794 7879	0.3446 6117	0.3130 7523	0.2584 1362
79	0.4132 1470	0.3747 9387	0.3399 8636	0.3084 4850	0.2539 6916
80	0.4086 1775	0.3701 6679	0.3353 7495	0.3038 9015	0.2496 0114
81	0.4040 7194	0.3655 9683	0.3308 2609	0.2993 9916	0.2453 0825
82	0.3995 7670	0.3610 8329	0.3263 3893	0.2949 7454	0.2410 8919
83	0.3951 3148	0.3566 2547	0.3219 1263	0.2906 1531	0.2369 4269
84	0.3907 3570	0.3522 2268	0.3175 4637	0.2863 2050	0.2328 6751
85	0.3863 8882	0.3478 7426	0.3132 3933	0.2820 8917	0.2288 6242
86	0.3820 9031	0.3435 7951	0.3089 9071	0.2779 2036	0.2249 2621
87	0.3778 3961	0.3393 3779	0.3047 9971	0.2738 1316	0.2210 5770
88	0.3736 3621	0.3351 4843	0.3006 6556	0.2697 6666	0.2172 5572
89	0.3694 7956	0.3310 1080	0.2965 8748	0.2657 7997	0.2135 1914
90	0.3653 6916	0.3269 2425	0.2925 6472	0.2618 5218	0.2098 4682
91	0.3613 0448	0.3228 8814	0.2885 9652	0.2579 8245	0.2062 3766
92	0.3572 8503	0.3189 0187	0.2846 8214	0.2541 6990	0.2026 9057
93	0.3533 1029	0.3149 6481	0.2808 2085	0.2504 1369	0.1992 0450
94	0.3493 7976	0.3110 7636	0.2770 1194	0.2467 1300	0.1957 7837
95	0.3454 9297	0.3072 3591	0.2732 5468	0.2430 6699	0.1924 1118
96	0.3416 4941	0.3034 4287	0.2695 4839	0.2394 7487	0.1891 0190
97	0.3378 4861	0.2996 9666	0.2658 9237	0.2359 3583	0.1858 4953
98	0.3340 9010	0.2959 9670	0.2622 8594	0.2324 4909	0.1826 5310
99	0.3303 7340	0.2923 4242	0.2587 2843	0.2290 1389	0.1795 1165
100	0.3266 9805	0.2887 3326	0.2552 1916	0.2256 2944	0.1764 2422

Table 9   *(Continued)*

$$v^n = (1 + i)^{-n}$$

n	2 %	2¼ %	2½ %	2¾ %	3 %
1	0.9803 9216	0.9779 9511	0.9756 0976	0.9732 3601	0.9708 7379
2	0.9611 6878	0.9564 7444	0.9518 1440	0.9471 8833	0.9425 9591
3	0.9423 2233	0.9354 2732	0.9285 9941	0.9218 3779	0.9151 4166
4	0.9238 4543	0.9148 4335	0.9059 5064	0.8971 6573	0.8884 8705
5	0.9057 3081	0.8947 1232	0.8838 5429	0.8731 5400	0.8626 0878
6	0.8879 7138	0.8750 2427	0.8622 9687	0.8497 8491	0.8374 8426
7	0.8705 6018	0.8557 6946	0.8412 6524	0.8270 4128	0.8130 9151
8	0.8534 9037	0.8369 3835	0.8207 4657	0.8049 0635	0.7894 0923
9	0.8367 5527	0.8185 2161	0.8007 2836	0.7833 6385	0.7664 1673
10	0.8203 4830	0.8005 1013	0.7811 9840	0.7623 9791	0.7440 9391
11	0.8042 6304	0.7828 9499	0.7621 4478	0.7419 9310	0.7224 2128
12	0.7884 9318	0.7656 6748	0.7435 5589	0.7221 3440	0.7013 7988
13	0.7730 3253	0.7488 1905	0.7254 2038	0.7028 0720	0.6809 5134
14	0.7578 7502	0.7323 4137	0.7077 2720	0.6839 9728	0.6611 1781
15	0.7430 1473	0.7162 2628	0.6904 6556	0.6656 9078	0.6418 6195
16	0.7284 4581	0.7004 6580	0.6736 2493	0.6478 7424	0.6231 6694
17	0.7141 6256	0.6850 5212	0.6571 9506	0.6305 3454	0.6050 1645
18	0.7001 5937	0.6699 7763	0.6411 6591	0.6136 5892	0.5873 9461
19	0.6864 3076	0.6552 3484	0.6255 2772	0.5972 3496	0.5702 8603
20	0.6729 7133	0.6408 1647	0.6102 7094	0.5812 5057	0.5536 7575
21	0.6597 7582	0.6267 1538	0.5953 8629	0.5656 9398	0.5375 4928
22	0.6468 3904	0.6129 2457	0.5808 6467	0.5505 5375	0.5218 9250
23	0.6341 5592	0.5994 3724	0.5666 9724	0.5358 1874	0.5066 9175
24	0.6217 2149	0.5862 4668	0.5528 7535	0.5214 7809	0.4919 3374
25	0.6095 3087	0.5733 4639	0.5393 9059	0.5075 2126	0.4776 0557
26	0.5975 7928	0.5607 2997	0.5262 3472	0.4939 3796	0.4636 9473
27	0.5858 6204	0.5483 9117	0.5133 9973	0.4807 1821	0.4501 8906
28	0.5743 7455	0.5363 2388	0.5008 7778	0.4678 5227	0.4370 7675
29	0.5631 1231	0.5245 2213	0.4886 6125	0.4553 3068	0.4243 4636
30	0.5520 7089	0.5129 8008	0.4767 4269	0.4431 4421	0.4119 8676
31	0.5412 4597	0.5016 9201	0.4651 1481	0.4312 8391	0.3999 8715
32	0.5306 3330	0.4906 5233	0.4537 7055	0.4197 4103	0.3883 3703
33	0.5202 2873	0.4798 5558	0.4427 0298	0.4085 0708	0.3770 2625
34	0.5100 2817	0.4692 9641	0.4319 0534	0.3975 7380	0.3660 4490
35	0.5000 2761	0.4589 6960	0.4213 7107	0.3869 3314	0.3553 8340
36	0.4902 2315	0.4488 7002	0.4110 9372	0.3765 7727	0.3450 3243
37	0.4806 1093	0.4389 9268	0.4010 6705	0.3664 9856	0.3349 8294
38	0.4711 8719	0.4293 3270	0.3912 8492	0.3566 8959	0.3252 2615
39	0.4619 4822	0.4198 8528	0.3817 4139	0.3471 4316	0.3157 5355
40	0.4528 9042	0.4106 4575	0.3724 3062	0.3378 5222	0.3065 5684
41	0.4440 1021	0.4016 0954	0.3633 4695	0.3288 0995	0.2976 2800
42	0.4353 0413	0.3927 7216	0.3544 8483	0.3200 0968	0.2889 5922
43	0.4267 6875	0.3841 2925	0.3458 3886	0.3114 4495	0.2805 4294
44	0.4184 0074	0.3756 7653	0.3374 0376	0.3031 0944	0.2723 7178
45	0.4101 9680	0.3674 0981	0.3291 7440	0.2949 9702	0.2644 3862
46	0.4021 5373	0.3593 2500	0.3211 4576	0.2871 0172	0.2567 3653
47	0.3942 6836	0.3514 1809	0.3133 1294	0.2794 1773	0.2492 5876
48	0.3865 3761	0.3436 8518	0.3056 7116	0.2719 3940	0.2419 9880
49	0.3789 5844	0.3361 2242	0.2982 1576	0.2646 6122	0.2349 5029
50	0.3715 2788	0.3287 2608	0.2909 4221	0.2575 7783	0.2281 0708

Table 9   *(Continued)*

$$v^n = (1 + i)^{-n}$$

n	2%	$2\frac{1}{4}\%$	$2\frac{1}{2}\%$	$2\frac{3}{4}\%$	3%
51	0.3642 4302	0.3214 9250	0.2838 4606	0.2506 8402	0.2214 6318
52	0.3571 0100	0.3144 1810	0.2769 2298	0.2439 7471	0.2150 1280
53	0.3500 9902	0.3074 9936	0.2701 6876	0.2374 4497	0.2087 5029
54	0.3432 3433	0.3007 3287	0.2635 7928	0.2310 9000	0.2026 7019
55	0.3365 0425	0.2941 1528	0.2571 5052	0.2249 0511	0.1967 6717
56	0.3299 0613	0.2876 4330	0.2508 7855	0.2188 8575	0.1910 3609
57	0.3234 3738	0.2813 1374	0.2447 5956	0.2130 2749	0.1854 7193
58	0.3170 9547	0.2751 2347	0.2387 8982	0.2073 2603	0.1800 6984
59	0.3108 7791	0.2690 6940	0.2329 6568	0.2017 7716	0.1748 2508
60	0.3047 8227	0.2631 4856	0.2272 8359	0.1963 7679	0.1697 3309
61	0.2988 0614	0.2573 5801	0.2217 4009	0.1911 2097	0.1647 8941
62	0.2929 4720	0.2516 9487	0.2163 3179	0.1860 0581	0.1599 8972
63	0.2872 0314	0.2461 5635	0.2110 5541	0.1810 2755	0.1553 2982
64	0.2815 7170	0.2407 3971	0.2059 0771	0.1761 8253	0.1508 0565
65	0.2760 5069	0.2354 4226	0.2008 8557	0.1714 6718	0.1464 1325
66	0.2706 3793	0.2302 6138	0.1959 8593	0.1668 7804	0.1421 4879
67	0.2653 3130	0.2251 9450	0.1912 0578	0.1624 1172	0.1380 0853
68	0.2601 2873	0.2202 3912	0.1865 4223	0.1580 6493	0.1339 8887
69	0.2550 2817	0.2153 9278	0.1819 9241	0.1538 3448	0.1300 8628
70	0.2500 2761	0.2106 5309	0.1775 5358	0.1497 1726	0.1262 9736
71	0.2451 2511	0.2060 1769	0.1732 2300	0.1457 1023	0.1226 1880
72	0.2403 1874	0.2014 8429	0.1689 9805	0.1418 1044	0.1190 4737
73	0.2356 0661	0.1970 5065	0.1648 7615	0.1380 1503	0.1155 7998
74	0.2309 8687	0.1927 1458	0.1608 5478	0.1343 2119	0.1122 1357
75	0.2264 5771	0.1884 7391	0.1569 3149	0.1307 2622	0.1089 4521
76	0.2220 1737	0.1843 2657	0.1531 0389	0.1272 2747	0.1057 7205
77	0.2176 6408	0.1802 7048	0.1493 6965	0.1238 2235	0.1026 9131
78	0.2133 9616	0.1763 0365	0.1457 2649	0.1205 0837	0.0997 0030
79	0.2092 1192	0.1724 2411	0.1421 7218	0.1172 8309	0.0967 9641
80	0.2051 0973	0.1686 2993	0.1387 0457	0.1141 4412	0.0939 7710
81	0.2010 8797	0.1649 1925	0.1353 2153	0.1110 8917	0.0912 3990
82	0.1971 4507	0.1612 9022	0.1320 2101	0.1081 1598	0.0885 8243
83	0.1932 7948	0.1577 4105	0.1288 0098	0.1052 2237	0.0860 0236
84	0.1894 8968	0.1542 6997	0.1256 5949	0.1024 0620	0.0834 9743
85	0.1857 7420	0.1508 7528	0.1225 9463	0.0996 6540	0.0810 6547
86	0.1821 3157	0.1475 5528	0.1196 0452	0.0969 9795	0.0787 0434
87	0.1785 6036	0.1443 0835	0.1166 8733	0.0944 0190	0.0764 1198
88	0.1750 5918	0.1411 3286	0.1138 4130	0.0918 7533	0.0741 8639
89	0.1716 2665	0.1380 2724	0.1110 6468	0.0894 1638	0.0720 2562
90	0.1682 6142	0.1349 8997	0.1083 5579	0.0870 2324	0.0699 2779
91	0.1649 6217	0.1320 1953	0.1057 1296	0.0846 9415	0.0678 9105
92	0.1617 2762	0.1291 1445	0.1031 3460	0.0824 2740	0.0659 1364
93	0.1585 5649	0.1262 7331	0.1006 1912	0.0802 2131	0.0639 9383
94	0.1554 4754	0.1234 9468	0.0981 6500	0.0780 7427	0.0621 2993
95	0.1523 9955	0.1207 7719	0.0957 7073	0.0759 8469	0.0603 2032
96	0.1494 1132	0.1181 1950	0.0934 3486	0.0739 5104	0.0585 6342
97	0.1464 8169	0.1155 2029	0.0911 5596	0.0719 7181	0.0568 5769
98	0.1436 0950	0.1129 7828	0.0889 3264	0.0700 4556	0.0552 0164
99	0.1407 9363	0.1104 9221	0.0867 6355	0.0681 7086	0.0535 9383
100	0.1380 3297	0.1080 6084	0.0846 4737	0.0663 4634	0.0520 3284

Table 9 (*Continued*)

$$v^n = (1 + i)^{-n}$$

n	$3\frac{1}{2}\%$	4%	$4\frac{1}{2}\%$	5%	$5\frac{1}{2}\%$
1	0.9661 8357	0.9615 3846	0.9569 3780	0.9523 8095	0.9478 6730
2	0.9335 1070	0.9245 5621	0.9157 2995	0.9070 2948	0.8984 5242
3	0.9019 4271	0.8889 9636	0.8762 9660	0.8638 3760	0.8516 1366
4	0.8714 4223	0.8548 0419	0.8385 6134	0.8227 0247	0.8072 1674
5	0.8419 7317	0.8219 2711	0.8024 5105	0.7835 2617	0.7651 3435
6	0.8135 0064	0.7903 1453	0.7678 9574	0.7462 1540	0.7252 4583
7	0.7859 9096	0.7599 1781	0.7348 2846	0.7106 8133	0.6874 3681
8	0.7594 1156	0.7306 9021	0.7031 8513	0.6768 3936	0.6515 9887
9	0.7337 3097	0.7025 8674	0.6729 0443	0.6446 0892	0.6176 2926
10	0.7089 1881	0.6755 6417	0.6439 2768	0.6139 1325	0.5854 3058
11	0.6849 4571	0.6495 8093	0.6161 9874	0.5846 7929	0.5549 1050
12	0.6617 8330	0.6245 9705	0.5896 6386	0.5568 3742	0.5259 8152
13	0.6394 0415	0.6005 7409	0.5642 7164	0.5303 2135	0.4985 6068
14	0.6177 8179	0.5774 7508	0.5399 7286	0.5050 6795	0.4725 6937
15	0.5968 9062	0.5552 6450	0.5167 2044	0.4810 1710	0.4479 3305
16	0.5767 0591	0.5339 0818	0.4944 6932	0.4581 1152	0.4245 8109
17	0.5572 0378	0.5133 7325	0.4731 7639	0.4362 9669	0.4024 4653
18	0.5383 6114	0.4936 2812	0.4528 0037	0.4155 2065	0.3814 6590
19	0.5201 5569	0.4746 4242	0.4333 0179	0.3957 3396	0.3615 7906
20	0.5025 6588	0.4563 8695	0.4146 4286	0.3768 8948	0.3427 2896
21	0.4855 7090	0.4388 3360	0.3967 8743	0.3589 4236	0.3248 6158
22	0.4691 5063	0.4219 5539	0.3797 0089	0.3418 4987	0.3079 2567
23	0.4532 8563	0.4057 2633	0.3633 5013	0.3255 7131	0.2918 7267
24	0.4379 5713	0.3901 2147	0.3477 0347	0.3100 6791	0.2766 5656
25	0.4231 4699	0.3751 1680	0.3327 3060	0.2953 0277	0.2622 3370
26	0.4088 3767	0.3606 8923	0.3184 0248	0.2812 4073	0.2485 6275
27	0.3950 1224	0.3468 1657	0.3046 9137	0.2678 4832	0.2356 0450
28	0.3816 5434	0.3334 7747	0.2915 7069	0.2550 9364	0.2233 2181
29	0.3687 4815	0.3206 5141	0.2790 1502	0.2429 4632	0.2116 7944
30	0.3562 7841	0.3083 1867	0.2670 0002	0.2313 7745	0.2006 4402
31	0.3442 3035	0.2964 6026	0.2555 0241	0.2203 5947	0.1901 8390
32	0.3325 8971	0.2850 5794	0.2444 9991	0.2098 6617	0.1802 6910
33	0.3213 4271	0.2740 9417	0.2339 7121	0.1998 7254	0.1708 7119
34	0.3104 7605	0.2635 5209	0.2238 9589	0.1903 5480	0.1619 6321
35	0.2999 7686	0.2534 1547	0.2142 5444	0.1812 9029	0.1535 1963
36	0.2898 3272	0.2436 6872	0.2050 2817	0.1726 5741	0.1455 1624
37	0.2800 3161	0.2342 9685	0.1961 9921	0.1644 3563	0.1379 3008
38	0.2705 6194	0.2252 8543	0.1877 5044	0.1566 0536	0.1307 3941
39	0.2614 1250	0.2166 2061	0.1796 6549	0.1491 4797	0.1239 2362
40	0.2525 7247	0.2082 8904	0.1719 2870	0.1420 4568	0.1174 6314
41	0.2440 3137	0.2002 7793	0.1645 2507	0.1352 8160	0.1113 3947
42	0.2357 7910	0.1925 7493	0.1574 4026	0.1288 3962	0.1055 3504
43	0.2278 0590	0.1851 6820	0.1506 6054	0.1227 0440	0.1000 3322
44	0.2201 0231	0.1780 4635	0.1441 7276	0.1168 6133	0.0948 1822
45	0.2126 5924	0.1711 9841	0.1379 6437	0.1112 9651	0.0898 7509
46	0.2054 6787	0.1646 1386	0.1320 2332	0.1059 9668	0.0851 8965
47	0.1985 1968	0.1582 8256	0.1263 3810	0.1009 4921	0.0807 4849
48	0.1918 0645	0.1521 9476	0.1208 9771	0.0961 4211	0.0765 3885
49	0.1853 2024	0.1463 4112	0.1156 9158	0.0915 6391	0.0725 4867
50	0.1790 5337	0.1407 1262	0.1107 0965	0.0872 0373	0.0687 6652

Table 9 *(Continued)*

$$v^n = (1 + i)^{-n}$$

n	$3\frac{1}{2}\%$	4%	$4\frac{1}{2}\%$	5%	$5\frac{1}{2}\%$
51	0.1729 9843	0.1353 0059	0.1059 4225	0.0830 5117	0.0651 8153
52	0.1671 4824	0.1300 9672	0.1013 8014	0.0790 9635	0.0617 8344
53	0.1614 9589	0.1250 9300	0.0970 1449	0.0753 2986	0.0585 6250
54	0.1560 3467	0.1202 8173	0.0928 3683	0.0717 4272	0.0555 0948
55	0.1507 5814	0.1156 5551	0.0888 3907	0.0683 2640	0.0526 1562
56	0.1456 6004	0.1112 0722	0.0850 1347	0.0650 7276	0.0498 7263
57	0.1407 3433	0.1069 3002	0.0813 5260	0.0619 7406	0.0472 7263
58	0.1359 7520	0.1028 1733	0.0778 4938	0.0590 2291	0.0448 0818
59	0.1313 7701	0.0988 6282	0.0744 9701	0.0562 1230	0.0424 7221
60	0.1269 3431	0.0950 6040	0.0712 8901	0.0535 3552	0.0402 5802
61	0.1226 4184	0.0914 0423	0.0682 1915	0.0509 8621	0.0381 5926
62	0.1184 9453	0.0878 8868	0.0652 8148	0.0485 5830	0.0361 6992
63	0.1144 8747	0.0845 0835	0.0624 7032	0.0462 4600	0.0342 8428
64	0.1106 1591	0.0812 5803	0.0597 8021	0.0440 4381	0.0324 9695
65	0.1068 7528	0.0781 3272	0.0572 0594	0.0419 4648	0.0308 0279
66	0.1032 6114	0.0751 2762	0.0547 4253	0.0399 4903	0.0291 9696
67	0.0997 6922	0.0722 3809	0.0523 8519	0.0380 4670	0.0276 7485
68	0.0963 9538	0.0694 5970	0.0501 2937	0.0362 3495	0.0262 3208
69	0.0931 3563	0.0667 8818	0.0479 7069	0.0345 0948	0.0248 6453
70	0.0899 8612	0.0642 1940	0.0459 0497	0.0328 6617	0.0235 6828
71	0.0869 4311	0.0617 4942	0.0439 2820	0.0313 0111	0.0223 3960
72	0.0840 0300	0.0593 7445	0.0420 3655	0.0298 1058	0.0211 7498
73	0.0811 6232	0.0570 9081	0.0402 2637	0.0283 9103	0.0200 7107
74	0.0784 1770	0.0548 9501	0.0384 9413	0.0270 3908	0.0190 2471
75	0.0757 6590	0.0527 8367	0.0368 3649	0.0257 5150	0.0180 3290
76	0.0732 0376	0.0507 5353	0.0352 5023	0.0245 2524	0.0170 9279
77	0.0707 2827	0.0488 0147	0.0337 3228	0.0233 5737	0.0162 0170
78	0.0683 3650	0.0469 2449	0.0322 7969	0.0222 4512	0.0153 5706
79	0.0660 2560	0.0451 1970	0.0308 8965	0.0211 8582	0.0145 5646
80	0.0637 9285	0.0433 8433	0.0295 5948	0.0201 7698	0.0137 9759
81	0.0616 3561	0.0417 1570	0.0282 8658	0.0192 1617	0.0130 7828
82	0.0595 5131	0.0401 1125	0.0270 6850	0.0183 0111	0.0123 9648
83	0.0575 3750	0.0385 6851	0.0259 0287	0.0174 2963	0.0117 5022
84	0.0555 9178	0.0370 8510	0.0247 8744	0.0165 9965	0.0111 3765
85	0.0537 1187	0.0356 5875	0.0237 2003	0.0158 0919	0.0105 5701
86	0.0518 9553	0.0342 8726	0.0226 9860	0.0150 5637	0.0100 0664
87	0.0501 4060	0.0329 6852	0.0217 2115	0.0143 3940	0.0094 8497
88	0.0484 4503	0.0317 0050	0.0207 8579	0.0136 5657	0.0089 9049
89	0.0468 0679	0.0304 8125	0.0198 9070	0.0130 0626	0.0085 2180
90	0.0452 2395	0.0293 0890	0.0190 3417	0.0123 8691	0.0080 7753
91	0.0436 9464	0.0281 8163	0.0182 1451	0.0117 9706	0.0076 5643
92	0.0422 1704	0.0270 9772	0.0174 3016	0.0112 3530	0.0072 5728
93	0.0407 8941	0.0260 5550	0.0166 7958	0.0107 0028	0.0068 7894
94	0.0394 1006	0.0250 5337	0.0159 6132	0.0101 9074	0.0065 2032
95	0.0380 7735	0.0240 8978	0.0152 7399	0.0097 0547	0.0061 8040
96	0.0367 8971	0.0231 6325	0.0146 1626	0.0092 4331	0.0058 5820
97	0.0355 4562	0.0222 7235	0.0139 8685	0.0088 0315	0.0055 5279
98	0.0343 4359	0.0214 1572	0.0133 8454	0.0083 8395	0.0052 6331
99	0.0331 8221	0.0205 9204	0.0128 0817	0.0079 8471	0.0049 8892
100	0.0320 6011	0.0198 0004	0.0122 5663	0.0076 0449	0.0047 2883

Table 9   *(Continued)*

$$v^n = (1 + i)^{-n}$$

n	6 %	6½ %	7 %	7½ %	8 %
1	0.9433 9623	0.9389 6714	0.9345 7944	0.9302 3256	0.9259 2593
2	0.8899 9644	0.8816 5928	0.8734 3873	0.8653 3261	0.8573 3882
3	0.8396 1928	0.8278 4909	0.8162 9788	0.8049 6057	0.7938 3224
4	0.7920 9366	0.7773 2309	0.7628 9521	0.7488 0053	0.7350 2985
5	0.7472 5817	0.7298 8084	0.7129 8618	0.6965 5863	0.6805 8320
6	0.7049 6054	0.6853 3412	0.6663 4222	0.6479 6152	0.6301 6963
7	0.6650 5711	0.6435 0621	0.6227 4974	0.6027 5490	0.5834 9040
8	0.6274 1237	0.6042 3119	0.5820 0910	0.5607 0223	0.5402 6888
9	0.5918 9846	0.5673 5323	0.5439 3374	0.5215 8347	0.5002 4897
10	0.5583 9478	0.5327 2604	0.5083 4929	0.4851 9393	0.4631 9349
11	0.5267 8753	0.5002 1224	0.4750 9280	0.4513 4319	0.4288 8286
12	0.4969 6936	0.4696 8285	0.4440 1196	0.4198 5413	0.3971 1376
13	0.4688 3902	0.4410 1676	0.4149 6445	0.3905 6198	0.3676 9792
14	0.4423 0096	0.4141 0025	0.3878 1724	0.3633 1347	0.3404 6104
15	0.4172 6506	0.3888 2652	0.3624 4602	0.3379 6602	0.3152 4170
16	0.3936 4628	0.3650 9533	0.3387 3460	0.3143 8699	0.2918 9047
17	0.3713 6442	0.3428 1251	0.3165 7439	0.2924 5302	0.2702 6895
18	0.3503 4379	0.3218 8969	0.2958 6392	0.2720 4932	0.2502 4903
19	0.3305 1301	0.3022 4384	0.2765 0833	0.2530 6913	0.2317 1206
20	0.3118 0473	0.2837 9703	0.2584 1900	0.2354 1315	0.2145 4821
21	0.2941 5540	0.2664 7608	0.2415 1309	0.2189 8897	0.1986 5575
22	0.2775 0510	0.2502 1228	0.2257 1317	0.2037 1067	0.1839 4051
23	0.2617 9726	0.2349 4111	0.2109 4688	0.1894 9830	0.1703 1528
24	0.2469 7855	0.2206 0198	0.1971 4662	0.1762 7749	0.1576 9934
25	0.2329 9863	0.2071 3801	0.1842 4918	0.1639 7906	0.1460 1790
26	0.2198 1003	0.1944 9579	0.1721 9549	0.1525 3866	0.1352 0176
27	0.2073 6795	0.1826 2515	0.1609 3037	0.1418 9643	0.1251 8682
28	0.1956 3014	0.1714 7902	0.1504 0221	0.1319 9668	0.1159 1372
29	0.1845 5674	0.1610 1316	0.1405 6282	0.1227 8761	0.1073 2752
30	0.1741 1013	0.1511 8607	0.1313 6712	0.1142 2103	0.0993 7733
31	0.1642 5484	0.1419 5875	0.1227 7301	0.1062 5212	0.0920 1605
32	0.1549 5740	0.1332 9460	0.1147 4113	0.0988 3918	0.0852 0005
33	0.1461 8622	0.1251 5925	0.1072 3470	0.0919 4343	0.0788 8893
34	0.1379 1153	0.1175 2042	0.1002 1934	0.0855 2877	0.0730 4531
35	0.1301 0522	0.1103 4781	0.0936 6294	0.0795 6164	0.0676 3454
36	0.1227 4077	0.1036 1297	0.0875 3546	0.0740 1083	0.0626 2458
37	0.1157 9318	0.0972 8917	0.0818 0884	0.0688 4729	0.0579 8572
38	0.1092 3885	0.0913 5134	0.0764 5686	0.0640 4399	0.0536 9048
39	0.1030 5552	0.0857 7590	0.0714 5501	0.0595 7580	0.0497 1341
40	0.0972 2219	0.0805 4075	0.0667 8038	0.0554 1935	0.0460 3093
41	0.0917 1905	0.0756 2512	0.0624 1157	0.0515 5288	0.0426 2123
42	0.0865 2740	0.0710 0950	0.0583 2857	0.0479 5617	0.0394 6411
43	0.0816 2962	0.0666 7559	0.0545 1268	0.0446 1039	0.0365 4084
44	0.0770 0908	0.0626 0619	0.0509 4643	0.0414 9804	0.0338 3411
45	0.0726 5007	0.0587 8515	0.0476 1349	0.0386 0283	0.0313 2788
46	0.0685 3781	0.0551 9733	0.0444 9859	0.0359 0961	0.0290 0730
47	0.0646 5831	0.0518 2848	0.0415 8747	0.0334 0428	0.0268 5861
48	0.0609 9840	0.0486 6524	0.0388 6679	0.0310 7375	0.0248 6908
49	0.0575 4566	0.0456 9506	0.0363 2410	0.0289 0582	0.0230 2693
50	0.0542 8836	0.0429 0616	0.0339 4776	0.0268 8913	0.0213 2123

Table 9 (*Continued*)

$$v^n = (1 + i)^{-n}$$

n	$8\frac{1}{2}\%$	9%	$9\frac{1}{2}\%$	10%	$10\frac{1}{2}\%$
1	0.9216 5899	0.9174 3119	0.9132 4201	0.9090 9091	0.9049 7738
2	0.8494 5529	0.8416 7999	0.8340 1097	0.8264 4628	0.8189 8405
3	0.7829 0810	0.7721 8348	0.7616 5385	0.7513 1480	0.7411 6204
4	0.7215 7428	0.7084 2521	0.6955 7429	0.6830 1346	0.6707 3487
5	0.6650 4542	0.6499 3139	0.6352 2767	0.6209 2132	0.6069 9989
6	0.6129 4509	0.5962 6733	0.5801 1659	0.5644 7393	0.5493 2116
7	0.5649 2635	0.5470 3424	0.5297 8684	0.5131 5812	0.4971 2323
8	0.5206 6945	0.5018 6628	0.4838 2360	0.4665 0738	0.4498 8527
9	0.4798 7968	0.4604 2778	0.4418 4803	0.4240 9762	0.4071 3599
10	0.4422 8542	0.4224 1081	0.4035 1419	0.3855 4329	0.3684 4886
11	0.4076 3633	0.3875 3285	0.3685 0611	0.3504 9390	0.3334 3788
12	0.3757 0168	0.3555 3473	0.3365 3526	0.3186 3082	0.3017 5374
13	0.3462 6883	0.3261 7865	0.3073 3813	0.2896 6438	0.2730 8031
14	0.3191 4178	0.2992 4647	0.2806 7410	0.2633 3125	0.2471 3150
15	0.2941 3989	0.2745 3804	0.2563 2337	0.2393 9205	0.2236 4842
16	0.2710 9667	0.2518 6976	0.2340 8527	0.2176 2914	0.2023 9676
17	0.2498 5869	0.2310 7318	0.2137 7651	0.1978 4467	0.1831 6449
18	0.2302 8450	0.2119 9374	0.1952 2969	0.1798 5879	0.1657 5972
19	0.2122 4378	0.1944 8967	0.1782 9195	0.1635 0799	0.1500 0879
20	0.1956 1639	0.1784 3089	0.1628 2370	0.1486 4363	0.1357 5456
21	0.1802 9160	0.1636 9806	0.1486 9744	0.1351 3057	0.1228 5481
22	0.1661 6738	0.1501 8171	0.1357 9675	0.1228 4597	0.1111 8082
23	0.1531 4965	0.1377 8139	0.1240 1530	0.1116 7816	0.1006 1613
24	0.1411 5176	0.1264 0494	0.1132 5598	0.1015 2560	0.0910 5532
25	0.1300 9378	0.1159 6784	0.1034 3012	0.0922 9600	0.0824 0301
26	0.1199 0210	0.1063 9251	0.0944 5673	0.0839 0545	0.0745 7286
27	0.1105 0885	0.0976 0781	0.0862 6185	0.0762 7768	0.0674 8675
28	0.1018 5148	0.0895 4845	0.0787 7795	0.0693 4335	0.0610 7398
29	0.0938 7233	0.0821 5454	0.0719 4333	0.0630 3941	0.0552 7057
30	0.0865 1828	0.0753 7114	0.0657 0167	0.0573 0855	0.0500 1861
31	0.0797 4035	0.0691 4783	0.0600 0153	0.0520 9868	0.0452 6571
32	0.0734 9341	0.0634 3838	0.0547 9592	0.0473 6244	0.0409 6445
33	0.0677 3586	0.0582 0035	0.0500 4193	0.0430 5676	0.0370 7190
34	0.0624 2936	0.0533 9481	0.0457 0039	0.0391 4251	0.0335 4923
35	0.0575 3858	0.0489 8607	0.0417 3552	0.0355 8410	0.0303 6129
36	0.0530 3095	0.0449 4135	0.0381 1463	0.0323 4918	0.0274 7628
37	0.0488 7645	0.0412 3059	0.0348 0788	0.0294 0835	0.0248 6542
38	0.0450 4742	0.0378 2623	0.0317 8802	0.0267 3486	0.0225 0264
39	0.0415 1836	0.0347 0296	0.0290 3015	0.0243 0442	0.0203 6438
40	0.0382 6577	0.0318 3758	0.0265 1156	0.0220 9493	0.0184 2930
41	0.0352 6799	0.0292 0879	0.0242 1147	0.0200 8630	0.0166 7810
42	0.0325 0506	0.0267 9706	0.0221 1093	0.0182 6027	0.0150 9330
43	0.0299 5858	0.0245 8446	0.0201 9263	0.0166 0025	0.0136 5910
44	0.0276 1160	0.0225 5455	0.0184 4076	0.0150 9113	0.0123 6118
45	0.0254 4848	0.0206 9224	0.0168 4087	0.0137 1921	0.0111 8658
46	0.0234 5482	0.0189 8371	0.0153 7979	0.0124 7201	0.0101 2361
47	0.0216 1734	0.0174 1625	0.0140 4547	0.0113 3819	0.0091 6163
48	0.0199 2382	0.0159 7821	0.0128 2692	0.0103 0745	0.0082 9107
49	0.0183 6297	0.0146 5891	0.0117 1408	0.0093 7041	0.0075 0323
50	0.0169 2439	0.0134 4854	0.0106 9779	0.0085 1855	0.0067 9026

Table 10

$$s_{\overline{n}|i} = \frac{(1 + i)^n - 1}{i}$$

n	$\frac{1}{4}\%$	$\frac{7}{24}\%$	$\frac{1}{3}\%$	$\frac{5}{12}\%$	$\frac{1}{2}\%$
1	1.0000 0000	1.0000 0000	1.0000 0000	1.0000 0000	1.0000 0000
2	2.0025 0000	2.0029 1667	2.0033 3333	2.0041 6667	2.0050 0000
3	3.0075 0625	3.0087 5851	3.0100 1111	3.0125 1736	3.0150 2500
4	4.0150 2502	4.0175 3405	4.0200 4448	4.0250 6952	4.0301 0013
5	5.0250 6258	5.0292 5186	5.0334 4463	5.0418 4064	5.0502 5063
6	6.0376 2523	6.0439 2051	6.0502 2278	6.0628 4831	6.0755 0188
7	7.0527 1930	7.0615 4861	7.0703 9019	7.0881 1018	7.1058 7939
8	8.0703 5110	8.0821 4480	8.0939 5816	8.1176 4397	8.1414 0879
9	9.0905 2697	9.1057 1772	9.1209 3802	9.1514 6749	9.1821 1583
10	10.1132 5329	10.1322 7606	10.1513 4114	10.1895 9860	10.2280 2641
11	11.1385 3642	11.1618 2853	11.1851 7895	11.2320 5526	11.2791 6654
12	12.1663 8277	12.1943 8387	12.2224 6288	12.2788 5549	12.3355 6237
13	13.1967 9872	13.2299 5082	13.2632 0442	13.3300 1739	13.3972 4018
14	14.2297 9072	14.2685 3818	14.3074 1510	14.3855 5913	14.4642 2639
15	15.2653 6520	15.3101 5475	15.3551 0648	15.4454 9896	15.5365 4752
16	16.3035 2861	16.3548 0936	16.4062 9017	16.5098 5520	16.6142 3026
17	17.3442 8743	17.4025 1089	17.4609 7781	17.5786 4627	17.6973 0141
18	18.3876 4815	18.4532 6822	18.5191 8107	18.6518 9063	18.7857 8791
19	19.4336 1727	19.5070 9025	19.5809 1167	19.7296 0684	19.8797 1685
20	20.4822 0131	20.5639 8593	20.6461 8137	20.8118 1353	20.9791 1544
21	21.5334 0682	21.6239 6422	21.7150 0198	21.8985 2942	22.0840 1101
22	22.5872 4033	22.6870 3412	22.7873 8532	22.9897 7330	23.1944 3107
23	23.6437 0843	23.7532 0463	23.8633 4327	24.0855 6402	24.3104 0322
24	24.7028 1770	24.8224 8481	24.9428 8775	25.1859 2053	25.4319 5524
25	25.7645 7475	25.8948 8373	26.0260 3071	26.2908 6187	26.5591 1502
26	26.8289 8619	26.9704 1047	27.1127 8414	27.4004 0713	27.6919 1059
27	27.8960 5865	28.0490 7417	28.2031 6009	28.5145 7549	28.8303 7015
28	28.9657 9880	29.1308 8397	29.2971 7062	29.6333 8622	29.9745 2200
29	30.0382 1330	30.2158 4904	30.3948 2786	30.7568 5866	31.1243 9461
30	31.1133 0883	31.3039 7860	31.4961 4395	31.8850 1224	32.2800 1658
31	32.1910 9210	32.3952 8188	32.6011 3110	33.0178 6646	33.4414 1666
32	33.2715 6983	33.4897 6811	33.7098 0154	34.1554 4090	34.6086 2375
33	34.3547 4876	34.5874 4660	34.8221 6754	35.2977 5524	35.7816 6686
34	35.4406 3563	35.6883 2666	35.9382 4143	36.4448 2922	36.9605 7520
35	36.5292 3722	36.7924 1761	37.0580 3557	37.5966 8268	38.1453 7807
36	37.6205 6031	37.8997 2883	38.1815 6236	38.7533 3552	39.3361 0496
37	38.7146 1171	39.0102 6970	39.3088 3423	39.9148 0775	40.5327 8549
38	39.8113 9824	40.1240 4966	40.4398 6368	41.0811 1945	41.7354 4942
39	40.9109 2673	41.2410 7814	41.5746 6322	42.2522 9078	42.9441 2666
40	42.0132 0405	42.3613 6461	42.7132 4543	43.4283 4199	44.1588 4730
41	43.1182 3706	43.4849 1859	43.8556 2292	44.6092 9342	45.3796 4153
42	44.2260 3265	44.6117 4961	45.0018 0833	45.7951 6547	46.6065 3974
43	45.3365 9774	45.7418 6721	46.1518 1436	46.9859 7866	47.8395 7244
44	46.4499 3923	46.8752 8099	47.3056 5374	48.1817 5357	49.0787 7030
45	47.5660 6408	48.0120 0056	48.4633 3925	49.3825 1088	50.3241 6415
46	48.6849 7924	49.1520 3556	49.6248 8371	50.5882 7134	51.5757 8497
47	49.8066 9169	50.2953 9566	50.7902 9999	51.7990 5581	52.8336 6390
48	50.9312 0842	51.4420 9057	51.9596 0099	53.0148 8521	54.0978 3222
49	52.0585 3644	52.5921 3000	53.1327 9966	54.2357 8056	55.3683 2138
50	53.1886 8278	53.7455 2371	54.3099 0899	55.4617 6298	56.6451 6299

Table 10   *(Continued)*

$$s_{\overline{n}|i} = \frac{(1 + i)^n - 1}{i}$$

n	$\frac{1}{4}\%$	$\frac{7}{24}\%$	$\frac{1}{3}\%$	$\frac{5}{12}\%$	$\frac{1}{2}\%$
51	54.3216 5449	54.9022 8149	55.4909 4202	56.6928 5366	57.9283 8880
52	55.4574 5862	56.0624 1314	56.6759 1183	57.9290 7388	59.2180 3075
53	56.5961 0227	57.2259 2851	57.8648 3154	59.1704 4502	60.5141 2090
54	57.7375 9252	58.3928 3747	59.0577 1431	60.4169 8854	61.8166 9150
55	58.8819 3650	59.5631 4991	60.2545 7336	61.6687 2600	63.1257 7496
56	60.0291 4135	60.7368 7577	61.4554 2194	62.9256 7902	64.4414 0384
57	61.1792 1420	61.9140 2499	62.6602 7334	64.1878 6935	65.7636 1086
58	62.3321 6223	63.0946 0756	63.8691 4092	65.4553 1881	67.0924 2891
59	63.4879 9264	64.2786 3350	65.0820 3806	66.7280 4930	68.4278 9105
60	64.6467 1262	65.4661 1285	66.2989 7818	68.0060 8284	69.7700 3051
61	65.8083 2940	66.6570 5568	67.5199 7478	69.2894 4152	71.1188 8066
62	66.9728 5023	67.8514 7209	68.7450 4136	70.5781 4753	72.4744 7507
63	68.1402 8235	69.0493 7222	69.9741 9150	71.8722 2314	73.8368 4744
64	69.3106 3306	70.2507 6622	71.2074 3880	73.1716 9074	75.2060 3168
65	70.4839 0964	71.4556 6429	72.4447 9693	74.4765 7278	76.5820 6184
66	71.6601 1942	72.6640 7664	73.6862 7959	75.7868 9183	77.9649 7215
67	72.8392 6971	73.8760 1353	74.9319 0052	77.1026 7055	79.3547 9701
68	74.0213 6789	75.0914 8524	76.1816 7352	78.4239 3168	80.7515 7099
69	75.2064 2131	76.3105 0207	77.4356 1243	79.7506 9806	82.1553 2885
70	76.3944 3736	77.5330 7437	78.6937 3114	81.0829 9264	83.5661 0549
71	77.5854 2345	78.7592 1250	79.9560 4358	82.4208 3844	84.9839 3602
72	78.7793 8701	79.9889 2687	81.2225 6372	83.7642 5860	86.4088 5570
73	79.9763 3548	81.2222 2791	82.4933 0560	85.1132 7634	87.8408 9998
74	81.1762 7632	82.4591 2607	83.7682 8329	86.4679 1499	89.2801 0448
75	82.3792 1701	83.6996 3186	85.0475 1090	87.8281 9797	90.7265 0500
76	83.5851 6505	84.9437 5578	86.3310 0260	89.1941 4880	92.1801 3752
77	84.7941 2797	86.1915 0840	87.6187 7261	90.5657 9108	93.6410 3821
78	86.0061 1329	87.4429 0030	88.9108 3519	91.9431 4855	95.1092 4340
79	87.2211 2857	88.6979 4210	90.2072 0464	93.3262 4500	96.5847 8962
80	88.4391 8139	89.9566 4443	91.5078 9532	94.7151 0435	98.0677 1357
81	89.6602 7934	91.2190 1797	92.8129 2164	96.1097 5062	99.5580 5214
82	90.8844 3004	92.4850 7344	94.1222 9804	97.5102 0792	101.0558 4240
83	92.1116 4112	93.7548 2157	95.4360 3904	98.9165 0045	102.5611 2161
84	93.3419 2022	95.0282 7314	96.7541 5917	100.3286 5253	104.0739 2722
85	94.5752 7502	96.3054 3893	98.0766 7303	101.7466 8859	105.5942 9685
86	95.8117 1321	97.5863 2980	99.4035 9527	103.1706 3312	107.1222 6834
87	97.0512 4249	98.8709 5659	100.7349 4059	104.6005 1076	108.6578 7968
88	98.2938 7060	100.1593 3022	102.0707 2373	106.0363 4622	110.2011 6908
89	99.5396 0527	101.4514 6160	103.4109 5947	107.4781 6433	111.7521 7492
90	100.7884 5429	102.7473 6169	104.7556 6267	108.9259 9002	113.3109 3580
91	102.0404 2542	104.0470 4150	106.1048 4821	110.3798 4831	114.8774 9048
92	103.2955 2649	105.3505 1203	107.4585 3104	111.8397 6434	116.4518 7793
93	104.5537 6530	106.6577 8436	108.8167 2614	113.3057 6336	118.0341 3732
94	105.8151 4972	107.9688 6957	110.1794 4856	114.7778 7071	119.6243 0800
95	107.0796 8759	109.2837 7877	111.5467 1339	116.2561 1184	121.2224 2954
96	108.3473 8681	110.6025 2312	112.9185 3577	117.7405 1230	122.8285 4169
97	109.6182 5528	111.9251 1382	114.2949 3089	119.2310 9777	124.4426 8440
98	110.8923 0091	113.2515 6206	115.6759 1399	120.7278 9401	126.0648 9782
99	112.1695 3167	114.5818 7912	117.0615 0037	122.2309 2690	127.6952 2231
100	113.4499 5550	115.9160 7627	118.4517 0537	123.7402 2243	129.3336 9842

Table 10 (*Continued*)

$$s_{\overline{n}|i} = \frac{(1 + i)^n - 1}{i}$$

n	$\tfrac{1}{4}\%$	$\tfrac{7}{24}\%$	$\tfrac{1}{3}\%$	$\tfrac{5}{12}\%$	$\tfrac{1}{2}\%$
101	114.7335 8038	117.2541 6482	119.8465 4439	125.2558 0669	130.9803 6692
102	116.0204 1434	118.5961 5614	121.2460 3287	126.7777 0589	132.6352 6875
103	117.3104 6537	119.9420 6159	122.6501 8632	128.3059 4633	134.2984 4509
104	118.6037 4153	121.2918 9261	124.0590 2027	129.8405 5444	135.9699 3732
105	119.9002 5089	122.6456 6063	125.4725 5034	131.3815 5675	137.6497 8701
106	121.2000 0152	124.0033 7714	126.8907 9217	132.9289 7990	139.3380 3594
107	122.5030 0152	125.3650 5365	128.3137 6148	134.4828 5065	141.0347 2612
108	123.8092 5902	126.7307 0173	129.7414 7402	136.0431 9586	142.7398 9975
109	125.1187 8217	128.1003 3294	131.1739 4560	137.6100 4251	144.4535 9925
110	126.4315 7913	129.4739 5891	132.6111 9208	139.1834 1769	146.1758 6725
111	127.7476 5807	130.8515 9129	134.0532 2939	140.7633 4859	147.9067 4658
112	129.0670 2722	132.2332 4177	135.5000 7349	142.3498 6255	149.6462 8032
113	130.3896 9479	133.6189 2205	136.9517 4040	143.9429 8697	151.3945 1172
114	131.7156 6902	135.0086 4391	138.4082 4620	145.5427 4942	153.1514 8428
115	133.0449 5820	136.4024 1912	139.8696 0702	147.1491 7754	154.9172 4170
116	134.3775 7059	137.8002 5951	141.3358 3904	148.7622 9911	156.6918 2791
117	135.7135 1452	139.2021 7693	142.8069 5851	150.3821 4203	158.4752 8704
118	137.0527 9830	140.6081 8328	144.2829 8170	152.0087 3429	160.2676 6348
119	138.3954 3030	142.0182 9048	145.7639 2498	153.6421 0401	162.0690 0180
120	139.7414 1888	143.4325 1050	147.2498 0473	155.2822 7945	163.8793 4681
121	141.0907 7242	144.8508 5532	148.7406 3741	156.9292 8894	165.6987 4354
122	142.4434 9935	146.2733 3698	150.2364 3953	158.5831 6098	167.5272 3726
123	143.7996 0810	147.6999 6755	151.7372 2766	160.2439 2415	169.3648 7344
124	145.1591 0712	149.1307 5912	153.2430 1842	161.9116 0717	171.2116 9781
125	146.5220 0489	150.5657 2383	154.7538 2848	163.5862 3887	173.0677 5630
126	147.8883 0990	152.0048 7386	156.2696 7458	165.2678 4819	174.9330 9508
127	149.2580 3068	153.4482 2141	157.7905 7349	166.9564 6423	176.8077 6056
128	150.6311 7575	154.8957 7872	159.3165 4207	168.6521 1616	178.6917 9936
129	152.0077 5369	156.3475 5808	160.8475 9721	170.3548 3331	180.5852 5836
130	153.3877 7308	157.8035 7179	162.3837 5587	172.0646 4512	182.4881 8465
131	154.7712 4251	159.2638 3221	163.9250 3506	173.7815 8114	184.4006 2557
132	156.1581 7062	160.7283 5172	165.4714 5184	175.5056 7106	186.3226 2870
133	157.5485 6604	162.1971 4274	167.0230 2335	177.2369 4469	188.2542 4184
134	158.9424 3746	163.6702 1774	168.5797 6676	178.9754 3196	190.1955 1305
135	160.3397 9355	165.1475 8921	170.1416 9931	180.7211 6293	192.1464 9062
136	161.7406 4304	166.6292 6968	171.7088 3831	182.4741 6777	194.1072 2307
137	163.1449 9464	168.1152 7172	173.2812 0111	184.2344 7680	196.0777 5919
138	164.5528 5713	169.6056 0793	174.8588 0511	186.0021 2046	198.0581 4798
139	165.9642 3927	171.1002 9095	176.4416 6779	187.7771 2929	200.0484 3872
140	167.3791 4987	172.5993 3346	178.0298 0669	189.5595 3400	202.0486 8092
141	168.7975 9775	174.1027 4819	179.6232 3937	191.3493 6539	204.0589 2432
142	170.2195 9174	175.6105 4787	181.2219 8351	193.1466 5441	206.0792 1894
143	171.6451 4072	177.1227 4530	182.8260 5678	194.9514 3214	208.1096 1504
144	173.0742 5357	178.6393 5331	184.4354 7697	196.7637 2977	210.1501 6311
145	174.5069 3921	180.1603 8475	186.0502 6190	198.5835 7865	212.2009 1393
146	175.9432 0655	181.6858 5254	187.6704 2944	200.4110 1023	214.2619 1850
147	177.3830 6457	183.2157 6961	189.2959 9753	202.2460 5610	216.3332 2809
148	178.8265 2223	184.7501 4894	190.9269 8419	204.0887 4800	218.4148 9423
149	180.2735 8854	186.2890 0354	192.5634 0747	205.9391 1778	220.5069 6870
150	181.7242 7251	187.8323 4647	194.2052 8550	207.7971 9744	222.6095 0354

Table 10 *(Continued)*

$$s_{\overline{n}|i} = \frac{(1 + i)^n - 1}{i}$$

n	$\frac{1}{4}\%$	$\frac{7}{24}\%$	$\frac{1}{3}\%$	$\frac{5}{12}\%$	$\frac{1}{2}\%$
151	183.1785 8319	189.3801 9081	195.8526 3645	209.6630 1910	224.7225 5106
152	184.6365 2965	190.9325 4970	197.5054 7857	211.5366 1501	226.8461 6382
153	186.0981 2097	192.4894 3631	199.1638 3017	213.4180 1757	228.9803 9464
154	187.5633 6627	194.0508 6383	200.8277 0960	215.3072 5931	231.1252 9661
155	189.0322 7469	195.6168 4551	202.4971 3530	217.2043 7289	233.2809 2309
156	190.5048 5538	197.1873 9465	204.1721 2575	219.1093 9111	235.4473 2771
157	191.9811 1752	198.7625 2455	205.8526 9950	221.0223 4691	237.6245 6435
158	193.4610 7031	200.3422 4858	207.5388 7517	222.9432 7336	239.8126 8717
159	194.9447 2298	201.9265 8014	209.2306 7142	224.8722 0366	242.0117 5060
160	196.4320 8479	203.5155 3266	210.9281 0699	226.8091 7118	244.2218 0936
161	197.9231 6500	205.1091 1963	212.6312 0068	228.7542 0939	246.4429 1840
162	199.4179 7292	206.7073 5456	214.3399 7135	230.7073 5193	248.6751 3300
163	200.9165 1785	208.3102 5102	216.0544 3792	232.6686 3256	250.9185 0866
164	202.4188 0914	209.9178 2258	217.7746 1938	234.6380 8520	253.1731 0121
165	203.9248 5617	211.5300 8290	219.5005 3478	236.6157 4389	255.4389 6671
166	205.4346 6831	213.1470 4564	221.2322 0323	238.6016 4282	257.7161 6154
167	206.9482 5498	214.7687 2452	222.9696 4390	240.5958 1633	260.0047 4235
168	208.4656 2562	216.3951 3330	224.7128 7605	242.5982 9890	262.3047 6606
169	209.9867 8968	218.0262 8577	226.4619 1897	244.6091 2514	264.6162 8989
170	211.5117 5665	219.6621 9577	228.2167 9203	246.6283 2983	266.9393 7134
171	213.0405 3605	221.3028 7718	229.9775 1467	248.6559 4787	269.2740 6820
172	214.5731 3739	222.9483 4390	231.7441 0639	250.6920 1432	271.6204 3854
173	216.1095 7023	224.5986 0991	233.5165 8674	252.7365 6438	273.9785 4073
174	217.6498 4415	226.2536 8919	235.2949 7537	254.7896 3340	276.3484 3344
175	219.1939 6876	227.9135 9578	237.0792 9195	256.8512 5687	278.7301 7561
176	220.7419 5369	229.5783 4377	238.8695 5626	258.9214 7044	281.1238 2648
177	222.2938 0857	231.2479 4727	240.6657 8811	261.0003 0990	283.5294 4562
178	223.8495 4309	232.9224 2045	242.4680 0741	263.0878 1120	285.9470 9284
179	225.4091 6695	234.6017 7751	244.2762 3410	265.1840 1041	288.3768 2831
180	226.9726 8987	236.2860 3269	246.0904 8821	267.2889 4379	290.8187 1245
181	228.5401 2159	237.9752 0029	247.9107 8984	269.4026 4772	293.2728 0601
182	230.1114 7190	239.6692 9462	249.7371 5914	271.5251 5875	295.7391 7004
183	231.6867 5058	241.3683 3007	251.5696 1634	273.6565 1358	298.2178 6589
184	233.2659 6745	243.0723 2103	253.4081 8172	275.7967 4905	300.7089 5522
185	234.8491 3237	244.7812 8196	255.2528 7566	277.9459 0217	303.2125 0000
186	236.4362 5520	246.4952 2737	257.1037 1858	280.1040 1010	305.7285 6250
187	238.0273 4584	248.2141 7178	258.9607 3098	282.2711 1014	308.2572 0531
188	239.6224 1420	249.9381 2978	260.8239 3341	284.4472 3977	310.7984 9134
189	241.2214 7024	251.6671 1600	262.6933 4652	286.6324 3660	313.3524 8379
190	242.8245 2392	253.4011 4508	264.5689 9101	288.8267 3842	315.9192 4621
191	244.4315 8523	255.1402 3176	266.4508 8765	291.0301 8316	318.4988 4244
192	246.0426 6419	256.8843 9077	268.3390 5727	293.2428 0892	321.0913 3666
193	247.6577 7085	258.6336 3691	270.2335 2080	295.4646 5396	323.6967 9334
194	249.2769 1528	260.3879 8501	272.1342 9920	297.6957 5669	326.3152 7731
195	250.9001 0756	262.1474 4997	274.0414 1353	299.9361 5567	328.9468 5369
196	252.5273 5783	263.9120 4670	275.9548 8491	302.1858 8965	331.5915 8796
197	254.1586 7623	265.6817 9017	277.8747 3453	304.4449 9753	334.2495 4590
198	255.7940 7292	267.4566 9539	279.8009 8364	306.7135 1835	336.9207 9363
199	257.4335 5810	269.2367 7742	281.7336 5359	308.9914 9134	339.6053 9760
200	259.0771 4200	271.0220 5135	283.6727 6577	311.2789 5589	342.3034 2459

Table 10 $(Continued)$

$$s_{\overline{n}|i} = \frac{(1 + i)^n - 1}{i}$$

n	$\frac{7}{12}\%$	$\frac{2}{3}\%$	$\frac{3}{4}\%$	$\frac{7}{8}\%$	1%
1	1.0000 0000	1.0000 0000	1.0000 0000	1.0000 0000	1.0000 0000
2	2.0058 3333	2.0066 6667	2.0075 0000	2.0087 5000	2.0100 0000
3	3.0175 3403	3.0200 4444	3.0225 5625	3.0263 2656	3.0301 0000
4	4.0351 3631	4.0401 7807	4.0452 2542	4.0528 0692	4.0604 0100
5	5.0586 7460	5.0671 1259	5.0755 6461	5.0882 6898	5.1010 0501
6	6.0881 8354	6.1008 9335	6.1136 3135	6.1327 9133	6.1520 1506
7	7.1236 9794	7.1415 6597	7.1594 8358	7.1864 5326	7.2135 3521
8	8.1652 5285	8.1891 7641	8.2131 7971	8.2493 3472	8.2856 7056
9	9.2128 8349	9.2437 7092	9.2747 7856	9.3215 1640	9.3685 2727
10	10.2656 2531	10.3053 9606	10.3443 3940	10.4030 7967	10.4622 1254
11	11.3265 1396	11.3740 9870	11.4219 2194	11.4941 0662	11.5668 3467
12	12.3925 8529	12.4499 2602	12.5075 8636	12.5946 8005	12.6825 0301
13	13.4648 7537	13.5329 2553	13.6013 9325	13.7048 8350	13.8093 2804
14	14.5434 2048	14.6231 4503	14.7034 0370	14.8248 0123	14.9474 2132
15	15.6282 5710	15.7206 3267	15.8136 7923	15.9545 1824	16.0968 9554
16	16.7194 2193	16.8254 3688	16.9322 8183	17.0941 2028	17.2578 6449
17	17.8169 5189	17.9376 0646	18.0592 7394	18.2436 9383	18.4304 4314
18	18.9208 8411	19.0571 9051	19.1947 1849	19.4033 2615	19.6147 4757
19	20.0312 5593	20.1842 3844	20.3386 7888	20.5731 0526	20.8108 9504
20	21.1481 0493	21.3188 0003	21.4912 1897	21.7531 1993	22.0190 0399
21	22.2714 6887	22.4609 2536	22.6524 0312	22.9434 5973	23.2391 9403
22	23.4013 8577	23.6106 6487	23.8222 9614	24.1442 1500	24.4715 8598
23	24.5378 9386	24.7680 6930	25.0009 6336	25.3554 7688	25.7163 0183
24	25.6810 3157	25.9331 8976	26.1884 7059	26.5773 3730	26.9734 6485
25	26.8308 3759	27.1060 7769	27.3848 8412	27.8098 8900	28.2431 9950
26	27.9873 5081	28.2867 8488	28.5902 7075	29.0532 2553	29.5256 3150
27	29.1506 1035	29.4753 6344	29.8046 9778	30.3074 4126	30.8208 8781
28	30.3206 5558	30.6718 6587	31.0282 3301	31.5726 3137	32.1290 9669
29	31.4975 2607	31.8763 4497	32.2609 4476	32.8488 9189	33.4503 8766
30	32.6812 6164	33.0888 5394	33.5029 0184	34.1363 1970	34.7848 9153
31	33.8719 0233	34.3094 4630	34.7541 7361	35.4350 1249	36.1327 4045
32	35.0694 8843	35.5381 7594	36.0148 2991	36.7450 6885	37.4940 6785
33	36.2740 6045	36.7750 9711	37.2849 4113	38.0665 8820	38.8690 0853
34	37.4856 5913	38.0202 6443	38.5645 7819	39.3996 7085	40.2576 9862
35	38.7043 2548	39.2737 3286	39.8538 1253	40.7444 1797	41.6602 7560
36	39.9301 0071	40.5355 5774	41.1527 1612	42.1009 3163	43.0768 7836
37	41.1630 2630	41.8057 9479	42.4613 6149	43.4693 1478	44.5076 4714
38	42.4031 4395	43.0845 0009	43.7798 2170	44.8496 7128	45.9527 2361
39	43.6504 9562	44.3717 3009	45.1081 7037	46.2421 0591	47.4122 5085
40	44.9051 2352	45.6675 4163	46.4464 8164	47.6467 2433	48.8863 7336
41	46.1670 7007	46.9719 9191	47.7948 3026	49.0636 3317	50.3752 3709
42	47.4363 7798	48.2851 3852	49.1532 9148	50.4929 3996	51.8789 8946
43	48.7130 9018	49.6070 3944	50.5219 4117	51.9347 5319	53.3977 7936
44	49.9972 4988	50.9377 5304	51.9008 5573	53.3891 8228	54.9317 5715
45	51.2889 0050	52.2773 3806	53.2901 1215	54.8563 3762	56.4810 7472
46	52.5880 8575	53.6258 5365	54.6897 8799	56.3363 3058	58.0458 8547
47	53.8948 4959	54.9833 5934	56.0999 6140	57.8292 7347	59.6263 4432
48	55.2092 3621	56.3499 1507	57.5207 1111	59.3352 7961	61.2226 0777
49	56.5312 9009	57.7255 8117	58.9521 1644	60.8544 6331	62.8348 3385
50	57.8610 5595	59.1104 1837	60.3942 5732	62.3869 3986	64.4631 8218

Table 10 $(Continued)$

$$s_{\overline{n}|i} = \frac{(1 + i)^n - 1}{i}$$

n	$\frac{7}{12}\%$	$\frac{2}{3}\%$	$\frac{3}{4}\%$	$\frac{7}{8}\%$	1%
51	59.1985 7877	60.5044 8783	61.8472 1424	63.9328 2559	66.1078 1401
52	60.5439 0381	61.9078 5108	63.3110 6835	65.4922 3781	67.7688 9215
53	61.8970 7659	63.3205 7009	64.7859 0136	67.0652 9489	69.4465 8107
54	63.2581 4287	64.7427 0722	66.2717 9562	68.6521 1622	71.1410 4688
55	64.6271 4870	66.1743 2527	67.7688 3409	70.2528 2224	72.8524 5735
56	66.0041 4040	67.6154 8744	69.2771 0035	71.8675 3443	74.5809 8192
57	67.3891 6455	69.0662 5736	70.7966 7860	73.4963 7536	76.3267 9174
58	68.7822 6801	70.5266 9907	72.3276 5369	75.1394 6864	78.0900 5966
59	70.1834 9791	71.9968 7706	73.8701 1109	76.7969 3900	79.8709 6025
60	71.5929 0165	73.4768 5625	75.4241 3693	78.4689 1221	81.6696 6986
61	73.0105 2691	74.9667 0195	76.9898 1795	80.1555 1519	83.4863 6655
62	74.4364 2165	76.4664 7997	78.5672 4159	81.8568 7595	85.3212 3022
63	75.8706 3411	77.9762 5650	80.1564 9590	83.5731 2362	87.1744 4252
64	77.3132 1281	79.4960 9821	81.7576 6962	85.3043 8845	89.0461 8695
65	78.7642 0655	81.0260 7220	83.3708 5214	87.0508 0185	90.9366 4882
66	80.2236 6442	82.5662 4601	84.9961 3353	88.8124 9636	92.8460 1531
67	81.6916 3580	84.1166 8765	86.6336 0453	90.5896 0571	94.7744 7546
68	83.1681 7034	85.6774 6557	88.2833 5657	92.3822 6476	96.7222 2021
69	84.6533 1800	87.2486 4867	89.9454 8174	94.1906 0957	98.6894 4242
70	86.1471 2902	88.8303 0633	91.6200 7285	96.0147 7741	100.6763 3684
71	87.6496 5394	90.4225 0837	93.3072 2340	97.8549 0671	102.6831 0021
72	89.1609 4359	92.0253 2510	95.0070 2758	99.7111 3714	104.7099 3121
73	90.6810 4909	93.6388 2726	96.7195 8028	101.5836 0959	106.7570 3052
74	92.2100 2188	95.2630 8611	98.4449 7714	103.4724 6618	108.8246 0083
75	93.7479 1367	96.8981 7335	100.1833 1446	105.3778 5025	110.9128 4684
76	95.2947 7650	98.5441 6118	101.9346 8932	107.2999 0644	113.0219 7530
77	96.8506 6270	100.2011 2225	103.6991 9949	109.2387 8063	115.1521 9506
78	98.4156 2490	101.8691 2973	105.4769 4349	111.1946 1996	117.3037 1701
79	99.9897 1604	103.5482 5726	107.2680 2056	113.1675 7288	119.4767 5418
80	101.5729 8939	105.2385 7898	109.0725 3072	115.1577 8914	121.6715 2172
81	103.1654 9849	106.9401 6950	110.8905 7470	117.1654 1980	123.8882 3694
82	104.7672 9723	108.6531 0397	112.7222 5401	119.1906 1722	126.1271 1931
83	106.3784 3980	110.3774 5799	114.5676 7091	121.2335 3512	128.3883 9050
84	107.9989 8070	112.1133 0771	116.4269 2845	123.2943 2855	130.6722 7440
85	109.6289 7475	113.8607 2977	118.3001 3041	125.3731 5393	132.9789 9715
86	111.2684 7710	115.6198 0130	120.1873 8139	127.4701 6903	135.3087 8712
87	112.9175 4322	117.3905 9997	122.0887 8675	129.5855 3301	137.6618 7499
88	114.5762 2889	119.1732 0397	124.0044 5265	131.7194 0642	140.0384 9374
89	116.2445 9022	120.9676 9200	125.9344 8604	133.8719 5123	142.4388 7868
90	117.9226 8367	122.7741 4328	127.8789 9469	136.0433 3080	144.8632 6746
91	119.6105 6599	124.5926 3757	129.8380 8715	138.2337 0994	147.3119 0014
92	121.3082 9429	126.4232 5515	131.8118 7280	140.4432 5491	149.7850 1914
93	123.0159 2601	128.2660 7685	133.8004 6185	142.6721 3339	152.2828 6933
94	124.7335 1891	130.1211 8403	135.8039 6531	144.9205 1455	154.8056 9803
95	126.4611 3110	131.9886 5859	137.8224 9505	147.1885 6906	157.3537 5501
96	128.1988 2103	133.8685 8298	139.8561 6377	149.4764 6903	159.9272 9256
97	129.9466 4749	135.7610 4020	141.9050 8499	151.7843 8814	162.5265 6548
98	131.7046 6960	137.6661 1380	143.9693 7313	154.1125 0153	165.1518 3114
99	133.4729 4684	139.5838 8790	146.0491 4343	156.4609 8592	167.8033 4945
100	135.2515 3903	141.5144 4715	148.1445 1201	158.8300 1955	170.4813 8294

Table 10 *(Continued)*

$$s_{\overline{n}|i} = \frac{(1 + i)^n - 1}{i}$$

n	$7/12\%$	$2/3\%$	$3/4\%$	$7/8\%$	1%
101	137.0405 0634	143.4578 7680	150.2555 9585	161.2197 8222	173.1861 9677
102	138.8399 0929	145.4142 6264	152.3825 1281	163.6304 5532	175.9180 5874
103	140.6498 0877	147.3836 9106	154.5253 8166	166.0622 2180	178.6772 3933
104	142.4702 6598	149.3662 4900	156.6843 2202	168.5152 6624	181.4640 1172
105	144.3013 4253	151.3620 2399	158.8594 5444	170.9897 7482	184.2786 5184
106	146.1431 0037	153.3711 0415	161.0509 0035	173.4859 3535	187.1214 3836
107	147.9956 0178	155.3935 7818	163.2587 8210	176.0039 3728	189.9926 5274
108	149.8589 0946	157.4295 3537	165.4832 2296	178.5439 7174	192.8925 7927
109	151.7330 8643	159.4790 6560	167.7243 4714	181.1062 3149	195.8215 0506
110	153.6181 9610	161.5422 5937	169.9822 7974	183.6909 1101	198.7797 2011
111	155.5143 0225	163.6192 0777	172.2571 4684	186.2982 0648	201.7675 1731
112	157.4214 6901	165.7100 0249	174.5490 7544	188.9283 1579	204.7851 9248
113	159.3397 6091	167.8147 3584	176.8581 9351	191.5814 3855	207.8330 4441
114	161.2692 4285	169.9335 0074	179.1846 2996	194.2577 7614	210.9113 7485
115	163.2099 8010	172.0663 9075	181.5285 1468	196.9575 3168	214.0204 8860
116	165.1620 3832	174.2135 0002	183.8899 7854	199.6809 1009	217.1606 9349
117	167.1254 8354	176.3749 2335	186.2691 5338	202.4281 1805	220.3323 0042
118	169.1003 8220	178.5507 5618	188.6661 7203	205.1993 6408	223.5356 2343
119	171.0868 0109	180.7410 9455	191.0811 6832	207.9948 5852	226.7709 7966
120	173.0848 0743	182.9460 3518	193.5142 7708	210.8148 1353	230.0386 8946
121	175.0944 6881	185.1656 7542	195.9656 3416	213.6594 4315	233.3390 7635
122	177.1158 5321	187.4001 1325	198.4353 7642	216.5289 6328	236.6724 6712
123	179.1490 2902	189.6494 4734	200.9236 4174	219.4235 9170	240.0391 9179
124	181.1940 6502	191.9137 7699	203.4305 6905	222.3435 4813	243.4395 8370
125	183.2510 3040	194.1932 0217	205.9562 9832	225.2890 5418	246.8739 7954
126	185.3199 9475	196.4878 2352	208.5009 7056	228.2603 3340	250.3427 1934
127	187.4010 2805	198.7977 4234	211.0647 2784	231.2576 1132	253.8461 4653
128	189.4942 0071	201.1230 6062	213.6477 1330	234.2811 1542	257.3846 0800
129	191.5995 8355	203.4638 8103	216.2500 7115	237.3310 7518	260.9584 5408
130	193.7172 4779	205.8203 0690	218.8719 4668	240.4077 2209	264.5680 3862
131	195.8472 6507	208.1924 4228	221.5134 8628	243.5112 8965	268.2137 1900
132	197.9897 0745	210.5803 9190	224.1748 3743	246.6420 1344	271.8958 5619
133	200.1446 4741	212.9842 6117	226.8561 4871	249.8001 3106	275.6148 1475
134	202.3121 5785	215.4041 5625	229.5575 6982	252.9858 8220	279.3709 6290
135	204.4923 1210	217.8401 8396	232.2792 5160	256.1995 0867	283.1646 7253
136	206.6851 8393	220.2924 5185	235.0213 4598	259.4412 5437	286.9963 1926
137	208.8908 4750	222.7610 6820	237.7840 0608	262.7113 6535	290.8662 8245
138	211.1093 7744	225.2461 4198	240.5673 8612	266.0100 8980	294.7749 4527
139	213.3408 4881	227.7477 8293	243.3716 4152	269.3376 7808	298.7226 9473
140	215.5853 3710	230.2661 0148	246.1969 2883	272.6943 8276	302.7099 2167
141	217.8429 1823	232.8012 0883	249.0434 0580	276.0804 5861	306.7370 2089
142	220.1136 6858	235.3532 1689	251.9112 3134	279.4961 6263	310.8043 9110
143	222.3976 6498	237.9222 3833	254.8005 6558	282.9417 5405	314.9124 3501
144	224.6949 8470	240.5083 8659	257.7115 6982	286.4174 9440	319.0615 5936
145	227.0057 0544	243.1117 7583	260.6444 0659	289.9236 4747	323.2521 7495
146	229.3299 0539	245.7325 2100	263.5992 3964	293.4604 7939	327.4846 9670
147	231.6676 6317	248.3707 3781	266.5762 3394	297.0282 5858	331.7595 4367
148	234.0190 5787	251.0265 4273	269.5755 5569	300.6272 5585	336.0771 3911
149	236.3841 6904	253.7000 5301	272.5973 7236	304.2577 4433	340.4379 1050
150	238.7630 7670	256.3913 8670	275.6418 5265	307.9199 9960	344.8422 8960

Table 10 (*Continued*)

$$s_{\overline{n}|i} = \frac{(1 + i)^n - 1}{i}$$

n	$7/12\%$	$2/3\%$	$3/4\%$	$7/8\%$	1%
151	241.1558 6131	259.1006 6261	278.7091 6655	311.6142 9959	349.2907 1250
152	243.5626 0383	261.8280 0036	281.7994 8530	315.3409 2472	353.7836 1962
153	245.9833 8569	264.5735 2036	284.9129 8144	319.1001 5781	358.3214 5582
154	248.4182 8877	267.3373 4383	288.0498 2880	322.8922 8419	362.9046 7038
155	250.8673 9546	270.1195 9279	291.2102 0251	326.7175 9167	367.5337 1708
156	253.3307 8860	272.9203 9008	294.3942 7903	330.5763 7060	372.2090 5425
157	255.8085 5153	275.7398 5935	297.6022 3613	334.4689 1384	376.9311 4480
158	258.3007 6808	278.5781 2507	300.8342 5290	338.3955 1684	381.7004 5624
159	260.8075 2256	281.4353 1257	304.0905 0979	342.3564 7761	386.5174 6081
160	263.3288 9978	284.3115 4799	307.3711 8862	346.3520 9679	391.3826 3541
161	265.8649 8503	287.2069 5831	310.6764 7253	350.3826 7764	396.2964 6177
162	268.4158 6411	290.1216 7137	314.0065 4608	354.4485 2607	401.2594 2639
163	270.9816 2331	293.0558 1584	317.3615 9517	358.5499 5067	406.2720 2065
164	273.5623 4945	296.0095 2128	320.7418 0714	362.6872 6274	411.3347 4008
165	276.1581 2982	298.9829 1809	324.1473 7069	366.8607 7629	416.4480 8826
166	278.7690 5225	301.9761 3754	327.5784 7597	371.0708 0808	421.6125 6915
167	281.3952 0505	304.9893 1179	331.0353 1454	375.3176 7765	426.8286 9484
168	284.0366 7708	308.0225 7387	334.5180 7940	379.6017 0733	432.0969 8179
169	286.6935 5770	311.0760 5770	338.0269 6499	383.9232 2227	437.4179 5161
170	289.3659 3678	314.1498 9808	341.5621 6723	388.2825 5046	442.7921 3112
171	292.0539 0475	317.2442 3074	345.1238 8349	392.6800 2278	448.2200 5243
172	294.7575 5252	320.3591 9228	348.7123 1261	397.1159 7298	453.7022 5296
173	297.4769 7158	323.4949 2022	352.3276 5496	401.5907 3774	459.2392 7549
174	300.2122 5392	326.6515 5303	355.9701 1237	406.1046 5670	464.8316 6824
175	302.9634 9206	329.8292 3005	359.6398 8821	410.6580 7245	470.4799 8492
176	305.7307 7910	333.0280 9158	363.3371 8737	415.2513 3058	476.1847 8477
177	308.5142 0864	336.2482 7886	367.0622 1628	419.8847 7972	481.9466 3262
178	311.3138 7486	339.4899 3405	370.8151 8290	424.5587 7154	487.7660 9895
179	314.1298 7247	342.7532 0028	374.5962 9677	429.2736 6080	493.6437 5994
180	316.9622 9672	346.0382 2161	378.4057 6900	434.0298 0533	499.5801 9754
181	319.8112 4345	349.3451 4309	382.2438 1226	438.8275 6612	505.5759 9951
182	322.6768 0904	352.6741 1071	386.1106 4086	443.6673 0733	511.6317 5951
183	325.5590 9042	356.0252 7145	390.0064 7066	448.5493 9627	517.7480 7710
184	328.4581 8512	359.3987 7326	393.9315 1919	453.4742 0348	523.9255 5787
185	331.3741 9120	362.7947 6508	397.8860 0559	458.4421 0276	530.1648 1345
186	334.3072 0731	366.2133 9685	401.8701 5063	463.4534 7116	536.4664 6159
187	337.2573 3269	369.6548 1949	405.8841 7676	468.5086 8904	542.8311 2620
188	340.2246 6713	373.1191 8496	409.9283 0808	473.6081 4007	549.2594 3746
189	343.2093 1102	376.6066 4619	414.0027 7039	478.7522 1129	555.7520 3184
190	346.2113 6534	380.1173 5716	418.1077 9117	483.9412 9314	562.3095 5216
191	349.2309 3163	383.6514 7288	422.2435 9961	489.1757 7946	568.9326 4768
192	352.2681 1207	387.2091 4936	426.4104 2660	494.4560 6753	575.6219 7415
193	355.3230 0939	390.7905 4369	430.6085 0480	499.7825 5812	582.3781 9390
194	358.3957 2694	394.3958 1398	434.8380 6859	505.1556 5550	589.2019 7584
195	361.4863 6868	398.0251 1941	439.0993 5410	510.5757 6749	596.0939 9559
196	364.5950 3917	401.6786 2021	443.3925 9926	516.0433 0545	603.0549 3555
197	367.7218 4356	405.3564 7767	447.7180 4375	521.5586 8437	610.0854 8490
198	370.8668 8765	409.0588 5419	452.0759 2908	527.1223 2286	617.1863 3975
199	374.0302 7783	412.7859 1322	456.4664 9855	532.7346 4319	624.3582 0315
200	377.2121 2112	416.5378 1931	460.8899 9729	538.3960 7131	631.6017 8518

Table 10   *(Continued)*

$$s_{\overline{n}|i} = \frac{(1+i)^n - 1}{i}$$

n	$1\frac{1}{8}\%$	$1\frac{1}{4}\%$	$1\frac{3}{8}\%$	$1\frac{1}{2}\%$	$1\frac{3}{4}\%$
1	1.0000 0000	1.0000 0000	1.0000 0000	1.0000 0000	1.0000 0000
2	2.0112 5000	2.0125 0000	2.0137 5000	2.0150 0000	2.0175 0000
3	3.0338 7656	3.0376 5625	3.0414 3906	3.0452 2500	3.0528 0625
4	4.0680 0767	4.0756 2695	4.0832 5885	4.0909 0338	4.1062 3036
5	5.1137 7276	5.1265 7229	5.1394 0366	5.1522 6693	5.1780 8939
6	6.1713 0270	6.1906 5444	6.2100 7046	6.2295 5093	6.2687 0596
7	7.2407 2986	7.2680 3762	7.2954 5893	7.3229 9419	7.3784 0831
8	8.3221 8807	8.3588 8809	8.3957 7149	8.4328 3911	8.5075 3045
9	9.4158 1269	9.4633 7420	9.5112 1335	9.5593 3169	9.6564 1224
10	10.5217 4058	10.5816 6637	10.6419 9253	10.7027 2167	10.8253 9945
11	11.6401 1016	11.7139 3720	11.7883 1993	11.8632 6249	12.0148 4394
12	12.7710 6140	12.8603 6142	12.9504 0933	13.0412 1143	13.2251 0371
13	13.9147 3584	14.0211 1594	14.1284 7745	14.2368 2960	14.4565 4303
14	15.0712 7662	15.1963 7988	15.3227 4402	15.4503 8205	15.7095 3253
15	16.2408 2848	16.3863 3463	16.5334 3175	16.6821 3778	16.9844 4935
16	17.4235 3780	17.5911 6382	17.7607 6644	17.9323 6984	18.2816 7721
17	18.6195 5260	18.8110 5336	19.0049 7697	19.2013 5539	19.6016 0656
18	19.8290 2257	20.0461 9153	20.2662 9541	20.4893 7572	20.9446 3468
19	21.0520 9907	21.2967 6893	21.5449 5697	21.7967 1636	22.3111 6578
20	22.2889 3519	22.5629 7854	22.8412 0013	23.1236 6710	23.7016 1119
21	23.5396 8571	23.8450 1577	24.1552 6663	24.4705 2211	25.1163 8938
22	24.8045 0717	25.1430 7847	25.4874 0155	25.8375 7994	26.5559 2620
23	26.0835 5788	26.4573 6695	26.8378 5332	27.2251 4364	28.0206 5490
24	27.3769 9790	27.7880 8403	28.2068 7380	28.6335 2080	29.5110 1637
25	28.6849 8913	29.1354 3508	29.5947 1832	30.0630 2361	31.0274 5915
26	30.0076 9526	30.4996 2802	31.0016 4569	31.5139 6896	32.5704 3969
27	31.3452 8183	31.8808 7337	32.4279 1832	32.9866 7850	34.1404 2238
28	32.6979 1625	33.2793 8429	33.8738 0220	34.4814 7867	35.7378 7977
29	34.0657 6781	34.6953 7659	35.3395 6698	35.9987 0085	37.3632 9267
30	35.4490 0769	36.1290 6880	36.8254 8602	37.5386 8137	39.0171 5029
31	36.8478 0903	37.5806 8216	38.3318 3646	39.1017 6159	40.6999 5042
32	38.2623 4688	39.0504 4069	39.8588 9921	40.6882 8801	42.4121 9955
33	39.6927 9829	40.5385 7120	41.4069 5907	42.2986 1233	44.1544 1305
34	41.1393 4227	42.0453 0334	42.9763 0476	43.9330 9152	45.9271 1527
35	42.6021 5987	43.5708 6963	44.5672 2895	45.5920 8789	47.7308 3979
36	44.0814 3417	45.1155 0550	46.1800 2835	47.2759 6921	49.5661 2949
37	45.5773 5030	46.6794 4932	47.8150 0374	48.9851 0874	51.4335 3675
38	47.0900 9549	48.2629 4243	49.4724 6004	50.7198 8538	53.3336 2365
39	48.6198 5906	49.8662 2921	51.1527 0636	52.4806 8366	55.2669 6206
40	50.1668 3248	51.4895 5708	52.8560 5608	54.2678 9391	57.2341 3390
41	51.7312 0934	53.1331 7654	54.5828 2685	56.0819 1232	59.2357 3124
42	53.3131 8545	54.7973 4125	56.3333 4072	57.9231 4100	61.2723 5654
43	54.9129 5879	56.4823 0801	58.1079 2415	59.7919 8812	63.3446 2278
44	56.5307 2957	58.1883 3687	59.9069 0811	61.6888 6794	65.4531 5367
45	58.1667 0028	59.9156 9108	61.7306 2810	63.6142 0096	67.5985 8386
46	59.8210 7566	61.6646 3721	63.5794 2423	65.5684 1398	69.7815 5908
47	61.4940 6276	63.4354 4518	65.4536 4131	67.5519 4018	72.0027 3637
48	63.1858 7097	65.2283 8824	67.3536 2888	69.5652 1929	74.2627 8425
49	64.8967 1201	67.0437 4310	69.2797 4128	71.6086 9758	76.5623 8298
50	66.6268 0002	68.8817 8989	71.2323 3772	73.6828 2804	78.9022 2468

Table 10 (*Continued*)

$$s_{\overline{n}|i} = \frac{(1 + i)^n - 1}{i}$$

n	$1\frac{1}{8}\%$	$1\frac{1}{4}\%$	$1\frac{3}{8}\%$	$1\frac{1}{2}\%$	$1\frac{3}{4}\%$
51	68.3763 5152	70.7428 1226	73.2117 8237	75.7880 7046	81.2830 1361
52	70.1455 8548	72.6270 9741	75.2184 4437	77.9248 9152	83.7054 6635
53	71.9347 2332	74.5349 3613	77.2526 9798	80.0937 6489	86.1703 1201
54	73.7439 8895	76.4666 2283	79.3149 2258	82.2951 7136	88.6782 9247
55	75.5736 0883	78.4224 5562	81.4055 0277	84.5295 9893	91.2301 6259
56	77.4238 1193	80.4027 3631	83.5248 2843	86.7975 4292	93.8266 9043
57	79.2948 2981	82.4077 7052	85.6732 9482	89.0995 0606	96.4686 5752
58	81.1868 9665	84.4378 6765	87.8513 0262	91.4359 9865	99.1568 5902
59	83.1002 4923	86.4933 4099	90.0592 5804	93.8075 3863	101.8921 0405
60	85.0351 2704	88.5745 0776	92.2975 7283	96.2146 5171	104.6752 1588
61	86.9917 7222	90.6816 8910	94.5666 6446	98.6578 7149	107.5070 3215
62	88.9704 2966	92.8152 1022	96.8669 5610	101.1377 3956	110.3884 0522
63	90.9713 4699	94.9754 0034	99.1988 7674	103.6548 0565	113.3202 0231
64	92.9947 7464	97.1625 9285	101.5628 6130	106.2096 2774	116.3033 0585
65	95.0409 6586	99.3771 2526	103.9593 5064	108.8027 7215	119.3386 1370
66	97.1101 7672	101.6193 3933	106.3887 9171	111.4348 1374	122.4270 3944
67	99.2026 6621	103.8895 8107	108.8516 3760	114.1063 3594	125.5695 1263
68	101.3186 9621	106.1882 0083	111.3483 4761	116.8179 3098	128.7669 7910
69	103.4584 3154	108.5155 5334	113.8793 8739	119.5701 9995	132.0204 0124
70	105.6224 4002	110.8719 9776	116.4452 2897	122.3637 5295	135.3307 5826
71	107.8106 9247	113.2578 9773	119.0463 5087	125.1992 0924	138.6990 4653
72	110.0235 6276	115.6736 2145	121.6832 3819	128.0771 9738	142.1262 7984
73	112.2613 2784	118.1195 4172	124.3563 8272	130.9983 5534	145.6134 8974
74	114.5242 6778	120.5960 3599	127.0662 8298	133.9633 3067	149.1617 2581
75	116.8126 6579	123.1034 8644	129.8134 4437	136.9727 8063	152.7720 5601
76	119.1268 0828	125.6422 8002	132.5983 7923	140.0273 7234	156.4455 6699
77	121.4669 8487	128.2128 0852	135.4216 0695	143.1277 8292	160.1833 6441
78	123.8334 8845	130.8154 6863	138.2836 5404	146.2746 9967	163.9865 7329
79	126.2266 1520	133.4506 6199	141.1850 5429	149.4688 2016	167.8563 3832
80	128.6466 6462	136.1187 9526	144.1263 4878	152.7108 5247	171.7938 2424
81	131.0939 3960	138.8202 8020	147.1080 8608	156.0015 1525	175.8002 1617
82	133.5687 4642	141.5555 3370	150.1308 2226	159.3415 3798	179.8767 1995
83	136.0713 9481	144.3249 7787	153.1951 2107	162.7316 6105	184.0245 6255
84	138.6021 9801	147.1290 4010	156.3015 5398	166.1726 3597	188.2449 9239
85	141.1614 7273	149.9681 5310	159.4507 0035	169.6652 2551	192.5392 7976
86	143.7495 3930	152.8427 5501	162.6431 4748	173.2102 0389	196.9087 1716
87	146.3667 2162	155.7532 8945	165.8794 9076	176.8083 5695	201.3546 1971
88	149.0133 4724	158.7002 0557	169.1603 3375	180.4604 8230	205.8783 2555
89	151.6897 4739	161.6839 5814	172.4862 8834	184.1673 8954	210.4811 9625
90	154.3962 5705	164.7050 0762	175.8579 7481	187.9299 0038	215.1646 1718
91	157.1332 1494	167.7638 2021	179.2760 2196	191.7488 4889	219.9299 9798
92	159.9009 6361	170.8608 6796	182.7410 6726	195.6250 8162	224.7787 7295
93	162.6998 4945	173.9966 2881	186.2537 5694	199.5594 5784	229.7124 0148
94	165.5302 2276	177.1715 8667	189.8147 4610	203.5528 4971	234.7323 6850
95	168.3924 3776	180.3862 3151	193.4246 9886	207.6061 4246	239.8401 8495
96	171.2868 5269	183.6410 5940	197.0842 8847	211.7202 3459	245.0373 8819
97	174.2138 2978	186.9365 7264	200.7941 9743	215.8960 3811	250.3255 4248
98	177.1737 3537	190.2732 7980	204.5551 1765	220.1344 7868	255.7062 3947
99	180.1669 3989	193.6516 9580	208.3677 5051	224.4364 9586	261.1810 9866
100	183.1938 1796	197.0723 4200	212.2328 0708	228.8030 4330	266.7517 6789

Table 10   (*Continued*)

$$s_{\overline{n}|i} = \frac{(1+i)^n - 1}{i}$$

n	2%	$2\frac{1}{4}\%$	$2\frac{1}{2}\%$	$2\frac{3}{4}\%$	3%
1	1.0000 0000	1.0000 0000	1.0000 0000	1.0000 0000	1.0000 0000
2	2.0200 0000	2.0225 0000	2.0250 0000	2.0275 0000	2.0300 0000
3	3.0604 0000	3.0680 0625	3.0756 2500	3.0832 5625	3.0909 0000
4	4.1216 0800	4.1370 3639	4.1525 1563	4.1680 4580	4.1836 2700
5	5.2040 4016	5.2301 1971	5.2563 2852	5.2826 6706	5.3091 3581
6	6.3081 2096	6.3477 9740	6.3877 3673	6.4279 4040	6.4684 0988
7	7.4342 8338	7.4906 2284	7.5474 3015	7.6047 0876	7.6624 6218
8	8.5829 6905	8.6591 6186	8.7361 1590	8.8138 3825	8.8923 3605
9	9.7546 2843	9.8539 9300	9.9545 1880	10.0562 1880	10.1591 0613
10	10.9497 2100	11.0757 0784	11.2033 8177	11.3327 6482	11.4638 7931
11	12.1687 1542	12.3249 1127	12.4834 6631	12.6444 1585	12.8077 9569
12	13.4120 8973	13.6022 2177	13.7955 5297	13.9921 3729	14.1920 2956
13	14.6803 3152	14.9082 7176	15.1404 4179	15.3769 2107	15.6177 9045
14	15.9739 3815	16.2437 0788	16.5189 5284	16.7997 8639	17.0863 2416
15	17.2934 1692	17.6091 9130	17.9319 2666	18.2617 8052	18.5989 1389
16	18.6392 8525	19.0053 9811	19.3802 2483	19.7639 7948	20.1568 8130
17	20.0120 7096	20.4330 1957	20.8647 3045	21.3074 8892	21.7615 8774
18	21.4123 1238	21.8927 6251	22.3863 4871	22.8934 4487	23.4144 3537
19	22.8405 5863	23.3853 4966	23.9460 0743	24.5230 1460	25.1168 6844
20	24.2973 6980	24.9115 2003	25.5446 5761	26.1973 9750	26.8703 7449
21	25.7833 1719	26.4720 2923	27.1832 7405	27.9178 2593	28.6764 8572
22	27.2989 8354	28.0676 4989	28.8628 5590	29.6855 6615	30.5367 8030
23	28.8449 6321	29.6991 7201	30.5844 2730	31.5019 1921	32.4528 8370
24	30.4218 6247	31.3674 0338	32.3490 3798	33.3682 2199	34.4264 7022
25	32.0302 9972	33.0731 6996	34.1577 6393	35.2858 4810	36.4592 6432
26	33.6709 0572	34.8173 1628	36.0117 0803	37.2562 0892	38.5530 4225
27	35.3443 2383	36.6007 0590	37.9120 0073	39.2807 5467	40.7096 3352
28	37.0512 1031	38.4242 2178	39.8598 0075	41.3609 7542	42.9309 2252
29	38.7922 3451	40.2887 6677	41.8562 9577	43.4984 0224	45.2188 5020
30	40.5680 7921	42.1952 6402	43.9027 0316	45.6946 0830	47.5754 1571
31	42.3794 4079	44.1446 5746	46.0002 7074	47.9512 1003	50.0026 7818
32	44.2270 2961	46.1379 1226	48.1502 7751	50.2698 6831	52.5027 5852
33	46.1115 7020	48.1760 1528	50.3540 3445	52.6522 8969	55.0778 4128
34	48.0338 0160	50.2599 7563	52.6128 8531	55.1002 2765	57.7301 7652
35	49.9944 7763	52.3908 2508	54.9282 0744	57.6154 8391	60.4620 8181
36	51.9943 6719	54.5696 1864	57.3014 1263	60.1999 0972	63.2759 4427
37	54.0342 5453	56.7974 3506	59.7339 4794	62.8554 0724	66.1742 2259
38	56.1149 3962	59.0753 7735	62.2272 9664	65.5839 3094	69.1594 4927
39	58.2372 3841	61.4045 7334	64.7829 7906	68.3874 8904	72.2342 3275
40	60.4019 8318	63.7861 7624	67.4025 5354	71.2681 4499	75.4012 5973
41	62.6100 2284	66.2213 6521	70.0876 1737	74.2280 1898	78.6632 9753
42	64.8622 2330	68.7113 4592	72.8398 0781	77.2692 8950	82.0231 9645
43	67.1594 6777	71.2573 5121	75.6608 0300	80.3941 9496	85.4838 9234
44	69.5026 5712	73.8606 4161	78.5523 2308	83.6050 3532	89.0484 0911
45	71.8927 1027	76.5225 0605	81.5161 3116	86.9041 7379	92.7198 6139
46	74.3305 6447	79.2442 6243	84.5540 3443	90.2940 3857	96.5014 5723
47	76.8171 7576	82.0272 5834	87.6678 8530	93.7771 2463	100.3965 0095
48	79.3535 1927	84.8728 7165	90.8595 8243	97.3559 9556	104.4083 9598
49	81.9405 8966	87.7825 1126	94.1310 7199	101.0332 8544	108.5406 4785
50	84.5794 0145	90.7576 1776	97.4843 4879	104.8117 0079	112.7968 6729

Table 10   (*Continued*)

$$s_{\overline{n}|i} = \frac{(1 + i)^n - 1}{i}$$

n	2%	2¼%	2½%	2¾%	3%
51	87.2709 8948	93.7996 6416	100.9214 5751	108.6940 2256	117.1807 7331
52	90.0164 0927	96.9101 5661	104.4444 9395	112.6831 0818	121.6961 9651
53	92.8167 3746	100.0906 3513	108.0556 0629	116.7818 9365	126.3470 8240
54	95.6730 7221	103.3426 7442	111.7569 9645	120.9933 9573	131.1374 9488
55	98.5865 3365	106.6678 8460	115.5509 2136	125.3207 1411	136.0716 1972
56	101.5582 6432	110.0679 1200	119.4396 9440	129.7670 3375	141.1537 6831
57	104.5894 2961	113.5444 4002	123.4256 8676	134.3356 2718	146.3883 8136
58	107.6812 1820	117.0991 8992	127.5113 2893	139.0298 5692	151.7800 3280
59	110.8348 4257	120.7339 2169	131.6991 1215	143.8531 7799	157.3334 3379
60	114.0515 3942	124.4504 3493	135.9915 8995	148.8091 4038	163.0534 3680
61	117.3325 7021	128.2505 6972	140.3913 7970	153.9013 9174	168.9450 3991
62	120.6792 2161	132.1362 0754	144.9011 6419	159.1336 8002	175.0133 9110
63	124.0928 0604	136.1092 7221	149.5236 9330	164.5098 5622	181.2637 9284
64	127.5746 6216	140.1717 3083	154.2617 8563	170.0338 7726	187.7017 0662
65	131.1261 5541	144.3255 9477	159.1183 3027	175.7098 0889	194.3327 5782
66	134.7486 7852	148.5729 2066	164.0962 8853	181.5418 2863	201.1627 4055
67	138.4436 5209	152.9158 1137	169.1986 9574	187.5342 2892	208.1976 2277
68	142.2125 2513	157.3564 1713	174.4286 6314	193.6914 2022	215.4435 5145
69	146.0567 7563	161.8969 3651	179.7893 7971	200.0179 3427	222.9068 5800
70	149.9779 1114	166.5396 1758	185.2841 1421	206.5184 2746	230.5940 6374
71	153.9774 6937	171.2867 5898	190.9162 1706	213.1976 8422	238.5118 8565
72	158.0570 1875	176.1407 1106	196.6891 2249	220.0606 2054	246.6672 4222
73	162.2181 5913	181.1038 7705	202.6063 5055	227.1122 8760	255.0672 5949
74	166.4625 2231	186.1787 1429	208.6715 0931	234.3578 7551	263.7192 7727
75	170.7917 7276	191.3677 3536	214.8882 9705	241.8027 1709	272.6308 5559
76	175.2076 0821	196.6735 0941	221.2605 0447	249.4522 9181	281.8097 8126
77	179.7117 6038	202.0986 6337	227.7920 1709	257.3122 2983	291.2640 7469
78	184.3059 9558	207.6458 8329	234.4868 1751	265.3883 1615	301.0019 9693
79	188.9921 1549	213.3179 1567	241.3489 8795	273.6864 9485	311.0320 5684
80	193.7719 5780	219.1175 6877	248.3827 1265	282.2128 7345	321.3630 1855
81	198.6473 9696	225.0477 1407	255.5922 8047	290.9737 2747	332.0039 0910
82	203.6203 4490	231.1112 8763	262.9820 8748	299.9755 0498	342.9640 2638
83	208.6927 5180	237.3112 9160	270.5566 3966	309.2248 3137	354.2529 4717
84	213.8666 0683	243.6507 9567	278.3205 5566	318.7285 1423	365.8805 3558
85	219.1439 3897	250.1329 3857	286.2785 6955	328.4935 4837	377.8569 5165
86	224.5268 1775	256.7609 2969	294.4355 3379	338.5271 2095	390.1926 6020
87	230.0173 5411	263.5380 5060	302.7964 2213	348.8366 1678	402.8984 4001
88	235.6177 0119	270.4676 5674	311.3663 3268	359.4296 2374	415.9853 9321
89	241.3300 5521	277.5531 7902	320.1504 9100	370.3139 3839	429.4649 5500
90	247.1566 5632	284.7981 2555	329.1542 5328	381.4975 7170	443.3489 0365
91	253.0997 8944	292.2060 8337	338.3831 0961	392.9887 5492	457.6493 7076
92	259.1617 8523	299.7807 2025	347.8426 8735	404.7959 4568	472.3788 5189
93	265.3450 2094	307.5257 8645	357.5387 5453	416.9278 3418	487.5502 1744
94	271.6519 2135	315.4451 1665	367.4772 2339	429.3933 4962	503.1767 2397
95	278.0849 5978	323.5426 3177	377.6641 5398	442.2016 6674	519.2720 2568
96	284.6466 5898	331.8223 4099	388.1057 5783	455.3622 1257	535.8501 8645
97	291.3395 9216	340.2883 4366	398.8084 0177	468.8846 7342	552.9256 9205
98	298.1663 8400	348.9448 3139	409.7786 1182	482.7790 0194	570.5134 6281
99	305.1297 1168	357.7960 9010	421.0230 7711	497.0554 2449	588.6288 6669
100	312.2323 0591	366.8465 0213	432.5486 5404	511.7244 4867	607.2877 3270

Table 10 (*Continued*)

$$s_{\overline{n}|i} = \frac{(1 + i)^n - 1}{i}$$

n	3½ %	4 %	4½ %	5 %	5½ %
1	1.0000 0000	1.0000 0000	1.0000 0000	1.0000 0000	1.0000 0000
2	2.0350 0000	2.0400 0000	2.0450 0000	2.0500 0000	2.0550 0000
3	3.1062 2500	3.1216 0000	3.1370 2500	3.1525 0000	3.1680 2500
4	4.2149 4288	4.2464 6400	4.2781 9113	4.3101 2500	4.3422 6638
5	5.3624 6588	5.4163 2256	5.4707 0973	5.5256 3125	5.5810 9103
6	6.5501 5218	6.6329 7546	6.7168 9166	6.8019 1281	6.8880 5103
7	7.7794 0751	7.8982 9448	8.0191 5179	8.1420 0845	8.2668 9384
8	9.0516 8677	9.2142 2626	9.3800 1362	9.5491 0888	9.7215 7300
9	10.3684 9581	10.5827 9531	10.8021 1423	11.0265 6432	11.2562 5951
10	11.7313 9316	12.0061 0712	12.2882 0937	12.5778 9254	12.8753 5379
11	13.1419 9192	13.4863 5141	13.8411 7879	14.2067 8716	14.5834 9825
12	14.6019 6164	15.0258 0546	15.4640 3184	15.9171 2652	16.3855 9065
13	16.1130 3030	16.6268 3768	17.1599 1327	17.7129 8285	18.2867 9814
14	17.6769 8636	18.2919 1119	18.9321 0937	19.5986 3199	20.2925 7203
15	19.2956 8088	20.0235 8764	20.7840 5429	21.5785 6359	22.4086 6350
16	20.9710 2971	21.8245 3114	22.7193 3673	23.6574 9177	24.6411 3999
17	22.7050 1575	23.6975 1239	24.7417 0689	25.8403 6636	26.9964 0269
18	24.4996 9130	25.6454 1288	26.8550 8370	28.1323 8467	29.4812 0483
19	26.3571 8050	27.6712 2940	29.0635 6246	30.5390 0391	32.1026 7110
20	28.2796 8181	29.7780 7858	31.3714 2277	33.0659 5410	34.8683 1801
21	30.2694 7068	31.9692 0172	33.7831 3680	35.7192 5181	37.7860 7550
22	32.3289 0215	34.2479 6979	36.3033 7795	38.5052 1440	40.8643 0965
23	34.4604 1373	36.6178 8858	38.9370 2996	41.4304 7512	44.1118 4669
24	36.6665 2821	39.0826 0412	41.6891 9631	44.5019 9887	47.5379 9825
25	38.9498 5669	41.6459 0829	44.5652 1015	47.7270 9882	51.1525 8816
26	41.3131 0168	44.3117 4462	47.5706 4460	51.1134 5376	54.9659 8051
27	43.7590 6024	47.0842 1440	50.7113 2361	54.6691 2645	58.9891 0943
28	46.2906 2734	49.9675 8298	53.9933 3317	58.4025 8277	63.2335 1045
29	48.9107 9930	52.9662 8630	57.4230 3316	62.3227 1191	67.7113 5353
30	51.6226 7728	56.0849 3775	61.0070 6966	66.4388 4750	72.4354 7797
31	54.4294 7098	59.3283 3526	64.7523 8779	70.7607 8988	77.4194 2926
32	57.3345 0247	62.7014 6867	68.6662 4524	75.2988 2937	82.6774 9787
33	60.3412 1005	66.2095 2742	72.7562 2628	80.0637 7084	88.2247 6025
34	63.4531 5240	69.8579 0851	77.0302 5646	85.0669 5938	94.0771 2207
35	66.6740 1274	73.6522 2486	81.4966 1800	90.3203 0735	100.2513 6378
36	70.0076 0318	77.5983 1385	86.1639 6581	95.8363 2272	106.7651 8879
37	73.4578 6930	81.7022 4640	91.0413 4427	101.6281 3886	113.6372 7417
38	77.0288 9472	85.9703 3626	96.1382 0476	107.7095 4580	120.8873 2425
39	80.7249 0604	90.4091 4971	101.4644 2398	114.0950 2309	128.5361 2708
40	84.5502 7775	95.0255 1570	107.0303 2306	120.7997 7424	136.6056 1407
41	88.5095 3747	99.8265 3633	112.8466 8760	127.8397 6295	145.1189 2285
42	92.6073 7128	104.8195 9778	118.9247 8854	135.2317 5110	154.1004 6360
43	96.8486 2928	110.0123 8169	125.2764 0402	142.9933 3866	163.5759 8910
44	101.2383 3130	115.4128 7696	131.9138 4220	151.1430 0559	173.5726 6850
45	105.7816 7290	121.0293 9204	138.8499 6510	159.7001 5587	184.1191 6527
46	110.4840 3145	126.8705 6772	146.0982 1353	168.6851 6366	195.2457 1936
47	115.3509 7255	132.9453 9043	153.6726 3314	178.1194 2185	206.9842 3392
48	120.3882 5659	139.2632 0604	161.5879 0163	188.0253 9294	219.3683 6679
49	125.6018 4557	145.8337 3429	169.8593 5720	198.4266 6259	232.4336 2696
50	130.9979 1016	152.6670 8366	178.5030 2828	209.3479 9572	246.2174 7645

Table 10   *(Continued)*

$$s_{\overline{n}|i} = \frac{(1 + i)^n - 1}{i}$$

n	$3\frac{1}{2}\%$	4%	$4\frac{1}{2}\%$	5%	$5\frac{1}{2}\%$
51	136.5828 3702	159.7737 6700	187.5356 6455	220.8153 9550	260.7594 3765
52	142.3632 3631	167.1647 1768	196.9747 6946	232.8561 6528	276.1012 0672
53	148.3459 4958	174.8513 0639	206.8386 3408	245.4989 7354	292.2867 7309
54	154.5380 5782	182.8453 5865	217.1463 7262	258.7739 2222	309.3625 4561
55	160.9468 8984	191.1591 7299	227.9179 5938	272.7126 1833	327.3774 8562
56	167.5800 3099	199.8055 3991	239.1742 6756	287.3482 4924	346.3832 4733
57	174.4453 3207	208.7977 6151	250.9371 0960	302.7156 6171	366.4343 2593
58	181.5509 1869	218.1496 7197	263.2292 7953	318.8514 4479	387.5882 1386
59	188.9052 0085	227.8756 5885	276.0745 9711	335.7940 1703	409.9055 6562
60	196.5168 8288	237.9906 8520	289.4979 5398	353.5837 1788	433.4503 7173
61	204.3949 7378	248.5103 1261	303.5253 6190	372.2629 0378	458.2901 4217
62	212.5487 9786	259.4507 2511	318.1840 0319	391.8760 4897	484.4960 9999
63	220.9880 0579	270.8287 5412	333.5022 8333	412.4698 5141	512.1433 8549
64	229.7225 8599	282.6619 0428	349.5098 8608	434.0933 4398	541.3112 7170
65	238.7628 7650	294.9683 8045	366.2378 3096	456.7980 1118	572.0833 9164
66	248.1195 7718	307.7671 1567	383.7185 3335	480.6379 1174	604.5479 7818
67	257.8037 6238	321.0778 0030	401.9858 6735	505.6698 0733	638.7981 1698
68	267.8268 9406	334.9209 1231	421.0752 3138	531.9532 9770	674.9320 1341
69	278.2008 3535	349.3177 4880	441.0236 1679	559.5509 6258	713.0532 7415
70	288.9378 6459	364.2904 5876	461.8696 7955	588.5285 1071	753.2712 0423
71	300.0506 8985	379.8620 7711	483.6538 1513	618.9549 3625	795.7011 2046
72	311.5524 6400	396.0565 6019	506.4182 3681	650.9026 8306	840.4646 8209
73	323.4568 0024	412.8988 2260	530.2070 5747	684.4478 1721	887.6902 3960
74	335.7777 8824	430.4147 7550	555.0663 7505	719.6702 0807	937.5132 0278
75	348.5300 1083	448.6313 6652	581.0443 6193	756.6537 1848	990.0764 2893
76	361.7285 6121	467.5766 2118	608.1913 5822	795.4864 0440	1045.5306 3252
77	375.3890 6085	487.2796 8603	636.5599 6934	836.2607 2462	1104.0348 1731
78	389.5276 7798	507.7708 7347	666.2051 6796	879.0737 6085	1165.7567 3226
79	404.1611 4671	529.0817 0841	697.1844 0052	924.0274 4889	1230.8733 5254
80	419.3067 8685	551.2449 7675	729.5576 9854	971.2288 2134	1299.5713 8693
81	434.9825 2439	574.2947 7582	763.3877 9497	1020.7902 6240	1372.0478 1321
82	451.2069 1274	598.2665 6685	798.7402 4575	1072.8297 7552	1448.5104 4294
83	467.9991 5469	623.1972 2952	835.6835 5680	1127.4712 6430	1529.1785 1730
84	485.3791 2510	649.1251 1870	874.2893 1686	1184.8448 2752	1614.2833 3575
85	503.3673 9448	676.0901 2345	914.6323 3612	1245.0870 6889	1704.0689 1921
86	521.9852 5329	704.1337 2839	956.7907 9125	1308.3414 2234	1798.7927 0977
87	541.2547 3715	733.2990 7753	1000.8463 7685	1374.7584 9345	1898.7263 0881
88	561.1986 5295	763.6310 4063	1046.8844 6381	1444.4964 1812	2004.1562 5579
89	581.8406 0581	795.1762 8225	1094.9942 6468	1517.7212 3903	2115.3848 4986
90	603.2050 2701	827.9833 3354	1145.2690 0659	1594.6073 0098	2232.7310 1660
91	625.3172 0295	862.1026 6688	1197.8061 1189	1675.3376 6603	2356.5312 2252
92	648.2033 0506	897.5867 7356	1252.7073 8692	1760.1045 4933	2487.1404 3976
93	671.8904 2073	934.4902 4450	1310.0792 1933	1849.1097 7680	2624.9331 6394
94	696.4065 8546	972.8698 5428	1370.0327 8420	1942.5652 6564	2770.3044 8796
95	721.7808 1595	1012.7846 4845	1432.6842 5949	2040.6935 2892	2923.6712 3480
96	748.0431 4451	1054.2960 3439	1498.1550 5117	2143.7282 0537	3085.4731 5271
97	775.2246 5457	1097.4678 7577	1566.5720 2847	2251.9146 1564	3256.1741 7611
98	803.3575 1748	1142.3665 9080	1638.0677 6976	2365.5103 4642	3436.2637 5580
99	832.4750 3059	1189.0612 5443	1712.7808 1939	2484.7858 6374	3626.2582 6237
100	862.6116 5666	1237.6237 0461	1790.8559 5627	2610.0251 5693	3826.7024 6680

Table 10   *(Continued)*

$$s_{\overline{n}|i} = \frac{(1 + i)^n - 1}{i}$$

n	6 %	6½ %	7 %	7½ %	8 %
1	1.0000 0000	1.0000 0000	1.0000 0000	1.0000 0000	1.0000 0000
2	2.0600 0000	2.0650 0000	2.0700 0000	2.0750 0000	2.0800 0000
3	3.1836 0000	3.1992 2500	3.2149 0000	3.2306 2500	3.2464 0000
4	4.3746 1600	4.4071 7463	4.4399 4300	4.4729 2188	4.5061 1200
5	5.6370 9296	5.6936 4098	5.7507 3901	5.8083 9102	5.8666 0096
6	6.9753 1854	7.0637 2764	7.1532 9074	7.2440 2034	7.3359 2904
7	8.3938 3765	8.5228 6994	8.6540 2109	8.7873 2187	8.9228 0336
8	9.8974 6791	10.0768 5648	10.2598 0257	10.4463 7101	10.6366 2763
9	11.4913 1598	11.7318 5215	11.9779 8875	12.2298 4883	12.4875 5784
10	13.1807 9494	13.4944 2254	13.8164 4796	14.1470 8750	14.4865 6247
11	14.9716 4264	15.3715 6001	15.7835 9932	16.2081 1906	16.6454 8746
12	16.8699 4120	17.3707 1141	17.8884 5127	18.4237 2799	18.9771 2646
13	18.8821 3767	19.4998 0765	20.1406 4286	20.8055 0759	21.4952 9658
14	21.0150 6593	21.7672 9515	22.5504 8786	23.3659 2066	24.2149 2030
15	23.2759 6988	24.1821 6933	25.1290 2201	26.1183 6470	27.1521 1393
16	25.6725 2808	26.7540 1034	27.8880 5355	29.0772 4206	30.3242 8304
17	28.2128 7976	29.4930 2101	30.8402 1730	32.2580 3521	33.7502 2569
18	30.9056 5255	32.4100 6738	33.9990 3251	35.6773 8785	37.4502 4374
19	33.7599 9170	35.5167 2176	37.3789 6479	39.3531 9194	41.4462 6324
20	36.7855 9120	38.8253 0867	40.9954 9232	43.3046 8134	45.7619 6430
21	39.9927 2668	42.3489 5373	44.8651 7678	47.5525 3244	50.4229 2144
22	43.3922 9028	46.1016 3573	49.0057 3916	52.1189 7237	55.4567 5516
23	46.9958 2769	50.0982 4205	53.4361 4090	57.0278 9530	60.8932 9557
24	50.8155 7735	54.3546 2778	58.1766 7076	62.3049 8744	66.7647 5922
25	54.8645 1200	58.8876 7859	63.2490 3772	67.9778 6150	73.1059 3995
26	59.1563 8272	63.7153 7769	68.6764 7036	74.0762 0112	79.9544 1515
27	63.7057 6568	68.8568 7725	74.4838 2328	80.6319 1620	87.3507 6836
28	68.5281 1162	74.3325 7427	80.6976 9091	87.6793 0991	95.3388 2983
29	73.6397 9832	80.1641 9159	87.3465 2927	95.2552 5816	103.9659 3622
30	79.0581 8622	86.3748 6405	94.4607 8632	103.3994 0252	113.2832 1111
31	84.8016 7739	92.9892 3021	102.0730 4137	112.1543 5771	123.3458 6800
32	90.8897 7803	100.0335 3017	110.2181 5426	121.5659 3454	134.2135 3744
33	97.3431 6471	107.5357 0963	118.9334 2506	131.6833 7963	145.9506 2044
34	104.1837 5460	115.5255 3076	128.2587 6481	142.5596 3310	158.6266 7007
35	111.4347 7987	124.0346 9026	138.2368 7835	154.2516 0558	172.3168 0368
36	119.1208 6666	133.0969 4513	148.9134 5984	166.8204 7600	187.1021 4797
37	127.2681 1866	142.7482 4656	160.3374 0202	180.3320 1170	203.0703 1981
38	135.9042 0578	153.0268 8259	172.5610 2017	194.8569 1258	220.3159 4540
39	145.0584 5813	163.9736 2996	185.6402 9158	210.4711 8102	238.9412 2103
40	154.7619 6562	175.6319 1590	199.6351 1199	227.2565 1960	259.0565 1871
41	165.0476 8356	188.0479 9044	214.6095 6983	245.3007 5857	280.7810 4021
42	175.9505 4457	201.2711 0981	230.6322 3972	264.6983 1546	304.2435 2342
43	187.5075 7724	215.3537 3195	247.7764 9650	285.5506 8912	329.5830 0530
44	199.7580 3188	230.3517 2453	266.1208 5125	307.9669 9080	356.9496 4572
45	212.7435 1379	246.3245 8662	285.7493 1084	332.0645 1511	386.5056 1738
46	226.5081 2462	263.3356 8475	306.7517 6260	357.9693 5375	418.4260 6677
47	241.0986 1210	281.4525 0426	329.2243 8598	385.8170 5528	452.9001 5211
48	256.5645 2882	300.7469 1704	353.2700 9300	415.7533 3442	490.1321 6428
49	272.9584 0055	321.2954 6665	378.9989 9951	447.9348 3451	530.3427 3742
50	290.3359 0458	343.1796 7198	406.5289 2947	482.5299 4709	573.7701 5642

Table 10 *(Continued)*

$$s_{\overline{n}|i} = \frac{(1 + i)^n - 1}{i}$$

n	$8\frac{1}{2}\%$	9%	$9\frac{1}{2}\%$	10%	$10\frac{1}{2}\%$
1	1.0000 0000	1.0000 0000	1.0000 0000	1.0000 0000	1.0000 0000
2	2.0850 0000	2.0900 0000	2.0950 0000	2.1000 0000	2.1050 0000
3	3.2622 2500	3.2781 0000	3.2940 2500	3.3100 0000	3.3260 2500
4	4.5395 1413	4.5731 2900	4.6069 5738	4.6410 0000	4.6752 5763
5	5.9253 7283	5.9847 1061	6.0446 1833	6.1051 0000	6.1661 5968
6	7.4290 2952	7.5233 3456	7.6188 5707	7.7156 1000	7.8136 0644
7	9.0604 9702	9.2004 3468	9.3426 4849	9.4871 7100	9.6340 3512
8	10.8306 3927	11.0284 7380	11.2302 0009	11.4358 8810	11.6456 0881
9	12.7512 4361	13.0210 3644	13.2970 6910	13.5794 7691	13.8683 9773
10	14.8350 9932	15.1929 2972	15.5602 9067	15.9374 2460	16.3245 7949
11	17.0960 8276	17.5602 9339	18.0385 1828	18.5311 6706	19.0386 6034
12	19.5492 4979	20.1407 1980	20.7521 7752	21.3842 8377	22.0377 1967
13	22.2109 3603	22.9533 8458	23.7236 3438	24.5227 1214	25.3516 8024
14	25.0988 6559	26.0191 8919	26.9773 7965	27.9749 8336	29.0136 0666
15	28.2322 6916	29.3609 1622	30.5402 3072	31.7724 8169	33.0600 3536
16	31.6320 1204	33.0033 9868	34.4415 5263	35.9497 2986	37.5313 3908
17	35.3207 3306	36.9737 0456	38.7135 0013	40.5447 0285	42.4721 2968
18	39.3229 9538	41.3013 3797	43.3912 8265	45.5991 7313	47.9317 0330
19	43.6654 4998	46.0184 5839	48.5134 5450	51.1590 9045	53.9645 3214
20	48.3770 1323	51.1601 1964	54.1222 3267	57.2749 9949	60.6308 0802
21	53.4890 5936	56.7645 3041	60.2638 4478	64.0024 9944	67.9970 4286
22	59.0356 2940	62.8733 3815	66.9889 1003	71.4027 4939	76.1367 3236
23	65.0536 5790	69.5319 3858	74.3528 5649	79.5430 2433	85.1310 8926
24	71.5832 1882	76.7898 1305	82.4163 7785	88.4973 2676	95.0698 5363
25	78.6677 9242	84.7008 9623	91.2459 3375	98.3470 5943	106.0521 8826
26	86.3545 5478	93.3239 7689	100.9142 9745	109.1817 6538	118.1876 6803
27	94.6946 9193	102.7231 3481	111.5011 5571	121.0999 4192	131.5973 7317
28	103.7437 4075	112.9682 1694	123.0937 6551	134.2099 3611	146.4150 9736
29	113.5619 5871	124.1353 5646	135.7876 7323	148.6309 2972	162.7886 8258
30	124.2147 2520	136.3075 3855	149.6875 0218	164.4940 2269	180.8814 9425
31	135.7729 7684	149.5752 1702	164.9078 1489	181.9434 2496	200.8740 5114
32	148.3136 7987	164.0369 8655	181.5740 5731	201.1377 6745	222.9658 2651
33	161.9203 4266	179.8003 1534	199.8235 9275	222.2515 4420	247.3772 3830
34	176.6835 7179	196.9823 4372	219.8068 3406	245.4766 9862	274.3518 4832
35	192.7016 7539	215.7107 5465	241.6884 8330	271.0243 6848	304.1587 9239
36	210.0813 1780	236.1247 2257	265.6488 8921	299.1268 0533	337.0954 6560
37	228.9382 2981	258.3759 4760	291.8855 3369	330.0394 8586	373.4904 8948
38	249.3979 7935	282.6297 8288	320.6146 5939	364.0434 3445	413.7069 9088
39	271.5968 0759	309.0664 6334	352.0730 5203	401.4477 7789	458.1462 2492
40	295.6825 3624	337.8824 4504	386.5199 9197	442.5925 5568	507.2515 7854
41	321.8155 5182	369.2918 6510	424.2393 9121	487.8518 1125	561.5129 9428
42	350.1698 7372	403.5281 3296	465.5421 3337	537.6369 9237	621.4718 5868
43	380.9343 1299	440.8456 6492	510.7686 3604	592.4006 9161	687.7264 0385
44	414.3137 2959	481.5217 7477	560.2916 5647	652.6407 6077	760.9376 7625
45	450.5303 9661	525.8587 3450	614.5193 6383	718.9048 3685	841.8361 3225
46	489.8254 8032	574.1860 2060	673.8987 0340	791.7953 2054	931.2289 2614
47	532.4606 4615	626.8627 6245	738.9190 8022	871.9748 5259	1030.0079 6339
48	578.7198 0107	684.2804 1107	810.1163 9284	960.1723 3785	1139.1587 9954
49	628.9109 8416	746.8656 4807	888.0774 5016	1057.1895 7163	1259.7704 7349
50	683.3684 1782	815.0835 5640	973.4448 0793	1163.9085 2880	1393.0463 7321

Table 11

$$a_{\overline{n}|i} = \frac{1 - (1 + i)^{-n}}{i}$$

n	$\frac{1}{4}\%$	$\frac{7}{24}\%$	$\frac{1}{3}\%$	$\frac{5}{12}\%$	$\frac{1}{2}\%$
1	0.9975 0623	0.9970 9182	0.9966 7774	0.9958 5062	0.9950 2488
2	1.9925 2492	1.9912 8390	1.9900 4426	1.9875 6908	1.9850 9938
3	2.9850 6227	2.9825 8470	2.9801 1056	2.9751 7253	2.9702 4814
4	3.9751 2446	3.9710 0261	3.9668 8760	3.9586 7804	3.9504 9566
5	4.9627 1766	4.9565 4602	4.9503 8631	4.9381 0261	4.9258 6633
6	5.9478 4804	5.9392 2328	5.9306 1759	5.9134 6318	5.8963 8441
7	6.9305 2174	6.9190 4274	6.9075 9228	6.8847 7661	6.8620 7404
8	7.9107 4487	7.8960 1270	7.8813 2121	7.8520 5970	7.8229 5924
9	8.8885 2357	8.8701 4146	8.8518 1516	8.8153 2916	8.7790 6392
10	9.8638 6391	9.8414 3726	9.8190 8487	9.7746 0165	9.7304 1186
11	10.8367 7198	10.8099 0836	10.7831 4107	10.7298 9376	10.6770 2673
12	11.8072 5384	11.7755 6297	11.7439 9442	11.6812 2200	11.6189 3207
13	12.7753 1555	12.7384 0928	12.7016 5557	12.6286 0283	12.5561 5131
14	13.7409 6314	13.6984 5545	13.6561 3512	13.5720 5261	13.4887 0777
15	14.7042 0264	14.6557 0963	14.6074 4364	14.5115 8766	14.4166 2465
16	15.6650 4004	15.6101 7994	15.5555 9167	15.4472 2422	15.3399 2502
17	16.6234 8133	16.5618 7447	16.5005 8970	16.3789 7848	16.2586 3186
18	17.5795 3250	17.5108 0130	17.4424 4821	17.3068 6654	17.1727 6802
19	18.5331 9950	18.4569 6848	18.3811 7762	18.2309 0443	18.0823 5624
20	19.4844 8828	19.4003 8402	19.3167 8832	19.1511 0815	18.9874 1915
21	20.4334 0477	20.3410 5594	20.2492 9069	20.0674 9359	19.8879 7925
22	21.3799 5488	21.2789 9222	21.1786 9504	20.9800 7661	20.7840 5896
23	22.3241 4452	22.2142 0080	22.1050 1167	21.8888 7297	21.6756 8055
24	23.2659 7957	23.1466 8962	23.0282 5083	22.7938 9839	22.5628 6622
25	24.2054 6591	24.0764 6659	23.9484 2275	23.6951 6853	23.4456 3803
26	25.1426 0939	25.0035 3960	24.8655 3763	24.5926 9895	24.3240 1794
27	26.0774 1585	25.9279 1651	25.7796 0561	25.4865 0517	25.1980 2780
28	27.0098 9112	26.8496 0516	26.6906 3682	26.3766 0266	26.0676 8936
29	27.9400 4102	27.7686 1337	27.5986 4135	27.2630 0680	26.9330 2423
30	28.8678 7134	28.6849 4894	28.5036 2925	28.1457 3291	27.7940 5397
31	29.7933 8787	29.5986 1963	29.4056 1055	29.0247 9626	28.6507 9997
32	30.7165 9638	30.5096 3320	30.3045 9523	29.9002 1205	29.5032 8355
33	31.6375 0262	31.4179 9738	31.2005 9325	30.7719 9540	30.3515 2592
34	32.5561 1234	32.3237 1986	32.0936 1454	31.6401 6139	31.1955 4818
35	33.4724 3126	33.2268 0834	32.9836 6898	32.5047 2504	32.0353 7132
36	34.3864 6510	34.1272 7046	33.8707 6642	33.3657 0128	32.8710 1624
37	35.2982 1955	35.0251 1388	34.7549 1670	34.2231 0501	33.7025 0372
38	36.2077 0030	35.9203 4621	35.6361 2960	35.0769 5105	34.5298 5445
39	37.1149 1302	36.8129 7503	36.5144 1488	35.9272 5416	35.3530 8900
40	38.0198 6336	37.7030 0792	37.3897 8228	36.7740 2904	36.1722 2786
41	38.9225 5697	38.5904 5244	38.2622 4147	37.6172 9033	36.9872 9141
42	39.8229 9947	39.4753 1610	39.1318 0213	38.4570 5261	37.7982 9991
43	40.7211 9648	40.3576 6641	39.9984 7389	39.2933 3040	38.6052 7354
44	41.6171 5359	41.2373 3086	40.8622 6633	40.1261 3816	39.4082 3238
45	42.5108 7640	42.1144 9691	41.7231 8903	40.9554 9028	40.2071 9640
46	43.4023 7047	42.9891 1200	42.5812 5153	41.7814 0111	41.0021 8547
47	44.2916 4137	43.8611 8355	43.4364 6332	42.6038 8492	41.7932 1937
48	45.1786 9463	44.7307 1895	44.2888 3387	43.4229 5594	42.5803 1778
49	46.0635 3580	45.5977 2559	45.1383 7263	44.2386 2832	43.3635 0028
50	46.9461 7037	46.4622 1081	45.9850 8900	45.0509 1617	44.1427 8635

Table 11 (*Continued*)
$$a_{\overline{n}|i} = \frac{1 - (1 + i)^{-n}}{i}$$

n	$\frac{1}{4}\%$	$\frac{7}{24}\%$	$\frac{1}{3}\%$	$\frac{5}{12}\%$	$\frac{1}{2}\%$
51	47.8266 0386	47.3241 8194	46.8289 9236	45.8598 3353	44.9181 9537
52	48.7048 4176	48.1836 4631	47.6700 9205	46.6653 9439	45.6897 4664
53	49.5808 8953	49.0406 1119	48.5083 9739	47.4676 1267	46.4574 5934
54	50.4547 5265	49.8950 8386	49.3439 1767	48.2665 0224	47.2213 5258
55	51.3264 3656	50.7470 7157	50.1766 6213	49.0620 7692	47.9814 4535
56	52.1959 4669	51.5965 8154	51.0066 3999	49.8543 5046	48.7377 5657
57	53.0632 8847	52.4436 2098	51.8338 6046	50.6433 3656	49.4903 0505
58	53.9284 6730	53.2881 9707	52.6583 3268	51.4290 4885	50.2391 0950
59	54.7914 8858	54.1303 1698	53.4800 6580	52.2115 0093	50.9841 8855
60	55.6523 5769	54.9699 8785	54.2990 6890	52.9907 0632	51.7255 6075
61	56.5110 7999	55.8072 1680	55.1153 5106	53.7666 7850	52.4632 4453
62	57.3676 6083	56.6420 1094	55.9289 2133	54.5394 3087	53.1972 5824
63	58.2221 0557	57.4743 7734	56.7397 8870	55.3089 7680	53.9276 2014
64	59.0744 1952	58.3043 2306	57.5479 6216	56.0753 2959	54.6543 4839
65	59.9246 0800	59.1318 5515	58.3534 5065	56.8385 0250	55.3774 6109
66	60.7726 7631	59.9569 8062	59.1562 6311	57.5985 0871	56.0969 7621
67	61.6186 2974	60.7797 0648	59.9564 0842	58.3553 6137	56.8129 1165
68	62.4624 7355	61.6000 3970	60.7538 9543	59.1090 7357	57.5252 8522
69	63.3042 1302	62.4179 8723	61.5487 3299	59.8596 5832	58.2341 1465
70	64.1438 5339	63.2335 5603	62.3409 2989	60.6071 2862	58.9394 1756
71	64.9813 9989	64.0467 5300	63.1304 9491	61.3514 9738	59.6412 1151
72	65.8168 5774	64.8575 8504	63.9174 3678	62.0927 7748	60.3395 1394
73	66.6502 3216	65.6660 5904	64.7017 6424	62.8309 8172	61.0343 4222
74	67.4815 2834	66.4721 8184	65.4834 8595	63.5661 2287	61.7257 1366
75	68.3107 5146	67.2759 6029	66.2626 1058	64.2982 1365	62.4136 4543
76	69.1379 0670	68.0774 0120	67.0391 4676	65.0272 6670	63.0981 5466
77	69.9629 9920	68.8765 1138	67.8131 0308	65.7532 9464	63.7792 5836
78	70.7860 3411	69.6732 9759	68.5844 8812	66.4763 1002	64.4569 7349
79	71.6070 1657	70.4677 6661	69.3533 1042	67.1963 2533	65.1313 1691
80	72.4259 5169	71.2599 2516	70.1195 7849	67.9133 5303	65.8023 0538
81	73.2428 4458	72.0497 7997	70.8833 0082	68.6274 0550	66.4699 5561
82	74.0577 0033	72.8373 3773	71.6444 8587	69.3384 9511	67.1342 8419
83	74.8705 2402	73.6226 0513	72.4031 4206	70.0466 3413	67.7953 0765
84	75.6813 2072	74.4055 8883	73.1592 7780	70.7518 3482	68.4530 4244
85	76.4900 9548	75.1862 9547	73.9129 0146	71.4541 0936	69.1075 0491
86	77.2968 5335	75.9647 3167	74.6640 2139	72.1534 6991	69.7587 1135
87	78.1015 9935	76.7409 0403	75.4126 4591	72.8499 2854	70.4066 7796
88	78.9043 3850	77.5148 1914	76.1587 8330	73.5434 9730	71.0514 2086
89	79.7050 7581	78.2864 8357	76.9024 4182	74.2341 8818	71.6929 5608
90	80.5038 1627	79.0559 0385	77.6436 2972	74.9220 1313	72.3312 9958
91	81.3005 6486	79.8230 8651	78.3823 5521	75.6069 8403	72.9664 6725
92	82.0953 2654	80.5880 3807	79.1186 2645	76.2891 1272	73.5984 7487
93	82.8881 0628	81.3507 6500	79.8524 5161	76.9684 1101	74.2273 3818
94	83.6789 0900	82.1112 7379	80.5838 3882	77.6448 9063	74.8530 7282
95	84.4677 3966	82.8695 7087	81.3127 9616	78.3185 6329	75.4756 9434
96	85.2546 0315	83.6256 6269	82.0393 3172	78.9894 4062	76.0952 1825
97	86.0395 0439	84.3795 5565	82.7634 5355	79.6575 3422	76.7116 5995
98	86.8224 4827	85.1312 5616	83.4851 6965	80.3228 5566	77.3250 3478
99	87.6034 3967	85.8807 7057	84.2044 8802	80.9854 1642	77.9353 5799
100	88.3824 8346	86.6281 0527	84.9214 1663	81.6452 2797	78.5426 4477

Table 11   (*Continued*)

$$a_{\overline{n}|i} = \frac{1 - (1 + i)^{-n}}{i}$$

n	$\frac{1}{4}\%$	$\frac{7}{24}\%$	$\frac{1}{3}\%$	$\frac{5}{12}\%$	$\frac{1}{2}\%$
101	89.1595 8450	87.3732 6657	85.6359 6342	82.3023 0172	79.1469 1021
102	89.9347 4763	88.1162 6081	86.3481 3630	82.9566 4901	79.7481 6937
103	90.7079 7768	88.8570 9429	87.0579 4315	83.6082 8117	80.3464 3718
104	91.4792 7948	89.5957 7328	87.7653 9185	84.2572 0947	80.9417 2854
105	92.2486 5784	90.3323 0406	88.4704 9021	84.9034 4511	81.5340 5825
106	93.0161 1755	91.0666 9287	89.1732 4606	85.5469 9928	82.1234 4104
107	93.7816 6339	91.7989 4595	89.8736 6717	86.1878 8310	82.7098 9158
108	94.5453 0014	92.5290 6950	90.5717 6130	86.8261 0765	83.2934 2446
109	95.3070 3256	93.2570 6971	91.2675 3618	87.4616 8397	83.8740 5419
110	96.0668 6539	93.9829 5276	91.9609 9951	88.0946 2304	84.4517 9522
111	96.8248 0338	94.7067 2482	92.6521 5898	88.7249 3581	85.0266 6191
112	97.5808 5126	95.4283 9201	93.3410 2224	89.3526 3317	85.5986 6856
113	98.3350 1372	96.1479 6046	94.0275 9692	89.9777 2598	86.1678 2942
114	99.0872 9548	96.8654 3627	94.7118 9062	90.6002 2504	86.7341 5862
115	99.8377 0123	97.5808 2553	95.3939 1092	91.2201 4112	87.2976 7027
116	100.5862 3564	98.2941 3430	96.0736 6536	91.8374 8493	87.8583 7838
117	101.3329 0338	99.0053 6864	96.7511 6149	92.4522 6715	88.4162 9690
118	102.0777 0911	99.7145 3458	97.4264 0680	93.0644 9841	88.9714 3970
119	102.8206 5747	100.4216 3814	98.0994 0877	93.6741 8929	89.5238 2059
120	103.5617 5308	101.1266 8531	98.7701 7486	94.2813 5033	90.0734 5333
121	104.3010 0058	101.8296 8207	99.4387 1248	94.8859 9203	90.6203 5157
122	105.0384 0457	102.5306 3438	100.1050 2905	95.4881 2484	91.1645 2892
123	105.7739 6965	103.2295 4820	100.7691 3195	96.0877 5918	91.7059 9893
124	106.5077 0040	103.9264 2945	101.4310 2852	96.6849 0541	92.2447 7505
125	107.2396 0139	104.6212 8404	102.0907 2610	97.2795 7385	92.7808 7070
126	107.9696 7720	105.3141 1786	102.7482 3199	97.8717 7479	93.3142 9921
127	108.6979 3237	106.0049 3679	103.4035 5348	98.4615 1846	93.8450 7384
128	109.4243 7144	106.6937 4670	104.0566 9782	99.0488 1506	94.3732 0780
129	110.1489 9894	107.3805 5342	104.7076 7225	99.6336 7475	94.8987 1423
130	110.8718 1939	108.0653 6278	105.3564 8397	100.2161 0764	95.4216 0619
131	111.5928 3730	108.7481 8058	106.0031 4016	100.7961 2379	95.9418 9671
132	112.3120 5716	109.4290 1263	106.6476 4800	101.3737 3323	96.4595 9872
133	113.0294 8345	110.1078 6469	107.2900 1462	101.9489 4596	96.9747 2509
134	113.7451 2065	110.7847 4253	107.9302 4713	102.5217 7191	97.4872 8365
135	114.4589 7321	111.4596 5187	108.5683 5262	103.0922 2099	97.9973 0214
136	115.1710 4560	112.1325 9346	109.2043 3816	103.6603 0306	98.5047 7825
137	115.8813 4224	112.8035 8800	109.8382 1079	104.2260 2794	99.0097 2960
138	116.5898 6758	113.4726 2617	110.4699 7754	104.7894 0542	99.5121 6876
139	117.2966 2601	114.1397 1866	111.0996 4538	105.3504 4523	100.0121 0821
140	118.0016 2196	114.8048 7112	111.7272 2131	105.9091 5708	100.5095 6041
141	118.7048 5981	115.4680 8919	112.3527 1227	106.4655 5061	101.0045 3772
142	119.4063 4395	116.1293 7850	112.9761 2519	107.0196 3547	101.4970 5246
143	120.1060 7875	116.7887 4466	113.5974 6696	107.5714 2121	101.9871 1688
144	120.8040 6858	117.4461 9327	114.2167 4448	108.1209 1739	102.4747 4316
145	121.5003 1778	118.1017 2989	114.8339 6460	108.6681 3350	102.9599 4344
146	122.1948 3071	118.7553 6009	115.4491 3415	109.2130 7900	103.4427 2979
147	122.8876 1168	119.4070 8941	116.0622 5995	109.7557 6332	103.9231 1422
148	123.5786 6502	120.0569 2338	116.6733 4879	110.2961 9584	104.4011 0868
149	124.2679 9503	120.7048 6752	117.2824 0743	110.8343 8590	104.8767 2506
150	124.9556 0601	121.3509 2732	117.8894 4262	111.3703 4280	105.3499 7518

Table 11 (Continued)

$$a_{\overline{n}|i} = \frac{1 - (1 + i)^{-n}}{i}$$

n	$\frac{1}{4}\%$	$\frac{7}{24}\%$	$\frac{1}{3}\%$	$\frac{5}{12}\%$	$\frac{1}{2}\%$
151	125.6415 0226	121.9951 0825	118.4944 6109	111.9040 7582	105.8208 7083
152	126.3256 8804	122.6374 1579	119.0974 6952	112.4355 9418	106.2894 2371
153	127.0081 6762	123.2778 5538	119.6984 7461	112.9649 0707	106.7556 4548
154	127.6889 4525	123.9164 3245	120.2974 8300	113.4920 2364	107.2195 4774
155	128.3680 2519	124.5531 5242	120.8945 0133	114.0169 5300	107.6811 4203
156	129.0454 1166	125.1880 2069	121.4895 3621	114.5397 0423	108.1404 3983
157	129.7211 0889	125.8210 4265	122.0825 9422	115.0602 8637	108.5974 5257
158	130.3951 2109	126.4522 2367	122.6736 8195	115.5787 0842	109.0521 9161
159	131.0674 5246	127.0815 6909	123.2628 0593	116.0949 7934	109.5046 6827
160	131.7381 0719	127.7090 8426	123.8499 7269	116.6091 0805	109.9548 9380
161	132.4070 8946	128.3347 7450	124.4351 8873	117.1211 0346	110.4028 7940
162	133.0744 0346	128.9586 4512	125.0184 6053	117.6309 7440	110.8486 3622
163	133.7400 5332	129.5807 0141	125.5997 9454	118.1387 2969	111.2921 7535
164	134.4040 4321	130.2009 4864	126.1791 9722	118.6443 7811	111.7335 0781
165	135.0663 7727	130.8193 9208	126.7566 7497	119.1479 2841	112.1726 4458
166	135.7270 5962	131.4360 3697	127.3322 3419	119.6493 8929	112.6095 9660
167	136.3860 9439	132.0508 8855	127.9058 8125	120.1487 6942	113.0443 7473
168	137.0434 8567	132.6639 5202	128.4776 2251	120.6460 7743	113.4769 8978
169	137.6992 3758	133.2752 3259	129.0474 6430	121.1413 2192	113.9074 5252
170	138.3533 5419	133.8847 3545	129.6154 1292	121.6345 1146	114.3357 7365
171	139.0058 3959	134.4924 6576	130.1814 7467	122.1256 5456	114.7619 6383
172	139.6566 9785	135.0984 2867	130.7456 5582	122.6147 5973	115.1860 3366
173	140.3059 3302	135.7026 2934	131.3079 6261	123.1018 3542	115.6079 9369
174	140.9535 4914	136.3050 7287	131.8684 0127	123.5868 9004	116.0278 5442
175	141.5995 5027	136.9057 6439	132.4269 7801	124.0699 3199	116.4456 2629
176	142.2439 4042	137.5047 0899	132.9836 9901	124.5509 6962	116.8613 1969
177	142.8867 2361	138.1019 1175	133.5385 7045	125.0300 1124	117.2749 4496
178	143.5279 0385	138.6973 7773	134.0915 9845	125.5070 6513	117.6865 1240
179	144.1674 8514	139.2911 1199	134.6427 8915	125.9821 3955	118.0960 3224
180	144.8054 7146	139.8831 1956	135.1921 4866	126.4552 4271	118.5035 1467
181	145.4418 6679	140.4734 0546	135.7396 8305	126.9263 8278	118.9089 6982
182	146.0766 7510	141.0619 7470	136.2853 9839	127.3955 6791	119.3124 0778
183	146.7099 0035	141.6488 3227	136.8293 0072	127.8628 0622	119.7138 3859
184	147.3415 4649	142.2339 8315	137.3713 9606	128.3281 0578	120.1132 7223
185	147.9716 1744	142.8174 3231	137.9116 9043	128.7914 7463	120.5107 1863
186	148.6001 1715	143.3991 8469	138.4501 8980	129.2529 2080	120.9061 8769
187	149.2270 4952	143.9792 4522	138.9869 0013	129.7124 5225	121.2996 8925
188	149.8524 1848	144.5576 1883	139.5218 2737	130.1700 7693	121.6912 3308
189	150.4762 2791	145.1343 1043	140.0549 7745	130.6258 0275	122.0808 2894
190	151.0984 8170	145.7093 2490	140.5863 5626	131.0796 3759	122.4684 8651
191	151.7191 8375	146.2826 6712	141.1159 6969	131.5315 8930	122.8542 1543
192	152.3383 3790	146.8543 4195	141.6438 2362	131.9816 6570	123.2380 2530
193	152.9559 4803	147.4243 5425	142.1699 2387	132.4298 7455	123.6199 2567
194	153.5720 1799	147.9927 0885	142.6942 7628	132.8762 2362	123.9999 2604
195	154.1865 5161	148.5594 1057	143.2168 8666	133.3207 2062	124.3780 3586
196	154.7995 5272	149.1244 6422	143.7377 6079	133.7633 7323	124.7542 6454
197	155.4110 2516	149.6878 7458	144.2569 0444	134.2041 8911	125.1286 2143
198	156.0209 7273	150.2496 4645	144.7743 2336	134.6431 7587	125.5011 1585
199	156.6293 9923	150.8097 8458	145.2900 2329	135.0803 4112	125.8717 5707
200	157.2363 0846	151.3682 9372	145.8040 0992	135.5156 9240	126.2405 5430

Table 11 (*Continued*)

$$a_{\overline{n}|i} = \frac{1 - (1 + i)^{-n}}{i}$$

n	$7/12\,\%$	$2/3\,\%$	$3/4\,\%$	$7/8\,\%$	$1\,\%$
1	0.9942 0050	0.9933 7748	0.9925 5583	0.9913 2590	0.9900 9901
2	1.9826 3513	1.9801 7631	1.9777 2291	1.9740 5294	1.9703 9506
3	2.9653 3732	2.9604 4004	2.9555 5624	2.9482 5570	2.9409 8521
4	3.9423 4034	3.9342 1196	3.9261 1041	3.9140 0813	3.9019 6555
5	4.9136 7722	4.9015 3506	4.8894 3961	4.8713 8352	4.8534 3124
6	5.8793 8083	5.8624 5205	5.8455 9763	5.8204 5454	5.7954 7647
7	6.8394 8384	6.8170 0535	6.7946 3785	6.7612 9323	6.7281 9453
8	7.7940 1874	7.7652 3710	7.7366 1325	7.6939 7098	7.6516 7775
9	8.7430 1780	8.7071 8917	8.6715 7642	8.6185 5859	8.5660 1758
10	9.6865 1314	9.6429 0315	9.5995 7958	9.5351 2624	9.4713 0453
11	10.6245 3667	10.5724 2035	10.5206 7452	10.4437 4348	10.3676 2825
12	11.5571 2014	11.4957 8180	11.4349 1267	11.3444 7929	11.2550 7747
13	12.4842 9509	12.4130 2828	12.3423 4508	12.2374 0202	12.1337 4007
14	13.4060 9288	13.3242 0028	13.2430 2242	13.1225 7945	13.0037 0304
15	14.3225 4470	14.2293 3802	14.1369 9495	14.0000 7876	13.8650 5252
16	15.2336 8156	15.1284 8148	15.0243 1261	14.8699 6656	14.7178 7378
17	16.1395 3427	16.0216 7035	15.9050 2492	15.7323 0885	15.5622 5127
18	17.0401 3350	16.9089 4405	16.7791 8107	16.5871 7111	16.3982 6858
19	17.9355 0969	17.7903 4177	17.6468 2984	17.4346 1820	17.2260 0850
20	18.8256 9315	18.6659 0242	18.5080 1969	18.2747 1445	18.0455 5297
21	19.7107 1398	19.5356 6466	19.3627 9870	19.1075 2361	18.8569 8313
22	20.5906 0213	20.3996 6688	20.2112 1459	19.9331 0891	19.6603 7934
23	21.4653 8738	21.2579 4723	21.0533 1473	20.7515 3300	20.4558 2113
24	22.3350 9930	22.1105 4361	21.8891 4614	21.5628 5799	21.2433 8726
25	23.1997 6732	22.9574 9365	22.7187 5547	22.3671 4547	22.0231 5570
26	24.0594 2070	23.7988 3475	23.5421 8905	23.1644 5647	22.7952 0366
27	24.9140 8852	24.6346 0406	24.3594 9286	23.9548 5152	23.5596 0759
28	25.7637 9968	25.4648 3847	25.1707 1251	24.7383 9060	24.3164 4316
29	26.6085 8295	26.2895 7464	25.9758 9331	25.5151 3319	25.0657 8530
30	27.4484 6689	27.1088 4898	26.7750 8021	26.2851 3823	25.8077 0822
31	28.2834 7993	27.9226 9766	27.5683 1783	27.0484 6417	26.5422 8537
32	29.1136 5030	28.7311 5662	28.3556 5045	27.8051 6894	27.2695 8947
33	29.9390 0610	29.5342 6154	29.1371 2203	28.5553 0998	27.9896 9255
34	30.7595 7524	30.3320 4789	29.9127 7621	29.2989 4422	28.7026 6589
35	31.5753 8549	31.1245 5088	30.6826 5629	30.0361 2809	29.4085 8009
36	32.3864 6445	31.9118 0551	31.4468 0525	30.7669 1757	30.1075 0504
37	33.1928 3955	32.6938 4653	32.2052 6576	31.4913 6810	30.7995 0994
38	33.9945 3808	33.4707 0848	32.9580 8016	32.2095 3467	31.4846 6330
39	34.7915 8716	34.2424 2564	33.7052 9048	32.9214 7179	32.1630 3298
40	35.5840 1374	35.0090 3209	34.4469 3844	33.6272 3350	32.8346 8611
41	36.3718 4465	35.7705 6168	35.1830 6545	34.3268 7335	33.4996 8922
42	37.1551 0653	36.5270 4803	35.9137 1260	35.0204 4446	34.1581 0814
43	37.9338 2588	37.2785 2453	36.6389 2070	35.7079 9947	34.8100 0806
44	38.7080 2904	38.0250 2437	37.3587 3022	36.3895 9055	35.4554 5352
45	39.4777 4221	38.7665 8050	38.0731 8136	37.0652 6944	36.0945 0844
46	40.2429 9143	39.5032 2566	38.7823 1401	37.7350 8743	36.7272 3608
47	41.0038 0258	40.2349 9238	39.4861 6775	38.3990 9535	37.3536 9909
48	41.7602 0141	40.9619 1296	40.1847 8189	39.0573 4359	37.9739 5949
49	42.5122 1349	41.6840 1949	40.8781 9542	39.7098 8212	38.5880 7871
50	43.2598 6428	42.4013 4387	41.5664 4707	40.3567 6047	39.1961 1753

Table 11 ($Continued$)

$$a_{\overline{n}|i} = \frac{1 - (1 + i)^{-n}}{i}$$

n	$\frac{7}{12}\%$	$\frac{2}{3}\%$	$\frac{3}{4}\%$	$\frac{7}{8}\%$	1%
51	44.0031 7907	43.1139 1775	42.2495 7525	40.9980 2772	39.7981 3617
52	44.7421 8301	43.8217 7260	42.9276 1812	41.6337 3256	40.3941 9423
53	45.4769 0108	44.5249 3967	43.6006 1351	42.2639 2324	40.9843 5072
54	46.2073 5816	45.2234 5000	44.2685 9902	42.8886 4757	41.5686 6408
55	46.9335 7895	45.9173 3444	44.9316 1193	43.5079 5298	42.1471 9216
56	47.6555 8802	46.6066 2362	45.5896 8926	44.1218 8647	42.7199 9224
57	48.3734 0980	47.2913 4796	46.2428 6776	44.7304 9465	43.2871 2102
58	49.0870 6856	47.9715 3771	46.8911 8388	45.3338 2369	43.8486 3468
59	49.7965 8846	48.6472 2289	47.5346 7382	45.9319 1939	44.4045 8879
60	50.5019 9350	49.3184 3334	48.1733 7352	46.5248 2716	44.9550 3841
61	51.2033 0754	49.9851 9868	48.8073 1863	47.1125 9198	45.5000 3803
62	51.9005 5431	50.6475 4836	49.4365 4455	47.6952 5846	46.0396 4161
63	52.5937 5739	51.3055 1161	50.0610 8640	48.2728 7084	46.5739 0258
64	53.2829 4024	51.9591 1749	50.6809 7906	48.8454 7296	47.1028 7385
65	53.9681 2617	52.6083 9486	51.2962 5713	49.4131 0826	47.6266 0777
66	54.6493 3836	53.2533 7238	51.9069 5497	49.9758 1984	48.1451 5621
67	55.3265 9986	53.8940 7852	52.5131 0667	50.5336 5039	48.6585 7050
68	55.9999 3358	54.5305 4158	53.1147 4607	51.0866 4227	49.1669 0149
69	56.6693 6230	55.1627 8965	53.7119 0677	51.6348 3745	49.6701 9949
70	57.3349 0867	55.7908 5064	54.3046 2210	52.1782 7752	50.1685 1435
71	57.9965 9520	56.4147 5230	54.8929 2516	52.7170 0374	50.6618 9539
72	58.6544 4427	57.0345 2215	55.4768 4880	53.2510 5699	51.1503 9148
73	59.3084 7815	57.6501 8756	56.0564 2561	53.7804 7781	51.6340 5097
74	59.9587 1896	58.2617 7573	56.6316 8795	54.3053 0638	52.1129 2175
75	60.6051 8869	58.8693 1363	57.2026 6794	54.8255 8253	52.5870 5124
76	61.2479 0922	59.4728 2811	57.7693 9746	55.3413 4575	53.0564 8638
77	61.8869 0229	60.0723 4581	58.3319 0815	55.8526 3520	53.5212 7364
78	62.5221 8952	60.6678 9319	58.8902 3141	56.3594 8966	53.9814 5905
79	63.1537 9239	61.2594 9654	59.4443 9842	56.8619 4762	54.4370 8817
80	63.7817 3229	61.8471 8200	59.9944 4012	57.3600 4721	54.8882 0611
81	64.4060 3044	62.4309 7549	60.5403 8722	57.8538 2623	55.3348 5753
82	65.0267 0798	63.0109 0281	61.0822 7019	58.3433 2216	55.7770 8666
83	65.6437 8590	63.5869 8954	61.6201 1930	58.8285 7215	56.2149 3729
84	66.2572 8507	64.1592 6114	62.1539 6456	59.3096 1304	56.6484 5276
85	66.8672 2625	64.7277 4285	62.6838 3579	59.7864 8133	57.0776 7600
86	67.4736 3007	65.2924 5979	63.2097 6257	60.2592 1321	57.5026 4951
87	68.0765 1706	65.8534 3687	63.7317 7427	60.7278 4457	57.9234 1535
88	68.6759 0759	66.4106 9888	64.2499 0002	61.1924 1097	58.3400 1520
89	69.2718 2197	66.9642 7041	64.7641 6875	61.6529 4768	58.7524 9030
90	69.8642 8033	67.5141 7591	65.2746 0918	62.1094 8965	59.1608 8148
91	70.4533 0273	68.0604 3964	65.7812 4981	62.5620 7152	59.5652 2919
92	71.0389 0910	68.6030 8574	66.2841 1892	63.0107 2765	59.9655 7346
93	71.6211 1923	69.1421 3815	66.7832 4458	63.4554 9210	60.3619 5392
94	72.1999 5284	69.6776 2068	67.2786 5467	63.8963 9861	60.7544 0982
95	72.7754 2950	70.2095 5696	67.7703 7685	64.3334 8066	61.1429 8002
96	73.3475 6869	70.7379 7049	68.2584 3856	64.7667 7141	61.5277 0299
97	73.9163 8975	71.2628 8460	68.7428 6705	65.1963 0375	61.9086 1682
98	74.4819 1193	71.7843 2245	69.2236 8938	65.6221 1028	62.2857 5923
99	75.0441 5436	72.3023 0707	69.7009 3239	66.0442 2333	62.6591 6755
100	75.6031 3606	72.8168 6132	70.1746 2272	66.4626 7492	63.0288 7877

Table 11   *(Continued)*

$$a_{\overline{n}|i} = \frac{1 - (1 + i)^{-n}}{i}$$

n	7/12 %	2/3 %	3/4 %	7/8 %	1 %
101	76.1588 7596	73.3280 0794	70.6447 8682	66.8774 9683	63.3949 2947
102	76.7113 9283	73.8357 6948	71.1114 5094	67.2887 2052	63.7573 5591
103	77.2607 0538	74.3401 6835	71.5746 4113	67.6963 7722	64.1161 9397
104	77.8068 3219	74.8412 2684	72.0343 8325	68.1004 9786	64.4714 7918
105	78.3497 9174	75.3389 6706	72.4907 0298	68.5011 1312	64.8232 4671
106	78.8896 0240	75.8334 1099	72.9436 2579	68.8982 5341	65.1715 3140
107	79.4262 8241	76.3245 8045	73.3931 7696	69.2919 4885	65.5163 6772
108	79.9598 4996	76.8124 9714	73.8393 8160	69.6822 2935	65.8577 8983
109	80.4903 2307	77.2971 8259	74.2822 6461	70.0691 2451	66.1958 3151
110	81.0177 1971	77.7786 5820	74.7218 5073	70.4526 6370	66.5305 2625
111	81.5420 5770	78.2569 4523	75.1581 6450	70.8328 7604	66.8619 0718
112	82.0633 5480	78.7320 6480	75.5912 3027	71.2097 9037	67.1900 0710
113	82.5816 2863	79.2040 3788	76.0210 7223	71.5834 3531	67.5148 5852
114	83.0968 9674	79.6728 8531	76.4477 1437	71.9538 3922	67.8364 9358
115	83.6091 7654	80.1386 2779	76.8711 8052	72.3210 3020	68.1549 4414
116	84.1184 8537	80.6012 8589	77.2914 9431	72.6850 3614	68.4702 4172
117	84.6248 4047	81.0608 8002	77.7086 7922	73.0458 8465	68.7824 1755
118	85.1282 5896	81.5174 3048	78.1227 5853	73.4036 0312	69.0915 0252
119	85.6287 5787	81.9709 5743	78.5337 5536	73.7582 1871	69.3975 2725
120	86.1263 5414	82.4214 8089	78.9416 9267	74.1097 5832	69.7005 2203
121	86.6210 6460	82.8690 2076	79.3465 9322	74.4582 4864	70.0005 1686
122	87.1129 0598	83.3135 9678	79.7484 7962	74.8037 1613	70.2975 4145
123	87.6018 9493	83.7552 2859	80.1473 7432	75.1461 8699	70.5916 2520
124	88.0880 4798	84.1939 3568	80.5432 9957	75.4856 8723	70.8827 9722
125	88.5713 8159	84.6297 3743	80.9362 7749	75.8222 4261	71.1710 8636
126	89.0519 1210	85.0626 5308	81.3263 3001	76.1558 7867	71.4565 2115
127	89.5296 5577	85.4927 0173	81.7134 7892	76.4866 2074	71.7391 2985
128	90.0046 2877	85.9199 0238	82.0977 4583	76.8144 9391	72.0189 4045
129	90.4768 4716	86.3442 7389	82.4791 5219	77.1395 2309	72.2959 8064
130	90.9463 2692	86.7658 3499	82.8577 1929	77.4617 3292	72.5702 7786
131	91.4130 8393	87.1846 0430	83.2334 6828	77.7811 4788	72.8418 5927
132	91.8771 3399	87.6006 0029	83.6064 2013	78.0977 9220	73.1107 5175
133	92.3384 9278	88.0138 4135	83.9765 9566	78.4116 8991	73.3769 8193
134	92.7971 7592	88.4243 4571	84.3440 1554	78.7228 6484	73.6405 7617
135	93.2531 9893	88.8321 3150	84.7087 0029	79.0313 4061	73.9015 6056
136	93.7065 7722	89.2372 1673	85.0706 7026	79.3371 4063	74.1599 6095
137	94.1573 2616	89.6396 1926	85.4299 4567	79.6402 8811	74.4158 0293
138	94.6054 6097	90.0393 5688	85.7865 4657	79.9408 0606	74.6691 1181
139	95.0509 9682	90.4364 4724	86.1404 9288	80.2387 1728	74.9199 1268
140	95.4939 4878	90.8309 0785	86.4918 0434	80.5340 4440	75.1682 3038
141	95.9343 3185	91.2227 5614	86.8405 0059	80.8268 0981	75.4140 8948
142	96.3721 6091	91.6120 0941	87.1866 0108	81.1170 3575	75.6575 1434
143	96.8074 5078	91.9986 8485	87.5301 2514	81.4047 4423	75.8985 2905
144	97.2402 1619	92.3827 9952	87.8710 9195	81.6899 5711	76.1371 5747
145	97.6704 7177	92.7643 7038	88.2095 2055	81.9726 9602	76.3734 2324
146	98.0982 3208	93.1434 1429	88.5454 2982	82.2529 8242	76.6073 4974
147	98.5235 1160	93.5199 4797	88.8788 3854	82.5308 3759	76.8389 6014
148	98.9463 2470	93.8939 8805	89.2097 6530	82.8062 8262	77.0682 7737
149	99.3666 8570	94.2655 5104	89.5382 2858	83.0793 3841	77.2953 2413
150	99.7846 0882	94.6346 5335	89.8642 4673	83.3500 2569	77.5201 2290

Table 11 (*Continued*)

$$a_{\overline{n}|i} = \frac{1 - (1 + i)^{-n}}{i}$$

n	$\frac{7}{12}\%$	$\frac{2}{3}\%$	$\frac{3}{4}\%$	$\frac{7}{8}\%$	1%
151	100.2001 0819	95.0013 1128	90.1878 3795	83.6183 6499	77.7426 9594
152	100.6131 9786	95.3655 4100	90.5090 2029	83.8843 7670	77.9630 6529
153	101.0238 9183	95.7273 5861	90.8278 1171	84.1480 8099	78.1812 5276
154	101.4322 0397	96.0867 8008	91.1442 2998	84.4094 9788	78.3972 7996
155	101.8381 4811	96.4438 2127	91.4582 9279	84.6686 4722	78.6111 6828
156	102.2417 3797	96.7984 9795	91.7700 1765	84.9255 4867	78.8229 3889
157	102.6429 8721	97.1508 2578	92.0794 2199	85.1802 2173	79.0326 1276
158	103.0419 0941	97.5008 2031	92.3865 2307	85.4326 8573	79.2402 1065
159	103.4385 1805	97.8484 9700	92.6913 3803	85.6829 5983	79.4457 5312
160	103.8328 2656	98.1938 7119	92.9938 8390	85.9310 6303	79.6492 6052
161	104.2248 4828	98.5369 5813	93.2941 7757	86.1770 1415	79.8507 5299
162	104.6145 9647	98.8777 7298	93.5922 3580	86.4208 3187	80.0502 5048
163	105.0020 8431	99.2163 3078	93.8880 7524	86.6625 3470	80.2477 7275
164	105.3873 2491	99.5526 4647	94.1817 1239	86.9021 4096	80.4433 3936
165	105.7703 3132	99.8867 3490	94.4731 6367	87.1396 6886	80.6369 6966
166	106.1511 1647	100.2186 1083	94.7624 4533	87.3751 3642	80.8286 8284
167	106.5296 9326	100.5482 8890	95.0495 7352	87.6085 6150	81.0184 9786
168	106.9060 7449	100.8757 8368	95.3345 6429	87.8399 6184	81.2064 3352
169	107.2802 7290	101.2011 0961	95.6174 3354	88.0693 5498	81.3925 0844
170	107.6523 0114	101.5242 8107	95.8981 9706	88.2967 5835	81.5767 4103
171	108.0221 7181	101.8453 1232	96.1768 7053	88.5221 8919	81.7591 4953
172	108.3898 9741	102.1642 1754	96.4534 6951	88.7456 6462	81.9397 5201
173	108.7554 9038	102.4810 1080	96.7280 0944	88.9672 0161	82.1185 6635
174	109.1189 6309	102.7957 0609	97.0005 0565	89.1868 1696	82.2956 1025
175	109.4803 2785	103.1083 1731	97.2709 7335	89.4045 2735	82.4709 0123
176	109.8395 9687	103.4188 5826	97.5394 2764	89.6203 4929	82.6444 5667
177	110.1967 8230	103.7273 4264	97.8058 8352	89.8342 9917	82.8162 9373
178	110.5518 9624	104.0337 8408	98.0703 5585	90.0463 9323	82.9864 2944
179	110.9049 5070	104.3381 9610	98.3328 5940	90.2566 4757	83.1548 8063
180	111.2559 5761	104.6405 9216	98.5934 0884	90.4650 7813	83.3216 6399
181	111.6049 2886	104.9409 8559	98.8520 1869	90.6717 0075	83.4867 9603
182	111.9518 7625	105.2393 8966	99.1087 0342	90.8765 3110	83.6502 9310
183	112.2968 1151	105.5358 1754	99.3634 7734	91.0795 8474	83.8121 7138
184	112.6397 4633	105.8302 8232	99.6163 5468	91.2808 7706	83.9724 4691
185	112.9806 9229	106.1227 9701	99.8673 4956	91.4804 2336	84.1311 3556
186	113.3196 6093	106.4133 7451	100.1164 7599	91.6782 3877	84.2882 5303
187	113.6566 6373	106.7020 2766	100.3637 4788	91.8743 3831	84.4438 1488
188	113.9917 1207	106.9887 6920	100.6091 7904	92.0687 3686	84.5978 3651
189	114.3248 1731	107.2736 1179	100.8527 8316	92.2614 4918	84.7503 3318
190	114.6559 9069	107.5565 6800	101.0945 7386	92.4524 8989	84.9013 1998
191	114.9852 4344	107.8376 5033	101.3345 6462	92.6418 7350	85.0508 1186
192	115.3125 8668	108.1168 7119	101.5727 6886	92.8296 1438	85.1988 2363
193	115.6380 3150	108.3942 4291	101.8091 9986	93.0157 2677	85.3453 6993
194	115.9615 8890	108.6697 7772	102.0438 7083	93.2002 2480	85.4904 6528
195	116.2832 6982	108.9434 8780	102.2767 9487	93.3831 2248	85.6341 2404
196	116.6030 8516	109.2153 8523	102.5079 8498	93.5644 3368	85.7763 6043
197	116.9210 4573	109.4854 8202	102.7374 5407	93.7441 7218	85.9171 8855
198	117.2371 6228	109.7537 9009	102.9652 1496	93.9223 5160	86.0566 2232
199	117.5514 4552	110.0203 2128	103.1912 8036	94.0989 8548	86.1946 7557
200	117.8639 0606	110.2850 8736	103.4156 6289	94.2740 8721	86.3313 6195

Table 11 *(Continued)*

$$a_{\overline{n}|i} = \frac{1 - (1 + i)^{-n}}{i}$$

n	$1\frac{1}{8}\%$	$1\frac{1}{4}\%$	$1\frac{3}{8}\%$	$1\frac{1}{2}\%$	$1\frac{3}{4}\%$
1	0.9888 7515	0.9876 5432	0.9864 3650	0.9852 2167	0.9828 0098
2	1.9667 4923	1.9631 1538	1.9594 9346	1.9558 8342	1.9486 9875
3	2.9337 4460	2.9265 3371	2.9193 5237	2.9122 0042	2.8979 8403
4	3.8899 8230	3.8780 5798	3.8661 9222	3.8543 8465	3.8309 4254
5	4.8355 8200	4.8178 3504	4.8001 8962	4.7826 4497	4.7478 5508
6	5.7706 6205	5.7460 0992	5.7215 1874	5.6971 8717	5.6489 9762
7	6.6953 3948	6.6627 2585	6.6303 5140	6.5982 1396	6.5346 4139
8	7.6097 3002	7.5681 2429	7.5268 5712	7.4859 2508	7.4050 5297
9	8.5139 4810	8.4623 4498	8.4112 0308	8.3605 1732	8.2604 9432
10	9.4081 0690	9.3455 2591	9.2835 5421	9.2221 8455	9.1012 2291
11	10.2923 1832	10.2178 0337	10.1440 7320	10.0711 1779	9.9274 9181
12	11.1666 9302	11.0793 1197	10.9929 2054	10.9075 0521	10.7395 4969
13	12.0313 4044	11.9301 8466	11.8302 5454	11.7315 3222	11.5376 4097
14	12.8863 6880	12.7705 5275	12.6562 3136	12.5433 8150	12.3220 0587
15	13.7318 8509	13.6005 4592	13.4710 0504	13.3432 3301	13.0928 8046
16	14.5679 9514	14.4202 9227	14.2747 2754	14.1312 6405	13.8504 9677
17	15.3948 0360	15.2299 1829	15.0675 4874	14.9076 4931	14.5950 8282
18	16.2124 1395	16.0295 4893	15.8496 1651	15.6725 6089	15.3268 6272
19	17.0209 2850	16.8193 0759	16.6210 7671	16.4261 6837	16.0460 5673
20	17.8204 4845	17.5993 1613	17.3820 7320	17.1686 3879	16.7528 8130
21	18.6110 7387	18.3696 9495	18.1327 4792	17.9001 3673	17.4475 4919
22	19.3929 0371	19.1305 6291	18.8732 4086	18.6208 2437	18.1302 6948
23	20.1660 3580	19.8820 3744	19.6036 9012	19.3308 6145	18.8012 4764
24	20.9305 6693	20.6242 3451	20.3242 3193	20.0304 0537	19.4606 8565
25	21.6865 9276	21.3572 6865	21.0350 0067	20.7196 1120	20.1087 8196
26	22.4342 0792	22.0812 5299	21.7361 2890	21.3986 3172	20.7457 3166
27	23.1735 0598	22.7962 9925	22.4277 4737	22.0676 1746	21.3717 2644
28	23.9045 7946	23.5025 1778	23.1099 8508	22.7267 1671	21.9869 5474
29	24.6275 1986	24.2000 1756	23.7829 6925	23.3760 7558	22.5916 0171
30	25.3424 1766	24.8889 0623	24.4468 2540	24.0158 3801	23.1858 4934
31	26.0493 6233	25.5692 9010	25.1016 7734	24.6461 4582	23.7698 7650
32	26.7484 4236	26.2412 7418	25.7476 4719	25.2671 3874	24.3438 5897
33	27.4397 4522	26.9049 6215	26.3848 5543	25.8789 5442	24.9079 6951
34	28.1233 5745	27.5604 5644	27.0134 2089	26.4817 2849	25.4623 7789
35	28.7993 6460	28.2078 5822	27.6334 6080	27.0755 9458	26.0072 5100
36	29.4678 5127	28.8472 6737	28.2450 9080	27.6606 8431	26.5427 5283
37	30.1289 0114	29.4787 8259	28.8484 2496	28.2371 2740	27.0690 4455
38	30.7825 9692	30.1025 0133	29.4435 7579	28.8050 5163	27.5862 8457
39	31.4290 2044	30.7185 1983	30.0306 5430	29.3645 8288	28.0946 2857
40	32.0682 5260	31.3269 3316	30.6097 6996	29.9158 4520	28.5942 2955
41	32.7003 7340	31.9278 3522	31.1810 3079	30.4589 6079	29.0852 3789
42	33.3254 6195	32.5213 1874	31.7445 4332	30.9940 5004	29.5678 0136
43	33.9435 9649	33.1074 7530	32.3004 1264	31.5212 3157	30.0420 6522
44	34.5548 5438	33.6863 9536	32.8487 4243	32.0406 2223	30.5081 7221
45	35.1593 1212	34.2581 6825	33.3896 3495	32.5523 3718	30.9662 6261
46	35.7570 4536	34.8228 8222	33.9231 9108	33.0564 8983	31.4164 7431
47	36.3481 2891	35.3806 2442	34.4495 1031	33.5531 9195	31.8589 4281
48	36.9326 3674	35.9314 8091	34.9686 9081	34.0425 5365	32.2938 0129
49	37.5106 4202	36.4755 3670	35.4808 2941	34.5246 8339	32.7211 8063
50	38.0822 1708	37.0128 7575	35.9860 2161	34.9996 8807	33.1412 0946

Table 11 (*Continued*)

$$a_{\overline{n}|i} = \frac{1 - (1 + i)^{-n}}{i}$$

n	$1\frac{1}{8}\%$	$1\frac{1}{4}\%$	$1\frac{3}{8}\%$	$1\frac{1}{2}\%$	$1\frac{3}{4}\%$
51	38.6474 3345	37.5435 8099	36.4843 6164	35.4676 7298	33.5540 1421
52	39.2063 6188	38.0677 3431	36.9759 4243	35.9287 4185	33.9597 1913
53	39.7590 7232	38.5854 1660	37.4608 5566	36.3829 9690	34.3584 4632
54	40.3056 3394	39.0967 0776	37.9391 9178	36.8305 3882	34.7503 1579
55	40.8461 1514	39.6016 8667	38.4110 3998	37.2714 6681	35.1354 4550
56	41.3805 8358	40.1004 3128	38.8764 8826	37.7058 7863	35.5139 5135
57	41.9091 0613	40.5930 1855	39.3356 2344	38.1338 7058	35.8859 4727
58	42.4317 4896	41.0795 2449	39.7885 3114	38.5555 3751	36.2515 4523
59	42.9485 7746	41.5600 2419	40.2352 9582	38.9709 7292	36.6108 5526
60	43.4596 5633	42.0345 9179	40.6760 0081	39.3802 6889	36.9639 8552
61	43.9650 4952	42.5033 0054	41.1107 2829	39.7835 1614	37.3110 4228
62	44.4648 2029	42.9662 2275	41.5395 5935	40.1808 0408	37.6521 3000
63	44.9590 3119	43.4234 2988	41.9625 7396	40.5722 2077	37.9873 5135
64	45.4477 4407	43.8749 9247	42.3798 5101	40.9578 5298	38.3168 0723
65	45.9310 2009	44.3209 8022	42.7914 6832	41.3377 8618	38.6405 9678
66	46.4089 1975	44.7614 6195	43.1975 0266	41.7121 0461	38.9588 1748
67	46.8815 0284	45.1965 0563	43.5980 2975	42.0808 9125	39.2715 6509
68	47.3488 2852	45.6261 7840	43.9931 2429	42.4442 2783	39.5789 3375
69	47.8109 5527	46.0505 4656	44.3828 5997	42.8021 9490	39.8810 1597
70	48.2679 4094	46.4696 7562	44.7673 0946	43.1548 7183	40.1779 0267
71	48.7198 4270	46.8836 3024	45.1465 4448	43.5023 3678	40.4696 8321
72	49.1667 1714	47.2924 7431	45.5206 3573	43.8446 6677	40.7564 4542
73	49.6086 2016	47.6962 7093	45.8896 5300	44.1819 3771	41.0382 7560
74	50.0456 0708	48.0950 8240	46.2536 6511	44.5142 2434	41.3152 5857
75	50.4777 3259	48.4889 7027	46.6127 3994	44.8416 0034	41.5874 7771
76	50.9050 5077	48.8779 9533	46.9669 4445	45.1641 3826	41.8550 1495
77	51.3276 1510	49.2622 1761	47.3163 4471	45.4819 0962	42.1179 5081
78	51.7454 7847	49.6416 9640	47.6610 0588	45.7949 8485	42.3763 6443
79	52.1586 9317	50.0164 9027	48.0009 9224	46.1034 3335	42.6303 3359
80	52.5673 1092	50.3866 5706	48.3363 6719	46.4073 2349	42.8799 3474
81	52.9713 8286	50.7522 5389	48.6671 9328	46.7067 2265	43.1252 4298
82	53.3709 5957	51.1133 3717	48.9935 3221	47.0016 9720	43.3663 3217
83	53.7660 9104	51.4699 6264	49.3154 4484	47.2923 1251	43.6032 7486
84	54.1568 2674	51.8221 8532	49.6329 9122	47.5786 3301	43.8361 4237
85	54.5432 1557	52.1700 5958	49.9462 3055	47.8607 2218	44.0650 0479
86	54.9253 0588	52.5136 3909	50.2552 2125	48.1386 4254	44.2899 3099
87	55.3031 4549	52.8529 7688	50.5600 2096	48.4124 5571	44.5109 8869
88	55.6767 8169	53.1881 2531	50.8606 8653	48.6822 2237	44.7282 4441
89	56.0462 6126	53.5191 3611	51.1572 7401	48.9480 0234	44.9417 6355
90	56.4116 3041	53.8460 6035	51.4498 3873	49.2098 5452	45.1516 1037
91	56.7729 3490	54.1689 4850	51.7384 3524	49.4678 3696	45.3578 4803
92	57.1302 1992	54.4878 5037	52.0231 1738	49.7220 0686	45.5605 3861
93	57.4835 3021	54.8028 1518	52.3039 3823	49.9724 2055	45.7597 4310
94	57.8329 0997	55.1138 9154	52.5809 5016	50.2191 3355	45.9555 2147
95	58.1784 0294	55.4211 2744	52.8542 0484	50.4622 0054	46.1479 3265
96	58.5200 5235	55.7245 7031	53.1237 5324	50.7016 7541	46.3370 3455
97	58.8579 0096	56.0242 6698	53.3896 4561	50.9376 1124	46.5228 8408
98	59.1919 9106	56.3202 6368	53.6519 3155	51.1700 6034	46.7055 3718
99	59.5223 6446	56.6126 0610	53.9106 5998	51.3990 7422	46.8850 4882
100	59.8490 6251	56.9013 3936	54.1658 7914	51.6247 0367	47.0614 7304

Table 11　(*Continued*)

$$a_{\overline{n}|i} = \frac{1 - (1 + i)^{-n}}{i}$$

n	2%	2¼%	2½%	2¾%	3%
1	0.9803 9216	0.9779 9511	0.9756 0976	0.9732 3601	0.9708 7379
2	1.9415 6094	1.9344 6955	1.9274 2415	1.9204 2434	1.9134 6970
3	2.8838 8327	2.8698 9687	2.8560 2356	2.8422 6213	2.8286 1135
4	3.8077 2870	3.7847 4021	3.7619 7421	3.7394 2787	3.7170 9840
5	4.7134 5951	4.6794 5253	4.6458 2850	4.6125 8186	4.5797 0719
6	5.6014 3089	5.5544 7680	5.5081 2536	5.4623 6678	5.4171 9144
7	6.4719 9107	6.4102 4626	6.3493 9060	6.2894 0806	6.2302 8296
8	7.3254 8144	7.2471 8461	7.1701 3717	7.0943 1441	7.0196 9219
9	8.1622 3671	8.0657 0622	7.9708 6553	7.8776 7826	7.7861 0892
10	8.9825 8501	8.8662 1635	8.7520 6393	8.6400 7616	8.5302 0284
11	9.7868 4805	9.6491 1134	9.5142 0871	9.3820 6926	9.2526 2411
12	10.5753 4122	10.4147 7882	10.2577 6460	10.1042 0366	9.9540 0399
13	11.3483 7375	11.1635 9787	10.9831 8497	10.8070 1086	10.6349 5533
14	12.1062 4877	11.8959 3924	11.6909 1217	11.4910 0814	11.2960 7314
15	12.8492 6350	12.6121 6551	12.3813 7773	12.1566 9892	11.9379 3509
16	13.5777 0931	13.3126 3131	13.0550 0266	12.8045 7315	12.5611 0203
17	14.2918 7188	13.9976 8343	13.7121 9772	13.4351 0769	13.1661 1847
18	14.9920 3125	14.6676 6106	14.3533 6363	14.0487 6661	13.7535 1308
19	15.6784 6201	15.3228 9590	14.9788 9134	14.6460 0157	14.3237 9911
20	16.3514 3334	15.9637 1237	15.5891 6229	15.2272 5213	14.8774 7486
21	17.0112 0916	16.5904 2775	16.1845 4857	15.7929 4612	15.4150 2414
22	17.6580 4820	17.2033 5232	16.7654 1324	16.3434 9987	15.9369 1664
23	18.2922 0412	17.8027 8955	17.3321 1048	16.8793 1861	16.4436 0839
24	18.9139 2560	18.3890 3624	17.8849 8583	17.4007 9670	16.9355 4212
25	19.5234 5647	18.9623 8263	18.4243 7642	17.9083 1795	17.4131 4769
26	20.1210 3576	19.5231 1260	18.9506 1114	18.4022 5592	17.8768 4242
27	20.7068 9780	20.0715 0376	19.4640 1087	18.8829 7413	18.3270 3147
28	21.2812 7236	20.6078 2764	19.9648 8866	19.3508 2640	18.7641 0823
29	21.8443 8466	21.1323 4977	20.4535 4991	19.8061 5708	19.1884 5459
30	22.3964 5555	21.6453 2985	20.9302 9259	20.2493 0130	19.6004 4135
31	22.9377 0152	22.1470 2186	21.3954 0741	20.6805 8520	20.0004 2849
32	23.4683 3482	22.6376 7419	21.8491 7796	21.1003 2623	20.3887 6553
33	23.9885 6355	23.1175 2977	22.2918 8094	21.5088 3332	20.7657 9178
34	24.4985 9172	23.5868 2618	22.7237 8628	21.9064 0712	21.1318 3668
35	24.9986 1933	24.0457 9577	23.1451 5734	22.2933 4026	21.4872 2007
36	25.4888 4248	24.4946 6579	23.5562 5107	22.6699 1753	21.8322 5250
37	25.9694 5341	24.9336 5848	23.9573 1812	23.0364 1609	22.1672 3544
38	26.4406 4060	25.3629 9118	24.3486 0304	23.3931 0568	22.4924 6159
39	26.9025 8883	25.7828 7646	24.7303 4443	23.7402 4884	22.8082 1513
40	27.3554 7924	26.1935 2221	25.1027 7505	24.0781 0106	23.1147 7197
41	27.7994 8945	26.5951 3174	25.4661 2200	24.4069 1101	23.4123 9997
42	28.2347 9358	26.9879 0390	25.8206 0683	24.7269 2069	23.7013 5920
43	28.6615 6233	27.3720 3316	26.1664 4569	25.0383 6563	23.9819 0213
44	29.0799 6307	27.7477 0969	26.5038 4945	25.3414 7507	24.2542 7392
45	29.4901 5987	28.1151 1950	26.8330 2386	25.6364 7209	24.5187 1254
46	29.8923 1360	28.4744 4450	27.1541 6962	25.9235 7381	24.7754 4907
47	30.2865 8196	28.8258 6259	27.4674 8255	26.2029 9154	25.0247 0783
48	30.6731 1957	29.1695 4777	27.7731 5371	26.4749 3094	25.2667 0664
49	31.0520 7801	29.5056 7019	28.0713 6947	26.7395 9215	25.5016 5693
50	31.4236 0589	29.8343 9627	28.3623 1168	26.9971 6998	25.7297 6401

Table 11 *(Continued)*

$$a_{\overline{n}|i} = \frac{1 - (1 + i)^{-n}}{i}$$

n	2%	$2\frac{1}{4}\%$	$2\frac{1}{2}\%$	$2\frac{3}{4}\%$	3%
51	31.7878 4892	30.1558 8877	28.6461 5774	27.2478 5400	25.9512 2719
52	32.1449 4992	30.4703 0687	28.9230 8072	27.4918 2871	26.1662 3999
53	32.4950 4894	30.7778 0623	29.1932 4948	27.7292 7368	26.3749 9028
54	32.8382 8327	31.0785 3910	29.4568 2876	27.9603 6368	26.5776 6047
55	33.1747 8752	31.3726 5438	29.7139 7928	28.1852 6879	26.7744 2764
56	33.5046 9365	31.6602 9768	29.9648 5784	28.4041 5454	26.9654 6373
57	33.8281 3103	31.9416 1142	30.2096 1740	28.6171 8203	27.1509 3566
58	34.1452 2650	32.2167 3489	30.4484 0722	28.8245 0806	27.3310 0549
59	34.4561 0441	32.4858 0429	30.6813 7290	29.0262 8522	27.5058 3058
60	34.7608 8668	32.7489 5285	30.9086 5649	29.2226 6201	27.6755 6367
61	35.0596 9282	33.0063 1086	31.1303 9657	29.4137 8298	27.8403 5307
62	35.3526 4002	33.2580 0573	31.3467 2836	29.5997 8879	28.0003 4279
63	35.6398 4316	33.5041 6208	31.5577 8377	29.7808 1634	28.1556 7261
64	35.9214 1486	33.7449 0179	31.7636 9148	29.9569 9887	28.3064 7826
65	36.1974 6555	33.9803 4405	31.9645 7705	30.1284 6605	28.4528 9152
66	36.4681 0348	34.2106 0543	32.1605 6298	30.2953 4409	28.5950 4031
67	36.7334 3478	34.4357 9993	32.3517 6876	30.4577 5581	28.7330 4884
68	36.9935 6351	34.6560 3905	32.5383 1099	30.6158 2074	28.8670 3771
69	37.2485 9168	34.8714 3183	32.7203 0340	30.7696 5522	28.9971 2399
70	37.4986 1929	35.0820 8492	32.8978 5698	30.9193 7247	29.1234 2135
71	37.7437 4441	35.2881 0261	33.0710 7998	31.0650 8270	29.2460 4015
72	37.9840 6314	35.4895 8691	33.2400 7803	31.2068 9314	29.3650 8752
73	38.2196 6975	35.6866 3756	33.4049 5417	31.3449 0816	29.4806 6750
74	38.4506 5662	35.8793 5214	33.5658 0895	31.4792 2936	29.5928 8107
75	38.6771 1433	36.0678 2605	33.7227 4044	31.6099 5558	29.7018 2628
76	38.8991 3170	36.2521 5262	33.8758 4433	31.7371 8304	29.8075 9833
77	39.1167 9578	36.4324 2310	34.0252 1398	31.8610 0540	29.9102 8964
78	39.3301 9194	36.6087 2675	34.1709 4047	31.9815 1377	30.0099 8994
79	39.5394 0386	36.7811 5085	34.3131 1265	32.0987 9685	30.1067 8635
80	39.7445 1359	36.9497 8079	34.4518 1722	32.2129 4098	30.2007 6345
81	39.9456 0156	37.1147 0004	34.5871 3875	32.3240 3015	30.2920 0335
82	40.1427 4663	37.2759 9026	34.7191 5976	32.4321 4613	30.3805 8577
83	40.3360 2611	37.4337 3130	34.8479 6074	32.5373 6850	30.4665 8813
84	40.5255 1579	37.5880 0127	34.9736 2023	32.6397 7469	30.5500 8556
85	40.7112 8999	37.7388 7655	35.0962 1486	32.7394 4009	30.6311 5103
86	40.8934 2156	37.8864 3183	35.2158 1938	32.8364 3804	30.7098 5537
87	41.0719 8192	38.0307 4018	35.3325 0671	32.9308 3994	30.7862 6735
88	41.2470 4110	38.1718 7304	35.4463 4801	33.0227 1527	30.8604 5374
89	41.4186 6774	38.3099 0028	35.5574 1269	33.1121 3165	30.9324 7936
90	41.5869 2916	38.4448 9025	35.6657 6848	33.1991 5489	31.0024 0714
91	41.7518 9133	38.5769 0978	35.7714 8144	33.2838 4905	31.0702 9820
92	41.9136 1895	38.7060 2423	35.8746 1604	33.3662 7644	31.1362 1184
93	42.0721 7545	38.8322 9754	35.9752 3516	33.4464 9776	31.2002 0567
94	42.2276 2299	38.9557 9221	36.0734 0016	33.5245 7202	31.2623 3560
95	42.3800 2254	39.0765 6940	36.1691 7089	33.6005 5671	31.3226 5592
96	42.5294 3386	39.1946 8890	36.2626 0574	33.6745 0775	31.3812 1934
97	42.6759 1555	39.3102 0920	36.3537 6170	33.7464 7956	31.4380 7703
98	42.8195 2505	39.4231 8748	36.4426 9434	33.8165 2512	31.4932 7867
99	42.9603 1867	39.5336 7968	36.5294 5790	33.8846 9598	31.5468 7250
100	43.0983 5164	39.6417 4052	36.6141 0526	33.9510 4232	31.5989 0534

Table 11   *(Continued)*

$$a_{\overline{n}|i} = \frac{1 - (1 + i)^{-n}}{i}$$

n	$3\frac{1}{2}\%$	4%	$4\frac{1}{2}\%$	5%	$5\frac{1}{2}\%$
1	0.9661 8357	0.9615 3846	0.9569 3780	0.9523 8095	0.9478 6730
2	1.8996 9428	1.8860 9467	1.8726 6775	1.8594 1043	1.8463 1971
3	2.8016 3698	2.7750 9103	2.7489 6435	2.7232 4803	2.6979 3338
4	3.6730 7921	3.6298 9522	3.5875 2570	3.5459 5050	3.5051 5012
5	4.5150 5238	4.4518 2233	4.3899 7674	4.3294 7667	4.2702 8448
6	5.3285 5302	5.2421 3686	5.1578 7248	5.0756 9207	4.9955 3031
7	6.1145 4398	6.0020 5467	5.8927 0094	5.7863 7340	5.6829 6712
8	6.8739 5554	6.7327 4487	6.5958 8607	6.4632 1276	6.3345 6599
9	7.6076 8651	7.4353 3161	7.2687 9050	7.1078 2168	6.9521 9525
10	8.3166 0532	8.1108 9578	7.9127 1818	7.7217 3493	7.5376 2583
11	9.0015 5104	8.7604 7671	8.5289 1692	8.3064 1422	8.0925 3633
12	9.6633 3433	9.3850 7376	9.1185 8078	8.8632 5164	8.6185 1785
13	10.3027 3849	9.9856 4785	9.6828 5242	9.3935 7299	9.1170 7853
14	10.9205 2028	10.5631 2293	10.2228 2528	9.8986 4094	9.5896 4790
15	11.5174 1090	11.1183 8743	10.7395 4573	10.3796 5804	10.0375 8094
16	12.0941 1681	11.6522 9561	11.2340 1505	10.8377 6956	10.4621 6203
17	12.6513 2059	12.1656 6885	11.7071 9143	11.2740 6625	10.8646 0856
18	13.1896 8173	12.6592 9697	12.1599 9180	11.6895 8690	11.2460 7447
19	13.7098 3742	13.1339 3940	12.5932 9359	12.0853 2086	11.6076 5352
20	14.2124 0330	13.5903 2634	13.0079 3645	12.4622 1034	11.9503 8248
21	14.6979 7420	14.0291 5995	13.4047 2388	12.8211 5271	12.2752 4406
22	15.1671 2484	14.4511 1533	13.7844 2476	13.1630 0258	12.5831 6973
23	15.6204 1047	14.8568 4167	14.1477 7489	13.4885 7388	12.8750 4239
24	16.0583 6760	15.2469 6314	14.4954 7837	13.7986 4179	13.1516 9895
25	16.4815 1459	15.6220 7994	14.8282 0896	14.0939 4457	13.4139 3266
26	16.8903 5226	15.9827 6918	15.1466 1145	14.3751 8530	13.6624 9541
27	17.2853 6451	16.3295 8575	15.4513 0282	14.6430 3362	13.8980 9991
28	17.6670 1885	16.6630 6322	15.7428 7351	14.8981 2726	14.1214 2172
29	18.0357 6700	16.9837 1463	16.0218 8853	15.1410 7358	14.3331 0116
30	18.3920 4541	17.2920 3330	16.2888 8854	15.3724 5103	14.5337 4517
31	18.7362 7576	17.5884 9356	16.5443 9095	15.5928 1050	14.7239 2907
32	19.0688 6547	17.8735 5150	16.7888 9086	15.8026 7667	14.9041 9817
33	19.3902 0818	18.1476 4567	17.0228 6207	16.0025 4921	15.0750 6936
34	19.7006 8423	18.4111 9776	17.2467 5796	16.1929 0401	15.2370 3257
35	20.0006 6110	18.6646 1323	17.4610 1240	16.3741 9429	15.3905 5220
36	20.2904 9381	18.9082 8195	17.6660 4058	16.5468 5171	15.5360 6843
37	20.5705 2542	19.1425 7880	17.8622 3979	16.7112 8734	15.6739 9851
38	20.8410 8736	19.3678 6423	18.0499 9023	16.8678 9271	15.8047 3793
39	21.1024 9987	19.5844 8484	18.2296 5572	17.0170 4067	15.9286 6154
40	21.3550 7234	19.7927 7388	18.4015 8442	17.1590 8635	16.0461 2469
41	21.5991 0371	19.9930 5181	18.5661 0949	17.2943 6796	16.1574 6416
42	21.8348 8281	20.1856 2674	18.7235 4975	17.4232 0758	16.2629 9920
43	22.0626 8870	20.3707 9494	18.8742 1029	17.5459 1198	16.3630 3242
44	22.2827 9102	20.5488 4129	19.0183 8305	17.6627 7331	16.4578 5063
45	22.4954 5026	20.7200 3970	19.1563 4742	17.7740 6982	16.5477 2572
46	22.7009 1813	20.8846 5356	19.2883 7074	17.8800 6650	16.6329 1537
47	22.8994 3780	21.0429 3612	19.4147 0884	17.9810 1571	16.7136 6386
48	23.0912 4425	21.1951 3088	19.5356 0654	18.0771 5782	16.7902 0271
49	23.2765 6450	21.3414 7200	19.6512 9813	18.1687 2173	16.8627 5139
50	23.4556 1787	21.4821 8462	19.7620 0778	18.2559 2546	16.9315 1790

Table 11 $(Continued)$

$$a_{\overline{n}|i} = \frac{1 - (1 + i)^{-n}}{i}$$

n	3½ %	4 %	4½ %	5 %	5½ %
51	23.6286 1630	21.6174 8521	19.8679 5003	18.3389 7663	16.9966 9943
52	23.7957 6454	21.7475 8193	19.9693 3017	18.4180 7298	17.0584 8287
53	23.9572 6043	21.8726 7493	20.0663 4466	18.4934 0284	17.1170 4538
54	24.1132 9510	21.9929 5667	20.1591 8149	18.5651 4556	17.1725 5486
55	24.2640 5323	22.1086 1218	20.2480 2057	18.6334 7196	17.2251 7048
56	24.4097 1327	22.2198 1940	20.3330 3404	18.6985 4473	17.2750 4311
57	24.5504 4760	22.3267 4943	20.4143 8664	18.7605 1879	17.3223 1575
58	24.6864 2281	22.4295 6676	20.4922 3602	18.8195 4170	17.3671 2393
59	24.8177 9981	22.5284 2957	20.5667 3303	18.8757 5400	17.4095 9614
60	24.9447 3412	22.6234 8997	20.6380 2204	18.9292 8953	17.4498 5416
61	25.0673 7596	22.7148 9421	20.7062 4118	18.9802 7574	17.4880 1343
62	25.1858 7049	22.8027 8289	20.7715 2266	19.0288 3404	17.5241 8334
63	25.3003 5796	22.8872 9124	20.8339 9298	19.0750 8003	17.5584 6762
64	25.4109 7388	22.9685 4927	20.8937 7319	19.1191 2384	17.5909 6457
65	25.5178 4916	23.0466 8199	20.9509 7913	19.1610 7033	17.6217 6737
66	25.6211 1030	23.1218 0961	21.0057 2165	19.2010 1936	17.6509 6433
67	25.7208 7951	23.1940 4770	21.0581 0684	19.2390 6606	17.6786 3917
68	25.8172 7489	23.2635 0740	21.1082 3621	19.2753 0101	17.7048 7125
69	25.9104 1052	23.3302 9558	21.1562 0690	19.3098 1048	17.7297 3579
70	26.0003 9664	23.3945 1498	21.2021 1187	19.3426 7665	17.7533 0406
71	26.0873 3975	23.4562 6440	21.2460 4007	19.3739 7776	17.7756 4366
72	26.1713 4275	23.5156 3885	21.2880 7662	19.4037 8834	17.7968 1864
73	26.2525 0508	23.5727 2966	21.3283 0298	19.4321 7937	17.8168 8970
74	26.3309 2278	23.6276 2468	21.3667 9711	19.4592 1845	17.8359 1441
75	26.4066 8868	23.6804 0834	21.4036 3360	19.4849 6995	17.8539 4731
76	26.4798 9244	23.7311 6187	21.4388 8383	19.5094 9519	17.8710 4010
77	26.5506 2072	23.7799 6333	21.4726 1611	19.5328 5257	17.8872 4180
78	26.6189 5721	23.8268 8782	21.5048 9579	19.5550 9768	17.9025 9887
79	26.6849 8281	23.8720 0752	21.5357 8545	19.5762 8351	17.9171 5532
80	26.7487 7567	23.9153 9185	21.5653 4493	19.5964 6048	17.9309 5291
81	26.8104 1127	23.9571 0754	21.5936 3151	19.6156 7665	17.9440 3120
82	26.8699 6258	23.9972 1879	21.6207 0001	19.6339 7776	17.9564 2767
83	26.9275 0008	24.0357 8730	21.6466 0288	19.6514 0739	17.9681 7789
84	26.9830 9186	24.0728 7240	21.6713 9032	19.6680 0704	17.9793 1554
85	27.0368 0373	24.1085 3116	21.6951 1035	19.6838 1623	17.9898 7255
86	27.0886 9926	24.1428 1842	21.7178 0895	19.6988 7260	17.9998 7919
87	27.1388 3986	24.1757 8694	21.7395 3009	19.7132 1200	18.0093 6416
88	27.1872 8489	24.2074 8745	21.7603 1588	19.7268 6857	18.0183 5466
89	27.2340 9168	24.2379 6870	21.7802 0658	19.7398 7483	18.0268 7645
90	27.2793 1564	24.2672 7759	21.7992 4075	19.7522 6174	18.0349 5398
91	27.3230 1028	24.2954 5923	21.8174 5526	19.7640 5880	18.0426 1041
92	27.3652 2732	24.3225 5695	21.8348 8542	19.7752 9410	18.0498 6769
93	27.4060 1673	24.3486 1245	21.8515 6499	19.7859 9438	18.0567 4662
94	27.4454 2680	24.3736 6582	21.8675 2631	19.7961 8512	18.0632 6694
95	27.4835 0415	24.3977 5559	21.8828 0030	19.8058 9059	18.0694 4734
96	27.5202 9387	24.4209 1884	21.8974 1655	19.8151 3390	18.0753 0553
97	27.5558 3948	24.4431 9119	21.9114 0340	19.8239 3705	18.0808 5833
98	27.5901 8308	24.4646 0692	21.9247 8794	19.8323 2100	18.0861 2164
99	27.6233 6529	24.4851 9896	21.9375 9612	19.8403 0571	18.0911 1055
100	27.6554 2540	24.5049 9900	21.9498 5274	19.8479 1020	18.0958 3939

Table 11   *(Continued)*

$$a_{\overline{n}|i} = \frac{1 - (1 + i)^{-n}}{i}$$

n	6 %	6½ %	7 %	7½ %	8 %
1	0.9433 9623	0.9389 6714	0.9345 7944	0.9302 3256	0.9259 2593
2	1.8333 9267	1.8206 2642	1.8080 1817	1.7955 6517	1.7832 6475
3	2.6730 1195	2.6484 7551	2.6243 1604	2.6005 2574	2.5770 9699
4	3.4651 0561	3.4257 9860	3.3872 1126	3.3493 2627	3.3121 2684
5	4.2123 6379	4.1556 7944	4.1001 9744	4.0458 8490	3.9927 1004
6	4.9173 2433	4.8410 1356	4.7665 3966	4.6938 4642	4.6228 7966
7	5.5823 8144	5.4845 1977	5.3892 8940	5.2966 0132	5.2063 7006
8	6.2097 9381	6.0887 5096	5.9712 9851	5.8573 0355	5.7466 3894
9	6.8016 9227	6.6561 0419	6.5152 3225	6.3788 8703	6.2468 8791
10	7.3600 8705	7.1888 3022	7.0235 8154	6.8640 8096	6.7100 8140
11	7.8868 7458	7.6890 4246	7.4986 7434	7.3154 2415	7.1389 6426
12	8.3838 4394	8.1587 2532	7.9426 8630	7.7352 7827	7.5360 7802
13	8.8526 8296	8.5997 4208	8.3576 5074	8.1258 4026	7.9037 7594
14	9.2949 8393	9.0138 4233	8.7454 6799	8.4891 5373	8.2442 3698
15	9.7122 4899	9.4026 6885	9.1079 1401	8.8271 1974	8.5594 7869
16	10.1058 9527	9.7677 6418	9.4466 4860	9.1415 0674	8.8513 6916
17	10.4772 5969	10.1105 7670	9.7632 2299	9.4339 5976	9.1216 3811
18	10.8276 0348	10.4324 6638	10.0590 8691	9.7060 0908	9.3718 8714
19	11.1581 1649	10.7347 1022	10.3355 9524	9.9590 7821	9.6035 9920
20	11.4699 2122	11.0185 0725	10.5940 1425	10.1944 9136	9.8181 4741
21	11.7640 7662	11.2849 8333	10.8355 2733	10.4134 8033	10.0168 0316
22	12.0415 8172	11.5351 9562	11.0612 4050	10.6171 9101	10.2007 4366
23	12.3033 7898	11.7701 3673	11.2721 8738	10.8066 8931	10.3710 5895
24	12.5503 5753	11.9907 3871	11.4693 3400	10.9829 6680	10.5287 5828
25	12.7833 5616	12.1978 7673	11.6535 8318	11.1469 4586	10.6747 7619
26	13.0031 6619	12.3923 7251	11.8257 7867	11.2994 8452	10.8099 7795
27	13.2105 3414	12.5749 9766	11.9867 0904	11.4413 8095	10.9351 6477
28	13.4061 6428	12.7464 7668	12.1371 1125	11.5733 7763	11.0510 7849
29	13.5907 2102	12.9074 8984	12.2776 7407	11.6961 6524	11.1584 0601
30	13.7648 3115	13.0586 7591	12.4090 4118	11.8103 8627	11.2577 8334
31	13.9290 8599	13.2006 3465	12.5318 1419	11.9166 3839	11.3497 9939
32	14.0840 4339	13.3339 2925	12.6465 5532	12.0154 7757	11.4349 9944
33	14.2302 2961	13.4590 8850	12.7537 9002	12.1074 2099	11.5138 8837
34	14.3681 4114	13.5766 0892	12.8540 0936	12.1929 4976	11.5869 3367
35	14.4982 4636	13.6869 5673	12.9476 7230	12.2725 1141	11.6545 6822
36	14.6209 8713	13.7905 6970	13.0352 0776	12.3465 2224	11.7171 9279
37	14.7367 8031	13.8878 5887	13.1170 1660	12.4153 6952	11.7751 7851
38	14.8460 1916	13.9792 1021	13.1934 7345	12.4794 1351	11.8288 6899
39	14.9490 7468	14.0649 8611	13.2649 2846	12.5389 8931	11.8785 8240
40	15.0462 9687	14.1455 2687	13.3317 0884	12.5944 0866	11.9246 1333
41	15.1380 1592	14.2211 5199	13.3941 2041	12.6459 6155	11.9672 3457
42	15.2245 4332	14.2921 6149	13.4524 4898	12.6939 1772	12.0066 9867
43	15.3061 7294	14.3588 3708	13.5069 6167	12.7385 2811	12.0432 3951
44	15.3831 8202	14.4214 4327	13.5579 0810	12.7800 2615	12.0770 7362
45	15.4558 3209	14.4802 2842	13.6055 2159	12.8186 2898	12.1084 0150
46	15.5243 6990	14.5354 2575	13.6500 2018	12.8545 3858	12.1374 0880
47	15.5890 2821	14.5872 5422	13.6916 0764	12.8879 4287	12.1642 6741
48	15.6500 2661	14.6359 1946	13.7304 7443	12.9190 1662	12.1891 3649
49	15.7075 7227	14.6816 1451	13.7667 9853	12.9479 2244	12.2121 6341
50	15.7618 6064	14.7245 2067	13.8007 4629	12.9748 1157	12.2334 8464

Table 11 (Continued)

$$a_{\overline{n}|i} = \frac{1 - (1 + i)^{-n}}{i}$$

n	$8\frac{1}{2}\%$	9%	$9\frac{1}{2}\%$	10%	$10\frac{1}{2}\%$
1	0.9216 5899	0.9174 3119	0.9132 4201	0.9090 9091	0.9049 7738
2	1.7711 1427	1.7591 1119	1.7472 5298	1.7355 3719	1.7239 6143
3	2.5540 2237	2.5312 9467	2.5089 0683	2.4868 5199	2.4651 2346
4	3.2755 9666	3.2397 1988	3.2044 8112	3.1698 6545	3.1358 5834
5	3.9406 4208	3.8896 5126	3.8397 0879	3.7907 8677	3.7428 5822
6	4.5535 8717	4.4859 1859	4.4198 2538	4.3552 6070	4.2921 7939
7	5.1185 1352	5.0329 5284	4.9496 1222	4.8684 1882	4.7893 0261
8	5.6391 8297	5.5348 1911	5.4334 3581	5.3349 2620	5.2391 8789
9	6.1190 6264	5.9952 4689	5.8752 8385	5.7590 2382	5.6463 2388
10	6.5613 4806	6.4176 5770	6.2787 9803	6.1445 6711	6.0147 7274
11	6.9689 8439	6.8051 9055	6.6473 0414	6.4950 6101	6.3482 1062
12	7.3446 8607	7.1607 2528	6.9838 3940	6.8136 9182	6.6499 6437
13	7.6909 5490	7.4869 0392	7.2911 7753	7.1033 5620	6.9230 4468
14	8.0100 9668	7.7861 5039	7.5718 5163	7.3666 8746	7.1701 7618
15	8.3042 3658	8.0606 8843	7.8281 7500	7.6060 7951	7.3938 2459
16	8.5753 3325	8.3125 5819	8.0622 6028	7.8237 0864	7.5962 2135
17	8.8251 9194	8.5436 3137	8.2760 3678	8.0215 5331	7.7793 8584
18	9.0554 7644	8.7556 2511	8.4712 6647	8.2014 1210	7.9451 4556
19	9.2677 2022	8.9501 1478	8.6495 5842	8.3649 2009	8.0951 5435
20	9.4633 3661	9.1285 4567	8.8123 8212	8.5135 6372	8.2309 0891
21	9.6436 2821	9.2922 4373	8.9610 7956	8.6486 9429	8.3537 6372
22	9.8097 9559	9.4424 2544	9.0968 7631	8.7715 4026	8.4649 4455
23	9.9629 4524	9.5802 0683	9.2208 9161	8.8832 1842	8.5655 6067
24	10.1040 9700	9.7066 1177	9.3341 4759	8.9847 4402	8.6566 1599
25	10.2341 9078	9.8225 7960	9.4375 7770	9.0770 4002	8.7390 1900
26	10.3540 9288	9.9289 7211	9.5320 3443	9.1609 4547	8.8135 9186
27	10.4646 0174	10.0265 7992	9.6182 9629	9.2372 2316	8.8810 7860
28	10.5664 5321	10.1161 2837	9.6970 7423	9.3065 6651	8.9421 5258
29	10.6603 2554	10.1982 8291	9.7690 1756	9.3696 0591	8.9974 2315
30	10.7468 4382	10.2736 5404	9.8347 1924	9.4269 1447	9.0474 4176
31	10.8265 8416	10.3428 0187	9.8947 2076	9.4790 1315	9.0927 0748
32	10.9000 7757	10.4062 4025	9.9495 1668	9.5263 7559	9.1336 7193
33	10.9678 1343	10.4644 4060	9.9995 5861	9.5694 3236	9.1707 4383
34	11.0302 4279	10.5178 3541	10.0452 5901	9.6085 7487	9.2042 9305
35	11.0877 8137	10.5668 2148	10.0869 9453	9.6441 5897	9.2346 5435
36	11.1408 1233	10.6117 6282	10.1251 0916	9.6765 0816	9.2621 3063
37	11.1896 8878	10.6529 9342	10.1599 1704	9.7059 1651	9.2869 9605
38	11.2347 3620	10.6908 1965	10.1917 0506	9.7326 5137	9.3094 9869
39	11.2762 5457	10.7255 2261	10.2207 3521	9.7569 5579	9.3298 6306
40	11.3145 2034	10.7573 6020	10.2472 4677	9.7790 5072	9.3482 9237
41	11.3497 8833	10.7865 6899	10.2714 5824	9.7991 3702	9.3649 7047
42	11.3822 9339	10.8133 6604	10.2935 6917	9.8173 9729	9.3800 6377
43	11.4122 5197	10.8379 5050	10.3137 6180	9.8339 9753	9.3937 2287
44	11.4398 6357	10.8605 0504	10.3322 0255	9.8490 8867	9.4060 8404
45	11.4653 1205	10.8811 9729	10.3490 4343	9.8628 0788	9.4172 7063
46	11.4887 6686	10.9001 8100	10.3644 2322	9.8752 7989	9.4273 9423
47	11.5103 8420	10.9175 9725	10.3784 6870	9.8866 1808	9.4365 5587
48	11.5303 0802	10.9335 7546	10.3912 9561	9.8969 2553	9.4448 4694
49	11.5486 7099	10.9482 3436	10.4030 0969	9.9062 9594	9.4523 5017
50	11.5655 9538	10.9616 8290	10.4137 0748	9.9148 1449	9.4591 4043

MATHEMATICS OF FINANCE

Table 12

$$\frac{1}{s_{\overline{n}|i}} = \frac{i}{(1+i)^n - 1} \qquad \left(\frac{1}{a_{\overline{n}|i}} = \frac{1}{s_{\overline{n}|i}} + i\right)$$

n	¼ % (0.0025)	⁷⁄₂₄ % (0.00291667)	⅓ % (0.00333333)	⁵⁄₁₂ % (0.00416667)	½ % (0.005)
1	1.0000 0000	1.0000 0000	1.0000 0000	1.0000 0000	1.0000 0000
2	0.4993 7578	0.4992 7190	0.4991 6805	0.4989 6050	0.4987 5312
3	0.3325 0139	0.3323 6300	0.3322 2469	0.3319 4829	0.3316 7221
4	0.2490 6445	0.2489 0890	0.2487 5347	0.2484 4291	0.2481 3279
5	0.1990 0250	0.1988 3673	0.1986 7110	0.1983 4026	0.1980 0997
6	0.1656 2803	0.1654 5552	0.1652 8317	0.1649 3898	0.1645 9546
7	0.1417 8928	0.1416 1200	0.1414 3491	0.1410 8133	0.1407 2854
8	0.1239 1035	0.1237 2953	0.1235 4895	0.1231 8845	0.1228 2886
9	0.1100 0462	0.1098 2111	0.1096 3785	0.1092 7209	0.1089 0736
10	0.0988 8015	0.0986 9451	0.0985 0915	0.0981 3929	0.0977 7057
11	0.0897 7840	0.0895 9106	0.0894 0402	0.0890 3090	0.0886 5903
12	0.0821 9370	0.0820 0496	0.0818 1657	0.0814 4082	0.0810 6643
13	0.0757 7595	0.0755 8607	0.0753 9656	0.0750 1866	0.0746 4224
14	0.0702 7510	0.0700 8426	0.0698 9383	0.0695 1416	0.0691 3609
15	0.0655 0777	0.0653 1613	0.0651 2491	0.0647 4378	0.0643 6436
16	0.0613 3642	0.0611 4409	0.0609 5223	0.0605 6988	0.0601 8937
17	0.0576 5587	0.0574 6297	0.0572 7056	0.0568 8720	0.0565 0579
18	0.0543 8433	0.0541 9094	0.0539 9807	0.0536 1387	0.0532 3173
19	0.0514 5722	0.0512 6341	0.0510 7015	0.0506 8525	0.0503 0253
20	0.0488 2288	0.0486 2870	0.0484 3511	0.0480 4963	0.0476 6645
21	0.0464 3947	0.0462 4499	0.0460 5111	0.0456 6517	0.0452 8163
22	0.0442 7278	0.0440 7804	0.0438 8393	0.0434 9760	0.0431 1380
23	0.0422 9455	0.0420 9958	0.0419 0528	0.0415 1865	0.0411 3465
24	0.0404 8121	0.0402 8606	0.0400 9159	0.0397 0472	0.0393 2061
25	0.0388 1298	0.0386 1767	0.0384 2307	0.0380 3603	0.0376 5186
26	0.0372 7312	0.0370 7767	0.0368 8297	0.0364 9581	0.0361 1163
27	0.0358 4736	0.0356 5180	0.0354 5702	0.0350 6978	0.0346 8565
28	0.0345 2347	0.0343 2783	0.0341 3299	0.0337 4572	0.0333 6167
29	0.0332 9093	0.0330 9521	0.0329 0033	0.0325 1307	0.0321 2914
30	0.0321 4059	0.0319 4482	0.0317 4992	0.0313 6270	0.0309 7892
31	0.0310 6449	0.0308 6869	0.0306 7378	0.0302 8663	0.0299 0304
32	0.0300 5569	0.0298 5987	0.0296 6496	0.0292 7791	0.0288 9453
33	0.0291 0806	0.0289 1222	0.0287 1734	0.0283 3041	0.0279 4727
34	0.0282 1620	0.0280 2037	0.0278 2551	0.0274 3873	0.0270 5586
35	0.0273 7533	0.0271 7951	0.0269 8470	0.0265 9809	0.0262 1550
36	0.0265 8121	0.0263 8541	0.0261 9065	0.0258 0423	0.0254 2194
37	0.0258 3004	0.0256 3428	0.0254 3957	0.0250 5336	0.0246 7139
38	0.0251 1843	0.0249 2271	0.0247 2808	0.0243 4208	0.0239 6045
39	0.0244 4335	0.0242 4767	0.0240 5311	0.0236 6736	0.0232 8607
40	0.0238 0204	0.0236 0642	0.0234 1194	0.0230 2644	0.0226 4552
41	0.0231 9204	0.0229 9648	0.0228 0209	0.0224 1685	0.0220 3631
42	0.0226 1112	0.0224 1562	0.0222 2133	0.0218 3637	0.0214 5622
43	0.0220 5724	0.0218 6181	0.0216 6762	0.0212 8295	0.0209 0320
44	0.0215 2855	0.0213 3321	0.0211 3912	0.0207 5474	0.0203 7541
45	0.0210 2339	0.0208 2813	0.0206 3415	0.0202 5008	0.0198 7117
46	0.0205 4022	0.0203 4504	0.0201 5118	0.0197 6743	0.0193 8894
47	0.0200 7762	0.0198 8254	0.0196 8880	0.0193 0537	0.0189 2733
48	0.0196 3433	0.0194 3933	0.0192 4572	0.0188 6263	0.0184 8503
49	0.0192 0915	0.0190 1425	0.0188 2077	0.0184 3801	0.0180 6087
50	0.0188 0099	0.0186 0620	0.0184 1285	0.0180 3044	0.0176 5376

Table 12 (*Continued*)

$$\frac{1}{s_{\overline{n}|i}} = \frac{i}{(1+i)^n - 1} \qquad \left(\frac{1}{a_{\overline{n}|i}} = \frac{1}{s_{\overline{n}|i}} + i \right)$$

n	$\frac{1}{4}\%$ (0.0025)	$\frac{7}{24}\%$ (0.00291667)	$\frac{1}{3}\%$ (0.00333333)	$\frac{5}{12}\%$ (0.00416667)	$\frac{1}{2}\%$ (0.005)
51	0.0184 0886	0.0182 1418	0.0180 2096	0.0176 3891	0.0172 6269
52	0.0180 3184	0.0178 3726	0.0176 4418	0.0172 6249	0.0168 8675
53	0.0176 6906	0.0174 7460	0.0172 8165	0.0169 0033	0.0165 2507
54	0.0173 1974	0.0171 2539	0.0169 3259	0.0165 5164	0.0161 7686
55	0.0169 8314	0.0167 8890	0.0165 9625	0.0162 1567	0.0158 4139
56	0.0166 5858	0.0164 6446	0.0162 7196	0.0158 9176	0.0155 1797
57	0.0163 4542	0.0161 5143	0.0159 5907	0.0155 7927	0.0152 0598
58	0.0160 4308	0.0158 4922	0.0156 5701	0.0152 7760	0.0149 0481
59	0.0157 5101	0.0155 5727	0.0153 6522	0.0149 8620	0.0146 1392
60	0.0154 6869	0.0152 7508	0.0150 8319	0.0147 0457	0.0143 3280
61	0.0151 9564	0.0150 0216	0.0148 1043	0.0144 3221	0.0140 6096
62	0.0149 3142	0.0147 3807	0.0145 4650	0.0141 6869	0.0137 9796
63	0.0146 7561	0.0144 8239	0.0142 9098	0.0139 1358	0.0135 4337
64	0.0144 2780	0.0142 3472	0.0140 4348	0.0136 6649	0.0132 9681
65	0.0141 8764	0.0139 9469	0.0138 0361	0.0134 2704	0.0130 5789
66	0.0139 5476	0.0137 6196	0.0135 7105	0.0131 9489	0.0128 2627
67	0.0137 2886	0.0135 3619	0.0133 4545	0.0129 6972	0.0126 0163
68	0.0135 0961	0.0133 1709	0.0131 2652	0.0127 5121	0.0123 8366
69	0.0132 9674	0.0131 0436	0.0129 1395	0.0125 3908	0.0121 7206
70	0.0130 8996	0.0128 9772	0.0127 0749	0.0123 3304	0.0119 6657
71	0.0128 8902	0.0126 9693	0.0125 0687	0.0121 3285	0.0117 6693
72	0.0126 9368	0.0125 0173	0.0123 1185	0.0119 3827	0.0115 7289
73	0.0125 0370	0.0123 1190	0.0121 2220	0.0117 4905	0.0113 8422
74	0.0123 1887	0.0121 2722	0.0119 3769	0.0115 6498	0.0112 0070
75	0.0121 3898	0.0119 4748	0.0117 5813	0.0113 8586	0.0110 2214
76	0.0119 6385	0.0117 7250	0.0115 8332	0.0112 1150	0.0108 4832
77	0.0117 9327	0.0116 0207	0.0114 1308	0.0110 4170	0.0106 7908
78	0.0116 2708	0.0114 3603	0.0112 4722	0.0108 7629	0.0105 1423
79	0.0114 6511	0.0112 7422	0.0110 8559	0.0107 1510	0.0103 5360
80	0.0113 0721	0.0111 1647	0.0109 2802	0.0105 5798	0.0101 9704
81	0.0111 5321	0.0109 6263	0.0107 7436	0.0104 0477	0.0100 4439
82	0.0110 0298	0.0108 1256	0.0106 2447	0.0102 5534	0.0098 9552
83	0.0108 5639	0.0106 6612	0.0104 7822	0.0101 0954	0.0097 5028
84	0.0107 1330	0.0105 2318	0.0103 3547	0.0099 6724	0.0096 0855
85	0.0105 7359	0.0103 8363	0.0101 9610	0.0098 2833	0.0094 7021
86	0.0104 3714	0.0102 4734	0.0100 6000	0.0096 9268	0.0093 3513
87	0.0103 0384	0.0101 1419	0.0099 2704	0.0095 6018	0.0092 0320
88	0.0101 7357	0.0099 8409	0.0097 9713	0.0094 3073	0.0090 7431
89	0.0100 4625	0.0098 5693	0.0096 7015	0.0093 0422	0.0089 4837
90	0.0099 2177	0.0097 3261	0.0095 4602	0.0091 8055	0.0088 2527
91	0.0098 0004	0.0096 1104	0.0094 2464	0.0090 5962	0.0087 0493
92	0.0096 8096	0.0094 9212	0.0093 0592	0.0089 4136	0.0085 8724
93	0.0095 6446	0.0093 7578	0.0091 8976	0.0088 2568	0.0084 7213
94	0.0094 5044	0.0092 6193	0.0090 7610	0.0037 1248	0.0083 5950
95	0.0093 3884	0.0091 5049	0.0089 6485	0.0086 0170	0.0082 4930
96	0.0092 2957	0.0090 4139	0.0088 5594	0.0084 9325	0.0081 4143
97	0.0091 2257	0.0089 3455	0.0087 4929	0.0083 8707	0.0080 3583
98	0.0090 1776	0.0088 2990	0.0086 4484	0.0082 8309	0.0079 3242
99	0.0089 1508	0.0087 2738	0.0085 4252	0.0081 8124	0.0078 3115
100	0.0088 1446	0.0086 2693	0.0084 4226	0.0080 8145	0.0077 319⁴

Table 12 (*Continued*)

$$\frac{1}{s_{\overline{n}|i}} = \frac{i}{(1+i)^n - 1} \qquad \left(\frac{1}{a_{\overline{n}|i}} = \frac{1}{s_{\overline{n}|i}} + i\right)$$

n	¼ % (0.0025)	⁷⁄₂₄ % (0.00291667)	⅓ % (0.00333333)	⁵⁄₁₂ % (0.00416667)	½ % (0.005)
101	0.0087 1584	0.0085 2848	0.0083 4400	0.0079 8366	0.0076 3473
102	0.0086 1917	0.0084 3198	0.0082 4769	0.0078 8782	0.0075 3947
103	0.0085 2439	0.0083 3736	0.0081 5327	0.0077 9387	0.0074 4610
104	0.0084 3144	0.0082 4457	0.0080 6068	0.0077 0175	0.0073 5457
105	0.0083 4027	0.0081 5357	0.0079 6987	0.0076 1142	0.0072 6481
106	0.0082 5082	0.0080 6430	0.0078 8079	0.0075 2281	0.0071 7679
107	0.0081 6307	0.0079 7670	0.0077 9340	0.0074 3589	0.0070 9045
108	0.0080 7694	0.0078 9075	0.0077 0764	0.0073 5061	0.0070 0575
109	0.0079 9241	0.0078 0638	0.0076 2346	0.0072 6691	0.0069 2264
110	0.0079 0942	0.0077 2356	0.0075 4084	0.0071 8476	0.0068 4107
111	0.0078 2793	0.0076 4225	0.0074 5972	0.0071 0412	0.0067 6102
112	0.0077 4791	0.0075 6239	0.0073 8007	0.0070 2495	0.0066 8242
113	0.0076 6932	0.0074 8397	0.0073 0184	0.0069 4720	0.0066 0526
114	0.0075 9211	0.0074 0693	0.0072 2500	0.0068 7083	0.0065 2948
115	0.0075 1626	0.0073 3125	0.0071 4952	0.0067 9582	0.0064 5506
116	0.0074 4172	0.0072 5688	0.0070 7535	0.0067 2213	0.0063 8195
117	0.0073 6846	0.0071 8380	0.0070 0246	0.0066 4973	0.0063 1013
118	0.0072 9646	0.0071 1196	0.0069 3082	0.0065 7857	0.0062 3956
119	0.0072 2567	0.0070 4135	0.0068 6041	0.0065 0863	0.0061 7021
120	0.0071 5607	0.0069 7192	0.0067 9118	0.0064 3988	0.0061 0205
121	0.0070 8764	0.0069 0365	0.0067 2311	0.0063 7230	0.0060 3505
122	0.0070 2033	0.0068 3652	0.0066 5617	0.0063 0584	0.0059 6918
123	0.0069 5412	0.0067 7048	0.0065 9034	0.0062 4049	0.0059 0441
124	0.0068 8899	0.0067 0552	0.0065 2558	0.0061 7621	0.0058 4072
125	0.0068 2491	0.0066 4162	0.0064 6188	0.0061 1298	0.0057 7808
126	0.0067 6186	0.0065 7874	0.0063 9919	0.0060 5078	0.0057 1647
127	0.0066 9981	0.0065 1686	0.0063 3751	0.0059 8959	0.0056 5586
128	0.0066 3873	0.0064 5595	0.0062 7681	0.0059 2937	0.0055 9623
129	0.0065 7861	0.0063 9601	0.0062 1707	0.0058 7010	0.0055 3755
130	0.0065 1942	0.0063 3699	0.0061 5825	0.0058 1177	0.0054 7981
131	0.0064 6115	0.0062 7889	0.0061 0035	0.0057 5435	0.0054 2298
132	0.0064 0376	0.0062 2168	0.0060 4334	0.0056 9782	0.0053 6703
133	0.0063 4725	0.0061 6534	0.0059 8720	0.0056 4216	0.0053 1197
134	0.0062 9159	0.0061 0985	0.0059 3191	0.0055 8736	0.0052 5775
135	0.0062 3675	0.0060 5519	0.0058 7745	0.0055 3339	0.0052 0436
136	0.0061 8274	0.0060 0135	0.0058 2381	0.0054 8023	0.0051 5179
137	0.0061 2952	0.0059 4830	0.0057 7097	0.0054 2787	0.0051 0002
138	0.0060 7707	0.0058 9603	0.0057 1890	0.0053 7628	0.0050 4902
139	0.0060 2539	0.0058 4453	0.0056 6760	0.0053 2546	0.0049 9879
140	0.0059 7446	0.0057 9377	0.0056 1704	0.0052 7539	0.0049 4930
141	0.0059 2425	0.0057 4373	0.0055 6721	0.0052 2604	0.0049 0055
142	0.0058 7476	0.0056 9442	0.0055 1809	0.0051 7741	0.0048 5250
143	0.0058 2597	0.0056 4580	0.0054 6968	0.0051 2948	0.0048 0516
144	0.0057 7787	0.0055 9787	0.0054 2195	0.0050 8224	0.0047 5850
145	0.0057 3043	0.0055 5061	0.0053 7489	0.0050 3566	0.0047 1252
146	0.0056 8365	0.0055 0401	0.0053 2849	0.0049 8975	0.0046 6718
147	0.0056 3752	0.0054 5805	0.0052 8273	0.0049 4447	0.0046 2250
148	0.0055 9201	0.0054 1272	0.0052 3760	0.0048 9983	0.0045 7844
149	0.0055 4712	0.0053 6800	0.0051 9309	0.0048 5580	0.0045 3500
150	0.0055 0284	0.0053 2390	0.0051 4919	0.0048 1238	0.0044 9217

Table 12   (*Continued*)

$$\frac{1}{s_{\overline{n}|i}} = \frac{i}{(1+i)^n - 1} \qquad \left(\frac{1}{a_{\overline{n}|i}} = \frac{1}{s_{\overline{n}|i}} + i\right)$$

n	¼ % (0.0025)	⁷⁄₂₄ % (0.00291667)	⅓ % (0.00333333)	⁵⁄₁₂ % (0.00416667)	½ % (0.005)
151	0.0054 5915	0.0052 8038	0.0051 0588	0.0047 6956	0.0044 4993
152	0.0054 1605	0.0052 3745	0.0050 6315	0.0047 2731	0.0044 0827
153	0.0053 7351	0.0051 9509	0.0050 2099	0.0046 8564	0.0043 6719
154	0.0053 3153	0.0051 5329	0.0049 7939	0.0046 4453	0.0043 2666
155	0.0052 9010	0.0051 1203	0.0049 3834	0.0046 0396	0.0042 8668
156	0.0052 4921	0.0050 7132	0.0048 9783	0.0045 6393	0.0042 4723
157	0.0052 0885	0.0050 3113	0.0048 5784	0.0045 2443	0.0042 0832
158	0.0051 6900	0.0049 9146	0.0048 1837	0.0044 8545	0.0041 6992
159	0.0051 2966	0.0049 5230	0.0047 7941	0.0044 4697	0.0041 3203
160	0.0050 9082	0.0049 1363	0.0047 4095	0.0044 0889	0.0040 9464
161	0.0050 5247	0.0048 7545	0.0047 0298	0.0043 7150	0.0040 5773
162	0.0050 1459	0.0048 3776	0.0046 6549	0.0043 3450	0.0040 2131
163	0.0049 7719	0.0048 0053	0.0046 2846	0.0042 9796	0.0039 8536
164	0.0049 4025	0.0047 6377	0.0045 9190	0.0042 6188	0.0039 4987
165	0.0049 0377	0.0047 2746	0.0045 5580	0.0042 2626	0.0039 1483
166	0.0048 6773	0.0046 9160	0.0045 2014	0.0041 9109	0.0038 8024
167	0.0048 3213	0.0046 5617	0.0044 8492	0.0041 5635	0.0038 4608
168	0.0047 9695	0.0046 2118	0.0044 5012	0.0041 2204	0.0038 1236
169	0.0047 6220	0.0045 8660	0.0044 1575	0.0040 8815	0.0037 7906
170	0.0047 2787	0.0045 5244	0.0043 8180	0.0040 5468	0.0037 4617
171	0.0046 9394	0.0045 1869	0.0043 4825	0.0040 2162	0.0037 1369
172	0.0046 6042	0.0044 8534	0.0043 1510	0.0039 8896	0.0036 8161
173	0.0046 2728	0.0044 5239	0.0042 8235	0.0039 5669	0.0036 4992
174	0.0045 9454	0.0044 1982	0.0042 4998	0.0039 2481	0.0036 1862
175	0.0045 6217	0.0043 8763	0.0042 1800	0.0038 9330	0.0035 8770
176	0.0045 3018	0.0043 5581	0.0041 8639	0.0038 6217	0.0035 5715
177	0.0044 9855	0.0043 2436	0.0041 5514	0.0038 3141	0.0035 2697
178	0.0044 6729	0.0042 9327	0.0041 2426	0.0038 0101	0.0034 9715
179	0.0044 3638	0.0042 6254	0.0040 9373	0.0037 7097	0.0034 6768
180	0.0044 0582	0.0042 3216	0.0040 6355	0.0037 4127	0.0034 3857
181	0.0043 7560	0.0042 0212	0.0040 3371	0.0037 1192	0.0034 0979
182	0.0043 4572	0.0041 7242	0.0040 0421	0.0036 8290	0.0033 8136
183	0.0043 1617	0.0041 4305	0.0039 7504	0.0036 5422	0.0033 5325
184	0.0042 8695	0.0041 1400	0.0039 4620	0.0036 2586	0.0033 2547
185	0.0042 5805	0.0040 8528	0.0039 1768	0.0035 9782	0.0032 9802
186	0.0042 2947	0.0040 5687	0.0038 8948	0.0035 7010	0.0032 7088
187	0.0042 0120	0.0040 2878	0.0038 6159	0.0035 4269	0.0032 4404
188	0.0041 7323	0.0040 0099	0.0038 3400	0.0035 1559	0.0032 1752
189	0.0041 4557	0.0039 7350	0.0038 0672	0.0034 8879	0.0031 9129
190	0.0041 1820	0.0039 4631	0.0037 7973	0.0034 6228	0.0031 6537
191	0.0040 9112	0.0039 1941	0.0037 5304	0.0034 3607	0.0031 3973
192	0.0040 6434	0.0038 9280	0.0037 2663	0.0034 1014	0.0031 1438
193	0.0040 3783	0.0038 6647	0.0037 0050	0.0033 8450	0.0030 8931
194	0.0040 1160	0.0038 4042	0.0036 7466	0.0033 5913	0.0030 6452
195	0.0039 8565	0.0038 1465	0.0036 4908	0.0033 3404	0.0030 4000
196	0.0039 5997	0.0037 8914	0.0036 2378	0.0033 0922	0.0030 1576
197	0.0039 3455	0.0037 6390	0.0035 9874	0.0032 8467	0.0029 9178
198	0.0039 0939	0.0037 3892	0.0035 7397	0.0032 6037	0.0029 6806
199	0.0038 8450	0.0037 1420	0.0035 4945	0.0032 3634	0.0029 4459
200	0.0038 5985	0.0036 8974	0.0035 2519	0.0032 1255	0.0029 2138

Table 12 *(Continued)*

$$\frac{1}{s_{\overline{n}|i}} = \frac{i}{(1+i)^n - 1} \qquad \left(\frac{1}{a_{\overline{n}|i}} = \frac{1}{s_{\overline{n}|i}} + i \right)$$

n	$7\!/_{12}\,\%$ (0.00583333)	$2\!/_3\,\%$ (0.00666667)	$3\!/_4\,\%$ (0.0075)	$7\!/_8\,\%$ (0.00875)	$1\,\%$ (0.01)
1	1.0000 0000	1.0000 0000	1.0000 0000	1.0000 0000	1.0000 0000
2	0.4985 4591	0.4983 3887	0.4981 3200	0.4978 2203	0.4975 1244
3	0.3313 9643	0.3311 2095	0.3308 4579	0.3304 3361	0.3300 2211
4	0.2478 2310	0.2475 1384	0.2472 0501	0.2467 4257	0.2462 8109
5	0.1976 8024	0.1973 5105	0.1970 2242	0.1965 3049	0.1960 3980
6	0.1642 5260	0.1639 1042	0.1635 6891	0.1630 5789	0.1625 4837
7	0.1403 7653	0.1400 2531	0.1396 7488	0.1391 5070	0.1386 2828
8	0.1224 7018	0.1221 1240	0.1217 5552	0.1212 2190	0.1206 9029
9	0.1085 4365	0.1081 8096	0.1078 1929	0.1072 7868	0.1067 4036
10	0.0974 0299	0.0970 3654	0.0966 7123	0.0961 2538	0.0955 8208
11	0.0882 8842	0.0879 1905	0.0875 5094	0.0870 0111	0.0864 5408
12	0.0806 9341	0.0803 2176	0.0799 5148	0.0793 9860	0.0788 4879
13	0.0742 6730	0.0738 9385	0.0735 2188	0.0729 6669	0.0724 1482
14	0.0687 5962	0.0638 8474	0.0680 1146	0.0674 5453	0.0669 0117
15	0.0639 8666	0.0636 1067	0.0632 3639	0.0626 7817	0.0621 2378
16	0.0598 1068	0.0594 3382	0.0590 5879	0.0584 9965	0.0579 4460
17	0.0561 2632	0.0557 4880	0.0553 7321	0.0548 1346	0.0542 5806
18	0.0528 5165	0.0524 7363	0.0520 9766	0.0515 3756	0.0509 8205
19	0.0499 2198	0.0495 4361	0.0491 6740	0.0486 0715	0.0480 5175
20	0.0472 8556	0.0469 0696	0.0465 3063	0.0459 7042	0.0454 1531
21	0.0449 0050	0.0445 2176	0.0441 4543	0.0435 8541	0.0430 3075
22	0.0427 3251	0.0423 5374	0.0419 7748	0.0414 1779	0.0408 6372
23	0.0407 5329	0.0403 7456	0.0399 9846	0.0394 3921	0.0388 8584
24	0.0389 3925	0.0385 6062	0.0381 8474	0.0376 2604	0.0370 7347
25	0.0372 7055	0.0368 9210	0.0365 1650	0.0359 5843	0.0354 0675
26	0.0357 3043	0.0353 5220	0.0349 7693	0.0344 1959	0.0338 6888
27	0.0343 0460	0.0339 2664	0.0335 5176	0.0329 9520	0.0324 4553
28	0.0329 8082	0.0326 0317	0.0322 2871	0.0316 7300	0.0311 2444
29	0.0317 4853	0.0313 7123	0.0309 9723	0.0304 4243	0.0298 9502
30	0.0305 9857	0.0302 2166	0.0298 4816	0.0292 9431	0.0287 4811
31	0.0295 2299	0.0291 4649	0.0287 7352	0.0282 2068	0.0276 7573
32	0.0285 1482	0.0281 3875	0.0277 6634	0.0272 1454	0.0266 7089
33	0.0275 6791	0.0271 9231	0.0268 2048	0.0262 6976	0.0257 2744
34	0.0266 7687	0.0263 0176	0.0259 3053	0.0253 8092	0.0248 3997
35	0.0258 3691	0.0254 6231	0.0250 9170	0.0245 4324	0.0240 0368
36	0.0250 4376	0.0246 6970	0.0242 9973	0.0237 5244	0.0232 1431
37	0.0242 9365	0.0239 2013	0.0235 5082	0.0230 0473	0.0224 6805
38	0.0235 8316	0.0232 1020	0.0228 4157	0.0222 9671	0.0217 6150
39	0.0229 0925	0.0225 3687	0.0221 6893	0.0216 2531	0.0210 9160
40	0.0222 6917	0.0218 9739	0.0215 3016	0.0209 8780	0.0204 5560
41	0.0216 6046	0.0212 8928	0.0209 2276	0.0203 8169	0.0198 5102
42	0.0210 8087	0.0207 1031	0.0203 4452	0.0198 0475	0.0192 7563
43	0.0205 2836	0.0201 5843	0.0197 9338	0.0192 5493	0.0187 2737
44	0.0200 0110	0.0196 3180	0.0192 6751	0.0187 3039	0.0182 0441
45	0.0194 9740	0.0191 2875	0.0187 6521	0.0182 2943	0.0177 0505
46	0.0190 1571	0.0186 4772	0.0182 8495	0.0177 5053	0.0172 2775
47	0.0185 5465	0.0181 8732	0.0178 2532	0.0172 9228	0.0167 7111
48	0.0181 1291	0.0177 4626	0.0173 8504	0.0168 5338	0.0163 3384
49	0.0176 8932	0.0173 2334	0.0169 6292	0.0164 3265	0.0159 1474
50	0.0172 8278	0.0169 1749	0.0165 5787	0.0160 2900	0.0155 1273

Table 12 (*Continued*)

$$\frac{1}{s_{\overline{n}|i}} = \frac{i}{(1+i)^n - 1} \qquad \left(\frac{1}{a_{\overline{n}|i}} = \frac{1}{s_{\overline{n}|i}} + i \right)$$

n	$7\frac{1}{12}\%$ (0.0058 3333)	$\frac{2}{3}\%$ (0.0066 6667)	$\frac{3}{4}\%$ (0.0075)	$\frac{7}{8}\%$ (0.00875)	1% (0.01)
51	0.0168 9230	0.0165 2770	0.0161 6888	0.0156 4142	0.0151 2680
52	0.0165 1694	0.0161 5304	0.0157 9503	0.0152 6899	0.0147 5603
53	0.0161 5585	0.0157 9266	0.0154 3546	0.0149 1084	0.0143 9956
54	0.0158 0824	0.0154 4576	0.0150 8938	0.0145 6619	0.0140 5658
55	0.0154 7337	0.0151 1160	0.0147 5605	0.0142 3430	0.0137 2637
56	0.0151 5056	0.0147 8951	0.0144 3478	0.0139 1449	0.0134 0824
57	0.0148 3918	0.0144 7885	0.0141 2496	0.0136 0611	0.0131 0156
58	0.0145 3863	0.0141 7903	0.0138 2597	0.0133 0858	0.0128 0573
59	0.0142 4836	0.0138 8949	0.0135 3727	0.0130 2135	0.0125 2020
60	0.0139 6787	0.0136 0973	0.0132 5836	0.0127 4390	0.0122 4445
61	0.0136 9666	0.0133 3926	0.0129 8873	0.0124 7575	0.0119 7800
62	0.0134 3428	0.0130 7763	0.0127 2795	0.0122 1644	0.0117 2041
63	0.0131 8033	0.0128 2442	0.0124 7560	0.0119 6557	0.0114 7125
64	0.0129 3440	0.0125 7923	0.0122 3127	0.0117 2273	0.0112 3013
65	0.0126 9612	0.0123 4171	0.0119 9460	0.0114 8754	0.0109 9667
66	0.0124 6515	0.0121 1149	0.0117 6524	0.0112 5968	0.0107 7052
67	0.0122 4116	0.0118 8825	0.0115 4286	0.0110 3879	0.0105 5136
68	0.0120 2383	0.0116 7168	0.0113 2716	0.0108 2459	0.0103 3889
69	0.0118 1289	0.0114 6150	0.0111 1785	0.0106 1677	0.0101 3280
70	0.0116 0805	0.0112 5742	0.0109 1464	0.0104 1506	0.0099 3282
71	0.0114 0906	0.0110 5919	0.0107 1728	0.0102 1921	0.0097 3870
72	0.0112 1567	0.0108 6657	0.0105 2554	0.0100 2897	0.0095 5019
73	0.0110 2766	0.0106 7933	0.0103 3917	0.0098 4411	0.0093 6706
74	0.0108 4481	0.0104 9725	0.0101 5796	0.0096 6441	0.0091 8910
75	0.0106 6690	0.0103 2011	0.0099 8170	0.0094 8966	0.0090 1609
76	0.0104 9375	0.0101 4773	0.0098 1020	0.0093 1967	0.0088 4784
77	0.0103 2517	0.0099 7993	0.0096 4328	0.0091 5426	0.0086 8416
78	0.0101 6099	0.0098 1652	0.0094 8074	0.0089 9324	0.0085 2488
79	0.0100 0103	0.0096 5733	0.0093 2244	0.0088 3645	0.0083 6983
80	0.0098 4514	0.0095 0222	0.0091 6821	0.0086 8374	0.0082 1885
81	0.0096 9316	0.0093 5102	0.0090 1790	0.0085 3494	0.0080 7179
82	0.0095 4496	0.0092 0360	0.0088 7136	0.0083 8992	0.0079 2851
83	0.0094 0040	0.0090 5982	0.0087 2847	0.0082 4854	0.0077 8887
84	0.0092 5935	0.0089 1955	0.0085 8908	0.0081 1067	0.0076 5273
85	0.0091 2168	0.0087 8266	0.0084 5308	0.0079 7619	0.0075 1998
86	0.0089 8727	0.0086 4904	0.0083 2034	0.0078 4497	0.0073 9050
87	0.0088 5602	0.0085 1857	0.0081 9076	0.0077 1691	0.0072 6418
88	0.0087 2781	0.0083 9115	0.0080 6423	0.0075 9190	0.0071 4089
89	0.0086 0255	0.0082 6667	0.0079 4064	0.0074 6982	0.0070 2056
90	0.0084 8013	0.0081 4504	0.0078 1989	0.0073 5060	0.0069 0306
91	0.0083 6047	0.0080 2616	0.0077 0190	0.0072 3413	0.0067 8832
92	0.0082 4346	0.0079 0994	0.0075 8657	0.0071 2031	0.0066 7624
93	0.0081 2903	0.0077 9629	0.0074 7382	0.0070 0908	0.0065 6673
94	0.0080 1709	0.0076 8514	0.0073 6356	0.0069 0033	0.0064 5971
95	0.0079 0757	0.0075 7641	0.0072 5571	0.0067 9401	0.0063 5511
96	0.0078 0038	0.0074 7001	0.0071 5020	0.0066 9002	0.0062 5284
97	0.0076 9547	0.0073 6588	0.0070 4696	0.0065 8829	0.0061 5284
98	0.0075 9275	0.0072 6394	0.0069 4592	0.0064 8877	0.0060 5503
99	0.0074 9216	0.0071 6415	0.0068 4701	0.0063 9137	0.0059 5936
100	0.0073 9363	0.0070 6642	0.0067 5017	0.0062 9604	0.0058 6574

Table 12 *(Continued)*

$$\frac{1}{s_{\overline{n}|i}} = \frac{i}{(1+i)^n - 1} \qquad \left(\frac{1}{a_{\overline{n}|i}} = \frac{1}{s_{\overline{n}|i}} + i \right)$$

n	$\frac{7}{12}\%$ (0.00583333)	$\frac{2}{3}\%$ (0.00666667)	$\frac{3}{4}\%$ (0.0075)	$\frac{7}{8}\%$ (0.00875)	1% (0.01)
101	0.0072 9711	0.0069 7069	0.0066 5533	0.0062 0271	0.0057 7413
102	0.0072 0254	0.0068 7690	0.0065 6243	0.0061 1133	0.0056 8446
103	0.0071 0986	0.0067 8501	0.0064 7143	0.0060 2184	0.0055 9668
104	0.0070 1901	0.0066 9495	0.0063 8226	0.0059 3418	0.0055 1073
105	0.0069 2994	0.0066 0668	0.0062 9487	0.0058 4830	0.0054 2656
106	0.0068 4261	0.0065 2013	0.0062 0922	0.0057 6416	0.0053 4412
107	0.0067 5696	0.0064 3527	0.0061 2524	0.0056 8169	0.0052 6336
108	0.0066 7294	0.0063 5205	0.0060 4291	0.0056 0086	0.0051 8423
109	0.0065 9052	0.0062 7042	0.0059 6216	0.0055 2162	0.0051 0669
110	0.0065 0965	0.0061 9033	0.0058 8297	0.0054 4393	0.0050 3069
111	0.0064 3028	0.0061 1175	0.0058 0527	0.0053 6774	0.0049 5620
112	0.0063 5237	0.0060 3464	0.0057 2905	0.0052 9301	0.0048 8317
113	0.0062 7590	0.0059 5895	0.0056 5425	0.0052 1971	0.0048 1155
114	0.0062 0081	0.0058 8465	0.0055 8084	0.0051 4780	0.0047 4133
115	0.0061 2708	0.0058 1171	0.0055 0878	0.0050 7724	0.0046 7245
116	0.0060 5466	0.0057 4008	0.0054 3803	0.0050 0799	0.0046 0488
117	0.0059 8353	0.0056 6974	0.0053 6858	0.0049 4003	0.0045 3860
118	0.0059 1365	0.0056 0065	0.0053 0037	0.0048 7331	0.0044 7356
119	0.0058 4499	0.0055 3278	0.0052 3338	0.0048 0781	0.0044 0974
120	0.0057 7751	0.0054 6609	0.0051 6758	0.0047 4350	0.0043 4709
121	0.0057 1120	0.0054 0057	0.0051 0294	0.0046 8035	0.0042 8561
122	0.0056 4602	0.0053 3618	0.0050 3942	0.0046 1832	0.0042 2525
123	0.0055 8194	0.0052 7289	0.0049 7702	0.0045 5740	0.0041 6599
124	0.0055 1894	0.0052 1067	0.0049 1568	0.0044 9754	0.0041 0780
125	0.0054 5700	0.0051 4951	0.0048 5540	0.0044 3874	0.0040 5065
126	0.0053 9607	0.0050 8937	0.0047 9614	0.0043 8096	0.0039 9452
127	0.0053 3615	0.0050 3024	0.0047 3788	0.0043 2418	0.0039 3939
128	0.0052 7721	0.0049 7208	0.0046 8060	0.0042 6838	0.0038 8524
129	0.0052 1922	0.0049 1488	0.0046 2428	0.0042 1352	0.0038 3203
130	0.0051 6216	0.0048 5861	0.0045 6888	0.0041 5960	0.0037 7975
131	0.0051 0602	0.0048 0325	0.0045 1440	0.0041 0659	0.0037 2837
132	0.0050 5077	0.0047 4878	0.0044 6080	0.0040 5446	0.0036 7788
133	0.0049 9639	0.0046 9518	0.0044 0808	0.0040 0320	0.0036 2825
134	0.0049 4286	0.0046 4244	0.0043 5621	0.0039 5279	0.0035 7947
135	0.0048 9016	0.0045 9052	0.0043 0516	0.0039 0321	0.0035 3151
136	0.0048 3828	0.0045 3942	0.0042 5493	0.0038 5444	0.0034 8437
137	0.0047 8719	0.0044 8911	0.0042 0550	0.0038 0646	0.0034 3801
138	0.0047 3688	0.0044 3959	0.0041 5684	0.0037 5926	0.0033 9242
139	0.0046 8733	0.0043 9082	0.0041 0894	0.0037 1281	0.0033 4759
140	0.0046 3853	0.0043 4280	0.0040 6179	0.0036 6711	0.0033 0349
141	0.0045 9046	0.0042 9551	0.0040 1536	0.0036 2213	0.0032 6012
142	0.0045 4311	0.0042 4893	0.0039 6965	0.0035 7787	0.0032 1746
143	0.0044 9645	0.0042 0305	0.0039 2464	0.0035 3430	0.0031 7549
144	0.0044 5048	0.0041 5786	0.0038 8031	0.0034 9141	0.0031 3419
145	0.0044 0518	0.0041 1333	0.0038 3664	0.0034 4918	0.0030 9356
146	0.0043 6053	0.0040 6947	0.0037 9364	0.0034 0761	0.0030 5358
147	0.0043 1653	0.0040 2624	0.0037 5127	0.0033 6668	0.0030 1423
148	0.0042 7316	0.0039 8364	0.0037 0954	0.0033 2638	0.0029 7551
149	0.0042 3040	0.0039 4166	0.0036 6841	0.0032 8669	0.0029 3739
150	0.0041 8825	0.0039 0029	0.0036 2790	0.0032 4760	0.0028 9988

Table 12 *(Continued)*

$$\frac{1}{s_{\overline{n}|i}} = \frac{i}{(1+i)^n - 1} \qquad \left(\frac{1}{a_{\overline{n}|i}} = \frac{1}{s_{\overline{n}|i}} + i\right)$$

n	$\frac{7}{12}\%$ (0.00583333)	$\frac{2}{3}\%$ (0.00666667)	$\frac{3}{4}\%$ (0.0075)	$\frac{7}{8}\%$ (0.00875)	1% (0.01)
151	0.0041 4670	0.0038 5950	0.0035 8797	0.0032 0910	0.0028 6294
152	0.0041 0572	0.0038 1930	0.0035 4862	0.0031 7177	0.0028 2659
153	0.0040 6532	0.0037 7967	0.0035 0984	0.0031 3381	0.0027 9079
154	0.0040 2548	0.0037 4059	0.0034 7162	0.0030 9701	0.0027 5554
155	0.0039 8617	0.0037 0206	0.0034 3395	0.0030 6075	0.0027 2084
156	0.0039 4741	0.0036 6407	0.0033 9681	0.0030 2502	0.0026 8666
157	0.0039 0917	0.0036 2661	0.0033 6019	0.0029 8981	0.0026 5300
158	0.0038 7146	0.0035 8966	0.0033 2409	0.0029 5512	0.0026 1986
159	0.0038 3425	0.0035 5321	0.0032 8849	0.0029 2093	0.0025 8721
160	0.0037 9753	0.0035 1727	0.0032 5340	0.0028 8724	0.0025 5504
161	0.0037 6131	0.0034 8181	0.0032 1878	0.0028 5402	0.0025 2336
162	0.0037 2556	0.0034 4683	0.0031 8465	0.0028 2128	0.0024 9215
163	0.0036 9029	0.0034 1232	0.0031 5098	0.0027 8901	0.0024 6141
164	0.0036 5547	0.0033 7827	0.0031 1777	0.0027 5720	0.0024 3111
165	0.0036 2111	0.0033 4467	0.0030 8502	0.0027 2583	0.0024 0126
166	0.0035 8720	0.0033 1152	0.0030 5270	0.0026 9490	0.0023 7185
167	0.0035 5372	0.0032 7880	0.0030 2083	0.0026 6441	0.0023 4286
168	0.0035 2067	0.0032 4652	0.0029 8938	0.0026 3434	0.0023 1430
169	0.0034 8804	0.0032 1465	0.0029 5834	0.0026 0469	0.0022 8614
170	0.0034 5583	0.0031 8319	0.0029 2772	0.0025 7544	0.0022 5840
171	0.0034 2403	0.0031 5215	0.0028 9751	0.0025 4660	0.0022 3105
172	0.0033 9262	0.0031 2150	0.0028 6769	0.0025 1816	0.0022 0409
173	0.0033 6160	0.0030 9124	0.0028 3827	0.0024 9010	0.0021 7751
174	0.0033 3098	0.0030 6137	0.0028 0922	0.0024 6242	0.0021 5132
175	0.0033 0073	0.0030 3187	0.0027 8056	0.0024 3512	0.0021 2549
176	0.0032 7085	0.0030 0275	0.0027 5226	0.0024 0818	0.0021 0003
177	0.0032 4134	0.0029 7399	0.0027 2433	0.0023 8161	0.0020 7492
178	0.0032 1219	0.0029 4560	0.0026 9676	0.0023 5539	0.0020 5016
179	0.0031 8340	0.0029 1755	0.0026 6954	0.0023 2952	0.0020 2575
180	0.0031 5495	0.0028 8985	0.0026 4267	0.0023 0399	0.0020 0168
181	0.0031 2684	0.0028 6250	0.0026 1613	0.0022 7880	0.0019 7794
182	0.0030 9908	0.0028 3548	0.0025 8993	0.0022 5394	0.0019 5453
183	0.0030 7164	0.0028 0879	0.0025 6406	0.0022 2941	0.0019 3144
184	0.0030 4453	0.0027 8242	0.0025 3851	0.0022 0520	0.0019 0867
185	0.0030 1774	0.0027 5638	0.0025 1328	0.0021 8130	0.0018 8621
186	0.0029 9126	0.0027 3065	0.0024 8837	0.0021 5771	0.0018 6405
187	0.0029 6509	0.0027 0523	0.0024 6376	0.0021 3443	0.0018 4219
188	0.0029 3923	0.0026 8011	0.0024 3945	0.0021 1145	0.0018 2063
189	0.0029 1367	0.0026 5529	0.0024 1544	0.0020 8876	0.0017 9936
190	0.0028 8841	0.0026 3077	0.0023 9173	0.0020 6637	0.0017 7838
191	0.0028 6343	0.0026 0653	0.0023 6830	0.0020 4425	0.0017 5768
192	0.0028 3875	0.0025 8258	0.0023 4516	0.0020 2242	0.0017 3725
193	0.0028 1434	0.0025 5892	0.0023 2230	0.0020 0087	0.0017 1710
194	0.0027 9021	0.0025 3552	0.0022 9971	0.0019 7959	0.0016 9721
195	0.0027 6636	0.0025 1240	0.0022 7739	0.0019 5857	0.0016 7759
196	0.0027 4277	0.0024 8955	0.0022 5534	0.0019 3782	0.0016 5822
197	0.0027 1945	0.0024 6696	0.0022 3355	0.0019 1733	0.0016 3911
198	0.0026 9639	0.0024 4464	0.0022 1202	0.0018 9709	0.0016 2026
199	0.0026 7358	0.0024 2256	0.0021 9074	0.0018 7711	0.0016 0164
200	0.0026 5103	0.0024 0074	0.0021 6972	0.0018 5737	0.0015 8328

Table 12   (*Continued*)

$$\frac{1}{s_{\overline{n}|i}} = \frac{i}{(1+i)^n - 1} \qquad \left(\frac{1}{a_{\overline{n}|i}} = \frac{1}{s_{\overline{n}|i}} + i\right)$$

n	$1\frac{1}{8}\%$ (0.01125)	$1\frac{1}{4}\%$ (0.0125)	$1\frac{3}{8}\%$ (0.01375)	$1\frac{1}{2}\%$ (0.015)	$1\frac{3}{4}\%$ (0.0175)
1	1.0000 0000	1.0000 0000	1.0000 0000	1.0000 0000	1.0000 0000
2	0.4972 0323	0.4968 9441	0.4965 8597	0.4962 7792	0.4956 6295
3	0.3296 1130	0.3292 0117	0.3287 9173	0.3283 8296	0.3275 6746
4	0.2458 2058	0.2453 6102	0.2449 0243	0.2444 4479	0.2435 3237
5	0.1955 5034	0.1950 6211	0.1945 7510	0.1940 8932	0.1931 2142
6	0.1620 4034	0.1615 3381	0.1610 2877	0.1605 2521	0.1595 2256
7	0.1381 0762	0.1375 8872	0.1370 7157	0.1365 5616	0.1355 3059
8	0.1201 6071	0.1196 3314	0.1191 0758	0.1185 8402	0.1175 4292
9	0.1062 0432	0.1056 7055	0.1051 3906	0.1046 0982	0.1035 5813
10	0.0950 4131	0.0945 0307	0.0939 6737	0.0934 3418	0.0923 7534
11	0.0859 0984	0.0853 6839	0.0848 2973	0.0842 9384	0.0832 3038
12	0.0783 0203	0.0777 5831	0.0772 1764	0.0766 7999	0.0756 1377
13	0.0718 6626	0.0713 2100	0.0707 7903	0.0702 4036	0.0691 7283
14	0.0663 5138	0.0658 0515	0.0652 6246	0.0647 2332	0.0636 5562
15	0.0615 7321	0.0610 2646	0.0604 8351	0.0599 4436	0.0588 7739
16	0.0573 9363	0.0568 4672	0.0563 0388	0.0557 6508	0.0546 9958
17	0.0537 0698	0.0531 6023	0.0526 1780	0.0520 7966	0.0510 1623
18	0.0504 3113	0.0498 8479	0.0493 4301	0.0488 0578	0.0477 4492
19	0.0475 0120	0.0469 5548	0.0464 1457	0.0458 7847	0.0448 2061
20	0.0448 6531	0.0443 2039	0.0437 8054	0.0432 4574	0.0421 9122
21	0.0424 8145	0.0419 3749	0.0413 9884	0.0408 6550	0.0398 1464
22	0.0403 1525	0.0397 7238	0.0392 3507	0.0387 0332	0.0376 5638
23	0.0383 3833	0.0377 9666	0.0372 6080	0.0367 3075	0.0356 8796
24	0.0365 2701	0.0359 8665	0.0354 5235	0.0349 2410	0.0338 8565
25	0.0348 6144	0.0343 2247	0.0337 8981	0.0332 6345	0.0322 2952
26	0.0333 2479	0.0327 8729	0.0322 5635	0.0317 3196	0.0307 0269
27	0.0319 0273	0.0313 6677	0.0308 3763	0.0303 1527	0.0292 9079
28	0.0305 8299	0.0300 4863	0.0295 2134	0.0290 0108	0.0279 8151
29	0.0293 5498	0.0288 2228	0.0282 9689	0.0277 7878	0.0267 6424
30	0.0282 0953	0.0276 7854	0.0271 5511	0.0266 3919	0.0256 2975
31	0.0271 3866	0.0266 0942	0.0260 8798	0.0255 7430	0.0245 7005
32	0.0261 3535	0.0256 0791	0.0250 8850	0.0245 7710	0.0235 7812
33	0.0251 9349	0.0246 6786	0.0241 5053	0.0236 4144	0.0226 4779
34	0.0243 0763	0.0237 8387	0.0232 6864	0.0227 6189	0.0217 7363
35	0.0234 7299	0.0229 5111	0.0224 3801	0.0219 3363	0.0209 5082
36	0.0226 8529	0.0221 6533	0.0216 5438	0.0211 5240	0.0201 7507
37	0.0219 4072	0.0214 2270	0.0209 1394	0.0204 1437	0.0194 4257
38	0.0212 3589	0.0207 1983	0.0202 1327	0.0197 1613	0.0187 4990
39	0.0205 6773	0.0200 5365	0.0195 4931	0.0190 5463	0.0180 9399
40	0.0199 3349	0.0194 2141	0.0189 1931	0.0184 2710	0.0174 7209
41	0.0193 3069	0.0188 2063	0.0183 2078	0.0178 3106	0.0168 8170
42	0.0187 5709	0.0182 4906	0.0177 5148	0.0172 6426	0.0163 2057
43	0.0182 1064	0.0177 0466	0.0172 0936	0.0167 2465	0.0157 8666
44	0.0176 8949	0.0171 8557	0.0166 9257	0.0162 1038	0.0152 7810
45	0.0171 9197	0.0166 9012	0.0161 9941	0.0157 1976	0.0147 9321
46	0.0167 1652	0.0162 1675	0.0157 2836	0.0152 5125	0.0143 3043
47	0.0162 6173	0.0157 6406	0.0152 7799	0.0148 0342	0.0138 8836
48	0.0158 2632	0.0153 3075	0.0148 4701	0.0143 7500	0.0134 6569
49	0.0154 0910	0.0149 1563	0.0144 3423	0.0139 6478	0.0130 6124
50	0.0150 0898	0.0145 1763	0.0140 3857	0.0135 7168	0.0126 7391

Table 12 (*Continued*)

$$\frac{1}{s_{\overline{n}|i}} = \frac{i}{(1+i)^n - 1} \qquad \left(\frac{1}{a_{\overline{n}|i}} = \frac{1}{s_{\overline{n}|i}} + i\right)$$

n	$1\frac{1}{8}\%$ (0.01125)	$1\frac{1}{4}\%$ (0.0125)	$1\frac{3}{8}\%$ (0.01375)	$1\frac{1}{2}\%$ (0.015)	$1\frac{3}{4}\%$ (0.0175)
51	0.0146 2494	0.0141 3571	0.0136 5900	0.0131 9469	0.0123 0269
52	0.0142 5606	0.0137 6897	0.0132 9461	0.0128 3287	0.0119 4665
53	0.0139 0149	0.0134 1653	0.0129 4453	0.0124 8537	0.0116 0492
54	0.0135 6043	0.0130 7760	0.0126 0797	0.0121 5138	0.0112 7672
55	0.0132 3213	0.0127 5145	0.0122 8418	0.0118 3018	0.0109 6129
56	0.0129 1592	0.0124 3739	0.0119 7249	0.0115 2106	0.0106 5795
57	0.0126 1116	0.0121 3478	0.0116 7225	0.0112 2341	0.0103 6606
58	0.0123 1726	0.0118 4303	0.0113 8287	0.0109 3661	0.0100 8503
59	0.0120 3366	0.0115 6158	0.0111 0380	0.0106 6012	0.0098 1430
60	0.0117 5985	0.0112 8993	0.0108 3452	0.0103 9343	0.0095 5336
61	0.0114 9534	0.0110 2758	0.0105 7455	0.0101 3604	0.0093 0172
62	0.0112 3969	0.0107 7410	0.0103 2344	0.0098 8751	0.0090 5892
63	0.0109 9247	0.0105 2904	0.0100 8076	0.0096 4741	0.0088 2455
64	0.0107 5329	0.0102 9203	0.0098 4612	0.0094 1534	0.0085 9821
65	0.0105 2178	0.0100 6268	0.0096 1914	0.0091 9094	0.0083 7952
66	0.0102 9758	0.0098 4065	0.0093 9949	0.0089 7386	0.0081 6813
67	0.0100 8037	0.0096 2560	0.0091 8682	0.0087 6376	0.0079 6372
68	0.0098 6985	0.0094 1724	0.0089 8082	0.0085 6033	0.0077 6597
69	0.0096 6571	0.0092 1527	0.0087 8122	0.0083 6329	0.0075 7459
70	0.0094 6769	0.0090 1941	0.0085 8773	0.0081 7235	0.0073 8930
71	0.0092 7552	0.0088 2941	0.0084 0009	0.0079 8727	0.0072 0985
72	0.0090 8896	0.0086 4501	0.0082 1806	0.0078 0779	0.0070 3600
73	0.0089 0779	0.0084 6600	0.0080 4140	0.0076 3368	0.0068 6750
74	0.0087 3177	0.0082 9215	0.0078 6991	0.0074 6473	0.0067 0413
75	0.0085 6072	0.0081 2325	0.0077 0336	0.0073 0072	0.0065 4570
76	0.0083 9442	0.0079 5910	0.0075 4157	0.0071 4146	0.0063 9200
77	0.0082 3269	0.0077 9953	0.0073 8435	0.0069 8676	0.0062 4285
78	0.0080 7536	0.0076 4436	0.0072 3151	0.0068 3645	0.0060 9806
79	0.0079 2226	0.0074 9341	0.0070 8290	0.0066 9036	0.0059 5748
80	0.0077 7323	0.0073 4652	0.0069 3836	0.0065 4832	0.0058 2093
81	0.0076 2812	0.0072 0356	0.0067 9772	0.0064 1019	0.0056 8828
82	0.0074 8678	0.0070 6437	0.0066 6086	0.0062 7583	0.0055 5936
83	0.0073 4908	0.0069 2881	0.0065 2762	0.0061 4509	0.0054 3406
84	0.0072 1489	0.0067 9675	0.0063 9789	0.0060 1784	0.0053 1223
85	0.0070 8409	0.0066 6808	0.0062 7153	0.0058 9396	0.0051 9375
86	0.0069 5654	0.0065 4267	0.0061 4843	0.0057 7333	0.0050 7850
87	0.0068 3215	0.0064 2041	0.0060 2847	0.0056 5584	0.0049 6636
88	0.0067 1081	0.0063 0119	0.0059 1155	0.0055 4138	0.0048 5724
89	0.0065 9240	0.0061 8491	0.0057 9756	0.0054 2984	0.0047 5102
90	0.0064 7684	0.0060 7146	0.0056 8641	0.0053 2113	0.0046 4760
91	0.0063 6403	0.0059 6076	0.0055 7799	0.0052 1516	0.0045 4690
92	0.0062 5387	0.0058 5272	0.0054 7222	0.0051 1182	0.0044 4882
93	0.0061 4629	0.0057 4724	0.0053 6902	0.0050 1104	0.0043 5327
94	0.0060 4119	0.0056 4425	0.0052 6829	0.0049 1273	0.0042 6017
95	0.0059 3851	0.0055 4366	0.0051 6997	0.0048 1681	0.0041 6944
96	0.0058 3816	0.0054 4541	0.0050 7397	0.0047 2321	0.0040 8101
97	0.0057 4007	0.0053 4941	0.0049 8022	0.0046 3186	0.0039 9480
98	0.0056 4418	0.0052 5560	0.0048 8866	0.0045 4268	0.0039 1074
99	0.0055 5041	0.0051 6391	0.0047 9921	0.0044 5560	0.0038 2876
100	0.0054 5870	0.0050 7428	0.0047 1181	0.0043 7057	0.0037 4880

Table 12 $(Continued)$

$$\frac{1}{s_{\overline{n}|i}} = \frac{i}{(1+i)^n - 1} \qquad \left(\frac{1}{a_{\overline{n}|i}} = \frac{1}{s_{\overline{n}|i}} + i \right)$$

n	2 % (0.02)	2¼ % (0.0225)	2½ % (0.025)	2¾ % (0.0275)	3 % (0.03)
1	1.0000 0000	1.0000 0000	1.0000 0000	1.0000 0000	1.0000 0000
2	0.4950 4950	0.4944 3758	0.4938 2716	0.4932 1825	0.4926 1084
3	0.3267 5467	0.3259 4458	0.3251 3717	0.3243 3243	0.3235 3036
4	0.2426 2375	0.2417 1893	0.2408 1788	0.2399 2059	0.2390 2705
5	0.1921 5839	0.1912 0021	0.1902 4686	0.1892 9832	0.1883 5457
6	0.1585 2581	0.1575 3496	0.1565 4997	0.1555 7083	0.1545 9750
7	0.1345 1196	0.1335 0025	0.1324 9543	0.1314 9747	0.1305 0635
8	0.1165 0980	0.1154 8462	0.1144 6735	0.1134 5795	0.1124 5639
9	0.1025 1544	0.1014 8170	0.1004 5689	0.0994 4095	0.0984 3386
10	0.0913 2653	0.0902 8768	0.0892 5876	0.0882 3972	0.0872 3051
11	0.0821 7794	0.0811 3649	0.0801 0596	0.0790 8629	0.0780 7745
12	0.0745 5960	0.0735 1740	0.0724 8713	0.0714 6871	0.0704 6209
13	0.0681 1835	0.0670 7686	0.0660 4827	0.0650 3252	0.0640 2954
14	0.0626 0197	0.0615 6230	0.0605 3652	0.0595 2457	0.0585 2634
15	0.0578 2547	0.0567 8852	0.0557 6646	0.0547 5917	0.0537 6658
16	0.0536 5013	0.0526 1663	0.0515 9899	0.0505 9710	0.0496 1085
17	0.0499 6984	0.0489 4039	0.0479 2777	0.0469 3186	0.0459 5253
18	0.0467 0210	0.0456 7720	0.0446 7008	0.0436 8063	0.0427 0870
19	0.0437 8177	0.0427 6182	0.0417 6062	0.0407 7802	0.0398 1388
20	0.0411 5672	0.0401 4207	0.0391 4713	0.0381 7173	0.0372 1571
21	0.0387 8477	0.0377 7572	0.0367 8733	0.0358 1941	0.0348 7178
22	0.0366 3140	0.0356 2821	0.0346 4661	0.0336 8640	0.0327 4739
23	0.0346 6810	0.0336 7097	0.0326 9638	0.0317 4410	0.0308 1390
24	0.0328 7110	0.0318 8023	0.0309 1282	0.0299 6863	0.0290 4742
25	0.0312 2044	0.0302 3599	0.0292 7592	0.0283 3997	0.0274 2787
26	0.0296 9923	0.0287 2134	0.0277 6875	0.0268 4116	0.0259 3829
27	0.0282 9309	0.0273 2188	0.0263 7687	0.0254 5776	0.0245 6421
28	0.0269 8967	0.0260 2525	0.0250 8793	0.0241 7738	0.0232 9323
29	0.0257 7836	0.0248 2081	0.0238 9127	0.0229 8935	0.0221 1467
30	0.0246 4992	0.0236 9934	0.0227 7764	0.0218 8442	0.0210 1926
31	0.0235 9635	0.0226 5280	0.0217 3900	0.0208 5453	0.0199 9893
32	0.0226 1061	0.0216 7415	0.0207 6831	0.0198 9263	0.0190 4662
33	0.0216 8653	0.0207 5722	0.0198 5938	0.0189 9253	0.0181 5612
34	0.0208 1867	0.0198 9655	0.0190 0675	0.0181 4875	0.0173 2196
35	0.0200 0221	0.0190 8731	0.0182 0558	0.0173 5645	0.0165 3929
36	0.0192 3285	0.0183 2522	0.0174 5158	0.0166 1132	0.0158 0379
37	0.0185 0678	0.0176 0643	0.0167 4090	0.0159 0953	0.0151 1162
38	0.0178 2057	0.0169 2753	0.0160 7012	0.0152 4764	0.0144 5934
39	0.0171 7114	0.0162 8543	0.0154 3615	0.0146 2256	0.0138 4385
40	0.0165 5575	0.0156 7738	0.0148 3623	0.0140 3151	0.0132 6238
41	0.0159 7188	0.0151 0087	0.0142 6786	0.0134 7200	0.0127 1241
42	0.0154 1729	0.0145 5364	0.0137 2876	0.0129 4175	0.0121 9167
43	0.0148 8993	0.0140 3364	0.0132 1688	0.0124 3871	0.0116 9811
44	0.0143 8794	0.0135 3901	0.0127 3037	0.0119 6100	0.0112 2985
45	0.0139 0962	0.0130 6805	0.0122 6751	0.0115 0693	0.0107 8518
46	0.0134 5342	0.0126 1921	0.0118 2676	0.0110 7493	0.0103 6254
47	0.0130 1792	0.0121 9107	0.0114 0669	0.0106 6358	0.0099 6051
48	0.0126 0184	0.0117 8233	0.0110 0599	0.0102 7158	0.0095 7777
49	0.0122 0396	0.0113 9179	0.0106 2348	0.0098 9773	0.0092 1314
50	0.0118 2321	0.0110 1836	0.0102 5806	0.0095 4092	0.0088 6549

Table 12 (*Continued*)

$$\frac{1}{s_{\overline{n}|i}} = \frac{i}{(1+i)^n - 1} \qquad \left(\frac{1}{a_{\overline{n}|i}} = \frac{1}{s_{\overline{n}|i}} + i\right)$$

n	2 % (0.02)	2¼ % (0.0225)	2½ % (0.025)	2¾ % (0.0275)	3 % (0.03)
51	0.0114 5856	0.0106 6102	0.0099 0870	0.0092 0014	0.0085 3382
52	0.0111 0909	0.0103 1884	0.0095 7446	0.0088 7444	0.0082 1718
53	0.0107 7392	0.0099 9094	0.0092 5449	0.0085 6297	0.0079 1471
54	0.0104 5226	0.0096 7654	0.0089 4799	0.0082 6491	0.0076 2558
55	0.0101 4337	0.0093 7489	0.0086 5419	0.0079 7953	0.0073 4907
56	0.0098 4656	0.0090 8530	0.0083 7243	0.0077 0612	0.0070 8447
57	0.0095 6120	0.0088 0712	0.0081 0204	0.0074 4404	0.0068 3114
58	0.0092 8667	0.0085 3977	0.0078 4244	0.0071 9270	0.0065 8848
59	0.0090 2243	0.0082 8268	0.0075 9307	0.0069 5153	0.0063 5593
60	0.0087 6797	0.0080 3533	0.0073 5340	0.0067 2002	0.0061 3296
61	0.0085 2278	0.0077 9724	0.0071 2294	0.0064 9767	0.0059 1908
62	0.0082 8643	0.0075 6795	0.0069 0126	0.0062 8402	0.0057 1385
63	0.0080 5848	0.0073 4704	0.0066 8790	0.0060 7866	0.0055 1682
64	0.0078 3855	0.0071 3411	0.0064 8249	0.0058 8118	0.0053 2760
65	0.0076 2624	0.0069 2878	0.0062 8463	0.0056 9120	0.0051 4581
66	0.0074 2122	0.0067 3070	0.0060 9398	0.0055 0837	0.0049 7110
67	0.0072 2316	0.0065 3955	0.0059 1021	0.0053 3236	0.0048 0313
68	0.0070 3173	0.0063 5500	0.0057 3300	0.0051 6285	0.0046 4159
69	0.0068 4665	0.0061 7677	0.0055 6206	0.0049 9955	0.0044 8618
70	0.0066 6765	0.0060 0458	0.0053 9712	0.0048 4218	0.0043 3663
71	0.0064 9446	0.0058 3816	0.0052 3790	0.0046 9048	0.0041 9266
72	0.0063 2683	0.0056 7728	0.0050 8417	0.0045 4420	0.0040 5404
73	0.0061 6454	0.0055 2169	0.0049 3568	0.0044 0311	0.0039 2053
74	0.0060 0736	0.0053 7118	0.0047 9222	0.0042 6698	0.0037 9191
75	0.0058 5508	0.0052 2554	0.0046 5358	0.0041 3560	0.0036 6796
76	0.0057 0751	0.0050 8457	0.0045 1956	0.0040 0878	0.0035 4849
77	0.0055 6447	0.0049 4808	0.0043 8997	0.0038 8633	0.0034 3331
78	0.0054 2576	0.0048 1589	0.0042 6463	0.0037 6806	0.0033 2224
79	0.0052 9123	0.0046 8784	0.0041 4338	0.0036 5382	0.0032 1510
80	0.0051 6071	0.0045 6376	0.0040 2605	0.0035 4342	0.0031 1175
81	0.0050 3405	0.0044 4350	0.0039 1248	0.0034 3674	0.0030 1201
82	0.0049 1110	0.0043 2692	0.0038 0254	0.0033 3361	0.0029 1576
83	0.0047 9173	0.0042 1387	0.0036 9608	0.0032 3389	0.0028 2284
84	0.0046 7581	0.0041 0423	0.0035 9298	0.0031 3747	0.0027 3313
85	0.0045 6321	0.0039 9787	0.0034 9310	0.0030 4420	0.0026 4650
86	0.0044 5381	0.0038 9467	0.0033 9633	0.0029 5397	0.0025 6284
87	0.0043 4750	0.0037 9452	0.0033 0255	0.0028 6667	0.0024 8202
88	0.0042 4416	0.0036 9730	0.0032 1165	0.0027 8219	0.0024 0393
89	0.0041 4370	0.0036 0291	0.0031 2353	0.0027 0041	0.0023 2848
90	0.0040 4602	0.0035 1126	0.0030 3809	0.0026 2125	0.0022 5556
91	0.0039 5101	0.0034 2224	0.0029 5523	0.0025 4460	0.0021 8508
92	0.0038 5859	0.0033 3577	0.0028 7486	0.0024 7038	0.0021 1694
93	0.0037 6868	0.0032 5176	0.0027 9690	0.0023 9850	0.0020 5107
94	0.0036 8118	0.0031 7012	0.0027 2126	0.0023 2887	0.0019 8737
95	0.0035 9602	0.0030 9078	0.0026 4786	0.0022 6141	0.0019 2577
96	0.0035 1313	0.0030 1366	0.0025 7662	0.0021 9605	0.0018 6619
97	0.0034 3242	0.0029 3868	0.0025 0747	0.0021 3272	0.0018 0856
98	0.0033 5383	0.0028 6578	0.0024 4034	0.0020 7134	0.0017 5281
99	0.0032 7729	0.0027 9489	0.0023 7517	0.0020 1185	0.0016 9886
100	0.0032 0274	0.0027 2594	0.0023 1188	0.0019 5418	0.0016 4667

Table 12 *(Continued)*

$$\frac{1}{s_{\overline{n}|i}} = \frac{i}{(1+i)^n - 1} \qquad \left(\frac{1}{a_{\overline{n}|i}} = \frac{1}{s_{\overline{n}|i}} + i \right)$$

n	$3\frac{1}{2}\%$ (0.035)	4% (0.04)	$4\frac{1}{2}\%$ (0.045)	5% (0.05)	$5\frac{1}{2}\%$ (0.055)
1	1.0000 0000	1.0000 0000	1.0000 0000	1.0000 0000	1.0000 0000
2	0.4914 0049	0.4901 9608	0.4889 9756	0.4878 0488	0.4866 1800
3	0.3219 3418	0.3203 4854	0.3187 7336	0.3172 0856	0.3156 5407
4	0.2372 5114	0.2354 9005	0.2337 4365	0.2320 1183	0.2302 9449
5	0.1864 8137	0.1846 2711	0.1827 9164	0.1809 7480	0.1791 7644
6	0.1526 6821	0.1507 6190	0.1488 7839	0.1470 1747	0.1451 7895
7	0.1285 4449	0.1266 0961	0.1247 0147	0.1228 1982	0.1209 6442
8	0.1104 7665	0.1085 2783	0.1066 0965	0.1047 2181	0.1028 6401
9	0.0964 4601	0.0944 9299	0.0925 7447	0.0906 9008	0.0888 3946
10	0.0852 4137	0.0832 9094	0.0813 7882	0.0795 0457	0.0776 6777
11	0.0760 9197	0.0741 4904	0.0722 4818	0.0703 8889	0.0685 7065
12	0.0684 8395	0.0665 5217	0.0646 6619	0.0628 2541	0.0610 2923
13	0.0620 6157	0.0601 4373	0.0582 7535	0.0564 5577	0.0546 8426
14	0.0565 7073	0.0546 6897	0.0528 2032	0.0510 2397	0.0492 7912
15	0.0518 2507	0.0499 4110	0.0481 1381	0.0463 4229	0.0446 2560
16	0.0476 8483	0.0458 2000	0.0440 1537	0.0422 6991	0.0405 8254
17	0.0440 4313	0.0421 9852	0.0404 1758	0.0386 9914	0.0370 4197
18	0.0408 1684	0.0389 9333	0.0372 3690	0.0355 4622	0.0339 1992
19	0.0379 4033	0.0361 3862	0.0344 0734	0.0327 4501	0.0311 5006
20	0.0353 6108	0.0335 8175	0.0318 7614	0.0302 4259	0.0286 7933
21	0.0330 3659	0.0312 8011	0.0296 0057	0.0279 9611	0.0264 6478
22	0.0309 3207	0.0291 9881	0.0275 4565	0.0259 7051	0.0244 7123
23	0.0290 1880	0.0273 0906	0.0256 8249	0.0241 3682	0.0226 6965
24	0.0272 7283	0.0255 8683	0.0239 8703	0.0224 7090	0.0210 3580
25	0.0256 7404	0.0240 1196	0.0224 3903	0.0209 5246	0.0195 4935
26	0.0242 0540	0.0225 6738	0.0210 2137	0.0195 6432	0.0181 9307
27	0.0228 5241	0.0212 3854	0.0197 1946	0.0182 9186	0.0169 5228
28	0.0216 0265	0.0200 1298	0.0185 2081	0.0171 2253	0.0158 1440
29	0.0204 4538	0.0188 7993	0.0174 1461	0.0160 4551	0.0147 6857
30	0.0193 7133	0.0178 3010	0.0163 9154	0.0150 5144	0.0138 0539
31	0.0183 7240	0.0168 5535	0.0154 4345	0.0141 3212	0.0129 1665
32	0.0174 4150	0.0159 4859	0.0145 6320	0.0132 8042	0.0120 9519
33	0.0165 7242	0.0151 0357	0.0137 4453	0.0124 9004	0.0113 3469
34	0.0157 5966	0.0143 1477	0.0129 8191	0.0117 5545	0.0106 2958
35	0.0149 9835	0.0135 7732	0.0122 7045	0.0110 7171	0.0099 7493
36	0.0142 8416	0.0128 8688	0.0116 0578	0.0104 3446	0.0093 6635
37	0.0136 1325	0.0122 3957	0.0109 8402	0.0098 3979	0.0087 9993
38	0.0129 8214	0.0116 3192	0.0104 0169	0.0092 8423	0.0082 7217
39	0.0123 8775	0.0110 6083	0.0098 5567	0.0087 6462	0.0077 7991
40	0.0118 2728	0.0105 2349	0.0093 4315	0.0082 7816	0.0073 2034
41	0.0112 9822	0.0100 1738	0.0088 6158	0.0078 2229	0.0068 9090
42	0.0107 9828	0.0095 4020	0.0084 0868	0.0073 9471	0.0064 8927
43	0.0103 2539	0.0090 8989	0.0079 8235	0.0069 9333	0.0061 1337
44	0.0098 7768	0.0086 6454	0.0075 8071	0.0066 1625	0.0057 6128
45	0.0094 5343	0.0082 6246	0.0072 0202	0.0062 6173	0.0054 3127
46	0.0090 5108	0.0078 8205	0.0068 4471	0.0059 2820	0.0051 2175
47	0.0086 6919	0.0075 2189	0.0065 0734	0.0056 1421	0.0048 3129
48	0.0083 0646	0.0071 8065	0.0061 8858	0.0053 1843	0.0045 5854
49	0.0079 6167	0.0068 5712	0.0058 8722	0.0050 3965	0.0043 0230
50	0.0076 3371	0.0065 5020	0.0056 0215	0.0047 7674	0.0040 6145

Table 12 (*Continued*)

$$\frac{1}{s_{\overline{n}|i}} = \frac{i}{(1+i)^n - 1} \qquad \left(\frac{1}{a_{\overline{n}|i}} = \frac{1}{s_{\overline{n}|i}} + i\right)$$

n	$3\frac{1}{2}\%$ (0.035)	4% (0.04)	$4\frac{1}{2}\%$ (0.045)	5% (0.05)	$5\frac{1}{2}\%$ (0.055)
51	0.0073 2156	0.0062 5885	0.0053 3232	0.0045 2867	0.0038 3495
52	0.0070 2429	0.0059 8212	0.0050 7679	0.0042 9450	0.0036 2186
53	0.0067 4100	0.0057 1915	0.0048 3469	0.0040 7334	0.0034 2130
54	0.0064 7090	0.0054 6910	0.0046 0519	0.0038 6438	0.0032 3245
55	0.0062 1323	0.0052 3124	0.0043 8754	0.0036 6686	0.0030 5458
56	0.0059 6730	0.0050 0487	0.0041 8105	0.0034 8010	0.0028 8698
57	0.0057 3245	0.0047 8932	0.0039 8506	0.0033 0343	0.0027 2900
58	0.0055 0810	0.0045 8401	0.0037 9897	0.0031 3626	0.0025 8006
59	0.0052 9366	0.0043 8836	0.0036 2221	0.0029 7802	0.0024 3959
60	0.0050 8862	0.0042 0185	0.0034 5426	0.0028 2818	0.0023 0707
61	0.0048 9249	0.0040 2398	0.0032 9462	0.0026 8627	0.0021 8202
62	0.0047 0480	0.0038 5430	0.0031 4284	0.0025 5183	0.0020 6400
63	0.0045 2513	0.0036 9237	0.0029 9848	0.0024 2442	0.0019 5258
64	0.0043 5308	0.0035 3780	0.0028 6115	0.0023 0365	0.0018 4737
65	0.0041 8826	0.0033 9019	0.0027 3047	0.0021 8915	0.0017 4800
66	0.0040 3031	0.0032 4921	0.0026 0608	0.0020 8057	0.0016 5413
67	0.0038 7892	0.0031 1451	0.0024 8765	0.0019 7758	0.0015 6544
68	0.0037 3375	0.0029 8578	0.0023 7487	0.0018 7986	0.0014 8163
69	0.0035 9453	0.0028 6272	0.0022 6745	0.0017 8715	0.0014 0242
70	0.0034 6095	0.0027 4506	0.0021 6511	0.0016 9915	0.0013 2754
71	0.0033 3277	0.0026 3253	0.0020 6759	0.0016 1563	0.0012 5675
72	0.0032 0973	0.0025 2489	0.0019 7465	0.0015 3633	0.0011 8982
73	0.0030 9160	0.0024 2190	0.0018 8606	0.0014 6103	0.0011 2652
74	0.0029 7816	0.0023 2334	0.0018 0159	0.0013 8953	0.0010 6665
75	0.0028 6919	0.0022 2900	0.0017 2104	0.0013 2161	0.0010 1002
76	0.0027 6450	0.0021 3869	0.0016 4422	0.0012 5709	0.0009 5645
77	0.0026 6390	0.0020 5221	0.0015 7094	0.0011 9580	0.0009 0577
78	0.0025 6721	0.0019 6939	0.0015 0104	0.0011 3756	0.0008 5781
79	0.0024 7426	0.0018 9007	0.0014 3434	0.0010 8222	0.0008 1243
80	0.0023 8489	0.0018 1408	0.0013 7069	0.0010 2962	0.0007 6948
81	0.0022 9894	0.0017 4127	0.0013 0995	0.0009 7963	0.0007 2884
82	0.0022 1628	0.0016 7150	0.0012 5197	0.0009 3211	0.0006 9036
83	0.0021 3676	0.0016 0463	0.0011 9663	0.0008 8694	0.0006 5395
84	0.0020 6025	0.0015 4054	0.0011 4379	0.0008 4399	0.0006 1947
85	0.0019 8662	0.0014 7909	0.0010 9334	0.0008 0316	0.0005 8683
86	0.0019 1576	0.0014 2018	0.0010 4516	0.0007 6433	0.0005 5593
87	0.0018 4756	0.0013 6370	0.0009 9915	0.0007 2740	0.0005 2667
88	0.0017 8190	0.0013 0953	0.0009 5522	0.0006 9228	0.0004 9896
89	0.0017 1868	0.0012 5758	0.0009 1325	0.0006 5888	0.0004 7273
90	0.0016 5781	0.0012 0775	0.0008 7316	0.0006 2711	0.0004 4788
91	0.0015 9919	0.0011 5995	0.0008 3486	0.0005 9689	0.0004 2435
92	0.0015 4273	0.0011 1410	0.0007 9827	0.0005 6815	0.0004 0207
93	0.0014 8834	0.0010 7010	0.0007 6331	0.0005 4080	0.0003 8096
94	0.0014 3594	0.0010 2789	0.0007 2991	0.0005 1478	0.0003 6097
95	0.0013 8546	0.0009 8738	0.0006 9799	0.0004 9003	0.0003 4204
96	0.0013 3682	0.0009 4850	0.0006 6749	0.0004 6648	0.0003 2410
97	0.0012 8995	0.0009 1119	0.0006 3834	0.0004 4407	0.0003 0711
98	0.0012 4478	0.0008 7538	0.0006 1048	0.0004 2274	0.0002 9101
99	0.0012 0124	0.0008 4100	0.0005 8385	0.0004 0245	0.0002 7577
100	0.0011 5927	0.0008 0800	0.0005 5839	0.0003 8314	0.0002 6132

Table 12 (*Continued*)

$$\frac{1}{s_{\overline{n}|i}} = \frac{i}{(1+i)^n - 1} \qquad \left(\frac{1}{a_{\overline{n}|i}} = \frac{1}{s_{\overline{n}|i}} + i \right)$$

n	6% (0.06)	6½% (0.065)	7% (0.07)	7½% (0.075)	8% (0.08)
1	1.0000 0000	1.0000 0000	1.0000 0000	1.0000 0000	1.0000 0000
2	0.4854 3689	0.4842 6150	0.4830 9179	0.4819 2771	0.4807 6923
3	0.3141 0981	0.3125 7570	0.3110 5167	0.3095 3763	0.3080 3351
4	0.2285 9149	0.2269 0274	0.2252 2812	0.2235 6751	0.2219 2080
5	0.1773 9640	0.1756 3454	0.1738 9069	0.1721 6472	0.1704 5645
6	0.1433 6263	0.1415 6831	0.1397 9580	0.1380 4489	0.1363 1539
7	0.1191 3502	0.1173 3137	0.1155 5322	0.1138 0032	0.1120 7240
8	0.1010 3594	0.0992 3730	0.0974 6776	0.0957 2702	0.0940 1476
9	0.0870 2224	0.0852 3803	0.0834 8647	0.0817 6716	0.0800 7971
10	0.0758 6796	0.0741 0469	0.0723 7750	0.0706 8593	0.0690 2949
11	0.0667 9294	0.0650 5521	0.0633 5690	0.0616 9747	0.0600 7634
12	0.0592 7703	0.0575 6817	0.0559 0199	0.0542 7783	0.0526 9502
13	0.0529 6011	0.0512 8256	0.0496 5085	0.0480 6420	0.0465 2181
14	0.0475 8491	0.0459 4048	0.0443 4494	0.0427 9737	0.0412 9685
15	0.0429 6276	0.0413 5278	0.0397 9462	0.0382 8724	0.0368 2954
16	0.0389 5214	0.0373 7757	0.0358 5765	0.0343 9116	0.0329 7687
17	0.0354 4480	0.0339 0633	0.0324 2519	0.0310 0003	0.0296 2943
18	0.0323 5654	0.0308 5461	0.0294 1260	0.0280 2896	0.0267 0210
19	0.0296 2086	0.0281 5575	0.0267 5301	0.0254 1090	0.0241 2763
20	0.0271 8456	0.0257 5640	0.0243 9293	0.0230 9219	0.0218 5221
21	0.0250 0455	0.0236 1333	0.0222 8900	0.0210 2937	0.0198 3225
22	0.0230 4557	0.0216 9120	0.0204 0577	0.0191 8687	0.0180 3207
23	0.0212 7848	0.0199 6078	0.0187 1393	0.0175 3528	0.0164 2217
24	0.0196 7900	0.0183 9770	0.0171 8902	0.0160 5008	0.0149 7796
25	0.0182 2672	0.0169 8148	0.0158 1052	0.0147 1067	0.0136 7878
26	0.0169 0435	0.0156 9480	0.0145 6103	0.0134 9961	0.0125 0713
27	0.0156 9717	0.0145 2288	0.0134 2573	0.0124 0204	0.0114 4810
28	0.0145 9255	0.0134 5305	0.0123 9193	0.0114 0520	0.0104 8891
29	0.0135 7961	0.0124 7440	0.0114 4865	0.0104 9811	0.0096 1654
30	0.0126 4891	0.0115 7744	0.0105 8640	0.0096 7124	0.0088 2743
31	0.0117 9222	0.0107 5393	0.0097 9691	0.0089 1628	0.0081 0728
32	0.0110 0234	0.0099 9665	0.0090 7292	0.0082 2599	0.0074 5081
33	0.0102 7293	0.0092 9924	0.0084 0807	0.0075 9397	0.0068 5163
34	0.0095 9843	0.0086 5610	0.0077 9674	0.0070 1461	0.0063 0411
35	0.0089 7386	0.0080 6226	0.0072 3396	0.0064 8291	0.0058 0326
36	0.0083 9483	0.0075 1332	0.0067 1531	0.0059 9447	0.0053 4467
37	0.0078 5743	0.0070 0534	0.0062 3685	0.0055 4533	0.0049 2440
38	0.0073 5812	0.0065 3480	0.0057 9505	0.0051 3197	0.0045 3894
39	0.0068 9377	0.0060 9854	0.0053 8676	0.0047 5124	0.0041 8513
40	0.0064 6154	0.0056 9373	0.0050 0914	0.0044 0031	0.0038 6016
41	0.0060 5886	0.0053 1779	0.0046 5962	0.0040 7663	0.0035 6149
42	0.0056 8342	0.0049 6842	0.0043 3591	0.0037 7789	0.0032 8684
43	0.0053 3312	0.0046 4352	0.0040 3590	0.0035 0201	0.0030 3414
44	0.0050 0606	0.0043 4119	0.0037 5769	0.0032 4710	0.0028 0152
45	0.0047 0050	0.0040 5968	0.0034 9957	0.0030 1146	0.0025 8728
46	0.0044 1485	0.0037 9743	0.0032 5996	0.0027 9354	0.0023 8991
47	0.0041 4768	0.0035 5300	0.0030 3744	0.0025 9190	0.0022 0799
48	0.0038 9765	0.0033 2505	0.0028 3070	0.0024 0527	0.0020 4027
49	0.0036 6356	0.0031 1240	0.0026 3853	0.0022 3247	0.0018 8557
50	0.0034 4429	0.0029 1393	0.0024 5985	0.0020 7241	0.0017 4286

Table 12 $(Continued)$

$$\frac{1}{s_{\overline{n}|i}} = \frac{i}{(1+i)^n - 1} \qquad \left(\frac{1}{a_{\overline{n}|i}} = \frac{1}{s_{\overline{n}|i}} + i \right)$$

n	$8\frac{1}{2}\%$ (0.085)	9% (0.09)	$9\frac{1}{2}\%$ (0.095)	10% (0.10)	$10\frac{1}{2}\%$ (0.105)
1	1.0000 0000	1.0000 0000	1.0000 0000	1.0000 0000	1.0000 0000
2	0.4796 1631	0.4784 6890	0.4773 2697	0.4761 9048	0.4750 5938
3	0.3065 3925	0.3050 5476	0.3035 7997	0.3021 1480	0.3006 5920
4	0.2202 8789	0.2186 6866	0.2170 6300	0.2154 7080	0.2138 9196
5	0.1687 6575	0.1670 9246	0.1654 3642	0.1637 9748	0.1621 7550
6	0.1346 0708	0.1329 1978	0.1312 5328	0.1296 0738	0.1279 8187
7	0.1103 6922	0.1086 9052	0.1070 3603	0.1054 0550	0.1037 9867
8	0.0923 3065	0.0906 7438	0.0890 4561	0.0874 4402	0.0858 6928
9	0.0784 2372	0.0767 9880	0.0752 0454	0.0736 4054	0.0721 0638
10	0.0674 0771	0.0658 2009	0.0642 6615	0.0627 4539	0.0612 5732
11	0.0584 9293	0.0569 4666	0.0554 3693	0.0539 6314	0.0525 2470
12	0.0511 5286	0.0496 5066	0.0481 8771	0.0467 6332	0.0453 7675
13	0.0450 2287	0.0435 6656	0.0421 5206	0.0407 7852	0.0394 4512
14	0.0398 4244	0.0384 3317	0.0370 6809	0.0357 4622	0.0344 6659
15	0.0354 2046	0.0340 5888	0.0327 4370	0.0314 7378	0.0302 4800
16	0.0316 1354	0.0302 9991	0.0290 3470	0.0278 1662	0.0266 4440
17	0.0283 1198	0.0270 4625	0.0258 3078	0.0246 6413	0.0235 4485
18	0.0254 3041	0.0242 1229	0.0230 4610	0.0219 3022	0.0208 6302
19	0.0229 0140	0.0217 3041	0.0206 1284	0.0195 4687	0.0185 3069
20	0.0206 7097	0.0195 4648	0.0184 7670	0.0174 5962	0.0164 9327
21	0.0186 9541	0.0176 1663	0.0165 9370	0.0156 2439	0.0147 0652
22	0.0169 3892	0.0159 0499	0.0149 2784	0.0140 0506	0.0131 3426
23	0.0153 7193	0.0143 8188	0.0134 4938	0.0125 7181	0.0117 4659
24	0.0139 6975	0.0130 2256	0.0121 3351	0.0112 9978	0.0105 1858
25	0.0127 1168	0.0118 0625	0.0109 5939	0.0101 6807	0.0094 2932
26	0.0115 8017	0.0107 1536	0.0099 0940	0.0091 5904	0.0084 6112
27	0.0105 6025	0.0097 3491	0.0089 6852	0.0082 5764	0.0075 9894
28	0.0096 3914	0.0088 5205	0.0081 2389	0.0074 5101	0.0068 2990
29	0.0088 0577	0.0080 5572	0.0073 6444	0.0067 2807	0.0061 4293
30	0.0080 5058	0.0073 3635	0.0066 8058	0.0060 7925	0.0055 2848
31	0.0073 6524	0.0066 8560	0.0060 6399	0.0054 9621	0.0049 7824
32	0.0067 4247	0.0060 9619	0.0055 0739	0.0049 7172	0.0044 8499
33	0.0061 7588	0.0055 6173	0.0050 0441	0.0044 9941	0.0040 4241
34	0.0056 5984	0.0050 7660	0.0045 4945	0.0040 7371	0.0036 4495
35	0.0051 8937	0.0046 3584	0.0041 3756	0.0036 8971	0.0032 8776
36	0.0047 6006	0.0042 3505	0.0037 6437	0.0033 4306	0.0029 6652
37	0.0043 6799	0.0038 7033	0.0034 2600	0.0030 2994	0.0026 7744
38	0.0040 0966	0.0035 3820	0.0031 1901	0.0027 4692	0.0024 1717
39	0.0036 8193	0.0032 3555	0.0028 4032	0.0024 9098	0.0021 8271
40	0.0033 8201	0.0029 5961	0.0025 8719	0.0022 5941	0.0019 7141
41	0.0031 0737	0.0027 0789	0.0023 5716	0.0020 4980	0.0017 8090
42	0.0028 5576	0.0024 7814	0.0021 4803	0.0018 5999	0.0016 0908
43	0.0026 2512	0.0022 6837	0.0019 5783	0.0016 8805	0.0014 5407
44	0.0024 1363	0.0020 7675	0.0017 8478	0.0015 3224	0.0013 1417
45	0.0022 1961	0.0019 0165	0.0016 2729	0.0013 9100	0.0011 8788
46	0.0020 4154	0.0017 4160	0.0014 8390	0.0012 6295	0.0010 7385
47	0.0018 7807	0.0015 9525	0.0013 5333	0.0011 4682	0.0009 7087
48	0.0017 2795	0.0014 6139	0.0012 3439	0.0010 4148	0.0008 7784
49	0.0015 9005	0.0013 3893	0.0011 2603	0.0009 4590	0.0007 9380
50	0.0014 6334	0.0012 2687	0.0010 2728	0.0008 5917	0.0007 1785

Table 13   Commissioners 1941 standard ordinary mortality table

Age x	Number living l_x	Number of deaths d_x	Yearly death rate q_x	Yearly rate of survival p_x	Age x	Number living l_x	Number of deaths d_x	Yearly death rate q_x	Yearly rate of survival p_x
1	1,000,000	5,770	.00577	.99423	51	800,910	10,628	.01327	.98673
2	994,230	4,116	.00414	.99586	52	790,282	11,301	.01430	.98570
3	990,114	3,347	.00338	.99662	53	778,981	12,020	.01543	.98457
4	986,767	2,950	.00299	.99701	54	766,961	12,770	.01665	.98335
5	983,817	2,715	.00276	.99724	55	754,191	13,560	.01798	.98202
6	981,102	2,561	.00261	.99739	56	740,631	14,390	.01943	.98057
7	978,541	2,417	.00247	.99753	57	726,241	15,251	.02100	.97900
8	976,124	2,255	.00231	.99769	58	710,990	16,147	.02271	.97729
9	973,869	2,065	.00212	.99788	59	694,843	17,072	.02457	.97543
10	971,804	1,914	.00197	.99803	60	677,771	18,022	.02659	.97341
11	969,890	1,852	.00191	.99809	61	659,749	18,988	.02878	.97122
12	968,038	1,859	.00192	.99808	62	640,761	19,979	.03118	.96882
13	966,179	1,913	.00198	.99802	63	620,782	20,958	.03376	.96624
14	964,266	1,996	.00207	.99793	64	599,824	21,942	.03658	.96342
15	962,270	2,069	.00215	.99785	65	577,882	22,907	.03964	.96036
16	960,201	2,103	.00219	.99781	66	554,975	23,842	.04296	.95704
17	958,098	2,156	.00225	.99775	67	531,133	24,730	.04656	.95344
18	955,942	2,199	.00230	.99770	68	506,403	25,553	.05046	.94954
19	953,743	2,260	.00237	.99763	69	480,850	26,302	.05470	.94530
20	951,483	2,312	.00243	.99757	70	454,548	26,955	.05930	.94070
21	949,171	2,382	.00251	.99749	71	427,593	27,481	.06427	.93573
22	946,789	2,452	.00259	.99741	72	400,112	27,872	.06966	.93034
23	944,337	2,531	.00268	.99732	73	372,240	28,104	.07550	.92450
24	941,806	2,609	.00277	.99723	74	344,136	28,154	.08181	.91819
25	939,197	2,705	.00288	.99712	75	315,982	28,009	.08864	.91136
26	936,492	2,800	.00299	.99701	76	287,973	27,651	.09602	.90398
27	933,692	2,904	.00311	.99689	77	260,322	27,071	.10399	.89601
28	930,788	3,025	.00325	.99675	78	233,251	26,262	.11259	.88741
29	927,763	3,154	.00340	.99660	79	206,989	25,224	.12186	.87814
30	924,609	3,292	.00356	.99644	80	181,765	23,966	.13185	.86815
31	921,317	3,437	.00373	.99627	81	157,799	22,502	.14260	.85740
32	917,880	3,598	.00392	.99608	82	135,297	20,857	.15416	.84584
33	914,282	3,767	.00412	.99588	83	114,440	19,062	.16657	.83343
34	910,515	3,961	.00435	.99565	84	95,378	17,157	.17988	.82012
35	906,554	4,161	.00459	.99541	85	78,221	15,185	.19413	.80587
36	902,393	4,386	.00486	.99514	86	63,036	13,198	.20937	.79063
37	898,007	4,625	.00515	.99485	87	49,838	11,245	.22563	.77437
38	893,382	4,878	.00546	.99454	88	38,593	9,378	.24300	.75700
39	888,504	5,162	.00581	.99419	89	29,215	7,638	.26144	.73856
40	883,342	5,459	.00618	.99382	90	21,577	6,063	.28099	.71901
41	877,883	5,785	.00659	.99341	91	15,514	4,681	.30173	.69827
42	872,098	6,131	.00703	.99297	92	10,833	3,506	.32364	.67636
43	865,967	6,503	.00751	.99249	93	7,327	2,540	.34666	.65334
44	859,464	6,910	.00804	.99196	94	4,787	1,776	.37100	.62900
45	852,554	7,340	.00861	.99139	95	3,011	1,193	.39621	.60379
46	845,214	7,801	.00923	.99077	96	1,818	813	.44719	.55281
47	837,413	8,299	.00991	.99009	97	1,005	551	.54826	.45174
48	829,114	8,822	.01064	.98936	98	454	329	.72467	.27533
49	820,292	9,392	.01145	.98855	99	125	125	1.00000	.00000
50	810,900	9,990	.01232	.98768					

Table 14 Commutation columns, commissioners 1941 standard
ordinary mortality table, $2\frac{1}{2}\%$

Age x	D_x	N_x	M_x	Age x	D_x	N_x	M_x
1	975 610	30 351 128	235 338.3	51	227 335	3 613 562.6	139 199.5
2	946 322	29 375 518	229 846.4	52	218 847	3 386 227.4	136 256.3
3	919 419	28 429 196	226 024.3	53	210 456	3 167 380.2	133 203.2
4	893 962	27 509 776	222 992.0	54	202 155	2 956 923.8	130 034.9
5	869 551	26 615 814	220 384.7	55	193 941	2 754 768.8	126 751.1
6	846 001	25 746 263	218 043.5	56	185 808	2 560 828.2	123 349.2
7	823 213	24 900 262	215 889.1	57	177 754	2 375 019.8	119 827.1
8	801 150	24 077 050	213 905.3	58	169 777	2 197 265.3	116 185.3
9	779 805	23 275 899	212 099.7	59	161 875	2 027 488.2	112 423.6
10	759 172	22 496 095	210 486.5	60	154 046	1 865 613.6	108 543.5
11	739 197	21 736 923	209 027.8	61	146 293	1 711 567.4	104 547.3
12	719 790	20 997 726	207 650.7	62	138 617	1 565 274.6	100 439.5
13	700 886	20 277 936	206 302.1	63	131 019	1 426 657.6	96 222.87
14	682 437	19 577 050	204 948.2	64	123 508	1 295 638.2	91 907.46
15	664 414	18 894 613	203 570.1	65	116 088	1 172 129.8	87 499.63
16	646 815	18 230 198	202 176.3	66	108 767	1 056 041.6	83 010.18
17	629 657	17 583 383	200 794.3	67	101 556	947 274.35	78 451.45
18	612 917	16 953 726	199 411.9	68	94 465.5	845 718.65	73 838.26
19	596 593	16 340 808	198 036.4	69	87 511.0	751 253.11	69 187.81
20	580 662	15 744 216	196 657.2	70	80 706.6	663 742.06	64 517.79
21	565 123	15 163 553	195 280.6	71	74 068.9	583 035.43	59 848.57
22	549 956	14 598 430	193 897.0	72	67 618.1	508 966.49	55 204.33
23	535 153	14 048 474	192 507.5	73	61 373.5	441 348.34	50 608.90
24	520 701	13 513 320	191 108.1	74	55 355.9	379 974.84	46 088.24
25	506 594	12 992 619	189 700.9	75	49 587.5	324 618.92	41 669.99
26	492 815	12 486 025	188 277.4	76	44 089.8	275 031.40	37 381.70
27	479 357	11 993 210	186 839.9	77	38 884.2	230 941.61	33 251.48
28	466 211	11 513 853	185 385.3	78	33 990.8	192 057.40	29 306.52
29	453 362	11 047 642	183 907.1	79	29 428.1	158 066.55	25 572.80
30	440 801	10 594 280	182 403.5	80	25 211.6	128 638.48	22 074.11
31	428 518	10 153 480	180 872.3	81	21 353.6	103 426.84	18 831.00
32	416 507	9 724 961.6	179 312.7	82	17 862.0	82 073.238	15 860.26
33	404 755	9 308 454.7	177 719.9	83	14 740.0	64 211.191	13 173.86
34	393 256	9 903 699.4	176 092.9	84	11 985.2	49 471.207	10 778.54
35	381 996	8 510 443.1	174 423.8	85	9 589.47	37 486.056	8 675.180
36	370 968	8 128 447.4	172 713.3	86	7 539.39	27 896.582	6 858.986
37	360 161	7 757 479.3	170 954.2	87	5 815.46	20 357.191	5 318.946
38	349 567	7 397 318.3	169 144.5	88	4 393.48	14 541.728	4 038.801
39	339 179	7 047 751.4	167 282.4	89	3 244.75	10 148.250	2 997.236
40	328 984	6 708 572.7	165 359.9	90	2 337.99	6 903.4959	2 169.615
41	318 976	6 379 589.0	163 376.4	91	1 640.03	4 565.5030	1 528.677
42	309 146	6 060 612.9	161 325.7	92	1 117.26	2 925.4721	1 045.904
43	299 485	5 751 467.4	159 205.3	93	737.236	1 808.2150	693.1335
44	289 986	5 451 982.4	157 011.2	94	469.916	1 070.9787	443.7944
45	280 639	5 161 996.0	154 736.6	95	288.366	601.06285	273.7056
46	271 437	4 881 357.0	152 379.4	96	169.865	312.69718	162.2378
47	262 372	4 609 920.2	149 935.2	97	91.6117	142.83260	88.12801
48	253 436	4 347 547.8	147 389.5	98	40.3754	51.220863	39.12613
49	244 624	4 094 111.6	144 767.6	99	10.8454	10.845444	10.58092
50	235 925	3 849 487.6	142 035.1				

Table 15   Mantissas for 1000–1050

N	0	1	2	3	4	5	6	7	8	9	Diff.
1000	000 0000	0434	0869	1303	1737	2171	2605	3039	3473	3907	435
01	4341	4775	5208	5642	6076	6510	6943	7377	7810	8244	434
02	8677	9111	9544	9977	$\overline{0411}$	$\overline{0844}$	$\overline{1277}$	$\overline{1710}$	$\overline{2143}$	2576	433
03	001 3009	3442	3875	4308	4741	5174	5607	6039	6472	6905	
04	7337	7770	8202	8635	9067	9499	9932	$\overline{0364}$	$\overline{0796}$	$\overline{1228}$	
05	002 1661	2093	2525	2957	3389	3821	4253	4685	5116	5548	432
06	5980	6411	6843	7275	7706	8138	8569	9001	9432	9863	
07	003 0295	0726	1157	1588	2019	2451	2882	3313	3744	4174	
08	4605	5036	5467	5898	6328	6759	7190	7620	8051	8481	431
09	8912	9342	9772	$\overline{0203}$	$\overline{0633}$	$\overline{1063}$	$\overline{1493}$	$\overline{1924}$	$\overline{2354}$	$\overline{2784}$	
1010	004 3214	3644	4074	4504	4933	5363	5793	6223	6652	7082	430
11	7512	7941	8371	8800	9229	9659	$\overline{0088}$	$\overline{0517}$	$\overline{0947}$	$\overline{1376}$	429
12	005 1805	2234	2663	3092	3521	3950	4379	4808	5237	5666	
13	6094	6523	6952	7380	7809	8238	8666	9094	9523	9951	
14	006 0380	0808	1236	1664	2092	2521	2949	3377	3805	4233	
15	4660	5088	5516	5944	6372	6799	7227	7655	8082	8510	428
16	8937	9365	9792	$\overline{0219}$	$\overline{0647}$	$\overline{1074}$	$\overline{1501}$	$\overline{1928}$	$\overline{2355}$	$\overline{2782}$	
17	007 3210	3637	4064	4490	4917	5344	5771	6198	6624	7051	427
18	7478	7904	8331	8757	9184	9610	$\overline{0037}$	$\overline{0463}$	$\overline{0889}$	$\overline{1316}$	
19	008 1742	2168	2594	3020	3446	3872	4298	4724	5150	5576	426
1020	6002	6427	6853	7279	7704	8130	8556	8981	9407	9832	425
21	009 0257	0683	1108	1533	1959	2384	2809	3234	3659	4084	
22	4509	4934	5359	5784	6208	6633	7058	7483	7907	8332	
23	8756	9181	9605	$\overline{0030}$	$\overline{0454}$	$\overline{0878}$	$\overline{1303}$	$\overline{1727}$	$\overline{2151}$	$\overline{2575}$	
24	010 3000	3424	3848	4272	4696	5120	5544	5967	6391	6815	424
25	7239	7662	8086	8510	8933	9357	9780	$\overline{0204}$	$\overline{0627}$	$\overline{1050}$	
26	011 1474	1897	2320	2743	3166	3590	4013	4436	4859	5282	423
27	5704	6127	6550	6973	7396	7818	8241	8664	9086	9509	
28	9931	$\overline{0354}$	$\overline{0776}$	$\overline{1198}$	$\overline{1621}$	$\overline{2043}$	$\overline{2465}$	$\overline{2887}$	$\overline{3310}$	$\overline{3732}$	
29	012 4154	4576	4998	5420	5842	6264	6685	7107	7529	7951	422
1030	8372	8794	9215	9637	$\overline{0059}$	$\overline{0480}$	$\overline{0901}$	$\overline{1323}$	$\overline{1744}$	$\overline{2165}$	
31	013 2587	3008	3429	3850	4271	4692	5113	5534	5955	6376	
32	6797	7218	7639	8059	8480	8901	9321	9742	$\overline{0162}$	$\overline{0583}$	421
33	014 1003	1424	1844	2264	2685	3105	3525	3945	4365	4785	
34	5205	5625	6045	6465	6885	7305	7725	8144	8564	8984	420
35	9403	9823	$\overline{0243}$	$\overline{0662}$	$\overline{1082}$	$\overline{1501}$	$\overline{1920}$	$\overline{2340}$	$\overline{2759}$	$\overline{3178}$	419
36	015 3598	4017	4436	4855	5274	5693	6112	6531	6950	7369	
37	7788	8206	8625	9044	9462	9881	$\overline{0300}$	$\overline{0718}$	$\overline{1137}$	$\overline{1555}$	
38	016 1974	2392	2810	3229	3647	4065	4483	4901	5319	5737	418
39	6155	6573	6991	7409	7827	8245	8663	9080	9498	9916	
1040	017 0333	0751	1168	1586	2003	2421	2838	3256	3673	4090	
41	4507	4924	5342	5759	6176	6593	7010	7427	7844	8260	
42	8677	9094	9511	9927	$\overline{0344}$	$\overline{0761}$	$\overline{1177}$	$\overline{1594}$	$\overline{2010}$	$\overline{2427}$	417
43	018 2843	3259	3676	4092	4508	4925	5341	5757	6173	6589	
44	7005	7421	7837	8253	8669	9084	9500	9916	$\overline{0332}$	$\overline{0747}$	
45	019 1163	1578	1994	2410	2825	3240	3656	4071	4486	4902	416
46	5317	5732	6147	6562	6977	7392	7807	8222	8637	9052	415
47	9467	9882	$\overline{0296}$	$\overline{0711}$	$\overline{1126}$	$\overline{1540}$	$\overline{1955}$	$\overline{2369}$	$\overline{2784}$	$\overline{3198}$	
48	020 3613	4027	4442	4856	5270	5684	6099	6513	6927	7341	414
49	7755	8169	8583	8997	9411	9824	$\overline{0238}$	$\overline{0652}$	$\overline{1066}$	$\overline{1479}$	
1050	021 1893	2307	2720	3134	3547	3961	4374	4787	5201	5614	
N	0	1	2	3	4	5	6	7	8	9	Diff.

Table 15   *(Continued)*   **Mantissas for 1050–1100**

N	0	1	2	3	4	5	6	7	8	9	Diff.
1050	021 1893	2307	2720	3134	3547	3961	4374	4787	5201	5614	414
51	6027	6440	6854	7267	7680	8093	8506	8919	9332	9745	
52	022 0157	0570	0983	1396	1808	2221	2634	3046	3459	3871	413
53	4284	4696	5109	5521	5933	6345	6758	7170	7582	7994	
54	8406	8818	9230	9642	0054	0466	0878	1289	1701	2113	412
55	023 2525	2836	3348	3759	4171	4582	4994	5405	5817	6228	
56	6639	7050	7462	7873	8284	8695	9106	9517	9928	0339	
57	024 0750	1161	1572	1982	2393	2804	3214	3625	4036	4446	411
58	4857	5267	5678	6088	6498	6909	7319	7729	8139	8549	
59	8960	9370	9780	0190	0600	1010	1419	1829	2239	2649	410
1060	025 3059	3468	3878	4288	4697	5107	5516	5926	6335	6744	
61	7154	7563	7972	8382	8791	9200	9609	0018	0427	0836	409
62	026 1245	1654	2063	2472	2881	3289	3698	4107	4515	4924	
63	5333	5741	6150	6558	6967	7375	7783	8192	8600	9008	
64	9416	9824	0233	0641	1049	1457	1865	2273	2680	3088	
65	027 3496	3904	4312	4719	5127	5535	5942	6350	6757	7165	408
66	7572	7979	8387	8794	9201	9609	0016	0423	0830	1237	
67	028 1644	2051	2458	2865	3272	3679	4086	4492	4899	5306	407
68	5713	6119	6526	6932	7339	7745	8152	8558	8964	9371	
69	9777	0183	0590	0996	1402	1808	2214	2620	3026	3432	406
1070	029 3838	4244	4649	5055	5461	5867	6272	6678	7084	7489	
71	7895	8300	8706	9111	9516	9922	0327	0732	1138	1543	
72	030 1948	2353	2758	3163	3568	3973	4378	4783	5188	5592	405
73	5997	6402	6807	7211	7616	8020	8425	8830	9234	9638	
74	031 0043	0447	0851	1256	1660	2064	2468	2872	3277	3681	404
75	4085	4489	4893	5296	5700	6104	6508	6912	7315	7719	
76	8123	8526	8930	9333	9737	0140	0544	0947	1350	1754	403
77	032 2157	2560	2963	3367	3770	4173	4576	4979	5382	5785	
78	6188	6590	6993	7396	7799	8201	8604	9007	9409	9812	
79	033 0214	0617	1019	1422	1824	2226	2629	3031	3433	3835	
1080	4238	4640	5042	5444	5846	6248	6650	7052	7453	7855	402
81	8257	8659	9060	9462	9864	0265	0667	1068	1470	1871	
82	034 2273	2674	3075	3477	3878	4279	4680	5081	5482	5884	401
83	6285	6686	7087	7487	7888	8289	8690	9091	9491	9892	
84	035 0293	0693	1094	1495	1895	2296	2696	3096	3497	3897	400
85	4297	4698	5098	5498	5898	6298	6698	7098	7498	7898	
86	8298	8698	9098	9498	9898	0297	0697	1097	1496	1896	
87	036 2295	2695	3094	3494	3893	4293	4692	5091	5491	5890	399
88	6289	6688	7087	7486	7885	8284	8683	9082	9481	9880	
89	037 0279	0678	1076	1475	1874	2272	2671	3070	3468	3867	
1090	4265	4663	5062	5460	5858	6257	6655	7053	7451	7849	
91	8248	8646	9044	9442	9839	0237	0635	1033	1431	1829	398
92	038 2226	2624	3022	3419	3817	4214	4612	5009	5407	5804	
93	6202	6599	6996	7393	7791	8188	8585	8982	9379	9776	
94	039 0173	0570	0967	1364	1761	2158	2554	2951	3348	3745	397
95	4141	4538	4934	5331	5727	6124	6520	6917	7313	7709	
96	8106	8502	8898	9294	9690	0086	0482	0878	1274	1670	396
97	040 2066	2462	2858	3254	3650	4045	4441	4837	5232	5628	
98	6023	6419	6814	7210	7605	8001	8396	8791	9187	9582	
99	9977	0372	0767	1162	1557	1952	2347	2742	3137	3532	395
1100	041 3927	4322	4716	5111	5506	5900	6295	6690	7084	7479	
N	0	1	2	3	4	5	6	7	8	9	Diff.

Table 15 (*Continued*)   **Mantissas for 100–149**

100	0	1	2	3	4	5	6	7	8	9
100	00 0000	0434	0868	1301	1734	2166	2598	3029	3461	3891
01	4321	4751	5181	5609	6038	6466	6894	7321	7748	8174
02	8600	9026	9451	9876	*0300	*0724	*1147	*1570	*1993	*2415
03	0i 2837	3259	3680	4100	4521	4940	5360	5779	6197	6616
04	7033	7451	7868	8284	8700	9116	9532	9947	*0361	*0775
05	02 1189	1603	2016	2428	2841	3252	3664	4075	4486	4896
06	5306	5715	6125	6533	6942	7350	7757	8164	8571	8978
07	9384	9789	*0195	*0600	*1004	*1408	*1812	*2216	*2619	*3021
08	03 3424	3826	4227	4628	5029	5430	5830	6230	6629	7028
09	7426	7825	8223	8620	9017	9414	9811	*0207	*0602	*0998
110	04 1393	1787	2182	2576	2969	3362	3755	4148	4540	4932
11	5323	5714	6105	6495	6885	7275	7664	8053	8442	8830
12	9218	9606	9993	*0380	*0766	*1153	*1538	*1924	*2309	*2694
13	05 3078	3463	3846	4230	4613	4996	5378	5760	6142	6524
14	6905	7286	7666	8046	8426	8805	9185	9563	9942	*0320
15	06 0698	1075	1452	1829	2206	2582	2958	3333	3709	4083
16	4458	4832	5206	5580	5953	6326	6699	7071	7443	7815
17	8186	8557	8928	9298	9668	*0038	*0407	*0776	*1145	*1514
18	07 1882	2250	2617	2985	3352	3718	4085	4451	4816	5182
19	5547	5912	6276	6640	7004	7368	7731	8094	8457	8819
120	9181	9543	9904	*0266	*0626	*0987	*1347	*1707	*2067	*2426
21	08 2785	3144	3503	3861	4219	4576	4934	5291	5647	6004
22	6360	6716	7071	7426	7781	8136	8490	8845	9198	9552
23	9905	*0258	*0611	*0963	*1315	*1667	*2018	*2370	*2721	*3071
24	09 3422	3772	4122	4471	4820	5169	5518	5866	6215	6562
25	6910	7257	7604	7951	8298	8644	8990	9335	9681	*0026
26	10 0371	0715	1059	1403	1747	2091	2434	2777	3119	3462
27	3804	4146	4487	4828	5169	5510	5851	6191	6531	6871
28	7210	7549	7888	8227	8565	8903	9241	9579	9916	*0253
29	11 0590	0926	1263	1599	1934	2270	2605	2940	3275	3609
130	3943	4277	4611	4944	5278	5611	5943	6276	6608	6940
31	7271	7603	7934	8265	8595	8926	9256	9586	9915	*0245
32	12 0574	0903	1231	1560	1888	2216	2544	2871	3198	3525
33	3852	4178	4504	4830	5156	5481	5806	6131	6456	6781
34	7105	7429	7753	8076	8399	8722	9045	9368	9690	*0012
35	13 0334	0655	0977	1298	1619	1939	2260	2580	2900	3219
36	3539	3858	4177	4496	4814	5133	5451	5769	6086	6403
37	6721	7037	7354	7671	7989	8303	8618	8934	9249	9564
38	9879	*0194	*0508	*0822	*1136	*1450	*1763	*2076	*2389	*2702
39	14 3015	3327	3639	3851	4263	4574	4885	5196	5507	5818
140	6128	6438	6748	7058	7367	7676	7985	8294	8603	8911
41	9219	9527	9835	*0142	*0449	*0756	*1063	*1370	*1676	*1982
42	15 2288	2594	2900	3205	3510	3815	4120	4424	4728	5032
43	5336	5640	5943	6246	6549	6852	7154	7457	7759	8061
44	8362	8664	8965	9266	9567	9868	*0168	*0469	*0769	*1068
45	16 1368	1667	1967	2266	2564	2863	3161	3460	3758	4055
46	4353	4650	4947	5244	5541	5838	6134	6430	6726	7022
47	7317	7613	7908	8203	8497	8792	9086	9380	9674	9968
48	17 0262	0555	0848	1141	1434	1726	2019	2311	2603	2895
49	3186	3478	3769	4060	4351	4641	4932	5222	5512	5802

Table 15 (*Continued*) Mantissas for 150–199

150	0	1	2	3	4	5	6	7	8	9
150	17 6091	6381	6670	6959	7248	7536	7825	8113	8401	8689
51	8977	9264	9552	9839	*0126	*0413	*0699	*0986	*1272	*1558
52	18 1844	2129	2415	2700	2985	3270	3555	3839	4123	4407
53	4691	4975	5259	5542	5825	6108	6391	6674	6956	7239
54	7521	7803	8084	8366	8647	8928	9209	9490	9771	*0051
55	19 0332	0612	0892	1171	1451	1730	2010	2289	2567	2846
56	3125	3403	3681	3959	4237	4514	4792	5069	5346	5623
57	5900	6176	6453	6729	7005	7281	7556	7832	8107	8382
58	8657	8932	9206	9481	9755	*0029	*0303	*0577	*0850	*1124
59	20 1397	1670	1943	2216	2488	2761	3033	3305	3577	3848
160	4120	4391	4663	4934	5204	5475	5746	6016	6286	6556
61	6826	7096	7365	7634	7904	8173	8441	8710	8979	9247
62	9515	9783	*0051	*0319	*0586	*0853	*1121	*1388	*1654	*1921
63	21 2188	2454	2720	2986	3252	3518	3783	4049	4314	4579
64	4844	5109	5373	5638	5902	6166	6430	6694	6957	7221
65	7484	7747	8010	8273	8536	8798	9060	9323	9585	9846
66	22 0108	0370	0631	0892	1153	1414	1675	1936	2196	2456
67	2716	2976	3236	3496	3755	4015	4274	4533	4792	5051
68	5309	5568	5826	6084	6342	6600	6858	7115	7372	7630
69	7887	8144	8400	8657	8913	9170	9426	9682	9938	*0193
170	23 0449	0704	0960	1215	1470	1724	1979	2234	2488	2742
71	2996	3250	3504	3757	4011	4264	4517	4770	5023	5276
72	5528	5781	6033	6285	6537	6789	7041	7292	7544	7795
73	8046	8297	8548	8799	9049	9299	9550	9800	*0050	*0300
74	24 0549	0799	1048	1297	1546	1795	2044	2293	2541	2790
75	3038	3286	3534	3782	4030	4277	4525	4772	5019	5266
76	5513	5759	6006	6252	6499	6745	6991	7237	7482	7728
77	7973	8219	8464	8709	8954	9198	9443	9687	9932	*0176
78	25 0420	0664	0908	1151	1395	1638	1881	2125	2368	2610
79	2853	3096	3338	3580	3822	4064	4306	4548	4790	5031
180	5273	5514	5755	5996	6237	6477	6718	6958	7198	7439
81	7679	7918	8158	8398	8637	8877	9116	9355	9594	9833
82	26 0071	0310	0548	0787	1025	1263	1501	1739	1976	2214
83	2451	2688	2925	3162	3399	3636	3873	4109	4346	4582
84	4818	5054	5290	5525	5761	5996	6232	6467	6702	6937
85	7172	7406	7641	7875	8110	8344	8578	8812	9046	9279
86	9513	9746	9980	*0213	*0446	*0679	*0912	*1144	*1377	*1609
87	27 1842	2074	2306	2538	2770	3001	3233	3464	3696	3927
88	4158	4389	4620	4850	5081	5311	5542	5772	6002	6232
89	6462	6692	6921	7151	7380	7609	7838	8067	8296	8525
190	8754	8982	9211	9439	9667	9895	*0123	*0351	*0578	*0806
91	28 1033	1261	1488	1715	1942	2169	2396	2622	2849	3075
92	3301	3527	3753	3979	4205	4431	4656	4882	5107	5332
93	5557	5782	6007	6232	6456	6681	6905	7130	7354	7578
94	7802	8026	8249	8473	8696	8920	9143	9366	9589	9812
95	29 0035	0257	0480	0702	0925	1147	1369	1591	1813	2034
96	2256	2478	2699	2920	3141	3363	3584	3804	4025	4246
97	4466	4687	4907	5127	5347	5567	5787	6007	6226	6446
98	6665	6884	7104	7323	7542	7761	7979	8198	8416	8635
99	8853	9071	9289	9507	9725	9943	*0161	*0378	*0595	*0813

Table 15   (*Continued*)   **Mantissas for 200–249**

200	0	1	2	3	4	5	6	7	8	9
200	30 1030	1247	1464	1681	1898	2114	2331	2547	2764	2980
01	3196	3412	3628	3844	4059	4275	4491	4706	4921	5136
02	5351	5566	5781	5996	6211	6425	6639	6854	7068	7282
03	7496	7710	7924	8137	8351	8564	8778	8991	9204	9417
04	9630	9843	*0056	*0268	*0481	*0693	*0906	*1118	*1330	*1542
05	31 1754	1966	2177	2389	2600	2812	3023	3234	3445	3656
06	3867	4078	4289	4499	4710	4920	5130	5340	5551	5760
07	5970	6180	6390	6599	6809	7018	7227	7436	7646	7854
08	8063	8272	8481	8689	8898	9106	9314	9522	9730	9938
09	32 0146	0354	0562	0769	0977	1184	1391	1598	1805	2012
210	2219	2426	2633	2839	3046	3252	3458	3665	3871	4077
11	4282	4488	4694	4899	5105	5310	5516	5721	5926	6131
12	6336	6541	6745	6950	7155	7359	7563	7767	7972	8176
13	8380	8583	8787	8991	9194	9398	9601	9805	*0008	*0211
14	33 0414	0617	0819	1022	1225	1427	1630	1832	2034	2236
15	2438	2640	2842	3044	3246	3447	3649	3850	4051	4253
16	4454	4655	4856	5057	5257	5458	5658	5859	6059	6260
17	6460	6660	6860	7060	7260	7459	7659	7858	8058	8257
18	8456	8656	8855	9054	9253	9451	9650	9849	*0047	*0246
19	34 0444	0642	0841	1039	1237	1435	1632	1830	2028	2225
220	2423	2620	2817	3014	3212	3409	3606	3802	3999	4196
21	4392	4589	4785	4981	5178	5374	5570	5766	5962	6157
22	6353	6549	6744	6939	7135	7330	7525	7720	7915	8110
23	8305	8500	8694	8889	9083	9278	9472	9666	9860	*0054
24	35 0248	0442	0636	0829	1023	1216	1410	1603	1796	1989
25	2183	2375	2568	2761	2954	3147	3339	3532	3724	3916
26	4108	4301	4493	4685	4876	5068	5260	5452	5643	5834
27	6026	6217	6408	6599	6790	6981	7172	7363	7554	7744
28	7935	8125	8316	8506	8696	8886	9076	9266	9456	9646
29	9835	*0025	*0215	*0404	*0593	*0783	*0972	*1161	*1350	*1539
230	36 1728	1917	2105	2294	2482	2671	2859	3048	3236	3424
31	3612	3800	3988	4176	4363	4551	4739	4926	5113	5301
32	5488	5675	5862	6049	6236	6423	6610	6796	6983	7169
33	7356	7542	7729	7915	8101	8287	8473	8659	8845	9030
34	9216	9401	9587	9772	9958	*0143	*0328	*0513	*0698	*0883
35	37 1068	1253	1437	1622	1806	1991	2175	2360	2544	2728
36	2912	3096	3280	3464	3647	3831	4015	4198	4382	4565
37	4748	4932	5115	5298	5481	5664	5846	6029	6212	6394
38	6577	6759	6942	7124	7306	7488	7670	7852	8034	8216
39	8398	8580	8761	8943	9124	9306	9487	9668	9849	*0030
240	38 0211	0392	0573	0754	0934	1115	1296	1476	1656	1837
41	2017	2197	2377	2557	2737	2917	3097	3277	3456	3636
42	3815	3995	4174	4353	4533	4712	4891	5070	5249	5428
43	5606	5785	5964	6142	6321	6499	6677	6856	7034	7212
44	7390	7568	7746	7924	8101	8279	8456	8634	8811	8989
45	9166	9343	9520	9698	9875	*0051	*0228	*0405	*0582	*0759
46	39 0935	1112	1288	1464	1641	1817	1993	2169	2345	2521
47	2697	2873	3048	3224	3400	3575	3751	3926	4101	4277
48	4452	4627	4802	4977	5152	5326	5501	5676	5850	6025
49	6199	6374	6548	6722	6896	7071	7245	7419	7592	7766

Table 15 *(Continued)* Mantissas for 250–299

250	0	1	2	3	4	5	6	7	8	9
250	39 7940	8114	8287	8461	8634	8808	8981	9154	9328	9501
51	9674	9847	*0020	*0192	*0365	*0538	*0711	*0883	*1056	*1228
52	40 1401	1573	1745	1917	2089	2261	2433	2605	2777	2949
53	3121	3292	3464	3635	3807	3978	4149	4320	4492	4663
54	4834	5005	5176	5346	5517	5688	5858	6029	6199	6370
55	6540	6710	6881	7051	7221	7391	7561	7731	7901	8070
56	8240	8410	8579	8749	8918	9087	9257	9426	9595	9764
57	9933	*0102	*0271	*0440	*0609	*0777	*0946	*1114	*1283	*1451
58	41 1620	1788	1956	2124	2293	2461	2629	2796	2964	3132
59	3300	3467	3635	3803	3970	4137	4305	4472	4639	4806
260	4973	5140	5307	5474	5641	5808	5974	6141	6308	6474
61	6641	6807	6973	7139	7306	7472	7638	7804	7970	8135
62	8301	8467	8633	8798	8964	9129	9295	9460	9625	9791
63	9956	*0121	*0286	*0451	*0616	*0781	*0945	*1110	*1275	*1439
64	42 1604	1768	1933	2097	2261	2426	2590	2754	2918	3082
65	3246	3410	3574	3737	3901	4065	4228	4392	4555	4718
66	4882	5045	5208	5371	5534	5697	5860	6023	6186	6349
67	6511	6674	6836	6999	7161	7324	7486	7648	7811	7973
68	8135	8297	8459	8621	8783	8944	9106	9268	9429	9591
69	9752	9914	*0075	*0236	*0398	*0559	*0720	*0881	*1042	*1203
270	43 1364	1525	1685	1846	2007	2167	2328	2488	2649	2809
71	2969	3130	3290	3450	3610	3770	3930	4090	4249	4409
72	4569	4729	4888	5048	5207	5367	5526	5685	5844	6004
73	6163	6322	6481	6640	6799	6957	7116	7275	7433	7592
74	7751	7909	8067	8226	8384	8542	8701	8859	9017	9175
75	9333	9491	9648	9806	9964	*0122	*0279	*0437	*0594	*0752
76	44 0909	1066	1224	1381	1538	1695	1852	2009	2166	2323
77	2480	2637	2793	2950	3106	3263	3419	3576	3732	3889
78	4045	4201	4357	4513	4669	4825	4981	5137	5293	5449
79	5604	5760	5915	6071	6226	6382	6537	6692	6848	7003
280	7158	7313	7468	7623	7778	7933	8088	8242	8397	8552
81	8706	8861	9015	9170	9324	9478	9633	9787	9941	*0095
82	45 0249	0403	0557	0711	0865	1018	1172	1326	1479	1633
83	1786	1940	2093	2247	2400	2553	2706	2859	3012	3165
84	3318	3471	3624	3777	3930	4082	4235	4387	4540	4692
85	4845	4997	5150	5302	5454	5606	5758	5910	6062	6214
86	6366	6518	6670	6821	6973	7125	7276	7428	7579	7731
87	7882	8033	8184	8336	8487	8638	8789	8940	9091	9242
88	9392	9543	9694	9845	9995	*0146	*0296	*0447	*0597	*0748
89	46 0898	1048	1198	1348	1499	1649	1799	1948	2098	2248
290	2398	2548	2697	2847	2997	3146	3296	3445	3594	3744
91	3893	4042	4191	4340	4490	4639	4788	4936	5085	5234
92	5383	5532	5680	5829	5977	6126	6274	6423	6571	6719
93	6868	7016	7164	7312	7460	7608	7756	7904	8052	8200
94	8347	8495	8643	8790	8938	9085	9233	9380	9527	9675
95	9822	9969	*0116	*0263	*0410	*0557	*0704	*0851	*0998	*1145
96	47 1292	1438	1585	1732	1878	2025	2171	2318	2464	2610
97	2756	2903	3049	3195	3341	3487	3633	3779	3925	4071
98	4216	4362	4508	4653	4799	4944	5090	5235	5381	5526
99	5671	5816	5962	6107	6252	6397	6542	6687	6832	6976

Table 15 (*Continued*) **Mantissas for 300–349**

300	0	1	2	3	4	5	6	7	8	9
300	47 7121	7266	7411	7555	7700	7844	7989	8133	8278	8422
01	8566	8711	8855	8999	9143	9287	9431	9575	9719	9863
02	48 0007	0151	0294	0438	0582	0725	0869	1012	1156	1299
03	1443	1586	1729	1872	2016	2159	2302	2445	2588	2731
04	2874	3016	3159	3302	3445	3587	3730	3872	4015	4157
05	4300	4442	4585	4727	4869	5011	5153	5295	5437	5579
06	5721	5863	6005	6147	6289	6430	6572	6714	6855	6997
07	7138	7280	7421	7563	7704	7845	7986	8127	8269	8410
08	8551	8692	8833	8974	9114	9255	9396	9537	9677	9818
09	9958	*0099	*0239	*0380	*0520	*0661	*0801	*0941	*1081	*1222
310	49 1362	1502	1642	1782	1922	2062	2201	2341	2481	2621
11	2760	2900	3040	3179	3319	3458	3597	3737	3876	4015
12	4155	4294	4433	4572	4711	4850	4989	5128	5267	5406
13	5544	5683	5822	5960	6099	6238	6376	6515	6653	6791
14	6930	7068	7206	7344	7483	7621	7759	7897	8035	8173
15	8311	8448	8586	8724	8862	8999	9137	9275	9412	9550
16	9687	9824	9962	*0099	*0236	*0374	*0511	*0648	*0785	*0922
17	50 1059	1196	1333	1470	1607	1744	1880	2017	2154	2291
18	2427	2564	2700	2837	2973	3109	3246	3382	3518	3655
19	3791	3927	4063	4199	4335	4471	4607	4743	4878	5014
320	5150	5286	5421	5557	5693	5828	5964	6099	6234	6370
21	6505	6640	6776	6911	7046	7181	7316	7451	7586	7721
22	7856	7991	8126	8260	8395	8530	8664	8799	8934	9068
23	9203	9337	9471	9606	9740	9874	*0009	*0143	*0277	*0411
24	51 0545	0679	0813	0947	1081	1215	1349	1482	1616	1750
25	1883	2017	2151	2284	2418	2551	2684	2818	2951	3084
26	3218	3351	3484	3617	3750	3883	4016	4149	4282	4415
27	4548	4681	4813	4946	5079	5211	5344	5476	5609	5741
28	5874	6006	6139	6271	6403	6535	6668	6800	6932	7064
29	7196	7328	7460	7592	7724	7855	7987	8119	8251	8382
330	8514	8646	8777	8909	9040	9171	9303	9434	9566	9697
31	9828	9959	*0090	*0221	*0353	*0484	*0615	*0745	*0876	*1007
32	52 1138	1269	1400	1530	1661	1792	1922	2053	2183	2314
33	2444	2575	2705	2835	2966	3096	3226	3356	3486	3616
34	3746	3876	4006	4136	4266	4396	4526	4656	4785	4915
35	5045	5174	5304	5434	5563	5693	5822	5951	6081	6210
36	6339	6469	6598	6727	6856	6985	7114	7243	7372	7501
37	7630	7759	7888	8016	8145	8274	8402	8531	8660	8788
38	8917	9045	9174	9312	9430	9559	9687	9815	9943	*0072
39	53 0200	0328	0456	0584	0712	0840	0968	1096	1223	1351
340	1479	1607	1734	1862	1990	2117	2245	2372	2500	2627
41	2754	2882	3009	3136	3264	3391	3518	3645	3772	3899
42	4026	4153	4280	4407	4534	4661	4787	4914	5041	5167
43	5294	5421	5547	5674	5800	5927	6053	6180	6306	6432
44	6558	6685	6811	6937	7063	7189	7315	7441	7567	7693
45	7819	7945	8071	8197	8322	8448	8574	8699	8825	8951
46	9076	9202	9327	9452	9578	9703	9829	9954	*0079	*0204
47	54 0329	0455	0580	0705	0830	0955	1080	1205	1330	1454
48	1579	1704	1829	1953	2078	2203	2327	2452	2576	2701
49	2825	2950	3074	3199	3323	3447	3571	3696	3820	3944

Table 15 (*Continued*)   Mantissas for 350–399

350	0	1	2	3	4	5	6	7	8	9
350	54 4068	4192	4316	4440	4564	4688	4812	4936	5060	5183
51	5307	5431	5555	5678	5802	5925	6049	6172	6296	6419
52	6543	6666	6789	6913	7036	7159	7282	7405	7529	7652
53	7775	7898	8021	8144	8267	8389	8512	8635	8758	8881
54	9003	9126	9249	9371	9494	9616	9739	9861	9984	*0106
55	55 0228	0351	0473	0595	0717	0840	0962	1084	1206	1328
56	1450	1572	1694	1816	1938	2060	2181	2303	2425	2547
57	2668	2790	2911	3033	3155	3276	3398	3519	3640	3762
58	3883	4004	4126	4247	4368	4489	4610	4731	4852	4973
59	5094	5215	5336	5457	5578	5699	5820	5940	6061	6182
360	6303	6423	6544	6664	6785	6905	7026	7146	7267	7387
61	7507	7627	7748	7868	7988	8108	8228	8349	8469	8589
62	8709	8829	8948	9068	9188	9308	9428	9548	9667	9787
63	9907	*0026	*0146	*0265	*0385	*0504	*0624	*0743	*0863	*0982
64	56 1101	1221	1340	1459	1578	1698	1817	1936	2055	2174
65	2293	2412	2531	2650	2769	2887	3006	3125	3244	3362
66	3481	3600	3718	3837	3955	4074	4192	4311	4429	4548
67	4666	4784	4903	5021	5139	5257	5376	5494	5612	5730
68	5848	5966	6084	6202	6320	6437	6555	6673	6791	6909
69	7026	7144	7262	7379	7497	7614	7732	7849	7967	8084
370	8202	8319	8436	8554	8671	8788	8905	9023	9140	9257
71	9374	9491	9608	9725	9842	9959	*0076	*0193	*0309	*0426
72	57 0543	0660	0776	0893	1010	1126	1243	1359	1476	1592
73	1709	1825	1942	2058	2174	2291	2407	2523	2639	2755
74	2872	2988	3104	3220	3336	3452	3568	3684	3800	3915
75	4031	4147	4263	4379	4494	4610	4726	4841	4957	5072
76	5188	5303	5419	5534	5650	5765	5880	5996	6111	6226
77	6341	6457	6572	6687	6802	6917	7032	7147	7262	7377
78	7492	7607	7722	7836	7951	8066	8181	8295	8410	8525
79	8639	8754	8868	8983	9097	9212	9326	9441	9555	9669
380	9784	9898	*0012	*0126	*0241	*0355	*0469	*0583	*0697	*0811
81	58 0925	1039	1153	1267	1381	1495	1608	1722	1836	1950
82	2063	2177	2291	2404	2518	2631	2745	2858	2972	3085
83	3199	3312	3426	3539	3652	3765	3879	3992	4105	4218
84	4331	4444	4557	4670	4783	4896	5009	5122	5235	5348
85	5461	5574	5686	5799	5912	6024	6137	6250	6362	6475
86	6587	6700	6812	6925	7037	7149	7262	7374	7486	7599
87	7711	7823	7935	8047	8160	8272	8384	8496	8608	8720
88	8832	8944	9056	9167	9279	9391	9503	9615	9726	9838
89	9950	*0061	*0173	*0284	*0396	*0507	*0619	*0730	*0842	*0953
390	59 1065	1176	1287	1399	1510	1621	1732	1843	1955	2066
91	2177	2288	2399	2510	2621	2732	2843	2954	3064	3175
92	3286	3397	3508	3618	3729	3840	3950	4061	4171	4282
93	4393	4503	4614	4724	4834	4945	5055	5165	5276	5386
94	5496	5606	5717	5827	5937	6047	6157	6267	6377	6487
95	6597	6707	6817	6927	7037	7146	7256	7366	7476	7586
96	7695	7805	7914	8024	8134	8243	8353	8462	8572	8681
97	8791	8900	9009	9119	9228	9337	9446	9556	9665	9774
98	9883	9992	*0101	*0210	*0319	*0428	*0537	*0646	*0755	*0864
99	60 0973	1082	1191	1299	1408	1517	1625	1734	1843	1951

Table 15 (*Continued*) **Mantissas for 400–449**

400	0	1	2	3	4	5	6	7	8	9
400	60 2060	2169	2277	2386	2494	2603	2711	2819	2928	3036
01	3144	3253	3361	3469	3577	3686	3794	3902	4010	4118
02	4226	4334	4442	4550	4658	4766	4874	4982	5089	5197
03	5305	5413	5521	5628	5736	5844	5951	6059	6166	6274
04	6381	6489	6596	6704	6811	6919	7026	7133	7241	7348
05	7455	7562	7669	7777	7884	7991	8098	8205	8312	8419
06	8526	8633	8740	8847	8954	9061	9167	9274	9381	9488
07	9594	9701	9808	9914	*0021	*0128	*0234	*0341	*0447	*0554
08	61 0660	0767	0873	0979	1086	1192	1298	1405	1511	1617
09	1723	1829	1936	2042	2148	2254	2360	2466	2572	2678
410	2784	2890	2996	3102	3207	3313	3419	3525	3630	3736
11	3842	3947	4053	4159	4264	4370	4475	4581	4686	4792
12	4897	5003	5108	5213	5319	5424	5529	5634	5740	5845
13	5950	6055	6160	6265	6370	6476	6581	6686	6790	6895
14	7000	7105	7210	7315	7420	7525	7629	7734	7839	7943
15	8048	8153	8257	8362	8466	8571	8676	8780	8884	8989
16	9093	9198	9302	9406	9511	9615	9719	9824	9928	*0032
17	62 0136	0240	0344	0448	0552	0656	0760	0864	0968	1072
18	1176	1280	1384	1488	1592	1695	1799	1903	2007	2110
19	2214	2318	2421	2525	2628	2732	2835	2939	3042	3146
420	3249	3353	3456	3559	3663	3766	3869	3973	4076	4179
21	4282	4385	4488	4591	4695	4798	4901	5004	5107	5210
22	5312	5415	5518	5621	5724	5827	5929	6032	6135	6238
23	6340	6443	6546	6648	6751	6853	6956	7058	7161	7263
24	7366	7468	7571	7673	7775	7878	7980	8082	8185	8287
25	8389	8491	8593	8695	8797	8900	9002	9104	9206	9308
26	9410	9512	9613	9715	9817	9919	*0021	*0123	*0224	*0326
27	63 0428	0530	0631	0733	0835	0936	1038	1139	1241	1342
28	1444	1545	1647	1748	1849	1951	2052	2153	2255	2356
29	2457	2559	2660	2761	2862	2963	3064	3165	3266	3367
430	3468	3569	3670	3771	3872	3973	4074	4175	4276	4376
31	4477	4578	4679	4779	4880	4981	5081	5182	5283	5383
32	5484	5584	5685	5785	5886	5986	6087	6187	6287	6388
33	6488	6588	6688	6789	6889	6989	7089	7189	7290	7390
34	7490	7590	7690	7790	7890	7990	8090	8190	8290	8389
35	8489	8589	8689	8789	8888	8988	9088	9188	9287	9387
36	9486	9586	9686	9785	9885	9984	*0084	*0183	*0283	*0382
37	64 0481	0581	0680	0779	0879	0978	1077	1177	1276	1375
38	1474	1573	1672	1771	1871	1970	2069	2168	2267	2366
39	2465	2563	2662	2761	2860	2959	3058	3156	3255	3354
440	3453	3551	3650	3749	3847	3946	4044	4143	4242	4340
41	4439	4537	4636	4734	4832	4931	5029	5127	5226	5324
42	5422	5521	5619	5717	5815	5913	6011	6110	6208	6306
43	6404	6502	6600	6698	6796	6894	6992	7089	7187	7285
44	7383	7481	7579	7676	7774	7872	7969	8067	8165	8262
45	8360	8458	8555	8653	8750	8848	8945	9043	9140	9237
46	9335	9432	9530	9627	9724	9821	9919	*0016	*0113	*0210
47	65 0308	0405	0502	0599	0696	0793	0890	0987	1084	1181
48	1278	1375	1472	1569	1666	1762	1859	1956	2053	2150
49	2246	2343	2440	2536	2633	2730	2826	2923	3019	3116

Table 15 *(Continued)* Mantissas for 450–499

450	0	1	2	3	4	5	6	7	8	9
450	65 3213	3309	3405	3502	3598	3695	3791	3888	3984	4080
51	4177	4273	4369	4465	4562	4658	4754	4850	4946	5042
52	5138	5235	5331	5427	5523	5619	5715	5810	5906	6002
53	6098	6194	6290	6386	6482	6577	6673	6769	6864	6960
54	7056	7152	7247	7343	7438	7534	7629	7725	7820	7916
55	8011	8107	8202	8298	8393	8488	8584	8679	8774	8870
56	8965	9060	9155	9250	9346	9441	9536	9631	9726	9821
57	9916	*0011	*0106	*0201	*0296	*0391	*0486	*0581	*0676	*0771
58	66 0865	0960	1055	1150	1245	1339	1434	1529	1623	1718
59	1813	1907	2002	2096	2191	2286	2380	2475	2569	2663
460	2758	2852	2947	3041	3135	3230	3324	3418	3512	3607
61	3701	3795	3889	3983	4078	4172	4266	4360	4454	4548
62	4642	4736	4830	4924	5018	5112	5206	5299	5393	5487
63	5581	5675	5769	5862	5956	6050	6143	6237	6331	6424
64	6518	6612	6705	6799	6892	6986	7079	7173	7266	7360
65	7453	7546	7640	7733	7826	7920	8013	8106	8199	8293
66	8386	8479	8572	8665	8759	8852	8945	9038	9131	9224
67	9317	9410	9503	9596	9689	9782	9875	9967	*0060	*0153
68	67 0246	0339	0431	0524	0617	0710	0802	0895	0988	1080
69	1173	1265	1358	1451	1543	1636	1728	1821	1913	2005
470	2098	2190	2283	2375	2467	2560	2652	2744	2836	2929
71	3021	3113	3205	3297	3390	3482	3574	3666	3758	3850
72	3942	4034	4126	4218	4310	4402	4494	4586	4677	4769
73	4861	4953	5045	5137	5228	5320	5412	5503	5595	5687
74	5778	5870	5962	6053	6145	6236	6328	6419	6511	6602
75	6694	6785	6876	6968	7059	7151	7242	7333	7424	7516
76	7607	7698	7789	7881	7972	8063	8154	8245	8336	8427
77	8518	8609	8700	8791	8882	8973	9064	9155	9246	9337
78	9428	9519	9610	9700	9791	9882	9973	*0063	*0154	*0245
79	68 0336	0426	0517	0607	0698	0789	0879	0970	1060	1151
480	1241	1332	1422	1513	1603	1693	1784	1874	1964	2055
81	2145	2235	2326	2416	2506	2596	2686	2777	2867	2957
82	3047	3137	3227	3317	3407	3497	3587	3677	3767	3857
83	3947	4037	4127	4217	4307	4396	4486	4576	4666	4756
84	4845	4935	5025	5114	5204	5294	5383	5473	5563	5652
85	5742	5831	5921	6010	6100	6189	6279	6368	6458	6547
86	6636	6726	6815	6904	6994	7083	7172	7261	7351	7440
87	7529	7618	7707	7796	7886	7975	8064	8153	8242	8331
88	8420	8509	8598	8687	8776	8865	8953	9042	9131	9220
89	9309	9398	9486	9575	9664	9753	9841	9930	*0019	*0107
490	69 0196	0285	0373	0462	0550	0639	0728	0816	0905	0993
91	1081	1170	1258	1347	1435	1524	1612	1700	1789	1877
92	1965	2053	2142	2230	2318	2406	2494	2583	2671	2759
93	2847	2935	3023	3111	3199	3287	3375	3463	3551	3639
94	3727	3815	3903	3991	4078	4166	4254	4342	4430	4517
95	4605	4693	4781	4868	4956	5044	5131	5219	5307	5394
96	5482	5569	5657	5744	5832	5919	6007	6094	6182	6269
97	6356	6444	6531	6618	6706	6793	6880	6968	7055	7142
98	7229	7317	7404	7491	7578	7665	7752	7839	7926	8014
99	8101	8188	8275	8362	8449	8535	8622	8709	8796	8883

Table 15   *(Continued)*   **Mantissas for 500–549**

500	0	1	2	3	4	5	6	7	8	9
500	69 8970	9057	9144	9231	9317	9404	9491	9578	9664	**9751**
01	9838	9924	*0011	*0098	*0184	*0271	*0358	*0444	*0531	*0617
02	70 0704	0790	0877	0963	1050	1136	1222	1309	1395	1482
03	1568	1654	1741	1827	1913	1999	2086	2172	2258	2344
04	2431	2517	2603	2689	2775	2861	2947	3033	3119	3205
05	3291	3377	3463	3549	3635	3721	3807	3893	3979	4065
06	4151	4236	4322	4408	4494	4579	4665	4751	4837	4922
07	5008	5094	5179	5265	5350	5436	5522	5607	5693	5778
08	5864	5949	6035	6120	6206	6291	6376	6462	6547	6632
09	6718	6803	6888	6974	7059	7144	7229	7315	7400	7485
510	7570	7655	7740	7826	7911	7996	8081	8166	8251	8336
11	8421	8506	8591	8676	8761	8846	8931	9015	9100	9185
12	9270	9355	9440	9524	9609	9694	9779	9863	9948	*0033
13	71 0117	0202	0287	0371	0456	0540	0625	0710	0794	0879
14	0963	1048	1132	1217	1301	1385	1470	1554	1639	1723
15	1807	1892	1976	2060	2144	2229	2313	2397	2481	2566
16	2650	2734	2818	2902	2986	3070	3154	3238	3323	3407
17	3491	3575	3659	3742	3826	3910	3994	4078	4162	4246
18	4330	4414	4497	4581	4665	4749	4833	4916	5000	5084
19	5167	5251	5335	5418	5502	5586	5669	5753	5836	5920
520	6003	6087	6170	6254	6337	6421	6504	6588	6671	6754
21	6838	6921	7004	7088	7171	7254	7338	7421	7504	7587
22	7671	7754	7837	7920	8003	8086	8169	8253	8336	8419
23	8502	8585	8668	8751	8834	8917	9000	9083	9165	9248
24	9331	9414	9497	9580	9663	9745	9828	9911	9994	*0077
25	72 0159	0242	0325	0407	0490	0573	0655	0738	0821	0903
26	0986	1068	1151	1233	1316	1398	1481	1563	1646	1728
27	1811	1893	1975	2058	2140	2222	2305	2387	2469	2552
28	2634	2716	2798	2881	2963	3045	3127	3209	3291	3374
29	3456	3538	3620	3702	3784	3866	3948	4030	4112	4194
530	4276	4358	4440	4522	4604	4685	4767	4849	4931	5013
31	5095	5176	5258	5340	5422	5503	5585	5667	5748	5830
32	5912	5993	6075	6156	6238	6320	6401	6483	6564	6646
33	6727	6809	6890	6972	7053	7134	7216	7297	7379	7460
34	7541	7623	7704	7785	7866	7948	8029	8110	8191	8273
35	8354	8435	8516	8597	8678	8759	8841	8922	9003	9084
36	9165	9246	9327	9408	9489	9570	9651	9732	9813	9893
37	9974	*0055	*0136	*0217	*0298	*0378	*0459	*0540	*0621	*0702
38	73 0782	0863	0944	1024	1105	1186	1266	1347	1428	1508
39	1589	1669	1750	1830	1911	1991	2072	2152	2233	2313
540	2394	2474	2555	2635	2715	2796	2876	2956	3037	3117
41	3197	3278	3358	3438	3518	3598	3679	3759	3839	3919
42	3999	4079	4160	4240	4320	4400	4480	4560	4640	4720
43	4800	4880	4960	5040	5120	5200	5279	5359	5439	5519
44	5599	5679	5759	5838	5918	5998	6078	6157	6237	6317
45	6397	6476	6556	6635	6715	6795	6874	6954	7034	7113
46	7193	7272	7352	7431	7511	7590	7670	7749	7829	7908
47	7987	8067	8146	8225	8305	8384	8463	8543	8622	8701
48	8781	8860	8939	9018	9097	9177	9256	9335	9414	9493
49	9572	9651	9731	9810	9889	9968	*0047	*0126	*0205	*0284

Table 15 *(Continued)* Mantissas for 550–599

550	0	1	2	3	4	5	6	7	8	9
550	74 0363	0442	0521	0600	0678	0757	0836	0915	0994	1073
51	1152	1230	1309	1388	1467	1546	1624	1703	1782	1800
52	1939	2018	2096	2175	2254	2332	2411	2489	2568	2647
53	2725	2804	2882	2961	3039	3118	3196	3275	3353	3431
54	3510	3588	3667	3745	3823	3902	3980	4058	4136	4215
55	4293	4371	4449	4528	4606	4684	4762	4840	4919	4997
56	5075	5153	5231	5309	5387	5465	5543	5621	5699	5777
57	5855	5933	6011	6089	6167	6245	6323	6401	6479	6556
58	6634	6712	6790	6868	6945	7023	7101	7179	7256	7334
59	7412	7489	7567	7645	7722	7800	7878	7955	8033	8110
560	8188	8266	8343	8421	8498	8576	8653	8731	8808	8885
61	8963	9040	9118	9195	9272	9350	9427	9504	9582	9659
62	9736	9814	9891	9968	*0045	*0123	*0200	*0277	*0354	*0431
63	75 0508	0586	0663	0740	0817	0894	0971	1048	1125	1202
64	1279	1356	1433	1510	1587	1664	1741	1818	1895	1972
65	2048	2125	2202	2279	2356	2433	2509	2586	2663	2740
66	2816	2893	2970	3047	3123	3200	3277	3353	3430	3506
67	3583	3660	3736	3813	3889	3966	4042	4119	4195	4272
68	4348	4425	4501	4578	4654	4730	4807	4883	4960	5036
69	5112	5189	5265	5341	5417	5494	5570	5646	5722	5799
570	5875	5951	6027	6103	6180	6256	6332	6408	6484	6560
71	6636	6712	6788	6864	6940	7016	7092	7168	7244	7320
72	7396	7472	7548	7624	7700	7775	7851	7927	8003	8079
73	8155	8230	8306	8382	8458	8533	8609	8685	8761	8836
74	8912	8988	9063	9139	9214	9290	9366	9441	9517	9592
75	9668	9743	9819	9894	9970	*0045	*0121	*0196	*0272	*0347
76	76 0422	0498	0573	0649	0724	0799	0875	0950	1025	1101
77	1176	1251	1326	1402	1477	1552	1627	1702	1778	1853
78	1928	2003	2078	2153	2228	2303	2378	2453	2529	2604
79	2679	2754	2829	2904	2978	3053	3128	3203	3278	3353
580	3428	3503	3578	3653	3727	3802	3877	3952	4027	4101
81	4176	4251	4326	4400	4475	4550	4624	4699	4774	4848
82	4923	4998	5072	5147	5221	5296	5370	5445	5520	5594
83	5669	5743	5818	5892	5966	6041	6115	6190	6264	6338
84	6413	6487	6562	6636	6710	6785	6859	6933	7007	7082
85	7156	7230	7304	7379	7453	7527	7601	7675	7749	7823
86	7898	7972	8046	8120	8194	8268	8342	8416	8490	8564
87	8638	8712	8786	8860	8934	9008	9082	9156	9230	9303
88	9377	9451	9525	9599	9673	9746	9820	9894	9968	*0042
89	77 0115	0189	0263	0336	0410	0484	0557	0631	0705	0778
590	0852	0926	0999	1073	1146	1220	1293	1367	1440	1514
91	1587	1661	1734	1808	1881	1955	2028	2102	2175	2248
92	2322	2395	2468	2542	2615	2688	2762	2835	2908	2981
93	3055	3128	3201	3274	3348	3421	3494	3567	3640	3713
94	3786	3860	3933	4006	4079	4152	4225	4298	4371	4444
95	4517	4590	4663	4736	4809	4882	4955	5028	5100	5173
96	5246	5319	5392	5465	5538	5610	5683	5756	5829	5902
97	5974	6047	6120	6193	6265	6338	6411	6483	6556	6629
98	6701	6774	6846	6919	6992	7064	7137	7209	7282	7354
99	7427	7499	7572	7644	7717	7789	7862	7934	8006	8079

Table 15 (*Continued*) Mantissas for 600–649

600	0	1	2	3	4	5	6	7	8	9
600	77 8151	8224	8296	8368	8441	8513	8585	8658	8730	8802
01	8874	8947	9019	9091	9163	9236	9308	9380	9452	9524
02	9596	9669	9741	9813	9885	9957	*0029	*0101	*0173	*0245
03	78 0317	0389	0461	0533	0605	0677	0749	0821	0893	0965
04	1037	1109	1181	1253	1324	1396	1468	1540	1612	1684
05	1755	1827	1899	1971	2042	2114	2186	2258	2329	2401
06	2473	2544	2616	2688	2759	2831	2902	2974	3046	3117
07	3189	3260	3332	3403	3475	3546	3618	3689	3761	3832
08	3904	3975	4046	4118	4189	4261	4332	4403	4475	4546
09	4617	4689	4760	4831	4902	4974	5045	5116	5187	5259
610	5330	5401	5472	5543	5615	5686	5757	5828	5899	5970
11	6041	6112	6183	6254	6325	6396	6467	6538	6609	6680
12	6751	6822	6893	6964	7035	7106	7177	7248	7319	7390
13	7460	7531	7602	7673	7744	7815	7885	7956	8027	8098
14	8168	8239	8310	8381	8451	8522	8593	8663	8734	8804
15	8875	8946	9016	9087	9157	9228	9299	9369	9440	9510
16	9581	9651	9722	9792	9863	9933	*0004	*0074	*0144	*0215
17	79 0285	0356	0426	0496	0567	0637	0707	0778	0848	0918
18	0988	1059	1129	1199	1269	1340	1410	1480	1550	1620
19	1691	1761	1831	1901	1971	2041	2111	2181	2252	2322
620	2392	2462	2532	2602	2672	2742	2812	2882	2952	3022
21	3092	3162	3231	3301	3371	3441	3511	3581	3651	3721
22	3790	3860	3930	4000	4070	4139	4209	4279	4349	4418
23	4488	4558	4627	4697	4767	4836	4906	4976	5045	5115
24	5185	5254	5324	5393	5463	5532	5602	5672	5741	5811
25	5880	5949	6019	6088	6158	6227	6297	6366	6436	6505
26	6574	6644	6713	6782	6852	6921	6990	7060	7129	7198
27	7268	7337	7406	7475	7545	7614	7683	7752	7821	7890
28	7960	8029	8098	8167	8236	8305	8374	8443	8513	8582
29	8651	8720	8789	8858	8927	8996	9065	9134	9203	9272
630	9341	9409	9478	9547	9616	9685	9754	9823	9892	9961
31	80 0029	0098	0167	0236	0305	0373	0442	0511	0580	0648
32	0717	0786	0854	0923	0992	1061	1129	1198	1266	1335
33	1404	1472	1541	1609	1678	1747	1815	1884	1952	2021
34	2089	2158	2226	2295	2363	2432	2500	2568	2637	2705
35	2774	2842	2910	2979	3047	3116	3184	3252	3321	3389
36	3457	3525	3594	3662	3730	3798	3867	3935	4003	4071
37	4139	4208	4276	4344	4412	4480	4548	4616	4685	4753
38	4821	4889	4957	5025	5093	5161	5229	5297	5365	5433
39	5501	5569	5637	5705	5773	5841	5908	5976	6044	6112
640	6180	6248	6316	6384	6451	6519	6587	6655	6723	6790
41	6858	6926	6994	7061	7129	7197	7264	7332	7400	7467
42	7535	7603	7670	7738	7806	7873	7941	8008	8076	8143
43	8211	8279	8346	8414	8481	8549	8616	8684	8751	8818
44	8886	8953	9021	9088	9156	9223	9290	9358	9425	9492
45	9560	9627	9694	9762	9829	9896	9964	*0031	*0098	*0165
46	81 0233	0300	0367	0434	0501	0569	0636	0703	0770	0837
47	0904	0971	1039	1106	1173	1240	1307	1374	1441	1508
48	1575	1642	1709	1776	1843	1910	1977	2044	2111	2178
49	2245	2312	2379	2445	2512	2579	2646	2713	2780	2847

Table 15 *(Continued)* **Mantissas for 650–699**

650	0	1	2	3	4	5	6	7	8	9
650	81 2913	2980	3047	3114	3181	3247	3314	3381	3448	3514
51	3581	3648	3714	3781	3848	3914	3981	4048	4114	4181
52	4248	4314	4381	4447	4514	4581	4647	4714	4780	4847
53	4913	4980	5046	5113	5179	5246	5312	5378	5445	5511
54	5578	5644	5711	5777	5843	5910	5976	6042	6109	6175
55	6241	6308	6374	6440	6506	6573	6639	6705	6771	6838
56	6904	6970	7036	7102	7169	7235	7301	7367	7433	7499
57	7565	7631	7698	7764	7830	7896	7962	8028	8094	8160
58	8226	8292	8358	8424	8490	8556	8622	8688	8754	8820
59	8885	8951	9017	9083	9149	9215	9281	9346	9412	9478
660	9544	9610	9676	9741	9807	9873	9939	*0004	*0070	*0136
61	82 0201	0267	0333	0399	0464	0530	0595	0661	0727	0792
62	0858	0924	0989	1055	1120	1186	1251	1317	1382	1448
63	1514	1579	1645	1710	1775	1841	1906	1972	2037	2103
64	2168	2233	2299	2364	2430	2495	2560	2626	2691	2756
65	2822	2887	2952	3018	3083	3148	3213	3279	3344	3409
66	3474	3539	3605	3670	3735	3800	3865	3930	3996	4061
67	4126	4191	4256	4321	4386	4451	4516	4581	4646	4711
68	4776	4841	4906	4971	5036	5101	5166	5231	5296	5361
69	5426	5491	5556	5621	5686	5751	5815	5880	5945	6010
670	6075	6140	6204	6269	6334	6399	6464	6528	6593	6658
71	6723	6787	6852	6917	6981	7046	7111	7175	7240	7305
72	7369	7434	7499	7563	7628	7692	7757	7821	7886	7951
73	8015	8080	8144	8209	8273	8338	8402	8467	8531	8595
74	8660	8724	8789	8853	8918	8982	9046	9111	9175	9239
75	9304	9368	9432	9497	9561	9625	9690	9754	9818	9882
76	9947	*0011	*0075	*0139	*0204	*0268	*0332	*0396	*0460	*0525
77	83 0589	0653	0717	0781	0845	0909	0973	1037	1102	1166
78	1230	1294	1358	1422	1486	1550	1614	1678	1742	1806
79	1870	1934	1998	2062	2126	2189	2253	2317	2381	2445
680	2509	2573	2637	2700	2764	2828	2892	2956	3020	3083
81	3147	3211	3275	3338	3402	3466	3530	3593	3657	3721
82	3784	3848	3912	3975	4039	4103	4166	4230	4294	4357
83	4421	4484	4548	4611	4675	4739	4802	4866	4929	4993
84	5056	5120	5183	5247	5310	5373	5437	5500	5564	5627
85	5691	5754	5817	5881	5944	6007	6071	6134	6197	6261
86	6324	6387	6451	6514	6577	6641	6704	6767	6830	6894
87	6957	7020	7083	7146	7210	7273	7336	7399	7462	7525
88	7588	7652	7715	7778	7841	7904	7967	8030	8093	8156
89	8219	8282	8345	8408	8471	8534	8597	8660	8723	8786
690	8849	8912	8975	9038	9101	9164	9227	9289	9352	9415
91	9478	9541	9604	9667	9729	9792	9855	9918	9981	*0043
92	84 0106	0169	0232	0294	0357	0420	0482	0545	0608	0671
93	0733	0796	0859	0921	0984	1046	1109	1172	1234	1297
94	1359	1422	1485	1547	1610	1672	1735	1797	1860	1922
95	1985	2047	2110	2172	2235	2297	2360	2422	2484	2547
96	2609	2672	2734	2796	2859	2921	2983	3046	3108	3170
97	3233	3295	3357	3420	3482	3544	3606	3669	3731	3793
98	3855	3918	3980	4042	4104	4166	4229	4291	4353	4415
99	4477	4539	4601	4664	4726	4788	4850	4912	4974	5036

Table 15 *(Continued)* **Mantissas for 700–749**

700	0	1	2	3	4	5	6	7	8	9
700	84 5098	5160	5222	5284	5346	5408	5470	5532	5594	5656
01	5718	5780	5842	5904	5966	6028	6090	6151	6213	6275
02	6337	6399	6461	6523	6585	6646	6708	6770	6832	6894
03	6955	7017	7079	7141	7202	7264	7326	7388	7449	7511
04	7573	7634	7696	7758	7819	7881	7943	8004	8066	8128
05	8189	8251	8312	8374	8435	8497	8559	8620	8682	8743
06	8805	8866	8928	8989	9051	9112	9174	9235	9297	9358
07	9419	9481	9542	9604	9665	9726	9788	9849	9911	9972
08	85 0033	0095	0156	0217	0279	0340	0401	0462	0524	0585
09	0646	0707	0769	0830	0891	0952	1014	1075	1136	1197
710	1258	1320	1381	1442	1503	1564	1625	1686	1747	1809
11	1870	1931	1992	2053	2114	2175	2236	2297	2358	2419
12	2480	2541	2602	2663	2724	2785	2846	2907	2968	3029
13	3090	3150	3211	3272	3333	3394	3455	3516	3577	3637
14	3698	3759	3820	3881	3941	4002	4063	4124	4185	4245
15	4306	4367	4428	4488	4549	4610	4670	4731	4792	4852
16	4913	4974	5034	5095	5156	5216	5277	5337	5398	5459
17	5519	5580	5640	5701	5761	5822	5882	5943	6003	6064
18	6124	6185	6245	6306	6366	6427	6487	6548	6608	6668
19	6729	6789	6850	6910	6970	7031	7091	7152	7212	7272
720	7332	7393	7453	7513	7574	7634	7694	7755	7815	7875
21	7935	7995	8056	8116	8176	8236	8297	8357	8417	8477
22	8537	8597	8657	8718	8778	8838	8898	8958	9018	9078
23	9138	9198	9258	9318	9379	9439	9499	9559	9619	9679
24	9739	9799	9859	9918	9978	*0038	*0098	*0158	*0218	*0278
25	86 0338	0398	0458	0518	0578	0637	0697	0757	0817	0877
26	0937	0996	1056	1116	1176	1236	1295	1355	1415	1475
27	1534	1594	1654	1714	1773	1833	1893	1952	2012	2072
28	2131	2191	2251	2310	2370	2430	2489	2549	2608	2668
29	2728	2787	2847	2906	2966	3025	3085	3144	3204	3263
730	3323	3382	3442	3501	3561	3620	3680	3739	3799	3858
31	3917	3977	4036	4096	4155	4214	4274	4333	4392	4452
32	4511	4570	4630	4689	4748	4808	4867	4926	4985	5045
33	5104	5163	5222	5282	5341	5400	5459	5519	5578	5637
34	5696	5755	5814	5874	5933	5992	6051	6110	6169	6228
35	6287	6346	6405	6465	6524	6583	6642	6701	6760	6819
36	6878	6937	6996	7055	7114	7173	7232	7291	7350	7409
37	7467	7526	7585	7644	7703	7762	7821	7880	7939	7998
38	8056	8115	8174	8233	8292	8350	8409	8468	8527	8586
39	8644	8703	8762	8821	8879	8938	8997	9056	9114	9173
740	9232	9290	9349	9408	9466	9525	9584	9642	9701	9760
41	9818	9877	9935	9994	*0053	*0111	*0170	*0228	*0287	*0345
42	87 0404	0462	0521	0579	0638	0696	0755	0813	0872	0930
43	0989	1047	1106	1164	1223	1281	1339	1398	1456	1515
44	1573	1631	1690	1748	1806	1865	1923	1981	2040	2098
45	2156	2215	2273	2331	2389	2448	2506	2564	2622	2681
46	2739	2797	2855	2913	2972	3030	3088	3146	3204	3262
47	3321	3379	3437	3495	3553	3611	3669	3727	3785	3844
48	3902	3960	4018	4076	4134	4192	4250	4308	4366	4424
49	4482	4540	4598	4656	4714	4772	4830	4888	4945	5003

Table 15   (*Continued*)   Mantissas for 750-799

750	0	1	2	3	4	5	6	7	8	9
750	87 5061	5119	5177	5235	5293	5351	5409	5466	5524	5582
51	5640	5698	5756	5813	5871	5929	5987	6045	6102	6160
52	6218	6276	6333	6391	6449	6507	6564	6622	6680	6737
53	6795	6853	6910	6968	7026	7083	7141	7199	7256	7314
54	7371	7429	7487	7544	7602	7659	7717	7774	7832	7889
55	7947	8004	8062	8119	8177	8234	8292	8349	8407	8464
56	8522	8579	8637	8694	8752	8809	8866	8924	8981	9039
57	9096	9153	9211	9268	9325	9383	9440	9497	9555	9612
58	9669	9726	9784	9841	9898	9956	*0013	*0070	*0127	*0185
59	88 0242	0299	0356	0413	0471	0528	0585	0642	0699	0756
760	0814	0871	0928	0985	1042	1099	1156	1213	1271	1328
61	1385	1442	1499	1556	1613	1670	1727	1784	1841	1898
62	1955	2012	2069	2126	2183	2240	2297	2354	2411	2468
63	2525	2581	2638	2695	2752	2809	2866	2923	2980	3037
64	3093	3150	3207	3264	3321	3377	3434	3491	3548	3605
65	3661	3718	3775	3832	3888	3945	4002	4059	4115	4172
66	4229	4285	4342	4399	4455	4512	4569	4625	4682	4739
67	4795	4852	4909	4965	5022	5078	5135	5192	5248	5305
68	5361	5418	5474	5531	5587	5644	5700	5757	5813	5870
69	5926	5983	6039	6096	6152	6209	6265	6321	6378	6434
770	6491	6547	6604	6660	6716	6773	6829	6885	6942	6998
71	7054	7111	7167	7223	7280	7336	7392	7449	7505	7561
72	7617	7674	7730	7786	7842	7898	7955	8011	8067	8123
73	8179	8236	8292	8348	8404	8460	8516	8573	8629	8685
74	8741	8797	8853	8909	8965	9021	9077	9134	9190	9246
75	9302	9358	9414	9470	9526	9582	9638	9694	9750	9806
76	9862	9918	9974	*0030	*0086	*0141	*0197	*0253	*0309	*0365
77	89 0421	0477	0533	0589	0645	0700	0756	0812	0868	0924
78	0980	1035	1091	1147	1203	1259	1314	1370	1426	1482
79	1537	1593	1649	1705	1760	1816	1872	1928	1983	2039
780	2095	2150	2206	2262	2317	2373	2429	2484	2540	2595
81	2651	2707	2762	2818	2873	2929	2985	3040	3096	3151
82	3207	3262	3318	3373	3429	3484	3540	3595	3651	3706
83	3762	3817	3873	3928	3984	4039	4094	4150	4205	4261
84	4316	4371	4427	4482	4538	4593	4648	4704	4759	4814
85	4870	4925	4980	5036	5091	5146	5201	5257	5312	5367
86	5423	5478	5533	5588	5644	5699	5754	5809	5864	5920
87	5975	6030	6085	6140	6195	6251	6306	6361	6416	6471
88	6526	6581	6636	6692	6747	6802	6857	6912	6967	7022
89	7077	7132	7187	7242	7297	7352	7407	7462	7517	7572
790	7627	7682	7737	7792	7847	7902	7957	8012	8067	8122
91	8176	8231	8286	8341	8396	8451	8506	8561	8615	8670
92	8725	8780	8835	8890	8944	8999	9054	9109	9164	9218
93	9273	9328	9383	9437	9492	9547	9602	9656	9711	9766
94	9821	9875	9930	9985	*0039	*0094	*0149	*0203	*0258	*0312
95	90 0367	0422	0476	0531	0586	0640	0695	0749	0804	0859
96	0913	0968	1022	1077	1131	1186	1240	1295	1349	1404
97	1458	1513	1567	1622	1676	1731	1785	1840	1894	1948
98	2003	2057	2112	2166	2221	2275	2329	2384	2438	2492
99	2547	2601	2655	2710	2764	2818	2873	2927	2981	3036

Table 15 (*Continued*) **Mantissas for 800–849**

800	0	1	2	3	4	5	6	7	8	9
800	90 3090	3144	3199	3253	3307	3361	3416	3470	3524	3578
01	3633	3687	3741	3795	3849	3904	3958	4012	4066	4120
02	4174	4229	4283	4337	4391	4445	4499	4553	4607	4661
03	4716	4770	4824	4878	4932	4986	5040	5094	5148	5202
04	5256	5310	5364	5418	5472	5526	5580	5634	5688	5742
05	5796	5850	5904	5958	6012	6066	6119	6173	6227	6281
06	6335	6389	6443	6497	6551	6604	6658	6712	6766	6820
07	6874	6927	6981	7035	7089	7143	7196	7250	7304	7358
08	7411	7465	7519	7573	7626	7680	7734	7787	7841	7895
09	7949	8002	8056	8110	8163	8217	8270	8324	8378	8431
810	8485	8539	8592	8646	8699	8753	8807	8860	8914	8967
11	9021	9074	9128	9181	9235	9289	9342	9396	9449	9503
12	9556	9610	9663	9716	9770	9823	9877	9930	9984	*0037
13	91 0091	0144	0197	0251	0304	0358	0411	0464	0518	0571
14	0624	0678	0731	0784	0838	0891	0944	0998	1051	1104
15	1158	1211	1264	1317	1371	1424	1477	1530	1584	1637
16	1690	1743	1797	1850	1903	1956	2009	2063	2116	2169
17	2222	2275	2328	2381	2435	2488	2541	2594	2647	2700
18	2753	2806	2859	2913	2966	3019	3072	3125	3178	3231
19	3284	3337	3390	3443	3496	3549	3602	3655	3708	3761
820	3814	3867	3920	3973	4026	4079	4132	4184	4237	4290
21	4343	4396	4449	4502	4555	4608	4660	4713	4766	4819
22	4872	4925	4977	5030	5083	5136	5189	5241	5294	5347
23	5400	5453	5505	5558	5611	5664	5716	5769	5822	5875
24	5927	5980	6033	6085	6138	6191	6243	6296	6349	6401
25	6454	6507	6559	6612	6664	6717	6770	6822	6875	6927
26	6980	7033	7085	7138	7190	7243	7295	7348	7400	7453
27	7506	7558	7611	7663	7716	7768	7820	7873	7925	7978
28	8030	8083	8135	8188	8240	8293	8345	8397	8450	8502
29	8555	8607	8659	8712	8764	8816	8869	8921	8973	9026
830	9078	9130	9183	9235	9287	9340	9392	9444	9496	9549
31	9601	9653	9706	9758	9810	9862	9914	9967	*0019	*0071
32	92 0123	0176	0228	0280	0332	0384	0436	0489	0541	0593
33	0645	0697	0749	0801	0853	0906	0958	1010	1062	1114
34	1166	1218	1270	1322	1374	1426	1478	1530	1582	1634
35	1686	1738	1790	1842	1894	1946	1998	2050	2102	2154
36	2206	2258	2310	2362	2414	2466	2518	2570	2622	2674
37	2725	2777	2829	2881	2933	2985	3037	3089	3140	3192
38	3244	3296	3348	3399	3451	3503	3555	3607	3658	3710
39	3762	3814	3865	3917	3969	4021	4072	4124	4176	4228
840	4279	4331	4383	4434	4486	4538	4589	4641	4693	4744
41	4796	4848	4899	4951	5003	5054	5106	5157	5209	5261
42	5312	5364	5415	5467	5518	5570	5621	5673	5725	5776
43	5828	5879	5931	5982	6034	6085	6137	6188	6240	6291
44	6342	6394	6445	6497	6548	6600	6651	6702	6754	6805
45	6857	6908	6959	7011	7062	7114	7165	7216	7268	7319
46	7370	7422	7473	7524	7576	7627	7678	7730	7781	7832
47	7883	7935	7986	8037	8088	8140	8191	8242	8293	8345
48	8396	8447	8498	8549	8601	8652	8703	8754	8805	8857
49	8908	8959	9010	9061	9112	9163	9215	9266	9317	9368

Table 15 *(Continued)* Mantissas for 850–899

850	0	1	2	3	4	5	6	7	8	9
850	92 9419	9470	9521	9572	9623	9674	9725	9776	9827	9879
51	9930	9981	*0032	*0083	*0134	*0185	*0236	*0287	*0338	*0389
52	93 0440	0491	0542	0592	0643	0694	0745	0796	0847	0898
53	0949	1000	1051	1102	1153	1204	1254	1305	1356	1407
54	1458	1509	1560	1610	1661	1712	1763	1814	1865	1915
55	1966	2017	2068	2118	2169	2220	2271	2322	2372	2423
56	2474	2524	2575	2626	2677	2727	2778	2829	2879	2930
57	2981	3031	3082	3133	3183	3234	3285	3335	3386	3437
58	3487	3538	3589	3639	3690	3740	3791	3841	3892	3943
59	3993	4044	4094	4145	4195	4246	4296	4347	4397	4448
860	4498	4549	4599	4650	4700	4751	4801	4852	4902	4953
61	5003	5054	5104	5154	5205	5255	5306	5356	5406	5457
62	5507	5558	5608	5658	5709	5759	5809	5860	5910	5960
63	6011	6061	6111	6162	6212	6262	6313	6363	6413	6463
64	6514	6564	6614	6665	6715	6765	6815	6865	6916	6966
65	7016	7066	7117	7167	7217	7267	7317	7367	7418	7468
66	7518	7568	7618	7668	7718	7769	7819	7869	7919	7969
67	8019	8069	8119	8169	8219	8269	8320	8370	8420	8470
68	8520	8570	8620	8670	8720	8770	8820	8870	8920	8970
69	9020	9070	9120	9170	9220	9270	9320	9369	9419	9469
870	9519	9569	9619	9669	9719	9769	9819	9869	9918	9968
71	94 0018	0068	0118	0168	0218	0267	0317	0367	0417	0467
72	0516	0566	0616	0666	0716	0765	0815	0865	0915	0964
73	1014	1064	1114	1163	1213	1263	1313	1362	1412	1462
74	1511	1561	1611	1660	1710	1760	1809	1859	1909	1958
75	2008	2058	2107	2157	2207	2256	2306	2355	2405	2455
76	2504	2554	2603	2653	2702	2752	2801	2851	2901	2950
77	3000	3049	3099	3148	3198	3247	3297	3346	3396	3445
78	3495	3544	3593	3643	3692	3742	3791	3841	3890	3939
79	3989	4038	4088	4137	4186	4236	4285	4335	4384	4433
880	4483	4532	4581	4631	4680	4729	4779	4828	4877	4927
81	4976	5025	5074	5124	5173	5222	5272	5321	5370	5419
82	5469	5518	5567	5616	5665	5715	5764	5813	5862	5912
83	5961	6010	6059	6108	6157	6207	6256	6305	6354	6403
84	6452	6501	6551	6600	6649	6698	6747	6796	6845	6894
85	6943	6992	7041	7090	7140	7189	7238	7287	7336	7385
86	7434	7483	7532	7581	7630	7679	7728	7777	7826	7875
87	7924	7973	8022	8070	8119	8168	8217	8266	8315	8364
88	8413	8462	8511	8560	8609	8657	8706	8755	8804	8853
89	8902	8951	8999	9048	9097	9146	9195	9244	9292	9341
890	9390	9439	9488	9536	9585	9634	9683	9731	9780	9829
91	9878	9926	9975	*0024	*0073	*0121	*0170	*0219	*0267	*0316
92	95 0365	0414	0462	0511	0560	0608	0657	0706	0754	0803
93	0851	0900	0949	0997	1046	1095	1143	1192	1240	1289
94	1338	1386	1435	1483	1532	1580	1629	1677	1726	1775
95	1823	1872	1920	1969	2017	2066	2114	2163	2211	2260
96	2308	2356	2405	2453	2502	2550	2599	2647	2696	2744
97	2792	2841	2889	2938	2986	3034	3083	3131	3180	3228
98	3276	3325	3373	3421	3470	3518	3566	3615	3663	3711
99	3760	3808	3856	3905	3953	4001	4049	4098	4146	4194

Table 15   (*Continued*)   **Mantissas for 900–949**

900	0	1	2	3	4	5	6	7	8	9
900	95 4243	4291	4339	4387	4435	4484	4532	4580	4628	4677
01	4725	4773	4821	4869	4918	4966	5014	5062	5110	5158
02	5207	5255	5303	5351	5399	5447	5495	5543	5592	5640
03	5688	5736	5784	5832	5880	5928	5976	6024	6072	6120
04	6168	6216	6265	6313	6361	6409	6457	6505	6553	6601
05	6649	6697	6745	6793	6840	6888	6936	6984	7032	7080
06	7128	7176	7224	7272	7320	7368	7416	7464	7512	7559
07	7607	7655	7703	7751	7799	7847	7894	7942	7990	8038
08	8086	8134	8181	8229	8277	8325	8373	8421	8468	8516
09	8564	8612	8659	8707	8755	8803	8850	8898	8946	8994
910	9041	9089	9137	9185	9232	9280	9328	9375	9423	9471
11	9518	9566	9614	9661	9709	9757	9804	9852	9900	9947
12	9995	*0042	*0090	*0138	*0185	*0233	*0280	*0328	*0376	*0423
13	96 0471	0518	0566	0613	0661	0709	0756	0804	0851	0899
14	0946	0994	1041	1089	1136	1184	1231	1279	1326	1374
15	1421	1469	1516	1563	1611	1658	1706	1753	1801	1848
16	1895	1943	1990	2038	2085	2132	2180	2227	2275	2322
17	2369	2417	2464	2511	2559	2606	2653	2701	2748	2795
18	2843	2890	2937	2985	3032	3079	3126	3174	3221	3268
19	3316	3363	3410	3457	3504	3552	3599	3646	3693	3741
920	3788	3835	3882	3929	3977	4024	4071	4118	4165	4212
21	4260	4307	4354	4401	4448	4495	4542	4590	4637	4684
22	4731	4778	4825	4872	4919	4966	5013	5061	5108	5155
23	5202	5249	5296	5343	5390	5437	5484	5531	5578	5625
24	5672	5719	5766	5813	5860	5907	5954	6001	6048	6095
25	6142	6189	6236	6283	6329	6376	6423	6470	6517	6564
26	6611	6658	6705	6752	6799	6845	6892	6939	6986	7033
27	7080	7127	7173	7220	7267	7314	7361	7408	7454	7501
28	7548	7595	7642	7688	7735	7782	7829	7875	7922	7969
29	8016	8062	8109	8156	8203	8249	8296	8343	8390	8436
930	8483	8530	8576	8623	8670	8716	8763	8810	8856	8903
31	8950	8996	9043	9090	9136	9183	9229	9276	9323	9369
32	9416	9463	9509	9556	9602	9649	9695	9742	9789	9835
33	9882	9928	9975	*0021	*0068	*0114	*0161	*0207	*0254	*0300
34	97 0347	0393	0440	0486	0533	0579	0626	0672	0719	0765
35	0812	0858	0904	0951	0997	1044	1090	1137	1183	1229
36	1276	1322	1369	1415	1461	1508	1554	1601	1647	1693
37	1740	1786	1832	1879	1925	1971	2018	2064	2110	2157
38	2203	2249	2295	2342	2388	2434	2481	2527	2573	2619
39	2666	2712	2758	2804	2851	2897	2943	2989	3035	3082
940	3128	3174	3220	3266	3313	3359	3405	3451	3497	3543
41	3590	3636	3682	3728	3774	3820	3866	3913	3959	4005
42	4051	4097	4143	4189	4235	4281	4327	4374	4420	4466
43	4512	4558	4604	4650	4696	4742	4788	4834	4880	4926
44	4972	5018	5064	5110	5156	5202	5248	5294	5340	5386
45	5432	5478	5524	5570	5616	5662	5707	5753	5799	5845
46	5891	5937	5983	6029	6075	6121	6167	6212	6258	6304
47	6350	6396	6442	6488	6533	6579	6625	6671	6717	6763
48	6808	6854	6900	6946	6992	7037	7083	7129	7175	7220
49	7266	7312	7358	7403	7449	7495	7541	7586	7632	7678

Table 15 *(Continued)* **Mantissas for 950–999**

950	0	1	2	3	4	5	6	7	8	9
950	97 7724	7769	7815	7861	7906	7952	7998	8043	8089	8135
51	8181	8226	8272	8317	8363	8409	8454	8500	8546	8591
52	8637	8683	8728	8774	8819	8865	8911	8956	9002	9047
53	9093	9138	9184	9230	9275	9321	9366	9412	9457	9503
54	9548	9594	9639	9685	9730	9776	9821	9867	9912	9958
55	98 0003	0049	0094	0140	0185	0231	0276	0322	0367	0412
56	0458	0503	0549	0594	0640	0685	0730	0776	0821	0867
57	0912	0957	1003	1048	1093	1139	1184	1229	1275	1320
58	1366	1411	1456	1501	1547	1592	1637	1683	1728	1773
59	1819	1864	1909	1954	2000	2045	2090	2135	2181	2226
960	2271	2316	2362	2407	2452	2497	2543	2588	2633	2678
61	2723	2769	2814	2859	2904	2949	2994	3040	3085	3130
62	3175	3220	3265	3310	3356	3401	3446	3491	3536	3581
63	3626	3671	3716	3762	3807	3852	3897	3942	3987	4032
64	4077	4122	4167	4212	4257	4302	4347	4392	4437	4482
65	4527	4572	4617	4662	4707	4752	4797	4842	4887	4932
66	4977	5022	5067	5112	5157	5202	5247	5292	5337	5382
67	5426	5471	5516	5561	5606	5651	5696	5741	5786	5830
68	5875	5920	5965	6010	6055	6100	6144	6189	6234	6279
69	6324	6369	6413	6458	6503	6548	6593	6637	6682	6727
970	6772	6817	6861	6906	6951	6996	7040	7085	7130	7175
71	7219	7264	7309	7353	7398	7443	7488	7532	7577	7622
72	7666	7711	7756	7800	7845	7890	7934	7979	8024	8068
73	8113	8157	8202	8247	8291	8336	8381	8425	8470	8514
74	8559	8604	8648	8693	8737	8782	8826	8871	8916	8960
75	9005	9049	9094	9138	9183	9227	9272	9316	9361	9405
76	9450	9494	9539	9583	9628	9672	9717	9761	9806	9850
77	9895	9939	9983	*0028	*0072	*0117	*0161	*0206	*0250	*0294
78	99 0339	0383	0428	0472	0516	0561	0605	0650	0694	0738
79	0783	0827	0871	0916	0960	1004	1049	1093	1137	1182
980	1226	1270	1315	1359	1403	1448	1492	1536	1580	1625
81	1669	1713	1758	1802	1846	1890	1935	1979	2023	2067
82	2111	2156	2200	2244	2288	2333	2377	2421	2465	2509
83	2554	2598	2642	2686	2730	2774	2819	2863	2907	2951
84	2995	3039	3083	3127	3172	3216	3260	3304	3348	3392
85	3436	3480	3524	3568	3613	3657	3701	3745	3789	3833
86	3877	3921	3965	4009	4053	4097	4141	4185	4229	4273
87	4317	4361	4405	4449	4493	4537	4581	4625	4669	4713
88	4757	4801	4845	4889	4933	4977	5021	5065	5108	5152
89	5196	5240	5284	5328	5372	5416	5460	5504	5547	5591
990	5635	5679	5723	5767	5811	5854	5898	5942	5986	6030
91	6074	6117	6161	6205	6249	6293	6337	6380	6424	6468
92	6512	6555	6599	6643	6687	6731	6774	6818	6862	6906
93	6949	6993	7037	7080	7124	7168	7212	7255	7299	7343
94	7386	7430	7474	7517	7561	7605	7648	7692	7736	7779
95	7823	7867	7910	7954	7998	8041	8085	8129	8172	8216
96	8259	8303	8347	8390	8434	8477	8521	8564	8608	8652
97	8695	8739	8782	8826	8869	8913	8956	9000	9043	9087
98	9131	9174	9218	9261	9305	9348	9392	9435	9479	9522
99	9565	9609	9652	9696	9739	9783	9826	9870	9913	9957

Index

Index